D1112350

INTERPERSONAL COMMUNICATION

Under the Advisory Editorship
of J. Jeffery Auer

INTERPERSONAL COMMUNICATION
Basic Text and Readings

BOBBY R. PATTON
The University of Kansas

KIM GIFFIN
The University of Kansas

HARPER & ROW, PUBLISHERS
New York, Evanston, San Francisco, London

Sponsoring Editor: *Voras D. Meeks*
Project Editor: *Holly Detgen*
Designer: *Jared Pratt*
Production Supervisor: *Stefania J. Taflinska*

Interpersonal Communication: Basic Text and Readings

Library of Congress Cataloging in Publication Data

Patton, Bobby R. 1935–
Interpersonal communication.
1. Interpersonal relations. I. Giffin, Kim,
1918– joint author. II. Title.
HM132.P36 001.5 73–7478
ISBN 0–06–042317–X

CONTENTS

PREFACE

Instructional programs in speech communication, business, education, psychology, social welfare, and minority studies are now realizing that knowledge and abilities in interpersonal communication are basic to student development. This realization is reflected by emphasis on interpersonal communication in courses on virtually every college and university campus. Such a development is understandable in terms of felt *needs* of students, as well as those of society at large, for increased awareness and improvements in abilities to relate to one another. In effect, we are witnessing a reaction to the impersonality of a large, automated, complex society.

We have been gratified by the response to our earlier writings and have drawn freely and liberally from our *Fundamentals of Interpersonal Communication* text and *Basic Readings in Interpersonal Communication* (Harper & Row, 1971). In the present volume, however, we feel that we have certainly gone far beyond merely combining the two books. Our own professional growth and perceptions have been greatly aided by our colleagues and students who have offered constructive criticism. To the best of our abilities we have endeavored to incorporate their suggestions into this book. Essentially we have made four improvements:

1. Balance between text and readings. *Combining text materials and readings provides greater cohesion than was possible with two separate volumes. The chapters preview the readings, which in turn serve to emphasize and reinforce—not merely repeat—key concepts in the text.*
2. Readability and easy comprehension. *We have attempted to use easily understandable language rather than confusing, specialized terminology. Similarly, the readings included do not require knowledge of professional jargon from a particular field.*
3. Updating of readings. *From the vast array of literature dealing with aspects of interpersonal communication, we have tried to select those that best illustrate our conception of the topic in a readable, interesting fashion. We have avoided basic research reports and any articles that required special educational background for understanding. Some readings are well*

known and are standard references, while others have received little circulation outside of specialized circles. We are gratified to have been able to obtain reprint permission from such a distinguished group of scholars from diverse fields.

4. Greater emphasis on applications. *Although our perspective is humanistic and requires the reader to make personalized choices in his/her interpersonal communication behaviors, we have been openly prescriptive at times. We have supplied supporting examples in both the text chapters and in the readings, to provide applications to the "real world." The Suggested Applications and Learning Experiences given at the end of each chapter are viewed as an integral part of the book in helping the reader make personal applications.*

The purposes of this book remain twofold: to present valid data on interpersonal communication to the student who possesses no specialized background, and to provide insights for improving our relationships with others.

We are greatly indebted to the researchers who have provided the foundations for our work and to our colleagues and associates who have encouraged us. Specifically we want to thank Ann Stuart, Marilyn Blubaugh, Lynna Froman, and Susan Harshaw for typing the manuscript; Dr. Bonnie Ritter Patton for her conceptual help, especially in Chapter 4; Doris Falen for assisting in proofreading and preparing the index; and Eddina Giffin for her general support, hot coffee, and providing a quiet place to work.

B. R. P.
K. G.

Section One
PERSPECTIVES ON INTERPERSONAL COMMUNICATION

During the last decade there has developed a new wave of human aspiration regarding the potential value of interpersonal communication as the means by which a person may reach a more satisfying relationship with other human beings. The older, more traditional view of communication usually focused on one (or a combination) of two objectives: (1) to tell them what I know or believe, or (2) to get them to see things as I do.

By comparison, the more recent view of interaction places much greater emphasis on the desire to relate to other persons. People with whom we are in daily contact are viewed as potential warm, personal friends, not just as coworkers or possible competitors. In this way new importance has been given to the phrase "human relations." There is an increased sense of personal justice. The other person has a right to be heard, not just a need to be informed or persuaded. The real potential of communication is seen in interaction, where listening as well as talking occurs. The emphasis on the human element reflects a very personal need of the individual in an automated and highly specialized society. It reflects one's need to be in personal touch with other people as well as a greater willingness to consider the needs of others. The hallmark of those who express increased interest in interpersonal communication is that they care about other people—they want to understand them, to know them better, and to reach out a friendly, helping hand to them.

In this section we shall examine the nature of communication and explore the role interpersonal communication plays in our lives.

Chapter 1
COMMUNICATING ABOUT COMMUNICATION

Communication. This word has become a twentieth-century "in" term. We like to have catch-all terms that allow us to disregard conceptual matters we don't care to deal with; thus we have "communication gaps," "communication breakdowns," and "failures to communicate," which tend to be abstractions of the highest order and do little to actually communicate.

We believe that this is an important preamble. When discussing communication we should be dealing with something specific. Such discussions should not be evasions or substitutes for looking at specific behaviors. Our goal in this chapter is to try to discuss communication generally, but in terms specific enough to bridge the gap between theory and an understanding of our personal behaviors.

THE NATURE OF COMMUNICATION

Communication is basic to human existence—indeed, to all life itself. Scholars have speculated for years attempting to formulate a definition for communication that both describes and delineates its essence. We, too, shall engage in such speculation, but in fundamental terms all life around us demonstrates communication. In human terms we suggest that death is denoted by the absence of communication. A renowned professor of molecular biology and bacteriology at the University of California at Berkeley stated recently: "The capacity to communicate is a fundamental feature of living cells." He proceeded to discuss the ways cells communicate by means of hormones and nerve fibers.[1] *To live is to communicate.*

Photosynthesis and rejuvenation in plant life have been discussed in terms of communication. Animals ranging from insects to mammals communicate by means of chemicals, movements, and sounds. People also use these modes of communication but add a unique kind of language based on symbols. Communications scientist John R. Pierce has stated:

> *Animals live without knowing how they live, and they communicate without knowing how they communicate. By and large, so do we. Unlike animals, however, we speculate about how we live and how we*

[1]S. Stent, "Cellular Communication," *Scientific American,* 227 (1972), 43–51.

> *communicate. Our better brain and our unique means of communication—language—make such speculation possible.*[2]

Pierce's value judgments reflect the fact that a human is making the description! Humans tend to attach meaning to the plant and animal kingdoms based on their own systems of communication.

COMMUNICATION AS PROCESS

Thus far we have done nothing to delineate communication. We should start by defining communication as a *process*, not a thing. This distinction is important; characteristic of our universe is the expectation of change—nothing is static. Communications scholar David Berlo has noted:

> *If we accept the concept of process, we view events and relationships as dynamic, ongoing, ever-changing, continuous. When we label something as a process, we also mean that it does not have a beginning,* an *end, a fixed sequence of events. It is not static, at rest. It is moving. The ingredients within a process interact; each affects all of the others.*[3]

Even to write about process tends to "freeze" it in static terms devoid of life and change. You are reading a textbook that is an object, that has a beginning and end. If these symbols written on the page generate thinking in you—and thereby change—then we have an operational process.

How can we then discuss this process? Berlo establishes a rationale when he states:

> *We have no alternative if we are to analyze and communicate about a process. The important point is that we must remember that we are not including everything in our discussion. The things we talk about do not have to exist in exactly the ways we talk about them, and they certainly do not have to operate in the order in which we talk about them. Objects which we separate may not always be separable, and they never operate independently—each affects and interacts with the others. This may appear obvious, but it is easy to overlook or forget the limitations that are necessarily placed on any discussion of a process.*[4]

We shall reiterate this problem of interdependency and mutual influence of all ingredients when we divide the process for purposes of discussion in Section Two.

[2] J. R. Pierce, "Communication," *Scientific American*, 227 (1972), 31.

[3] D. K. Berlo, *The Process of Communication* (New York: Holt, Rinehart and Winston, 1960), p. 24. An excerpt from this book is included as a reading in this volume, pp. 68–84.

[4] *Ibid.*, p. 26.

Conceptions of Communication

In the readings that follow this chapter, both Boulding and Barnlund view communication as the process that promotes change among humans. People attempt to interpret the world and their role—to make sense out of the influx of perceptions—to order and assign significance to the various components of their environment.

We define communication as *the generation and attribution of meaning*. This definition is broad enough to encompass nonhuman communication. Thus bees may perform a dance that signals other bees to go for nectar. A dog may show hunger by walking back and forth to the dog bowl. People may attribute meaning to elements in nature; for example, dark clouds signal the prospect of rain or bad weather; an unusual noise in the night stirs us to investigate. As we assign significance to phenomena or events around us, communication is taking place.

The source of the "communique" or *message* is the generator or sender. Such generation may be intentional or unintentional. People are unique in the extent to which their communication behaviors are intentional—that is, planned with an expectation of achieving a desired effect or eliciting a desired response. However, even between people the unintentional messages may carry more meaning than the planned ones. Other limitations on human communication will be noted subsequently.

The preceding definition is broad enough to be applied to mechanistic, schematic models of communication. Two mathematicians developed a model in the late 1940s that proved useful in analyzing such nonhuman communication as that involving computers, electrical circuiting, and energy transmission. Their model is shown in Figure 1.1.

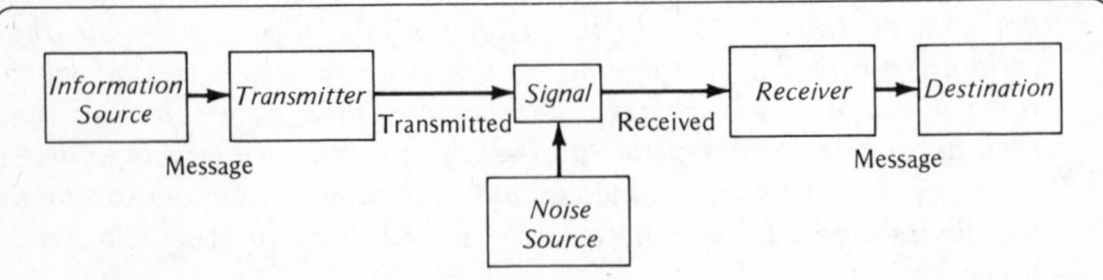

Figure 1.1 Shannon–Weaver Model of Communication. (From C. E. Shannon and W. Weaver, *The Mathematical Theory of Communication*, p. 98. Copyright 1949. Reprinted by permission of the University of Illinois Press, Urbana, Illinois.)

One limitation of the Shannon-Weaver model is that it presents communication as a linear concept, having a beginning and an end. Largely as a result of the work of Norbert Wiener in cybernetics, the importance of *feedback* was noted.[5] Wiener pointed out that communication should be viewed as circular rather than linear, since input and output of circuits are mutually linked as a means of controlling the performance. In his reading following Chapter 2, Berlo illustrates this concept by citing the examples of a thermostat in a house and the furnace engaged in mutual interaction. He states: "Continual communication occurs between the furnace and the thermostat. Each transmits messages, each receives messages. Each reacts to the message it receives."[6]

PEOPLE AS COMMUNICATORS

The Shannon-Weaver model was flexible enough to suggest to students modifications of human communication through simple terminology adaptation. The "Information Source" became the "Sender of the Message" or the "Speaker." Sometimes a stimulus was introduced to show that the speaker was motivated to send the message. The "Transmitter" was taken to represent the "Encoder of the Message," whereas the "Receiver" became the "Decoder." The "Signal" became "Meaning." "Noise" was interpreted in a variety of ways ranging from simple situational disturbances to the more systematic problems of meaning embodied in semantics. The "Destination" was made in turn the "Receiver of the Message," with notations of potential response sometimes added. Feedback was also noted to be important in human communication as a means for a sender to check the success of his intended message by observing the reactions of the receiver.

At approximately the same time that Shannon and Weaver were constructing their model, political scientist Harold Lasswell, interested in mass-media analysis, proposed five questions to indicate what he felt to be the important variables in communication:

Who?
Says What?
In Which Channel?
To Whom?
With What Effect?[7]

These five variables have become accepted criteria for describing and evaluating human communication.

In terms of our definition of communication, the "Who?" is the generator of the message, and the "To Whom?" is the attributor of

[5]N. Wiener, *The Human Use of Human Beings* (Boston: Houghton Mifflin, 1954).

[6]Berlo, *op. cit.*, p. 70 of this volume.

[7]H. D. Lasswell, "The Structure and Function of Communications in Society," in L. Bryson, ed., *The Communication of Ideas* (New York: Harper & Row, 1948), p. 37.

meaning. A frequently told story illustrates the application to human communication:

> *A plumber wrote the U.S. Bureau of Standards about using hydrochloric acid to clean drain pipes. . . . Several days later he received this reply: "The efficacy of hydrochloric acid is indisputable, but the corrosive residue is incompatible with metallic permanence." Confused, he wrote again and asked if the acid "is okay to use or not."*
>
> *A second letter advised him, "We cannot assume responsibility for the production of toxic and noxious residue, and suggest that you use an alternative procedure."*
>
> *Still baffled, he wrote, "Do you mean it's okay to use hydrochloric acid?"*
>
> *A final letter resolved the question. "Don't use hydrochloric acid. It eats the hell out of pipes."*

Communication in this story involved the messages generated and the meanings attributed by the plumber. Basic to the problem was the difference in meanings between source and receiver.

The Search for "Meaning"

If communication is concerned with the process of sending and receiving messages, intrinsic to human communication is the attempt to interchange meanings. The very process in which we arbitrarily make certain sounds or symbols stand for other things is societal in essence. We can, by mutual agreement, make anything stand for anything. This elementary "meaning-of-words" aspect of communication is important because arguments or disagreements may arise simply because A uses a word one way, and B receives the word as if it meant something entirely different. This could happen when A says, "I was only a little late," and B responds, "You were not!"

Social psychologist Roger Brown has offered a reasonable definition of "meaning" as ". . . the total disposition to make use of or react to a linguistic form." To concentrate on all the possible components in a word or phrase in a literal or absolute fashion, however, presents an unsurmountable problem, as Brown continues: "A man might give all his productive years to spelling out the . . . meaning of a single utterance and find the task unfinished in the end."[8]

Problems resulting from confusion of meanings attached to words are countless, ranging from the attempt of the U.S. Bureau of Standards to communicate with the plumber to situations with far more serious consequences. In a report in *Harper's Magazine* in 1953, there is a startling suggestion that the mistranslation of a single word may have caused the bombing of Hiroshima and Nagasaki. The word *mokusatsu* has two meanings in Japanese. One is "to ignore," with intent to affront, and the other is "to ignore," meaning a mere with-

[8]R. Brown, *Words and Things* (New York: Free Press, 1958), pp. 100, 103.

holding of comment. To a surrender ultimatum from the Allies, a message with the "no comment" meaning was prepared; the translator, however, applied the meaning of "refused to notice" as the message was passed on. The first interpretation could have led to surrender with face, while the second forced the Allies to take the drastic action required to end the conflict. According to Coughlin's report, if the misinterpretation of that one word had not occurred, the atom bombs would never have been dropped and Russia would never have entered the Pacific theater, paving the way for the Korean War.[9]

Similar types of problems can also be cited over misunderstanding nonverbal communication. We shall discuss the problems of sending and receiving messages in greater detail in Chapter 6.

Characteristics of the Human Communication Act

We have already suggested characteristics of communication in general that must also apply to human communication; in the words of Dean Barnlund: "1. Communication is not a thing, it is a process," and "2. Communication is not linear; it is circular."[10] He goes on to cite three additional "principles" with examples tied to human behaviors:

> *3. Communication is complex. Someone once said that whenever there is communication there are at least six "people" involved: The person you think yourself to be; the man your partner thinks you are; the person you believe your partner thinks you are; plus the three equivalent "persons" at the other end of the circuit. If, with as few as four constants, mathematicians must cope with approximately fifty possible relations, then we, in studying communication, where an even greater number of variables is concerned, ought to expound with considerable humility. In this age of Freudian and non-Freudian analysts, of information theory specialists, of structural linguists, and so on, we are just beginning to unravel the mysteries of this terribly involved, and therefore fascinating, puzzle.*
>
> *4. Communication is irreversible and unrepeatable. The distinction being suggested here is between systems that are deterministic and mechanical, and those that are spontaneous and evolutionary. One can start a motor, beat a rug, or return a book. But you cannot start a man thinking, beat your son, or return a compliment with the same consequences. The words of a teacher, even when faithfully repeated, do not produce the same effect, but may lead to new insight, increased tension, or complete boredom. A moment of indifference or interest, a disarming or tangential remark, leave indelible traces.*
>
> *5. Communication involves the total personality. Despite all ef-*

[9]W. J. Coughlin, "The Great MOKUSATSU Mistake: Was This the Deadliest Error of Our Time?" *Harper's Magazine*, March 1953.

[10]D. C. Barnlund, "Toward a Meaning-Centered Philosophy of Communication," *Journal of Communication*, 11 (1962), 198–202. Reprinted in K. Giffin and B. R. Patton, eds., *Basic Readings in Interpersonal Communication* (New York: Harper & Row, 1971), pp. 40–47.

> *forts to divide body and mind, reason and emotion, thought and action, meanings continue to be generated by the whole organism. This is not to say that some messages do not produce greater or lesser dissonance, or shallower or deeper effects on the personality; it is only to hold that eventually every fact, conclusion, guilt, or enthusiasm must somehow be accommodated by the entire personality. The deeper the involvement produced by any communication, the sooner and more pervasive its effects upon behavior.*[11]

Barnlund posits another basic characteristic of human communication in his reading following this chapter: Communication is the basis of change in our views of the world and of ourselves. "Aside from common social rituals, *men nearly always talk in a context of change.* What prompts communication is the desire for someone else to see our facts, appreciate our values, share our feelings, accept our decision. Communication is initiated, consciously or unconsciously, to change the other person."[12]

In Chapter 2 we shall suggest additional characteristics that apply directly to our interpersonal communication.

Levels of Human Communication

Before moving operationally into a discussion of interpersonal communication, we should suggest by way of contrast alternative levels or kinds of human communication.

1. Intrapersonal Communication. Signals are presently going from all parts of your body to your brain. A throbbing in your stomach may suggest that you are hungry or that you have overeaten. Intrapersonal communication refers to the communication that transpires inside a person.

Other forms of intrapersonal communication include the perceptual notes we make, the rationalizations and attitudes that determine our overt behaviors. Basic to all levels of communication is a developed consciousness of self. As psychologist Rollo May has observed:

> *The capacity for consciousness of ourselves gives us the ability to see ourselves as others see us and to have empathy with others. It underlies our remarkable capacity to transport ourselves into someone else's parlor where we will be in reality next week, and then in imagination to think and plan how we will act. And it enables us to imagine ourselves in someone else's place, and to ask how we would feel and what we would do if we were this other person. No matter how poorly we use or fail to use or even abuse these capacities, they are the rudiments*

[11] *Ibid.*

[12] D. C. Barnlund, "Communication: The Context of Change," in C. E. Larson and F. E. X. Dance, eds., *Perspectives on Communication* (Milwaukee: University of Wisconsin Communication Research Center, 1968), p. 27. Reprinted in this volume, pp. 25–41.

of our ability to begin to love our neighbor, to have ethical sensitivity, to see truth, to create beauty, to devote ourselves to ideals, and to die for them if need be.[13]

May goes on to develop the thesis that fulfilling these potentialities is the key to becoming a person.

Deep internal problems are the province of the psychologist and psychoanalyst. Our concerns are the intrapersonal influences on our overt behaviors with others. In Chapters 3 and 4 we shall discuss our needs to communicate and our interpersonal perceptions and orientations as they *affect* our interpersonal communication. Although interpersonal communication will be our central focus, other levels of the process cannot be ignored.

2. One-Way Communication. This level suggests the absence of feedback. While we have opposed the linear view of the communication process, we should note that on one level the roles of sender and receiver tend to be fixed. For example, in a large lecture hall the speaker has a preplanned message and the members of the audience accept the role of listeners. Feedback in such a situation is less direct and dependent upon the speaker's inferential abilities. Applause or lack of attentiveness provides clues to the audience's receptiveness to the speaker.

Other types of one-way communication involve mass media. As we watch a speaker on television or listen to the radio, our feedback to the sender is indirect (ratings, letters, and reviews). Written communication also fits this category. As you are now reading this page, your means of providing feedback are limited. We are on the sender end of a continuum, and you are on the receiving end. In such one-way situations the receiver determines whether or not communication is to occur. It is your choice whether to continue reading, or to listen (in an attempt to attribute meaning) to the words of the teacher.

In contrast to two-way communication (involving direct feedback, give-and-take, between sender and receiver), researchers have concluded the following:

1. *Two-way communication takes much longer.*
2. *Two-way communication results in greater mutual understanding.*
3. *In one-way communication, the sender feels relatively confident; the receiver, uncertain or frustrated.*
4. *In two-way communication, the sender often feels frustrated or angry; the receiver, relatively confident.*[14]

While one-way communication is obviously required in certain situa-

[13]R. May, *Man's Search for Himself* (New York: Norton, 1953), p. 75.

[14]H. J. Leavitt, *Managerial Psychology* (Chicago: University of Chicago Press, 1958), pp. 118–128.

tions, Barnlund presents a persuasive case for two-way communication in situations requiring understanding and a cooperative relationship.[15]

Interpersonal Communication. This two-way level of communication is the focus of this text. With "interpersonal communication" we are concerned with the face-to-face interactions between people who are consistently aware of each other. Each person assumes the roles of both sender and receiver of messages, which involves constant adaptation and spontaneous adjustment to the other person.

The Role of Communication in Our Lives

The child is born into a world of strange sensory sensations. Lights, visual images, and strange sounds bombard the nervous system. The child's early days are spent sorting out these sensations. The presence of certain people becomes recognized as signals that physical needs will be fulfilled. Sounds also begin to take on meaning as words are repeated over and over again to him. Eventually the child begins to behave in certain ways that exert influence over the environment. Babbling, cooing, and finally vocalizing "ma-ma" or "pa-pa" gain warm approving signals of positive acceptance from the elders. Thus it is with our communication behaviors. As we develop we become more sophisticated and discriminating as we attach meaning to phenomena, and are more able to control our environments by initiating communication with others.

We expand our experiences and our expectations of others in terms of our cultural surroundings and the models of behaviors that we encounter. Communication, with its intrinsic feedback on our own behaviors, is the means by which we adjust ourselves to our environment and adjust our environment to suit us. We don't think we overstate in saying that communication is the most important process in our lives. As human beings, we no longer live simply as a result of the products of our own hands, but through our dealings with others.

Barnlund has stated clearly and concisely the role and goal of communication in our lives:

> *Communication arises out of the need to reduce uncertainty, to act effectively, to defend or strengthen the ego. On some occasions words are used to ward off anxiety. On other occasions they are means of evolving more deeply satisfying ways of expressing ourselves.* The aim of communication is to increase the number and consistency of our meanings within the limits set by patterns of evaluation that have proven successful in the past, our emerging needs and drives, and the demands of the physical and social setting of the moment. *Communication*

[15]See pp. 25–41.

> *ceases when meanings are adequate; it is initiated as soon as new meanings are required. However, since man is a homeostatic, rather than static, organism, it is impossible for him to discover any permanently satisfying way of relating all his needs; each temporary adjustment is both relieving and disturbing, leading to successively novel ways of relating to himself and his environment.*[16]

[16]Barnlund, "Toward a Meaning-Centered Philosophy of Communication," *op. cit.*

SUMMARY AND PREVIEW OF READINGS

We have noted the process nature of communication and the difficulty of holding a process up for examination. We defined communication as the generation and attribution of meaning. Since meaning is personal, difficulties can arise in the communication process when different people may attribute different meanings to the generated message. In subsequent chapters we shall explore the elements in the process as it relates to face-to-face spontaneous interaction between people.

In the first reading that follows this chapter, Kenneth Boulding presents in a personalized fashion the ways that the individual develops his "image" and the impact of messages on the image, which can take several forms. Growth is the key.

Dean C. Barnlund extends Boulding's personalized view into theoretical communication constructs. The threat of change and the problems intrinsic to personal communication—such as defensive behaviors—are discussed.

Together these two articles provide us with an excellent overview of the process of communication and suggest a philosophy that warrants the serious study of human communication. In Chapter 2 we shall attempt to relate this process and philosophy specifically to the study of interpersonal communication.

SUGGESTED APPLICATIONS AND LEARNING EXPERIENCES

1. Meet with a group of students and share your views on definitions of communication. Discuss the definition given in this chapter and determine whether it encompasses the views of your group.

2. Decide on three isolated, ambiguous words (e.g., mail, dream, march). Have other members of the class make up sentences incorporating the three words. Read the sentences and compare variations in the themes of the sentences, different ways in which specific words are interpreted, etc.

3. Compare one-way and two-way communication by having someone give a report with his or her back turned to the group and no feedback permitted. Have a second report given with interaction permitted. Compare your results with the research findings reported in this chapter.

4. In this chapter Barnlund was quoted as stating that "communication ceases when meanings are adequate." Cite examples that either illustrate or refute this observation.

5. In the reading that follows, Boulding discusses the nature of knowledge. Discuss what specific learning in your life has made significant differences. Compare your views on education with others to see if you agree with Boulding's conclusions.

6. Barnlund suggests some barriers to communication in his essay that follows. Draw up a list of such barriers to your communication and see if other problems should be added. Discuss which barriers cause you the greatest difficulties.

INTRODUCTION TO *THE IMAGE*

Kenneth E. Boulding

As I sit at my desk, I know where I am. I see before me a window; beyond that some trees; beyond that the red roofs of the campus of Stanford University; beyond them the trees and the roof tops which mark the town of Palo Alto; beyond them the bare golden hills of the Hamilton Range. I know, however, more than I see. Behind me, although I am not looking in that direction, I know there is a window, and beyond that the little campus of the Center for the Advanced Study in the Behavioral Sciences; beyond that the Coast Range; beyond that the Pacific Ocean. Looking ahead of me again, I know that beyond the mountains that close my present horizon, there is a broad valley; beyond that a still higher range of mountains; beyond that other mountains, range upon range, until we come to the Rockies; beyond that the Great Plains and the Mississippi; beyond that the Alleghenies; beyond that the eastern seaboard; beyond that the Atlantic Ocean; beyond that is Europe; beyond that is Asia. I know, furthermore, that if I go far enough I will come back to where I am now. In other words, I have a picture of the earth as round. I visualize it as a globe. I am a little hazy on some of the details. I am not quite sure, for instance, whether Tanganyika is north or south of Nyasaland. I probably could not draw a very good map of Indonesia, but I have a fair idea where everything is located on the face of this globe. Looking further, I visualize the globe as a small speck circling around a bright star which is the sun, in the company of many other similar specks, the planets. Looking still further, I see our star the sun as a member of millions upon millions of others in the Galaxy. Looking still further, I visualize the Galaxy as one of millions upon millions of others in the universe.

I am not only located in space, I am located in time. I know that I came to California about a year ago, and I am leaving it in about three weeks. I know that I have lived in a number of different places at different times. I know that about ten years ago a great war came to an end, that about forty years ago another great war came to an end. Certain dates are meaningful: 1776, 1620, 1066. I have a picture in my mind of the formation of the earth, of the long history of geological time, of the brief history of man. The great civilizations pass before my mental screen. Many of the images are vague, but Greece follows Crete, Rome follows Assyria.

I am not only located in space and time, I am located in a field of personal relations. I not only know where and when I am, I know to some extent who I am. I am a professor at a great state university. This means that in September I shall go into a classroom and expect to find some students in it and begin to talk to them, and nobody will be surprised. I expect, what is perhaps even more agreeable, that regular salary checks will arrive from the university. I expect that when I open my mouth on certain occasions people will listen. I know, furthermore, that I am a husband and a father, that there are people who will respond to me affectionately and to whom I will respond in like manner. I know, also, that I have friends, that there are houses here, there, and everywhere into which I may go and I will be welcomed and recognized and received as a guest. I belong to many societies. There are places into which I go, and it will be recognized that I am expected to behave in a certain manner. I may sit down to worship, I may make a speech, I may listen to a concert, I may do all sorts of things.

I am not only located in space and in time and in personal relationships, I am also located in the world of nature, in a world of how things operate. I know that when I get into my car there are some things I must do to start it; some things I must do to back out of the parking lot; some things I must do to drive home. I know that if I jump off a high place I will probably hurt myself. I know that there are some things that would probably not be good for me to eat or to drink. I know certain precautions that are advisable to take to maintain good health. I know that if I lean too far backward in my chair as I sit here at my desk, I will probably fall over. I live, in other words, in a world of reasonably stable relationships, a world of "ifs" and "thens," of "if I do this, then that will happen."

Finally, I am located in the midst of a world of subtle intimations and emotions. I am sometimes elated, sometimes a little depressed, sometimes happy, sometimes sad, sometimes inspired, sometimes pedantic. I am open to subtle intimations of a presence beyond the world of space and time and sense.

What I have been talking about is knowledge. Knowledge, perhaps, is not a good word for this. Perhaps one would rather say my *Image* of the world. Knowledge has an implication of validity, of truth. What I am talking about is what I believe to be true: my subjective knowledge. It is this Image that largely governs my behavior. In about an hour I shall rise, leave my office, go to a car, drive down to my home, play with the children, have supper, perhaps read a book, go to bed. I can predict this behavior with a fair degree of accuracy because of the knowledge which I have: the knowledge that I have a home not far away, to which I am accustomed to go. The prediction, of course, may not be fulfilled. There may be an earthquake, I may have an accident with the car on the way home, I may get home to find that my family has been suddenly called away. A hundred and one things may happen. As each event occurs, however, it alters my knowledge structure or my image. And as it alters my image, I behave accordingly. *The first proposition of this work, therefore, is that behavior depends on the image.*

What, however, determines the image? This is the central question of this work. It is not a question which can be answered by it. Nevertheless, such answers as I shall give will be quite fundamental to the understanding of how both life and society really operate. One thing is clear. The image is built up as a result of all past experience of the possessor of the image.

Part of the image is the history of the image itself. At one stage the image, I suppose, consists of little else than an undifferentiated blur and movement. From the moment of birth if not before, there is a constant stream of messages entering the organism from the senses. At first, these may merely be undifferentiated lights and noises. As the child grows, however, they gradually become distinguished into people and objects. He begins to perceive himself as an object in the midst of a world of objects. The conscious image has begun. In infancy the world is a house and, perhaps, a few streets or a park. As the child grows his image of the world expands. He sees himself in a town, a country, on a planet. He finds himself in an increasingly complex web of personal relationships. Every time a message reaches him his image is likely to be changed in some degree by it, and as his image is changed his behavior patterns will be changed likewise.

We must distinguish carefully between the image and the messages that reach it. The messages consist of *information* in the sense that they are structured experiences. *The meaning of a message is the change which it produces in the image.*

When a message hits an image one of three things can happen. In the first place, the image may remain unaffected. If we think of the image as a rather loose structure, something like a molecule, we may imagine that the message is going straight through without hitting it. The great majority of messages is of this kind. I am receiving messages all the time, for instance, from my eyes and my ears as I sit at my desk, but these messages are ignored by me. There is, for instance, a noise of carpenters working. I know, however, that a building is being built nearby and the fact that I now hear this noise does not add to this image. Indeed, I do not hear the noise at all if I am not listening for it, as I have become so accustomed to it. If the noise stops, however, I notice it. This information changes my image of the universe. I realize that it is now five o'clock, and it is time for me to go home. The message has called my attention, as it were, to my position in time, and I have re-evaluated this position. This is the second possible effect or impact of a message on an image. It may change the image in some rather regular and well-defined way that might be described as simple addition. Suppose, for instance, to revert to an earlier illustration, I look at an atlas and find out exactly the relation of Nyasaland to Tanganyika. I will have added to my knowledge, or my image; I will not, however, have very fundamentally revised it. I still picture the world much as I had pictured it before. Something that was a little vague before is now clearer.

There is, however, a third type of change of the image which might be described as a revolutionary change. Sometimes a message hits some sort of nucleus or supporting structure in the image, and the whole thing changes in a quite radical way. A spectacular instance of such a change is conversion. A man, for instance, may think himself a pretty good fellow and then may hear a preacher who convinces him that, in fact, his life is worthless and shallow, as he is at present living it. The words of the preacher cause a radical reformulation of the man's image of himself in the world, and his behavior changes accordingly. The psychologist may say, of course, that these changes are smaller than they appear, that there is a great mass of the unconscious which does not change, and that the relatively small change in behavior which so often follows intellectual conversion is a testimony to this fact. Nevertheless, the phenomenon of reorganization of the image is an important one, and it occurs to all of us and in ways that are much less spectacular than conversion.

The sudden and dramatic nature of these reorganizations is perhaps a result of the fact that our image is in itself resistant to change. When it receives messages which conflict with it, its first impulse is to reject them as in some sense untrue. Suppose, for instance, that somebody tells us something which is inconsistent with our picture of a certain person. Our first impulse is to reject the proffered information as false. As we continue to receive messages which contradict our image, however, we begin to have doubts, and then one day we receive a message which overthrows our previous image and we revise it completely. The person, for instance, whom we saw as a trusted friend is now seen to be a hypocrite and a deceiver.

Occasionally, things that we see, or read, or hear, revise our conceptions of space and time, or of relationships. I have recently read, for instance, Vasiliev's *History of the Byzantine Empire*. As a result of reading this book I have considerably revised my image of at least a thousand years of history. I had not given the matter a great deal of thought before, but I suppose if I had been questioned on my view of the period, I would have said that Rome fell in the fifth century and that it was succeeded by a little-known empire centering in Constantinople and a confused medley of tribes, invasions, and successor states. I now see that Rome did not fall, that in a sense it merely faded away, that the history of the Roman Empire and of Byzantium is continuous, and that from the time of its greatest extent the Roman Empire lost one piece after another until only Constantinople was left; and then in 1453 that went. There are books, some of them rather bad books, after which the world is never quite the same again. Veblen, for instance, was not, I think, a great social scientist, and yet he invented an undying phrase: "conspicuous consumption." After reading Veblen, one can never quite see a university campus or an elaborate house in just the same light as before. In a similar vein, David Riesman's division of humanity into inner-directed and other-directed people is no doubt open to serious criticism by the methodologists. Nevertheless, after reading Riesman one has a rather new view of the universe and one looks in one's friends and acquaintances for signs of inner-direction or other-direction.

One should perhaps add a fourth possible impact of the messages on the image. The image has a certain dimension, or quality, of certainty or uncertainty, probability or improbability, clarity or vagueness. Our image of the world is not uniformly certain, uniformly probable, or uniformly clear. Messages, therefore, may have the effect not only of adding to or of reorganizing the image. They may also have the effect of clarifying it, that is, of making something which previously was regarded as less certain more certain, or something which was previously seen in a vague way, clearer.

Messages may also have the contrary effect. They may introduce doubt or uncertainty into the image. For instance, the noise of carpenters has just stopped, but my watch tells me it is about four-thirty. This has thrown a certain amount of confusion into my mental image. I was under the impression that the carpenters stopped work at five o'clock. Here is a message which contradicts that impression. What am I to believe? Unfortunately, there are two possible ways of integrating the message into my image. I can believe that I was mistaken in thinking that the carpenters left work at five o'clock and that in fact their day ends at four-thirty. Or, I can believe that my watch is wrong. Either of these two modifications of my image gives meaning to the message. I shall not know for certain which is the right one, however, until I have an opportunity of comparing my watch with a timepiece or with some other source of time which I regard as being more reliable.

The impact of messages on the certainty of the image is of great importance in the interpretation of human behavior. Images of the future must be held with a degree of uncertainty, and as time passes and as the images become closer to the present, the messages that we receive inevitably modify them, both as to content and as to certainty.

The subjective knowledge structure or image of any individual or organization consists not only of images of "fact" but also images of "value." We shall subject the concept of a "fact" to severe scrutiny in the course of the discussion. In the meantime, however, it is clear that there is a certain difference between the image which I have of physical objects in space and time and the valuations which I put on these objects or on the events which concern them. It is clear that there is a certain difference between, shall we say, my image of Stanford University existing at a certain point in space and time, and my image of the value of Stanford University. If I say "Stanford University is in California," this is rather different from the statement "Stanford University is a good university, or is a better university than X, or a worse university than Y." The latter statements concern my image of values, and although I shall argue that the process by which we obtain an image of values is not very different from the process whereby we obtain an image of fact, there is clearly a certain difference between them.

The image of value is concerned with the *rating* of the various parts of our image of the world, according to some scale of betterness or worseness. We, all of us, possess one or more of these scales. It is what the economists call a welfare function. It does not extend over the whole universe. We do not now, for instance, generally regard Jupiter as a better planet than Saturn. Over that part of the universe which is closest to ourselves, however, we all erect these scales of valuation. Moreover, we change these scales of valuation in response to messages received much as we change our image of the world around us. It is almost certain that most people possess not merely one scale of valuation but many scales for different purposes. For instance, we may say A is better than B for me but worse for the country, or it is better for the country but worse for the world at large. The notion of a hierarchy of scales is very important in determining the effect of messages on the scales themselves.

One of the most important propositions of this theory is that the value scales of any individual or organization are perhaps the most important single element determining the effect of the messages it receives on its image of the world. If a message is perceived that is neither good nor bad it may have little or no effect on the image. If it is perceived as bad or hostile to the image which is held, there will be resistance to accepting it. This resistance is not usually infinite. An often repeated message or a message which comes with unusual force or authority is able to penetrate the resistance and will be able to alter the image. A devout Moslem, for instance, whose whole life has been built around the observance of the precepts of the Koran will resist vigorously any message which tends to throw doubt on the authority of his sacred work. The resistance may take the form of simply ignoring the message, or it may take the form of emotive response: anger, hostility, indignation. In the same way, a "devout" psychologist will resist strongly any evidence presented in favor of extrasensory perception, because to accept it would overthrow his whole image of the universe. If the resistances are very strong, it may take very strong, or often repeated, messages to penetrate them, and when they are penetrated, the effect is a realignment or reorganization of the whole knowledge structure.

On the other hand, messages which are favorable to the existing image of the world are received easily and even though they may make minor modifications of the knowledge structure, there will not be any fundamental reorganization. Such messages either will make no impact on the knowledge structure or their impact will be one of rather simple addition or accretion. Such messages may also have the effect of increasing the stability, that is to say, the resistance to unfavorable messages, which the knowledge structure or image possesses.

The stability or resistance to change of a knowledge structure also depends on its internal consistency and arrangement. There seems to be some kind of principle of minimization of internal strain at work which makes some images stable and others unstable for purely internal reasons. In the same way, some crystals or molecules are more stable than others because of the minimization of internal strain. It must be emphasized that it is not merely logical consistency which gives rise to internal cohesiveness of a knowledge structure, although this is an important element. There are important qualities of a nonlogical nature which also give rise to stability. The structure may, for instance, have certain aesthetic relationships among the parts. It may represent or justify a way of life or have certain consequences which are highly regarded in the value system, and so on. Even in mathematics, which is of all knowledge structures the one whose internal consistency is most due to logic, is not devoid of these nonlogical elements. In the acceptance of mathematical arguments by mathematicians there are important criteria of elegance, beauty, and simplicity which contribute toward the stability of these structures.

Even at the level of simple or supposedly simple sense perception we are increasingly discovering that the message which comes through the senses is itself mediated through a value system. We do not perceive our sense data raw; they are mediated through a highly learned process of interpretation and acceptance. When an object apparently increases in size on the retina of the eye, we interpret this not as an increase in size but as movement. Indeed, we only get along in the world because we consistently and persistently disbelieve the plain evidence of our senses. The stick in water is not bent; the movie is not a succession of still pictures; and so on.

What this means is that for any individual organism or organization, there are no such things as "facts." There are only messages filtered through a changeable value system. This statement may sound rather startling. It is inherent, however, in the view which I have been propounding. This does not mean, however, that the image of the world possessed by an individual is a purely private matter or that all knowledge is simply subjective knowledge, in the sense in which I have used the word. Part of our image of the world is the belief that this image is shared by other people like ourselves who also are part of our image of the world. In common daily intercourse we all behave as if we possess roughly the same image of the world. If a group of people are in a room together, their behavior clearly shows that they all think they are in the same room. It is this shared image which is "public" knowledge as opposed to "private" knowledge. It follows, however, from the argument above that if a group of people are to share the same image of the world, or to put it more exactly, if the various images of the world which they have are to be roughly identical, and if this group of people are exposed to much the same set of messages in building up images of the world, the value systems of all individuals must be approximately the same.

The problem is made still more complicated by the fact that a group of individuals does not merely share messages which come to them from "nature." They also initiate and receive messages themselves. This is the characteristic which distinguishes man from the lower organisms—the art of conversation or discourse. The human organism is capable not only of having an image of the world, but of talking about it. This is the extraordinary gift of language. A group of dogs in a pack pursuing a stray cat clearly share an image of the world in the sense that each is aware to some degree of the situation which they are all in, and is likewise aware of his neighbors. When the chase is over, however, they do not, as far as we know, sit around and talk about it and say, "Wasn't that a fine chase?" or, "Isn't it too bad the cat got away?" or even, "Next time you ought to go that way and I'll go this way and we can corner it." It is discourse or conversation which makes the human image public in a way that the image of no lower animal can possibly be. The term, "universe of discourse" has been used to describe the growth and development of common images in conversation and linguistic intercourse. There are, of course, many such universes of discourse, and although it is a little awkward to speak of many universes, the term is well enough accepted so that we may let it stay.

Where there is no universe of discourse, where the image possessed by the organism is purely private and cannot be communicated to anyone else, we say that the person is mad (to use a somewhat old-fashioned term). It must not be forgotten, however, that the discourse must be received as well as given, and that whether it is received or not depends upon the value system of the recipient. This means that insanity is defined differently from one culture to another because of these differences in value systems and that the schizophrenic of one culture may well be the shaman or the prophet of another.

Up to now I have sidestepped and I will continue to sidestep the great philosophical arguments of epistemology. I have talked about the image. I have maintained that images can be public as well as private, but I have not discussed the question as to whether images are *true* and how we know whether they are true. Most epistemological systems seek some philosopher's stone by which statements may be tested in order to determine their "truth," that is, their correspondence to outside reality. I do not claim to have any such philosopher's stone, not even the touchstone of science. I have, of course, a great respect for science and scientific method —for careful observation, for planned experience, for the testing of hypotheses and for as much objectivity as semirational beings like ourselves can hope to achieve. In my theoretical system, however, the scientific method merely stands as one among many of the methods whereby images change and develop. The development of images is part of the culture or the subculture in which they are developed, and it depends upon all the elements of that culture or subculture. Science is a subculture among subcultures. It can claim to be useful. It may claim rather more dubiously to be good. It cannot claim to give validity.

In summation, then, my theory might well be called an organic theory of knowledge. Its most fundamental proposition is that knowledge is what somebody or something knows, and that without a knower, knowledge is an absurdity. Moreover, I argue that the growth of knowledge is the growth of an "organic" structure. I am not suggesting here that knowledge is simply an arrangement of neuronal circuits or brain cells, or something of that kind. On the question of the relation between the physical and chemical structure of an organism and its knowledge structure, I am quite prepared to be agnostic. It is, of course, an article of faith among physical scientists that there must be somewhere a one-to-one correspondence between the structures of the physical body and the structures of knowledge. Up to now, there is nothing like empirical proof or even very good evidence for this hypothesis. Indeed, what we know about the brain suggests that it is an extraordinarily unspecialized and, in a sense, unstructured object; and that if there is a physical and chemical structure corresponding to the knowledge structure, it must be of a kind which at present we do not understand. It may be, indeed, that the correspondence between physical structure and mental structure is something that we will never be able to determine because of a sort of "Heisenberg principle" in the investigation of these matters. If the act of observation destroys the thing observed, it is clear that there is a fundamental obstacle to the growth of knowledge in that direction.

All these considerations, however, are not fundamental to my position. We do not have to conceive of the knowledge structure as a physicochemical structure in order to use it in our theoretical construct. It can be inferred from the behavior of the organism just as we constantly infer the images of the world which are possessed by those around us from the messages which they transmit to us. When I say that knowledge is an organic structure, I mean that it follows principles of growth and development similar to those with which we are familiar in complex organizations and organisms. In every organism or organization there are both internal and external factors affecting growth. Growth takes place through a kind of metabolism. Even in the case of knowledge structures, we have a certain intake and output of messages. In the knowledge structure, however, there are important violations of the laws of conservation. The accumulation of knowledge is not merely the difference between messages taken in and messages given out. It is not like a reservoir; it is rather an organization which grows through an active internal organizing principle much as the gene is a principle or entity organizing the growth of bodily structures. The gene, even in the physico-chemical sense may be thought of as an inward teacher imposing its own form and "will" on the less formed matter around it. In the growth of images, also, we may suppose similar models. Knowledge grows also because of inward teachers as well as outward messages. As every good teacher knows, the business of teaching is not that of penetrating the student's defenses with the violence or loudness of the teacher's messages. It is, rather, that of co-operating with the student's own inward teacher whereby the student's image may grow in conformity with that of his outward teacher. The existence of public knowledge depends, therefore, on certain basic similarities among men. It is literally because we are of one "blood," that is, genetic constitution, that we are able to communicate with each other. We cannot talk to the ants or bees; we cannot hold conversations with them, although in a very real sense they communicate to us. It is the purpose of this work, therefore, to discuss the growth of images, both private and public, in individuals, in organizations, in society at large, and even, with some trepidation, among the lower forms of life. Only thus can we develop a really adequate theory of behavior.

COMMUNICATION: THE CONTEXT OF CHANGE

Dean C. Barnlund

Among the few universals that apply to man is this: That all men—no matter of what time or place, of what talent or temperament, of what race or rank—are continually engaged in making sense out of the world about them. Man, according to Nicholas Hobbs, "has to build defenses against the absurd in the human condition and at the same time find a scheme that will make possible reasonably accurate predictions of his own behavior and of the behavior of his wife, his boss, his professor, his physician, his neighbor, and of the policeman on the corner."[1] Although men may tolerate doubt, few can tolerate meaninglessness.

To survive psychically, man must conceive a world that is fairly stable, relatively free of ambiguity, and reasonably predictable. Some structure must be placed on the flow of impressions; events must be viewed from some perspective. Incoming sensations will be categorized, organized around some theme. Some facts will be noted and others neglected; some features will be emphasized and others minimized; certain relationships will appear reasonable, others unlikely or impossible. Meaning does not arise until experience is placed in some context.

Man is not a passive receptor, but an active agent in giving sense to sensation. The significance that any situation acquires is as much a result of what the perceiver brings to it as it is of the raw materials he finds there. Terms such as "personal constructs," "social schema," or "perceptual sets" have been used to identify the cognitive processes by which men render experience intelligible. As George Kelly notes, "Man looks at this world through transparent patterns or templets which he created and then attempted to fit over the realities of which the world is composed. The fit is not always good. But without such patterns the world appears to be such an undifferentiated homogeneity that man is unable to make any sense out of it. Even a poor fit is more helpful to him than nothing at all."[2]

As the infant matures into adulthood he gradually acquires a picture of the world he inhabits and his place within it. Pervasive orientations—of trust or suspicion, of affection or hostility—are learned early, often at considerable pain, and through communication with significant other people. Every success or failure contributes in some way to his accumulating assumptions about the world and how it operates. Such cognitive predisposi-

From Dean C. Barnlund, "Communication: The Context of Change," Carl E. Larson and Frank E. X. Dance, eds., *Perspectives on Communication*, Shorewood, Wis.: Helix Press, 1968, pp. 24–40. Reprinted by permission of the publisher.

[1] Nicholas Hobbs, "Sources of Gain in Psychotherapy," *American Psychologist*, (17, 1962), 74.

[2] George A. Kelly, *The Psychology of Personal Constructs* (New York: W. W. Norton, 1955), 8–9.

tions are learned unconsciously, and most people are only vaguely aware of their profound effects. Yet they are, in the view of Roger Harrison, "the most important survival equipment we have."[3] Thus it is not events themselves, but how men construe events, that determines what they will see, how they will feel, what they will think, and how they will respond.

Such perceptual biases, taken together, constitute what has been called the assumptive world of the individual. The world men get inside their heads is the only world they know. It is this symbolic world, not the real world, that they talk about, fight about, argue about, laugh about. It is this world that drives them to cooperate or compete, to love or hate. Unless this symbolic world is kept open and responsive to continuing experience, men are forced to live out their lives imprisoned within the constructs of their own invention.

The worlds men create for themselves are distinctive worlds, not the same world. Out of similar raw materials each fabricates meanings according to the dictates of his own perceptual priorities. It is not surprising that nurtured in different families, informed by different sources, frightened by different dreams, inspired by different teachers, rewarded for different virtues, men should view the world so differently. The way men project private significance into the world can be readily illustrated. Here is a group of people asked to respond to an ordinary photograph showing adults of various ages, standing together, and looking up at a distant object. The experimenter asks, "What do you see?" "What does it mean?" Some of the viewers comment on the mood of the figures, reporting "grief," "hope," "inspiration," or "despair." Others notice the identity of the persons, describing them as "peasants," "members of a minority," "Mexicans," or "Russians." Still others see the "ages of man," a "worshipping family," or "three generations." Even at the objective level there is disagreement; some report three persons, some four, some five. When shown before lunch "hunger" is one of the first interpretations; after lunch this meaning is never assigned. A similar process of projection would seem to fit the varying reactions people have to a peace demonstration, Charles de Gaulle, a labor contract, the Hippies, or the Pill.

Two behavioral scientists, Hastorf and Cantril, studied the conflicting reactions of Princeton and Dartmouth students to a hotly contested game between their football teams. The students seemed not to have attended the same game, their perceptions were subservient to their personal loyalties. The investigators conclude: "It is inaccurate and misleading to say that different people have different attitudes toward the same 'thing.' " For the 'thing' is *not* the same for different people whether the 'thing' is a football game, a presidential candidate, Communism, or spinach. . . . We behave according to what we bring to the occasion, and what each of us brings to the occasion is more or less unique. And except for these significances which we bring to the occasion, the happenings around us would be meaningless occurrences, would be 'inconsequential.' "[4]

[3]Roger Harrison, "Defenses and the Need to Know," in Paul Lawrence and George V. Seiler, *Organizational Behavior and Administration* (Homewood, Illinois: Irwin and Dorsey), 267.

[4]Albert Hastorf and Hadley Cantril, "They Saw a Game: A Case Study," *Journal of Abnormal and Social Psychology*, (49, 1954), 129–134.

While we are continually engaged in an effort after meaning, every perception is necessarily a private and incomplete one. No one ever sees all, for each abstracts in accordance with his past experience and emerging needs. Where men construe events similarly, they can expect to understand and agree readily; where they construe events differently, agreement is more difficult. In exploring the impact of cognitive styles upon communication, Triandis found that pairs of subjects who categorized objects similarly communicated more effectively than those who categorized them differently.[5]

Paradoxically, it is these differences in perception that make communication inevitable. If men saw the same facts in the same way, there would be no reason to talk at all. Certain rituals of recognition or flattery might interrupt the silence, but there would be no occasion for serious talk. There would be no experiences to share, no conflicts to negotiate. A simple experiment will demonstrate this idea. At the next conversational opportunity, agree completely, both in fact and feeling, with the person who has just expressed an opinion. (This is more difficult than many people imagine.) In a matter of seconds following this restatement, the conversation will grind to a halt, or someone will change the subject. The reason is clear: Where men see and feel alike there is nothing to share. Talk is primarily a means of confronting and exploring differences. Conversation moves from disagreement to disagreement, interrupted only occasionally to note areas of momentary concurrence.

It is not only inevitable that men communicate, but fortunate that they do so. The exposure to differences through communication, painful as it sometimes is, provides the only opportunity to test our private perceptions, to construct a total picture out of our separate visions, and to find new ways of negotiating unresolved problems.

Research on decision making illustrates how important communication is in improving human performance. Subjects in one of these studies solved a set of problems working alone, then through majority vote, and finally by discussing them in small groups.[6] The problems resembled those in everyday life; that is, they were difficult, emotionally involving, and presented a range of possible solutions. The results indicated that voting did not improve the quality of solutions reached by solitary effort, but group decisions were clearly superior to individual decisions. In some instances, groups of the least competent subjects were, through discussion, able to surpass the decisions made by the most talented person working alone. Subsequent research using executives in labor, government, education, and business confirmed these findings. Even groups composed of persons who were unable to solve *any* of the problems by themselves, made better group decisions than the most effective person working alone. That is, administrators with no ability to solve the test problems by themselves showed superior judgment when allowed to confer. Maximizing communicative opportunity produced superior judgments.

[5] Harry Triandis, "Cognitive Similarity and Communication in a Dyad," *Human Relations*, (13, 1969), 175–183.

[6] Dean C. Barnlund, "A Comparative Study of Individual, Majority and Group Judgment," *Journal of Abnormal and Social Psychology*, (58, 1959), 55–60.

How can we account for these results? Careful study of the recorded conversations revealed a number of contributing factors: Groups had a wider range of information so that each person benefited from the knowledge of others. Every person had his own view of the problem, and sharing these perspectives enlarged the number of possible approaches. More solutions were proposed in the groups, supplying more alternatives from which to choose. The different biases of participants prevented any subject from suffering the consequences of his own prejudices. Finally, sharing opinions led to more critical examination of proposals. Where persons worked alone they could remain blind to their own errors, but groups quickly identified mistakes that would lead to wrong decisions.

After finishing the analysis, one further question arose: Why were the groups not infallible? Although this smacked of asking why men are not perfect, the question led to new findings. Two conditions accounted for most of the group errors. In some cases the groups lacked conflict, and, assuming that unanimity proved they were correct, did not discuss the problem. In others, despite the occurrence of conflict, the subjects lacked the patience or skill to resolve it, and compromised to avoid interpersonal antagonism. The absence of conflict or the inability to explore it prevented communication and thereby diminished the quality of decisions. In the vocabulary of science, communication among mature persons may be a necessary if not a sufficient condition for personal growth and social progress.

What, then, prevents men from transforming their differences into agreements? Why are facts so often distorted and disputed? What inhibits the flow of new ideas? What produces friction? Why is there so often an undercurrent of resistance when men talk? It is, I believe, because communication nearly always implies change. Aside from common social rituals, *men nearly always talk in a context of change*. What prompts communication is the desire for someone else to see our facts, appreciate our values, share our feelings, accept our decisions. Communication is initiated, consciously or unconsciously, to change the other person. If difference is the raw material of conversation, influence is its intent.

For most people, change is theatening. It is the old and familiar that is trusted; the novel and unknown that arouses alarm. "No one," John Dewey once wrote, "discovers a new world without forsaking an old one."[7] To change is to give up cherished values, to be left defenseless and forced to assume responsibility for a new organization of experience. The degree to which fear is aroused is usually proportional to the extent to which core values are placed in question. In some cases the fears may be quite specific, and can be articulated. More commonly, the threatened person is unable to identify the reason for his anxiety. Ordinarily threat arises from the source, the content, or the manner of communicating.

The mere presence of some people produces tension. Persons who are superior in age, power, wealth, appearance, esteem may create apprehension. Secretaries and lathe operators, medical interns and practice teachers are often incapable of accurate work while supervisors are observing their

[7]John Dewey, *Experience and Nature* (Chicago: Open Court Publishing Company, 1925), 246.

performance. There is evidence that people who control the destiny of others, such as parents, teachers, supervisors, provoke ego defensive reactions, quite apart from what they may say. The same seems to be the case for those who interrupt or reverse the direction of self-growth.[8] Threatening people, Landfield found, are those who perceive us as we once were, or now are and no longer wish to be.[9] Even status signs—the policeman's uniform, the judge's gavel, the executive's desk, the physician's stethoscope, the psychologist's tests—can arouse fear before or during interpersonal encounters. The presence of threat, of course, affects the depth and accuracy of communication. A number of studies demonstrate that where superiors are feared, information is withheld or distorted.[10] Thus where human institutions proliferate status differences or personal habits aggravate them, communication may be more difficult because of the repressive context in which it occurs.

The substance of communication, that is, the subject being discussed, may also trigger defenses. A new fact tests an old fact; a new attitude challenges an existing one. New proposals may provoke fear of an unknown future, fear of possible failure, fear of loss of power or prestige. No matter how frustrating the present, its dangers are palpable and familiar. Time has permitted some adjustment to them. But to turn in new directions is to face a host of uncertainties. Even consideration of a new program implies an attack on those who created or support an existing program. "We tend to maintain our cognitive structures in relatively stable form," writes Joseph Precker, "and select and interact with those who do not attack these structures." When such encounters were unavoidable he found they aroused defensiveness or rejection of the attacker.[11] Any new or unassimilated thought challenges the assumptions on which behavior is based, and no one is so secure that he cannot be aroused at the thought of revising favored values. Thus, even where people are not initially hostile and try to avoid unnecessary friction, the topic, because of its emotional significance, may trigger resistance.

Beyond the source and content lies the manner in which men talk. One cannot separate who is speaking and what is talked about from the way differences are expressed. Matter and manner interact to produce meaning. Although all men have their own rhetoric, preferring some interpersonal strategies to others, a number of techniques that complicate communication can be identified.[12] Since interpersonal attitudes are conveyed

[8]Jacob Hurwitz, Alvin Zander, and Bernard Hymovitch, "Some Effects of Power on the Relations Among Group Members," in D. Cartwright and A. Zander, *Group Dynamics: Research and Theory* (New York: Row Peterson, 1960).

[9]A. Landfield, "A Movement Interpretation of Threat," *Journal of Abnormal and Social Psychology*, (49, 1954), 529–532.

[10]See, for example, John Thibaut and Henry Riecken, "Authoritarianism, Status, and the Communication of Aggression," *Human Relations*, (8, 1955), 113–133; Arthur Cohen, "Upward Communication in Experimentally Created Hierarchies," *Human Relations*, (11, 1958), 41–53; William Read, "Upward Communication in Industrial Hierarchies," *Human Relations*, (15, 1962), 3–16.

[11]Joseph Precker, "The Automorphic Process and the Attribution of Values," *Journal of Personality*, (21, 1953), 356–363.

[12]Efforts to identify nonfacilitating techniques may be found in Jack Gibb, "Defensive Communication," *Journal of Communication*, (11, 1961), 141–148; in Frank

both by verbal and nonverbal codes, any discrepancy in these codes may be regarded as a warning signal. Warm words are spoken in a cold voice. Frank statements are offset by calculating glances. Expressions of respect are contradicted with every interruption. Against the deceit that is evident in a confusion of codes, men become apprehensive and guarded in their own messages.

An attitude of infallibility discourages communication. The dogmatic assertion of difference leaves no opportunity for influence to move in both directions. Where men claim, "There is only one conclusion," "It all boils down to," "The only course of action is," there will be negligible exploration of differences. The person who is impervious to the words of others while demanding sympathetic consideration of his own denies his associates any significant role in communication. They are forced to disregard their experience, deny their feelings, censor their thoughts. Since unquestioned statements are untested statements, the dogmatic person appears to be more interested in triumph than in truth.

Messages that convey a manipulative purpose also subvert communication. A calculated use of argument, a carefully phrased idea, a solicitous manner, a restrained reaction, all indicate that someone is being maneuvered into a predetermined position. Sooner or later the manipulated recognizes his manipulator. He begins to feel regarded as an object, not as a person. He becomes suspicious, emotionally tense, and verbally devious himself. That the manipulator is sometimes unaware of his own desires to control others, does not reduce the threat he poses for them.

Information normally flows between communicants in both directions: The man who speaks also listens. But often, through deliberate design or personal preference, interaction is blocked so that one person sends all the messages, the other only receives them. The captain commands, the soldier obeys; the teacher lectures, the student takes notes. A letter from a friend who is an educational consultant in India illustrates how far it is possible to carry this kind of communicative irresponsibility. His daughter, raised in one of the great cattle provinces of Western Canada, is attending school in India.

> *Thora came home the other day doggedly repeating to herself, "A cow is a big animal with four legs and two horns. It is the most useful of all animals. The feet of the cow are called hoofs." I asked what she was doing, repeating this over and over again, and she replied that this was nature study and she had to memorize the cow. The teacher will not tolerate improvised replies, but the students must jump up smartly beside their desks and repeat exactly what was copied from the blackboard the day before. It sounds fantastic, but the end of the system is to stifle initiative, destroy creativity and engender a violent dislike for learning.*[13]

One-way communication implies, of course, that meanings in the nervous system of one person can be deposited in the nervous system of another.

Miyamoto, Laura Crowell, and Allan Katcher, "Communicant Behavior in Small Groups," *Journal of Communication*, (7, 1957), 151–160; and in Phillip Lichtenberg, "Emotional Maturity as Manifest in Ideational Interaction," *Journal of Abnormal and Social Psychology*, (51, 1955), 298–301.

[13]Personal correspondence.

Unfortunately communication is not this simple. Men differ not only in experience, but in their habits of speech as well. The only way to arrive at common meanings is through mutual accommodation. Each must share some responsibility for calibrating his words and intentions with the other.

Limiting communication to the sending of messages impoverishes the process and renders at least one participant impotent. Studies by Leavitt and Mueller illustrate some of the difficulties that attend one-way communication.[14] Persons attempting to give even the simplest instructions found their orders were inaccurately executed, that errors of interpretation could not be corrected, and that this condition produced extremely low morale. It is not difficult to estimate the cause of the low morale: For someone to receive confusing or complicated information and to be unable to clarify it, especially when it affects his performance or status, can be unnerving. Since all messages are ambiguous in some respect, cutting off efforts to confirm their meaning leaves the receiver without protection in a potentially punishing situation.

A threatening atmosphere is probable, also, in encounters in which one of the communicants maintains considerable emotional distance. The person who is coldly objective or who refuses to disclose his own feelings is likely to be viewed with suspicion. To be treated as a set of facts or as a problem to be solved, rather than as a human being, seldom contributes to interpersonal rapport. Such emotional distancing creates, to use a phrase of Martin Buber's, an I-It rather than an I-Thou relation. One is not likely to approach or expose himself to an unresponsive façade. It is safer to remain on guard in the company of those who are themselves guarded. Any verbal indiscretion or spontaneous revelation may give an advantage or be used against one. As interaction continues, participants draw farther and farther apart from any real confrontation with their differences.

The most familiar form of threat is found in a highly evaluative communication context. There is continual appraisal. Remarks are judged rather than understood. Conversation becomes cross-examination. Criticism may be given directly through attack, or indirectly through sarcasm or innuendo. (The latter, because of its ambiguity, is far harder to handle.) Compliments seem only slightly less corrupting than insults, for in one case the receiver modifies his behavior to gain further rewards and in the other to avoid further punishments. In either case he is encouraged to distort his judgment. It becomes hazardous to be honest, to be open, to be original. Ideas are suppressed and remarks tailored to fit the expectations of others. The result is to diminish honest contribution to the conversation, and to isolate men from their own experience.

A more subtle form of threat occurs when conversation is converted into a struggle over identity. At one level, talk flows around a common interest or problem; at another, communication becomes a competition for status. Participants present their credentials and challenge those of others. In organizational life these claims relate to the respective power, intelligence, skill, or rank of the communicants. But even in ordinary en-

[14]Harold Leavitt and Ronald Mueller, "Some Effects of Feedback on Communication," *Human Relations*, (4, 1951), 401–410.

counters, men verbally compete to determine who is in better physical condition, who has the more talented children, who can consume more alcohol, or who is more attractive to the opposite sex. Communication becomes an occasion for asserting and validating personal identity rather than for testing what we know. Status-reminding phrases, such as "I've devoted years to this matter," "I've had much more experience," or "You wouldn't be able to appreciate," are likely to invite reaction in kind. "Once the 'proving' syndrome is present," according to Paul Goodman, "the boys are quite out of touch with the simplest realities."[15] People who constantly remind us of who they are and of who we are—especially when who they are is superior, and who we are is inferior—threaten the concept we have of ourselves. When identity is challenged, few have enough insight or strength to resist. What might have become a productive conversation turns in to an interaction of roles and of façades. Even the expression of affection can turn into a competitive affair:

> *"I love you," she said.*
> *"I adore you," he said.*
> *"I love you more," she said.*
> *"More than what?" he said.*
> *"Than you love me," she said.*
> *"Impossible," he said.*
> *"Don't argue," she said.*
> *"I was only . . ." he said.*
> *"Shut up," she said.*[16]

In short, the prospect of communication may threaten people for a number of reasons: because such interactions occur with persons endowed with considerable power and status; because the underlying purpose is to change perceptions that have personal significance; because the communicative approach prevents a full and sympathetic exploration of differences. Any one of these factors alone can produce an undercurrent of tension in human affairs; but in many instances all three combine to arouse deeper anxiety.

Through all there runs a common theme. Though manifested differently, there is always a challenge to the personal integrity and self-respect of the person in communication. To talk to some people is dangerous because they control what it is possible for us to be and do. To talk about some topics is hazardous for it exposes one to differences in attitude and feeling. To talk in some ways is disturbing for one must guard continually against being exposed and attacked. But it is at the intersection of all three that men are most vulnerable: where a sensitive topic must be discussed with a powerful person in an emotionally charged atmosphere.

During a lifetime of painful encounters people acquire an extensive repertoire of defensive strategies.[17] At low levels of stress men tend to

[15]Paul Goodman, *Growing Up Absurd* (New York: Random House, 1960), 206.

[16]John Ciardi, "Manner of Speaking," *Saturday Review*, (December 23, 1967).

[17]Men defend themselves intrapersonally as well as interpersonally. The principal forms of such inner defense—introjection, identification, repression, denial, regression, reaction-formation, displacement—will not be treated here. It is the character of defensive behavior in interpersonal relationships that is our major concern.

remain open to new facts, flexible in interpretation, creative in response. As the perceived threat increases, they narrow their vision, resist certain kinds of information, distort details to fit their own biases, even manufacture evidence to bolster their preconceptions. The old, whether appropriate or not, is favored over the new. Anxiety is aroused when a person, in encounters with others, confronts perceptions that are beyond his capacity to assimilate. As Gregory Bateson has suggested, "This is a terrifying moment . . . , you've been climbing up a ladder, you knew it was an unsound ladder and now you're asked to step off it and you don't really know there's going to be another ladder—even if the ladder you were on was a rather unsound one. This is terror."[18] Defenses protect the individual against facts that might otherwise undermine the system of assumptions that give stability and significance to his experience.

Not all defending behavior, of course, is defensive. Most men hold tentative conclusions about many issues. We believe that certain ways of looking at the world and at ourselves have some credibility. At any time we may voice these opinions. If, when confronted with opinions that differ from our own, we can explore these differences quietly, comfortably, thoroughly, and with the aim of testing the validity of our own beliefs, then we are only defending an opinion to reach more reliable conclusions. However, if when confronted with disagreement, we find it difficult to examine that thought or feeling, find the opposing view arousing us emotionally, find our hearts racing and our minds frantically seizing upon arguments, find we cannot reply calmly and without antagonism, the reaction is probably defensive. Words are being used to protect rather than to test private judgment.

Some defensive techniques are conscious; most of them are unconscious. Each person has his own hierarchy of tactics to which he retreats when faced with inadmissable perceptions. These defenses, provoked in a context of change, constitute the major barriers to communication among men. When attacked, as Paul Tournier notes, "Each of us does his best to hide behind a shield."

> *For one it is a mysterious silence which constitutes an impenetrable retreat. For another it is facile chit-chat so that we never seem to get near him. Or else, it is erudition, quotations, abstractions, theories, academic argument, technical jargon; or ready-made answers, trivialities, or sententious and patronizing advice. One hides behind his timidity, so that we cannot find anything to say to him; another behind a fine self-assurance which renders him less vulnerable. At one moment we have recourse to our intelligence, to help us to juggle with words. Later on we pretend to be stupid so that we cannot reply. . . . It is possible to hide behind one's advanced years, or behind one's university degree, one's political office, or the necessity of nursing one's reputation. A woman can hide behind her startling beauty, or behind her husband's notoriety; just as, indeed, a husband can hide behind his wife.*[19]

One of the principal forms of defense is to avoid communicative contact altogether. It is unlikely that anyone reading these words has not, on some occasion, deliberately avoided certain persons. It may have been a

[18] Gregory Bateson, Lecture at San Francisco State College, 1959.

[19] Paul Tournier, *The Meaning of Persons* (New York: Harper & Row, 1957), 219.

teacher, a parent, a supervisor, or, depending on circumstances, anyone with the ability to contradict, to embarrass, to attack us. Selective communication—Whites talking with Whites, Republicans with Republicans, Generation with Generation, Physicians with Physicians—greatly reduces the prospect of having to cope with discrepant or damaging points of view.

Even when contact cannot be avoided, it is possible to resist exposure by remaining silent. If a person does not speak he cannot expose himself or his judgments to public scrutiny. By retreating into his own private world he can remain untouched by the worlds of others. Theodore Newcomb has identified the process of communicative avoidance, whether of persons or topics, as "autistic hostility."[20] Confrontation is avoided to protect prevailing attitudes. In talking together people run the risk of understanding one another, hence of having to alter existing prejudices. Fraternizing with the enemy or socializing with competitors is traditionally avoided lest one become incapable of manipulating and mistreating them on other occasions.

A kind of psychic withdrawal is also possible. In this case the person never really presents himself as he is. According to Ronald Laing, "He never quite says what he means or means what he says. The part he plays is always not quite himself."[21] Where this withdrawal occurs, there is often an undercurrent of nonverbal signs that express defensive feelings. Recent research shows that people who wish to avoid communication choose to sit at a greater distance from others than those who wish to interact.[22] Tension-reducing body movements and gestures which serve no instrumental purpose increase.[23] Any act, from smoking a cigarette to doodling on a note pad, may reflect developing resistance. Research on mutual glances shows that eye contact is reduced when persons are in competitive, embarrassing, or critical encounters with others.[24] Thus many nonverbal indicators may convey the defensive attitudes of another person.

Just short of the verbal forms of resistance lies the noncommittal reply. Such phrases as "Uh-huh," "I guess so," "Maybe," and "Oh yeah," fill the void left by a preceding question, but reveal little of the thought or feeling of the respondent. They provide an escape route, for at the moment of utterance they convey only an ambiguous neutrality; later, according to the shifting intent of the speaker, they may be given a variety of meanings.

Yet men also talk to protect themselves from confronting differences. Words become a substitute for, rather than a means to, understanding. People spin verbal cocoons around themselves that disquieting ideas cannot penetrate. One person describes it this way: "If, for example, I can

[20]Theodore Newcomb, "Autistic Hostility and Social Reality," *Human Relations*, (1,1947), 69–86.

[21]Ronald Laing, *The Divided Self* (Chicago: Quadrangle, 1960).

[22]Howard Rosenfeld, "Effect of Approval-Seeking Induction on Interpersonal Proximity," *Psychological Reports*, (17, 1965), 120–122.

[23]Maurice Krout, "An Experimental Attempt to Determine the Significance of Unconscious Manual Symbolic Movements," *Journal of General Psychology*, (51, 1954), 121–152.

[24]Ralph Exline and Lewis Winters, "Affective Relations and Mutual Glances in Dyads," in S. Tomkins and C. Izard (eds.), *Affect, Cognition, and Personality* (New York: Springer, 1965).

talk at such an abstract level that few can determine what I am saying, then I must have high intelligence. This is especially true if no one can understand me. The reason I could not communicate was that I did not want to."[25] Men often talk compulsively, and through long and frequent repetitions leave others no chance to reflect on what was said, to explore their own reactions, or to answer objections. Opponents are overwhelmed and defeated in a rush of words. Sometimes this takes the form of counter-attacks, with the defensive person placing the burden of proof upon the opposition. By turning attention to others and exposing their weakness he hopes to hide his own vulnerability.

Conversational detours around painful topics are not uncommon. This may be done consciously, as in the case of the hostess who steers talk away from religious or political topics. More commonly it is done unconsciously by people who are unaware of the threat they seek to avoid. The essential point of a remark is disregarded, and some tangential or entirely new thought is introduced. Parents who fear discussing sex with their children, or supervisors who prefer not to know about critical failures of their subordinates, often rely upon topical control to neutralize communication. Each time a threatening or sensitive comment is made talk is turned abruptly in a new direction. Men have become so skillful at defensively diverting conversation into painless channels that some are able to avoid meaningful interaction on nearly every vital issue that touches their lives.

Men also hide from each other through communicating by formula. Talk is prompted not by inner necessity, but by social convention. Everyone is familiar with the meaningless phrases used in social greetings. But this same verbal game may be extended to cover more serious encounters. Phrases are uttered and repeated, but when examined turn out to be empty. Flattery substitutes for frankness. There is much moralizing and sloganizing. Instead of examining differences, communicants obscure them in large abstractions that permit a multitude of interpretations. A kind of double-talk preserves the illusion of confrontation while preventing it from ever occurring. There is often an interaction of roles rather than of persons. When people speak as parents, professors, as physicians, or as political candidates, listeners are likely to discount or mistrust much of what is said. Their remarks are seen as a consequence of their position, not of their personal experience. Of all the defenses, this currently seems most disruptive of efforts to reach across races and generations.

There is also the use of indirection. Instead of speaking frankly, men speak in double meanings. At the explicit level, one idea is transmitted; at the implicit level another idea, often the opposite. The most familiar forms include kidding and sarcasm. Humor, despite its high reputation as a form of recreational communication, often serves defensive and destructive ends. Verbal indirection is almost an unassailable stratagem, for anyone who takes the implied meaning seriously may be accused of projecting false interpretations of it. With a few oblique comments, efforts to openly explore differences may be totally blocked.

Defensive behavior is characteristic of some men all of the time, and

[25]Personal correspondence.

of all men some of the time. Everyone must build the house of his own consciousness to interpret events around him. It is this "personal cosmology" that stands between us and the unknown and unacceptable. With such a guidance system events become recognizable and comprehensible. Those who perceive reality of different terms—as everyone does—alarm us because they shake the stability of our system. Defenses, note Kahn and Cannell, "are designed in large part to help us to protect ourselves against making some undesirable revelation or against putting ourselves in an unfavorable light. They are man's methods of defending himself against the possibility of being made to look ridiculous or inadequate. And in most cases we are not content merely to avoid looking inadequate, we also want to appear intelligent, thoughtful, or in possession of whatever other virtues are relevant to the situation from our point of view."[26] Confronted with difference, men may deny it, obscure it, confuse it, or evade it in order to protect their own assumptive world against the meanings of others.

Unfortunately, to the extent that men insulate themselves from the worlds that others know, they are imprisoned within their own defenses. They become blind to the limits of their own knowledge, and incapable of incorporating new experience. They are forced to repeat the same old ways of thinking because they result from the same old ways of seeing. Interaction loses the significance it might have. "This shutup self, being isolated," writes Ronald Laing, "is unable to be enriched by outer experience, and so the whole inner world comes to be more and more impoverished, until the individual may come to feel he is merely a vacuum."[27] Without access to the experience and perceptions of others, the individual deprives himself of the raw material of growth. Defenses corrupt the only process by which we might extend and deepen our experience. Until we can hear what others say, we cannot grow wiser ourselves.

To appreciate the full significance of incomplete communication in organizational life, another factor must be added. It is this: The higher men rise, the fewer the problems with which they have direct contact, and the more they must rely on the words of others. Unfortunately, as men assume greater power their higher status increases the difficulty in obtaining reliable accounts from others, and increases their own capacity to shield themselves from unpleasant information. Given a superior who prefers reassurance and a subordinate who fears to speak out, there is every reason to expect censored and distorted reports. Yet it is imperative that those in high places cope with realities rather than defensive fantasies.

What, then, can be done to create conditions in which men are not afraid to communicate? How can the destructive cycle of threat and defense be broken? Are there conditions that encourage men to respond to each other more creatively, so that differences can widen and deepen human experience? Can self-protective encounters be converted into self-enriching ones?

To reduce defenses, threat must be reduced. Such threats, as sug-

[26]Robert Kahn and Charles Cannell, *The Dynamics of Interviewing* (New York: Wiley, 1957), 6.

[27]Laing, *op. cit.*, 75.

gested earlier, spring from the source, the content, or the manner of communicating. Where it is the person who threatens, it is usually because differences in status exist, are introduced, or accentuated. For this reason groups and organizations ought regularly to review their internal structure to see if differences in authority are essential to or destructive of effective performance. Differences in rank are often multiplied or emphasized without regard for their inhibiting and distorting effects on the flow of information and ideas. Studies of organizational behavior suggest that those marked by severe competition for status often have serious problems of communication.[28] Status barriers, however, may dissolve in the face of facilitating interpersonal attitudes.

Where the threat arises from different perceptions of problems and policies, there are ways of rendering these differences less disruptive. Proposals can be made as specific as possible to counteract fears of an uncertain future; they can be introduced gradually to reduce the amount of risk involved; they can be initiated experimentally so that failure can be remedied; they can include guarantees against the loss of personal prestige and power. Every new idea, since it is an implicit criticism of an old idea, may disturb those responsible for the prevailing view; but it is possible to innovate without attacking unnecessarily those associated with former policies.

Neither the source nor the subject, however, is as critical as the climate in which interaction occurs. Communication as a physical fact produces no magic; words can lead toward destructive or productive outcomes depending on the attitudes that surround them. Where the object is to secure as complete, as frank, as creative an interaction of experience as possible, the following attitudes would seem to promote communication in a context of change.

Human understanding is facilitated where there is a willingness to become involved with the other person. It means to treat him as a person, not as an object; to see him as a man, not as a number, a vote, or a factor in production. It is to regard him as a value in himself, rather than a means to some other value. It is to prize his experience and his needs. Most of all, it is to consider and explore his feelings. In practical terms it means one is willing to take time, to avoid interruptions, to be communicatively accessible. Dozens of superficial and fragmentary conversations do not encourage a meeting of minds. There must be as much respect for his experience as we expect for our own. Since it is the loss of self-esteem that men fear most, such respect can do much to reduce the motivation for defensive interaction.

Communication is facilitated when there is a frank and full exposure of self. It is when men interact in roles, speaking as they believe they should rather than as they feel, that communication is often corrupted. In the words of Sidney Jourard, "We say that we feel things we do not feel. We say that we did things we did not do. We say that we believe things we do not believe."[29] We present, in short, persons that we are not. As one person retreats behind his false self—performing his lines, weighing

[28]Read, *op. cit.*

[29]Sidney Jourard, *The Transparent Self* (New York: Van Nostrand, 1964).

his words, calculating his movements—the danger signs are recognized. Rarely does the other person fail to detect them. In an atmosphere of deceit, his suspicion is aroused and defenses go up. He begins to edit his thoughts, censor his feelings, manipulate his responses, and assume the rituals and mask of his office. Not only does communication stop, but mistrust lingers on to corrupt future encounters. Afterwards each says to himself, "I don't believe him," "I don't trust him," "I will avoid him in the future." This pattern accounts for much of the communicative isolation of parent and child, teacher and student, Black and White. It may also be the reason why interaction is so often accompanied by an undercurrent of strain, for it takes considerable energy to sustain both a false and a real self.

In contrast, defenses tend to disintegrate in an atmosphere of honesty. There are no inconsistent messages. What is said is what is known, what is felt, what is thought. Pretenses are dropped and contrivance ceases. Instead the effort is to express, as spontaneously and accurately as possible, the flow of thought and feeling. In the absence of deceit, there is less reason to distort or deny in reply. A genuine interaction of experience can occur. Much of the tension goes out of personal relationships. Communication becomes something to seek rather than something to avoid. Through talk it becomes possible to learn more about ourselves and more about the issues we face as men.

The willingness to be transparent leads to a further condition that promotes healthy interaction. In social encounters men see their purposes in many ways: some as manipulative, some as dominating, some as competitive, some as impressive, some as protective. People seldom talk for more than a few moments without exposing their underlying communicative strategy. Most of our defenses are designed to prevent damage to the symbolic self that occurs in the face of these depreciating motives. But an attitude of mutuality can also be heard, and heard loud and clear. This attitude is manifest in many ways: whenever there is patience rather than impatience, whenever there is a tentative rather than dogmatic assertion of opinion, whenever there is curiosity rather than indifference for alternative views, whenever there is a creative rather than inflexible approach to arguments. Where there is a feeling of mutual involvement among communicative equals, defenses are unlikely to interfere with the pursuit of new meanings.

Understanding is also promoted when people assume their full communicative responsibilities. Now what does that mean? Simply that one will listen as well as speak, that he will try to understand as well as try to be understood. There is little doubt among specialists that listening is by far the harder communicative task. Then why is it so often assigned to the younger, the weaker, the less competent? Usually it is the student who must understand the teacher, the employee who must understand the supervisor, the patient who must understand the doctor, the young who must understand the old. In response to an essay "On Being an American Parent," one college student wrote the following lines as part of a "Letter to the Editor."

> *Your paragraph under "Listen" very well sums up what I'm trying to say. I could never tell my parents anything, it was always "I'm too busy . . . too*

> *tired . . . that's not important . . . that's stupid . . . can't you think of better things. . . . " As a result, I stopped telling my parents anything. All communication ceased.*
>
> *I have only one important plea to parents. . . .* Listen, listen, *and* listen again. *Please, I know the consequences and I'm in hell.*[30]

In instance after instance, the heavier communicative burden is forced upon the weaker, and the easier load is assumed by the stronger. It is not surprising that such exploitation should occasionally arouse defensive reactions.

Research in the behavioral sciences gives consistent support to the principle that two-way, as compared with one-way, communication produces more accurate understanding, stimulates a greater flow of ideas, corrects misunderstandings more efficiently, and yields a higher level of morale. Why, then, do men so often block feedback? Partly out of habit. In many interpersonal encounters listening means no more than a passive monitoring of the conversation, a time in which men prepare their next remarks. Partly we prevent feedback because of fear. It is upsetting to find how confusing our instructions have been, how inconsistent our words and deeds, how irritating our actions sometimes are. Where receivers have been given a chance to talk back after long periods of following orders, they usually respond at first with hostility. Yet the easing of communicative restrictions, in most instances, quickly restores a constructive and cooperative relationship.

On the national scene these days we hear much about the need for more dialogue. Many are skeptical of this demand. Has there not always been the right of free speech, free access to the platform for every advocate? True, but freedom to speak is not freedom to influence. For genuine dialogue there must be someone to talk, but also someone to listen. To speak is an empty freedom—as racial clashes and political demonstrations should remind us–unless there is someone willing to hear. And to reply in ways that prove that what was said has made a difference.

Within the intimacy of the therapeutic relationship—where communicative principles are tested at every moment—this premise seems equally valid. Again, it is not the talking that appears to accomplish the cure but association with someone capable of hearing. To be with someone who is truly willing to listen, who concentrates sensitively on all that is said, is no longer to need defenses. Such listening, of course, involves the risk of change. No one can leave the safety and comfort of his own assumptive world and enter that of another without running the risk of having his own commitments questioned. Not only questioned, but perhaps altered. To communicate fully with another human being, since it entails the risk of being changed oneself, is to perform what may be the most courageous of all human acts.

Communication is facilitated when there is a capacity to create a nonevaluative atmosphere. Defenses are provoked not so much by the expectation of difference, as by the expectation of criticism. "The major barrier to interpersonal communication," Carl Rogers has suggested, "is

[30] *Time*, December 22, 1967, 7.

our very natural tendency to judge, to evaluate, to approve, or disapprove the statement of the other person or group." Under the surface of many, if not most, conversations there runs an undercurrent of censure. If we differ, one of us, usually the other fellow, must be wrong, must be stupid, must be incompetent, must be malicious. In so polarized a setting, where conversation becomes cross-examination, it is not surprising that men speak cautiously, incompletely, ambiguously; it is not surprising that with such critical preoccupations they listen suspiciously, partially, vaguely, to what is actually said. "The stronger our feelings," continues Rogers, "the more likely it is there will be no mutual element in the communication. There will be just two ideas, two feelings, two judgments, missing each other in psychological space."[31] When people recognize that they will not be forced beyond their own limits, when they see that their meanings will be respected and understood, when they feel that others will help in exploring difficult or dangerous experiences, they can begin to drop their defenses.

As the atmosphere becomes less evaluative, men are more likely to express and examine a wider range of differences without distortion. Where the intent is to comprehend rather than to attack, communication becomes a source of benefit rather than harm. In a permissive climate people feel comfortable, feel respected, feel secure enough to talk openly. "Conveying assurance of understanding," writes Anatol Rapoport, "is the first step in the removal of threat."[32] Research done on the attributes of helpful people indicates that they are easy to talk with, maximize areas open to discussion, minimize embarrassment, and seldom disapprove.[33]

In such trusting relationships men can develop empathy. They can participate in each other's experience, sharing the assumptions, the perspectives, and the meanings that events hold for them. This is not to insist that evaluation always be avoided, for decisions must be made about facts, theories, policies, even people. It is only to argue that mutual understanding should precede mutual evaluation. Problems cannot be solved until they are understood, and highly critical attitudes inhibit the communication of problems.

It appears that whether communication promotes understanding and affection, or blocks understanding and builds defenses, depends more on the assumptions than on the techniques of the communicator.[34] Or, rather, it is to say that technique cannot be divorced from assumption: As men assume, so will they communicate. Where men presume their knowledge to be complete or infallible, there is no communication or only a manipulative concern for others. Where men presume—as we know to be the case—that their knowledge is fragmentary and uncertain, genuine communication can occur. To recognize the limits of one's own facts and feelings

[31]Carl Rogers, *On Becoming a Person* (Boston: Houghton Mifflin, 1961), 54.

[32]Anatol Rapoport, *Fights, Games and Debates* (Ann Arbor: University of Michigan Press, 1960).

[33]Edwin Thomas, Norman Polansky and Jacob Kounin, "The Expected Behavior of a Potentially Helpful Person," *Human Relations*, (8, 1955), 165–174.

[34]Dean C. Barnlund, *Interpersonal Communication* (Boston: Houghton Mifflin, 1968), 613–641.

is to become curious about the facts and feelings of others. At such moments men are likely to be open, honest, trusting, empathic, not because of some altruistic motive, but because it is the only way to correct and to extend their own perceptions of the world. Each stands to gain; the speaker because he can test what he believes and because it is rewarding to be understood; the listener because he can broaden his experience and because it is stimulating to understand.

Every significant human crisis begins or ends in a communicative encounter of one kind or another. It is here that differences are voiced. It is here that differences threaten. It is here that defenses are raised, and men embittered. But it is here, too, that differences may be welcomed. It is here that words may be heard. It is here that understanding may be reached, that men may cross the distance that divides them. "In my civilization," wrote Antoine de Saint Exupéry, "he who is different from me does not impoverish me—he enriches me."[35]

[35]Antoine de Saint Exupéry, *Airman's Odyssey* (New York: Reynal and Hitchcock, 1939), 420.

Chapter 2
THE NATURE OF INTERPERSONAL COMMUNICATION

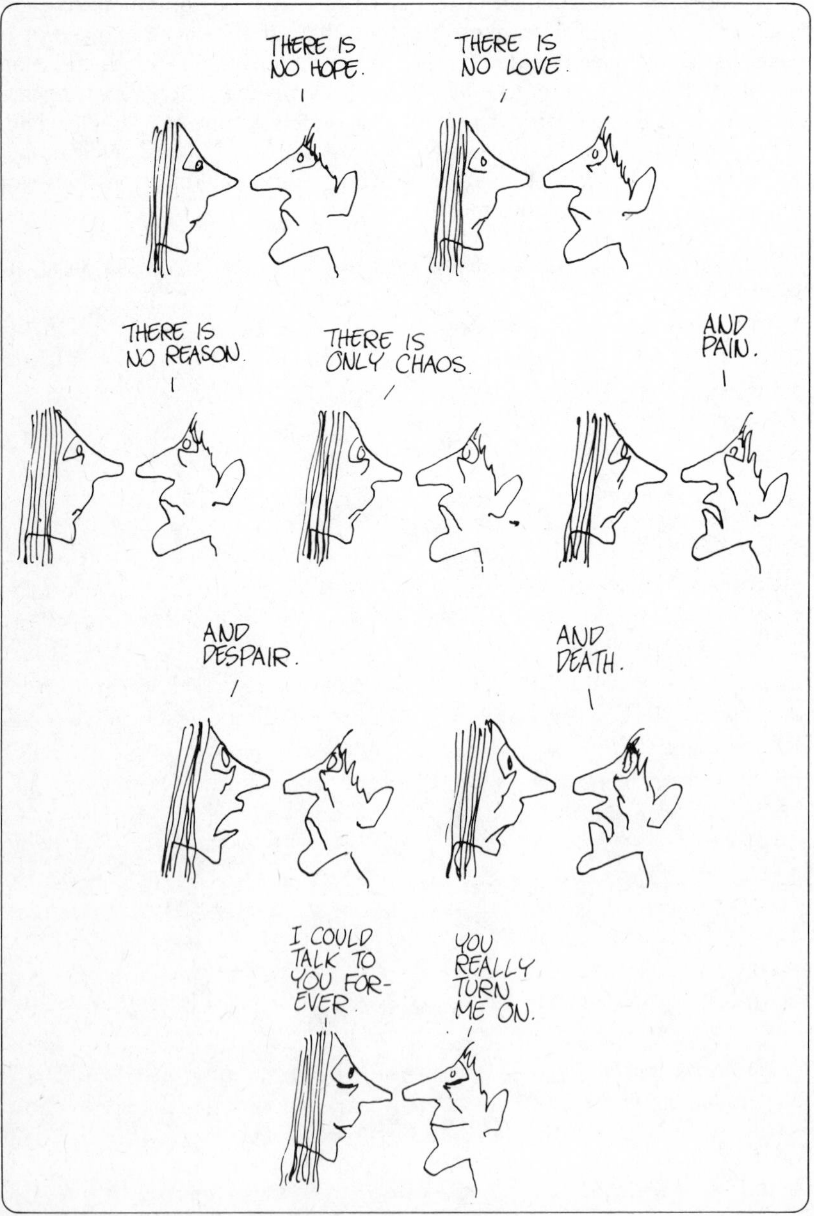

INTERCEPTED LETTER[1]

Dear Gail,

You wouldn't believe my first day on the university campus. The bus got in at 9:30 this morning. The trip *wasn't* pleasant. The hard-hat next to me wanted to talk about "young" people. I was lucky I had a book. I just told him I didn't have any opinions and read *Open Marriage.* When I got tired of the book, I found out he worked at the university and asked him some questions. He really talked down to me. I now know one thing he thinks about "young" people—we're dumb.

The next thing I did *was* dumb. I had a taxi take me to campus. The driver took me to the Student Union and asked if this was where I wanted to go. My money and the meter reading convinced me it was. After walking about a mile uphill to my dorm, I knew I should have admitted my mistake.

I arrived at the dorm to find that my housing letter and the dorm records didn't agree at all. The lady at the desk kept insisting that no Stacey Clegg was preregistered. It was obvious I couldn't talk to her so I asked for the housing director. They told me I'd need an appointment and recommended I speak to my college advisor. When I arrived at his office, I was told this was not his office hour. After I created a scene, they sent me to the Dean of Women's office and someone there helped me. She had to make five phone calls before finding that I had been assigned to the men's wing. When I suggested that might be fun, she wasn't amused. I decided "I was not amused" and told her what I thought about such mistakes and the time I had been forced to waste.

By the time I got unpacked, lunch had been served. I'd had it. I told the man at the cafeteria that that is no way to accommodate students. He finally arranged for me to get something to eat. It just goes to show that you have to stand up for your rights.

Had to rush then to get to my 2:30 medical examination. You wouldn't believe the hassle and all the incompetency. I filled out a questionnaire with a lot of ridiculous questions; I left the crazy ones blank. Some nurse then asked a lot more and by then I was sick and tired of answering questions so I told her so. She got all uptight and said that the information was

[1]Thanks to the students in Ms. Doris Falen's honors class in interpersonal communciation at the University of Kansas, Fall 1972, for contributing ideas for this hypothetical narrative.

important when they had to treat me. I told her the only thing I was sick of was stupid questions and nosy people like her. She let me go on to the next line. From there on I didn't have to worry about talking to people. I just stripped down, as was suggested, and followed arrow after arrow while "silent" machines and people recorded things. They even had a sign saying "drink this before next test." It was some orange stuff and I was not about to. I wonder what happened to that test? I had real fun at the hearing table playing deaf with the examiner. I kept saying "huh?" when he'd ask questions. I think maybe he believed me!

I cut the last few lines because I needed to get to a snack bar before meeting my academic advisor at 4:00. It turned out I had plenty of time because he was behind schedule. When he got to me about 4:20 he asked to see my class preference forms. In the hustle and bustle of getting ready to move I forgot to fill them out. He was nice about it though (I was really surprised at how nice a chemistry prof. could be!); he went through the options with me several times. I ended up enrolled in courses in English, French, American History, Sociology, and a Speech class in interpersonal communication. I told him I didn't think I needed the speech course because I've been talking all my life! Oh well, we'll see.

When I got back to the dorm, my apartment mates were in—a Roberta Brown from the Deep South and a girl from Thailand who's name I can neither pronounce nor spell. I really like southern drawls but I find the Thailand girl easier to understand. I told them so. It took a little doing but I got everyone organized and I think we'll be OK together.

Dinner in the cafeteria—met a few fellows who seem promising but who knows?? We had a meeting with our wing counselors (I slept through it), then this letter home. I'm ready for sleep now; tomorrow is enrollment and I'm really looking forward to that.

Love,
Stacey

THE STUDY OF INTERPERSONAL COMMUNICATION

Stacey's question concerning the need to study interpersonal communication is basic to this chapter. So thoroughly do we take our interpersonal communication for granted that it scarcely ever occurs to us to examine the nature of it. We usually learn to communicate without much conscious effort, and by the time we are mature enough to understand the symbolism of actions and sounds that provide the basis for our interaction with others, it has become so much like reflex behavior, such as breathing, coughing, or chewing, that it hardly occurs to us that there is anything to be understood.

Social and behavioral scientists have long been interested in human communication behaviors. There is the tacit admission that communication is the foundation for all of our interpersonal relationships

—its relevancy and significance for our lives can hardly be overemphasized. Yet only recently have attempts been made to translate behavioral theories into research-based foundations for personalized growth and development.

We have the capacity for controlling and choosing among alternative patterns of communication behaviors. By understanding the interactive, ongoing, process nature of interpersonal communication, it becomes possible to alter elements within the process with more predictable results. The article by Jurgen Ruesch that follows this chapter provides an excellent overview of the dimensions of interpersonal communication. This psychiatrist's view of the effects of messages on the behavior of people describes the characteristics of normal communication behaviors as a backdrop for analysis of deviant behaviors. The channnels, contexts, and systems that he discusses distinguish the broad area for interdisciplinary academic concern. He reflects the philosophy of communication that we have articulated, emphasizing communication as the basis of change in people.

Self-Awareness

One major goal of studying interpersonal communication is to become more aware of ourselves and our potentials as communicators. This use of interpersonal communication as the avenue of awareness of self is graphically demonstrated in a model prepared by Joseph Luft and Harry Ingham labeled the "Johari Window" after their first names. Human interaction was depicted in terms of a single individual and his or her relation to others.

The four quadrants of the Johari Window represent the whole person in relation to others:

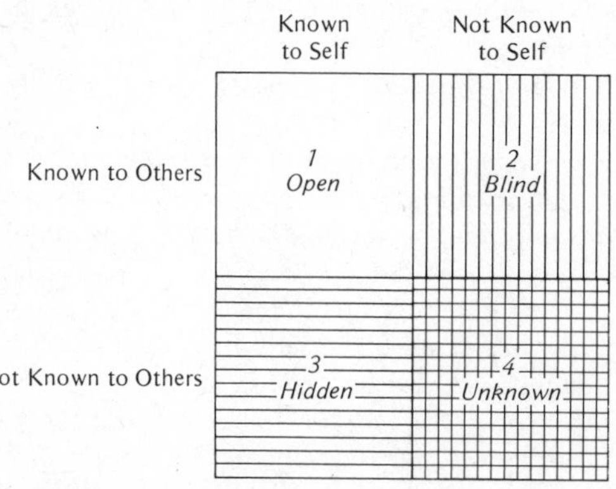

Figure 2.1 The Johari Window. (From Joseph Luft, *Group Processes*, p. 11. Copyright © 1963, 1970 by Joseph Luft. Reprinted by permission of National Press Books.)

Area 1 *is the behavior and motivation known to self and known to others. It shows the extent to which two or more persons can give and take, work together and enjoy experiences together. The larger this area, the greater is the individual's contact with the real world and the more available are his/her abilities and needs to self and others.*

Area 2, *the blind area, represents behavior and motivation not known to self but apparent to others. The simplest illustration is a mannerism in speech or gesture of which the person is unaware (such as a repeated reliance on a phrase such as "You know?") but which is quite obvious to other people. Similarly a person may demonstrate a need to dominate others and not be as aware of this as others are.*

Area 3 *is behavior and motivation open to self but kept away, "hidden" from others. With a new acquaintance this is a large quadrant because we don't feel safe in revealing our true selves and feelings. For example, we may resent a particular remark, but keep it to ourself.*

Area 4 *represents the inner sphere of behaviors and motivations unknown either to self or to others. This area is assumed to exist because both the individual and the persons with whom he or she is associated discover from time to time new behaviors or motives that were likely there all the time. For example, an individual may surprise himself/herself and others by showing abilities in bringing warring factions together although he/she was never previously thought to be a peacemaker.*

Based upon his work in examining personal growth through group dynamics, Luft states the following twelve "principles of change" in terms of the four quadrants:

1. *A change in any one quadrant will affect all other quadrants.*
2. *It takes energy to hide, deny, or be blind to behavior which is involved in interaction.*
3. *Threat tends to decrease awareness; mutual trust tends to increase awareness.*
4. *Forced awareness (exposure) is undesirable and usually ineffective.*
5. *Interpersonal learning means a change has taken place so that Q1 is larger and one or more of the other quadrants has grown smaller.*
6. *Working with others is facilitated by a large enough area of free activity. An increased Q1 means more of the resources and skills in the membership can be applied to a task.*
7. *The smaller the first quadrant, the poorer the communication.*
8. *There is universal curiosity about the unknown area, but this is held in check by custom, social training, and diverse fears.*
9. *Sensitivity means appreciating the covert aspects of behavior, in quadrants 2, 3, and 4, and respecting the desire of others to keep them so.*

10. *Learning about group processes as they are being experienced helps to increase awareness (enlarge Q1) for the group as a whole as well as for individual members.*
11. *The value system of a group and its membership may be noted in the way unknowns in the life of the group are confronted.*
12. *A centipede may be perfectly happy without awareness, but after all, he restricts himself to crawling under rocks.*[2]

Interpersonal communication is the means by which we expand our Quadrant 1. As Luft suggests, some people may get along fine with other people without insight or awareness (like the happy centipede that doesn't worry about which foot to put forward), but such lack of awareness inhibits our communication effectiveness and impedes our personal growth. We think Stacey could have profited from an expansion of her Quadrant 1.

Functional Applications. In terms of specific objectives for students like Stacey, we believe that the study of interpersonal communication should contribute to personal development in three significant areas:

1. *Functional intelligence—the capability of converting personal experience, knowledge, and insights into social currency; learning to translate what one knows into value and utility for others.*
2. *Social decision making—the capability to participate effectively in the dynamic interchange of ideas with others; the capacity to both process data and work with people through discussion and open exchange of ideas.*
3. *Self-expression—development of a realistic and positive sense of self in human interaction; strengthening personal identity and social involvement through our interpersonal communication.*

Such development obviously requires both theory and practice. The educated and aware individual requires more data than simply to know that certain behaviors "work" in obtaining our goals; theory should provide an understanding of the "whys" of interpersonal communication.

Knowledge of theory alone, however, is of little value unless a person has opportunities to engage in experiences that provide feedback and insights into his or her interpersonal communication. Analogies can be made to any personal behavioral skill—writing (composition), driving an automobile, or hitting a golf ball. The study of interpersonal communication is somewhat different, however, in that

[2]J. Luft, *Group Processes* (Palo Alto, Calif.: National Press Books, 1970), p. 15.

each individual must make personal judgments and choices about his or her behaviors. In some areas the criteria of excellence are not as specifically defined as in the case of other disciplines; there are no *absolute* rules of conduct. Personal growth and self-actualization must be generated within each individual. At this moment you are making a decision whether or not to continue reading; in this instance you are in control of your communicative behaviors. We would hope that Stacey would gain such an awareness of her interpersonal behaviors and the choices available to her.

CHARACTERISTICS OF INTERPERSONAL COMMUNICATION

In Chapter 1 we discussed communication in general and posited (from Barnlund) six characteristics of the human communication act. All of these characteristics obviously apply to interpersonal communication; there are additional characteristics that further delineate the essence of interpersonal communication.

1. In Interpersonal Communication, Both the Generator and Attributor of Meaning Must Be Present. In other types of human communication the mutual presence of the message generator (sender) and receiver is not required. In one-way communication I may write alone, and you may read my message alone; I may record a message for you and you may hear it in my absence. In a large public meeting your presence or absence likely makes no difference to the speaker. Such is not the case with interpersonal communication.

We defined interpersonal communication as the face-to-face interactions between people who are consistently aware of each other. Thus, if I overhear a conversation unknown to the sender, we are not engaging in interpersonal communication. A mutual awareness of the other person makes communication inevitable. This factor will be later developed in greater detail. The important point here is that interpersonal communication cannot transpire without the presence and awareness of the parties involved.

2. Each Person Assumes Roles as Both Sender and Receiver of Messages in Interpersonal Communication. As opposed to one-way communication, interpersonal communication requires constant adaptation and spontaneous adjustment to the other person. This give-and-take of *verbal* and *nonverbal* messages poses special problems for both parties. Based on personal experience, perceptions of the other person, and personal capabilities, the sender of the message selects and utilizes symbols in an attempt to elicit a desired response from the other person (or persons). The receiver, based on his/her knowledge of this person and similarities of experiences, attaches meaning to the symbols that may or may not correspond to the meaning intended by the sender. Ideally there would be total congruence between the two sets of meanings, but such is rarely the case.

3. In Interpersonal Communication, the Sender and the Receiver Are Interdependent. Again in contrast to one-way communication where sender and receiver function independently, the behaviors of the participants in interpersonal communication are so intertwined in the process that it is difficult to separate sender from receiver. The circular nature of interpersonal communication means that as we are attributing meaning to messages generated by the sender, we are simultaneously generating feedback messages to the sender that in turn influence subsequent message generation. We shall attempt to clarify this interdependency in the next section.

David Berlo distinguishes four levels of communicative interdependency in the reading that follows this chapter. He utilizes the term "interaction" to exemplify the highest level of interdependency. At this ideal level of interpersonal communication, Berlo states:

> *When two people interact, they put themselves into each other's shoes, try to perceive the world as the other person perceives it, try to predict how the other will respond. Interaction involves reciprocal role-taking, the mutual employment of empathic skills. The goal of interaction is the merger of self and other, a complete ability to anticipate, predict, and behave in accordance with the joint needs of self and other.*[3]

4. Since Interpersonal Communication Relies on Behaviors, We Must Be Satisfied with Degrees of Mutual Understanding. At this point we should distinguish between our behaviors, the overt actions of a person that we can see and hear, and the intrapersonal experiences that are invisible. Behavior would be what is recorded on a videotape machine. Alone it provides no interpretation of movements or sounds; the meanings are attached by the viewer-receiver. Like an iceberg, behavior is merely the manifestation of a unique intrapersonal experience. As we use words like interpersonal imperatives, perceptions, orientations, and relationships, we are evoking aspects of our experience, but they merge together in such ways as to make differentiation difficult. R. D. Laing, who has written extensively on the distinction between behavior and internalized experience, puts it this way: "Experience is man's invisibility to man."[4]

[3]D. K. Berlo, *The Process of Communication* (New York: Holt, Rinehart and Winston, 1960). Reprinted in this volume, pp. 68–84.

[4]R. D. Laing, *The Politics of Experience* (New York: Ballantine, 1967), p. 18. Another of Laing's works, *The Divided Self* (London: Tavistock, 1960), is devoted to describing versions of the split between experience and behavior.

This distinction is important because while we are in effect cut off from one another in our private worlds of experience, interpersonal communication becomes the bridge of contact between people. Since we feel that we can attach personal meanings to our own behaviors, we have some control on the way others experience us. My behavior becomes your experience of me. You cannot see my inner life (my experience), and your perceptions, thoughts, and feelings about me are simply projective aspects of your own inner life. Thus the impact we have on other people is the personal meanings we attach to behaviors.

As we attribute meaning to the behavior of others, we are inferring with some degree of probability what is going on inside the person. We attach meanings to the behaviors that may or may not be valid. For example, an acquaintance fails to acknowledge and speak to us. We may infer that she is angry at us, while in reality she has just received disturbing news (the death of a loved one) and is not "seeing" anyone at that moment. We shall discuss this problem in greater detail in Chapter 4.

5. Interpersonal Communication Involves Mutual Needs to Communicate. You may want to share with me the latest news about your brother in New Orleans. Unless I have some interest in the information I may merely feign interest as I permit my mind to wander to subjects that are interesting me. Since we both have controls over communicative behaviors, we choose whether to initiate contact, speak, or listen.

If you want to talk about you, and I only want to talk about me, we may be encoding words to reflect our ideas and feelings, with neither of us working at decoding. The receiver ultimately determines whether genuine, functional communication is to transpire. Just as we may daydream or sleep during a dull lecture, we employ the same capabilities of "cutting off" the sender in an interpersonal situation. Such a reliance upon listening and responding to visual cues as receivers can be distinguished from a one-way system in two ways.

First, receiving interpersonal messages, unlike reading or watching television, is a socialized activity. Instead of being able to shut out distractions and focus our attention, we are forced to respond to a variety of signals. While we may choose the time and place to read or watch television, we have no such control over our interpersonal environment. Even after we have received shocking or distressing news, we are still placed in situations when messenger reception is important. A wide variety of emotional and social pressures influence our capacity to attribute meaning.

A second distinction is that in interpersonal communication, again unlike reading, the sender controls the production of a message. While we are each able to read at our own individual speed, we have no such control over the listening process. The speaker may rush and slur over important words that are vital to the message, yet we may have no opportunity to "rerun" the speech in order to correct our listening errors. For social reasons we respond as if we understand completely. These problems will be discussed in greater detail in Chapter 6.

With this background on the characteristics of interpersonal communication, we should now look at the total process.

THE PROCESS OF INTERPERSONAL COMMUNICATION—OVERVIEW

In Chapter 1 we discussed in some detail the process nature of communication and presented a couple of models that identified some of the ingredients. Probably no one model will ever be able to identify all the potential variables in human communication, for even if it were possible to apply labels to all conceivable elements, the size and complexity of the model would make it useless. For our purposes, we must recognize that communication is a dynamic process, constantly changing, never static. All variables are constantly interacting with one another, modifying and adapting to all situational modifications. Although we may focus attention on one or another of the variables, we must remember the fluid nature of the total process. As we examine interpersonal communication from a number of perspectives, different models will be utilized to help clarify views of particular variables.

At this point, we have prepared a model that will hopefully help provide an overview of our conception of the major ingredients in the process of interpersonal communication. This model is shown in Figure 2.2. Our model attempts to identify the elements in the interpersonal communication process comprising the heart of this book. Discussion of any one element at a given time is arbitrary, since all are interdependent and since a change in any one affects all others. We have elected to discuss them in the following order in this book:

1. *We desire and seek out communication with others*—the communication imperative. *Each of us has personal needs that can only be satisfied by interaction with others. Personal growth and development as well as our needs of controlling our environment can be accomplished only with the help of other people. This basic imperative to communicate is the topic of Chapter 3.*
2. *We* perceive *the other person, and, based upon our habitual* orientation *to this person, we choose whether or not to initiate interaction. Is this person able to fulfill our personal needs of the moment? This topic will be discussed in Chapter 4.*

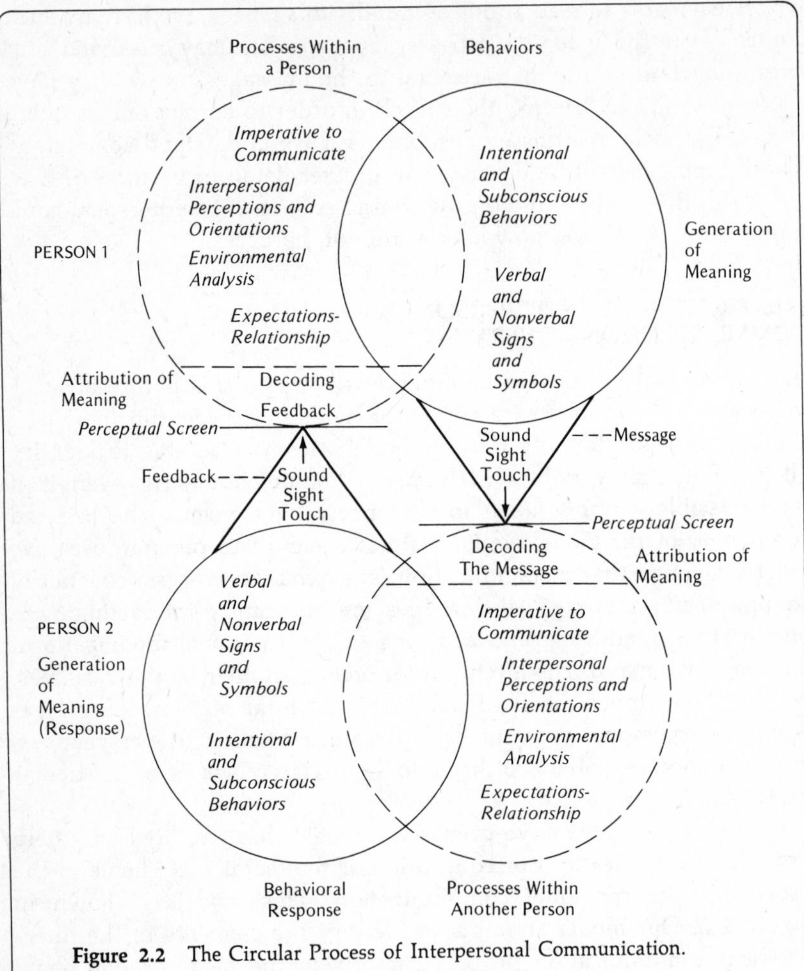

Figure 2.2 The Circular Process of Interpersonal Communication.

3. *We make an* environmental analysis *of such matters as the physical environment (place, time, space) and the social context (presence of others, cultural influences, etc.) and decide on appropriate behaviors. We will discuss the interpersonal environment in Chapter 5.*
4. *We attempt to share ideas by means of attributing meaning to* verbal and nonverbal messages. *Based on the mutual understandings of the code, we infer the thoughts of the other person and work for rapport. This topic, interpersonal semantics, is the focus of Chapter 6.*
5. *Based on the degree of mutual understandings,* relationships *tend to stabilize over time and we develop certain expectations. We evaluate these relationships in terms of cost/reward to our*

needs and decide to maintain, change, or terminate the relationships. The nature of the interpersonal relationship is discussed in Chapter 7.

Looking back at our model of interpersonal communication, we see that processes are occurring within Person 1 that are reflected in his or her overt behaviors. An attempt is made to encode meanings by verbal and nonverbal signs and symbols. These messages are transmitted by means of sound, sight, and touch to Person 2. There are not only a variety of complex motivations on the part of the communicator and a variety of messages generated by him/her at each moment, but the receiver of the message attributes meaning from an equally complex motivational system.

Each of us has a perceptual screen or filter through which we perceive the behavior of others. We "hear" what we want to hear, either laudatory or critical. Thus the complexity of both sending and receiving sets makes communication a difficult human act. Of the many messages the individual may communicate, many of which he or she is unaware, he/she cannot know which are received by the other, or whether the perceptual screen of the other distorts the message he/she attempted to convey.

The behavioral response of Person 2 generates a message back to Person 1 in the form of feedback that serves to monitor his/her subsequent communication. For example, an apparent lack of interest in the subject may cause the speaker to change subjects or adjust the message if he/she decodes the feedback with awareness. Thus we see the circular nature of the process.

SUMMARY AND PREVIEW OF READINGS

We have examined the nature of interpersonal communication by looking at reasons for concern, basic characteristics, and an overview of the ingredients in the process.

We believe that the study of interpersonal communication is important in promoting awareness of our capabilities as communicators and should contribute to personal development in at least three areas: functional intelligence, social decision making, and self-expression. Such development requires both theory and the opportunity for practice of behaviors with feedback.

To delineate further the nature of interpersonal communication, we suggested that both the generator and attributor of meaning must be present, assuming roles of both sender and receiver interchangeably and interdependently. Since interpersonal communication relies upon interpretations given to behaviors, we rarely if ever achieve total mutual understanding; and mutual needs of the parties involved must be fulfilled if interpersonal communication is to transpire.

Finally, we have presented a model in an attempt to identify significant ingredients in the interpersonal communication process. These elements provide the chapter topics in the next section of this book. In the book's final section we will explore specific ways of improving our interpersonal communication by examining significant interpersonal barriers and utilizing an understanding of the process to effect personal growth and actualization.

The article by psychiatrist Jurgen Ruesch that follows provides an excellent overview of the dimensions of interpersonal communication. He opens with a case example of situations involving different types of communication, cites the problems of the "observing reporter" of social situations, and presents a compelling case for our needs to master the tools of communication.

In the second selection, Berlo identifies interaction as the primary goal of interpersonal communication. This interaction is viewed as interdependent: A person acts (communicates), and another person reacts; in turn, the first person then reacts, too. This interaction (or, perhaps, interreaction) is viewed as the primary goal of the communication process. As we react, we tell the other person both something about ourselves and something of our view of him. Through this feedback process we come to know ourselves as well as to know others.

When we respond to such new information, we grow and develop, thus satisfying a deep personal need.

From these perspectives on interpersonal communication, in the next section we shall examine the interpersonal communication process in detail by focusing attention on the significant elements we have identified.

SUGGESTED APPLICATIONS AND LEARNING EXPERIENCES

1. Discuss with your classmates the letter from Stacey. Have you encountered any similar types of interpersonal problems? What would you anticipate for her at enrollment?

2. A great deal of data in interpersonal communication can be labeled "common sense." Discuss whether what is common sense to one person is necessarily that to another. Select examples of common sense statements from this book and compare your views.

3. Working in small groups, examine the Johari Window and discuss your individual quadrants. Are members of your group motivated to enlarge Quadrant 1? Relate this model to your personal expectations in this class.

4. In groups of two or three, design a situation involving hidden conflict. Who you are, where you are, and what you are doing must be agreed upon. Each of you is to decide on a point of conflict that you will never verbalize as you role-play with the other participants.

Example: Where—kitchen; Who—husband and wife; What—breakfast.

Hidden conflict: *Husband:* I'm not going to work today.
Wife: I want him to leave. I'm expecting a visitor.

Diagnose your capabilities to interpret the basis for conflict and discuss situations involving such problems.

5. Compare the significant components of communication cited by Ruesch in the reading that follows with the model of interpersonal communication shown in this chapter. Where would the components fit into the model?

6. In the reading that follows, Berlo makes the point that a person does not just talk to another person, but interacts; that is, the other person's responses and behavior influence what the first person says and the way he/she says it. How does this principle relate to our efforts to satisfy our need to interact with others? Does it influence our attempts to initiate interaction? To choose to talk with some persons and not others? To ignore some persons who seem to want to talk with us? Relate this view to Stacey's interpersonal behaviors and to your own.

COMMUNICATION AND HUMAN RELATIONS: AN INTERDISCIPLINARY APPROACH

Jurgen Ruesch

The field of communication is concerned with human relatedness. Every person, plant, animal, and object emits signals which, when perceived, convey a message to the receiver. This message changes the information of the receiver and hence may alter his behavior. Change in behavior of the receiver, in turn, may or may not perceptibly influence the sender. Sometimes the effect of a message is immediate; at other times the message and its effect are so far apart in time and space that the observer fails to connect the two events. For purposes of our presentation however, we shall be concerned more with the immediate effects of messages and their influence upon the behavior of people.

CHANNELS OF COMMUNICATION IN EVERYDAY LIFE

In order to familiarize the reader with the varieties of human communication, let us view the experiences of Mr. A as he proceeds with his daily activities. In the morning when Mr. A enters his office he reads his incoming mail (written communication). In sorting his mail he encounters a number of pamphlets which are designed to describe the merits of various business machines (pictorial communication). Through the open window the faint noise of a radio is heard, as the voice of an announcer clearly praises the quality of a brand of toothpaste (spoken communication). When his secretary enters the room she gives him a cheerful "good morning," which he acknowledges with a friendly nod of his head (gestural communication) while he continues with his conversation on the telephone (spoken communication) with a business associate. Later in the morning he dictates a number of letters to his secretary, then he holds a committee meeting (group communication), where he gathers the advice of his associates. In this meeting a number of new governmental regulations (mass communication) and their effect upon the policies of the firm are discussed. Later in the meeting a resolution to the employees of the firm concerning the annual bonus (mass and group communication) is considered. After the committee has adjourned, Mr. A, engaged in thoughts concerning unfinished business (communication with self), slowly crosses the street to his restaurant for lunch. On the way he sees his friend Mr. B, who in a great hurry enters the same luncheon place (communication through action), and Mr. A decides to sit by himself rather than to join his friend, who will probably gulp down his coffee and hurry on (communication with self). While waiting, Mr. A studies the menu (communication through printed word) but the odor of a juicy steak deflects his gaze (chemical communication); it is so appetizing that he orders one himself. After lunch he decides to buy a pair of gloves. He enters a men's store and with the tips of his fingers carefully examines the various qualities of leather (communication through touch). After leisurely concluding the purchase, he decides to take the afternoon off and to escort his son on a promised trip to the zoo. On the way there, John, watching his father drive through the streets, asks him why he always stops at a red light and why he does not stop at a green light (communication by visual symbol). As they approach the zoo, an ambulance screams down the street, and Mr. A pulls over to the side of the road and stops (communication by sound). As they sit there he explains to his son that the church across the street is the oldest in the state, built many years ago, and still standing as a landmark in the community (communication through material culture). After paying admission to the zoo (communication through action), they leisurely stroll over to visit the elephants. Here John laughs at the antics of an elephant who sprays water through his trunk at one of the spectators (communication through action), sending him into near flight. Later on in the afternoon Mr. A yields to the pressure of his son, and they enter a movie house to see a cartoon (communication through pictures). Arriving home, Mr. A dresses in order to attend a formal dinner and theater performance (communication through the arts).

These examples may suffice to illustrate the varieties of social situations in which communication occurs. Let us next consider how a scientist can conceptualize these various events in a more systematized fashion.

THE CONTEXT IN WHICH COMMUNICATION OCCURS

The scientific approach to communication has to occur on several levels of complexity. In a first step we shall be concerned with the definition of the context in which communication occurs. This context is summarized by the label which people give to specific social situations. Identification of a social situation is important both for the participant who wishes to communicate and for the scientist who aims at conceptualizing the processes of communication.

The Perception of the Perception

A social situation is established as soon as an exchange of communication takes place; and such exchange begins with the moment in which the actions of the other individual are perceived as responses—that is, as evoked by the sender's message and therefore as comments upon that message, giving the sender an opportunity of judging what the message meant to the receiver. Such communication about communication is no doubt difficult, because it is usually implicit rather than explicit, but it must be present if an exchange of messages is to take place. The perception of the perception, as we might call this phenomenon, is the sign that a silent agreement has been reached by the participants, to the effect that mutual influence is to be expected.

The mutual recognition of having entered into each other's field of perception equals the establishment of a system of communication. The criteria of mutual awareness of perception are in all cases instances of communication about communication. If a person "A" raises his voice to attract person "B's" attention, he is thereby making a statement about communication. He may, for example, be saying, "I am communicating with you," or he may be saying, "I am not listening to you; I am doing the talking"—and so on. Similarly, all punctuations of the stream of emitted signals are statements about how that stream is to be broken down into sections, and significantly all modifications of the stream of signals, which implicitly or explicitly assign roles either to the self or to the other, are statements about communication. If "A" adds the word "please" to a verbal request, he is making a statement about that request; he is giving instructions about the mood or role which he desires the listener to adopt when he interprets the verbal stream. He is adding a signal to cause a modification in the receiver's interpretation. In this sense the added signal is a communication about communication as well as a statement about the relationship between two persons.

The Position of the Observer Within the System of Communication

Dependent upon whether an observer is a participant in a group discussion, or remains a scientific observer who, rather aloof and with a minimum of participation, proceeds to make scientific notes, the information about what happens is going to vary. The position of the observer, his viewpoints and foci of interest, his degree of participation, and his lucidity in interpreting rules, roles, and situations will determine that which he is going to report.

When a scientist endeavors to study such complicated matters as human relations, he conveniently divides the universe into segments small enough so that the events which occur within such a subdivision can be observed and recorded in a satisfactory manner. In proceeding from the larger to the smaller units of consideration, the scientist has to guard against pitfalls which may arise from his personal focus of endeavor, his personal views, and his particular perspectives. His position may be likened to that of a visitor to a museum of art, who never succeeds in seeing the front and back views of a statue at the same moment. From a position in back of the statue, for example, he will be unable to predict the facial expression until he has seen it from the front. To obtain a complete impression, he has to walk around the statue; and as he moves, a new perspective will open at every step until the combination of all impressions will enable the visitor to construct within himself a small-scale model of the marble figure. Matters get even more complicated if one considers that not all visitors go to the museum with the same purpose in mind. Some wish to obtain a quick impression of the treasures on hand; others want to undertake detailed studies in preparation for an artist's career; some want to meet people who have the same interests. Thus, varying with their purpose, any of several persons gathered around the statue might retain within himself a different view of the marble figure.

The scientist is very much in the same position as the spectator of the statue, with the exception that, to achieve a more complete understanding of what he is doing and of what happens in nature, he does not limit himself to perception and observation only. In order to satisfy his curiosity, he compensates for his human limitations of perception by creating a theory. In brief, he proceeds about as follows: First, he postulates that there are events. An event is defined as an occurrence which occupies a small part of the general four-dimensional, space-time continuum. If the scientist happens to observe such an event and if it can be verified by others, he refers to his statement of it as a fact. Sometimes he adds to his observations certain physical measurements; he makes observations on the relations between measurements; he makes observations on the relations between the event and his own measuring rod. In order to be able to measure or to experiment, however, the scientist needs a hypothesis; it is nothing but a provisional, tentative theory, a supposition that he adopts temporarily in order to add to the already well-established knowledge a series of new facts. Hypotheses thus guide all future research work. When a hypothesis—that is, an assumption without proof—can be substantiated by fact, it becomes a theory. The latter can be described as being the result of reasoning with the intent to derive from a body of known facts some general or abstract principles. Such principles can then be applied to other bodies of knowledge in order to finally interconnect the information about events in a larger time-space continuum. The scientist has to rely upon theory, because only few events are accessible to direct observation or measurement. The majority of processes in nature or within the human being himself are either so slow or so fast that they escape perception. Theory is then used to combine the known facts into a network, allowing for interpolation and extrapolation, reconstruction of past and prediction of future events.

At this point the reader will recognize that as soon as we talk or think about a social situation we have to define our own position as observers. Therefore, every individual becomes a scientific observer as soon as he engages in communication.

To evaluate daily events and to guide future actions, every single human being possesses a private scientific system. To students of human behavior, the private systems of others are accessible only in a rather restricted manner. That which is assimilated by the human being in terms of stimuli—be it food, oxygen, sound, or light—and that which the individual produces in heat, waste materials, or purposive action is accessible to investigation. Whatever happens between intake and output is known on a restricted scale only; through introspection and, in recent years, by means of X-rays and radioactive tracer substances, scientists have been able to follow some of the processes which take place within the organism. For practical purposes, however, events occurring in other persons are accessible to an observer in terms of inference alone; all he observes is the stimuli which reach the other person and the latter's reactions; the rest is subject to conjecture. Furthermore, the observer, being a social stimulus for others, possesses knowledge about the origin and the nature of some of the stimuli which he feeds to other individuals. In such a system, which includes the observer as an integral part, the actions of the first person are stimuli for the second person and the responses of the second person are stimuli for the first person.

Identification of Roles and Rules

Once the position of the observing reporter is clearly defined and a social situation has been established because people have entered into communication, it is left to the participants to identify the social situation. The label which a person is going to give to a social situation is intimately connected with the rules which govern the situation, as well as the roles which the various participants are to assume. It is obvious that each person has his own views regarding the label of the situation and that much confusion results when people disagree as to what a situation is about. Through communication with others, roles are mutually assigned, and by means of mutual exploration agreement is frequently reached as to the nature of the situation. Used in connection with communication, the term "role" refers to nothing but the code which is used to interpret the flow of messages. For example, the statements of a person who wishes to see an automobile are going to be interpreted in a sense quite different from that which they would have if the person were to make the same statements in the role of an automobile buyer. Awareness of a person's role in a social situation enables others to gauge correctly the meaning of his statements and actions.

Once the roles of the self and of all other participants have been established, the code for interpreting the conversation is given. The number of roles which people can assume is limited, and elsewhere we have calculated that their number is probably about twenty-five.[1] A mature individual is capable of mastering this number of roles in the course of a lifetime.

Any social situation is governed by explicit or implicit rules; these rules may be created on the spur of the moment for a particular situation, or they may be the result of centuries of tradition. In the context of communication, rules can be viewed as directives which govern the flow of messages from one person to another. Inasmuch as rules are usually restrictive, they limit the possibilities of communication between people, and above all, they restrict the actions of the participating persons. Rules can be viewed as devices which either stabilize or disrupt a given communication system, and they provide directives for all eventualities. The meaning of rules, regulations, and laws can be understood best if one thinks of a card game in which several persons participate: The channels of communication are prescribed, the sequence of messages is regulated, and the effects of messages are verifiable. The rules also explain that certain messages, at certain times, addressed to certain people, are not admissible, and that known penalties are imposed upon those who break the rules. Furthermore, regulations pertaining to the beginning of the game, the division of functions in terms of roles, and the termination of the game are always included.[2]

[1] J. Ruesch and A. R. Prestwood, "Interactive Processes and Personal Codification," *Journal of Personality*, 18 (1950), 391–430, p. 405.

[2] *Ibid.*, p. 401. See also J. Von Neumann and O. Morgenstern, *Theory of Games and Economic Behavior* (Princeton, N.J.: Princeton University Press, 1941).

The Label of the Social Situation

A social situation is established when people have entered into communication; the state of communication is determined by the fact that a person perceives that his perception has been noted by others. As soon as this fact has been established, a system of communication can be said to exist. At that point selective reception, purposive transmission, and corrective processes take place and the circular characteristics and self-corrective mechanisms of the system of communication become effective. This implies that roles have been assigned and rules established. The participants in a social situation experience these events more or less consciously, and the experience induces them to label a social situation. Such a label specifies not only the status assignment (roles) of the participants and the rules pertaining to the gathering, but also the task or the purpose to which a social situation is devoted. A funeral, for example, serves another purpose than a wedding, and communications vary accordingly. Elsewhere[3] we have advanced the idea that the social situations encountered by the average person number less than forty, a figure which the normally gifted person can master easily.

In identifying social labels it is obvious that external criteria are extremely helpful. If people are dressed in mourning, and others know the significance of the special clothing, they will all agree as to the label of the situation, and communications are therefore limited and interpreted under the seal of the situation. Different and difficult is the situation, however, when two strangers meet—for example, in a western frontier setting, around 1850. External cues of behavior might not have helped them recognize each other's roles. One man, for example, might have been intent on murder, or persecution, or trade. In such cases the label has to be worked out as time goes on, and new rules created. The interval which elapses between the establishment of a social situation and its definite label may vary. Some persons are very skillful in bringing about a clarification of the situation; others, especially neurotics, may experience great anxiety until roles, rules, and purpose have been defined.

THE SIMPLER SYSTEMS OF COMMUNICATION

When a person is alone, the system of communication is confined to that one organism. If there are two people, then the communication network embraces both organisms. If there are many people, the network embraces the whole group, and if we consider many groups, we may talk about a cultural network. In a one-person communication system the signals travel along the established pathways of the body. In a two-or-more-person system the signals travel both along the pathways of the body and through the media which separate the bodies.

Let us now consider first the human instruments of communication and the bodily pathways used for communication. A man's organism as a whole can be conceived of as an instrument of communication, equipped with sense organs, the receivers; with effector organs, the senders; with internal transmitters, the humoral and nervous pathways; and with a cen-

[3]Ruesch, *op. cit.*, 398.

ter, the brain. However, the reader is warned not to think in anatomical terms when considering the internal network of communication; more appropriate is the comparison of the individual with a social organization. Within the organized confines of a state, for example, messages from the borders and from all parts of the nation are transmitted to the capital and to all other points by means of an intricate network. The messages can be conveyed by radio, telephone, telegraph, or word of mouth; printed messages may be carried by air, ship, rail, on wheels, on foot, or on horseback. The person that first reports an event usually does not engage in any extensive traveling to spread the news. Instead, through a system of relays the message is transmitted to other places and people. Each relay station may alter, amplify, condense, or abstract the original message for local use; and frequently after long transit any resemblances between the first and the last report are purely coincidental. This analogy applies well to the consideration of the human organism.

The sense organs, for example, are found scattered from head to toe on the external surface of the body and in or around internal organs as well. Sensitive to stimuli which originate in the surroundings as well as in the body itself, the end organs act as stations of impulse transformation. Regardless of whether the original stimulus consists of a series of light or sound waves or of a chemical reagent, the sense organs transform that which is perceived into impulses which are suitable for internal transmission within the organism. Likewise, it does not matter whether these impulses are conducted along afferent pathways from peripheral and cranial nerves to the brain or along humoral pathways, or perhaps contiguously from cell to cell within a given organ. The essence of the matter is that all living tissue is equipped with the ability to respond to the impact of specific stimuli; such responsiveness may be called irritability. The nature of this responsiveness is determined in part by the type of stimulus which is perceived and in part by the nature of the reacting tissues, organs, and systems of organs. For greater economy and efficiency the stimulus perceived on the surface of the body or within the organism itself is transformed in such a way that it can be transmitted properly; and likewise, the impulses originating in the brain and other regulatory centers are transformed in several stations before they reach the effector organs or, even more remotely, the sense organs of another person.

Our effector organs, the striped and smooth muscles of the body, react to stimuli originating in the organism itself. The irritability of the muscles, when stimulated, results in contractions which in turn may give rise to movements of the limbs, to motions of the body in space, to passage of air through the windpipe, and subsequently to sound or to internal movements of the intestinal tract or the circulatory system. Whenever activities of an organ or of the whole organism are perceived by the self or by others, they constitute communicative acts which warrant interpretation. The higher centers of the nervous systems and perhaps certain glands evaluate messages originating in single organs, and a person may respond automatically, sometimes not being consciously aware of this transmission. Such automatic responses are termed reflexes if the circuit, with the exception of the stimulus, is located entirely within one organism. In transmission of messages from person to person information pertaining to the state of the organism of the speakers is frequently transmitted without the awareness of the participants. In social situations, for example, people automatically evaluate the other person's attitude—that is, whether it is friendly or hostile. Without being conscious of their own responses they will be more cautious and alert when facing a hostile individual than when they encounter an apparently harmless person. More complex interpersonal messages, especially when coded in verbal form, require a more conscious evaluation and interpretation. But regardless of the complexity of the message or the extent of the network, the basic principles remain the same.

A neutral observer, for example, when perceiving that a person tumbles downstairs and remains motionless at the end of the fall, might be impressed by several different communicative aspects of this incident. Referring to the physical sphere, the conclusion may be warranted that the person was injured. With reference to the intrapersonal system of the victim, the inference is made that certain processes within the mind of the accident-bearer may have been altered or arrested, and that the person has lost consciousness. Pertinent to the interpersonal relation, the conclusion is warranted that the person needs help; and in social terms, though not immediately, certain repercussions can be expected which might deal with lawsuits, establishment of rules for accident prevention, and the like. Thus any change in the state of an organism can be viewed from varied standpoints and can be registered consciously or unconsciously.

If actions of human beings and animals have communicative aspects, so also do plants and objects convey a message to the person who perceives them. It takes but the fraction of a second for our organism to perceive a multitude of stimuli, and most scientific descriptions of perceptive phenomena run into insurmountable difficulties when an attempt is made to describe the processes involved. A brief illustration may serve as an example. When our attention is attracted by the sight of a red rose, we conceive its splendor under the influence of messages transmitted to us through several channels. First we see, then we smell, and eventually after approaching the rose, we can touch the flower. The scientific description of these three steps would run into many hundreds of pages. Starting with the assessment of the color, the wave length of the reflected light, for example, could be specified as being around 7,000 Angstrom units. Thereafter the tint or shade of the color, the angle of reflection, the position and nature of the original source of light, its brightness, the surface texture and the color of the contrasting background, and many other features would have to be studied to complete the scientific description of the processes related to light alone. Botanical specifications of the family and species of the rose bush, identification of the time and duration of the process of blooming, would embrace some of the plant biological aspects of the investigation. Specifications of the odor emitted by the blossom, the number and type of insects attracted, and their effectiveness in seed dispersion might follow next. Chemical analysis of the constituent parts of the rose tissues or an assessment of the soil or weather conditions might head other chapters of the scientific study. Finally, after exhausting consideration of the rose, and of the conditions under which it bloomed, the investigation would finally reach the human being who perceives the rose. Name, age, sex, and other specifications would be needed to identify us, the individual observer. Study of our physical health and assessment of our vital apparatus would probably precede the psychological investigation of our past experiences, in particular those with flowers and roses. Psychological probing might reveal traces of previous events which enabled us to focus upon the rose rather than upon the structure of the wall in the background or upon a dog playing nearby. Further elaboration might reveal the purposes that we might have had in focusing upon roses, either as decoration of the buttonhole in the lapel, as an arrangement on our desk, or maybe as a present for a beloved one. And after all this long and tedious scientific preparation and accumulation of information regarding the rose and the human being who perceived it, we would have to be concerned with that split second which it took to see the rose, and those few seconds more which were necessary to walk towards it.

The reader will readily understand that no scientist is able to describe all the things that might have acted as stimuli or all the possible reactions that a person might have had in that situation. Nevertheless, a neutral observer, sitting on a bench nearby and observing the act of approach and of picking the rose, might infer a number of things from his own experiences in similar situations. He might conclude that we possess a readiness —or shall we say a preference—for that particular rose at that particular time in that particular situation. Let us say that the act of picking the rose had for us the significance of satisfying a desire and of providing us with a present, while for the observer it constituted an expressive act which transmitted to him information about ourself and the rose as well as about the total situation which was conducive to this act. To him, the observer, the only thing that was obvious was the combination of a particular stimulus, the rose, with a particular kind of response, the picking. This combination of a particular stimulus with a particular response we have called a value. For the observer, the choice of this act indicated to him that at that particular moment no other act could take place, though, for example, we might have walked by, heading for the dog without even noticing the rose. For ourselves who proceeded to pick the rose, the act created a precedent which might influence future actions and which in itself was a sequel to previous experiences of ours. Regardless of whether we were aware of our choice, and regardless of whether we knew the motivating reasons for our actions, we, as well as any observer, would agree that at the instant we picked the rose we conveyed a message to others. And this message certainly carried the meaning that within the context of this situation we valued—above all—a rose.

For purposes of communication, then, any action constitutes a message to ourselves as well as to others. Within the framework of communication, the expression and transmission of values—that is, actions denoting a choice—occupy a central place. A value conveys not only information about the choice made, but also relays information about the things that could have been chosen but were not selected. The ability to select, to maximize or minimize certain aspects of perception, are features which characterize our communication center. Furthermore, this center possesses the faculty of retaining traces of past experiences. Obviously not the action itself, but a symbolic representation, is retained, which has the function of representing within the human organism a small-scale model of all the events which have been experienced in the past.

Creation of new things and adaptation through molding of the surroundings distinguishes man from all other creatures. This gift, which the organicist calls "brain" and which the mentalist refers to as "psyche," is localized nowhere. With no anatomical structure of its own, nonetheless it needs for its functioning the sum total of all the cells and properties of the organism. To integrate parts into a whole, to magnify, minimize, or discard events, to evaluate the past and to anticipate the future, to create that which never before existed, such are the functions of the center. The infant, when born, is vested with all these potentialities; their exploitation, however, depends upon experiences and circumstances. Equipped with an insatiable desire for a search for the new, the exploration of things and people grinds permanent and indelible grooves into the center of the child. Imprints become experiences when events are registered, and traces remain available for future reference. Little by little, information is acquired through representation of outside events in the mind of the child. Happenings in and around a person are recorded in codified form, and complementation of immediate impressions with traces of the past facilitates a selective response. The individual is said to have learned when discriminating reactions as well as anticipation of events indicate mastery of self and surroundings.

The expansion of the maturing individual is controlled by biological limitations which in turn delineate the extension in space of the system of communication. Man's genetic endowment forces him to seek social relations, while his early development and his first social contacts will in part determine the way he is going to use[4] and eventually refine his means of communication. Man is born of a mother. After his birth, certain death would embrace the infant unless it were fed, clothed, and sheltered. The severance of the umbilical cord is but the first step towards achieving independence. The infant's struggle to acquire an identity of his own requires some fifteen or twenty years. During this time, the growing child, at first helpless and immobilized, little by little learns to explore the world and to undertake ventures on his own. Tedious codification of events leading to the accumulation of a vast mass of information and acquisition of the "know-how" pertaining to the use of this information enables the child to relinquish gradually the help received from parents and protectors. When biological maturation and social learning have progressed sufficiently, the child is equipped to set out on his own and to continue the battle for life with a reasonable chance of survival. Now even more than before, communication with fellow men becomes a necessity, since information about the self, others, and the surroundings has to be kept up to date.

[4]J. Ruesch, "Individual Social Techniques," *Journal of Social Psychology*, 29 (1949), 3–28.

The state of maturity has been reached when finally communication and cooperation with contemporaries has replaced the former reliance upon physical and emotional assistance from elders.

Man's concept of the world is acquired through social interaction[5] and communication, and these acquired views are the foundations upon which will rest the future organization of his surroundings. The shaping of things in the environment distinguishes man from all other living creatures. Man has mastered his physical limitations by extension in space and time. His voice, audible within a few hundred yards at best, now can encompass the globe and perhaps beyond. His movements in space, under primitive conditions, perhaps extended a few hundred miles; now they embrace the whole world and possibly more. The creation of script, the construction of man-made shelters, and the use of design enables messages from times past to reach future generations. The invention of time-binding mass communication led to the formation of a cumulative body of knowledge. Information accumulated in the course of centuries became the ground upon which were erected new object systems and events which eventually developed an existence of their own. In contrast to the animal, the human being has to face not only other people but messages and productions of the past as well. The inventions of man, frequently designed in the name of progress and survival, may undermine his biological foundations. Whether in the end the creations of man will improve his lot or result in his own modification or in his total annihilation remains to be seen. Be that as it may, at the root of all man-made events stands his ability to communicate, which is the foundation upon which cooperation is built.

Cooperation is closely linked to those characteristics which make man a gregarious creature. Thus man does not live alone. Usually he is surrounded by parents, mate, and offspring, and he seeks the company of contemporaries. In the fold of the family, the clan, the group, or, in the widest sense of the word, the herd, he feels secure. Here, the threatening experiences can be shared, and through pooling of information and cooperation of forces he can master adverse events. Reliance upon other members of the group increases his chances for survival in a troubled world. The first experience of being helped and raised by the mother or other members of the group induces man to trust or fear people. If trust and confidence prevail, he will seek the help of others; if fear predominates he will dominate or avoid others. But regardless of the motive, be it for the sake of sharing, avoiding, conquering, or destroying, he always needs other people.

Man has to move. As the infant acquires mastery of space, locomotion is soon supplemented by other means of transportation. In boats, on the backs of animals, on wheels, or on wings, the exploration of the world is carried on. Movement in space facilitates the acquisition and dissemination of information and the satisfaction of needs. Transportation and communication are thus so intimately linked that distinction is hardly possible.

In his exploration of space, in his quest for mastery, and in his need

[5]N. E. Miller and J. Pollard, *Social Learning and Imitation* (New Haven, Conn.: Yale University Press, 1941).

for food, shelter, and a mate, man will meet dangers and perhaps interference from others. Man and animal alike are alarmed at the sight of danger, and anything is threatening which, by their experience, is not known to be harmless. In animals, alarm—that is, impending readiness for events to come—is told in many ways: the lion tosses his mane and roars, the fiddler crab brandishes a bright red claw, while the moor hen utters a harsh "krek." A cat when chased by a dog seeks refuge in a tree, its fur erect, claws thrust into the bark, hissing at the growling canine below. The cat's body spells readiness for any future action if a change in the situation should occur; when prowling and stalking a mouse, it will patiently wait for hours for the opportune jump which will spell doom to the outwitted rodent.

While the alarmed animal has the choice of fight, flight, or playing possum, the human being has one additional opportunity. Constructive action, designed to eliminate the source of danger, long-term planning with the intent of preventing a recurrence of the danger, and pooling of information with subsequent cooperation with other humans are the unique privileges of man. Communication for the purpose of sharing and transmission of information to obtain the views of others provides help for the alarmed person. When fight, flight, playing possum, and communication are barred, the readiness of the body for action cannot be consummated. The continuous alarm becomes a permanent state, which is referred to as anxiety. Eventually the overtaxation of mind and body will gradually lead to a breakdown of integrated functioning. The individual is then psychologically and physically sick; the focusing of protracted attention upon the impending danger monopolizes the mental resources and perpetual readiness of the body results in anxiety and fatigue. Unawareness of other circumstances which might require immediate attention and the inability to mobilize the worn-out body for maximal effort eventually defeat the individual in situations which otherwise he could easily have mastered. Even then, communication is a helpful procedure. The process of talking, though not an act of great physical expenditure for the individual, will absorb the overflow of readiness, and eventually a person is again enabled to find his bearings. This interpersonal process constitutes the core of any type of psychotherapy.

The human being's need for social action is the moving force which compels him to master the tools of communication. Without these his ability to gather information is imperiled and gratification of vital needs is threatened. The superiority of a person within his group is determined in the first instance by skillful use of his means of communication; to receive information and to give that which others need, to possess a workable concept of events, and to act accordingly, marks the successful man.

INTERACTION: THE GOAL OF INTERPERSONAL COMMUNICATION

David K. Berlo

We have spent a good deal of time talking about the ways in which communication sources and receivers behave. At the beginning, we defined communication as a process, and pointed out that it is on-going, dynamic, without starting and stopping points. This is true. Yet, we necessarily have talked at times as if communication were static, nondynamic. This has not been intentional, but it is impossible to avoid when we *talk about* communication, when we take it apart to see how it works.

At this point, we might profit from another look at the process viewpoint of communication. The behaviors of the source do not occur independently of the behaviors of the receiver or vice versa. *In any communication situation, the source and the receiver are interdependent.*

The concept of interdependence is itself complex and can be illustrated by defining the possible relationships between any two concepts, such as *A* and *B*. A *and* B *are independent if and only if neither affects the other.* For example, the color of a person's hair *(A)* and his left- or right-handedness *(B)* are independent. They do not affect each other. Blondes are just as likely to be right-handed as they are left-handed. So are brunettes or red-heads. Right-handed people are just as likely to be blondes as they are to be brunettes or red-heads. The same is true for left-handed people. Neither affects the other.

There is a dependency relationship between A *and* B *if* A *affects* B *but* B *does not affect* A, *or vice versa.* For example, the production of the ragweed flower (*A*) and the incidence of hay-fever (*B*) are dependently related. The presence of ragweed affects some people by producing hay-fever. Hay-fever is dependent on the existence of ragweed. Ragweed is not dependent on the existence of hay-fever. People who have hay-fever do not affect the existence of ragweed. *A* is not affected by *B*, but *B* is affected by *A;* therefore, *A* and *B* are dependently related.

Interdependence can be defined as *reciprocal* or *mutual* dependence. If *A* affects *B* and *B* affects *A*, then *A* and *B* are interdependent. For example, in this country the farmer and the grocer are interdependent. The food the farmer grows affects the product the grocer can sell. On the other hand, the sales of the grocer affect the kind and amount of crops the farmer will grow. Each is dependent on the other, each affects the other.

There are varying levels of interdependence among concepts or events. Maximum interdependence is found in concepts that we have referred to as dyadic. For example, the concepts of father and child are interdependent for their existence, neither can exist without the other. The same is true for husband-wife, leader-follower, supervisor-supervisee, etc. This can be called *definitional interdependence*. Dyadic concepts refer to relationships between events which cannot exist alone.

Communication between two or more people requires an interdependent relationship; however, the levels of communicative interdependence vary from situation to situation. How do these levels differ?

LEVELS OF COMMUNICATIVE INTERDEPENDENCE

For purposes of discussion, we shall distinguish four levels of communicative interdependence. Again, it must be emphasized that we are distorting the process of communication when we do this. The four levels discussed are themselves not independent. Any communication situation probably includes some aspect of each; however, there are differences in emphasis from situation to situation.

If we remember that we are distinguishing among levels to point out differences in emphasis rather than differences in kind, we will not be misled. If we assume that communication at one level of interdependence is *not* related to the other levels we will *not* be taking the process aspect of communication into account.

Definitional-Physical Interdependence

If we reflect for a moment, it becomes clear that the communication concepts of source and receiver are dyadic. They depend on each other for their very definition. You cannot define a source without defining a receiver. You cannot define a receiver without defining a source.

In addition to their definitional interdependence, the functions of the source and receiver are *physically* interdependent, although the functions may be performed at different points in time and space. When two people are communicating, they rely on the physical existence of the other for the production or reception of messages. Occasionally, this is the only kind of mutual interdependence involved to any appreciable extent. For example, let us look at the following hypothetical conversation between an industrial foreman (Harry) and a plant worker (John). John and Harry work in the same department. They meet when they get to work in the morning, and have the following "conversation":

John: Harry, let me tell you about what happened last night at home. . . .
Harry: Fine, John. You know, things aren't going well on that experimental assembly job on the line. . . .
John: I came in last night, and everything hit me. The wife said that the kids had ruined some of the plants in the yard . . .
Harry: If we don't get into full production pretty soon on that job, I don't see how . . .
John: The plumbing stopped up in the basement . . .
Harry: We can fulfill the contract we're working on.
John: And the dog tried to bite the little boy down the street.
Harry: Things are sure rough.
John: They sure are.

This set of messages is exaggerated slightly to demonstrate a point, but most of us have heard conversations like this one, or even participated in a few. John and Harry were interdependent. Without the presence of the other, neither would have encoded the messages that he did; however, their major functions were to serve as receivers for the other's messages.

The kind of interdependence emphasized in this kind of situation is merely definitional-physical. The two communicators were not even reacting to each other's message. They were only waiting their turn to encode.

We probably would not want to label this "good" or "effective" communication. It *is a* frequent kind of communication.

When we communicate this way, we are not talking *to* each other, we are merely talking. We do not feel right in encoding certain messages unless we are in the presence of another. We cannot continue to do this when we are with another unless he puts up with it, or uses the situation for his own purposes. We are interdependent—but only because of the dyadic nature of the concepts of source and receiver.

Action-Reaction Interdependence

In explaining what is meant by action-reaction interdependence, we can use any of several servo-mechanisms as an illustration. For example, take the relationship between the modern furnace and the thermostat which we keep in our living rooms. We can look on thermostat-furnace behaviors as a communication relationship. Both the thermostat and the furnace serve as a source and a receiver. Each encodes messages, each receives messages from the other. Each affects the other. They are interdependent, and this relationship is more than mere physical interdependence. The responses that each makes are determined by the responses of the other. We can describe the communication situation between the thermostat and the furnace as follows: The thermostat has an intention, a purpose: to maintain the temperature of the room at a specific level, such as 68°. As long as the temperature remains at that level, the thermostat is silent. It encodes no message. When the temperature drops below that level, the thermostat transmits a message to the furnace—"turn on." *The thermostat acts.*

When the furnace receives the message "turn on," it decodes it and *reacts* to the message. The furnace allows oil or gas to enter its chambers, it increases the force of the pilot, it produces heat. When the air at the top of the furnace reaches a certain level, such as 150°, another thermostat starts.

None of these messages are transmitted to the thermostat. They are internal (covert) responses of the furnace. When the blower starts, however, the furnace begins to transmit a message to the thermostat—heat. The thermostat receives this message (a reaction by the furnace), decodes it and decides that its original purpose has been accomplished. The room temperature is now at the desired level.

On making this decision, the thermostat reacts to the heat it received by encoding another message—"turn off." The furnace reacts to this message by reducing oil or gas flow, lowering the pilot, shutting off the blower, and stopping the transmission of heat. In time, the thermostat reacts to the absence of heat, decides the temperature has dropped below the desirable level, and encodes another message—"turn on." The cycle begins again. Continual communication occurs between the furnace and the thermostat. Each transmits messages, each receives messages. Each reacts to the messages it receives.

The thermostat-furnace relationship is illustrative of many communication situations. Take the . . . example of the dinner table discussion between Bill and John. Bill had a purpose, he wanted John to pass him the salt. He encoded a message ("Pass me the salt, please"). He performed some *action.* John decoded the message and *reacted* to it. He responded by producing the salt. His action was taken as a result of decoding Bill's message.

When Bill perceived John's reaction, he reacted to it by reaching his hand out for the salt and saying "Thank you" to John. Each of these behaviors was dependent on the behavior preceding it. Bill acted, John reacted, Bill reacted, and so on. Bill and John were interdependent. Each was affected by the action of the other.

Feedback. Communication terminology includes a term related to action-reaction interdependence to which we have already referred: "feedback." It is correct to say that the furnace reacted to the thermostat; however, if we analyze the situation from the thermostat's point of view we can say that the reaction of the furnace was *fed back* to the thermostat. The thermostat can utilize the reaction of the furnace in determining its next message.

Feedback from the furnace was useful because it affected the next message that the thermostat produced. Without feedback from the furnace, the thermostat would not be able to determine whether it should tell the furnace to keep providing heat or to turn itself off. The thermostat needed feedback to ascertain whether it was being successful in its communication, whether it was having the desired effect.

The term "feedback" names a special aspect of receiver reaction. It names the use which the source can make of this reaction in determining its own success. For example, when Bill asked John to pass the salt, he could watch John to see if he did it. John's response was useful to Bill as feedback. It told him whether he had been successful in accomplishing his objective. If John did not pass the salt, Bill could have asked him again. If the furnace did not turn on, the thermostat would have repeated its message.

The source can use the reaction of the receiver as a check of his own effectiveness and a guide to his own future actions. The reaction of the receiver is a *consequence* of the response of the source. As a response consequence, it serves as feedback to the source.

Feedback provides the source with information concerning his success in accomplishing his objective. In doing this, it exerts control over future messages which the source encodes.

In the thermostat-furnace example, the reaction of each to the behavior of the other serves as feedback; however, these reactions can be utilized only in a limited way. The thermostat can repeat its message of "turn on" or "turn off." The furnace can repeat its message of "heat" or "no heat." No other alternative is available to either. Neither can communicate a different message, neither can alter the code, content or treatment of its message. All feedback can do in this illustration is affect the repetition of a message.

In human communication we can utilize feedback to a much greater extent. John's response to Bill was usable by Bill as feedback. It told him whether he had been successful or not. If John did not pass the salt, Bill could have changed his message, changed the code, the content, or the treatment. Bill could have changed receivers and asked someone else. He even could have changed his purpose and eaten his food without salt.

John also could get feedback. When he passed Bill the salt, he could observe Bill's response. If Bill smiled, and said "Thanks," or began to use the salt, that would be one thing. If Bill frowned, looked confused, said "What's that for," that would be another thing. All these responses could be used by John as feedback. *One consequence of a communication response is that it serves as feedback—to both the source and the receiver.*

In summary, communication often involves an action-reaction interdependence. The action of the source affects the reaction of the receiver, the reaction of the receiver affects the subsequent reaction of the source, etc. The source or the receiver can make use of the reactions of the other. Reactions serve as feedback. They allow the source or receiver to check up on himself, to determine how well he is doing in accomplishing his purpose. Feedback also affects subsequent behavior, if the source and receiver are sensitive to it.

When a source receives feedback that is rewarding, he continues to produce the same kind of message. When he gets nonrewarding feedback, he eventually will change his message. In responding to a message, the receiver exerts control over the source. The kind of feedback he provides determines in part the next set of behaviors of the source. Speakers and audiences, actors and theatre-goers, sources and receivers generally can be interdependent through the mutual effects of their reactions on the other.

For example, suppose you are giving a talk, making a speech. At one point in your talk, you tell a joke. The audience is supposed to laugh. If they laugh, this can serve as feedback to you. It tells you that you were successful. It tells you to keep going, your messages are having an effect. On the other hand, suppose the audience does not laugh. Suppose it just sits. This, too, serves as feedback. It tells you that you are not getting what you want, your messages are not meeting with success. You might change your jokes, or stop telling jokes. *The audience exerts control over your future messages by the responses it makes.* These are fed back to you. You are dependent on the audience for feedback.

At the same time, members of the audience are dependent on feedback. If one person does not laugh at your jokes and all the other members of the audience do, these responses are fed back to the nonlaughing receiver. He begins to question his sense of humor—and often begins to laugh at succeeding jokes, whether they strike him as funny or not. Eventually, they may even begin to strike him as funny.

Communication sources and receivers are mutually interdependent, for existence and for feedback. Each of them continually exerts influence over himself and others by the kinds of responses that he makes to the messages he produces and receives. A newspaper affects its readers by selecting the news they are allowed to read. On the other hand the readers also affect the newspaper (although probably not as much as some publishers would have us believe). If readers do not buy the paper (negative feedback), it may change its selection and presentation of news.

Advertisers control the reasons given to the public for buying this or that product. But the consumer affects the advertiser—through feedback. If the public buys more (positive feedback), the advertiser keeps his messages. If the public quits buying the product (negative feedback), the advertiser changes his messages—or the stockholders get a new advertising manager.

We can separate one communication situation from another by the ease with which feedback is obtained. Clearly, person-to-person communication permits maximum feedback. All available communication channels can operate. The source has an opportunity to change his message on the spot as a result of the feedback he gets. On the other hand, communication forms that we refer to as the public media (newspaper, television, magazines, etc.) have minimum opportunities for feedback. The source and the receiver are separated in time and space. They have little opportunity to get feedback from the responses of the other.

The difficulty of obtaining feedback for sources who use the public media has given rise to an entire industry: the public opinion pollster, the audience rating service, people who measure the amount of readership of a magazine, researchers who study the impact of advertising copy, organizations that interview receivers to check their responses to the source's message in an immediate and personal way. All these professionals attempt to provide feedback for a communication source. They are paid to help the source determine who is receiving his messages and what reactions are being made.

As communication receivers we often overlook our affecting power on the source. In a competitive market, it is amazing how much influence ten letters to the manager of a television station can have on his future policy decisions. Our decisions to turn off the television set affect future program decisions; i.e., audience ratings serve as feedback. The battle of audience ratings is of great importance in the broadcasting industry. Major policy decisions are often made solely on the basis of feedback on how many people are listening to or viewing a given program.

Even in our own person-to-person communication situations, we overlook the importance of feedback. As students, we fail to realize the extent to which we can affect the teacher. When we indicate that we do not understand, he repeats, if he is sensitive to feedback. When we let him know we think he is a good teacher, he may become a better teacher. Any performer would testify that he gives a better performance when his audience reacts favorably, when they make responses which he can use as positive feedback.

We underestimate the value of feedback when we communicate with our friends and families. We neglect to tell them when we think they have done a good job or when we like them. These kinds of responses are useful to them as feedback. They affect future actions toward us.

Action-reaction relationships are significant in analyzing communication. Feedback is an important instrument of affect. The reactions of the receiver are useful to the source in analyzing his effectiveness. They also affect his subsequent behaviors because they serve as consequences of his prior responses. If the feedback is rewarding, he perseveres. If it is not rewarding, he changes his message to increase the chances of being successful.

An awareness and utilization of feedback increase the communication effectiveness of the individual. The ability to observe carefully the reactions others make to our messages is one of the characteristics of the person we designate as being good at "human relations," or "sensitive as a communicator."

It is true to say that one can find communication situations that fit this action-reaction level of interdependence between the source and the receiver. Granted, too, that it is useful to retain the action-reaction concept and the corresponding concept of communication feedback. Yet there are at least two possible pitfalls into which this kind of analysis can lead.

First, the concept of feedback is used to reflect a *source orientation* to communication, rather than a receiver orientation or a process orientation. When we talk about the receiver's responses as feedback for the source, we are observing communication situations from the point of view of the source. We are perceiving through his eyes, not as an external observer.

As we shall show, there are levels of interdependence higher than action-reaction. We do not have to look at the source-receiver relationship as a one-way relationship; however, the feedback concept emphasizes one-wayness, at the expense of a two-way analysis. When people are taught about feedback, they are likely to take a source orientation to communication. We talk about "getting feedback" to the source, or "using the receiver's behavior" as feedback for the source.

The term "feedback" implies a point of view. We have said that one individual makes a response, performs an act. This response is perceived by a second individual and responded to. We say that the second individual reacts to the original message. When we call this reaction "feedback," we are structuring it as if we were the original source. We are talking about a use we can make of a reaction, not the reaction itself. There is nothing inherently wrong with this kind of terminology. In fact, it is useful to think this way. Nevertheless, if we are not careful, we begin to think about all of the processes from the source's point of view, and ignore the basic interdependence that produced the term "feedback" in the first place.

The second pitfall in the use of the action-reaction concept is concerned with our continuing reference to communication as a process. The terms "action" and "reaction" deny the concept of process. They imply that there is a beginning to communication (the act), a second event in communication (reaction), subsequent events, etc., with a final end. They imply an interdependence of events within the sequence, but they do not imply the kind of dynamic interdependence that is involved in the communication process.

People are not thermostats or furnaces. They have the capacity to make trial responses within the organism, to use symbols to anticipate how others will respond to their messages, to develop expectations about their own behavior and the behavior of others. The concept of *expectations* is crucial to human communication. It requires analysis at a third level of communication interdependence.

Interdependence of Expectations: Empathy

All human communication involves predictions by the source and receiver about how other people will respond to a message. Even in the minimal-interdependence situation that we have called physical interdependence, Bill and John had some expectations about each other. They made predictions about the language facility of the other, the length of time the other would tolerate listening rather than speaking, the social relationships that existed between them, etc. We can analyze expectations as a distinctive level of interdependence; however, to some extent this kind of interdependence is involved in all communication.

Every communicator carries around with him an image of his receiver. He takes his receiver (as he pictures him to be) into account when he produces a message. He anticipates the possible responses of his receiver and tries to predict them ahead of time. These images affect his own message behaviors. For example, the Madison Avenue advertiser has an image (accurate or inaccurate) of the American public. The Hollywood producer has an image of the movie-goer. Newspapers have expectations about how their readers will react to messages. Magazines can be distinguished on the basis of the images they have of their subscribers. Personnel managers have an image of the typical factory worker. Teachers have expectations about students.

The development of expectations of the receiver by the source has its counterpart in the development of expectations of the source by the receiver. Receivers have expectations about sources. When we observe the President, we expect him to behave in certain ways and not in others—because he is the President. Magazine readers have an image of the magazines they read. The public image of the *Ladies' Home Journal* is not the same as the image of *Fortune, Playboy*, or *True Story*. We expect different message treatments.

Communication receivers select and attend to messages in part because of their images of the sources and their expectations as to the kind of message these sources would produce. The public has an image of business corporations, labor union leaders, educators, doctors, etc. One of the major missions of the public relations expert is the development of expectations about his client. People in this profession are paid to manipulate the receiver's image of a company, a public figure, a product.

As sources and receivers, we have expectations about each other that affect our communication behaviors. Behavior is also affected by our images of *ourselves*. Our self-images influence the kinds of messages we create and the treatment we give our messages. Our expectations about our own behavior affect which messages we attend to. Subscribers to *Harper's* may have self-images different from those of subscribers to *The Reader's Digest.* Republicans have different expectations about their own behavior than do Democrats—at least in some behavioral areas.

As sources and receivers, we carry around images of ourselves and a set of expectations about other people. We use these expectations in encoding, decoding, and responding to messages. We take other people into account in framing messages. We frame messages to influence a receiver, but our expectations about the receiver influence us and our messages.

Some of the more interesting studies in communication analyze the images which individuals or communicative organizations have of their receivers, and how these expectations affect the source's behavior. For example, what image does Madison Avenue have of the typical Iowa farmer, of Madison Avenue itself? What image does the corporation executive have of himself, of the average factory worker, etc.? These are research questions, and important ones. Their answers can help us explain why people treat their messages as they do, because a source's expectations influence the way he communicates.

In approaching the concept of expectations, we can return to our basic model of the communication process. The communication source and receiver each possess certain communication skills, attitudes, and knowledges. Each exists within a social system and a cultural context. These affect how they will react to messages. Communication represents an attempt to couple these two individuals, these two psychological systems. Messages are used to accomplish this coupling of the organisms.

In one sense, messages are all that the organisms have available to them. By using messages, we come to "know" other men, to know ourselves. We believe that we can understand in part what is going on *within* another person. We develop expectations about what is going on within others and what will go on within ourselves. The basic question is, how do we develop these expectations?

To put it another way, we often make statements of the order, "I know John," or "He won't accept that argument—I know him inside and out." How do we come to "know" other people, inside and out? For that matter, how do we come to "know" ourselves? What is the process underlying our ability to develop expectations about others, to predict how they will behave before a situation arises?

Clearly, we frequently face decisions requiring this kind of knowledge. We decide whether we should promote Jones, whether we should marry Mary, whether we should recommend Bill for a responsible job. When we make these kinds of decisions, we operate on the assumption that we "know" Jones or Mary or Bill. We make decisions which imply that we understand people, that we can predict how they will behave.

When we say that we "know" somebody, we mean more than that we can recognize him physically when we see him. We mean that we can predict correctly that he will believe certain things and not others, he will behave in certain ways and not in others, he will react in certain ways and not in others.

When we say we "know" somebody, including ourselves, we are saying that we understand how he operates as a psychological entity—as a person with thoughts, feelings, emotions, etc. In making these predictions, we have physical behaviors as our basic data. Each of us perceives how others behave. We can observe these behaviors. They are overt, public. Expectations involve more than this. They involve the private behaviors of man, his covert responses, his internal states, his beliefs, his meanings. When we develop expectations, when we make predictions, we are assuming that we have skill in what the psychologists call *empathy—the ability to project ourselves into other people's personalities.* How do we develop empathic ability?

This is a basic question for students of communication. Unfortunately, there is no definitive answer to the question. In any complete sense, we are still without enough research evidence to substantiate one position or another. There are theories of empathy which are plausible—and at least consistent with research evidence. Tomorrow may provide an adequate answer—but we have to operate on what we know today. *We can define empathy as the process through which we arrive at expectations, anticipations of the internal psychological states of man.* How does this occur?

There are three major points of view on empathy. One school of thought argues that there is no such thing, that we cannot develop expectations. Supporters of this position for the most part are believers in a simple one-stage (S-R) theory of learning. This kind of learning theorist argues that all we have in communication is a set of messages. A message is produced by one person, and perceived by another. In other words, there are stimuli and responses. And that is that. . . . A simple S-R theory of learning may account for nonhuman animal learning, but not for the more complex learning behaviors of man. By the same argument, a simple S-R theory of empathy does not seem to account for man's communication behavior.

We *do* develop expectations, we *do* have the ability to project ourselves into the internal states of others. We cannot accept the argument that empathy does not have meaning for us, that we cannot develop expectations and predictions. Some kind of *interpretative* process occurs.

The development of expectations requires a special kind of talent. We need to be able to think about objects that are not available. *Expectations require decisions about the not-here and the not-now.* In order to have expectations, to talk about the not-here and the not-now, we create arbitrary symbols to represent the objects that are not available. We need to be able to produce these symbols and manipulate them.

Man is distinguished from other animals in that he has developed both of these talents. He can receive and manipulate arbitrary symbols. He can produce these symbols to serve his purposes. Because of this, he can represent the nonavailable, the not-here and not-now. As Thorndike put it, the use of arbitrary symbols allows "humans to think *about* things, not merely to think things." Man clearly has these talents, although there are individual differences among people.

Some of our games involve this kind of skill, the development of empathic ability. Chess is an example. A successful chess-player cannot rely on action-reaction. He develops expectations about the consequences of his behavior, and operates under those expectations. He predicts how the other man will react—often several events in advance. He debates moving a pawn. He reasons, if I move this pawn, my opponent probably will take my knight with his bishop—but if he does that, then I will checkmate his king with my queen, etc.

The same thing occurs in contract bridge. The good bidder anticipates possible answering bids from his partner or opponents before he makes his own bid. He also predicts how others will play their hands. The inclusion of this kind of skill is what prevents bridge from becoming a mechanical game that can be described in books. We differ in empathic ability. Some of us are better predictors than others.

We can reject the argument that we have no meaning for the concept of empathy. All of us anticipate the future, we make predictions about the relationships between (a) certain behaviors on our parts, (b) subsequent behaviors of other people, and (c) subsequent behaviors of our own. We do more than act and react. We develop expectations about others which affect our actions—before we take them. This is what we mean by empathy.

THEORIES OF EMPATHY

There are two popular theories about the basis for empathy. Both theories agree that the basic data of expectations are physical behaviors produced by man, i.e., messages. Both theories agree that man's predictions about the internal psychological states of man are based on observable physical behaviors. Both agree that man makes these predictions by using symbols to represent these physical behaviors and by manipulating these symbols. At this point, the two theories of empathy differ sharply. We can best discuss them separately.

Inference Theory of Empathy[1]

An inference theory of empathy is psychologically oriented. It argues that man can observe his own physical behavior directly, and can relate his behavior symbolically to his own internal psychological states—his feelings, thoughts, emotions, etc. Through this process, man comes to have meanings (interpretations) for his own physical behavior. He develops a concept of *self*, by himself, based on his observations and interpretations of his own behavior.

Given a self-concept, he communicates with other people. He observes their physical behaviors. On the basis of his prior interpretations of himself, he makes *inferences* about the internal states of others. In other words, he argues to himself that if behavior on his part represented such and such a feeling, a similar behavior produced by somebody else would represent a similar feeling.

This view of empathy assumes that man has first-hand knowledge of himself and second-hand knowledge of other people. It argues that man

[1]The major source of this theory is Solomon Asch, *Social Psychology*, Prentice-Hall, 1952, pp. 139–169.

has the ability to understand himself, through analysis of his own behaviors. From this analysis, man can make inferences about other people based on the similarities between their behavior and his own.

Let us take a simple example of this argument. Suppose you observe yourself making certain gestures; e.g., you repeatedly pound your hand on a table. You analyze how you felt when you performed this behavior. You conclude that you were angry, that you were upset. You discover a relationship between your overt behavior (table-pounding) and an internal state or feeling of anger. Then you observe somebody else pounding his hand on the table. From this behavior, you infer that he too is angry. You make assumptions about his internal state from (a) observing his behavior, and (b) comparing his behavior with similar behavior on your part which reflected anger in you.

This is the position of an *inference* theory of empathy. What are its assumptions?

1. *Man has first-hand evidence of his own internal states. He can only have second-hand evidence of other people's internal states.*
2. *Other people express a given internal state by performing the same behaviors that you perform to express the same state.*
3. *Man cannot understand internal states in other people which he has not experienced himself. Man cannot understand emotions which he has not felt, thoughts which he has not had, etc.*

Let us take these assumptions one at a time. First, an inference theory of empathy says that man's first-hand knowledge is of himself. All other knowledge is second-hand. As we shall find, the other major view of empathy contradicts this assumption directly. From currently available research evidence, we cannot resolve this issue; the assumption can be neither accepted nor rejected.

There is considerable evidence that conflicts with the second assumption, that all people express the same purposes by the same behaviors, that all people mean the same things by the behaviors they perform. Many breakdowns in communication stem from this belief. We often assume that another person attaches the same meaning to a word that we do, that a smile by another person expresses the same internal state as does a smile by us, that other people see the world in the same way that we do —just because they perform many of the physical behaviors that we perform.

It is true that we often get our ideas about the internal states of other people by inferring them from our own internal states, as related to our own behavior. But in so doing, we often err. We often fail to "know" the internal workings of others when we assume they are the same as ours.

When we look at the success we have in predicting and anticipating the behavior of others, it seems likely that we need to add another approach to empathy to provide a complete explanation of our success. We need an approach which does not assume that man's first-hand knowledge is always of use. People are not the same.

There also is evidence that contradicts the third assumption of inference theory: that we cannot understand internal states which we have not experienced ourselves. Few theorists would dispute the point that man understands best those things which he has experienced himself. Yet we can find many examples of the understanding (at least in part) of emotions which have not been experienced. For instance, we can empathize with a mother who has just lost her baby. We can have expectations about how she will behave, what her internal states are, even though we have never lost a baby. We can empathize with people who are in a state of great happiness over their coming marriage, even though we have not been married ourselves. Experience increases our understanding, but it does not seem to be essential to understanding.

These are the essential arguments of an inference theory of empathy. There seems to be some merit in the arguments; however, inference theory does not seem to explain empathy in terms that are completely satisfying. We can turn our attention to the second point of view, popularized by Mead and usually considered to be a sociological point of view. Mead labeled his theory as *role-taking.*

Role-Taking Theory of Empathy[2]

Let us not assume that man's first-hand knowledge is of himself, or even that man *has* a concept of self before he communicates with other people. We can examine some of the behaviors of man, and try to interpret their implications for empathy.

Let us look at the very young child, the infant. How does he behave, how does he develop his ability to empathize? The basic data that are observable to the infant are physical behaviors, message behaviors. The infant, like everyone else, can observe and produce physical behavior. The question is, how does the child develop interpretations of self and others, given observable physical behaviors?

Role-taking theorists argue that the new-born infant cannot distinguish himself from other people, cannot tell one person from another. In order to develop the concept of self, the infant must first look on himself as an object—must act toward himself as he acts toward other objects, other people. *In other words, the concept of self does not precede communication. It is developed through communication.*

The young child exhibits a good deal of imitative behavior. He observes other people's behavior. He tries to repeat the behavior as well as he can. Some of the behavior he imitates is behavior directed toward him. His mother makes sounds (speaks) in his presence. He begins to imitate the sounds. The father moves his face (smiles) in his presence. He begins to imitate these facial movements.

In imitating behaviors directed toward him, the infant begins to act toward himself as others act toward him, but he has no interpretation for these actions, no meaning for the actions. This is the beginning of role-taking, the beginning of the development of a concept of self. *In the first stage of role-taking, the infant actually plays other people's roles without*

[2]The major source of this theory is the work of George H. Mead. Much of the discussion is taken from George H. Mead, *Mind, Self and Society*, University of Chicago Press, 1934.

interpretation. He imitates the behavior of others. He is rewarded for these role-playing responses; therefore he retains them.

As the child develops, he increases his role-playing behavior. He increasingly acts toward himself in the same way that other people act toward him. At the same time, he learns to produce and manipulate a set of symbols, significant symbols, symbols for which he and other people have meanings. Equipped with a set of significant symbols, the infant can begin to understand the roles that he takes. He can understand how other people behave toward him. He can begin really to put himself in other people's shoes, to look at himself as other people do.

Those of you who have watched small children know what is meant by this. The child at age two or three will play by having a make-believe tea party. At the tea party, he will reprimand himself—produce messages such as "Todd, you mustn't do that or I'll send you up to bed," or "No, no, Sandy, that's not the way to sit at the table." When the child behaves like this, he is looking at himself as an object of behavior—as an external object. He is playing the role of the parent, putting himself in the shoes of the parent. *This is the second stage of role-taking, in which the infant plays other people's roles—with understanding.*

As the child matures, he engages in more complex roleplaying. He begins to play games with several other people. In playing games, the child must take a large number of roles at the same time. In hide-and-seek, the child must put himself in the shoes of the person who is "it," must, simultaneously, take the roles of all the other children who are hiding.

It now becomes impossible physically to *play* all these roles. The child cannot imitate all the related behaviors. Through the use of symbols, however, he hypothesizes what it would be like to behave as the other children do. He infers their roles, he takes their roles in his own mind, rather than playing the roles physically. *This is the third stage of role-taking, in which the child begins to put himself in other people's shoes symbolically, rather than physically.*

By putting himself in the places of all the other children, the child develops expectations about his own behavior—about what is expected of him in this situation. He then behaves according to his expectations, as determined by *taking* the roles of others. If he has done a good job of role-taking, his behavior conforms to the expectations the others have, and they reward him, they let him play, they like him. If he has not done a good job of role-taking, his behavior does not conform to the expectations of the other children and he is not rewarded. He is rejected, punished.

As the child continues to participate in group activity, he takes the roles of many other people. In so doing, he looks on himself as a receiver, as an object of behavior. Gradually, he begins to *generalize* the roles of others. He starts to get a general concept of how other people behave, how they interpret and how they act toward him. We can call this the concept of the generalized other. *The generalized other is an abstract role that is taken, the synthesis of what an individual learns of what is general or common to the individual roles of all other people in his group.*

Each of us develops a concept of the generalized other, based on our experiences in a specific social environment and in the successive roles of other people that we take. The generalized other provides us with a set of expectations as to how we should behave. This is our meaning for the concept of self. *Our self-concept is the set of expectations that we have as to how we should behave in a given situation.* How do we develop a self-concept? Through communication, through taking the roles of others, through acting toward ourselves as an object of communication, through the development of a generalized other.

Inference theory *assumes* a concept of self, and suggests that we empathize by using the self-concept to make inferences about the internal states of other people. Inference theory suggests that the self-concept determines how we empathize. Role-taking theory argues the other way around. It suggests that the concept of self does not determine empathy. Rather, communication produces the concept of self and role-taking allows for empathy. Both theories place great importance on the nature of language, significant symbols, in the process of empathy and the development of a concept of self.

Which are we to believe? How does man empathize? Here, we will take the position that *man utilizes both these approaches to empathy.* We can argue that man's first approach is through role-taking. Each of us takes roles of other people. Each of us develops a concept of the generalized other. The way that we look on ourselves, our definition of ourselves, is determined by our concept of the generalized other, the social context in which we exist, the expectations which we perceive others to have about our own behaviors.

As we develop and mature, we construct a concept of self. Then we operate on it. We now begin to make inferences about other people, based on our concept of self. We lessen our use of role-taking, and increase our use of inferences. We make the assumption that other people are like us, and that their behaviors reflect the same internal states that our behavior reflects. We do this until we do not find it rewarding.

When we empathize by making inferences and are not rewarded, we are forced to do one of two things. Either (1) we distort the behaviors of others that we perceive, and make them correspond to our expectations, or (2) we take another look at our images of ourselves, we redefine self, we return to role-taking.

If we take the first solution, distorting the world that we perceive, we become mentally ill, we have "delusions," we end up in an institution. This is not desirable. Yet we can predict that much of the problem of mental health is related to man's inability or unwillingness to change his own image of himself when he finds that it is not rewarded in his social environment.

What about the second alternative, a redefinition of self? To do this, we have to return to role-taking, we again have to take the role of others, to develop a new concept of the generalized other, a new set of expectations for our own behavior. In so doing, we redefine ourselves, change our behaviors accordingly, and again begin to make inferences about other people.

We often engage in role-playing when we are revising our role-taking or self concepts. Again, the mentally ill can use role-playing as a technique to increase their ability to make useful hypotheses about how others would react, and how they should react in a given situation.

As we play the role of another, we combine the inference and role-taking points of view. When we role-play, we actually perform certain behaviors. From these, we can infer our own internal states, we can make inferences from our own behavior which are pertinent to the behavior of another. We then can use these inferences in taking the role of another.

This process of role-taking, inference, role-taking, inference goes on continually. It is what we mean when we say that man is adjustable, adaptable, able to alter his behavior to fit the situation, the social environment in which he finds himself. He develops expectations by taking the roles of others, or by making inferences about himself, or both.

When do we often find it necessary to redefine self? When we enter a new social situation, a new group, a different social environment. For example, when a teen-ager enters the university, he finds himself in a new social situation. His inferences about other people are no longer valid. He makes false predictions, has hazy expectations. Often, he begins to ask himself who he really is.

What does the teen-ager begin to do? He reverts to role-playing, often at a primitive stage. He begins to imitate the behavior of others—without meaning. Gradually, he takes the roles of others (students, teachers, etc.) and is able to put himself in other people's shoes, to look at himself through their eyes. In so doing, he develops a new concept of the generalized other, a new set of expectations about his own behavior. He redefines self and begins to behave in accord with his new definition.

This kind of process is required of us many times in our lives. When we enter a new community, join a new group, travel to a different culture, our predictive power is weakened. We find it difficult to make inferences from self-knowledge. If we are to operate effectively in a changing social situation, we need to be able to take other people's roles, to redefine ourselves. In part, this is the mark of the adjusted man.

INTERACTION: THE GOAL OF HUMAN COMMUNICATION

One necessary condition for human communication is an interdependent relationship between the source and the receiver. Each affects the other. At one level of analysis, communication involves only a physical interdependence; i.e., source and receiver are dyadic concepts, each requires the other for its very definition, each requires the other for its existence.

At a second level of complexity, interdependence can be analyzed as an action-reaction sequence. An initial message affects the response that is made to it, the response affects the subsequent response, etc. Responses affect subsequent responses because they are utilized by communicators as feedback—as information that helps them determine whether they are achieving the desired effect.

At a third level of complexity, communication analysis is concerned with empathic skills, the interdependence produced by expectations about how others will respond to a message. Empathy names the process in which we project ourselves into the internal states or personalities of others in order to predict how they will behave. We infer the internal states of others by comparing them to our own attitudes and predispositions.

At the same time, we engage in role-taking. We try to put ourselves in the other person's shoes, to perceive the world as he sees it. In doing this, we develop the concept of self that we use to make inferences about others. In communicating, we shift from inferences to role-taking as a basis for our predictions. The expectations of the source and receiver are interdependent. Each affects the other, each is in part developed by the other.

A final level of interdependent complexity is interaction. The term *interaction* names the process of reciprocal role-taking, the mutual performance of empathic behaviors. *If two individuals make inferences about their own roles and take the role of the other at the same time, and if their communication behavior depends on the reciprocal taking of roles, then they are communicating by interacting with each other.*

Interaction differs from action-reaction in that the acts of each participant in communication are interrelated with each other, they affect each other through the development of hypotheses about what these acts will be, how they fit the purposes of the source and receiver, etc.

The concept of interaction is central to an understanding of the concept of process in communication. Communication represents an attempt to couple two organisms, to bridge the gap between two individuals through the production and reception of messages which have meanings for both. At best, this is an impossible task. Interactive communication approaches this ideal.

When two people interact, they put themselves into each other's shoes, try to perceive the world as the other person perceives it, try to predict how the other will respond. Interaction involves reciprocal role-taking, the mutual employment of empathic skills. The goal of interaction is the merger of self and other, a complete ability to anticipate, predict, and behave in accordance with the joint needs of self and other.

We can define interaction as the ideal of communication, the goal of human communication. All communication is not interactional, or at least does not emphasize this level of interdependence. . . . Much of our social behavior involves attempts to find substitutes for interaction, to find less energy-consuming bases for communication.

We can communicate without interacting to any appreciable extent; however, to the extent that we are in an interactional situation, our effectiveness, our ability to affect and be affected by others increases. As interaction develops, expectations become perfectly interdependent. The concepts of source and receiver as separate entities become meaningless, and the concept of process becomes clear.

Section Two
THE PROCESS OF INTERPERSONAL COMMUNICATION

In this section (Chapters 3–7) we shall discuss the basic elements of the process of interpersonal communication in some detail. Our analysis of an interpersonal communication event produces these five process elements:

1. *We sense a need for interaction with another person (or persons); two needs are apparent: personal development and control of our environment (Chapter 3, The Interpersonal Imperative).*
2. *We perceive the other person as he or she relates to these needs (Chapter 4, Interpersonal Perception and Orientations).*
3. *We analyze the situation in which we encounter another person in terms of spatial and temporal conditions; we note social conventions versus a behavior imposed by these conditions (Chapter 5, The Interpersonal Environment).*
4. *We employ signs and symbols to convey our thoughts to the other person (Chapter 6, Sharing Ideas: Interpersonal Semantics).*
5. *We establish, evaluate, and sometimes modify a relationship; by the term "relationship" we mean routinized ways of interacting with another person (Chapter 7, The Interpersonal Relationship).*

As we have emphasized, these five basic elements of the interpersonal communication process are all interactive; each one influences each other one. As people generate and attribute meanings to messages, each element is present. One or another frequently changes, sometimes without our conscious awareness. Each one influences the way we interact with others; they are usually different from one communication event to another. And each comprises differences that matter—"differences that make a difference."

Although there is constant interactive influence between each of these basic elements, each must be discussed separately; we will attempt to do so for purposes of clarity of analysis. However, we must remember that none of them operates in isolation.

The order for discussing each of the basic elements is arbitrary; in any interpersonal communication event each one is present and influences the others. We will start with a person's need for interacting with others because, to some extent, it is primary, both in time and importance. We carry our interpersonal needs around with us. As we start life, or when we first meet another person, we bring these needs with us to the encounter.

Chapter 3
THE INTERPERSONAL IMPERATIVE

Interaction with other people is imperative if we are to achieve a sense of personal well-being. The quality of our interpersonal communication heavily influences our personal growth, psychological health, and our success in influencing our environment. In our culture interaction is imperative because we cannot avoid people, and when we are with them we cannot *not* communicate; if we try to ignore the presence of others we only succeed in giving them a message that is disconfirming to them.

In this chapter we look at ways in which interpersonal communication contributes to our personal development and our efforts to control our social and physical environment. Such behavior is so automatic that, as adults, we rarely stop to analyze our motives. Such an analysis should be helpful to our understanding of the process of interpersonal communication. Our study of this process thus begins with an investigation of our motives for interacting with others. Such motivations are the essential first steps in the process and greatly influence ways in which we respond to each other.

PERSONAL DEVELOPMENT

As we grow we strive to make sense of the world around us, to determine what is real and what is not real (illusory, imaginary), and we depend upon other people to check our views. All of us want to have an identity, to be sombody, a person with a distinct feeling of who he or she is. As our self-image develops, we constantly evaluate it; if to us it seems to be good, we gain self-esteem--a very comfortable feeling. To the extent that our personal interaction with others is successful and confirming, we are able to grow, find our identity, gain self-esteem, and feel that we are firmly in touch with reality.

The Search for Self-Identity

As very small children we become aware of parts of the world around us. We particularly become aware of our relationships to other people and tend to experience ourselves by noting their responses to us. Thus, a major need is to obtain a clear reflection of ourselves from others.

Relating to Other People. Ordinarily we are most comfortable and happy when we feel that our relationships with others are dependable and friendly—that is, that we can count on being understood and warmly accepted. As very small children we find ourselves greatly dependent upon persons immediate to us, usually our parents or those who take care of us. The satisfaction of our needs almost entirely depends upon our ability to establish a workable relationship with them. At this stage our thoughts about ourselves are greatly colored by the quality of this relationship.[1] As we grow older this factor continues to influence our view of ourselves.[2]

Most of us have been able to establish relationships with others that meet our needs and give us a fairly satisfactory self-image. The importance of this process may be demonstrated by looking at some persons who, for one reason or another, are unable to establish such an acceptable relationship. Such persons frequently develop great anxiety over their inability to relate adequately to others; they tend to feel helpless in the face of this problem without really knowing why.[3] They cling to unproductive ways of reaching out to others and seem unable to change to more productive methods.[4] They tend to be afraid, feeling inadequate, helpless, and alone.[5]

An illustrative case of this problem is presented by Sidney Jourard in his book, *Disclosing Man to Himself*. A man in his late twenties consulted Professor Jourard for help when he found he couldn't complete a thesis. They met a number of times; the young man was quite obsessed with his manliness, and very tense. He told about his earlier life and an unsatisfactory relationship with his father. Then, during one session there was a prolonged silence, and the young man sat there with a look of desperation on his face. Jourard writes:

> *I felt an impulse to take his hand and hold it. I pondered . . . and debated whether I should do such a thing. I did it. I took his hand and gave it a firm squeeze. He grimaced; and with much effort not to do so, he burst into deep, racking sobs.*[6]

Experiencing Ourselves Through Other People's Responses to Us. As we interact with other people we note their responses to us, and, as a result, we experience ourselves in terms of their reactions. As long as these reactions are positive and supportive we get along pretty well;

[1]Cf. Frieda Fromm-Reichmann's review of this process in *An Outline of Psychoanalysis* (New York: Random House, 1955), pp. 113–120.

[2]See E. Erikson, *Identity: Youth and Crisis* (New York: Norton, 1968), pp. 91–141.

[3]Cf. R. May, *The Meaning of Anxiety* (New York, Ronald Press), 1951.

[4]See, for example, H. S. Sullivan, "The Meaning of Anxiety in Psychiatry and in Life," *Psychiatry*, 11 (1948), 1–13.

[5]Fromm-Reichmann, *op. cit.*, pp. 115–126.

[6]S. Jourard, *Disclosing Man to Himself* (New York: Van Nostrand Reinhold, 1968), p. 98.

if they are varied, we tend to try to pay more attention to those that are pleasant.[7]

When most or all responses to us are negative, we suffer from unhappy feelings about ourself. In some cases we may be driven to make up, create, or imagine responses that are more pleasing. Erik Erikson describes a rather inventive high school girl who secretly sought the company of Scottish immigrant neighbors, assimilating their dialect and social habits. With travel guides and history books, she reconstructed for herself a childhood in an actual Scottish township and made it quite convincing in her talks with newly arrived immigrants from that country. She referred to her American-born parents as "the people who brought me over here." In her discussions with Erikson she was calm and almost convincing. Finally, when he asked her how she managed to work out all the details of life in Scotland, she said, in a pleading Scottish brogue, "Bless you, sir, I needed a past." Her own unhappy childhood and her near-delusional attempts to create one that was more to her liking eventually came to be viewed in better perspective. The basis of the invention came to be seen as her attachment to one of the immigrant women who had given her more of the kind of love she needed than had her parents.[8]

Most of us don't go as far as this young woman in trying to improve our self-image. Some of us encourage a favorite nickname or paint a slightly enlarged or brighter picture of our past. In so doing, we are attempting to give ourselves a better self-image by encouraging more favorable responses from others.

In our youth or adolescence we seem to be desperately struggling to define ourselves. Some of us seem to know what we are, while others are most concerned about what they might hope to become. With respect to this process of identity formation, it is useful to note the contribution of George Herbert Mead; perhaps more than any other theorist he viewed the development of self-identity as the product of social interaction. Mead emphasized the importance of face-to-face interpersonal communication—how we respond to others and how they in turn respond to us. In this way we learn about ourselves; each interchange gives us cues about how others see us, and this shapes our view of ourselves. From the time we are small children this process goes on; virtually all communication to us gives us indications of our importance, capabilities, potential, and inadequacies.[9]

The following description of this process of identity formation has been given by Erikson:

[7]Cf. Erikson, *op. cit.*, pp. 96–107.

[8]*Ibid.*, p. 174.

[9]G. H. Mead, *Mind, Self and Society* (Chicago: University of Chicago Press, 1934), pp. 144–164.

> *Identity formation . . . is a lifelong development largely unconscious to the individual and to his society. Its roots go back all the way to the first self-recognition: in the baby's earliest exchange of smiles there is something of a self-realization coupled with a mutual recognition.*[10]

The process of identity formation via interaction with others, suggested by Mead and Erikson, is largely a reflection of others' perception of us. Cooley coined the phrase "the looking-glass self" and Sullivan spoke of "reflected self-appraisal." These are graphic labels for this process.[11] A more detailed discussion of the theories of Cooley, Mead, and Erikson is included in an essay on the summary of identity theory by Bennis and his associates, presented as a reading at the conclusion of this chapter.

Obtaining a Clear Reflection from Others. The images of us reflected by others are sometimes vague or distorted. Our psychological comfort is greatly increased if from such reflections we can develop a clear and accurate picture of ourselves. It is particularly important to us that you and I each see ourself as *an individual,* somehow different from people around us. In a sense we tend to feel that we are real to the extent that we are unique.

An illustrative example is the case of a pair of identical twins often described in the literature on child development. In typical fashion identical twins of the same sex are dressed alike and treated alike by their parents, with friends and relatives doting on "How cute they are" and "How much they look alike." The search for identity is well illustrated when one or the other objects to being dressed like, treated like, and especially *confused with* the other. In one such case a twin girl said, "I don't want to be like her; I want to be like me."

Handling Inconsistent Reflections. Sometimes other people reflect images of us that are inconsistent. For example, one of our actions may be characterized by two other people as two different behaviors, so incompatible that both *views* cannot be correct. Occasionally these inconsistent reflections of us are produced by understandably different views of others based on their perceptions. These differing ways of seeing us may be influenced by different backgrounds or experiences

[10] E. Erikson, "The Problem of Ego Identity," *Psychological Issues,* 1 (1959), 47.

[11] Not all psychologists are in agreement on theories of the development of the self-concept. Here we are following the widely accepted theories developed by William James, C. H. Cooley, G. H. Mead, and Erik Erikson. For a detailed treatment of theories of self-concept, see C. Gordon and K. J. Gergen, eds., *The Self in Social Interaction* (New York: Wiley 1968); see also M. R. Stein, A. J. Vidich, and D. M. White, eds., *Identity and Anxiety* (New York: Free Press, 1960).

on the part of our friends or relatives. For example, a brother may admire one of our actions as a show of "independence," while a parent may criticize us for being "disobedient." As we grow and more frequently take a stand, we may be applauded by some for our "determination" and resented by others for our "stubbornness."

Inconsistent or contradictory reflections of our image ordinarily cause us to be uncomfortable. We seek to organize these reflections somehow into a unified picture, composed of elements that seem to us to belong together. Requesting and receiving clarification or explanation frequently can help to reduce inconsistencies. In this way direct interpersonal communication can reduce tension and anxiety concerning our self-image.

Using "Reference" Persons or Groups. As we compare reflections of our image from various other persons, we tend to pay more attention to some people and less to others. We select those whose approval is more important to us—more credible as well as desirable. Sometimes these are individuals; more frequently they are groups, sometimes called *primary* or *reference groups.*[12] For most of us an important reference group is our immediate family.

In his book, *Self and Society,* Nevitt Sanford reports a large in-depth study of college students and the influences of others on their lives. An illustrative example of the positive influence of a father is taken from interviews with a rather successful sophomore:

> *"Mother was sick in bed a great deal of the time. I remember her reading and singing to us. She devoted her last strength to us kids. I don't have those early recollections of my father. My first recollection of him as a father was one spring morning, when mother passed away. He came back to tell us. Of course, there is such a disparity between his age and mine. He is 77 now. Mother had 3 operations. The third time she left I was very distressed. It was like a premonition. The aunt across the street helped take care of us, when we got sick. Father spent all of his time with us after mother died. . . ."*
>
> (What things did you admire especially in your father?) *"Mostly, his attention to us kids was very admirable. He's very honest, so much so that he won't condone charge accounts. He's known throughout the country as a man whose word is as good as his bond. His greatest contribution was denying himself pleasures to take care of us kids."*
>
> (What disagreements have you had with your father?) *"There haven't been any to any great extent. I had a mind of my own at a very early age. He has too. We've had arguments, but I can't remember any lickings by him. He scolded but usually talked things over. Our arguments were usually about things I wanted that he didn't want*

[12]For a detailed discussion see H. H. Kelley, "Two Functions of Reference Groups," in G. E. Swanson, T. M. Newcomb, and E. L. Hartley, eds., *Readings in Social Psychology* (New York: Holt, Rinehart and Winston, 1952), pp. 410–414.

me to have—like the .22 rifle I wanted when I was 10, or a bicycle. He had to be very careful about money. He wouldn't let me work—he thought it was beneath me. He was afraid I would hurt myself with the rifle. But he never denied me anything I needed."

(What have been the effects of the age discrepancy?) *"Well, I've had to shift for myself a lot. I would have welcomed instruction that he wasn't able to give me. My first venture socially was in the DeMolay. I was a charter member and later a master counselor. I was vice-president of the student body in high school and president of the student body at business school. He was pleased and encouraged me.*[13]

By way of contrast we may look at parts of an autobiography reported by Sanford given by a young man, who, at the age of 21, had begun to serve a sentence of 10 to 20 years for armed robbery:

"My first memory has to do with Dad beating Mother. It seems that Mother and Aunt Catherine, who in the meantime had arrived from Greece, were having an argument. I do not recall its exact nature. However, Dad entered the room cursing Mother. He called her a son of a bitch and an old whore, and kicked her in the stomach. I began to cry and felt extremely sorry for Mother, who with her hands pressed to her abdomen had fallen into one of the dining room chairs. . . .

Dad came home angry one night. Business had fallen off; he was discouraged and was thinking of closing the store. Mother said that it was too bad. If she said anything else, I cannot remember it. Dad swore at her. She ran from the table. Dad kicked back his chair and started for her. She ran out in the hall toward the piazza. Dad ran and kicked her. She cried, 'Don't.' He stood there and cursed. 'You son of a bitch of a whore, you dirty bastard.' I ran and put my hand on his leg and between sobs asked him not to hit Mother. He told me to get away from him and struck at me. I ran up the hall. Poor Mother, heavy with child, stayed on the piazza until he had become quiet and then with a red nose and a drawn, haggard face crept into bed, afraid to speak, afraid to open her mouth for fear that her husband would kick her. Years later, when he would begin to curse, this scene would unfold itself, and I would rise and for every vile epithet he used, call him one in return, while four young children sat and listened."[14]

Sanford suggests that the young offender has transferred his hatred of his father to the police and other authority figures in general, and has come to view himself as a compulsively "bad" person, unable to behave in ways that will win social approval.[15]

These cases illustrate ways in which our relating to individuals can influence our self-concept. In similar ways groups can exercise such an influence. Groups can be healthy or unhealthy; they can stimulate undue fear or distrust, inadequate or distorted interpersonal

[13]N. Sanford, *Self and Society* (New York: Atherton, 1966), pp. 141–142.
[14]*Ibid.*, p. 123.
[15]*Ibid.*, pp. 123–124.

communication, vague or unsatisfying goals, and conflict over power or interpersonal influence. As such, they can exercise damaging influence on our self-image.[16] Most of us have some opportunity to choose the groups with which we will identify, although sometimes, perhaps in school or at work, our choices are limited. In such cases our best hope may be to try to improve those groups with which we are associated. An essay by Jack and Lorraine Gibb, "Humanistic Elements in Group Growth," following this chapter, identifies those group characteristics that enhance personal growth and a satisfactory self-concept.

Regardless of whatever else it is, interpersonal communication is a very human process, with direct impact of other people on ways you identify yourself. Your own program for personal development should consider the impact on you of those groups with whom you associate. Such groups will tend to reflect major ethics of the surrounding society. In this decade our society's hallmarks are approval of scientific technology, a market economy, and a warfare state. You should consider these potential influences on your self-image. In so doing, you will need to reevaluate your reference groups with care. And after this has been accomplished, you will need to employ interpersonal communication for further evaluation of your own self-image as it is reflected by those in whom you have the greatest confidence.

To the extent that our efforts are successful in providing us with a self-image that is clear, unique, and consistent, we know who we are and what we are. To the extent that we are not so successful, we continue to search for our personal identity. For most of us this search continues more or less throughout our lives. Each new experience, each change of environment, each unexpected reflection of our image from a new acquaintance can cause us to reconsider various parts of our self-concept. Inconsistencies can produce significant feelings of discomfort, even anxiety.

In succeeding chapters we will consider problems of interpersonal communication—problems that interfere with the reflection of our image as seen by others. For these reflections to be perceived accurately and interpreted correctly, it is imperative that we make optimum use of the process of interpersonal communication.

The Pursuit of Self-Esteem

Of all the factors that combine to make our lives worth living, it appears that self-esteem is one of the most important. Almost all of us are concerned about a feeling that we are seen, both in our own eyes and in the view of others, as admirable people. The specific criteria

[16]J. R. Gibb, "Defense Level and Influence Potential in Small Groups," in L. Petrullo and B. M. Bass, eds., *Leadership and Interpersonal Behavior* (New York: Holt, Rinehart and Winston, 1961), pp. 66–81.

for esteem may vary considerably from one person to another, but the desire for approval is almost universal. In large measure the "pursuit of happiness" is the pursuit of self-esteem.

Numerous examples may be cited of persons who have given up wealth, position, and even life itself in order to achieve or maintain self-esteem. The ordinary basis of self-esteem is a self-image that is satisfying to us as individuals, even though this self-concept is heavily influenced by our image as it is reflected to us by others.

An astute observer of this process was George Bernard Shaw; at the same time he refused to allow himself to become completely trapped by it, maintaining his own personal position of judgment. A rather humorous description of Shaw's insight into the process as it affected himself is given by Erikson with brief quotations from Shaw's own writings:[17]

> *G. B. S. (for this is the public identity which was one of his masterpieces) describes young Shaw as an "extremely disagreeable and undesirable" young man, "not at all reticent of diabolical opinion," while inwardly "suffering . . . from simple cowardice . . . and horribly ashamed of it." "The truth is," he concludes, "that all men are in a false position in society until they have realized their possibilities and imposed them on their neighbors. They are tormented by a continual shortcoming in themselves; yet they irritate others by a continual overweening. This discord can be resolved by acknowledged success or failures only: everyone is ill at ease until he had found his natural place, whether it be above or below his birthplace." But Shaw must always exempt himself from any universal law which he inadvertently pronounces, so he adds: "This finding of one's place may be very puzzling by the fact that there is no place in ordinary society for extraordinary individuals."*
>
> *Shaw proceeds to describe a crisis at the age of twenty. This crisis was not caused by lack of success or the absence of a defined role, but by too much of both: "I made good in spite of myself, and found, to my dismay, the Business, instead of expelling me as the worthless imposter I was, was fastening upon me with no intention of letting me go. Behold me, therefore, in my twentieth year, with a business training, in an occupation which I detested as cordially as any sane person lets himself detest anything he cannot escape from. In March 1876 I broke loose." Breaking loose meant to leave family and friends, business and Ireland, and to avoid the danger of success unequal to "the enormity of my unconscious ambition."*[18]

Seeking Approval of Others. As we develop a concept of ourselves, some elements will please us and likely some will not. What we tend to seek most from others is approval that bolsters our belief in the

[17] G. B. Shaw, *Selected Prose* (New York: Dodd, Mead, 1952).
[18] Erikson, *Identity: Youth and Crisis, op. cit.*, 143.

desirable elements of our view of ourselves. Occasionally we find approval of those elements about which we have some misgivings, and may conclude that they are more or less admirable after all. If, in the long run, the balance appears to be favorable, our self-esteem grows and becomes more secure.

In some cases a favorable balance is achieved only at great personal risk—or so it would appear. Most high school and college students are acquainted with the game of "chicken" usually played with speeding autos aimed for a head-on collision—until one or both drivers swerve, with special social notoriety (approval) for the one who does not (if he lives to collect his reward). Occasionally the "chicken" game is played by people with guns, as reported in Fresno, California:

> *A barmaid and a bandit played a game of "chicken" with loaded pistols early yesterday and, although no shots were fired, the barmaid won.*
>
> *The action took place at The Bit, a proletarian beer and wine oasis on the southern fringe of town, where lovely Joan O'Higgins was on duty behind the bar.*
>
> *Suddenly a towering bandit walked into the establishment, ordered a beer, flashed a small pistol and commanded Miss O'Higgins to clean out the cash register.*
>
> *The barmaid placed $11 on the bar, an amount that failed to satisfy the bandit, whose height was estimated at six feet five.*
>
> *"Give me the rest," he demanded.*
>
> *Barmaid O'Higgins reached into a drawer for the main money bag and the .22 caliber pistol beneath it.*
>
> *She pointed the gun at the man and asked:*
>
> *"Now, what do you want to do?"*
>
> *The bandit, realizing that he had met his match in The Bit, blinked at the sight of the gun and left, leaving his beer and the $11 behind.*[19]

Sorting Out Approval and Disapproval. Situations occur. We act or react, always hoping for approval from those whose opinion is important to us. However, responses from others usually include both some approval and some disapproval—a mixed picture of our success.

In many cases we have a serious problem of determining when, if any, approval of us is being given. A response to our behavior may be inappropriate, apparently unrelated to our intention and unmeasurable in terms of its approval to us. In other cases it may appear that our actions have produced no response whatsoever. Occasionally we are praised for things we did not do, or did not know we did. Sometimes a response is given in such a nonchalant fashion that we are totally unable to decide whether or not we are being approved.

[19] *San Francisco Chronicle*, July 14, 1966.

We sort our way through mirages and reality of reflected approval and disapproval—an uneasy task at best. Difficult as it may be, we find ourselves doing it as best we can because it is of great importance to us. All in all, we seek for a favorable balance: Are we generally liked, occasionally loved, sometimes admired, and ordinarily respected?

Putting On an Act. Since maintenance of self-esteem is important to us, and our primary device for evaluating our behavior is the approval of persons important to us, we tend to behave whenever we can in ways that produce approval, and we avoid acting in ways that bring disapproval. Many times we are tempted to act in ways that win approval but are not true to our own inner feelings or beliefs—to present a front, acting out something we are not. One young woman described her behavior as follows:

> *I somehow developed a sort of knack, I guess, of-well-a-habit-of trying to make people feel at ease around me, or to make things go along smoothly. . . . At a small meeting, I could help things go along nicely and appear to be having a good time. And sometimes I'd surprise myself by arguing against what I really thought when I saw that the person in charge would be quite unhappy about it if I didn't. . . . I just didn't stand up for my own convictions, until I don't know whether I have any convictions to stand up for. I haven't been really honestly being myself, or actually knowing what my real self is, and I've been just playing a sort of false role.*[20]

We are often tempted to act as if we are something we are not in two ways: hiding parts of ourselves, and pretending we are more than we really are. Neither deception works very well; both have serious consequences for our self-image. In the long run, although frequently tried, both are self-defeating.

When we perceive that parts of ourselves are eliciting disapproval, we may attempt to hide those parts—if we think it can be done. We then relate to others as "part-persons" rather than whole persons. For example, we may attempt to show no fear except when we are alone. Generally such attempts are ineffective; people usually see nonverbal signs of tension which are beyond our control, and these are communicated to persons close to us despite our efforts to "say nothing." However, there are two important considerations when we are thus successful at hiding such parts of ourselves. The first consideration is that our anger or fear is stored up inside us, possibly influencing our later responses to communication from others. These feelings may break out in ways we don't understand and which are

[20]Reported by C. Rogers, "What It Means to Become a Person," in C. E. Moustakas, ed., *The Self* (New York: Harper & Row, 1959), p. 197.

not understood by others. Such "breakouts" (or "outbreaks") may not even be perceived by us but are easily seen by others.[21] In this fashion, later communication not related to the focus of our anger or fear may be influenced in such a way that others (and we) are confused. At best, such internalized anger and fear contribute to our problem of fighting off an early ulcer.[22] Improved habits of being open and frank in our interpersonal communication can be personally helpful.

A second possibly damaging effect of hiding parts of ourselves is that we cause apprehension in those persons with whom we relate. Suppose as your employer I must tell you that you have failed to do your job in an adequate manner. Suppose I tell you, and you show no reaction—you smile, remain calm, say nothing, and go your way. My interpretation is that you are a cool one, that you maintain your calmness through stiff self-discipline, and do not easily go out of control. But I also wonder if you'll "lay low and stab me in the back" when I'm not expecting it—I become suspicious of you! I wonder how many emotional stimuli you can take before you react; do you remain calm under stress until at a certain point you "break" and cannot be depended upon at all? The point is this: You have given me no way to assess your emotional behavior—I perceive only part of you and suspect there is more. I have experienced you as only a "part-person," and as such you do not seem to be real. I am confused and will be suspicious until I learn more about you. In the meantime, this attitude will tend to distort my perceptions of even your ordinary, everyday communication which may be totally unrelated to the earlier event. In such fashion interpersonal communication and personal relationships are distorted by attempts to hide part of ourselves.

Often we try to hide parts of our true selves by staying close to the "straight and narrow" ritualized patterns of interaction. We don't really believe in these rituals, but they appear to be very safe, sometimes winning approval but seldom bringing disapproval. We try to be cautious, to pursue only the "tried and true" forms of interpersonal behavior. "I can't receive negative feedback if I only do as everybody else does." The effect on the other person is one of appraising you as only a "part-person"—too cautious, unnatural, and somewhat unreal. In some cases the other person becomes somewhat apprehensive, wondering when your real self may show and what it will be like—and to what extent it may prove to be a threat.[23]

The second form of deceptive interaction is to pretend that we

[21] C. Rogers, *On Becoming a Person* (Boston: Houghton Mifflin, 1961), pp. 338–346.

[22] S. Jourard, *The Transparent Self* (New York: Van Nostrand Reinhold, 1964), pp. 184–185.

[23] Cf. E. Goffman, "On Face-Work: An Analysis of Ritual Elements in Social Interaction," *Psychiatry*, 18 (1955), 213–231.

are something we are not. This approach includes attempts to communicate false messages about ourselves—to wear masks or to erect facades. This game can be carried to incredible extremes; we can even put forth a little of that part of ourselves that produces undesired responses and then deride, derogate, or castigate such behavior! Erving Goffman has carefully analyzed such forms of pretense in his book, *The Presentation of Self in Everyday Life.*[24] He draws a distinction between "expressions given" (genuine communication) and "expressions given off" (artificial communication) and cites an insightful and humorous example taken from a novel by William Sansom in which Preedy, a vacationing Englishman, makes his first appearance on the beach at a summer resort:

> *But in any case he took care to avoid catching anyone's eye. First of all, he had to make it clear to those potential companions of his holiday that they were of no concern to him whatsoever. He stared through them, around them, over them—eyes lost in space. The beach might have been empty. If by chance a ball was thrown his way, he looked surprised; then let a smile of amusement lighten his face (Kindly Preedy), looked around dazed to see that there were people on the beach, tossed it back with a smile to himself and not a smile at the people, and then resumed carelessly his nonchalant survey of space. But it was time to institute a little parade of the Ideal Preedy. By devious handlings he gave any who wanted to look a chance to see the title of his book—a Spanish translation of Homer, classic thus, but not daring, cosmopolitan too—and then gathered together his beachwrap and bag into a neat sand-resistant pile (Methodological and Sensible Preedy), rose slowly to stretch at ease his huge frame (Big-Cat Preedy), and tossed aside his sandals (Carefree Preedy after all).*
>
> *The marriage of Preedy and the sea! There were alternative rituals. The first involved the stroll that turns into a run and a dive straight into the water, thereafter smoothing into a strong splashless crawl towards the horizon, but of course not really to the horizon. Quite suddenly he would turn on his back and thrash great white splashes with his legs, somehow thus showing that he could have swum further had he wanted to, and then stand up a quarter out of water for all to see who it was. The alternative course was simpler, it avoided the cold-water shock and it avoided the risk of appearing too high-spirited. The point was to appear to be so used to the sea, the Mediterranean, and this particular beach, that one might as well be in the sea as out of it. It involved a stroll down and into the edge of the water—not even noticing his toes were wet, land and water all the same to him!—with his eyes up at the sky gravely surveying portents, invisible to others, of the weather (Local Fisherman Preedy).*[25]

[24]E. Goffman, *The Presentation of Self in Everyday Life* (Garden City, N.Y.: Doubleday, 1959).

[25]W. Sansom, *A Contest of Ladies* (London: Hogarth, 1956), pp. 230–232.

It is quite possible for most of us to recall times when we have behaved in a manner somewhat similar to Preedy's. We all play roles of one kind or another at various times. The important thing is to know when we are doing it, and to note the relative portion of our time devoted to such behavior. Are we ever truly ourselves?

Pretense and Self-Defeat. A number of points may be made about pretending to be what we are not. In the first place, it takes much energy and concentration; while focusing on our performance, we may miss many clues to the way people are perceiving us. Goffman makes the point that many times people eventually discover that nobody is really watching these performances and in reality could not care less.[26] Such performances, when ignored, can amount to a severe loss of time and effort—time during which a genuinely rewarding interpersonal relationship might have been achieved.

In the second place, such play-acting must be good. Many a television comedy is based on a character's pretense to be something he is not, with himself being the only member of the group who does not know that all others see through his façade. We may laugh at a comic character in a play, but we hardly want people laughing at our silly performance in real life. We shall mention more damaging effects later, but it seems bad enough to have people meet us and go away saying to themselves, "What an ass!"

Most of us are incapable of carrying off our deception on the nonverbal level. By muscular tension, changes of posture, facial expressions, jerky gestures, tone of voice, or other behaviors usually beyond our control, we signal our anger, fear, surprise, elation, and other real feelings and attitudes.[27] Few of us are adept at maintaining "poker faces" in our interactions. People may tolerate our pretense but they usually know it for what it is if they care at all to look. How, for example, would you be able to carry off a pretense that would deny the messages described below:

> *In a sheltered corner of the room we stopped dancing altogether and talked, and what I distinctly remember is how her hands, beneath steady and opaque appraisal of her eyes, in nervous slurred agitation blindly sought mine and seized and softly gripped, with infantile instinct, my thumbs. Just my thumbs she held, and as we talked she moved them this way and that as if she were steering me. When I closed my eyes, the red darkness inside my lids was trembling, and when I rejoined my wife, and held her to dance, she asked, "Why are you panting?"*[28]

[26]Goffman, *The Presentation of Self in Everyday Life, op. cit.*, pp. 6–14.

[27]P. Watzlawick, J. H. Beavin, and D. D. Jackson, *Pragmatics of Communication* (New York: Norton, 1967), pp. 62–67.

[28]J. Updike, *Pigeon Feathers* (New York: Crest Books, 1953), p. 176.

A more damaging consequence of another person's penetration of our "cover" is that they cannot further depend upon anything we do or say—suspicion haunts their every observation of our behavior–"What a phony!" He or she may never give us a very *obvious* clue of this suspicion, while a *subtle show* of a clue is lost by us in our "performance." But when we need his or her confidence most—when we very much want real trust and accurate estimate of our potential, when we ask sincerely to be given a try—they will try others first, and we may be left alone with our pretenses, a lonely phony.

Even when our pretenses successfully win approval they tend to provide shallow satisfaction. Inside we know that we are a fraud; such self-knowledge is damaging to our self-esteem and eventually to our self-concept. Even if we successfully use such deception in our interpersonal communication, we have only misused such interaction to defeat ourselves.

In our final estimation, the most severe consequence of pretending to be something we are not is that it becomes a way of life. The more we pretend, the better we become at "playing a part." And the better we are at "playing parts," the more we will try to solve our problems of interpersonal relations by pretense rather than by honestly facing issues and working out solutions based on reality. One phony bit of behavior thus produces another, and even if we convince many other people, we will be faced with the problem of trying to find our real self. "Who are you?" is the basic question asked of persons thought to be mentally disturbed. Unlimited pursuit of pretense in life can produce the seeds of madness.[29]

Changing Our Behavior. Instead of pretense, a better alternative for maintaining or increasing self-esteem is to attempt to make personal changes in our behavior, changes that honestly win approval and at the same time make our self-image more satisfying to us.

We are usually able to make adjustments to *severe* demands in our environment without too much difficulty; such changes are required for personal survival, and although not easy to make, they are eventually handled by most of us. However, over a period of time we develop certain ways of relating to other people. These relationship patterns are discussed in detail in Chapter 4 under the heading, Interpersonal Orientations. The point to be emphasized here is that once such habitual patterns have become established, they are difficult to change. Only through firm resolve and deliberate effort on our part can such changes ordinarily be accomplished.

[29]H. Deutsch, "The Imposter: Contribution to Ego Psychology of a Type of Psychopath," *Psychoanalytical Quarterly*, 24 (1955), 483–505.

In any case, an attempt to change our behavior should be our own decision, firmly based on our own personal conviction. We should carefully evaluate those persons whose responses to us have fostered consideration of such changes. In no case should we try to change just to please someone else if our own sensitivities are thus violated; this would be very similar to the pretense approach previously discussed. In the long run, violation of our own values to please someone else will diminish our own self-esteem.

Identification of changes that we wish to make can be helped by discussing our actions with persons we trust. We can thus gain a clearer picture of ourself through interpersonal communication. However, we must try to make sure that these images of ourselves are accurately perceived and honestly reflected back to us; thus, the process of interpersonal communication discussed in this book must be employed in optimal fashion. Effective maintenance or improvement in self-esteem requires that we openly discuss our own behavior and that we seek and obtain honest feedback. And we must carefully evaluate any suggestions for change.

There can be no guarantee of continued self-esteem as we attempt changes. We must risk our self-esteem with each attempt to improve it. Our doubts about our self-worth can only be dissipated by putting them to the test of self-exposure and feedback. *In the long run, probably the best type of self-esteem is confidence in our ability to use this approach—confidence that we can maintain our self-esteem by using self-exposure and feedback.*

This procedure involves exposure of ourselves through initiation of communication or by responding to communication of others. It also involves *evaluative* feedback. By evaluative feedback we mean reflected appraisals of ourselves as exposed. These are useful for self-evaluation and making decisions to attempt self-change. Persons with excessive fears and very low self-esteem will be able to accept *only* feedback that is reassuring. Those with higher self-esteem can risk the acceptance of feedback that shows some weaknesses or unacceptable aspects of themselves. They can test their assumptions about real worth, acceptability, lovability, and value to other persons.

There are two general classes of communication feedback useful for evaluating self-worth. When people communicate, however impersonally, they give off subtle cues in the form of *indirect* feedback. *Direct* feedback consists of verbal statements explicitly describing one person's reactions to another.

Indirect feedback is often ambiguous. A smile may be a polite social habit. Aloofness may indicate disapproval, or it may indicate the other person's fear of his own self-exposure and consequent evaluation. The problem is magnified by a person's tendency to see what he expects to see, to be sensitive only to those cues that confirm his expectations.[30] Thus, if we are suspicious of our self-worth, we are more likely to note cues confirming our suspicions.[31]

Indirect feedback tends to be overgeneralized. It is frequently difficult to associate our feeling of rejection by another person with any one of our own specific acts. We tend to interpret such rejection of some minor part of our behavior as rejection of our whole self, or all parts of ourselves about which we have doubts. Indirect feedback does not provide for explanation, specificity, or justification. In addition, indirect feedback may reveal more about the other person than about us; consequently, when we are fearful we may rationalize a negative response from another person by attributing it to *their* weakness, injustice, narrowness, or malice.[32] Such indirect feedback may be easily misinterpreted.

Direct feedback is potentially more useful for evaluating self-worth; however, it is useless, even harmful, if it is not frank and honest. Frank evaluations are difficult to obtain because of our cultural taboos. We tend to approve people who look for and respond to "some good in everyone." We think it is somehow wrong to look critically at and to speak openly to another person. Maslow has noted that even our definitions of love do not ordinarily include an obligation to give open and honest interpersonal evaluation; he points out the irony of our willingness to let someone go on doing damage to himself and others, ostensibly "out of kindness."[33] Probably our own fear of hurting someone and receiving retaliation is our real motivation.[34] Requesting frank and honest evaluation of ourself from another person requires courage.

Increasing self-esteem requires positive reevaluation of oneself. This reevaluation requires exposure plus awareness and honest responses on the part of another person. We may thus conclude that it is difficult for a person to achieve change in interpersonal behavior without interaction with honest persons.[35] Such relationships are to be prized and protected with great care.

We have given extensive consideration to the development of self-image and the achievement of self-esteem. We have done so de-

[30]M. Deutsch and L. Soloman, "Reactions to Evaluations by Others as Influenced by Self-Evaluations," *Sociometry*, 22 (1959), 93–122.

[31]J. W. Thibault and H. W. Rieken, "Some Determinants and Consequences of the Perception of Social Causality," *Journal of Personality*, 24 (1955), 113–133.

[32]F. Heider, *The Psychology of Interpersonal Relations* (New York: Wiley, 1958), pp. 169–173.

[33]A. H. Maslow, "Summer Notes on Social Psychology of Industry and Management," Non-Linear Systems, Inc., Del Mar, Calif., unpublished manuscript, 1962.

[34]W. G. Bennis et al., *Interpersonal Dynamics*, rev. ed. (Homewood, Ill.: Dorsey, 1968), pp. 35–39.

[35]*Ibid.*, pp. 505–523.

liberately because, in all of the areas in which interpersonal communication influences people, we can think of nothing more important. We believe that these elements are fundamental to most, if not all, human interaction.

Reaching for Reality

In our development as people we are constantly trying to ascertain what is real, to find solid ground, to determine its dependability, and to penetrate those appearances of reality that are illusory products of our imagination. It is not by accident that a long-running Coca-Cola advertisement neglects to discuss the contents of the product but joyously proclaims that "It's the real thing," and in another commercial we are advised that "When you're out of Schlitz—you're out of beer," regardless of what other brands may be on hand.

Many questions concerning reality in the world around us can be answered by our physical senses: We can reach out and touch the soft surface of a leaf; smell the perfume of a rose; see a fleecy, floating cloud; and feel a summer breeze gently on our skin. Other questions of reality cannot be answered simply by sight, smell or touch. They concern the reality of interpersonal relationships and social competence. It is important to us to determine the reality of our relationships with other people, the quality of their opinion of us, and our competence in dealing with them. One writer on human relations has said that it takes two to see one.[36]

The quality of a relationship is difficult to assess, and many times we express our concern about how well we are doing at getting along with others. For example, young people frequently ask: Does he (or she) "really" love me? Can I count on it—is it "for real"? Such questions are neither naïve nor inconsequential; they are intensely important to all of us.

Perceiving Social Reality. From the time we are small children we need to know how to get along in the world, to determine what other people are like, how they view us, and how they tend to respond to our efforts to make our way through life. In effect, we are motivated to discover all we can about ourselves and the people around us through interpersonal communication. We are particularly concerned about learning to get along with others.

In 1954 Leon Festinger wrote an essay that provided the basis for a large number of research studies.[37] In this essay Festinger describes his view of the way a person confirms his impressions of his environ-

[36]S. A. Culbert, "The Interpersonal Processes of Self-Disclosure: It Takes Two to See One," in J. T. Hart and T. M. Tomlinson, eds., *New Directions in Client-Centered Therapy* (Boston: Houghton Mifflin, 1968).

[37]L. Festinger, "A Theory of Social Comparison Processes," *Human Relations*, 7 (1954), 117–140.

ment. Festinger identifies a continuum on which he places "physical reality" at one end and "social reality" on the other. Physical reality is said to involve such things as objects or surfaces, the perceptions of which an individual can validate with his physiological senses. Social reality is said to involve perceptions of such things as appropriate social behavior, judgments of a moral or ethical nature—those elements of reality we usually associate with attitudes, opinions, or beliefs. An opinion, attitude, or belief is said to be perceived by the individual as valid to the extent that it is anchored in (or reflected by) an approved reference group. For example, the validation of one's perception of himself as an "adequate communicator" would require, at least in part, positive feedback from other people.

There are many areas in which our perceptions of social reality need to be checked by comparison with those of others through interpersonal communication. We do this each time we change to a new environment; for example, when we enter a different school, take a new job, or become a new member of a group, we ask others about norm-expectancies. In groups and organizations certain people may be identified as "norm givers"—those who take responsibility for giving us orientations. Frequently such people tell us how we are doing as we adjust to the new environment.

In thus comparing ourselves with others we tend to seek information about persons who are somewhat similar to us. We seek information about people similar to us or even a little above us when the characteristic in question is highly valued—for example, the ability to do well on an examination.[38] We tend to seek information about those a little less confident than ourselves when evaluating our fear or our behavior in a situation we see as threatening.[39] We tend to seek information about others who are closely similar to us when we have some reason to be unsure of our ability.[40] And in the absence of information about other persons, we tend to make inaccurate and unstable self-evaluations.[41] This process of discovering socially approved norms of behavior never ends. We continuously want to be sure we are doing the right thing, and doing it well—that is, doing it in a way that will win the continued cooperation of others in satisfying such needs.

As we search for socially approved norms, we find it necessary

[38] L. Wheeler, "Motivation as a Determinant of Upward Comparison," *Journal of Experimental Social Psychology Supplement*, 1 (1966), 27–32.

[39] J. M. Darley and E. Aronson, "Self-Evaluation vs. Direct Anxiety Reduction as Determinants of the Fear-Affiliation Relationship," *Journal of Experimental Social Psychology Supplement*, 1 (1966), 66–70.

[40] K. Hakmiller, "Need for Self-Evaluation, Perceived Similarity and Comparison Choice," *Journal of Experimental Social Psychology Supplement*, 1 (1966), 6–26.

[41] R. Radloff, "Social Comparison and Ability Evaluation," *Journal of Experimental Social Psychology Supplement*, 1 (1966), 6–26.

to resolve our confusion when receiving conflicting feedback from others regarding our behavior. Studies of this problem have generally been reported under the rubric of *resolving cognitive dissonance.* This general concept applies to all of our perceptions, those related to physical reality as well as the ones directly relating to our self-evaluations.

Three theories of cognitive consistency have received wide attention: the "balance theory" of Heider,[42] the "congruity theory" of Osgood,[43] and the "cognitive dissonance theory" of Festinger.[44] The three consistency theories are somewhat different but have one thing in common: They assert that the normal condition of a person's attitudes is that of internal consistency between elements perceived as related, and that attitude change is the reduction of dissonance generated by new communications about, or new perceptions of, an attitude object.

Perhaps an example taken from a research report can illustrate the use of interpersonal communication to resolve problems of conflicting feedback about our behavior. In a manufacturing plant that was part of a nationally known industrial complex, a small item was being produced under a federal government contract. This contract required that all workmen at the plant wear conspicuous identification badges at all times. Compliance with this ruling had been lacking; some of the men said they thought the brightly colored official badges "looked silly." Interviews showed that company officials were telling the men that the badges must be worn. An inventory of attitudes toward wearing the badges showed that most of the men held negative attitudes. The experimenters arranged for discussion of the topic by randomly selected groups of workmen; workmen not selected were treated as a "control" group—the basis for comparison. The experimental groups were asked to "meet and discuss the topic of identification badges"—no additional instructions or leadership were provided. The kind of communication employed was not controlled by the experimenter (nor by management); details of the discussion sessions reflected the decisions of the individuals involved. It was inferred that there was sufficient cognitive dissonance to motivate group interaction; the group members did talk about the badges and related considerations—federal contracts, rulings, need for individual identification, etc.

The results showed that the persons in the experimental groups

[42]F. Heider, "Attitudes and Cognitive Organization," *Journal of Psychology,* 21 (1946), 107–112; see also F. Heider, *The Psychology of Interpersonal Relations* (New York: Wiley, 1958).

[43]C. E. Osgood, G. J. Suci, and P. H. Tannenbaum, *The Measurement of Meaning* (Urbana: University of Illinois Press, 1957).

[44]L. Festinger, *A Theory of Cognitive Dissonance* (New York: Harper & Row, 1957).

who had discussed the badges for about an hour showed significant changes in attitudes (favorable) as measured by post-testing. Their post-test attitudes were significantly different from the post-test attitudes of the control group, and the members of the experimental group were later reported by the company officials to have significantly increased the amount of wearing the badges. Postexperiment interviews indicated that the men found that although the individual's evaluation of *himself* when he wore the badge was that he "looked silly," most persons' evaluation of the looks of another person's wearing the badge was that he did not "look silly"—given the contract conditions existing at that plant. In this experiment it appeared that cognitive dissonance regarding badges was reduced by interpersonal communication.[45]

Determining the Quality of a Relationship. It is not easy to assess the quality of one's relationship to another person. Relationships seem to be full of little surprises. In the first place, we must interact in order to test a relationship, to produce evidence of its nature, its strength and dependability; and we must weigh this evidence with care. When we have noted the responses of others, we will need to compare our impressions with those of other observers. Such interaction requires a good working relationship.

Over time it is quite possible for people to change and consequently for a relationship to change. Because of new experiences or association people can change their degree of expertness on some operation, or their amount of power or social influence, or even the nature of their own self-image. Usually such changes occur only in response to major environmental changes, but they do occur. Recently we were exposed to a changing perception of President Nixon during the Watergate hearings.

When former associates meet following a period of separation, it is quite important to reaffirm the previous relationship before continuing interaction. An assumption that a prior relationship is still in effect is inappropriate; a brief exploration of how the relationship currently is viewed can expose new and different perceptions or indicate that the old basis is a solid one, still in effect. Businessmen seem to find this procedure a bit awkward; however, teenagers in love seem to make it a daily occurrence—in fact, sometimes they seem to do little else as they interact with each other. This problem is particularly pertinent in a leader-follower relationship. People in authority roles (e.g., parents) seem to take for granted that a relationship with a subordinate will never change; such an assumption holds real danger

[45]K. Giffin and L. Ehrlich, "The Attitudinal Effects of a Group Discussion on a Proposed Change in Company Policy," *Speech Monographs*, 30 (1963), 337–379.

in terms of interpersonal cooperation and personal satisfaction. An authority relationship needs to be reaffirmed periodically if the relationship is to be functionally effective.

Predictable changes in a relationship need to be identified and affirmed. Such a situation is the new relationship between a husband and wife at the birth of their first child. Probable changes in such a relationship need to be explored, and mutual agreement and understanding need to be achieved and then reaffirmed periodically as social conditions change (e.g., as the baby becomes a young child, etc.).

To reaffirm a prior relationship is simply to fulfill a social expectation; a mutually agreeable relationship is easily renewed. On the other hand, if events have transpired calling for a new relationship, the participants logically should start interaction with a discussion of required changes in their mode of interacting with each other.

The nature of one's relationships to other people—subservient or influential, warmly accepted or coldly tolerated—can have considerable impact on one's view of oneself. One's psychological development, sense of well-being, and personal self-esteem can be severely influenced. Accurate determination of the quality of such relationships depends heavily on effective use of interpersonal communication. On the basis of this line of reasoning, we see it supporting our theory that interpersonal communication must be viewed as a basic human imperative.

The Quest for Confirmation

We have noted that as very small children our sense of self-identity is influenced by the way other people respond to us. As we grow and develop, we need to feel that our relationships with others are dependable, that we can count on them, and that they are friendly—that we are accepted. For our personal sense of well-being we need the responses of others to confirm our belief in ourselves—that we are acceptable persons.

At the very least it is necessary that we receive confirmation from a few persons significant to us; confirmation that we exist as human beings, with senses, feelings, and thoughts similar to those of other people. In this way we must feel that we are human. Without this degree of confirmation, life itself loses significance.

The Implicit Issue of Validation. Whenever one person attempts to initiate interpersonal communication with another, he or she has made an implicit request: "Please validate me as a person." Ostensibly there is a surface request for recognition of the person's message, admission that his/her ideas are worth considering. However, beneath the surface there is the implicit issue of the value of that person as a human being.

Suppose you are alone at a table in a crowded café. Another person *acts as if* he would like a place to eat—perhaps at your table. Note that this behavior, without any verbal interchange, has already implicitly raised the question of your recognition of his needs and feelings as a person. If you *act as if* you don't see him, you have implicitly answered his request, "Please validate me," in a negative way.

Note that in an interpersonal situation where two people are face-to-face, each aware of the presence of the other, if one even *acts out* a message, it is impossible for the other to ignore that overture without giving an implied message in response. Ignoring him/her, attempting to make *no response* in such a situation, *is a response*. Denial of the opportunity to talk with you implies that, for you, he/she does not exist as a person worthy of your consideration. The implicit issue of validation of a person as a human being is always present whenever two or more people are together, face-to-face, and their presence is obvious to anyone who is awake.

Confirmation of another human being as a person consists of responses indicating that he or she is a normal, healthy individual. *Disconfirmation* consists of responses suggesting they are ignorant, inept, unhealthy, unimportant, or, at worst, that they do not exist. Disconfirmation by communication denial constitutes a major barrier between people, and will be discussed in detail in Chapter 8.

As children we like to have our parents give us things, but most of all we want them to *communicate* with us. We do not know for certain what we are until others (significant to us) tell us. We even prefer mild punishment to total indifference; in later life we can tolerate hate better than we can accept total neglect.[46] Even in the pain of being hated we can at least know that we really exist. Socrates, condemned to death, faced condemnation with pride and honor; he believed that his death would affect important future acts of his countrymen. But if no one responds to our acts or thoughts, while yet we cannot live without thinking and acting, the incongruity between our needs and our world becomes unbearable. Under such circumstances children aggress against their parents and teenagers test authority by violating rules. In extreme circumstances a person may behave in extreme ways in order to obtain a response—any response—to establish his existence, regardless of the degree of antagonism or hostility his/her behavior will produce.

An unprovoked attack upon another person can never be condoned; however, the terrible sense of loneliness, neglect, and the need for some kind of attention from others that instigates such an attack is pertinent to the study of interpersonal communication. Attempted

[46]H. D. Duncan, *Communication and Social Order* (New York: Oxford University Press, 1962), pp. 271–273.

destruction of oneself may be a call for "help"—attention from and consequential interaction with others; it may also be the despondent conclusion that this need will never be met, that rewarding human interaction for such a person is impossible.

The important point to be understood is that almost every time we initiate communication, even on a nonverbal level, we are making an implied request: "Please confirm my viewpoint." Sometimes this request is actually spoken; usually, however, it is implied on the unspoken, nonverbal level. Sometimes it concerns our understanding of factual data or information; frequently, it involves confirmation of an opinion. Always there is an implicit request for evaluation of us as a person. In this fashion we use interpersonal communication to form an impression of our self-identity.

If there is consistent social confirmation, a strong integrated self-identity will be developed and sustained. In such a case there is less need to seek confirmatory responses or to shield oneself from possible disconfirmation. This condition provides greater freedom for the individual to be spontaneous, creative—to live; there is no great need to be concerned about every little criticism or evaluation of one's behavior. Such a person can dare to hear feedback about who and what he is and can frequently test the validity of his beliefs about himself.

On the other hand, a person whose self-image is frequently disconfirmed will have a great need for information about it; he will need to hear feedback, but will fear it; he will seek it, and at the same time try to avoid it. His self-image will suffer either way: If he hears negative evaluation no matter how slight, he will likely feel anxiety; if he avoids evaluation he will derogate himself for being a coward —he's "damned if he does and damned if he doesn't." A wise person once said, "To him who hath shall be given and from him who hath not shall be taken away." This principle applies to the maintenance of one's self-image. To a large extent theories of nondirective counseling developed by Carl Rogers are attempts to break this vicious circle of need, fear, and avoidance of possible image-building feedback.[47]

There is little question of the importance to the individual of the continuing need for interpersonal communication that confirms one's self-image. Once is never enough. Men have developed elaborate social rituals to reduce the probability of disconfirmation. Children are taught to become "tactful," responding to other people in a way that does not challenge the validity of the self-image they present in public.

Confirmation by Pleasant Recognition. The purpose of much small talk is to acknowledge in a pleasant way the presence of another per-

[47]Rogers, *On Becoming a Person, op. cit.*

son. Commonly used greetings and friendly chatter are examples of a type of communication labeled "phatic communion."[48] We use such pleasant noises to signal that we welcome interaction, that we are friendly, or that we at least recognize the presence of the other person. In our culture such courtesies tend to be rather unimaginative: "Hello," "Nice day," "Howdy," "Hi." We call these greetings "noises" because no literal meaning is usually intended. If someone asks, "How are you?" he would indeed be surprised by even a brief medical report, however accurate. A precise response could be humorous, as when James Thurber was once asked, "How's your wife?" and he replied, "Compared to what?"

It should be obvious that pleasantries upon encountering another person are small but effective measures of confirmation. If you as a reader do not think this is true, stroll down the nearest campus walkway, giving each person you meet a warm, friendly smile. Check your own feelings when this overture is ignored—rewarded with a cold stare that in effect says, "Who (or what) do you think you are?" And you only thought you were another human being out for a stroll.

Studies have shown that simple failure to acknowledge a person's presence is painful if not insulting; few persons find comfort in situations lacking sociability.[49] The democratic act of social recognition may appear to be somewhat perfunctory or even artificial, but it is the action of individuals desiring to create little moments of pleasurable interaction, moments when the stresses of life are temporarily set aside and two persons may simply enjoy being together on a friendly basis. Such brief encounters are important to an individual's psychological well-being and enjoyment of life.

Confirmation by Sharing Personal Growth. If two people have fairly good self-images and if their self-esteem is reasonably secure, they may engage in interpersonal communication that is growth producing and mutually confirming. Interpersonal exchange is then exhilarating; ideas bounce back and forth; response and feedback are openly given and easily accepted. The pleasure lies in the interaction, not simply in talking or listening. When such an instance occurs we are struck by the feeling, "Isn't he (or she) a wonderful person?" Such experiences actually *are* wonderful.

There can be a certain pleasure in exposing some of our more protected thoughts and feelings to trusted others. We take pleasure in articulating such thoughts; some of them may have been little understood by us until we started to express them, and they may take

[48]B. Malinowski, "The Problem of Meaning in Primitive Languages," Supplement I in C. K. Ogden and I. A. Richards, *The Meaning of Meaning* (New York: Harcourt Brace Jovanovich, 1923), pp. 296–336.

[49]Duncan, *op. cit.*, pp. 20–24.

shape in ways we had not quite planned or even suspected. There is pleasure in having such thoughts and feelings become clearer as we gain honest feedback. Sometimes we feel that they must be reassessed or reshaped by us; sometimes we achieve solid confirmation from other persons.

There is also pleasure in seeing this happen to the other person, joy in participating in his/her personal growth and development. There is gratification in giving honest feedback when you feel it will not be misused. It is our belief that most families would like to have such a relationship, and that interpersonal communication of this order between parents and children would make parenthood worthy of the name.

Confirmation Through Shared Silence. When personal growth and development have been shared and enjoyed, frequently moments of silent communion are the result. In such cases interpersonal communication has not stopped; the persons so involved are quite aware of each other's presence and feelings. There is an atmosphere of shared trust and confidence, one in which one's own feelings are secure and one's feelings about the other person are also secure. There is also a willing tolerance of the other person's need for silence, with security in knowing that their thoughts will give them pleasure. There is a ready willingness to offer independence to the other person—freedom to think as he wishes, to develop thoughts and feelings that may be shared at some future time or perhaps never shared.

Such nonverbal interpersonal communion is usually restful, frequently much more so than merely being alone. Occasionally an autobiography or diary will attest the value of such moments. Our own personal experiences corroborate this principle. Sometimes there was an environmental element, such as a sunset or the shadows creeping along the basin of the valley below. Sometimes such conditions seemed to offer an excuse to enjoy shared silence. But the thing that was later recalled with greatest pleasure was not the sunset or the valley, but the restful comfort of the moment of silence enjoyed together. Such moments of silent communion provide a yardstick to judge the quality of an interpersonal relationship.

INTERPERSONAL NEGOTIATION

In the foregoing section of this chapter we have discussed ways in which interpersonal communication aids us in our personal development. We have suggested that optimal use of this process is necessary in our struggle for personal identity, self-esteem, a sense of reality, and confirmation as human beings.

The second primary contribution of interpersonal communication is that it is useful in negotiating with other people as we seek to control our social and physical environment. Of course, other forms of communication assist us in this task—written communication, the mass media, and "one-way" speaker presentations to audiences. Even so, most significant negotiations are carried out in face-to-face, two-way interactions.

Consideration of interpersonal negotiation exposes clearly one of man's basic dilemmas: *How can I maintain my own personal freedom and obtain your needed assistance in achieving my personal goals?* Perhaps, with the single exception of the need for personal growth and development, there is no more important question for us to face in all of our life struggles. It is also a most difficult question because it is truly a dilemma: To the extent that assistance is obtained, almost always some element of personal liberty is given up; and to the extent that personal independence is achieved, assistance from others is lost. Small wonder that people throughout history have tried to slide between the horns of this dilemma by manipulation and even brainwashing the minds of others. We view such manipulative use of interpersonal communication as unethical—beneath the dignity of people's potential for relating to each other.

Achieving Our Personal Independence

In some ways it appears that every new generation must win its independence from the older generations that precede it. To a large extent this is true of every individual person. We start with other people doing things for us and keeping us from doing things that might hurt us. Later we are kept from doing things that might hurt others.

Achieving one's individual independence essentially consists of negotiating with others (1) to reduce their attempts to restrict us and (2) to diminish their efforts to keep us dependent on them. There are few arguments against these individual goals as such; interpersonal conflicts arise on how far they should be carried out. Interpersonal communication is useful in establishing agreement on fine lines of distinction concerning these boundaries.

If the people around us—parents, teachers, and other authority figures—are willing to allow us more and more freedom, our interactions with them will be cooperative. Our interpersonal communication can be exploratory, agreeable, and productive, giving them and us a deep sense of personal satisfaction. To the extent that they seem determined to keep us restricted or reliant upon their help, we find ourselves attempting to persuade them that they are wrong and we are right. Exactly at this point optimal use of interpersonal communication can be of great value.

It is important to discuss with others your needs and desires for increased freedom in a tentative, exploratory way before commitments have been made, "sides" have been chosen, and an atmosphere of conflict has settled on the scene. If we assume too early that they will never negotiate, that in no way can they be persuaded, one's struggle for personal independence may take the form of a "resistance movement," with heavy commitments on both sides and no expectation of resolution through interpersonal communication. Personal freedom is generally won in small stages—little incidents and persistence. In negotiating with others, we should work on small items one at a time and not expect large gates to open all at once. But the keynote must be that voiced by Winston Churchill as he reviewed his early life and struggle: "Never give in!"[50] In the struggle for personal freedom, one must not give up just because progress is not rapid. As we get older we find that this struggle is continuous throughout life.

Achieving Freedom from Restrictions. In attempting to diminish personal restrictions placed on us, we must recognize that liberty does not mean absolute license; at no time in our lives will we be allowed to do whatever we please without consideration of the effect on others if they can help it. Thus, in attempting to reduce restrictions placed on us by others, we should seek to identify those restrictions that we will, in turn, place upon ourselves. Our negotiation will thus consist of our offering to provide self-discipline as a replacement for their discipline. Such a trade—a substitution of one policy for another—can hardly be worked out with another person at long distance unless interpersonal communication has previously set the stage for such negotiation.

Negotiation of a trade, giving something in return for something received, appears to be almost a universally common form of social interaction. The process essentially consists of offers and responses, counteroffers and counterresponses, until either an agreement is reached, or one or both of the participants decide that no agreement is possible. Here again is life's basic dilemma: To get something new, I must give up something owned. If I cannot receive without giving, how can I avoid giving without receiving? Only by negotiation can the answer be obtained.

Reducing Our Reliance on Others. A difficult and sensitive problem in achieving personal independence is diminishing one's dependency upon others. In early life we can't seem to wait until we are *capable* of doing things for ourselves. A little girl, 2 years old, fell asleep while playing in the basement. Her parents carried her upstairs and tucked her into bed, whereupon she awoke, jumped out of bed, said,

[50]Churchill in his speech at The Harrow School, reported in D. Price and D. Walley, eds., *Never Give In* (Kansas City, Mo.: Hallmark Cards, 1967), p. 30.

"Me get in mine own bed," crawled back in and went to sleep. Achieving capability is only part of the problem; being allowed to use this capacity, to do for oneself that which one can do, may be even more difficult. It seems that many people like to have others rely upon them; such dependant-seeking behavior has been identified as a primary function of a major personality variable.[51]

As we increasingly do more for ourselves, many persons are content to let us do so. A simple show of initiative can diminish some other's efforts to keep us reliant upon them. Some of our associates will be most happy that we are no longer their burden and will encourage our efforts. But those few who want to keep us tied to them may be persistent; frequently they are persons about whom we care very much. The sensitive part of the problem is our desire to consider their feelings while simultaneously considering our own. It is in precisely this kind of situation that interpersonal communication may be the only way we can make any progress—exposing our feelings and needs, showing concern for the sensitivities of the other person, offering suggestions, asking for feedback, and searching for possible areas of agreement.

A short time ago a man 35 years old came to inquire about our graduate program. He was pleased with our program but hesitated to leave his present job, working in his father's small business. We asked if his fear was that his father could not get along without his help, whereupon he said that was not the case; rather, he feared he would hurt his father's feelings if he ceased to depend upon his father's help and made his professional success on his own. We listened while he mulled over his problem and suggested he talk it over with his father. A few days later we received a letter saying that he just couldn't do it; that his father couldn't accept his son's being on his own, and that, although he would very much like to become part of our graduate program, he would stay where he was. We later thought that perhaps in his father's business is really where this man belongs; without more courage he probably is not capable of being free.

Negotiating Mutual Assistance

A great amount of our time is spent in working out ways in which we, with one or more other persons, try to achieve desired goals that each of us individually cannot hope to accomplish. Usually such activities are identified as problem solving. People work with each other in two basic ways: (1) cooperating to solve mutual problems—resolving shared concerns, and (2) trading help and resources. Both approaches involve the use of interpersonal communication.

[51]R. B. Cattell, H. W. Eber, and M. W. Tatsvoka, *Handbook for the Sixteen Personality Factor Questionnaire (16PF)* (Champaign, Ill.: Institute for Personality and Ability Testing, 1970), pp. 85–86.

Many times people share a mutual concern; they talk it over, hoping to cooperate in reaching a resolution. This simple process is the essence of democratic action. It is cooperative in that all different viewpoints are allowed to be voiced. It is purposive in that an attempt is made to identify and resolve a problem felt by two or more people. In many cases, who takes part in these discussions—and who does not—is influenced primarily by the degree of concern mutually shared by the participants.

Cooperating to Solve Mutual Problems. A concern shared with another person ordinarily involves the need for reaching agreement on a program of action that commits you and them to a way of assisting each other—sharing a load or responsibility. Such commitment allows each person to rely upon the other for behaving in a way that is mutually beneficial. In many cases the mutual concern requires pooling of resources—material, energy, time, money.

Types of problems that require mutual assistance cover a wide range of conditions. A group of students and teachers may try to develop a new set of required courses for a major academic program. Two or three students living in an apartment may reach an agreement on tasks of cooking and cleaning, and perhaps ways of providing each individual some minimum personal privacy. Two families may share their resources and build a cabin on a lake. Six commuters may arrange a program of taking turns driving as well as schedules for picking up each member of the carpool. In each of these examples there are certain common factors: Two or more people are identifying a mutual concern, analyzing a situation, and producing a desired program of action requiring certain behavior on the part of each individual.

Much of our lives are spent working with others, working out arrangements with them, developing new procedures for mutual benefit. The interpersonal problem-solving process involves two major types of behavior: (1) task-oriented behavior—identifying and analyzing a mutual problem, evaluating various possible ways of trying to resolve it, and preparing to implement a selected solution; and (2) relating to each other in a decent human way—noting the way a person *feels* about his/her ideas as well as just hearing the idea, and listening for indications regarding the way they feel about us as well as how they feel about our ideas. *Task-oriented behavior* focuses on dealing with the problem. *Relating interpersonally* focuses on understanding each other as human beings.

Both types of behavior are essential for working out programs of mutual assistance. Neither type can be neglected if we are to be effective in resolving concerns shared with others. And a particularly vexing problem arises when elements of the two are confused; a common example being when open, honest *disagreement* on ideas is perceived as *personal dislike*. It is extremely unfortunate that the two are frequently confused. Only by efficient use of the process of interpersonal communication can such confusion ordinarily be dispelled.[52]

Honest *disagreement* can reasonably occur on any step in the problem-solving process—on the nature or causes of the problem, on possible values of alleged solutions, on who can best do what in implementing a plan of action. Ample reason for sincere disagreement can include different sources or amounts of information, different personal experiences or observations, and different personal value systems.

Honest disagreement should be voiced, heard, and discussed; only in this way can the full value of different backgrounds and resources be used. However, when such disagreement is misperceived as personal *dislike*, it usually elicits defense of oneself *as a person*. The true value of the source of disagreement is lost entirely, and the problem-solving process is contravened—"shot down." *And for no adequate reason!* In addition, considerable interpersonal difficulty usually results. Sometimes this takes the form of retaliatory behavior—a show of *retaliatory* personal dislike. This, of course, is usually perceived correctly and reacted to immediately. Hostilities may consume endless time and energy in friction; they may ebb and flow for minutes, sometimes days, even years. We should be deeply concerned about such waste of human potential. As authors of this book we are highly aware of this problem because we have observed it happen so often.

Proper use of the process of interpersonal communication can contribute greatly to the achievement of shared effort in solving mutual problems. Even more important, in our estimation, it is practically the only way that confusion of honest disagreement with personal dislike can be resolved.

Trading Help and Resources. A second way of negotiating mutual assistance is that of working out a trade. Such a trade requires giving something in return for something received. There are many interpersonal situations in which the persons involved are not likely to be entirely cooperative. More often than not the goal of one or another individual contains both cooperative and competitive motivations. For example, suppose your car will not start on a cold morning. The relationship between you as owner and a mechanic as repairman is both cooperative and competitive. Both of you can benefit from negotiating an agreement in which the mechanic earns a fee and you achieve an

[52]For a detailed treatment of this and other factors in negotiating mutual assistance, see B. R. Patton and K. Giffin, *Problem-Solving Group Interaction* (New York: Harper & Row, 1973).

auto that functions in cold weather. To this extent both of your motivations are cooperative. On the other hand, the terms of the agreement are competitive: The higher the mechanic's fee, the greater the relative cost to you (assuming the quality of his workmanship remains the same). Such interpersonal situations have been studied under the label of "mixed-motive negotiations." Many human interactions fall into this category.

The study of such negotiation or bargaining has usually focused on two questions: (1) For a specified set of conditions, what procedures are likely to be used by the participants, and (2) what decision will likely be the outcome? The theory of games has been used to find answers to these questions.[53] Game theory as applied to negotiation situations rests on the assumption that individuals attempt to achieve the highest possible returns (in terms of each individual's value system) by interacting with others. If the theory of games is to provide insight into mixed-motive interactions, communication between the participants must be considered. In recent research, direct verbal communication has been studied as a part of the negotiation process. Research by Beisecker[54] has explored the role of communication in mixed-motive negotiations.

Beisecker has concluded that the potential impact of communication on the outcome of a negotiation is related to the degree that each participant can estimate the other's position. When participants have only limited knowledge of each other's utility values, or when these tend to change during interaction, understanding of such values can be achieved only with the aid of communication; estimates will tend to be valid to the extent that such communication is effective. Beisecker has also developed a theoretical analysis of the ways in which communication can aid participants in pursuit of both cooperative and competitive goals.[55] Communication can be employed cooperatively by two or more persons to produce a group decision that gives maximum satisfaction to all participants. The role of cooperative communication is to discover and increase areas of common interest; it provides a search process through which the participants identify previously unnoticed alternatives, reconsider criteria for evaluating alternatives, and strive for greater logical consistency among their utility (evaluative) systems. Most scholars who study this process have labeled it "problem-solving" discussion or interaction.

[53]For an introductory treatment of game theory, see A. Rapoport, *Two-Person Game Theory: The Essential Ideas* (Ann Arbor: University of Michigan Press, 1966).

[54]T. Beisecker, "The Use of Persuasive Strategies in Dyadic Interaction," unpublished Ph.D. dissertation, University of Wisconsin, 1968.

[55]T. Beisecker, *The Role of Verbal Communication in Interpersonal Interaction: An Analysis from the Point of View of Games* (Lawrence, Kans.: Communication Research Center, University of Kansas, 1969).

Communication can also be employed competitively to distort the other person's perceptions of the situation in order to gain an individual bargaining advantage. Strategies for accomplishing this are numerous, including the following: (1) misrepresentation of available alternatives, (2) misrepresentation of utility (value) of various alternatives, (3) rejection of additional alternatives, (4) rejection of additional criteria for estimating utilities of alternatives, (5) insisting on the other person's need to achieve an agreement, and (6) indicating high commitment to a demand for resolution. There are additional strategies that could be identified; however, in each case the purpose is to alter the other person's perception of the outcome when a specific agreement is reached. Mothers and fathers seem to be altogether too adept at the use of these strategies in negotiating with their offspring.[56]

In this discussion it should be noted that competitive communication strategies are here viewed (deliberately) as unjust or "unfair" whenever attempts are made to distort another person's perception of a situation or the value system involved. On the other hand, *mutual efforts* in search of new alternatives, new value systems, or greater internal consistency are considered to be just and fair. Although they may produce differences of opinion, *efforts toward accurate or objective perception of a bargaining situation* are viewed broadly as a cooperative effort.

In our culture, deliberate distortion of the perceptions of another person is unethical. However, from time to time one may find it practiced. In many situations the participants possess simultaneous motivations to be both cooperative and competitive; sometimes one or the other is uppermost, and sometimes the individual himself would be hard pressed to analyze his interpersonal motivations objectively. *In any case, to provide an opportunity for another person to alter his perceptions in a mutual search for a negotiated agreement is not unethical; however, to distort deliberately the perceptions of others is an irresponsible and unethical use of communication in an interpersonal situation.*

Cooperative communication can serve the participants' purposes in a mixed-motive situation by providing information needed by them. One of these purposes is to indicate to each other the utility values attached to each possible bargaining alternative; data can be given concerning such values and the firmness with which such is held. Procedurally this may take the form of one person offering to "settle" for certain considerations by the other, followed by the other person telling what he thinks of the offer.

[56]For a very insightful and interesting analysis of parental competitive communication strategies, see C. Russell and W. M. S. Russell, *Human Behavior* (Boston: Little, Brown, 1961), pp. 189–247.

A second purpose is served when each person indicates his perception of the interpersonal relationship between the participants: Can the other person be trusted as a source of pertinent information (e.g., does he bluff); does he view himself as a subordinate or superior to the other; and is one person heavily dependent upon the other for needed information, or does he have access to a reliable "outside" source?

Finally, a useful purpose is served by discussion of the negotiation process itself: Determination of an agenda, speaking order, speaker responsibilities, and data desired.

Much of the discussion above seems to imply that people negotiate mainly on matters of material value, and indeed much of the research on negotiation focuses upon this type of bargaining. However, it should be made perfectly clear that a large amount of interpersonal negotiation concerns matters less tangible, such as criteria for gaining personal regard, standards for determining status, procedures for showing recognition, and a host of other areas requiring social contracts or agreements if people are to achieve personal satisfaction from their interaction with others. It is fairly safe to assume that almost anything is likely to have utility value for someone somewhere. If it has such a value, one may have to negotiate with others in order for such value to be enjoyed.

THE INEVITABILITY OF INTERPERSONAL COMMUNICATION

There appears to be very little room for disagreement with the conclusion that interpersonal communication is inevitable. In the first place, we can hardly succeed in avoiding people even if we so desire. In the second place, if we are in the presence of others, we cannot "*not* communicate."

We Cannot Avoid People

In our culture it is difficult to be alone, to achieve privacy. Daily more people are pressed together in tightly compact areas—apartment complexes, dormitories, suburban development. Increased specialization of occupational roles makes us more interdependent, each upon the other. Advances in technology make people more mobile, make communication easier, make others more available to us—and conversely, make us more available to them. A day alone at the seashore is for most of us a romantic dream; even an afternoon alone in one's room will require special measures involving telephone, signs on the door, and a bit of luck.

A major ethic of parenthood in our society is the socialization of children: Make sure that little Johnny learns to play and work with the other children. This project is often programmed to boundless limits—preschool, parties, dancing lessons, swimming teams, Webelos, etc., until parent and child are nearly exhausted.

Much of this activity is desirable and beneficial. Our point is not that it can be overdone; rather, that at least some of it cannot *not* be done. A child in our culture is going to be with people; when he becomes an adult, probably even more so. This fact alone is important; it holds great significance for this chapter as it relates to this principle: When we are with other people, we cannot *not* communicate.

We Cannot Avoid Responding to Others

There is no more important recent observation in the study of interpersonal communication than this: When we are with other people, and they are aware of our presence, we cannot *not* communicate. Its importance is more fully realized because of new investigations of nonverbal communication, body language, vocal intonations, and facial expression. We now know that when people try to communicate least they may be communicating most. In terms of personal disconfirmation, such messages frequently have more impact on interpersonal relations than do occasional overt, verbal statements.

"No Response" Is *a Response.* Perhaps we can best make this point visible by describing the experiences of people who have deliberately tried to give other people "no response." In the literature on child development there are careful studies of children who are identified as "autistic"—children who have shut themselves off from interaction with all other human beings. These children are typically passive, usually mute, frequently inert—almost deathlike.[57] It has often been noted that they give an impression of lonely desperation combined with an appearance of little old men or women possessing an inner silent wisdom. Most of them exhibit a profound withdrawal from contact with people, behaving as if others were not there, perhaps crouching in a corner, indifferent to all that goes on about them. Some of them endlessly repeat snatches of songs, phrases, or even lists of items (sometimes heard only once), patiently refraining from expressing their own thoughts or making any personal commitments. Others make clucking or clicking noises, unused, however, for interpersonal communication.[58] Occasionally, when approached (e.g., for medical attention) these children fight with inordinate strength and the violence of utter desperation. For the most part, however, they are unresponsive to the world around them. In many cases bodily functions

[57] B. Bettelheim, *The Empty Fortress* (New York: Free Press, 1967), pp. 56–60.

[58] *Ibid.*, pp. 100, 364–365.

are so constricted that special measures are necessary for feeding or elimination.[59] It would appear that they have attempted to blot out all stimuli, inner or outer, in order to avoid giving any response to their environment.[60]

Careful diagnostic examination separates these autistic children from those that are feebleminded or brain-damaged. Their central nervous systems are normally and fully developed, and they possess all the necessary potential for human communication.[61] With treatment, they demonstrate that they understand language but fear people. With extended treatment the majority of them take their place in society pretty much like normal people. Most autistic persons are children; without special treatment they rarely live to be adults.[62]

Autism has been identified as a massive response to a catastropic threat in early childhood. In almost every case the early development of these children included the ordinary beginnings of speech, most of them functioning in a fairly normal way at least for awhile. Then something happened that to them was frightening, and it involved, in some way, other people.[63] The perceived threat may have involved either physical or psychological danger. Consequently these children have tried to shut out the world, sometimes closing their ears (and even their nostrils) with their fingers when approached by others.[64]

In their attempt to close out other people, autistic children have tried at a great price to avoid the inevitability of interpersonal communication; they seem to be saying, "If I don't respond, they can't hurt me."[65] Actually, they are aware of others, but "passionately indifferent."[66]

We Cannot Not *Communicate When We Are with Others.* Although the autistic children have tried almost beyond endurance, they have not succeeded in giving "no response" to those about them.[67] Their response is negative and mostly nonverbal. But their unspoken message is clear to strangers seeing them on the street whenever they stray from home or institutions.[68] They are readily seen as "different" and in trouble. Their autism is very real and easily identified, not by what they say verbally but by what they say nonverbally in bodily

[59] *Ibid.*, pp. 57–60.
[60] *Ibid.*, pp. 160–161, 205.
[61] *Ibid.*, pp. 4–5.
[62] *Ibid.*, pp. 89–90, 413–421.
[63] *Ibid.*, pp. 43–45.
[64] *Ibid.*, pp. 161–162.
[65] *Ibid.*, p. 46.
[66] *Ibid.*, p. 89.
[67] *Ibid.*, pp. 89–90. To some extent Kanner disagrees, saying that they *do not relate* to persons. See L. Kanner, "Early Infantile Autism," *Journal of Pediatrics*, 25 (1944), 211–217.
[68] Bettelheim, *op. cit.*, pp. 356–357.

expression and behavior. Studies by Spitz and others have well documented the principle that if small children are denied human warmth and attention they will sicken and die.[69] The same is generally true of autistic children. Formal treatment generally consists of a demonstration of warmth and acceptance, along with efforts to reduce the source of fear or anxiety. The road to recovery actually commences, however, when these children *initiate* interaction—that is, when they actively start to try to deal with the world around them.[70]

We opened this chapter with the statement that personal development and psychological health require human interaction. The experiences of those who have tried to deny its principle serve to prove its merit. Fortunately most of us readily acknowledge the dictum that interaction with others is unavoidable and interpersonal communication inevitable. We strive to use and improve it for purposes suggested in the earlier sections of this chapter.

[69]See R. A. Spitz, "The Psychogenic Diseases in Infancy," in *The Psychoanalytical Study of the Child* (New York: International Universities Press, 1951), vol. 6, pp. 255–275.

[70]Bettelheim, *op. cit.*, pp. 89–94, 405–413.

SUMMARY AND PREVIEW OF READINGS

We may briefly summarize this chapter by reviewing the ways in which interpersonal communication is used to achieve personal growth and development. In addition, we will briefly preview the readings that follow.

We try to achieve a personal identity by relating to other people, experiencing ourselves through their responses to us. We strive to obtain a clear reflection of our image from others, comparing and evaluating inconsistent or contradictory reflections. We learn to rely primarily upon "reference" persons or groups in whom we have the most confidence. The essay by Bennis and his associates presents in some detail the ways in which our interactions with others influence the development of our self-concept.

We try to achieve self-esteem by developing a self-image that is pleasing to us. A pleasing self-concept is one that elicits approval of those persons we trust. We tend to monitor and modify our behavior in ways that obtain more approval and less disapproval. We are frequently tempted to "put on acts" that gain applause, hiding parts of our true selves or acting as if we are something that we are not. Careful consideration of such performances show them likely to be self-defeating. Instead, sincere efforts to change our ways of relating to others may lead to personal growth and increased self-esteem. To some extent the Bennis essay expands upon these concepts.

As we grow and develop we are always in search of reality—"the real thing"—especially in terms of our relationships to other people. To test social reality we need to make optimal use of the process of interpersonal communication. We must expose our true selves to a trusted other person, request and obtain honest feedback, and check our perceptions of this feedback with the person giving it. Through this process of exposure, feedback, and checking of our impressions, we can assess the reality of our relations with others, at least to the extent that they and we are honest.

The quest for confirmation of ourselves as persons—human beings—is a lifelong process. Each time we are in the presence of another person, we implicitly ask for validation of ourself as an acceptable person. If the other person is important to us, denial by him can seriously discredit our belief in ourself. Conversely, confirmation may be derived from pleasant recognition by others, from sharing our personal growth with another trusted person, and by spending with that person comfortable moments in silent communion. Special attention is given to this problem of self-confirmation in the Bennis essay.

The second major contribution of interpersonal communication is its use in negotiating with others. Through interpersonal negotiation we seek to control our social and physical environment. We negotiate to achieve our personal freedom—freedom from restrictions placed on us by others, and reduction of our reliance upon them. We also negotiate with others in cooperative efforts to solve mutual problems. In mixed-motive (partially cooperative, partially competitive) situations we negotiate "trades" of help and resources. The article by Jack and Lorraine Gibb following this chapter gives special attention to problems of negotiating with others in groups.

For reasons summarized above, interpersonal communication is a basic human imperative. In our culture it is inevitable. As our society is presently constituted we cannot avoid people; and when two or more people meet, the implicit issue of personal confirmation is raised. This implied request cannot be avoided: "Please respond to me as a human being." Any effort to avoid giving a response *becomes* a response, even if not intended as such. In this way the human imperative of interpersonal communication is unavoidable; it is bound to happen. The attendant question thus arises: How well do we understand and use this process?

SUGGESTED APPLICATIONS AND LEARNING EXPERIENCES

1. With two or three of your closest friends, discuss actual people you know who try to act as if they are smarter, better educated, or more experienced than they really are. After about twenty or thirty minutes, ask your friends to give you some feedback on whether or not they see you sometimes behaving in a similar way. Offer such feedback to them if they ask for it.

2. Attend a meeting of some campus problem-solving group, such as a planning group for a dormitory or house party. While you are participating in this group, as an experiment follow very carefully "straight and narrow" patterns that reflect generally "what everybody believes." After you have done this for one meeting, if one member of the group is a good friend tell him what you have been doing and how you plan to be different during the next meeting. Ask for his help and support during the next meeting as you attempt to do more than "just what everybody expects."

3. With two of your classmates write a three-person skit in which one "actor" presents only a small part of himself and the other "actors" try to obtain more information from him about himself. Ask your teacher if you may present this skit to the class. Have the class give you feedback on whether or not they know people who behave this way in real life and how they respond to such persons.

4. With a particularly good friend or helpful classmate, mutually attempt to share some of your more protected thoughts and feelings about yourself. Strive especially for clarity as you try to express these thoughts and feelings. Listen very carefully to the responses the other person gives as you talk about yourself. Pay close attention to responses that indicate that some of your notions about yourself seem to be unwarranted. Discuss ways in which you can achieve growth and maturity by behaving differently. Note new perceptions of yourself as you begin to think about adopting some of these new behaviors.

5. Note the ways in which a person's self-identity can be confirmed as described in the article by Bennis et al., "Some Interpersonal Aspects of Self-Confirmation." Have lunch with a friend and, in as many ways as possible, try to confirm his self-image. Note his responses. Note your responses to his responses. At the end of an hour or so ask him if he has had a good time. At a later time reflect back upon the encounter and ask yourself if you had a good time.

6. Make a list of the behaviors described in the reading, "Humanistic Elements in Group Growth," following this chapter. Arrange to observe two meetings of a campus group. Determine the different behaviors on your list exhibited by this group. Give them the benefit of your observations only if they ask for them, but discuss your findings with one of your classmates.

SOME INTERPERSONAL ASPECTS OF SELF-CONFIRMATION

Warren G. Bennis, Edgar H. Schein, Fred I. Steele, and David E. Berlew

INTRODUCTION

American psychology has only recently acknowledged the important role played by human relationships in man's search for a sense of personal identity and personal worth. Perhaps Harry Stack Sullivan and Carl Rogers more than any other writers have been responsible for this humanizing trend in our psychological tradition. One of the most important contributions of this trend has been the emphasis it has placed on the individual's potential for personal development and growth. This essay will examine some of the interpersonal processes relevant to such personal development.

In this essay we shall discuss what we believe to be two major components or subprocesses of self-confirmation. We shall call the first of these the process of *self-evaluation.* All of us have beliefs about our relative and our ultimate worth. We feel superior to some persons but inferior to others. We may or may not feel "worthy." Most of us expend considerable energy trying to maintain or change our beliefs about how good we are. It is this continual process of self-evaluation and re-evaluation that determines an individual's level of self-esteem or sense of personal worth.

We shall refer to the second major component of self-confirmation as the process of *self-definition.* Just as we have beliefs about our worth, so we also have beliefs about who we are and what we are. Some persons, particularly adolescents, seem to be engaged in a desperate struggle to define themselves. Others appear to be concerned primarily with maintaining or preserving beliefs about themselves. Still other persons seem to know what they are now, but are intent on discovering what they might become. In every case, however, attempts to define the self result in certain beliefs about the self, or what we shall refer to as a "self-image" or "identity."[1]

The first section of this essay will examine some of the interpersonal aspects of *self-evaluation.* Our primary focus will be on *re-evaluation* of self, or the possibility of change in level of self-esteem after adolescence. However, the section begins with a discussion of the initial development of self-esteem, and an examination of some critical elements of parent-child interaction. After a description of several possible outcomes of early relationships, we turn to a consideration of strategies for maintaining self-esteem. The first section closes with a consideration of self-exposure as a strategy for testing possibly invalid assumptions about self-worth, and an

From Warren G. Bennis et al., *Interpersonal Dynamics,* rev. ed., Homewood, Ill.: The Dorsey Press, 1968, pp. 207–226. Reprinted by permission of the publisher.

[1] "Identity," "self-concept," and "self-image" are used interchangeably in this essay.

examination of some problems involved in obtaining useful "evaluative" feedback.

The second section of the essay examines the relevance of interpersonal relationships to the process of *self-definition*. The section begins with a brief examination of some ways an identity is formed, and then takes up problems of maintaining an identity or self-image. The second section closes with consideration of the possibility of enlarging or extending one's personal identity. The concept of "selflessness" and the role of "descriptive" feedback from other persons are discussed in this context.

SELF-EVALUATION

A. The Development of Self-Esteem

The basic unit of interaction that concerns us is a very simple one. One person acts and in doing so intentionally or unintentionally exposes a part of his self—something of what he is, or thinks he is, or hopes he is. A second person responds to the first person's act and to his exposed self. Very frequently his reactions convey approval or disapproval, acceptance or rejection. In this simple unit of social interaction lies one of the keys of the process of self-evaluation.

The process of learning about ourselves begins very early in life. Clearly not all of it involves social interaction. The infant explores his body and experiences recurrent organic sensations which lead to the evalution of a sense of bodily self. He interacts with his physical environment and learns the distinction between what is himself and what is not himself. But the infant also learns very quickly that some of his actions elicit responses of approval, attention, love. Others seem to go unnoticed. Still others are responded to with withdrawal, coldness, or irritation. As he progresses from infancy to young childhood, he discovers more and more evaluative elements in the responses of others to his behavior or to his self.

The result of these different responses to his acts soon becomes quite apparent. Acts that elicit responses of attention or approval or affection tend to occur more and more frequently. Behavior that elicits withdrawal or coldness or rejection occurs less and less frequently.[2] Gradually the overt personality of the child, as manifested in his behavior, is shaped by the people with whom he interacts.

However, because of the human capacity for self-consciousness, the process of personality formation is not entirely a matter of simple reinforcement. The child's patterns of behavior arouse responses *within himself* leading to a set of perceptions of himself which become stable. Once a self as a stabilizing concept begins to emerge, the child associates certain of his acts with this self, even if others ignore or punish them. In this case the acts may become a covert part of the child's self, and others' responses to those acts become judgments of parts of the child's self.

[2]There are, of course, exceptions to this general tendency, such as when a child resists or aggresses against his parents, or tests their love by being "bad," or more pathological cases where the child acts in order to obtain a response—any response—in order to establish an *existence*, regardless of the evaluation of these elicitative acts.

Most of us who are parents set an impossible task for ourselves: we want our children to believe that our love for them is unconditional but we also want them to behave in a reasonably acceptable manner. To accomplish the latter we must respond differentially to their behaviors, to the different parts of their selves that are manifested in their behavior. We must communicate approval in response to some, disapproval in response to others. A child must inevitably experience our disapproval as a withholding or withdrawal of love, *and therefore our love as conditional*, regardless of our intentions and real feelings.

It may be helpful to think rather crudely of the evolution of a "good self" and a "bad self." We behave, and in doing so we always manifest or expose a part of our self. In some cases our behavior elicits a response from others that we perceive as accepting, approving, loving. Thus we learn that certain parts of our selves are acceptable and lovable. Subjectively, we experience these parts of our self as our "good self." In other instances, our acts elicit reactions we perceive as disapproving, rejecting, unloving. When this happens we learn that certain parts of our self are not acceptable or lovable to others. These we experience as our "bad self."[3]

What we have described is congruent with Freud's notions about self-esteem or self-love as outlined in his paper, "On Narcissism: An Introduction."[4] Freud argued that the infant cathects his ego, or loves himself as he is. Thus he is completely acceptable to himself and his self-love or self-esteem is maximal. However, as the infant becomes a child he learns the difference between what he is and what his parents (and society) want him to be. He learns that certain parts of himself are no longer acceptable and lovable to his parents. Two things then happen. First, his libido deserts his ego and cathects an idealized image of his self that he feels would be completely accepted and loved by his parents, i.e., his ego ideal. He no longer loves and accepts himself for what he is, but rather loves and accepts himself only to the extent that he approximates his ego ideal. Effectively, then, the acceptance or rejection of others determines his acceptability to himself, or his self-esteem. Second, he tends to repress or suppress those parts of his self that are not consonant with his ego ideal. They become his "bad" self, unacceptable and unlovable to others and thus to himself.

Types of Outcomes of Parental Strategies. Generally speaking, we can conceive of three types of outcomes of early experiences with acceptance and rejection:

1. A person may learn that no matter how he behaves or tries to "be," he cannot be assured of the love and esteem of other people. He becomes convinced of his own worthlessness, or at the very least, has serious doubts about his lovability. Maternally deprived and rejected children will often fall in this category.

[3]Those parts of the "bad self" which we selectively *inattend-to* would comprise what Sullivan calls the "not self."

[4]S. Freud, "On Narcissism: An Introduction," in *Collected Papers*, Vol. IV, Joan Riviere (trans.) (London: Hogarth Press, 1956).

There are several behavior patterns we might expect from the individual with very low self-esteem. He may simply give up. This might take the form of deep depression and suicidal tendencies, or of acting out good and bad impulses alike without regard for the reactions of other people or of society generally. Such a person might exhibit his "bad self," either to confirm his feelings of worthlessness or to receive the punishment he feels he deserves.

The person who has not given up, who has accepted himself as a person with some worth, will behave quite differently. He may expose to other people as little of his self as possible to avoid the feedback that will confirm his fears. Or he may behave narcissistically by exposing only the best things about his self, or things that are not really his self at all, and demand the approval and love of others. But as long as there is a glimmer of hope, exposing much of his real self is a terrible risk because one bit of negative feedback, real or perceived, may serve to extinguish that glimmer.

2. A second outcome of early experience, at the opposite extreme from the first, is to learn that love is unconditional, that whatever one does or feels—or *is*—he is loved and is therefore worthy of love. In our society, given the socialization practices we employ, this outcome is rarely observed. A person with such high self-esteem will be capable of responding naturally and spontaneously, as a whole person, in any situation. The possibility that relationships after childhood can lead to such an outcome will be discussed later in this essay.

3. It is with the third outcome, somewhere between the first and second, that most of us must live. We have learned that we are loved and are worthy of love at certain times but not at other times. Whether we are loved or not depends on how we are behaving, what parts of ourselves we are exposing. As we pass childhood this becomes translated into a feeling that certain things about us are acceptable and lovable, whereas other things are not. This outcome tends to be associated with several behavioral strategies designed to maintain or preserve self-esteem.

B. Maintaining Self-Esteem

The feeling or expectancy that if someone knew everything about us they could not accept or love us has profound implications for behavior. There appear to be three primary effects. First, it leads to a tendency to *hide* those parts of our self which we feel are less than totally acceptable. We relate to others as part persons rather than whole persons.

Second, the feeling that parts of our self are unlovable often results in a tendency to *pretend* we are something we are not, to wear masks, to erect façades.[5] Pretending has a number of advantages over hiding. For one thing it includes hiding; we can play a part that does not include "bad"

[5]Carl Rogers in *On Becoming a Person* (Boston: Houghton Mifflin, 1961), chap. 18, subsumes both hiding and pretending under the more general heading of "incongruence." People are incongruent, according to Rogers, when there is a lack of correspondence or match between (1) what they are experiencing and their awareness of it, or (2) their awareness and what they communicate about their awareness to other persons. In the first instance, they are hiding from or deluding themselves; in the second they are hiding from or deluding others.

parts of our self. We can even act out or expose our "bad self," but as part of the role we are playing, not as part of us.[6] If we are rejected while playing a part we are comforted by our belief that it is not our real self that has been found wanting.[7]

Third, doubts concerning self-worth encourage *cautious and ritualized behavior*. To respond spontaneously and naturally involves the risk of unintentional exposure of "bad" parts of the self and the possibility that fears of unacceptability will be confirmed. Thus there is a tendency not to be spontaneous or natural but to be guarded and deliberate in any new situation that may arise. Often persons who are reserved or aloof are in fact exercising caution.

All three of the effects described above are essentially strategies designed to avoid the rejection anticipated if more of the self were visible to others. Fear of rejection in this case stems not so much from the possible frustration of affiliative needs as from possible confirmation of the person's fears of being unacceptable to others. Maintaining self-esteem is a lifelong concern for most of us, and for many of us the possibility of even a single instance of rejection by another presents a terrible threat and one to be carefully guarded against.

C. Re-evaluation of Self

1. *Self-Exposure.* The same strategies or behavior tendencies that serve to maintain self-esteem also prevent any real self-growth. There can be no basic change in self-esteem without testing the assumption that if others knew certain things about us we would be unloved. That assumption cannot be tested except by exposing all of the self to others and observing their reaction. We may discover that others accept and love us even after we have exposed our "bad self" to them. If so, relearning or re-evaluation of self can occur, leading to a greater sense of personal worth. Of course, we may also have our fear that we are unworthy of love confirmed by others and thus experience a loss of self-esteem.

2. *Validity of Assumptions About Self-Worth.* What chance is there that a person's doubts about his self-worth are realistic? If his doubts are unwarranted, testing through self-exposure should logically lead to their dissipation or extinction. But if they are realistic fears, greater exposure of self may lead only to their reinforcement and a further loss of self-esteem.

There are several reasons for expecting doubts about self-worth to be unrealistic, mostly stemming from the fact that the most serious of these doubts originate in infancy and early childhood. First, some of the most persistent assumptions about the acceptability or unacceptability of parts of the self are formed before the child's faculties for making fine dis-

[6]Erving Goffman focuses on impression making and pretense in his book, *The Presentation of Self in Everyday Life* (Garden City, N.Y.: Doubleday Anchor, 1959). In his brilliant paper, "On Face-Work: An Analysis of Ritual Elements in Social Interaction," . . . he analyzes social rituals that facilitate both "hiding" and "pretending."

[7]Helene Deutsch analyzes some of the subtle dynamics of pretending and being exposed in her excellent paper, "The Impostor: Contribution to Ego Psychology of a Type of Psychopath."

criminations have fully developed, resulting in a tendency for him to overgeneralize.[8] For example, a child who feels threatened with loss of love for hitting other children may "learn" to believe that any of the aggressive impulses he feels make him unworthy of love.

Second, a child cannot be objective about his parent's love for him and may see the threat of loss of love where in fact it does not exist. His perceptions may be distorted or autistic due to immature notions of causality, a vague conception of time, intense affect, or a simple lack of experience and the perspective it provides. This can lead to invalid assumptions, as when a child assumes that something he did caused his mother to desert him, when in fact she had to go to the hospital.

A third reason we can expect many assumptions about self-worth to be invalid is that they are frequently based on the reactions of just one or two persons, usually the parents. Parents may find something about their child unacceptable because they are intolerant and not capable of loving any other human unconditionally, or because the child has become involved in his parents' neuroses.[9] In other cases, changing standards of behavior make it impossible for parents to accept their children, and for their children to accept themselves. Because of changed attitudes toward sex in our society, for example, strictly brought up young people often experience guilt and loss of self-esteem for behaving in ways that are unacceptable to their parents but perfectly acceptable among their peers.

Finally, the simple fact that what may be quite unacceptable in a child may be acceptable or even desirable in an adolescent or adult may lead to incorrect assumptions about self-worth. A child may feel threatened by loss of love if he is willful or overly independent as a child. However, this same independence in the male adult may lead to acceptance and success.

To summarize, the probability that an individual's doubts about his self-worth are based on adequate evidence of his unacceptability to a number of relatively unconflicted persons who know him well is very low.

3. *Evaluative Feedback.* By "evaluative feedback" we mean social cues or "reflected self-appraisals" useful for evaluation or re-evaluation of the self. Not all persons are concerned with self-improvement. Persons with low-self-esteem, for example, are primarily concerned with *reassurance.* They tend to search others' responses to them only for clues of approval or disapproval, acceptance or rejection. Narcissists seek the compliments, admiration, and applause of other persons in a desperate and continuous effort to dispel doubts about their ultimate worth as human beings. There is little concern among such people for realistic self-appraisal or self-improvement.

For most persons, however, evaluative feedback serves a potentially

[8]For an illuminating and thorough discussion of the characteristics of learning that occurs during infancy and early childhood, see D. C. McClelland, *Personality* (New York: Holt, Rinehart and Winston, 1951), pp. 441–58.

[9]For an enlightening discussion of neurotic interaction between parent and child, see E. Vogel and N. Bell, "The Emotionally Disturbed Child as the Family Scapegoat."

useful function. Through self-exposure and feedback persons can test assumptions about their acceptability or lovability and thereby develop greater self-esteem. Evaluative feedback makes it possible to develop and maintain a realistic conception of one's competencies and liabilities, strengths and weaknesses. Finally, evaluative feedback serves as a basis for self-improvement; unless we become aware of our weaknesses and shortcomings, we cannot set about overcoming them.

There are two general classes of social responses that people tend to use as feedback for purposes of evaluating self-worth. When people interact, however formally or impersonally, they frequently give off very subtle cues regarding their feelings about the other person. We can call this *indirect feedback*. The second class, which we will call *direct feedback,* consists of verbal statements explicitly describing one person's perceptions of or reactions to another.

There are several points of interest concerning the nature and use of indirect feedback. It is often ambiguous. A smile may be a polite social habit, but it may also convey warmth and approval. Aloofness may indicate disapproval, but it may also indicate an individual's fear of intimacy. The problem of ambiguous feedback is magnified by the fact that people tend to see what they expect to see, to be particularly sensitive to those cues in their environment which confirm their expectancies. Thus, if a person expects others to find him unacceptable, he will tend to see smiles as polite only and aloofness as rejection.

Indirect feedback tends to be overgeneralized. The feeling that we are being rejected, if the cues are subtle, may develop gradually. If so, it is difficult to associate someone's rejection of us with a specific act, or one small part of our self that we exposed. Rather, we tend to experience the incident as a rejection of our whole self, or all those parts of our self about which we have doubts.

Indirect feedback does not allow for justification or explanation. It frequently happens that we find something about another person unacceptable until we understand why he is that way, until he has a chance to explain his self to us.

Just as frequently the feedback may reveal more about the giver than the receiver. If inaccurate feedback is communicated indirectly, there is little chance it will be questioned or corrected by others. If the reason for another's reaction to us cannot be openly explored, there is no way to determine whether or not the feedback was justified.

It should be clear that indirect feedback is not very useful, and can be harmful, for purposes of self-evaluation. The person receiving the feedback must draw inferences from subtle, often ambiguous, cues without the opportunity to explore the exact meaning of or reasons for the feedback.

Direct feedback is potentially more useful for evaluating self-worth. However, even direct feedback can be useless if it does not reflect frank appraisals or reactions.

One major reason for lack of frankness is our cultural taboo on criticizing another person, particularly to his face. We tend to admire people who claim, "There is some good in everyone, and I look for that," or, "If

I do not have something good to say about someone, I do not say anything at all."[10] These are high-sounding sentiments, but they also convey the message that it is wrong to look critically at another person and even worse to communicate criticism. Maslow has noted that even our definitions of love do not ordinarily include the obligation to feedback or criticize.[11]

One result of our tendency to say only positive things to each other is that we cannot really trust others to be honest with us. If people suppress their criticism and look for something polite or tactful to say, even positive feedback becomes suspect and therefore of little benefit. It is little wonder that we often are not comforted by others' reassurances that they accept and love us despite what we have exposed of our self.

Because of the taboo we place on face-to-face criticism, negative feedback tends to be accompanied by strong emotions on the part of both giver and receiver. Many persons will level criticism only if they first become angry. As a result we learn to react defensively or strike back, responding to the threat we have learned to associate with criticism. Because of our emotional response we tend to experience the criticism as a rejection of our whole self and thus something to be warded off or discredited at all costs.

We cannot blame the scarcity of direct evaluative feedback entirely on social custom. Frequently people ask others to evaluate them, but at the same time give off subtle cues that they do not really want to hear anything other than reassurance. On the other hand, we sometimes withhold feedback because we do not want another person to change. We get used to others being the way they are, our relationships with them stabilize and become comfortable, and we may even obtain satisfaction from their weaknesses and imperfections. In fact it is likely that we use other people, particularly hated or scapegoat targets, in a defensive way to keep our own anxiety at a minimum. Evaluative feedback, even though it might be helpful to the other person, would only upset a satisfying relationship. Finally, people are frequently *afraid* to offer even helpful criticism. They are afraid that they might hurt the other person and/or might be hurt themselves by an act of retaliation on his part.

4. *Facilitating Relationships.* The prototype of a relationship that facilitates positive self-re-evaluation or increased self-esteem is one in which unconditional love is combined with direct feedback.

[10]A parallel to this is the anti-intellectual component: "What I don't know won't hurt me"; "Let sleeping dogs lie," etc.

[11]A. H. Maslow, "Summer Notes on Social Psychology of Industry and Management at Non-Linear System, Inc., Del Mar, California," unpublished manuscript (1962). Maslow goes on to point out the irony of our willingness to let someone go on making the same mistake over and over, ostensibly out of kindness, but really because we are afraid of hurting him and being struck back. As contrast, he cites the Bruderhof where one aspect of Christian love is to be honest with others, even when it hurts. If a faculty member is a bad teacher because he mumbles on and on it is considered to be a brotherly duty, and an expression of caring, to tell him so (*ibid.*, pp. 5–6).

Retaliation is one main factor that inhibits feedback. Another is the danger that if

Some relationships between adults come to approximate this state. A relationship of this sort begins when people trust each other enough to start exposing more and more of themselves to each other. Each person exposes his self in small increments, tentatively, waiting for a response. If the response is disapproval or rejection, the relationship freezes at that point, is terminated, or the testing begins anew. If each exposure is met with acceptance, there is a continual build-up of trust, a growing confidence that they will not hurt each other intentionally. The process is mutually reinforcing, since when one person trusts enough to make himself vulnerable by exposing himself, trust is generated in the other person.

A successful relationship from the standpoint of an increase in self-esteem is one where the individuals are committed to openness and trust in their human transactions, and find themselves accepted or loved. There is concrete evidence of each individual's acceptability, with a corresponding increase in self-esteem.

Let us briefly summarize what we have said about the process of self-evaluation. Experiences with acceptance and rejection during infancy and childhood are basic to the development of our self-esteem as adults. However, re-evaluation of self with a consequent increase in self-esteem can occur after childhood, usually as a result of testing assumptions about self-worth through exposing the self to others and obtaining feedback. Relearning of this type depends primarily on direct feedback that is both honest and unambiguous. Thus, while exposure of self can be an effective strategy for confirming self-worth, it must occur in the context of a relationship that can tolerate honest expression of feelings.

SELF-DEFINITION

In this section we are concerned with a second major component of self-confirmation—the process of self-definition. Every person has certain beliefs about who or what he is; taken together, these beliefs are a person's self-image, or identity. Here we shall focus on interpersonal processes that bear on how such beliefs are formed, how they are maintained, and how they change.

A. Identity Formation

Erik Erikson has defined identity formation in the following manner: ". . . identity formation . . . is a lifelong development largely unconscious to the individual and to his society. Its roots go back all the way to the first self-recognition: in the baby's earliest exchange of smiles there is something of a self-realization coupled with a mutual recognition."[12]

With respect to identity formation, it may be useful to examine some ideas of G. H. Mead, who perhaps more than any other theorist before or since views the self as predominantly a social product. Mead[13] emphasized

---

one exposes a perception or feeling about another, he *may* have to change it. Or even more: he may have to get *closer* to the target of criticism. . . .

[12]E. Erikson, "The Problem of Ego Identity," in *Identity and Anxiety*, Stein, Vidich, and White (eds.), (Glencoe, Ill.: Free Press, 1960), p. 47.

[13]G. H. Mead, *Mind, Self, and Society* (Chicago: Univ. of Chicago Press, 1934).

the importance of face-to-face interaction with others: from the time we are very young children, we constantly act toward others and they respond to us. One result of the continuous exchange between ego and alter is that we learn about our selves; each act directed toward us contains cues about how others see and experience us as individuals. Thus our beliefs about our self, our self-image, are in large measure a reflection of others' perceptions of us. The phrases "looking-glass self" coined by Cooley and "reflected self-appraisal" by Sullivan are graphic statements of this process.

Not all beliefs about self are formed as a result of face-to-face interaction. Festinger[14] has used the term "social comparison process" to describe another way people appraise and evaluate different aspects of their selves. In some cases it may be more efficient, or less risky, to compare our self to another person whose social stimulus value is known to us. In this way, we may develop certain beliefs about our selves without benefit of direct feedback from other persons. It seems probable that as we pass from childhood into adolescence and adulthood, more and more of our beliefs about our self are formed indirectly, through some form of social comparison process.

B. Maintaining an Identity

Festinger[15] has distinguished between what he calls *physical* and *social* reality. Beliefs and opinions about physical reality can be validated by physical measurement: we can test our belief that glass is fragile by striking it with a hammer. Social reality cannot be tested by physical means. There is no physical measurement, for example, that can tell us decisively whether Republicans or Democrats are most adept at handling problems of foreign policy. Festinger goes on to assert that beliefs, attitudes, or opinions about social reality are correct, valid, or proper only to the extent they are anchored in a group of people with similar beliefs.

Many beliefs about self fall into the category of social reality. There are no physical means of determining whether we are in fact a leader of men, good-looking, or exceptionally tactful. Therefore, validation or confirmation of many beliefs about who or what we are must ultimately depend upon social consensus.

There are at least two varieties of beliefs that must be socially validated and confirmed if an individual's self-image or identity is to remain secure: (1) beliefs about the self, about who and what we are, and (2) beliefs about the nature of social reality.

1. *Beliefs About Self.* An individual's self-image is confirmed when other persons' responses to him indicate that their beliefs about who and what he is correspond with his own. There is a mutual recognition of his self, and the validity of his self-image is confirmed. Under conditions that provide consistent social confirmation of all aspects of the self, a strong and

[14]L. Festinger, "A Theory of Social Comparison Processes," *Human Relations*, Vol. 7 (1954), pp. 117–40.

[15]L. Festinger, "Informal Social Communication," *Psychological Review*, Vol. 57 (1950), pp. 271–82.

integrated identity or self-image will develop and be sustained. As a result there is less need to search for responses that confirm the self, or to shield one's self from disconfirming responses. There is greater freedom to respond spontaneously to a situation, to *be*, without a binding concern for the consistency or recognizability of the self-image that is presented. Operating from such a position of strength, a person can dare to *hear* feedback about who he is and what he is, and thus can continually test the validity of his beliefs about his self.

The psychological importance of maintaining a consistent self-image is evident from the existence of elaborate social rituals that function primarily to reduce the probability of disconfirmation, particularly in casual social contacts. "Being tactful," for example, consists essentially of responding to other people in a way that does not challenge the validity of the self they are publicly presenting.

The "identity diffusion" and uncertainty that results when the self is not confirmed by others, or when it is disconfirmed, has been described by a number of authors. In his moving essay, "The Therapeutic Despair,"[16] Leslie Farber writes of his *despair* when a patient refuses to confirm him in his role as therapist or healer by getting well. Erik Erikson has suggested that *identity crises* result when other people, or society, are willing to recognize a person only as something he cannot or does not want to be. He points out that social confirmation of *some* identity, even a negative one, is often preferable to a lack of confirmation and the uncertainty and confusion that results: ". . . many a late adolescent, if faced with continuing diffusion, would rather be nobody or somebody bad, or indeed, dead—and this totally, and by free choice—than be not-quite-somebody."[17]

Finally, in his perceptive and fascinating tale about a young British Colonial officer, George Orwell graphically illustrates the relationship between identity diffusion and *susceptibility to influence*. Unhappy with his role but desperate ". . . to avoid looking a fool," the young officer acts out the oft-quoted wisdom that "people become what you expect them to be."

2. *Beliefs About Reality.*[18] It is important to most people to believe that they are rational and objective, that their world view is "realistic" and accurate. This element of self-image is confirmed through validation of various beliefs or assumptions about the world. When these beliefs and assumptions involve social reality, their validation depends upon interaction with other persons who share a common image of the nature of reality.

Confidence in one's self as someone who has valid beliefs about the nature of reality is prerequisite for discovery, for daring to see the world in new ways. We depend on people with such confidence to lead in defining and redefining social reality, to raise questions even about beliefs supported by social consensus. Persons who lack confidence in the validity

[16]L. Farber, "The Therapeutic Despair," *Psychiatry*, Vol. 1 (1958), pp. 7–20.
[17]Erikson, *op. cit.*, p. 62.
[18]In this part we are focusing on social processes relevant to definition of self.

of their perceptions and beliefs will feel pressures to conform, to accept the beliefs of others as more valid than their own. However, in a heterogeneous society no man can be a complete conformist; the validity of many of our beliefs is challenged by the different beliefs of other people, other groups. Nevertheless, the effort we expend to make sure we have some social support for our views is evidence of our dependence on shared perceptions and beliefs for confirmation of a core part of the self.

One of the most common ways we confirm our views that are not universally held is by associating with people who *do* share and thus confirm our perceptions, attitudes, opinions, and beliefs. Persons who have lived for an extended period in an alien culture often speak of their relief at having their world view confirmed upon their return home. Festinger, Riecken, and Schachter[19] and Hardyck and Braden have provided penetrating descriptions of the reactions of apocalyptic groups to disconfirmations of some important beliefs and expectations. In the case of members of the "Lake City" group described by Festinger *et al.*, the reaction to disconfirmation was to proselytize and attract new members to the group in order to restore the individual's confidence in his beliefs and thus prevent identity-diffusion, if not disintegration. In contrast, the highly cohesive "True Word" group discussed by Hardyck and Braden apparently provided the social confirmation required for individual members to maintain their beliefs in the face of physical disconfirmation without proselytizing. In both cases, however, one clear implication is that lack of confirmation of important beliefs about the environment threatens certain beliefs about the self and leads to defensive rather than reality-testing strategies.

People also respond to a lack of social support or confirmation of their perceptions and beliefs by changing them to conform to those of their most salient reference group. The paper by Schachter provides unusual documentation of the way people use very subtle social cues to "test reality" and to adjust the appropriateness of their emotional responses.

C. Identity Extension

In this section we are concerned with identity change, specifically the growth or extension of identity or self-image.

1. *Self-Realization.* The verb "to realize" has more than one meaning. Among other things, it implies both *knowing* and *making concrete or real,* suggesting two ways that a self-image might be extended. Self-realization, as we conceive of it, involves both becoming consciously aware of the self as it presently exists, and extending the self to include latent potentialities. The discussion of self-esteem in an earlier section of the essay is directly relevant to the first aspect of self-realization: self-awareness. There we suggested that doubts about self-worth can lead to repression as well as suppression of certain parts of the self; hiding, pretending, and caution are strategies for self-delusion as well as for deluding others. Here we are more

[19]L. Festinger, H. W. Riecken, Jr., and S. Schachter, *When Prophecy Fails* (Minneapolis: Univ. of Minnesota, 1956).

concerned with self-realization in the sense of discovering what the self *can* be.

2. *Self-Realization Through "Selflessness."* For us, the key to self-realization, to discovering what the self *can* be is selflessness: we become our self only as we can forget our self. Fingarette has described selflessness in the following terms:

> . . . *"Selflessness" is a characteristic mystic concept associated with the "enlightened" state. . . . It does not mean the absence of a self in the psychoanalytic sense of that term, nor does it refer to the absence of the ego or of the "self-representations," or to the loss of ability to distinguish "inner" and "outer" as in hallucination or estrangement. . . . "Selflessness," being a term in a "subjective" language, expresses the lack of conscious awareness of self. But this is true in a sense which cannot be made unambiguous in ordinary language. We can point to the unawareness in question by referring to its psychological conditions: it is that "normal" unselfconciousness characteristic of experience which is primarily nonanxious and motivated by neutralized drives functioning within the non-conflictful portions of the ego. It is an unselfconsciousness akin to the normal unawareness of our breathing.*[20]

A person capable of selflessness must be sure enough of his worth as an individual, self-accepting enough, that he does not need to hide, or pretend, or be cautious; instead he can respond openly, spontaneously, and naturally to new situations and new people. Only by temporarily suspending the conscious desire for consistency, the need to be what we know we can be successfully and safely, can we find out what *else* we might be. Only by responding *unselfconsciously*, momentarily freed from too great dependence on what we have been, can we discover what variety there is within us.

It should be emphasized that while selflessness connotes a lack of conscious awareness of self in action, it is a *suspension* of awareness, not the incapacity to be aware. It is this distinction that differentiates the person capable of selflessness from the schizophrenic. Although the term "selflessness" often has been used to describe only the rather esoteric states of the religious mystic or drug addict, it is probable that most persons with some "nonconflictful portions of the ego" can behave selflessly, or unselfconsciously, in some situations.

Selflessness also implies the capacity to observe one's self in a detached and objective fashion. A person's first impulse in the face of critical feedback from the environment is to defend the self, to preserve the status quo, to look out for his self-interests. Under these conditions it is difficult, if not impossible, to evaluate feedback objectively and use it constructively. Selflessness, on the other hand, suggests the capacity to become temporarily detached from one's self, to stand back and look at the self as another person might. If the ability to behave unselfconsciously is the first step toward identity extension, then the capacity to view our behavior objectively is certainly the second.

[20] H. Fingarette, "The Ego and Mystic Selflessness," in *Identity and Anxiety*, Stein, Vidich, and White (eds.) (Glencoe, Ill.: Free Press, 1960), pp. 580–81.

3. *Facilitating Relationships.* Selflessness and self-realization can occur to the degree that a person feels worthy in a relationship. The parties to the relationship will feel that they are accepted, that the other has made a positive decision concerning their value of them. There will be a feeling that this decision is final and will stand in the face of any new aspects of the self that might emerge.

Furthermore, the persons involved will feel they are accepted for what they are; their images of each other will be neither too grandiose nor too modest. Expectations of each other will be realistic.

Finally, there will be an implicit assumption that one person will not deliberately hurt the other to satisfy his own needs, a quality of a relationship often called *trust.*

It appears, therefore, that self-definition and self-evaluation interact with each other. The person has to be something in order to be evaluated, and the person has to be positively evaluated in order to be something new.

4. *Descriptive Feedback.* Learning about our self from others' responses to us does not stop with the end of childhood and the initial development of a sense of identity. During our discussion of self-evaluation, we suggested that low self-esteem is associated with a tendency to perceive only the evaluative elements in others' responses to us—the approval or disapproval, acceptance or rejection. The need to maintain a certain level of self-esteem seems to take precedence over all else, and doubt about self-worth stimulates "selfishness" or "selfconsciousness," rather than selflessness. Most people, however, at least in some areas, can become temporarily self-detached to observe the reactions of others to their self. They can go beyond the evaluated feedback to the descriptive cues that can help them discover *what* they are rather than just how acceptable they are.

The distinction between indirect and direct feedback, made in connection with evaluative feedback, is also relevant here. However, whereas indirect feedback is of little use, and may even be harmful, for purposes of self-evaluation, it plays an extremely important role in self-definition. Others' responses to our behavior, often nonverbal, may contain information they might not be able to express more directly. Nevertheless, it frequently is not enough. Persons who attend human relations training laboratories such as those sponsored by the National Training Laboratories[21] almost invariably express a desire to be told point blank how other people perceive them. This is particularly true of persons with a relatively strong sense of personal worth who are not worried about, or even particularly interested in, others' *evaluations* of them.

The shortage of useful descriptive feedback stems partly from difficulty in predicting whether the person to receive the descriptive feedback will respond to it as just that, or whether he will scan it only for its evaluative content. Psychologists face this problem when they try to feed back the results of psychological tests; teachers face a similar dilemma

[21]E. H. Schein and W. G. Bennis, *Personal and Organizational Change Through Group Methods* (New York: Wiley, 1964).

when they discuss a student's work with him, or counsel a student on possible careers. All too often persons who want and can make good use of descriptive feedback are denied it because the person who might help them has had a bad experience with someone who could hear only the evaluative elements in the feedback he was given.

SUMMARY

This essay represents an attempt to point up some of the interpersonal aspects of self-confirmation. We have focused on self-evaluation and self-definition as two processes critical to self-confirmation and having important interpersonal ramifications. Rather than try to draw conclusions, it seems more appropriate to close with an illustration that dramatizes many of the points we have made.

> *As part of a research project, forty-five young managers in a large utility company were interviewed extensively about their career problems. Nearly all of the men had been hired right out of college as management trainees, and had been working for this particular organization for six years. As one might expect, a variety of complaints and problems were unearthed, but one in particular stood out because of the intense frustration associated with it.*
>
> *Several of the young managers had been quite successful up to the time they began their business careers, and as a result they had no reason to believe they would not continue to be successful. Each had, at the beginning of his career, rather high expectations of what he would accomplish. The image each had of himself was that of a highly competent person who would rise to the top among a group of his peers.*
>
> *Before long, however, their experiences in the company began to challenge their self-images. They did not move ahead particularly fast, only keeping pace with or falling behind the majority of their peers. This experience was quite at odds with the expectations they had. The environment offered several possible rationalizations for failure. Because of a period of business regression, promotions were frozen. The company was automating various functions, cutting back on the total number of employees and thus the number of management positions. The company was consolidating small work units into larger ones, giving more responsibility to individual managers, but eliminating managerial positions in the process.*
>
> *The basic dilemma these men expressed was whether or not in the face of feedback from their environment they should re-evaluate themselves and re-adjust their self-images to be more consistent with the cues they were receiving. Many of their colleagues were quick to perceive and accept the evaluative cues contained in the company's response to them and to re-evaluate themselves accordingly. Others, less confident of their worth as individuals, sought only reassurance, rationalizing or denying their predicament. These men could do neither, at least not on the basis of the impersonal and frequently ambiguous feedback available to them. They did express a desperate need for respected superiors to give them absolutely objective, point-blank feedback on their potential as managers. With honest, direct feedback they could trust, they felt they could decide whether to modify their self-image appropriately, or to try to confirm their self-image in another company. However, they were unable to persuade their superiors to be absolutely honest and open with them; the superiors apparently either felt they would be hurting rather than helping their subordinate by leveling with him, or they had been taught it was poor management. In any case, the organization failed to recognize the capacity these men had to use direct feedback constructively, with the result that the men in question were unable to resolve their dilemma.*

Clearly there are no simple solutions to the dilemmas the young managers are confronting. Self-esteem and self-image are the hardcore of personality, but we have little control over their development, and lack the knowledge and techniques to influence or alter them reliably. Recently, however, there has been an increasing awareness of the importance of interpersonal processes, and a growing concern with "creative human relationships," or relationships that facilitate personal growth. This section . . . is a reflection of that concern.

HUMANISTIC ELEMENTS IN GROUP GROWTH

Jack R. Gibb and
Lorraine M. Gibb

Some groups seem to grow. They appear healthy—and seem to get more healthy as time goes on. In such groups the human being seems to emerge as having great worth and great potential. It is difficult to separate feelings of personal growth and well-being from feelings of membership and interdependent fulfillment. Members of the group feel free, emergent, and creative.

Some groups appear to stagnate. They seem unhealthy. Members may speak defensively about their membership. In such groups the human being may appear as less than he is, as having little worth and little potential. Members may wonder whether the group is ever really going to amount to much or whether it will ever accomplish its aims. Members may feel restricted by the demands of the group. Persons may feel that they give more to the group than they get from it.

What distinguishes sick from healthy groups is a significant question. For most of us, groups are important elements in the structure of our culture. Some groups grow, and become, in a sense, actualized. Other groups progress slowly or fail to develop in meaningful dimensions. Therapy groups can provide a setting for therapy and remedial help, or they can be useless to the members. Classroom groups can be environments where growth and learning are easy, or they can be of little help and actually inhibit such growth. YMCA clubs can be climates which foster healthy spirituality and character formation, or they can hamper such formation. Families, regardless of such variables as economic welfare or presence or absence of fathers, can foster healthy growth in parents and children, or they can be festering grounds for juvenile delinquency, neurotic habits, or unhappiness. Research teams can be creative atmospheres for innovation and productivity, or they can lead to mediocrity, stagnation, and low productivity.

Research Base of Observation

In our research on group growth,[1] we have obtained a revealing and even inspiring view of man as he might become, and we have had occasional glimpses of groups in peak experiences of sustained creativity and trust,

[1]Since 1951 the authors have conducted a series of experimental and field studies designed to investigate longitudinal changes in small groups, particularly as these changes are associated with the arousal and maintenance of defensive or productive behavior. These studies were financed mainly by a series of grants from the Group Psychology Branch of the Office of Naval Research.

i.e., group actualization. These group experiences have occurred most often (1) when groups have been in sensitivity training in semiweekly sessions for eight or nine consecutive months, (2) when groups have been in around-the-clock "marathon" sessions for 90 to 120 hours with little or no sleep, or (3) when groups have been in twelve-hour sessions daily for twelve or thirteen consecutive days. In our experience, this optimal growth occurs most frequently in groups which have no professional leader present and in which emergent and interdependent strength is maximized.

Under these conditions, the groups are qualitatively different from the groups usually met in natural settings. The groups attain and often maintain states of creativity, depth of communication, and trust that are impressive and memorable, both to those participating and to those observing. We have seen this state of affairs in occasional natural groups in organizational settings, usually after the group has undergone a training experience of appropriate duration and intensity.

Group and Person Potentials

Research from several different disciplines has indicated that man grows at a fraction of his potential growth rate. This underdevelopment is even more startling when one examines the growth rate of groups in our culture. In our research program, we made systematic observations of groups in natural settings—YMCA clubs, management teams, national boards, therapy groups, work groups, and families. We made use of a number of methods in comparing the groups under depth training with natural groups: group interviews, individual depth interviews, coded group observations, questionnaires, expert opinions, and analysis of taped recordings (Gibb, 1955; Gibb, 1963; Gibb, 1964).

In this chapter, we shall present informal summaries of our general impressions from the longitudinal research and of our conclusions about a humanistic theory of personal and group growth.

Our impression is that man's capacity for creativity, happiness, and personal growth is greatly underrated, both by himself and by many scientists who study man. Behavioral scientists in evaluating potential have looked at persons and groups in the natural setting and judged what they might become. It is as if, wishing to determine how well men could hit golf balls, we lined up fifty average adult males at a golf tee, had each hit two balls, measured the distances, and concluded that the average man's driving potential was 30 yards. After practice and effort, perhaps the average man could hit the ball 155 yards. However, after experiencing a refined instruction process, the average person could possibly be trained to hit the ball 225 yards. The above analogy is relevant to the testing of the group's capability for creative growth. There is a qualitative difference between the average management team in the usual organizational setting and the same group after it receives the kind of training that is now possible. This significant fact has led to a new look at human potential in persons and groups, to new organizational theories, and to new theories of individual and group development.

BASIC DIMENSIONS OF GROUP LIFE

The process aspects of the group, *qua* group, are a relatively recent object of scientific study. Knowing little about groups and often fearing them, man has sometimes felt that they were a hindrance to human growth. It now seems likely that man can reach new satisfactions and significant functional levels of living in group action.

Our research indicates four significant dimensions in which groups differ. These dimensions are interdependent, and as yet we have no clear comprehension of that interdependence, but we do have some convincing evidence of the relevance of each of these factors in group growth, health, or actualization

Groups differ in (1) the degree of *reciprocal trust* among members; (2) the *validity, depth, and quality of the feedback system;* (3) the degree of *directionality toward group-determined goals*; and (4) the degree of *real interdependence in the system.* A schematic picture of these four variables is given in Table 1. Let us examine each of these factors in some detail.

THE FORMATION OF TRUST

Trust is the pacemaker variable in group growth. From it stem all the other significant variables of health. That is, to the extent that trust develops, people are able to communicate genuine feelings and perceptions on relevant issues to all members of the system. To the degree that trust is present, people are able to communicate with themselves and others to form consensual goals. To the degree that trust is present, people can be truly interdependent. Each of the four group-growth variables is dependent upon the prior variable in the hierarchy. Feedback is dependent upon

Table 1 Personal and Group Growth

Key Areas of Social Behavior	*Directions of Personal Growth*	*Directions of Group Growth*
Climate (membership)	Acceptance of self; acceptance of others	Climate of trust; climate of support
Data flow (decision making)	Awareness (input); openness (output)	Valid feedback system; consensual decision making
Goal formation (productivity)	Goal integration in self; self-determination; self-assessment	Goal integration in group; group determination and assessment of goals
Control (organization)	Interdependence (inner, emergent control and value system)	Interdependence (inner, emergent control and norm system)

trust. Goal formation is dependent upon feedback and trust. Interdependence is dependent upon goal formation, feedback, and trust.

As is indicated in Table 1, the four factors in group growth are related to parallel factors in personal growth. There is some agreement among psychologists on the criteria of mental health in personal growth.[2] There is considerably less agreement among group scientists on the criteria of group health and development. The schema outlined here provides a framework for analyzing group actualization.

The Dynamic of Fear

The most impressive dynamic of early group life is the presence of fear. Fear grows out of distrust. We tend to fear events, people, and stimuli for which we feel we have no adequate response. Many factors in the new or immature group increase the normal residual fear that all people share. Great uncertainty increases fear, and individuals have many ways of trying to reduce this uncertainty. They put other people into categories which they feel they can understand and predict. "If I know she is a nurse, then I know what nurses are like and can respond to what I know they will do." They get the group to agree upon some ground rules. "If we take turns talking around the circle, then I know when my turn comes." Individuals also try to find out what the other members think of them and about the world.

Some of these efforts to lessen uncertainty are unsuccessful, while others are fairly effective. Even if I can reduce the ambiguity in my own perceptual world, this gets shattered when I realize that growth in me and in the group can come only with ambiguity, tension, conflict, and unfreezing. I cannot truly become safe from my fears by building my perceptual world into safe and predictable categories.

Growth turns out to be something more.

The group in its early stages will attempt to cling to and create fragile structural stabilities to reduce fear. These apparently secure structures turn out to be made of sand. A group may assign a timekeeper so that one person will not monopolize the group; it may appoint a chairman, or it may decide in what order people will speak. This supposedly "rules in" order and control and "rules out" chaos and threatening situations.

For some people, moving quickly lessens fear by reducing the tension and turmoil of decision making in depth. "Let's do anything," "Let's get something done," "We are wasting time," and other impatient expressions aimed at speeding up direct movement are common in the early stages of group development. Later observations show that these frantic demands for movement are fear-based.

Other Group Evidences of Fear

Politeness and formality are early indications of fear. Politeness prevents retaliation, keeps people at a safe distance, makes it unnecessary to face members in such a way that intimidating negative feelings would be re-

[2]See a helpful analysis of contemporary agreement and disagreement on criteria of personal growth in Jahoda (1958).

vealed, discourages the other person from giving negative feedback, and in general serves the unanalyzed needs of the fearful person.

Another response to fear in early stages of group life is the use of humor. It is ambiguous enough to serve as a presumably safe camouflage for hostile feedback to another person. Humor tends to encourage people to keep things from getting too sentimental, too intimate, and too close to embarrassing or painful exposure or confrontation. By using humor, a person can "hedge his bets" and deny the hostile intent if the listener accuses him of being unfriendly.

In its early stages, the group is sometimes work-addicted. The group can avoid fearsome confrontation, interpersonal conflict, and exposure by hard, safe work upon a seemingly legitimate task. Groups can make long lists, engage in routine tasks, and attempt to look busy to themselves and others, in order to avoid depth relationships. A group may engage in an unending warm-up session, talking in an apparently serious, work-oriented vein about the factors determining today's weather. Of course, all the defense mechanisms are relevant here.

People who are afraid distrust the motivations of other members and tend to step in and try to control the situation in order to prevent those whom they fear from exerting prior influence. This is often done in subtle ways, such as nominating a less-feared person to be chairman. This apparent cleanly motivated act can hopefully be seen as selfless and group-oriented rather than as a disguised manipulation for control.

Signs of Group Growth

Thus, fear and distrust characterize behavior in the early stages of group development. As groups grow, these fears gradually become reduced. Trust grows. People learn to tolerate greater degrees of ambiguity. They become more spontaneous and less cautious. Members make allowances for greater differences, both in themselves and in others. People are allowed to hold a wider variety of opinions. They are permitted to be themselves—to dress differently, to be unpredictable, and perhaps even to be disloyal. The boundaries of acceptance widen. Whereas in the early stages of development, the group boxes in or punishes persons who deviate from the group norms, in the later stages, nonconformists are encouraged. Radical ideas are used to test reality or to create new solutions. Deviation is perhaps even welcomed as a creative contribution to possible group productivity.

Fear reduction allows people to feel and to express publicly the warmth that wells up. People are able to show affection in a number of spontaneous, often gestural, ways without the need for exaggerated or showy expressions. There is a great deal of warmth in the group. In addition, there is an easy expression of "I feel this way," on the assumption that other members will permit the voicing of individualistic feelings. It is also common to hear people spontaneously say and feel "we," rather than "you." (The use of "you" in referring to the group is a sign of membership denial.)

The problem of trust formation is the problem of attaining membership. One achieves genuine belonging by trusting himself and the group. The critical index of group health is trust development. As the group grows, fear decreases and trust increases. Thus, group actualization is a process of attaining increasingly higher levels of trust.

COMMUNICATION AND DECISION MAKING

In the early stages of group development, the customary fear and distrust make it difficult for a valid feedback system to occur, for people to talk honestly with one another, and for the group to integrate these feelings and perception data into appropriate decisions for the group.

The processes of ambiguity, strategy, façade building, and gamesmanship, mentioned in the earlier paragraph as resulting from fears, also tend to reduce the effectiveness of the communication system. With the presence of fear and the lack of trust, there is little encouragement for open exploration of one's own inner world of motivations and attitudes. People give off mixed messages: There is a difference between facial expression and verbal content, between tone of voice and what one says, between what one has courage enough to say in a subgroup and what one says publicly in the total group, and between what one says the first time and what one says when challenged to repeat or clarify the message. Thus, such differences further increase the distortion of data.

In low trust, a great number of concealing skills develop. People become adept at consciously or unconsciously withholding feelings. Especially in situations of actual or supposed power differences, the weaker person, the person lower in the hierarchy, or the person with the lowest status may deliberately treat a disliked person with great friendliness in order to cover his real negative feelings. Secretaries may develop complicated strategies for seeming busy. Using façades, bosses may camouflage favoritism or degrees of differential feelings about employees.

People spread rumors in order to test reactions. This feedback distortion is used to hurt others or to explore the depth of feeling. There are elaborate skills for learning one's way in the maze of distortion in the usual organization.

A common process which suppresses relevant information in the group is the ignoring of known or suspected experts. People are jealous of those with knowledge and are suspicious of their motives. The expert is frequently articulate and persuasive, so he overstates his case in an imposing manner and rebreeds resentment and resistance. Thus,. there are many reasons why people with information are discouraged from sharing it.

Another source of distortion occurs because of inadequate methods of problem solving. In its early stages, the group seldom adequately defines the problem, and because problem definition may cause conflict, the participants find it safer to philosophize about nonpersonal items.

As the group develops, the members learn that it is possible to deal with many deep-seated feelings and concerns without undue fear and anxiety about being hurt. The participants discover that, although long-withheld feelings are sometimes disturbing to everyone present, the alternative of holding back the feelings has even worse consequences for the group. It becomes clear to the group that feelings can, in a genuine sense, be integrated into work, creativity, and problem solving.

Effective groups, with development, are able to develop consensual decision making about significant problems that the group faces. This is the payoff of data processing and the feedback system of the group.

GOAL FORMATION AND PRODUCTIVITY

Group health is related to the integration of group goals. Unhealthy groups are unable to decide what they want to be or want to do. Lacking an adequate system of communication, members may not know that they, as a group, are not doing what they want to do. The difficulties in goal formation arise rather directly from partial data processing, which in turn grows out of fear and distrust. When members distrust the motivations of other members, it is difficult to share goals in a meaningful way. The problem that the group faces is somehow to create out of the available data a satisfying goal which would adequately include the real goals of the members and which would be more fulfilling than any of the half-verbalized goals that the individuals have.

One of the early errors that groups make is to force the expression of a few goals that come "off the top of the head," separate these into some alternatives, and then vote on a goal. This process necessitates a compromise, so that participants often feel that they are now doing something less satisfying than they would have done alone. They say that they are going along to satisfy others, to appear flexible, to avoid being seen as stubborn or rebellious, and to please authorities. In our early research, we found a high "reservation score" in early stages of group growth; that is, a large number of members were seen by the rest of the group as consenting, but were found (when data were later gathered by better means such as depth interviews) to have a number of unverbalized reservations about the decisions that had been made by the group (Gibb, 1963).

Coercion and Resistance

One error made by unhealthy groups is the attempt to impose control mechanisms and to verbalize public goals before the group has worked through its fears and data-processing problems. Verbal, anxious, or dominant people are prone to do this. For various reasons, weak, uninterested, or nonverbal individuals often go along with these coercive members. Members combat persuasion by using various forms of resistance, often little understood by the high persuaders. Thus, members, consciously or not, will be withdrawn and apathetic and will show a low commitment to verbalize any goals. Then, too, there are those who really do not know what they want to do. Perhaps because they have so often gone along with persuasive or dynamic leadership, they have never developed the capacity to examine their own goals and plan life activities that will accomplish these aims.

One of the first tasks in training groups or teams in natural situations is to learn to examine the motivations of individuals. This may be a lengthy task, calling for long-dormant skills and feelings. The general stagnation of self and the lack of personal identity in our withdrawn culture are evident in immature groups. In the developing group, members can seek their identity; they can learn to explore previously half-formulated desires, repressed wishes, and formerly unrealizable goals in an atmosphere of trust and listening. Sharpening of this inner quest takes place in the caring group.

The apparent reverse of apathy is a condition of frenetic work at tasks that the group uses to respond to duty motivations, loyalty to the organization, compulsive needs, and the desire to prove to themselves and to others that they can work hard. This busywork can easily be misunderstood and seen as productive or creative work.

Public Goals and Real Goals

A common error is the declaring of public "motherhood-and-the-flag" kinds of goals. There is no real commitment to these goals, and they are used as a cover-up. Learning groups, for instance, will set up as a goal a two-hour discussion of foremen training because this seems like something that the company would want or that the group should be interested in. In reality, though, the people come to the meeting to complain about the company, air personal grudges, or get a vacation, or because of a whole variety of motivations that are unrelated to the public statement.

When a group of people have worked through the fear, trust, and data-flow problems to the point where they can communicate in high trust or "speak the truth in love," it is possible to work to a reasonable consensus on major problems of goal formation and decision making.

The members integrate tasks, groups, and individual goals. (We are assuming that all people are achievement-motivated and that work, when self-determined, is intrinsically satisfying.) In order for personal and group needs to be met, the group must select a task and make some kind of visible progress toward accomplishing it. In effective groups, *esprit de corps*, individual satisfaction over group achievement, and commitment to the group are vital. Group members must also feel some sense of belonging, fulfillment, self-worth, influence, and linkage to whatever goals are currently important to them as individuals. As high trust and a valid communication system develop, it becomes possible to mesh these needs in satisfying ways without undue group pressures to conform for the sake of conformity. The creation of this state of affairs gives people a sense of freedom

A well-known vice-president of one of America's largest corporations once said, after observing a T-group in a highly cooperative session, that he had never seen a group in which people listened to one another so deeply and were so well able to integrate what they said into a creative and satisfying discussion. He was so impressed that he had a deep emotional experience just observing the session! A minister stated, after spending a day in such a group, "This is the first time that I have ever really had a religious experience!" When the average organization works at from 20 to 40 percent effectiveness, it is a dramatic and memorable occasion to see a group working at a 70 percent efficiency level. Those of us who have seen participative groups in action, both in training and in the natural organizational setting, are aware of the exciting and awesome potential of people who are engaged in creative interaction on group-initiated tasks.

Group actualization occurs with the productive integration of deeply personal needs into a genuine consensus on goals. The group continues to form goals that are a creative synthesis of personal goals—new, exciting, and fulfilling (Gibb, 1961a; Gibb, 1965).

CONTROL SYSTEMS AND ORGANIZATION

Most all of us in the process of socialization develop authority and influence problems that stem from our early relations with our parents and teachers. When a group of people meet in the early stages, problems of mutual influence become immediately visible to the observer and to the more sensitive members. This is true of all groups, whether their purpose is work or recreation. Distrust, distorted communication, and imposed or ambiguous goals tend to make these feelings more severe and to limit growth.

One of our T-groups, composed of upper-middle management people from governmental, industrial, educational, and religious organizations, was discussing what seemed to be an innocent problem of whether or not to take a coffee break. The issue was brought up by a member in the first three minutes of the opening session as an apparently harmless and minor goal. The member's proposal was followed by a few, apparently frivolous, comments about the absence of cream, some mild wishes for tea, some weak resistance to taking time from the group for an unnecessary break, a few jokes, and laughter. This then led a few of the more vigorous members to try to push for a quick decision. These tactics snowballed into a mild resistance, and a long conversation developed. The discussion became more heated and continued for two hours and twenty minutes, until the group was actually late for lunch and yet still deadlocked over whether to waste time taking a morning coffee break! People shouted, developed hurt feelings, withdrew occasionally to sulk, and argued violently about apparently trivial issues. The group broke up at someone's suggestion and went to lunch. After lunch, one of the observers interpreted the discussion as a power struggle. This meaning was violently rejected by those engaged in the fight, but three days later, the group laughed together in recognition that it had been just that.

In undeveloped groups we often see such camouflaged and displaced battles for power and authority. Members are aware to various degrees of these interpersonal feelings in themselves and others. When communication and trust are low and facades are high, people pretend that there is no struggle, that the argument is "purely intellectual," that mixed feelings toward powerful members are inevitable and nonintrusive, and that there is nothing they can do about the matter.

Feelings of Impotence

A sense of powerlessness or impotence is a dominant characteristic of the early life of groups. Because people seldom listen, because the group has a difficult time finding a satisfying direction, and for a number of other reasons explored above, individuals in the group feel that it is very difficult to influence other individuals or "the group." Both the quiet and the talkative people have these feelings.

Resistance to induction takes many forms. The aggressive, high initiators are responded to with apathy or passive listening. Persuasion leads to resistance. Quiet, low-status, mild people are often ignored and thought to be idealists or uninterested in initiation. A recent study indicated that, in general, during the early stages of group life, members thought that unusually restrained people were stupid, uninterested, afraid, or lazy! Another factor that leads to the feeling of powerlessness is the tendency of people, especially during the early fear and distrust stages, to be suspicious of the motivations of other people. Thus, our study indicated that quiet members thought that the aggressive members were insecure, manipulative, domineering, and showing off their knowledge! It is also true that some of the noninitiators saw the initiators as helpful, full of ideas, and courageous. Some of the talkative members saw quiet individuals as good listeners, flexible, and courteous. As people trust and communicate better, the initiators are more apt to be seen as wanting to help, and the quiet members are more apt to be seen as receptive listeners. Ironically, in early stages the same behavior is viewed as dominance, manipulation, or uninterested resistance (Gibb, 1959; Gibb, 1961b; Gibb, 1964).

When people are afraid and feel powerless to influence their own important development or goal setting, they try to sway the group in a number of ways. People may not wish to admit to themselves or to the other members of the group that they do desire to influence, because this unrelieved need for power, as such, is looked down on in our aspiring-to-be-democratic society. Direct influence efforts are fairly easy to deal with, but camouflaged or devious attempts are more difficult for the group to examine and handle. Covert strategies are used by individuals with varying degrees of consciousness. Some may deliberately try to use strategies and manipulative gimmicks. Others may unconsciously use tricky means of getting their way (Gibb, 1961a).

Sometimes the opposition may be conscious and take the form of strategies such as appointing committees, using parliamentary maneuvers, calling for a summary, or apparently innocent or useful list making, in order to prevent an impending decision that is being pushed by a person who is thought to be seeking power.

Desires to influence are apparently characteristic of all of us. These needs are troublesome only when they are covered up and are thus difficult for the group to handle or when they are denied (although overpowering because of fear and anxiety), so that the group cannot deal with the behavior for what it is. The wish to influence and be influenced is a productive and creative one and is necessary for group growth.

The Fear of Uncontrolled Groups

Groups in early stages of development seem unmanageable. This gives rise to the feeling that special procedures are necessary to control the group. The organization tries rules, regulations, appointed leaders, span of control, parliamentary procedure, channels of communication, tight organization, and "articles of war" formally to control the behavior of people in groups. It seems to members that it would be unthinkable for the group to operate without strong formal leadership and regulations. Thus, tight controls arise which tend to be self-deceiving. People resist the rules by various forms of displaced rebellion, by apathy, or by a kind of unimaginative obedience. Conflict, spontaneity, and vigorous interplay are all productive in a high-trust and high-feedback situation. These factors, however, produce disruptions and unproductive organizations in a low-trust and low-feedback condition.

Another state of affairs characteristic of the early stages of group life and related to control and organization may be the calm of the orderly, obedient, peace-at-any-price atmosphere. The deadly politeness may be interpreted by members or observers as productive work. "Sweetness and light" can be a cover-up for the group's uncertainty about the handling of the control and authority problems.

Permissiveness is another uncertain concept in this connection. What is called "permissiveness" may be many things. In low-trust and low-communication groups, it may be a kind of unrelated, undigestible disorder in which people look as if they are doing what they want to do, but are in fact responding to impulse, play, and resistance. Lacking formal leadership, the group is thus confused and structureless. Permissiveness in high-trust, high-feedback groups can be realized in exciting, spontaneous, and playful integration of creative efforts in the group. Opponents of permissiveness are thinking about low-trust groups, while the advocates of permissiveness are thinking about the high-trust situation that occurs in the relatively well-developed group.

It has been our observation that developed groups can operate in a leaderless situation without formal, prepared agenda, without organizational coercion in the formal sense, and without the parliamentary procedures which are thought to make decision making easier.

EXTRINSIC SOLUTIONS TO GROUP PROBLEMS

Because of low trust and low communication, groups have invented mechanisms for solving the problems on these four dimensions. A legal system of formal laws has been invented to solve the fear and distrust problem. Membership requirements such as college entrance examinations and racial and religious codes for housing, clubs, and jobs have been developed.

A great many mechanisms have been produced to solve the low-communication, poor-data-flow problems. Communication channels are organized. Parliamentary procedures which guarantee minimal opportunity for people to talk are set up. Formal rules for making decisions by majority vote are used. Company newspapers, written memoranda, multiple copy systems, and many tools of the communications and public relations professions have arisen.

Various mechanisms are devised during the early stages of group development to solve the passivity toward the goal-formation dimension. Most of these involve the artificial creation of motivation by extrinsic reward systems: competition, grades, piecework, and praise and merit systems.

All these mechanisms are control systems which arise as a result of recognition of membership, decision, and motivation problems. Mechanisms for handling control problems, of course, are also used. Rules of way, bargaining contracts, codes of gentlemen, punishments for nonconformity, formal job prescriptions, and tables of organizations are all examples. As groups grow, the necessity for these formal control systems disappears.

Conflict

Conflicts will occur in living and in active and creative people. Resolving the conflict, by finding alternatives that are creative solutions rather than deadening compromises, can be a productive process. The motivation to build something new can come from the dissatisfaction revealed by the discord. The deliberate creation of conflict is likely to occur in the early stages of group development, when frantic leaders have no other way for creating excitement or when playful members are bored. However, when conflict does exist, the best way to handle it is to look at it and resolve it. The mature group is able to do this. A process analysis of the way the conflict arose and was solved is potentially meaningful and is likely to be cathartic. The aftermath of conflict can also be productive. People can learn about themselves, about the group, and about the reality of the world by the way that they, as individuals or as a group, have handled the discord.

CONCLUSION

Groups are often unhealthy and add little to the lives of their members. Such groups might well be discontinued or certainly changed. Grouping can become a fetish, and many groups are preserved long beyond their day. As we have seen, signs of ill health include undue fear and distrust, inadequate and distorted communication, undigested and dysfunctional goal systems, and unresolved dependency problems.

Groups *can* be healthy. Groups can be creative, fulfilling, and satisfying to all their members. We have seen groups that can be appropriately described as actualizing. Such groups develop a high degree of trust, valid communication in depth, a consensual goal system, and a genuine interdependence. Our research has shown promising data that provide a way for therapists, parents, managers, and teachers to aid in the process of creating groups which are in themselves healthy organisms and which provide a climate for member growth and fulfillment (Gibb, 1964; Gibb, 1965). It is such groups that can provide the framework for a better world.

REFERENCES

Gibb, J. R. Factors producing defensive behavior within groups. II. *Annual Technical Report, Office of Naval Research*, Contract Nonr–1147(03), NR 170–226, 1955.

Gibb, J. R. Factors producing defensive behavior within groups. VI. *Final Technical Report, Office of Naval Research*, Contract Nonr–2285(01), 1959.

Gibb, J. R. Defensive communication. *Journal of Communication*, 1961, 11, 141–148, (a).

Gibb, J. R., Defense level and influence potential in small groups. In L. Petrullo & B. M. Bass (eds.), *Leadership and interpersonal behavior.* New York: Holt, Rinehart and Winston, 1961, pp. 66–61, (b).

Gibb, J. R. Factors producing defensive behavior within groups. VII. *Final Technical Report, Office of Naval Research*, Contract Nonr–3088(00), 1963.

Gibb, J. R. Climate for trust formation. In L. P. Bradford, J. R. Gibb, & K. D. Benne (eds.), *T-group theory and laboratory method.* New York: Wiley, 1964, pp. 279–309.

Gibb, J. R. Fear and façade: Defensive management. In R. E. Farson (ed.), *Science and human affairs.* Palo Alto, Calif.: Science and Behavior Books, 1965, pp. 197–214.

Jahoda, Marie. *Current concepts of positive mental health.* (A report by the Joint Commission on Mental Illness and Health.) New York: Basic Books, 1958.

Chapter 4
INTERPERSONAL PERCEPTION AND ORIENTATIONS

The first step in communicating with another person is to form some impression of him/her. This impression directs our reactions to that person and thus influences the course of our interpersonal communication. This process of forming impressions of others and making judgments about them we have labeled interpersonal perception; our characteristic responses to people are our orientations. In this chapter we shall examine these processes of interpersonal perception and making characteristic responses in keeping with our personal needs.

THE PROCESS OF INTERPERSONAL PERCEPTION

We tend to take our perceptions of others for granted without considering why and how we form them and whether they are right. We thus select our friends without conscious realizations of why; we choose whom to ask for a date, and even marriage partners, without analyzing why we find ourselves attracted to each other.

The significance of attention to interpersonal perception has been stated by British psychologist Mark Cook:

> *Everyday "informal" judgments of others can have far-reaching effects such as marriage; the same is even more true of "professional" judgments. People are selected for jobs or higher education, etc., often on the basis of an interview in which the interviewer forms, on the basis of a fifteen-minute encounter, an opinion of the person's suitability, and, in the process, affects that person's life for years to come. Interviewers often never consider whether they are right or not, but rather have a firm belief in their own infallibility. Is this justified? If not, does it not follow that the interviewer should be abandoned as a form of assessment? The interviewer is the most important single type of "professional" perception of others, but there are many more. Psychiatrists decide what is wrong with patients, and have complete confidence in the correctness of the (often highly unlikely) conclusions they draw. Social workers do the same for their "clients." School teachers give assessments of their pupils' ability and often of their behaviors, with complete confidence in their own judgment. The police and the courts decide whether someone has committed an offense or whether witnesses are telling the truth, and are confident that their verdicts are correct.*[1]

[1]M. Cook, *Interpersonal Perception* (Middlesex, England: Penguin, 1971), pp. 13–14.

The process of perception is generally believed to accomplish two things:

1. *People recode the diversity of data they encounter in a form simple enough to be retained by their limited memory; and*
2. *They mentally go beyond the data given to predict future events, and thereby minimize surprise.*[2]

These two accomplishments of perception, selective recoding and prediction, become the basis for forming our impressions of other people. In forming our impression of others, we observe their actions and expressive movements, we notice their voices, and we note what they say and do as they respond to us and other stimuli. From this data we make inferences about their cognitions, needs, emotions and feelings, goals, and attitudes. Our actions toward them and prediction of future interactions are guided by these judgments. Simultaneously the other person is making judgments about us that will direct subsequent communications to us. If our judgments of each other are correct, genuine communication can be established and effective interaction becomes possible. If, however, our observations or predictions of each other are incorrect, communication is hampered and difficulties may develop in our interpersonal relations.

As with the other variables in the process of interpersonal communication, our person perceptions (i.e., our perception of another's personality) are never static; we are constantly in a state of modification and reevaluation. The flawless boyfriend of last week may now be the most despicable villain of the twentieth century. As we have greater and more diverse opportunities for interaction, our perceptions undergo change.

In essence, the process can be outlined as follows: We process the available data (our sensory bases of judgment); we define the other person and build expectations of future behavior (encoding simplification—stereotyping); in an attempt to achieve consistency of beliefs, expectations, and predictions, we choose what we see, process, and internalize (congruency and selective perception); our expectations help determine our behavior toward the other person (estimated relationship potential); and our behavior often significantly affects the behavior of the other person (reciprocal perspectives). We shall now examine this process in greater detail.

Our Sensory Bases of Judgment

Sight, sound, touch, and smell are our avenues of contact with other people. While other animals rely heavily upon odors, people tend to

[2]J. S. Bruner, "Social Psychology and Perception," in E. Maccoby, T. M. Newcomb, and E. L. Hartley, eds., *Readings in Social Psychology* (New York: Holt, Rinehart and Winston, 1958), pp. 85–94.

place greater emphasis on the other sensors. As Mark Knapp has observed,

> *Generally, Americans do not rely on their sense of smell for interpersonal cues unless perspiration odor, breath, or some other smell is unusually strong. Ironically, however, hundreds of thousands of dollars are spent by American men and women each year on deodorant sprays and soaps, mouth washes, breath mints, perfumes, aftershave lotions, and other artificial scents. The so-called "natural" scent seems to have low priority at this time point in our cultural development.*[3]

In the absence of systematic studies of human perceptual responses to odor, we shall turn our attention to the other sensory bases of judgment.

Sight. As we have already suggested, visual communication is inevitable when people are together and basic to the establishment of a relationship. The study of nonverbal communication is tied closely to the visual signals exchanged between people.

Eye contact between people may establish the initial contact. As one sociologist has suggested:

> *Of the special sense organs, the eye has a uniquely sociological function. The union and interaction of individuals is based upon mutual glances. This is perhaps the most direct and purest reciprocity which exists anywhere. . . .*
>
> *This mutual glance between persons, in distinction from the simple sight or observation of the other, signifies a wholly new and unique union between them. . . . By the glance which reveals the other, one discloses himself. By the very act in which the observer seeks to know the observed, he surrenders himself to be understood by the observer. The eye cannot take unless at the same time it gives.*[4]

Thus the dynamic nature of the visual interaction is indicated. We have all traded glances with a stranger across a room. Our desire for communication will depend upon whether we seek or avoid this visual contact.

In recent years, the role of eye contact in interpersonal communication has been the subject of considerable research. Knapp has summarized the research as follows:

> *Eye contact is influenced by a number of different conditions: whether we are seeking feedback, need for certain markers in the conversation, whether we wish to open or close the communication channel, whether the other party is too near or too far, whether we wish to induce*

[3]M. L. Knapp, *Nonverbal Communication in Human Interaction* (New York: Holt, Rinehart and Winston, 1972), p. 76.

[4]G. Simmel, "Sociology of the Senses: Visual Interaction," in R. E. Park and E. W. Burgess, eds., *Introduction to the Science of Sociology* (Chicago: University of Chicago Press, 1921), p. 358.

anxiety, whether we are rewarded by what we see, whether we are in competition with another or wishing to hide something from him, and whether we are with members of a different sex or status. Personality characteristics such as introversion/extroversion may also influence eye behavior.[5]

Another part of our impression of another person is based on his/her facial features and expressions. Studies confirm that people tend to agree in attributing certain personality traits to faces. This perceptual agreement amounts to a sort of cultural stereotyping. For example, the use of cosmetics and other grooming aids has been demonstrated to affect our judgment of women. At the time of the research, the amount of lipstick worn was perceived as related to sexuality, while bowed lips gave the impression of being conceited, demanding, immoral, and receptive to the attentions of men.[6] These perceptual judgments change, as evidenced by our culture's altered response to long-haired men.

Some facial expressions are so fleeting that we respond to them subconsciously. These have been labeled "micromomentary" expressions and have been studied by film or video-tape run in slow motion. At 4 frames per second instead of the usual 24, psychologists have noticed as many as 2½ times as many changes of expression, some lasting only ⅕ of a second. These expressions seem especially significant in conflict situations. If a person wishes to appear confident but feels fearful, some of the fear is released through these flickering expressions.[7] In the current vernacular, this person would thus give off "*bad vibes.*" Someone truly confident and consistent in the micromomentary expressions would be a source of "*good vibes.*" Such research lends support for our thesis of the need for genuineness and lack of artificiality in our interpersonal relations.

In addition to facial expressions, other visual cues are given us in a person's gestures and other expressive movements. Subtle cues tend to be tied to individual cultures, but certain acts seem to have near-universal meaning. The elocutionists of the nineteenth century worked out detailed scientific analyses of the overt expressions of our various feelings and emotions. This mechanistic approach for training public speakers has long been disdained as artificial and unnatural, but the fact remains that visually we are constantly communicating, either reinforcing or distracting from any messages being sent vocally.

[5]Knapp, *op. cit.*, p. 138.

[6]P. F. Secord, "Facial Features and Inference Processes in Interpersonal Perception," in R. Tagiuri and L. Petrullo, eds., *Person Perception and Interpersonal Behavior* (Stanford, Calif.: Stanford University Press, 1958), pp. 300–318.

[7]E. A. Haggard and K. S. Isaacs, "Micromomentary Facial Expressions as Indicators of Ego Mechanisms in Psychotherapy," in L. A. Gottschalk and A. H. Auerback, eds., *Methods of Research in Psychotherapy* (New York: Appleton, 1966).

Some people are more expressive than others in their visual communication. The highly animated person may appear more open and involved in the act of communicating, but even the stiff, rigid, aloof person cannot conceal himself for long. The person who shrugs his shoulders or waves his hands while speaking without facial emotion may only be reflecting a cultural heritage, yet the receiver of the message will react as if these expressive movements are cues to the personality. The animated talker is likely to be judged as "forceful," while the immobile speaker is thought to be "controlled" and "cold."

Jurgen Ruesch has defined three classifications of a nonverbal codification system that indicate the scope of behaviors constituting nonverbal communication:

> Sign language *includes all those forms of codification in which words, numbers, and punctuation signs have been supplanted by gestures; these vary from the monosyllabic gesture of the hitchhiker to such complete systems as the language of the deaf.*
>
> Action language *embraces all movements that are not used exclusively as signals. Such acts as walking and drinking, for example, have a dual function: on one hand, they serve personal needs, and on the other, they constitute statements to those who perceive them.*
>
> Object language *comprises all intentional and nonintentional display of material things, such as implements, machines, art objects, architectural structures and—last but not least—the human body and whatever clothes or covers it. The embodiment of letters as they occur in books and on signs has a material substance, and this aspect of words has to be considered as object language.*[8]

Of the three classes named, action language is probably the least consciously performed and the richest source of communication in interpersonal relationships. Although we communicate often by gesture and material objects, we tend to be more conscious of these than we are of the natural stream of movements we perform when we go about our business of living. This topic will be discussed in greater detail in Chapter 6.

Sound. We hear a voice for the first time on the telephone or radio and quickly assess our response to the speaker. Low, deep voices of males are perceived as indicators of strength, sophistication, maturity, and general appeal. The male with a high-pitched voice has a burden in our society. U.S. soldiers serving in Vietnam sometimes laughed at the orders delivered in a falsetto voice by a Vietnamese officer. In one study 18 male speakers read uniform manuscripts from prepared texts to an audience of 600 people by means of audio recording. The audi-

[8]J. Ruesch and J. Kees, *Nonverbal Communication* (Berkeley: University of California Press, 1956).

ence, which did not know the speakers and could not see them, was asked to match certain personality data including photographs and sketches of people to the voices of the speakers. The experimenters concluded that the voice alone conveys some correct information in choosing among age and general personality sketches. Individual personality traits and photographs were matched less accurately. Members of the audience tended to respond in a uniform manner if incorrect in their judgments, and when stereotypes were perceived from the voice (as through accents), all features of the stereotype were attributed to the speaker.[9]

A subsequent study verified that whether we like it or not, our voices do elicit stereotyped personality judgments that may or may not be valid. In response to tape-recorded voices, freshmen students at the University of Iowa attributed personality characteristics to the speakers in terms of vocal attributes. Among the many findings,

> *thinness in female voices cued perceptions of increased immaturity on four levels: social, physical, emotional, and mental, while no significant traits were correlated to thinness in the male voice. Males with throaty voices were stereotyped as being older, more realistic, mature, sophisticated, and well adjusted; females with throatiness were perceived as being less intelligent, more masculine, lazier, more boorish, unemotional, ugly, sickly, careless, inartistic, naïve, humble, neurotic, quiet, uninteresting, and apathetic. As both male and female speakers increased their rates of speaking they were perceived as more animated and extroverted.*[10]

In the face-to-face encounter, the vocal communication, rather than the fact of being isolated, is but one of the ingredients of the interaction. The question then becomes one of congruency. As with the micromomentary expression studies, we unconsciously note if the words, vocal signals, and movements carry the same message. If there is conflict, the nonverbal aspects tend to speak closer to the truth because they are, to a great extent, unconsciously performed. We shall note later the potential inaccuracies of such judgment.

Touch. Tactile communication plays an ambivalent role in the lives of most of us. On the one hand, it is critical in our interpersonal relations as we affirm, encourage, support, and show love and tenderness. Moreover, widespread positive responses to exercises involving touch in encounter groups reflect a yearning for physical contact. A study controlling the conditions for interaction revealed the following comparative descriptions:

[9] G. W. Allport and H. Cantril, "Judging Personality from Voice," *Journal of Social Psychology*, 5 (1934), 37–55.

[10] D. W. Addington, "The Relationship of Selected Vocal Characteristics to Personality Perception," *Speech Monographs*, 35 (1968), 499–502.

Verbal—"*distant, noncommunicative, artificial, insensitive, and formal.*"
Visual—"*artificial, childish, arrogant, comic, and cold.*"
Touch—"*trustful, sensitive, natural, mature, serious, and warm.*"[11]

Touch thus seems to be trusted in interpersonal relations more than do other modes of communication.

On the other hand, however, our culture places strict limitations on tactile interactions. A handshake and pat on the back are acceptable among business associates. Affectionate pats and embraces are reserved for intimate moments. Ashley Montagu has suggested, "Perhaps it would be . . . accurate to say that the taboos on interpersonal tactuality grew out of a fear closely associated with the Christian tradition in its various denominations, the fear of bodily pleasure."[12] This attitude restricting touch is a cultural one. Montagu states:

> *There are clearly contact people and non-contact people, the Anglo-Saxon peoples being among the latter. Curious ways in which non-contactuality expresses itself are to be seen in the behavior of members of the non-contact cultures in various situations. It has, for example, been observed that the way an Anglo-Saxon shakes hands constitutes a signal to the other to keep his proper distance. In crowds this is also observable. For example, in a crowded vehicle like a subway, the Anglo-Saxon will remain stiff and rigid, with a blank expression on his face which seems to deny the existence of other passengers. The contrast on the French Metro, for example, is striking. Here the passengers will lean and press against others, if not with complete abandon, at least without feeling the necessity either to ignore or apologize to the other against whom they may be leaning or pressing. Often the learning and lurching will give rise to good-natured laughter and joking, and there will be no attempt to avoid looking at the other passengers.*[13]

Interpersonal perception by touch, then, is quite restricted. The handshake is the most common contributor to first impressions. One college administrator has suggested that the handshake is his most significant signal in whether he is interested in getting to know a new acquaintance. A firm, natural handshake from a warm hand is his expectation. The problem with such judgments is that, like other responses to nonverbal communication, they are intuitive and without validation; the validity of such judgments must therefore be questioned.

[11]J. P. Bardeen, "Interpersonal Perception Through the Tactile, Verbal and Visual Modes," paper presented to the International Communication Association, Phoenix, Ariz., 1971.

[12]A. Montagu, *Touching: The Human Significance of the Skin* (New York: Perennial Library, 1972), p. 273.

[13]*Ibid.*, pp. 303–304.

The Accuracy of Our Judgments

As we have suggested, few people realize that they are constantly making judgments about others, and even fewer consider that they may be wrong about others much of the time. A basic fact to consider is that we differ in our perceptions of people. Just as witnesses at an accident note different phenomena, we may respond to different aspects of a person. William V. Haney, in the reading that follows this chapter, suggests and discusses five variables that affect our responses: differing environments, differing stimuli, differing sensory receptors, differing internal states, and differing evoked sets. Thus we vary in our ability to perceive the attitudes, intentions, feelings, needs, and wishes of others. Since even slight misjudgments may cause difficulties in communicating, it is truly amazing that we do as well as we do.

As we observe the behavior of others, we are merely inferring with some degree of probability what is going on inside the person. How well we infer depends upon the quality of the cues, how well we know the person, and our capabilities as judges. We have all likely known people about whom we could not tell in certain situations whether they were serious or joking; the cues supplied were inadequate for our purposes.

A college instructor felt ill and abruptly left class early in the middle of a discussion. At the next class meeting the students were asked by the instructor why they thought he had left. Responses included such reactions as: The instructor was angered over the low quality of the discussion and left in disgust; he had an appointment; he thought he had arrived at a good stopping point; he wanted to give the class more preparation time; and he was reacting emotionally to one of the comments made by a member of the class. None of the class guessed the true reason, but all were willing to make inferences concerning the behavior witnessed.

It seems that experience, and the learning that accompanies it, are vital in making accurate judgments of others. Small children become quite adept at "reading" their parents for indications of "how far to go" before actual punishment becomes imminent. Cues of punishment threat are often interpreted with great accuracy. The child, however, is not yet a discriminating observer and may try unsuccessfully to generalize from his parents to all adults. In kindergarten, attempts to cajole the teacher through baby talk and acting "cute" may prove inappropriate responses to threatened discipline.

Intelligence as well as maturity should obviously be related to our skill in judging people. Two kinds of capacity (relevant to our judgment of others) are correlated with intelligence: the ability to draw inferences about people from observations of their behavior; and the ability to account for observations in terms of general principles, or concepts. A researcher arranged to have some seven hundred pupils in elementary and secondary public schools observe a silent movie. Two scenes of the film depicted a boy engaged in "good" activities, while two others reflected "bad" behavior. The children were asked to write their opinions of the boy. Expert judges then classified these responses as inferences if the student attempted to go beyond the action shown on the screen, and concepts if the student attempted to explain both the good and the bad behavior by introducing conceptual notions that accounted for the diversity. This analysis revealed that the older the child, the greater the number of inferences and conceptual applications. On the average, the girls slightly exceeded the boys at all ages in the number of inferences made.[14]

There is also abundant evidence that, other things being equal, one can judge people with whom he has a common background of experience more accurately than he can judge unknown persons. Members of the same sex or age category, or the same national, ethnic, or religious groups are better judges of one another than would be an outsider. This advantage may result from sharing the same sets of norms, including the meanings attached to special gestures and speech mannerisms, as well as other forms of interpersonal responses. For example, the "straight" social scientist may have difficulty interpreting responses in an interview with groups of students who label themselves "freaks." Facetious and satirical responses may be accepted as genuine unless the interviewer becomes adept at recognizing the subtle nonverbal signals. Similarly, an American who first-names everyone as soon as he meets him will probably be more fully understood by another American who recognizes him as a compatriot and who has similar habits than by an Englishman to whom such habits may be strange. Such familiarity goes beyond mere stereotyped accuracy; the more one knows about any set of phenomena the more sensitive one becomes to small differences within that set. This fact would account for the ability of men and women to understand the behavior of members of their own sex better than members of the opposite sex.

Our backgrounds also affect the ways that we simplify data about people for determining our response to them. We shall now look into this process.

Encoding Simplification—Stereotyping

The following sign is on the Mexican border entrance at Tijuana (1972):

[14]E. S. Gollin, "Organizational Characteristics of Social Judgment: A Developmental Investigation," *Journal of Personality*, 26 (1958), 139–154.

NOTICE

MEN WITH LONG HAIR
ARE NOT ALLOW TO
ENTER MEXICO, DUE TO
PROBLEMS CAUSED
BY LONG HAIR
PEOPLE. DON'T
INSIST ON COMING
ACROSS. AVOID
BEING SENT TO
JAIL.

As we perceive other people and proceed to encode our impressions, the necessity of classifying the data for memory storage forces us to generalize and simplify. These classifications of people are commonly called "stereotypes." These "pictures in the head," as Walter Lippmann once described stereotypes, permit us to classify quickly and easily, providing ready-made compartments in which to place people. This phenomenon of stereotyping helps to explain why we may be "unjust" or "biased" in our reactions to social practices, institutions, and other cultures, as well as to people. The simplification involved may blind us to the innumerable differences among the members of our self-imposed classification based on such categories as age, race, socioeconomic status, national origin, or sex.

The sign leading into Mexico says a great deal about police experiences with "long-hairs" in Tijuana. The conclusion was reached that long hair is the signal that there is likely to be trouble. Before we dismiss this example for its naïveté and grammatical errors, consider the techniques currently employed by airlines to detect potential "sky-jackers." Surveilance and searches of people with certain characteristics are the current rule.

An important point to remember concerning stereotyping is that this categorical mode of perceiving people is not a fault found only among prejudiced people. It is done by all of us, due to the very nature of our perceptual processes. Our judgment of the competitiveness of a particular Jew, the intelligence of someone with a thick southern accent, or the honesty of a used car dealer, is merely the application to specific individuals of traits associated in our minds with a group. For example, consider your inferences about the driver of a car with a bumper-sticker proclaiming: "America—Love it or leave it." The attorney who refuses to accept bearded men on a jury, the school board that refuses to hire unmarried men over 30, the employer who restricts applicants to white, Anglo-Saxon Protestants, and the Black who views all policemen as brutal, are all engaged in stereotyping, applying categories, and predicting about future behavior based on these categories.

Stereotyping simplifies perceptual judgments by extending generalizations concerning one aspect of a person (long hair) to force him/her to assume all characteristics that we associate with this grouping. Obviously, with all the differences among people, such judgments ignore the differences among people that we feel make us unique individuals. It involves a "probabilities" game that tends to govern our first impressions until additional behavioral data are generated. While all of us are guilty of stereotyping according to some human dimensions, the practice has two serious adverse effects.

1. Stereotyping Limits Our Perceptions of the Gradations of Differences Among People. We are forced to think in "allness" terms; rather than looking for differences, we fit people into a category and use it as a basis for explaining all their behaviors. One such limitation is based on bipolar dichotomies. It is much easier to dismiss an individual totally for one character trait of which we disapprove than to consider the divergent facets of each individual that we encounter. Thus, all drinkers may be viewed as sinners, and the President of the United States is either a "good" or a "bad" President, a judgment often based on party label.

In many ways our society promotes this two-valued orientation of other people. Our television and movie heroes are typically portrayed as all good, while villains are viewed without redeeming qualities (although we have gained some overt sophistication in dispensing with the white hats on our cowboy heroes and the black hats on the villains). Our two-party political system and our fraternity-sorority-independent splits are facets of such an orientation. When we are in the habit of viewing people as either American or un-American, saved or damned, wholesome or degenerate, we narrow our perceptual capacities by these labels we apply. To force a person into honest-dishonest, dependable-undependable, clean-dirty, sane-insane, liberal-conservative categories ignores the numerous possible degrees between the two extremes.

Similar to this dichotomized view of people is a special category of perception behavior known typically as "the halo effect." Acting as a type of filter to our sense perceptions, a strong, favorable view of a person gives us a mental set for judging all his behaviors. As a hypothetical example, consider the behavior of Will Gray, a young history professor and basketball enthusiast. Professor Gray was elated to learn that the university's new basketball star—known for his speed and ball handling—had enrolled in his European history course.

Gray took every opportunity to discuss basketball with the young man, and so great was his admiration for his student's basketball talent that he failed to notice that the young man's work was below the standards of most of the other students in the class. When other students complained, Professor Gray attributed their reactions entirely to jealousy. Conversely, if we have a generally unfavorable impression of a person (labelel by an undergraduate student "the horns effect"), we may judge him/her unusually low in all personality traits. In both cases we are exaggerating the homogeneity of the personality of an individual. We are guilty of oversimplifying our perceptions.

2. *Stereotyping Serves to Perpetuate Self-Fulfilling Myths About People.* If we perceive a person as untrustworthy and treat him/her as such, we tend to *make* the person less trustworthy. This phenomenon of forcing people to fit our definition of them will be discussed later in greater detail, but here we should note how by forcing people into categories we perpetuate erroneous "truths" about them.

A contemporary case in point is the claim that women, by nature, are the "weaker sex," that they are not built to perform physical labor. As a result we encourage women to spend their lives reinforcing this "weakness" rather than trying to compensate for it. We do this by teaching women not to be aggressive and not to be physically competitive in such activities as baseball, track, weight lifting, and tree climbing. Political scientist Warren Farrell cites some of the effects:

> *To create a myth of weak women when that myth suits economic purposes and destroy it when it does not is a highly cynical use of human potential and aspiration. If this is a form of cynicism, it perpetuates every socializing agent: television commercials of women with whiter wash for the satisfaction of role number one (woman as a fulfilled washing machine) and the soap manufacturer's budget; for role number two (woman as a fulfilled sex object) our woman is transformed into a seductive tigress to be had along with an over-horsepowered, convertible sports car—"a machine made for a man." The system of education (for equal opportunity) continues the process with school books rife with men as astronauts, doctors, lawyers, and manual laborers and women as secretaries, mothers, elementary school teachers, and nurses. At the end of this process we declare that these positions are what women want, and ask "shouldn't women have the freedom to do whatever they want—nobody is preventing them from becoming a doctor or anything else." To still other observers these career patterns appear as natural outgrowths of the biological differences between men and women. We do not look beyond us, even to Sweden, where 75% of the crane operators are women, to Rumania where over 40,000*

women hold political office or to Czechoslovakia where 70% of the judges at the district level are women.[15]

This self-fulfilling myth extends to our interpretations of behaviors of men and women who are essentially alike. When a man has a picture of his family on his desk it is a reflection of a solid family man. A picture on a woman's desk reflects a woman more concerned with her home than her job—"a doting mother at heart." When a man's desk is cluttered it is interpreted as a busy, overburdened executive; when a woman's desk is cluttered it is a disorganized, scatterbrained female. When a man talks about his colleagues *he* is engaged in constructive criticism or office politics; when a woman does the same, *she* is catty.

Such myths help account for antifeminine prejudice even among women. In a 1968 study at the University of Connecticut, forty college girls were given the same writing selection to evaluate, but half of them were told that it was by John T. McKay, while the other half were told it was by Joan T. McKay. John was rated as much more intelligent and persuasive than Joan, even though there was no difference in the material other than the author's name.[16] Since we do have a penchant to react initially on the bases of stereotypes, it is important that we recognize this tendency and realize that our perceptions of people are filtered.

Selective Perception and Congruency

"We see what we want to see and hear what we want to hear." This exaggerated simplification does have an element of truth. Selective perception refers to the choices we make in attributing meaning to the infinite number of signals generated by another person; congruency is the term we have used to indicate an accurate matching of experiencing and awareness. A number of studies bear on these phenomena.

A significant experiment by Solomon Asch attempted to determine how people form impressions of personality. The experimenter read to some college students a number of characteristics that were said to belong to an unknown person. For example, one list included such adjectives as "energetic," "assured," "cold," "inquisitive," "talkative," "ironical," and "persuasive." After the list was repeated a second time, the subjects were instructed to write a description of their impression of this person. One student wrote:

[15]W. T. Farrell, "The Resocialization of Men's Attitudes Toward Women's Role in Society," paper presented to the American Political Science Association, Los Angeles, September 9, 1970.

[16]P. A. Goldberg, "Are Women Prejudiced Against Women?" *Transaction,* April, 1968, 28–30.

> *He impresses people as being more capable than he really is. He is popular and never ill at ease. Easily becomes the center of attraction at any gathering. He is likely to be a jack-of-all-trades. Although his interests are varied, he is not necessarily well versed in any of them. He possesses a sense of humor. His presence stimulates enthusiasm and very often he does arrive at a position of importance.*

Another subject reported:

> *He is the type of person you meet all too often: sure of himself, talks too much, always trying to bring you around to his way of thinking, and with not much feeling for the other fellow.*

Thus, the discrete terms on the list were organized into a single, unified personality. The subjects even gained impressions about characteristics not mentioned ("He possesses a sense of humor"). Asch summarized his study as follows:

> *When a task of this kind is given, a normal adult is capable of responding to the instruction by forming a unified impression. Though he hears a sequence of discrete terms, his resulting impression is not discrete.*[17]

The complexities and contradictions in people may be too great, however, to permit a unified impression to emerge. Another experiment involved a motion picture showing a young woman in five different scenes, designed to portray divergent aspects of her personality. In the first scene she is shown being "picked up" in front of a shabby hotel; in the second she is going to a bar with a man different from the one who had "picked her up"; the third scene shows her giving aid to a woman who has fallen down a public stairway; the fourth shows her giving money to a beggar; and the final scene shows her walking and talking with another young woman. The film was shown to a group of college students, and they were asked to write their impression of the woman's personality. The investigators then divided the responses into three categories:

1. Unified. *The major character qualities of sexual promiscuity and kindliness were able to be integrated by 23 percent of the respondents.*
2. Simplified. *Forty-eight percent of the subjects retained only one of the two major character qualities.*
3. Aggregated. *Twenty-nine percent of the subjects kept both major character qualities but failed to unify their impression.*

[17] S. E. Asch, "Forming Impressions of Personality," *Journal of Abnormal and Social Psychology*, 41 (1946), 258–290.

Then, less than 1/4 of the students were able to achieve an organized impression of the divergent bits of information.[18]

The importance of first impression in our interpersonal relationships was confirmed by a series of studies by social psychologist Abraham S. Luchins. In one study Luchins composed two separate paragraphs about a person named Jim:

> 1. *Jim left the house to get some stationery. He walked out into the sun-filled street with two of his friends, basking in the sun as he walked. Jim entered the stationery store, which was full of people. Jim talked with an acquaintance while he waited for the clerk to catch his eye. On his way out, he stopped to chat with a school friend who was just coming into the store. Leaving the store, he walked toward school. On his way out he met the girl to whom he had been introduced the night before. They talked for a short while, and then Jim left for school.*
>
> 2. *After school Jim left the classroom alone. Leaving the school, he started on his long walk home. The street was brilliantly filled with sunshine. Jim walked down the street on the shady side. Coming down the street toward him, he saw the pretty girl whom he had met on the previous evening. Jim crossed the street and entered a candy store. The store was crowded with students, and he noticed a few familiar faces. Jim waited quietly until the counterman caught his eye and then gave his order. Taking a drink, he sat down at a side table. When he had finished the drink he went home.*

When the two paragraphs were read separately to different groups of subjects, those who heard the first paragraph pictured Jim as friendly and somewhat extroverted; subjects hearing only the second paragraph viewed Jim as more introverted. To determine the importance of the first impression of a person, the two paragraphs were combined into two patterns—one citing the extrovertive data first and the other citing the introvertive first. Consistently the data presented first had the greater impact on the subjects' perception of Jim. On the trait of "friendliness," for example, 90 percent of the people who heard the first paragraph noted Jim to be friendly, as did 71 percent of the subjects hearing the combined paragraph with the extrovertive data first. Only 25 percent of the subjects who heard only the second paragraph thought Jim to be friendly; 54 percent of the people who heard that paragraph combined with the introvertive data considered Jim friendly. Thus, with the only variable being the order of the data presentation, the composite impression of Jim differed markedly.[19]

Possibly the first information perceived about a person gives us

[18]E. S. Gollin, "Forming Impressions of Personality," *Journal of Personality*, 23 (1954), 65–76.

[19]A. S. Luchins, "Definitiveness of Impression and Primacy-Recency in Communication," *Journal of Social Psychology*, 48 (1958), 275–290.

a "mental set" that we consider more basic than subsequent data. If in our minds we initially accept Jim as friendly, we may create special circumstances to account for his latter actions. Perhaps he had a bad day at school or is otherwise bothered by something. We try to fit the conflicting pieces of data together by inferring what is going on inside Jim. On the other hand, if we initially react to Jim as unfriendly, we may view his later actions as merely fulfilling some ulterior base motive. Consider how our impression of Jim would greatly affect our response to him and communication with him.

Since we have a stake in avoiding dissonance, our expectation/prediction helps us choose what we see, process, and believe. Thus we can better account for the findings comparing the work of John McKay and Joan McKay.

Estimated Relationship Potential

When we encounter new people, we process our perceptions consciously and unconsciously and decide whether a relationship is possible and desirable. Look around you in class. By now you may have formed some friendships that mean a greal deal to you, while there may be other members of the class that you would like to get to know better. Conversely, there may be members of the class that do not interest you in the least. In each case you have calculated an ERP (estimated relationship potential).

What sort of people have the greatest attraction to you? Even folk adages offer contradictory general rules: "Opposites attract," while "Birds of a feather flock together."

While there are also conflicting data from social researchers, there is a general finding of a positive relationship between similarities and attraction. Perception plays a major role here: People will tend to like those who possess attitudes similar to their own; concurrently, people will *perceive* themselves as being more similar to those they like, and less similar to those they abhor, than they really are.[20]

The relationship must be by mutual agreement; people tend to like those who like them. One study attempted to determine why people seek out people like themselves and avoid dissimilar ones.[21] The researchers reasoned that individuals might more often choose to associate with people different from themselves if they were not afraid of being disliked. When the other person is unknown, we are afraid that our behavior will be unacceptable and fear "being ourselves." In the study, college students were informed that they had been assigned to one of several groups set up to discuss why people dream. The students could elect to participate in a group of students similar to

[20]E. Berscheid and E. H. Walster, *Interpersonal Attraction* (Reading, Mass.: Addison-Wesley, 1969), pp. 69–70.

[21]E. Walster and G. W. Walster, "Effect of Expecting to Be Liked on Choice of Associates," *Journal of Abnormal and Social Psychology*, 67 (1963), 402–404.

themselves or in a group of such people as psychologists, factory workers, etc., quite different from the student population. The variable was the information given the students as to whether or not members of the dissimilar group would probably like or dislike them; some were told to select a group in which the members were likely to like them. As we might guess, those students who had been assured that everyone would find them likeable were more willing to join with dissimilar people, greatly preferring dissimilar groups. Those students told that they would probably not be liked were more anxious to join student groups made up of people like themselves. It was also found that if students were told that it was important to talk with people who would like them, they more often chose to interact with similar than with dissimilar people. Apparently they assumed that similar people were more likely to like them than dissimilar people.

The ERP with a given person is generated by our own feelings of self-esteem and our interpersonal needs as well as qualities, traits, behaviors, or inferred attitudes of the other person. Sara Kiesler devised an experiment to determine the relationship of male self-esteem to his choice of a romantic partner. The male subjects were paid to participate in the study that involved initially taking an intelligence test. Impressions of raised or lowered self-esteem were created by the experimenter's response to the test performance. During a planned break in the experiment, a girl who was a confederate in the experiment was introduced to each subject as a coed from a nearby college. The girl's physical appearance was altered to fit one of two conditions —attractive or unattractive—by such techniques as makeup, clothing, and heavy glasses (in the unattractive condition). The girl would be friendly and show interest in the boy subject. If the subject asked for a date or behaved in such a way as to suggest future interest, he was rated upward on an index of "romantic behavior." The conclusions were as predicted: Subjects with raised self-esteem displayed more romantic behavior toward the girl when she appeared to be highly attractive than when she was made to appear unattractive; the lowered-self-esteem subjects displayed more romantic behavior toward the girl when she seemed unattractive than when she was made to appear highly attractive.[22] Another study has shown that individuals who consider themselves (and are judged to be) socially desirable (physically attractive, personable, wealthy, famous, etc.) require that a romantic partner also be more socially desirable than the average.[23]

[22]S. B. Kiesler and R. L. Baral, "The Search for a Romantic Partner: The Effects of Self-Esteem and Physical Attractiveness on Romantic Behavior," in K. Gergen and D. Marlow, eds., *Personality and Social Behavior* (Reading, Mass.: Addison-Wesley, 1970).

[23]E. Walster, V. Aronson, D. Abrahams, and L. Rottmann, "Importance of Physical Attractiveness in Dating Behavior," *Journal of Personality and Social Psychology*, 5 (1966), 508–516.

This emphasis on physical attractiveness and social status in determining the degree of acceptance on the ERP scale makes it difficult for less-attractive people in our society. A university coed has stated:

> *One of the greatest troubles is that men here, as everywhere, I guess, are easily overwhelmed by physical beauty. Campus glamor girls have countless beaux flocking around them, whereas many companionable, sympathetic girls who want very much to be companions and, eventually wives and mothers, but who are not dazzling physically, go without dates and male companionship. Many who could blossom out and be very charming never have the opportunity. Eventually, they decide that they are unattractive and become discouraged to the point that often they will not attend no-date functions where they have their best (and perhaps only) opportunity to meet men. I will never understand why so many men (even, or maybe particularly, those who are the least personally attractive themselves) seem to think they may degrade themselves by dating or even dancing with a girl who does not measure up to their beauty standards.*[24]

We may agree cognitively that "beauty is only skin-deep," but the evidence suggests that physical attractiveness is a major contributor to the ERP of new acquaintances.

Reciprocal Perspectives

A few years ago a popular song pondered whether "she looked back to see if I looked back to see if she looked back." Communication problems can occur when people disagree in their interpretations of their responses to one another. We are here concerned with the question: Do you see me responding to you in the same way I see me responding to you? Further, will how I see you accepting (or not accepting) my views of me affect my further responses to you? To complicate matters more, you are also responding to your view of my perception of you. Thus we are greatly affected by our reciprocal perspectives.

Our behavior as response to other people significantly affects their subsequent behaviors in our presence. R. D. Laing and his associates have constructed a hypothetical example of how perceptions of greed and meanness "spiral":

> *Jack feels Jill is greedy. Jill feels Jack is mean. That is, Jack feels Jill wants too much from him whereas Jill feels Jack does not give her enough. Moreover Jack feels that Jill is mean as well as greedy. And Jill feels that Jack is greedy as well as mean. Each feels that the other has and is withholding what he or she needs. Moreover, Jack does not feel he is either greedy or mean himself, nor does Jill. Jack, however, realizes that Jill thinks he is mean, and Jill realizes that Jack thinks she*

[24]Quoted in E. W. Burgess, P. Wallin, and G. D. Schultz, *Courtship, Engagement and Marriage* (Philadelphia: Lippincott, 1953), pp. 63–64.

is greedy. In view of the fact that Jack feels he is already overgenerous, he resents being regarded as mean. In view of the fact that Jill feels that she puts up with so little, she resents being regarded as greedy. Since Jack feels generous but realizes that Jill thinks he is mean, and since Jill feels deprived and realizes that Jack thinks she is greedy, each resents the other and retaliates. If, after all I've put up with, you feel that I'm greedy, then I'm not going to be so forbearing in the future. If, after all I've given you, you feel I'm mean, then you're not getting anything from me any more. The circle is whirling and becomes increasingly vicious. Jack becomes increasingly exhausted by Jill's greed and Jill becomes increasingly starved by Jack's meanness. Greed and meanness are now so confused in and between each and both that they appear to take on a life of their own. Like two boxers dominated by the fight that they are themselves fighting, the dyad, the system, the marriage, becomes "the problem" to each of the persons who comprise it, rather than they themselves.[25]

Both parties are thus caught in a spiral that destroys the potential for the relationship.

Responding to people in terms of stereotyped roles promotes a similar spiral of adversity. Betty and Theodore Roszak have depicted in vivid terms the mutually destructive effects of reciprocal responses in terms of masculine/feminine roles:

He is playing masculine. She is playing feminine. He is playing masculine because she is playing feminine. She is playing feminine because he is playing masculine. He is playing the kind of man that she thinks the kind of woman she is playing ought to admire. She is playing the kind of woman that he thinks the kind of man he is playing ought to desire. If he were not playing masculine, he might well be more feminine than she is—except when she is playing very feminine. If she were not playing feminine, she might well be more masculine than he is—except when he is playing very masculine. So he plays harder. And she plays . . . softer.[26]

Envy poisons any opportunity for love. The spiral continues until:

Her femininity, growing more dependently supine, becomes contemptible. His masculinity, growing more oppressively domineering, becomes intolerable. At last she loathes what she has helped his masculinity to become. At last he loathes what he has helped her femininity to become.[27]

Thus the reciprocal perspectives force both parties into roles and behaviors that destroy the relationship.

[25]R. D. Laing, H. Phillipson, and A. R. Lee, "The Spiral of Reciprocal Perspectives," reprinted in K. Giffin and B. R. Patton, eds., *Basic Readings in Interpersonal Communication* (New York: Harper & Row, 1971), p. 219.

[26]B. Roszak and T. Roszak, *Masculine/Feminine* (New York: Harper & Row, 1969), p. vii.

[27]*Ibid.*, p. viii.

On a more positive level, the Jack Gibb study of defensive and supportive behaviors discussed in the Haney reading that follows suggests how the characteristic climates of small groups influence individual behaviors. Defensive behaviors increase general defensiveness that serves to impair the accuracy of our perceptions. As we become emotionally involved, we tend to lose perspective. Conversely, as Gibb states:

> *The more "supportive" or defense reductive the climate, the less the receiver reads into the communication distorted loadings which arise from projections of his own anxieties, motives, and concerns. As defenses are reduced, the receivers become better able to concentrate upon the structure, the content and the cognitive meanings of the message.*[28]

Thus to a great extent we create the "other" person in our relationships. This phenomenon will be discussed further in Chapter 7.

INTERPERSONAL ORIENTATIONS

Closely related to our perception of others is our system of typical responses. In our modern environment most of our actions immediately or ultimately are reactions to other people. We must be able to anticipate, for example, how an instructor views the process of living —what his experiences mean to him, and how he goes about relating to us and to others.

Our purpose here is to review systematic approaches to the analysis of interpersonal orientations—that is, ways in which individuals are usually oriented toward other people as they attempt to communicate with them. There are several systematic approaches. Each is slightly different, indicating that this field of study is in process of being explored and has not as yet become well stabilized; each systematic approach, however, provides some additional insight into possible improvement of one's interpersonal-communication habits.

Open- and Closed-Mindedness

Milton Rokeach theorized one framework for examining a given person's interpersonal orientation—a continuum extending from closed-mindedness to open-mindedness, depending upon the characteristic way in which an individual receives and processes messages from others.[29] The general degree to which a person will change his/her attitude toward an object or concept after hearing another person's orientation toward that object or concept is the basis of a scale from

[28] J. R. Gibb, "Defensive Communication," *Journal of Communication*, 11, No. 3 (September 1961), 142.

[29] M. Rokeach, *The Open and Closed Mind* (New York: Basic Books, 1960).

open- to closed-mindedness. Extreme closed-mindedness is identified as dogmatism. A dogmatic person is described as follows:

1. *Likely to evaluate messages on the basis of irrelevant inner drives or arbitrary reinforcements from external authority, rather than on the basis of considerations of logic;*
2. *Primarily seeking information from sources within his/her own belief system—for example, "the more closed-minded a Baptist, the more likely it is that he/she will know what he/she knows about Catholicism or Judaism through Baptist sources";*
3. *Less likely to differentiate among various messages coming from belief systems other than his/her own—for example, an "extremely radical rightist may perceive all nonrightists as communist sympathizers";*
4. *Less likely to distinguish between information and the source of the information and likely to evaluate the message in terms of his perceptions of the belief system of the other person.*

Essentially the "closed" person is one who rigidly maintains a system of beliefs, who sees a wide discrepancy between his/her belief system and those belief systems that are different from his/hers and who evaluates messages in terms of the "goodness-of-fit" with his/her own belief system.

It should be readily apparent that the "openness" or "closed-mindedness" of an individual is an index to his/her interpersonal orientation. In like manner it is an indicator of the way this person will interpret another person's attempts to communicate with him/her.

Cooperative–Uncooperative Behavior

Another conceptual framework for examining our characteristic responses to people is in terms of attempts to be either cooperative or uncooperative. In Chapter 3 we noted the interpersonal needs of all people. Some of us attempt to fulfill these needs with the *help* of others, while some of us move at the *expense* of others.

Obviously all situations do not call for cooperative behaviors. When we are engaged in purchasing an automobile, we are in effect competing to reduce the margin of potential profit for the salesperson. In such situations our gain is at the expense of the other party. Other situations, however, involve the potential for mutual gain since we are seeking compatible goals; for example, planning a vacation with the family may involve conflicting ideas, but the outcome of the best possible trip for all is shared mutually. Regardless of situation, some people display orientations of willingness to cooperate or an inherent tendency to compete.

Basic to this orientation is the degree of trust that we feel toward other people. If we fear others and their motives, we are likely to respond in a defensive, uncooperative manner. Only when we trust—are willing to rely on people in order to achieve a desired objective in a risky situation[30]—is cooperation possible. Such trust can be shown from a classic example that has been labeled "the prisoner's dilemma":

> *Two suspects are taken into custody and separated. The district attorney . . . points out to each that he has two alternatives: to confess to the crime the police are sure they have done or not to confess. If they both do not confess then the district attorney states that he will book them on some trumped-up charge . . . if they both confess, they will be prosecuted, but he will recommend less than the most severe sentence; but if one confesses and the other does not, then the confessor will receive lenient treatment for turning state's evidence, whereas the latter will get the "book" slapped at him.*[31]

Compare the above situation with disarmament talks. Trust is essential if we are going to be cooperative and disarm. The risk is high, and if we misjudge the loss will be gigantic! The difference is one of fighting a war or negotiating for peace. Willingness to cooperate is obviously then tied to the amount of risk involved and the desirability of the goal.

Some people are more competitive than others and tend to view all interpersonal relationships in terms of winning or losing. Morton Deutsch studied this orientation in a game situation with college students that rewarded cooperative behavior.[32] To cooperate meant mutual gain for both parties, while individual gains as a result of a competitive orientation were made at the other's expense.

As an illustration, in the design below used by Deutsch, Person 1 has to choose between rows X and Y, and Person 2 has to choose between Columns A and B:

		Possible Choices of Person 2	
		A	B
Possible Choices of Person 1	X	(+$9, +$9)	(−$10, +$10)
	Y	(+$10, −$10)	(−$9, −$9)

Person 1's payoffs are the first numbers in the parentheses, and Person 2's are the second numbers. The amount of money won or lost by each on any specified trial is thus determined by the combination of

[30]For a detailed discussion of the dimensions of trust, see K. Giffin, "Interpersonal Trust in Small Group Communication," *Quarterly Journal of Speech*, 53 (1967), 224–234.

[31]R. D. Luce and H. Raiffa, *Games and Decisions: Introduction and Critical Survey* (New York: Wiley, 1957), p. 95.

[32]M. A. Deutsch, "Trust and Suspicion," *Journal of Conflict Resolution*, 2 (1958), 265–279.

the choices made by each of the two persons. For example, if Person 1 chooses row Y (in an attempt to win $10), and Person 2 chooses Column B (in a similar attempt to win $10), they each lose $9. Examination of the possibilities of choice for Person 1 shows that he can win most and lose least by choosing Y, as Person 2 can do by choosing B. But if Person 1 chooses Y and Person 2 chooses B they both lose. Both can win only with the AX arrangement.

From Deutsch's work and that of his students, the following inferences can be drawn concerning interpersonal cooperation:

1. *A cooperative (or noncooperative) orientation on the part of the individual will influence his tendency toward actual cooperative behavior.*[33]
2. *Communication between the speaker and listener will tend to increase the likelihood of cooperation between them, especially if they express their intentions and expectations of each other and indicate their plan of reacting to violations of their expectations.*[34]
3. *Increased social power over another person increases the likelihood of the powerful person cooperating with the person over whom he has power.*[35]
4. *A person will tend to cooperate with another person if he knows they both dislike a specified third person.*[36]
5. *Cooperative persons tend to have personalities which can be characterized as below average in authoritative or dogmatic orientations.*[37]

This basic interpersonal orientation applies to many social situations where mutual trust and cooperation are vital, as in husband-wife relations, pupil-teacher interactions, and in a theatre where there is a fire.

Interpersonal Response Traits

A slightly more elaborate classification of interpersonal styles has been developed by Karen Horney.[38] She classified people into three

[33]M. A. Deutsch, "The Effect of Motivational Orientation upon Trust and Suspicion," *Human Relations*, 13 (1960), 123–139.

[34]J. Loomis, "Communication, the Development of Trust, and Cooperative Behavior," *Human Relations*, 12 (1959), 305–315.

[35]L. Solomon, "The Influence of Some Types of Power Relationships and Game Strategies upon the Development of Interpersonal Trust," *Journal of Abnormal and Social Psychology*, 61 (1960), 223–230.

[36]J. N. Farr, "The Effects of a Disliked Third Person upon the Development of Mutual Trust," paper presented to the American Psychological Association Annual Conference, New York, 1957.

[37]M. Deutsch, "Trust, Trustworthiness, and the F Scale," *Journal of Abnormal and Social Psychology*, 61 (1960), 138–140.

[38]K. Horney, *Our Inner Conflicts* (New York: Norton, 1945).

types according to their interpersonal response traits: (1) moving toward others; (2) moving against others; and (3) moving away from others. According to Horney's system, going toward others ranges from mild attraction to affiliation, trust, and love. Such a person shows a marked need for affection and approval and a special need for a partner—that is, a friend, lover, husband, or wife who is to fulfill all expectations of life and to take responsibility for good and evil. This person "needs to be liked, wanted, desired, loved; to feel accepted, welcome, approved of, appreciated; to be needed, to be of importance to others, especially to one particular person; to be helped, protected, taken care of, guided."[39]

Behavior identified as going against others ranges from mild antagonism to hostility, anger, and hate. Such a person perceives that the world is an arena where, in the Darwinian sense, only the fittest survive and the strong overcome the weak. Such behavior is typified by a callous pursuit of self-interest. The person with this interpersonal orientation needs to excel, to achieve success, prestige, or recognition in any form. According to Horney, such a person has "a strong need to exploit others, to outsmart them, to make them of use to himself." Any situation or relationship is viewed from the standpoint of "what can I get out of it?"[40]

Behavior characterized as going away from others ranges from mild alienation to suspicion, withdrawal, and fear. With this orientation the underlying principle is that one never becomes so attached to anybody or anything that he or it becomes indispensable. There is a pronounced need for privacy. When such a person goes to a hotel, he rarely removes the "Do Not Disturb" sign from outside his door. Self-sufficiency and privacy both serve his outstanding need, the need for utter independence. His independence and detachment have a negative orientation, aimed at not being influenced, coerced, tied, or obligated. To such a person, according to Horney, "to conform with accepted rules of behavior or to additional sets of values is repellant. . . . He will conform outwardly in order to avoid friction, but in his own mind he stubbornly rejects all conventional rules and standards."[41]

Horney summarizes the three types as follows:

> *Where the compliant type looks at his fellow men with a silent question, "Will he like me?"—and the aggressive type wants to know, "How strong an adversary is he?" or "Can he be useful to me?"—the detached person's concern is "Will he interfere with me? Will he want to influence me or (will he) leave me alone?"*[42]

[39]*Ibid.*, pp. 50–51.
[40]*Ibid.*, p. 65.
[41]*Ibid.*, p. 78.
[42]*Ibid.*, pp. 80–81.

Most of us display more than one of these interpersonal response patterns at different times toward various people. However, it is quite surprising how easily we can classify our acquaintances on the basis of their choice of words: "Will they like me?"—"I wonder if I can beat him (or use him)?"—or, "Will they interfere with me or let me alone?"

Orientations Based on Interpersonal Needs

Although all the orientations discussed relate to the needs of the people involved, a more elaborate and systematic approach has been advanced by William Schutz.[43] The major premise of this theory is that people need people; and each person, from childhood on, develops a fundamental interpersonal-relations orientation. Schutz posited three fundamental dimensions of interpersonal behavior: inclusion, control, and affection. His analysis of the results of a large number of research studies—parental, clinical, small group—shows convergence in their discovery of the importance of these three areas, and demonstrates how a measure of these three variables can be used both to test a wide variety of hypotheses about interpersonal relations and to understand and predict interpersonal communication behavior.

Schutz's theory is the topic of his article that follows this chapter. We believe that his theory is significant because it establishes the groundwork for understanding the basis of a relationship between people. From his theory, we can infer that others respond to us within a framework of the role we indicate they should play in our interpersonal relationship. They can then make a choice to play that role or not to respond to us in the way that we intend. For example, if we show a desire to control other people, they will respond according to their willingness to be controlled or refuse to respond to our messages. Of course, they may initiate new communication concerning the role we have identified for them to play.

[43]W. C. Schultz, *FIRO: A Three-Dimensional Theory of Interpersonal Behavior* (New York: Holt, Rinehart and Winston, 1958).

SUMMARY AND PREVIEW OF READINGS

As we come into contact with one another, we receive sensory signals that establish the basis for our communication. The attempts at communication will be guided by our interpretation of these signals. These signals and the interpretations establish the basis of our "interpersonal perception." By interpersonal perception we mean the way individuals view and evaluate each other in direct interaction; this encompasses the interrelationships between the perceiver, the person perceived, and the external contextual variables to be discussed in the next chapter.

While all of our sense receptions form the basis for a variety of perceptual cues, interpersonal perception differs from our perception of objects in at least two ways: First, unlike objects, other people are perceived as having motives that influence their behaviors; and second, the person being perceived is simultaneously perceiving the other person and may alter his behaviors accordingly. The essay by William V. Haney provides a model of perception that identifies the interrelated variables and the behavioral results.

When one person responds in a specific way to another person, this manner of response might be termed a type of interpersonal orientation. However, the concern of this chapter has been with the way in which a person or persons generally respond to other people—an interpersonal lifestyle, so to speak. We might say our interest is on the wholesale, rather than the retail, level. Sets of typical interpersonal responses may be identified, classified, observed, and analyzed. Basic classifications of interpersonal response sets are commonly recognized by all of us: We note that a person is generally cooperative or competitive, generally open to new friends and ideas, or usually closed to these situations. The article by Schutz outlines the ways in which individuals may orient themselves toward other people in order to satisfy interpersonal needs. These basic needs are identified as inclusion, control, and affection. A case is made for the proposition that these needs, as described, constitute a conceptual system that is helpful in the prediction and explanation of interpersonal behavior.

SUGGESTED APPLICATIONS AND LEARNING EXPERIENCES

1. With one of your classmates play the two-person (Prisoner's Dilemma) game used and described in the Deutsch experiments. Play for matches and then play for pennies; note ways in which your own thinking differs, if at all, as you raise the value of the "stakes." Note the degree to which it seems to be important for you to "beat" the other person; compare this with your motivation to cooperate in order that both you and the other person may win from the "bank." (Note: For the game you and the other player will need to contribute initially to a "bank" that can pay off if both of you "cooperate" and both "win.")

2. Working in groups, prepare a brief questionnaire that you think can categorize members of the class. Some categories may be: What jobs have you held? What are your hobbies? What are your career plans? How serious are you? Compare your evaluations of one another and identify cues that might be misleading from your behavior.

3. Eye behavior is one of the most potent elements in our nonverbal behavior. Our normal eye contacts last only about a second, and we are quite careful about how and when we look someone directly in the eye. Intercultural communication researchers have noted the differences between cultures and subcultures on the amount and types of interpersonal eye contacts. What have you noted of these differences? As an exercise, work in pairs and sit facing each other for a period of about three minutes, saying nothing and looking each other intently in the eyes. Discuss your reactions. What were you able to communicate?

4. Compile a list of current bumper-stickers. Put them in various combinations and determine your stereotype of the driver. What stickers are considered totally contradictory?

5. What are the assumptions concerning "reality" and the "nature of the world" that underlie Haney's analysis of perception theory? Relate this view back to Chapter 1 and the readings from Boulding and Barnlund.

6. Note Schutz's table entitled "Matrix of Relevant Interpersonal Data." To what extent is graphic representation inadequate as a model of personal needs for human interaction and useful ways of meeting these needs? Can you suggest additional personal needs for interaction with others not included among those postulated by Schutz—inclusion, control, and affection?

PERCEPTION AND COMMUNICATION
William V. Haney

"This is nothing. When I was your age the snow was so deep it came up to my chin!" (Reprinted by permission of *Redbook*.)

Dad is right, of course—*as he sees it.* And in this seemingly innocuous self-deception lies one of the most interesting and perhaps terrifying aspects of human experience: *We never really come into direct contact with reality.* Everything we experience is a manufacture of our nervous system.

For practical purposes we should acknowledge that there is a considerable range of similarity between reality and one's perception of it. When an engineer is measuring, testing, and the like, usually with the aid of precise gauges and instruments, his perceptions may be an extremely close approximation of reality. This is basically why bridges, tunnels, and skyscrapers not only get built but generally stay built.

But when the engineer, or anyone else, is relating to and communicating with other human beings—when he is operating in a world of feelings, attitudes, values, aspirations, ideals, and emotions—he is playing in a very

From William V. Haney, *Communication and Organizational Behavior*, rev. ed., Homewood, Ill.: Richard D. Irwin, Inc., 1967, pp. 51–77. Reprinted by permission of the publisher.

different league and the match between reality and perceptions may be far from exact.

Just what is going on and just what is this concept "perception" we have been alluding to so casually? "Perception" is a term we perhaps shouldn't be using at all. There seems to be very little agreement as to what it entails. It evidently is a complex, dynamic, interrelated composite of processes which are incompletely and variously understood. Allport, for example, describes some 13 *different* schools of thought on the nature of perception, listing, among others, core-context theory, gestalt theory, topological field theory, cell-assembly, and sensory-tonic field theory.[1] In the face of such irresolution I will be so bold as to define perception in unsophisticated language as the process of *making sense out of experience—of imputing meaning to experience.*[2]

Obviously what kind of "sense" one makes of a situation will have great bearing on how he responds to that situation, so let us examine the phenomenon more closely.

A MODEL OF PERCEPTION

March and Simon suggest a model (see Figure 1) which seems well supported by research. First of all, they regard man as a complex, information-

[1]F. H. Allport, *Theories of Perception and the Concept of Structure* (New York: John Wiley & Sons, Inc., 1955).

[2]Perception has been defined as "the more complex process [as distinguished from sensation] by which people select, organize, and interpret sensory stimulation into a meaningful and coherent picture of the world." B. Berelson and G. A. Steiner, *Human Behavior: An Inventory of Scientific Findings* (New York: Harcourt, Brace & World, Inc., 1964), p. 88.

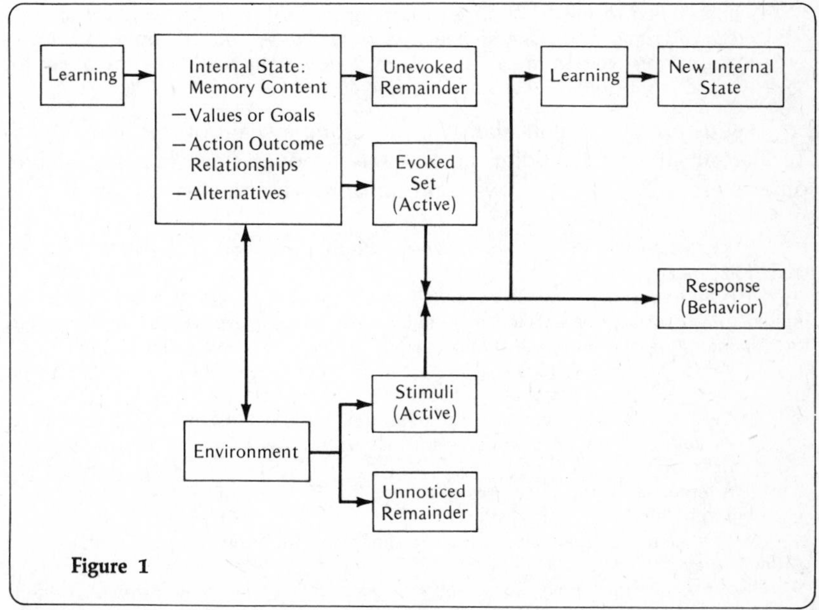

Figure 1

processing system—"a choosing, decision-making, problem-solving organism that can do only one or a few things at a time, and that can attend to only a small part of the information in its memory and presented by the environment."[3]

They argue that one's behavior, through a short interval of time, is determined by the interaction between his *internal state*[4] (which is largely a product of one's previous *learning*) at the beginning of the interval and his *environment*.

When the interval is very short only a small part of one's internal state and a small part of his environment will be active, i.e., will significantly influence his behavior during the interval. In information theory terms, the eye can handle about 5 million bits per second, but the resolving power of the brain is approximately 500 bits per second. *Selection* is inevitable. How, then, are these active parts determined? As stated above, they are selected through the interaction of one's internal state and his environment at the beginning of the time interval. The active part of the internal state is called the *set*[5] which is evoked by the environment, leaving the *unevoked remainder* which plays no significant role in affecting the behavior at that time. Similarly, the active part of the environment is selected by the internal state and is called the *stimuli*; the residue is the "unnoticed" remainder. Munn gives a relevant illustration:

> *I once had a colony of white rats in the attic of the psychology building. One afternoon I found several rats outside of their cages. Some were dead and partly eaten. It occurred to me that, however the rats had escaped, they must have been eaten by wild rats. I went downstairs to get some water and was climbing the stairs again when I saw before me, and directly in front of the cages, a large wild gray rat. It was standing tense and trembling, apparently having heard me ascend the stairs. Very slowly I raised a glass jar that was in my right hand, and aimed it at the rat. Much to my surprise, the animal failed to move. Upon approaching the object, I discovered it to be a piece of crumpled-up-grayish paper. Without the set induced by my suspicion that gray rats were in the attic, I should undoubtedly have seen the paper for what it was, assuming that I noticed it at all.*[6]

Let us examine Munn's behavior, asserting a chain of *sets* and *stimuli*. To start at an arbitrary point, he was *set* to notice the white rats among other reasons because they were presumably why he went to the attic in

[3]J. G. March and H. A. Simon, *Organizations* (New York: John Wiley & Sons, Inc., 1958), p. 11.

[4]His internal state is mostly contained in his memory which "includes [but is not limited to] all sorts of partial and modified records of past experiences and programs for responding to environmental stimuli." Thus, the memory consists, in part, of:

a) Values or goals: criteria that are applied to determine which courses of action are preferred among those considered.
b) Relations between actions and their outcome; beliefs, perceptions, and expectations as to the consequences that will follow from one course of action or another. . . .
c) Alternatives: possible courses of action.

Ibid., pp. 10–11.

[5]Set is generally regarded as the readiness of the organism to respond in a particular way.

[6]Norman L. Munn, *Psychology: The Fundamentals of Human Adjustment* (Boston: Houghton Mifflin Co., 1947), p. 327.

the first place. Thus, the partly eaten white rats readily became *stimuli* which in turn triggered still another *set*—the expectation of wild gray rats. Any part of his environment which bore a reasonable resemblance to a wild gray rat thus became a candidate for becoming his new *stimuli*. The crumpled paper qualified. It was not only selected as a *stimulus* (supposedly it had been part of the "unnoticed remainder" of the environment on his first trip to the attic) but was interpreted as a wild gray rat.

The result of the interplay of environment and internal state is one's *response* (behavior) and his *internal state* at the beginning of the next time interval. This new internal state can be considered as modified by the *learning* derived from the experience of the previous interval.

Just what is active or passive in one's internal state and environment is a function of time, among other factors. For a very short period, there will be very few active elements in set and stimuli. For a longer period, a larger portion of the memory content will likely be evoked and a large number of environmental events will influence behavior at some time during the interval. Thus, phrases such as "definition of the situation" and "frame of reference" are more appropriate than "set" in discussing longer time periods.

If one's response is a function of interrelated variables it follows that a variation in any or all of them would normally affect the response. Therefore we shall examine some of these variables in greater detail.

Differing Environments

Hold up a die between us. If you see three dots I will see four. As obvious as it should be, the phenomenon of differing environments, which would preclude our receiving the same stimuli, seems to contribute to a great deal of unnecessary and destructive conflict.

I have had the rewarding experience of serving for several years as a consultant to the Federal Mediation and Conciliation Service. Any number of the commissioners, men who are constantly concerned with union-management controversies, have asserted to me that a significant portion of the lack of communication, understanding, and harmony between the two parties stems from the simple fact that neither side is given full and direct access to the private environment—including the pressures, complexities, and restrictions—of the other. Thus, from the very outset of the negotiation the parties are exposed to substantially different environments and therefore, are, in many respects, responding to different stimuli.

Differing Stimuli

Presume a mutual environment and there is still no guarantee that your responses and mine will be influenced by the same stimuli. Our respective evoked sets will have a considerable bearing on which parts of the environment will significantly impinge upon us as stimuli. Munn's story of the rat is a case in point.

Differing Sensory Receptors

Another reason why parts of the environment either never become stimuli or are experienced differently is that our sensory "equipment" varies. It has long been recognized that individuals differ markedly in sensory thresholds and acuity. While there has been gratifying progress in the prevention, correction, and amelioration of sensory limitations there is still much to be learned.

An interesting demonstration of differing sensory equipment is to give a bit of paper to each person in a group and request each to determine the taste of the paper. The group does not know it but the paper is impregnated with phenylthiocarbamide (PTC). If the group is representative, a significant portion will experience a distinctly bitter sensation. But some will taste it as sweet, others as sour, and still others as salty. And about half will find it utterly tasteless!

PTC, a chemical used by geneticists to trace hereditary traits, reveals dramatically that we simply do not all inherit identical sensory apparatus. Add to this variations of the nervous system due to disease and injury and it is clear that our senses are inclined to be neither infallible nor uniform. I have a personal example to contribute in this regard. I have had a few mild disputes with my wife who "alleged" a shrill whistle in the television set. Since I did not hear it I denied that it existed. Somewhat later I had an audiometric examination and discovered that, like many others who were around artillery during the war, I had lost the capacity to hear tones of extremely high pitch.

Differing Internal States

One's *internal state* is the product of his *learning processes* and it is obvious that the "lessons" acquired by one person can differ markedly from those of another. Imagine a number of individuals observing a man drinking liquor. If the observers are candid and sufficiently representative we can expect a gamut of reactions. Some will regard the man as sinful; others as extravagant. Others will associate his drinking with friendliness and congeniality. Some will view it as a character flaw—a way of avoiding unpleasantness, running from problems. Still others may perceive it as a relaxant. And people in the distilling industry—and the Alcohol and Tobacco Tax Division of the Internal Revenue Service—may relate it to a job!

For a more dramatic example of the role of learning compare cultures. One's culture is an extraordinarily effective teacher. First, it teaches us unrelentingly—every waking moment. Second, it is a most subtle, even insidious teacher—which detracts not at all from its effectiveness. Immersed in it constantly, we are seldom conscious of what it has been teaching us until we contrast its lessons with those taught by other cultures. The perceptive traveler, for example, as he visits countries learns a good deal about *himself* and the special lessons his culture has taught him.

For example, anthropologists tell us that we learn from our respective cultures how to perceive a misbehaving child. This is revealed by how we speak to the child. English-speaking people generally consider misbehavior as "bad" or "naughty," a suggestion of immorality, and admonish the child with "Johnny, be *good*!" Italian- and Greek-speaking people say the equivalent. The French, however, tend to say "Jean, sois sage!"—be *wise*. Their culture teaches that the child who misbehaves is being stupid, foolish, imprudent, injudicious. The Scandinavians have another concept expressed by the Swedish, "Jan, var snell!" and the Norwegian, "Jan, ble snil!"—be *friendly*, be *kind*. Germans have learned still differently. With them it is "Hans, sei artig!"—*get back in step. Sei artig* is literally "be of your own kind"—in other words, "conform to your role as a child."[7]

Clearly, individuals from these various cultures could observe the same child misbehaving but regard him very differently because they had been *trained* to do so. Grant that different people learn different "lessons" from life and it is readily apparent that individualized learning plays a subtle but critical role in one's communication with others.

Differing Evoked Sets

One's set, according to the model, is dependent upon three other variables: that which is available in the internal state, the stimuli which trigger the set, and, though less directly, the processes of learning. March and Simon clarify the role of learning in this regard:

> *When one of these elements (values or goals, action-outcome relationships and alternatives) is evoked by a stimulus, it may also bring into the evoked set a number of other elements with which it has become associated through the learning process. Thus, if a particular goal has been achieved on previous occasions by execution of a particular course of action, then evocation of that goal will be likely to evoke that course of action again. Habitual responses are extreme instances of this in which the connecting links between stimulus and response may be suppressed from consciousness. In the same way, the evocation of a course of action will lead by association to evocation of consequences that have been associated with the action.*[8]

This helps to account for the apparent self-perpetuating nature of sets which others have observed.

> *Our concept of causal texture implies that definitions and relations, once they have been adopted, influence interpretations of subsequent events. Early definitions of the conditions under which a task will be accomplished are apt to take precedence over later definitions.*[9]
>
> *. . . the tendency to distort messages in the direction of identity with previous inputs is probably the most pervasive of the systematic biases.*[10]

Sebald confirmed a hypothesis "that largely only those meanings are being perceived and recalled which reinforce images."[11] He also suggested "that selective distortion takes place in order to screen out dissonant features—features which are apt to disturb pre-conceived images."[12]

The concept of differing sets helps to explain the abyss which so fre-

[7]L. Sinclair (ed.), "A Word in Your Ear," *Ways of Mankind* (Boston: Beacon Press, 1954), pp. 28–29. For a fascinating account of cultural differences interfering with interpersonal communication see E. T. Hall, *The Silent Language* (Garden City, N.Y.: Doubleday & Co., Inc., 1959).

[8]March and Simon, *op. cit.*, p. 11.

[9]H. B. Pepinsky, K. E. Weick, and J. W. Riner, *Primer for Productivity* (Columbus, Ohio: The Ohio State University Research Foundation, March, 1964), p. 54.

[10]D. T. Campbell, "Systematic Error on the Part of Human Links in Communication Systems," *Information and Control*, Vol. 1 (1958), p. 346.

[11]H. Sebald, "Limitations of Communication: Mechanisms of Image Maintenance in the Form of Selective Perception, Selective Memory and Selective Distortion," *Journal of Communication*, Vol. XII, No. 3 (September, 1962), p. 149.

[12]*Ibid.*

quently separates superiors and subordinates. A man looking downward in an organization may often have a very different set from the man below him looking up. For example, Likert reports that 85 percent of a sampling of foremen estimated that their men "felt very free to discuss important things about the job with my superior." However, only 51 percent of their men shared this view.[13] Seventy-three percent of the foremen felt they "always or almost always get subordinates' ideas" on the solution of job problems. Only 16 percent of their subordinates agreed with this appraisal.[14] Ninety-five percent of the foremen said they understood their men's problems well but only 34 percent of the men felt that they did.[15]

The gulf between superiors' and subordinates' sets is documented further by Maier[16] who reports a study of 35 pairs from four large firms. A pair consisted of a manager, third echelon from the top, and one of his immediate subordinates. Each partner in each pair was questioned regarding the subordinate's job. On only one aspect was there substantial agreement—the content of the subordinate's duties. However, there was little agreement on the order of importance of these duties. There was only fair agreement on the job's requirements and almost complete disagreement on their priority ranking. Finally, there was virtually no agreement on the problems and obstacles of the subordinate. These findings were discussed with all participants. Several months later a questionnaire was sent to each participant asking if the superior and his respective subordinate had gotten together to discuss their differences. Only 22 pairs replied. Six of them agreed that they had gotten together; nine agreed that they had not; and seven pairs could not agree on whether they had or had not gotten together![17]

In Summation

The perception model suggests why it is impossible for one to be in simple, direct contact with reality, why he lives in a personalized world and why, in the words of St. Paul, "We see through a glass darkly." Indeed, there are a number of interrelated variables (differing environments, stimuli, sensory receptors, internal states, and evoked sets) which intervene between perception and reality. Thus, individuals are led to respond differently to events and, in general, complicate the process of communication enormously—particularly *if the role of such factors is ignored or misunderstood.*

> *. . . The prime obstacle of every form of communications . . . is simply the* fact of difference. *On this point most serious students of communication are in agreement, the great gap in background, experience, and motivations be-*

[13]Rensis Likert, *New Patterns in Management* (New York: McGraw-Hill Book Co., 1961), p. 47.

[14]*Ibid.*, p. 53.

[15]*Ibid.*, p. 52.

[16]N. R. F. Maier, "Breakdown in Boss-Subordinate Communication," *Communication in Organizations* (Ann Arbor, Mich.: The Foundation for Research on Human Behavior, 1959).

[17]The reader may wish to test the influence of sets upon him by viewing perceptual (*not optical*) illusions.

tween ourselves and those with whom we would communicate.

It is a gap that will remain. . . . But if we cannot close the gap, we must at least acknowledge it. For this acknowledgement of difference is the vital preface to all the efforts that follow. . . .[18]

DEFENSIVENESS

The "acknowledgement of difference"—a simple phrase but how difficult to practice! Perhaps the most appropriate adjective to describe much of the behavior of people communicating and relating to one another in organizational settings would be *defensive.* A fundamental reason for defensive behavior appears to be the inability of so many people to *acknowledge differences*—differences between their perceptions and reality and differences between their perceptions and those of others. Their prevailing, albeit largely unconscious, presumption is that "the world is as I see it." He who harbors this notion will find life continuously threatening for there are many others who share his notion—but not *his "world!"* Such people find it perpetually necessary to protect their "worlds" and to deny or attack the other fellow's.

Admittedly, the premise that one deals only indirectly and often unreliably with reality can be disturbing. To those who crave a certain, definite, and dependable world (and that includes all of us in varying degrees) the admission that we respond only to *what it appears to be* rather than *what it is* necessarily lessens our *predictability* about the "real world." Even those who *intellectually accept* the perception model and the roles that stimuli, set, learning, and so on, play in determining responses may have difficulty converting the concept into performance. A good test of the extent to which one has truly internalized such awareness occurs when he becomes emotionally involved with others.

For instance, suppose you and I work in the same organization and we observe one of our colleagues taking home company supplies—such as paper pads, paper clips, and pencils—not in large quantities but it is obvious to us that he will not use them exclusively for official purposes. He will let the children have them, use them for his private affairs, and so on.

Now, let us say that you are the product of a rigorous, religious upbringing. It is likely that you will be *set* to regard Joe as dishonest. But suppose that I have had none of your training and that the only part of my background that is particularly relevant was the three years I spent in the Army in World War II. There I learned a code that was unwritten but very pervasive. It was in effect, "You may rob the Army blind! but you must not steal a nickel from another serviceman." I would be quite inclined to regard Joe as honest and could readily consider his acquisitions as normal perquisites.

Let us examine the *communication* issue. (Permit me to disregard the moral issue without denying that there is one.) Consider the tremendous difficulty you and I would have in discussing Joe if in our increasingly

[18]"Is Anybody Listening," *Fortune*, September 1950, p. 83. The emphasis is mine.

vehement statements—"Joe's dishonest!" "No, he's not!"—we failed to realize that neither of us was talking about *Joe*. We were talking about *you* and *me* and our *respective* "inside-the-skin" experiences. Our respective worlds were different from the outset and there was no reason to expect them to be identical—and no *rational* reason to have to protect them. Why, then, did we protect them so ardently?

Let us begin with an assertion: Most reasonably mature people can tolerate fairly well differences in value judgments, opinions, attitudes, points of view—*so long as they can recognize them as such.* If I can realize that your "reality" is not the same as mine then your statement about *your* "reality" is no threat to *mine*.

But no one can tolerate differences on matters of objectivity—matters which submit to corrobable measurement and are capable of general agreement. To illustrate, suppose you and I have a mutual superior and he comes to us and says: "This may sound silly but I'm serious. I want you two to estimate the length of that 2×4 over there (about 20 feet away) on the ground. You have to estimate because you can't use any kind of measuring device and you can't get any closer to it than you are now. Now, I want a good estimate and only one between you—so get to it!"

(Now suppose the piece of lumber is actually 7 feet long but neither of us knows this.) So we start sizing up the situation and you say, "Looks about 6½ or 7 feet." And I say, "No, no—you're way short—that's a lot closer to 14 feet!" Unless you had admirable constraint you would probably blurt out. "You're crazy!"

Now, why were you moved to feel I was crazy?

Was it not partly because my statement was at least a slight threat to your sense of reality and, therefore, your sanity? In other words if (I said *if*) I were indeed right—i.e., if the board actually were 14 feet and everything were twice as big as you perceive it—would you not begin to have serious misgivings about *your* "contact with reality"? "You're crazy!", then, is your understandable if impulsive way of defending yourself against an attack on your sanity.

Actually, we would be unlikely to have such a disparity (unless one or both of us *were* losing touch with reality) because our perceptual lessons, when we initially learned to perceive the inch, the foot, and the yard, were likely to have been very similar regardless of where or when we learned them. And even if we were to disagree on matters such as distance, speed, and weight we could resolve our differences by using standardized measuring devices.

But when we encounter Cezanne and Dali, Tolstoi and Faulkner, Mozart and Cole Porter, we are unlikely to have had identical learning experiences and where is the "standardized measuring device"? Will someone resolve a controversy with "Why, that Van Gogh is 87 percent beautiful"? Even professional critics are unable to provide universally acceptable and applicable criteria.

The point is that not only can we not tolerate differences in matters of objectivity (but what differences there may be are generally minor or resolvable by objective measurement) but we cannot accept differences on matters of subjectivity (value judgments, opinions, and so on) if we unconsciously *treat them* as matters of objectivity. There are many important aspects of our lives such as art, music, architecture, religion, politics, morals, fashions, food, economic and political theory, which (1) are taught to us in standardized lessons and (2) are not, by and large, measurable by standardized scales or gauges. It is in such areas that we find it easiest to threaten one another. And when one is threatened he tends, if he does not run, to fight back—the threatener is now threatened and bootless conflict generally follows.

Defensiveness appears to be so pervasive and potentially so destructive to organizational communication and interpersonal relationships that we shall examine it in more detail in terms of the communicator's *frame of reference.*

Frame of Reference

Frame of reference is the term March and Simon used for longer intervals of time in lieu of "set." It has been defined as:

> *A system of standards or values, usually merely implicit, underlying and to some extent controlling an action, or the expression of any attitude, belief, or idea.*[19]

Carl Rogers offers several propositions[20] which serve as a rationale for the validity and utility of the frame of reference construct.

1. *Every individual exists in a continually changing world of experience of which he is the center.*

Rogers holds that each of us is at the core of his own world and everything else is happening, developing, occurring about him (not unlike Ptolemy's homocentric notion of the earth as the center of the universe). It is painfully obvious that man is the most egocentric organism on earth, and surely no one can be more self-centered than the human infant. The baby will outgrow much of this, of course, but hardly all of it. But it would seem that one who is approaching emotional maturity has already recognized that egocentrism is a substantial part of being human. Once one accepts this frailty he is in an excellent state to begin to compensate for it and to grow beyond it. The truly arrogant person, however, is the man or woman who has never made and perhaps cannot make this admission. For so long as one can shield himself from a recognition of his fallibility, he need not expend energy in growing and he need not submit to the unknowns and possible pain of change.

2. *The individual reacts to his world as he experiences and perceives it and thus this perceptual world is, for the individual, "reality."*

Rogers put quotes around *reality* to indicate that it is not the "real" reality. Consider these definitions of perception: "The point of reality contact, the door to reality appraisal,"[21] the "structuring of stimuli"[22] and the "organ-

[19]H. B. English and A. C. English, *A Comprehensive Dictionary of Psychological and Psychoanalytical Terms* (New York: Longmans, Green & Co., 1958).

[20]Paraphrased from C. R. Rogers, *Client-Centered Therapy* (Boston, Mass.: Houghton Mifflin Co., 1951), pp. 483, 484, 487, 494.

[21]G. S. Klein, "The Personal World Through Perception," *Perception, An Approach to Personality*, eds. R. R. Blake and G. V. Ramsey (New York: The Ronald Press Co., 1951), pp. 328–329.

[22]C. M. Solley and G. Murphy, *Development of the Perceptual World* (New York: Basic Books, Inc., Publishers, 1960), p. 26.

ization of stimuli";[23] and "the way in which the person structures his world and himself."[24] But regardless of how invalid and incomplete it may be, one's personalized reality is the only one he has and therefore the only one to which he responds.

3. *The individual has one basic tendency and striving which is to actualize, maintain, and enhance himself.*

Rogers writes of the *actualizing tendency* as "the inherent tendency of the organism to develop all its capacities in ways to serve to maintain or enhance the organism. It involves not only the tendency to meet . . . 'deficiency needs' for air, food, water, and the like, but also more generalized activities. . . . It is development toward autonomy and away from heteronomy, or control by external forces."[25] He subscribes to Angyal's statement: "Life is an autonomous event which takes place between the organism and the environment. Life processes do not merely tend to preserve life but transcend the momentary status quo of the organism, expanding itself continually and imposing its autonomous determination upon an ever-increasing realm of events."[26]

More specifically, Rogers refers to *self*-actualization. We will discuss his concept of the self-image later in this chapter and for the moment will merely suggest that much of the individual's perceiving is in the service of preserving or enhancing his self-image.

According to Frenkel-Brunswik:

> *It would appear that we do not always see ourselves as we are but instead perceive the environment in terms of our own need. Self-perception and perception of the environment actually merge in the service of these needs. Thus, the perceptual distortions of ourselves and the environment fulfill an important function in our psychological household.*[27]

The role of *needs* and *motivation* in influencing perception and therefore behavior is clearly important. . . .

4. *Therefore, the best vantage point for understanding another's behavior is from that person's internal frame of reference.*

This conclusion follows logically from Rogers' preceding propositions but this does not necessarily make it easy to utilize the frame of reference concept. The individual's internal frame of reference *is* his subjective world. "Only he knows it fully. It can never be known to another except through empathic inference and then can never be perfectly known."[28]

Probably the greatest single deterrent to one's accurately visualizing another's frame of reference is his *own*. An analogy will suggest why this is so.

[23]F. A. Beach, "Body Chemistry and Perception," Blake and Ramsey, *op. cit.*, p. 56.

[24]U. Bronfenbrenner, "Toward an Integrated Theory of Personality," *ibid.*, p. 207.

[25]C. R. Rogers, "A Theory of Therapy, Personality, and Interpersonal Relationships, as Developed in the Client-Centered Framework," *Psychology: The Study of a Science*, Vol. 3, *Formulations of the Person and the Social Context*, ed. Sigmund Koch (New York: McGraw-Hill Book Co., 1959), p. 196.

[26]A. Angyal, *Foundations for a Science of Personality* (New York: Commonwealth Fund, 1941).

[27]Else Frenkel-Brunswik, "Personality Theory and Perception," chap. 13 in Blake and Ramsey, *op. cit.*, p. 379.

[28]C. R. Rogers, "A Theory of Therapy . . . ," *op. cit.*, p. 210.

Analogy of the Box

Visualize each of us as the sole and constant tenant of a box with a top, a bottom, and four sides. There is just one window in this box—one's frame of reference, loosely speaking—through which he views the outside world.

A Restricted Window. This suggests immediately that one's view is restricted—he cannot see what is happening in back of him, above, to the sides, and so forth. One obviously cannot be ubiquitous and therefore his view is inevitably limited. But there is another restriction that he can overcome to an extent—the *size* of the window. We all have our "narrownesses"—our areas of naïveté. I, for example, was born and reared in a suburb. Suppose you are a country boy and we go out to a farm. We could share the same environment but I would expect that your stimuli and evoked sets would greatly outnumber mine. You would have the preparation, the memory content, to make so much more significance out of the experience than I.

But I have the capacity to learn. Given the time and provided I have the motivation I can acquire some of your sophistication. In short I can *expand* my window.

Stained-Glass Window. Not only is one's window frame restricted (but expandable largely at his will) but it also does not contain a pane of clear glass. It is rather like a stained-glass church window with various, peculiarly shaped, tinted, and refracting lenses. In one's frame of reference these lenses are his experiences, biases, values, needs, emotions, aspirations, and the like. They may all be distorting media to an extent but are we powerless to overcome these distortions? Hardly, but let us establish one point first.

Does anyone grow up with a clear window? Can anyone be without bias for example? Quite unlikely, for everyone had to be born at a particular time and in a particular place. Thus he was exposed to particular people and situations all of whom and which taught him *special* lessons regarding values, customs, mores, codes, and so on.

But again man has viability and the capacity to adjust and compensate—he can *clarify* his window. A pencil in a glass of water appears to bend abruptly but if one *understands* something about the nature of refraction he can compensate for the distortion, aim at where the pencil appears not to be, and hit it. So it is more profoundly with a man himself—if he can *understand himself* he can *compensate* for his distorted frame of reference and, in effect, clarify his window.

The Self-Image

But there is at least one extremely formidable obstacle in the way of a man's truly understanding himself. We return to Carl Rogers for this. A key concept of the Rogerian therapeutic approach is the premise that as a person grows up he develops a *self-image* or *self-concept*—a picture of himself. Hayakawa asserted: "The mode of human behavior is not self-preservation but self-concept. The self-concept is who you think you are and the self is who you are. Values determine people's self-concept and self-concept determines social experience."[29] Rogers uses *self, concept of self,* and *self-structure* as terms to refer to

> *the organized, consistent conceptual gestalt composed of perceptions of the characteristics of the "I" or "me" and the perceptions of the relationships of the "I" or "me" to others and to various aspects of life, together with the values attached to these perceptions. It is a fluid and changing gestalt, a process. . . . The term self or self-concept is more likely to be used when we are talking of the person's view of himself, self-structure when we are looking at this gestalt from an external frame of reference.*[30]

On Coping with Guilt. The self-image helps to explain how one copes with guilt.

One of man's most compelling needs is the need to justify himself. Moreover, most of us tolerate guilt very poorly. Guilt is painful—acutely so. Therefore, as pain-avoidance organisms most of us have highly facile and sophisticated means for eliminating or diminishing the pain of guilt. Test this assertion, if you can tread a painful route, by tracing back to an event in which you did something that you *knew* was *wrong;* that you *could not justify* by rationalizing that the end warranted the means; and that was *not beyond your control.*

Most of us have great difficulty remembering such events objectively and yet almost all of us have been guilty of them. The pain of guilt is so noisome that we have developed great skill in justifying our behavior before, during, or after the act.

At the core of this behavior appears to be the overriding motive to "actualize, maintain, and enhance" one's self-image. It is clear that the individual can distort experience to satisfy this powerful need. For example, suppose Mike treats Tom unjustly—at least as Tom perceives it. Tom will likely become angry and want revenge. If Tom were to analyze himself he might find that what he wants most of all is for Mike to experience remorse, true contrition—the pain of guilt—at least commensurate with the pain he inflicted upon Tom. However, Mike as a pain-avoider has already begun to justify his behavior and is unlikely, therefore, to tender a sincere apology. Failing to receive evidence of Mike's acceptance of his own guilt, Tom may be moved to retaliate in kind or to attempt to wrench an apology from Mike. In either event, Tom's behavior, as Mike perceives it, is sufficiently obnoxious to complete his self-justification. "You see how Tom is acting? That ——— deserved to be treated that way in the first place!"

No matter how unreasonable, irrational, or immoral another's behavior may appear to us it is generally a good assumption that it is quite reasonable, rational and moral *in his world.* Epictetus wrote: "The appearances of things to the mind is the standard of action of every man."

One's self-image is perhaps most profoundly important to the individual in the sense that it serves as *his contact with himself.* In fact, when he talks or thinks about *himself* he is usually not referring to his limbs,

[29]S. I. Hayakawa, participating in the 1965 Student Symposium, "Spectrum of Perspectives," Northwestern University.

[30]C. R. Rogers, "A Theory of Therapy . . ," *op. cit.,* p. 200.

torso, and head but rather to an abstraction he usually labels as "my *self.*" Thus, it is by his self-image that he *knows* himself.

Images of Others. But we also need to know and understand others and thus we form images of them as well—particularly those with whom we are most interdependent—parents, spouse, children, superiors, subordinates. Such image formation, whether one is conscious of it or not, requires considerable energy output and the marshaling of much psychological intelligence about the individual of whom one is forming an image. The prime motive for the effort is that we need to build a good base for understanding and predicting the behavior of the other person. And only by predicting the other's behavior reasonably accurately can we confidently control our own behavior and deal effectively with the other person.[31] This helps to explain why one becomes confused and upset when another's behavior suddenly contradicts his image of that other person. He has lost or risks the loss of his base for predicting and thus for controlling himself in dealing with the other.

And this holds even when the other's behavior is *more favorable* than anticipated. Suppose you have a superior—a father, a teacher, a boss—who is a versatile tyrant. And suppose one day he greets you with a broad smile, a friendly clap on the back, and an encouraging comment. Is your initial response—"Wonderful, the old buzzard has finally turned over a new leaf!" Or is it—"What's he up to now!" As a friend in business put it, "You can work for an s.o.b.—provided he's a *consistent* s.o.b.! It's the one who turns it on and off unpredictably that gives you the ulcers!"

Self-Image Challenged. Now if we are troubled by another person's jeopardizing our predictability about him, then how much more traumatic is it for one to have his *own self*-image challenged. He stands the risk of losing the ability to predict, control and *know himself.* It is difficult to imagine a greater internal upheaval than suddenly not to *know oneself*—

[31]The process we call *forming impressions of personality* is sometimes called *person perception.* Bruner [J. S. Bruner, "Social Psychology and Perception," *Readings in Social Psychology*, eds. E. Maccoby, T. M. Newcomb, and E. L. Hartley (3rd ed.; New York: Henry Holt, Inc., 1958), pp. 85–94] has argued that the "process of perception tends, in general, to accomplish two things: (1) a recording of the diversity of data we encounter into a simpler form that brings it within the scope of our limited memory; (2) a going beyond the information given to predict future events and thereby minimize surprise." Roger Brown, *Social Psychology* (New York: The Free Press, 1965), p. 611.

Social psychologists, in particular, have been concerned with how we perceive or infer the traits and intentions of others. For a sampling of experimental and theoretical works in "social perception" or "person perception" see: I. E. Bender and A. H. Hastorf, "On Measuring Generalized Empathic Ability (Social Sensitivity)," *Journal of Abnormal and Social Psychology*, Vol. 48 (1958), pp. 503–506; V. B. Cline and J. M. Richards, Jr., "Accuracy of Interpersonal Perception—A General Trait?", *Journal of Abnormal and Social Psychology*, Vol. 60 (1960), pp. 1–7; F. Heider, *The Psychology of Interpersonal Relations* (New York: John Wiley & Sons, Inc., 1958); W. C. Schutz, *FIRO: A Three-Dimensional Theory of Interpersonal Behavior* (New York: Holt, Rinehart & Winston, Inc., 1960); R. Taft, "The Ability to Judge People," *Psychological Bulletin*, Vol. 52 (1955), pp. 1–23; R. Tagiuri and L. Petrullo (eds.), *Person Perception and Interpersonal Behavior* (Stanford, Calif.: Stanford University Press, 1958).

to lose contact with oneself. It may not be inaccurate to say that our mental institutions are filled with people who have lost contact with themselves more or less permanently.

It is no wonder, then, that the loss of a self-image is generally warded off at almost any cost. And yet few of us have gone through life unscathed. Anyone who has experienced a deeply traumatic experience at one time or another—whether related to a parent, a spouse, a child, school, religion, vocation, narcotics, alcoholism, job security, illness, injury, lawsuit—will probably find on restrospection that his self-image was being severely threatened.

A Personal Case. My own experience is a case in point. As a high school freshman I hit upon chemical research for a career. I suppose this was encouraged by an older boy I admired who also aspired to chemistry. He had built a laboratory in his basement so, of course, I had to have one too. I remember collecting hundreds of jars and bottles and scores of other treasures that might somehow be useful in my lab. I can also recall spending hour after hour thoroughly enjoying mixing potions of every description—and some beyond description. (I recall without quite so much relish the time I brewed some chlorine and nearly gassed myself unconscious!)

I *devoured* the chemistry course in my junior year. I must admit feeling rather smug during this period for I had a ready answer to the recurrent question, What are you going to be? Most of my friends had either a hazy answer or none at all. My self-image in this regard was forming and solidifying.

I was graduated from high school during World War II and immediately entered the service. Somehow the Army gave little shrift to young men who were long on aspiration but short on experience and consequently I had three years of singularly nonchemical experience—but this did not dissuade me. Finally, the war ended and I was discharged. I immediately enrolled in a chemical technology program at a university reputed for this field.

Suddenly, reality began to catch up with my self-image. I had not realized that a chemist was also expected to be a pretty fair mathematician. I had done well enough in high school math courses but the last three years were nonmathematical as well as nonchemical. At any rate I foolishly disregarded the math refresher course (my self-image said I didn't need a "crutch") and charged headlong into college algebra where I was in competition with fellows fresh from high school math. While I was rusty, it would be unfair to say that I didn't get the math; I did get it but about a week after the exams, which is poor timing! Net result—the first *D* I had ever received in my life. What was the consequence—did I trade in my self-image for a new model? Hardly; rather than yield, I fought tenaciously and found a ready explanation for my plight: Aside from the Army's causing me to "forget my math" the instructor "had it in for me." Among other evidences he had a Scottish name and I was convinced he was anti-Irish!

I was practicing what some writers call "perceptual defense," a form of perceptual distortion which "demonstrates that when confronted with a fact inconsistent with a stereotype already held by a person, the perceiver is able to distort the data in such a way as to eliminate the inconsistency. Thus, by perceiving inaccurately, he defends himself from having to change his stereotypes."[32] Haire and Grunes suggest that we "blinder" ourselves to avoid seeing that which might trouble us.[33] As communication authority David K. Berlo paraphrased the Bible—"Seek and ye shall find—whether it is there or not!"

The next quarter? A *C* in math. This instructor had an Irish name but he didn't like me either! In the middle of the third quarter and another math *D*, my self-image had withstood all the onslaught from harsh reality that it could. And for two to three weeks (at the time it seemed like six months) I was in a state of unrelieved depression. I became very nervous and had difficulty eating, sleeping, and studying (which only intensified my problem). Figuratively, a large section of my self-image had been shot away and *I had nothing to replace it.* The most appalling aspect of the experience was that I realized that *I didn't know myself.* To give the story a happy ending I took a battery of aptitude tests, changed to another major, and very gradually began to construct another self-image.

Resistance to Image Change. Anyone who has undergone such a trauma will understand why the individual generally resists image change—particularly sudden change. And herein lies one of the greatest obstacles to the full development of an effective communicator and, for that matter, an effective person. The central premise of an excellent book[34] by psychiatrist Karen Horney is that the neurotic process is a special form of human development which is the antithesis of healthy growth. Optimally, man's energies are directed toward realizing his own potentialities. But, under inner stress, he becomes estranged from his *real self* and spends himself creating and protecting a false, idealized self, based on pride, but threatened by doubts, self-contempt, and self-hate. Throughout the book the goal of liberation for the forces that lead to true self-realization is emphasized.

Take the case of a high school friend. After graduation he, too, went into the service but was more fortunate (in a sense), for the Army put him through three years of an engineering curriculum. Then the war was over and he was discharged. But he decided he did not care for engineering and could not bring himself to take a final year of course work to earn an engineering degree. And yet he could not bear the thought of starting all over again in another field. The net result was that, for all practical purposes, he did nothing. He took a clerical job in a nearby insurance firm

[32]S. S. Zalkind and T. W. Costello, "Perception: Some Recent Research and Implications for Administration," *Administrative Science Quarterly*, September, 1962, p. 227.

[33]M. Haire and W. F. Grunes, "Perceptual Defenses: Processes Protecting an Original Perception of Another Personality," *Human Relations*, Vol. 3 (1958), pp. 403–412.

[34]Karen Horney, *Neurosis and Human Growth: The Struggle Toward Self-Realization* (New York: W. W. Norton & Co., Inc., 1950).

and has been there for 20 years. Through the years, his perhaps largely unconscious philosophy of life has evidently been: "I can't stand another failure [he probably regarded not completing the engineering degree as a failure] and one sure way not to lose a race is not to enter it." In sum, here is a man who apparently has protected his self-image at the cost of a stunted life.

The handicap of inaccurate self-knowledge and the unwillingness to reconstruct a more realistic self-image seem to be very widespread. In 15 years of organizational research and consulting I have known scores, if not hundreds of men, particularly in the middle echelons of their organizations, who seemed to have all the requisites for continued success: intelligence, education, experience, drive, ability, ambition. But they lacked one vital thing—*they did not know themselves*. The image they held of themselves was pitifully out of phase with that which they were projecting to others. They seemed chronically annoyed and/or bewildered by the reactions of others to them. What was happening? As unrealistic as their self-images were it was nevertheless too threatening to entertain contrary cues from other people. Fending off the reactions of others variously as "those malicious/crazy/misinformed/ornery/perverse/stupid people!" they had been successful in perpetuating and even reinforcing their respective self-myths. Thus, they ineffectualized themselves; squandered their nervous energies in a kind of internal conflict, protecting their fallacious self-images.[35] The masterful Robert Burns captured the poignancy of self-deception almost two centuries ago.

Oh wad some power the giftie gie us
To see oursels as ithers see us!
It wad frae monie a blunder free us,
An' foolish notion.

ON COPING WITH DEFENSIVENESS

We have discussed defensive behavior as a critical obstacle to effective interpersonal communication. What, in the final analysis, are people defending *against*? In a word, *perceived threat*—the threat of change or harm to their self-images, to their personalized worlds. This would suggest that whatever reduced perceived threat would reduce the need to defend against it—to enable one to reduce his defenses accordingly. What threat-reducing techniques or approaches, then, are available to us?

After an eight-year study of recordings of interpersonal discussions, Jack Gibb delineated two communication climates—one threatening ("defensive"); the other nonthreatening ("supportive"). (See Table 1.) Incidentally, Gibb's "supportive climate" is quite in keeping with Likert's "supportive relationship" and McGregor's Theory Y.
Gibb defined his paired categories of perceived behavior as follows.[36]

[35]This is why Brouwer was moved to write: "Manager development means change in the manager's self-image." Paul J. Brouwer, "The Power to See Ourselves," *Harvard Business Review*, Vol. 42, No. 6 (November–December, 1964), p. 156.

[36]"Defensive Communication," *Journal of Communication*, Vol. 11, No. 3, Sept., 1961, pp. 142–148.

Table 1 Categories of Behavior Characteristic of Supportive and Defensive Climates in Small Groups

Defensive Climates	*Supportive Climates*
1. Evaluation	1. Description
2. Control	2. Problem orientation
3. Strategy	3. Spontaneity
4. Neutrality	4. Empathy
5. Superiority	5. Equality
6. Certainty	6. Provisionalism

Source: Jack R. Gibb. "Defensive Communication," *Journal of Communication*, Vol. 11, No. 3 (Sept., 1961), p. 143.

Evaluation. *To pass judgment on another; to blame or praise; to make moral assessments of another; to question his standards, values and motives and the affect loadings of his communications.*

Description. *Nonjudgmental; to ask questions which are perceived as genuine requests for information; to present "feelings, events, perceptions, or processes which do not ask or imply that the receiver change behavior or attitude."*

Control. *To try to do something to another; to attempt to change an attitude or the behavior of another—to try to restrict his field of activity; "implicit in all attempts to alter another person is the assumption of the change agent that the person to be altered is inadequate."*

Problem Orientation. *The antithesis of persuasion; to communicate "a desire to collaborate in defining a mutual problem and in seeking its solution" (thus tending to create the same problem orientation in the other); to imply that he has no preconceived solution, attitude, or method to impose upon the other; to allow "the receiver to set his own goals, make his own decisions, and evaluate his own progress—or to share with the sender in doing so."*

Strategy. *To manipulate others; to use tricks to "involve" another, to make him think he was making his own decisions, and to make him feel that the speaker had genuine interest in him; to engage in a stratagem involving ambiguous and multiple motivation.*

Spontaneity. *To express guilelessness; natural simplicity; free of deception; having a "clean id"; having unhidden, uncomplicated motives; straightforwardness and honesty.*

Neutrality. *To express lack of concern for the welfare of another; "the clinical, detached, person-is-an-object-of-study attitude."*

Empathy. *To express respect for the worth of the listener; to identify with his problems, share his feelings, and accept his emotional values at face value.*

Superiority. *To communicate the attitude that one is "superior in position, power, wealth, intellectual ability, physical characteristics, other ways" to another; to tend to arouse feelings of inadequacy in the other; to impress the other that the speaker "is not willing to enter into a shared problem-solving relationship, that he probably does not desire feedback, that he does not require help and/or that he will be likely to try to reduce the power, the status, or the worth of the receiver."*

Equality. *To be willing to enter into participative planning with mutual trust and respect; to attach little importance to differences in talent, ability, worth, appearance, status, and power.*

> Certainty. *To appear dogmatic; "to seem to know the answers, to require no additional data"; and to regard self as teacher rather than as co-worker; to manifest inferiority by* needing to be right, *wanting to win an argument rather than solve a problem, seeing one's ideas as truths to be defended.*
>
> Provisionalism. *To be willing to experiment with one's own behavior, attitudes, and ideas; to investigate issues rather than taking sides on them, to problem solve rather than debate, to communicate that the other person may have some control over the shared quest or the investigation of ideas. "If a person is genuinely searching for information and data, he does not resent help or company along the way."*

It would appear that if one were to offer another the most supportive climate possible his behavior should be descriptive, problem oriented, spontaneous, and so on, and should avoid attempting to evaluate, control, employ stratagems, and so forth. But the situation is a bit more complex.

First of all, the above are *perceived* behaviors. Therefore, the *perceptions* of the *perceiver* rather than the *intentions* of the perceived will be the final arbiter as to how defensive or supportive the perceiver regards the climate. Moreover, as a person become more defensive he becomes less able to assess accurately the motives, values, and emotions of the other person. Conversely, as he grows less defensive, the more accurate his perceptions become.[37]

> *The more "supportive" or defense reductive the climate, the less the receiver reads into the communication distorted loadings which arise from projections of his own anxieties, motives, and concerns. As defenses are reduced, the receivers become better able to concentrate upon the structure, the content and the cognitive meanings of the message.*[38]

Another qualification on Gibb's classifications is that while the defensive categories *generally* arouse defensiveness and the supportive categories *ordinarily* generate defense reduction, the degree to which these responses occur depends upon the *individual's level of defensiveness* as well as the *general climate of the group at the time.*[39]

Still another qualification is that the behavior categories are *interactive*. For example, when a speaker's behavior appears *evaluative* it ordinarily increases defensiveness. But if the listener feels the speaker regards him as an *equal* and was being direct and *spontaneous*, the evaluativeness of the message might be neutralized or not even perceived. Again, attempts to *control* will stimulate defensiveness depending upon the degree of *openness* of the effort. The suspicion of hidden motives heightens resistance. Still another example, the use of *stratagems* becomes especially threatening when one attempt seems to be trying to make strategy *appear spontaneous*.

[37] J. R. Gibb, "Defense Level and Influence Potential in Small Groups," L. Petrullo and B. M. Bass (eds.), *Leadership and Interpersonal Behavior* (New York: Holt, Rinehart, and Winston, 1961), pp. 66–81.

[38] J. R. Gibb, "Defensive Communication," *op. cit.*, p. 142.

[39] J. R. Gibb, "Sociopsychological Processes of Group Instruction," N. B. Henry (ed.), *The Dynamics of Instructional Groups* (Fifty-ninth Yearbook of the National Society for the Study of Education) (1960), Part II, pp. 115–135.

Openness

A central theme running throughout Gibb's findings is the importance of *openness*—the willingness to be receptive to experience. Rogers considered openness as the polar opposite of defensiveness.

> *In the hypothetical person who is completely open to his experience, his concept of self would be a symbolization in awareness which would be completely congruent with his experience. There would, therefore, be no possibility of threat.*[40]

One who is open to experience evaluates threat more accurately and tolerates change more graciously. This is why the frame of reference concept can be so helpful in reducing defenses and in keeping them low. Because the frame of reference obviates the mine-is-the-only-valid-world presumption it makes defense of one's personalized world unnecessary. Nondefensive, one is not compelled to attack or counterattack—thus he is more able to contribute to a supportive climate in his relations with others.

In a supportive climate people are more able to explore their own and each other's decision premises[41] and thus get down to the real grounds of controversy (or to discover that there was no real basis for conflict). Even if there are genuine differences, under conditions of openness people find themselves more capable of dealing with them maturely.

Rogers offers this practical suggestion:

> *The next time you get into an argument with your wife, or your friend, or with a small group of friends, just stop the discussion for a moment and for an experiment, institute this rule. "Each person can speak up for himself only after he has first restated the ideas and feelings of the previous speaker accurately, and to that speaker's satisfaction." You see what this would mean? It would be necessary for you to really achieve the other speaker's frame of reference–to understand his thoughts and feelings so well that you could summarize them for him. Sounds simple, doesn't it? But if you try it you will discover it one of the most difficult things you have tried to do. However, once you have been able to see the other's point of view, your own comments will have to be drastically revised. You will also find the emotion going out of the discussion, the differences being reduced, and those differences which remain being of a rational and understandable sort.*[42]

SUMMARY

We have depicted human behavior as the product of the internal state of the individual and the environment in which he finds himself. His behavior, then, is only indirectly a response to reality. One who cannot tolerate this basic uncertainty of life and assumes *his world is the only real world* may find that "world" in almost constant jeopardy. Closed and defensive he may respond to the "threats" with irrational attack and/or flight.

[40]C. R. Rogers, "A Theory . . . ," *op. cit.*, p. 206.

[41]H. A. Simon, *Administrative Behavior* (2d ed.; New York: The Macmillan Co., 1957).

[42]C. R. Rogers, "Communication: Its Blocking and Its Facilitation," a paper originally prepared for delivery at the Northwestern University Contennial Conference on Communications, held in Evanston, Illinois, October 11–13, 1951. Reproduced here from the Northwestern University *Information*, Vol. XX, No. 25.

We have conceded that many organizations are populated to an extent with more or less defensive (and thus often aggressive) people. Therefore, the challenge to anyone who aspires to be an effective leader or member of an organization (or more broadly, wishes to live an emotionally mature and deeply satisfying life) might be phrased as follows:

1. *Can he come to accept that* his *and everyone else's "reality" is subjective, incomplete, distorted, and unique? Can he, therefore, muster the courage to become open and nondefensive—to permit even contrary cues to reach him and to begin to revise, update, and make more valid his self-image?*
2. *Having clarified his own frame of reference can he learn to assess accurately the frames of reference of others? Can the manager, for example, realize the simple but profound truth that his subordinates' worlds have him in it as a boss—his world does not?*

THE POSTULATE OF INTERPERSONAL NEEDS: DESCRIPTION

William C. Schutz

Postulate 1. The Postulate of Interpersonal Needs.

(a). Every individual has three interpersonal needs: inclusion, control, and affection.

(b). Inclusion, control, and affection constitute a sufficient set of areas of interpersonal behavior for the prediction and explanation of interpersonal phenomena.

Explanation: In studying interpersonal behavior it is important to isolate the relevant variables. "People need people" serves as a good starting point, but, if the frontiers of knowledge are to recede, the next question must be investigated: "*In what ways* do people need people?"

The literature is not lacking in contestants for the mantle of "basic interpersonal variables." French[1] in a recent report summarizes the factors found in the factor analysis of various personality tests; he was able to reduce the number of apparently unrelated factors to forty-nine! Clearly this number is unmanageable for use in future investigation.

If the strictly statistical techniques for reducing variables still leaves forty-nine, some other exploratory method must be employed or at least added. A developmental approach to isolating variables has several appealing features. It seems promising to attempt to trace the developing individual through his sequence of typical interpersonal dealings, as a method of identifying the most basic interpersonal areas from which others are derivable. A consideration of this developmental process (discussed in more detail below), and some formulations presented by certain investigators, notably Bion, led the author to the conclusion that three interpersonal areas seemed to cover most interpersonal behavior. Later analysis of certain relevant literature lent weight to the proposition that three areas would prove adequate for fruitful investigation.

As the description of these three areas, here called inclusion, control, and affection, progressed, the fable came to mind of the blind men who disagreed over the characteristics of an elephant because each was exploring a different sector. It seems that various investigators are describing different aspects of the elephant—the three need areas—but apparently

From William C. Schutz, *The Interpersonal Underworld*, Palo Alto, California: Science and Behavior Books, pp. 13–33.

[1] T. French, *Summary of Factor Analytic Studies of Personality* (Princeton, N.J. Educational Testing Service, 1956).

they are describing the same elephant. Thus clinicians discuss unconscious forces, small-group investigators describe overt behavior, child psychologists report on early interpersonal relations, and sociologists are interested in roles and group structures. But there seems to be heartening convergence toward the same set of variables, even though the approaches differ. The problem, then, is to give a complete description of the "elephant" and point out which aspects are being described by each observer. This chapter attempts to provide a complete description of the three basic interpersonal areas as basic needs, by showing how they appear in personality structure, in overt behavior, and in pathological behavior.

INTERPERSONAL NEED

The concept of interpersonal need, often called "social need," has been discussed by many authors[2] but because it forms the central part of this book it is important to describe in what sense the term will be used.

The term "interpersonal" refers to relations that occur between people as opposed to relations in which at least one participant is inanimate. It is assumed that, owing to the psychological presence of other people, interpersonal situations lead to behavior in an individual that differs from the behavior of the individual when he is not in the presence of other persons. An optimally useful definition of "interpersonal" is one such that all situations classified as interpersonal have important properties in common—properties that are in general different from those of noninterpersonal situations. With this criterion for a definition in mind, the following specifies the meaning of "interpersonal situation." (The term "interpersonal" shall be used as equivalent to the term "group.")

An *interpersonal situation* is one involving two or more persons, in which these individuals take account of each other for some purpose, or decision, *D*. It is described from a particular point of reference, usually either that of one of the participants or of an outside observer. It is also specified as existing during a stated time interval. Thus a complete statement of an interpersonal situation has the form:

"From the standpoint of *O* (or *A*, or *B*), *A* takes account of *B* for decision *D* during time interval t_1 to t_n."

"*A* takes account of *B* for decision *D*" means that when *A* considers what alternative to select for decision *D* one criterion for his choice is his expectation of *B*'s response to his choice. This expectation does not require that *A* make a different decision because of the influence of *B*; it simply means that his criteria for making the decision are supplemented.

For example, if a man who is sitting on a bus trying to decide whether or not to give up his seat to an elderly lady considers the reaction of the attractive young woman across the aisle, he is taking account of the young woman whether or not he gives up his seat. From *his* point of view the relation is interpersonal, since he takes account of her. From the standpoint of the young woman the situation may not be interpersonal at all, since

[2]N. E. Miller and J. Pollard, *Social Learning and Imitation* (New Haven, Conn.: Yale University Press, 1941).

she may not even be aware of his presence. Further, *A* may take account of *B* for one decision, for example, giving up a bus seat, as in the previous example, but not for another, for example, deciding which cobbler to patronize a week later. In addition, the degree to which *A* takes account of *B* varies with time. Our bus rider may be taking account of the lady during the bus ride (i.e., t_1 to t_n) but not at all when watching television that evening (i.e., after t_n).

The type of investigation will determine which point of reference for defining the term "interpersonal" will be most useful. Sometimes it is useful to consider an interpersonal situation from the standpoint of an individual, as when we speak of an interpersonal need. Sometimes it is more advantageous to consider a situation interpersonal only if the "taking account of" relation is reciprocal, that is, perceived by both members of a dyadic (two-person) relation. Sometimes the point of view of observers will decide whether a situation is interpersonal, regardless of the reports of the individuals involved in the relation. For conceptual clarity the important requirement in describing an interpersonal relation is that the point of reference be specified.

The phrase "face-to-face" used frequently by other writers when defining "interpersonal" or "group" has been omitted from the present definition. As shall be elaborated below, the property of physical presence is an important variable within the scope of interpersonal behavior, closely related to the area of inclusion. Further, it is often useful to consider situations as interpersonal in which behavior is determined by *expectations* of the behavior of others, even if the others are not physically present. It therefore seems more useful to leave the term "interpersonal" free of the face-to-face condition and consider as a separate problem the effect of that condition on behavior.

The other term in the phrase under discussion is "need." A "need" is defined in terms of a situation or condition of an individual the nonrealization of which leads to undesirable consequences. An interpersonal need is one that may be satisfied only through the attainment of a satisfactory relation with other people. The satisfaction of a need is a necessary condition for the avoidance of the undesirable consequences. An interpersonal need is one that may be satisfied only through the attainment of a satisfactory relation with other people. The satisfaction of a need is a necessary condition for the avoidance of the undesirable consequences of illness and death. A discrepancy between the satisfaction of an interpersonal need and the present state of an organism engenders a feeling in the organism that shall be called *anxiety*.

There is a close parallel between biological needs and interpersonal needs, in the following respects:

1. A biological need is a requirement to establish and maintain a satisfactory relation between the organism and its *physical* environment. An interpersonal need is a requirement to establish a satisfactory relation between the individual and his *human* environment. A biological need is not satisfied by providing unlimited gratification. An organism may take in too much water and drown, as well as too little water and die of thirst. The

need is satisfied by establishing an equilibrium between the amount of water inside and outside the organism. The same is true for the "commodities" exchanged between people. An individual's needs may be unfulfilled either by having, for example, too much control over his human environment and hence too much responsibility, or too little control, hence not enough security. He must establish a satisfactory relation with his human environment with respect to control.

2. Nonfulfillment of a biological need leads to physical illness and sometimes death. Nonfulfillment of an interpersonal need leads to mental (or interpersonal) illness and sometimes death. Unsatisfactory personal relations lead directly to difficulties associated with emotional illness. Death, either through suicide or resulting from the more general loss of motivation for life, results when interpersonal dissatisfaction is prolonged.

3. The organism has characteristic modes, which are temporarily successful, of adapting to lack of complete satisfaction of biological needs. The organism also has characteristic ways, which are temporarily successful, of adapting to nonsatisfaction of interpersonal needs. For the interpersonal situation the terms "conscious" and "unconscious" needs are sometimes used to describe the phenomena at issue.

The distinction between a conscious and an unconscious need finds a parallel in a biological condition such as drug addiction. In drug addiction the immediate (conscious) need is to satisfy the immediate craving and to adjust the body chemistry so that the pain is reduced. The more basic (unconscious) need is to adjust the body chemistry back to the state where the drug is no longer required. The pain or anxiety felt when the organism is in a situation which does not allow for the satisfaction of these two needs is different in each case. In the first there is the immediate deprivation, analogous to an interpersonal situation in which an individual's characteristic psychological adjustment mechanisms (for example, defenses) cannot operate. To illustrate, if denial were the defense used by an individual in the affection area and he were placed in a situation in which close personal relations were called for, he would feel an *immediate anxiety* caused by the discrepancy between the demands of the situation and his most comfortable behavior pattern. The more *basic anxiety* or interpersonal imbalance stemming from the general inadequacy of the defense to ward off the need for affection is analogous to the physical discomfort caused by the discrepancy between the chemical balance produced by the drug addiction and the normal chemical balance.

This analogy assumes a particular interpersonal relation that optimally satisfies interpersonal needs, parallel to an optimal chemical balance. This assumption is made, although it is difficult to test. Perhaps it parallels the condition in which the psychoanalyst attempts to place his patient. The analyst has a conception of an optimal psychological condition for a given individual toward which the person strives. This condition goes deeper than the reinforcement of the patient's defense mechanisms, which protect him from undesirable impulses. The optimal state is one in which defenses are only minimally required. It is this psychological state that is analogous to the concept of an optimal interpersonal relation.

These parallels between the interpersonal and biological needs will be specified more precisely in the following discussion. Other aspects of this problem could be mentioned at this point, such as the phylogenetic continuity of interpersonal needs, their universality cross-culturally, and possible physiological correlates. However, this would take the discussion too far afield. The main point is that in many important ways interpersonal needs have properties closely parallel to those of biological needs.

INCLUSION, CONTROL, AND AFFECTION

Now comes the problem of describing the elephant, that is, providing a complete description of interpersonal variables sufficient to provide a framework for integration and future investigation in the field.

To construct such a schema it is necessary to determine the most relevant parameters for describing important aspects of the interpersonal variables. These parameters may then be used as the classification variables for generating a matrix to encompass the interpersonal behavior of interest. This process is called "substructing" by Lazarsfeld and Barton,[3] and "facet analysis" by Guttman.[4] It has the virtue of providing all possible combinations of parameter values so that omissions or duplications are easily recognized.

The parameters chosen should delineate salient differences worthy of preservation in personality description. Differences on these parameters represent important behavioral differences which are helpful, even necessary, when behavioral characteristics are related to external factors, for example, childhood experiences, productivity, compatibility, leadership. The matrix generated by the parameters represents the *types of available data*. The methods of obtaining the data (such as introspection, questionnaire, observation, projective test) are independent of the matrix. Any method of data collection is permissible for any type of data. The parameters:

1. Observability—*the degree to which an action of an individual is observable by others. This parameter is dichotomized into* action and feeling. *An action is usually more observable to outsiders, a feeling usually more observable to the self.*
2. Directionality—*the direction of the interaction with respect to originator and target. This parameter is trichotomized into (a) self toward other, (b) other toward self, and (c) self toward self. The last category is interpersonal in the sense that it represents interaction between the self and others who have been interiorized early in life.*

[3]P. Lazarsfeld and A. Barton, "Qualitative Measurement in the Social Sciences," in D. Lerner and H. Lasswell, *The Policy Sciences* (Stanford, Calif.: Stanford University Press, 1951).

[4]L. Guttman, "Principal Components of Scalable Attitudes," in *Mathematical Thinking in the Social Sciences*, ed. by P. Lazarsfeld (Glencoe, Ill.: Free Press, 1954).

Table 1 Matrix of Relevant Interpersonal Data—"The Elephant"

<table>
<tr><td colspan="6">Inclusion</td></tr>
<tr><td colspan="3"></td><td>Self to Other (Actions)</td><td>Other to Self (Reactions)</td><td>Self to Self</td></tr>
<tr><td colspan="2" rowspan="2">Desired Interpersonal Relations (Needs)</td><td>Act</td><td colspan="2">Satisfactory relation re interaction and inclusion behavior 1</td><td rowspan="4">Feeling that I am significant
15</td></tr>
<tr><td>Feel</td><td colspan="2">Satisfactory relation re feelings of mutual interest 2</td></tr>
<tr><td colspan="2" rowspan="2">Ideal Interpersonal Relations</td><td>Act</td><td>Social 3</td><td>People include me 4</td></tr>
<tr><td>Feel</td><td>I am interested in people 5</td><td>People are interested in me 6</td></tr>
<tr><td rowspan="4">Anxious Interpersonal Relations (Anxieties)</td><td rowspan="2">Too much activity</td><td>Act</td><td>Over-social 7</td><td>Social-compliant 8</td><td rowspan="4">I am insignificant (I don't know who I am; I am nobody)
16</td></tr>
<tr><td>Feel</td><td>I am not really interested in people 9</td><td>People aren't really interested in me 10</td></tr>
<tr><td rowspan="2">Too little activity</td><td>Act</td><td>Under social 11</td><td>Counter-social 12</td></tr>
<tr><td>Feel</td><td>I am not interested in people 13</td><td>People are not interested in me 14</td></tr>
<tr><td rowspan="2">Pathological Interpersonal Relations</td><td colspan="4">Too Much</td><td>17</td></tr>
<tr><td colspan="2">Too Little</td><td colspan="2">Psychotic (Schizophrenia)</td><td>18</td></tr>
</table>

Control			*Affection*		
Self to Other (Actions)	*Other to Self (Reactions)*	*Self to Self*	*Self to Other (Actions)*	*Other to Self (Reactions)*	*Self to Self*
Satisfactory relation re power and control behavior 19		Feeling that I am responsible 33	Satisfactory relation re love and affection behavior 37		Feeling that I am lovable 51
Satisfactory relation re feelings of mutual respect 20			Satisfactory relation re feelings of mutual affection 38		
Democrat 21	People respect me 22		Personal 39	People are friendly to me 40	
I respect people 23	People respect me 24		I like people 41	People like me 42	
Autocrat 25	Rebel 26	I am incompetent (I am stupid, irresponsible) 34	Overpersonal 43	Personal-compliant 44	I am unlovable (I am no good, rotten bastard) 52
I don't trust people 27	People don't trust me 28		I don't *really* like people 45	People don't *really* like me 46	
Abdicrat 29	Submissive 30		Underpersonal 47	Counterpersonal 48	
I don't *really* respect people 31	People don't *really* respect me 32		I don't like people 49	People don't like me 50	
Obsessive-compulsive 35			Neurotic 53		
Psychopath 36			Neurotic 54		

3. Status of Action—*whether the behavior is in the inclusion, control, or affection area.*
4. State of Relation—*whether the relation is desired, ideal, anxious or pathological.*

Table 1 summarizes the terms and concepts discussed. . . . This table, in a sense, is the "elephant."

THE THREE INTERPERSONAL NEEDS

The interpersonal need for inclusion is defined behaviorally as the need to establish and maintain a satisfactory relation with people with respect to interaction and association. "Satisfactory relation" includes (1) a psychologically comfortable relation with people somewhere on a dimension ranging from originating interaction with all people to not initiating interaction with anyone; (2) a psychologically comfortable relation with people with respect to eliciting behavior from them somewhere on a dimension ranging from always initiating interaction with the self to never initiating interaction with the self.

On the level of feelings the need for inclusion is defined as the need to establish and maintain a feeling of mutual interest with other people. This feeling includes (1) being able to take an interest in other people to a satisfactory degree and (2) having other people interested in the self to a satisfactory degree.

With regard to the self-concept, the need for inclusion is the need to feel that the self is significant and worth while.

The interpersonal need for control is defined behaviorally as the need to establish and maintain a satisfactory relation with people with respect to control and power. "Satisfactory relation" includes (1) a psychologically comfortable relation with people somewhere on a dimension ranging from controlling all the behavior of other people to not controlling any behavior of others and (2) a psychologically comfortable relation with people with respect to eliciting behavior from them somewhere on a dimension ranging from always being controlled by them to never being controlled by them.

With regard to feelings, the need for control is defined as the need to establish and maintain a feeling of mutual respect for the competence and responsibleness of others. This feeling includes (1) being able to respect others to a satisfactory degree and (2) having others respect the self to a satisfactory degree.

The need for control, defined at the level of perceiving the self, is the need to feel that one is a competent, responsible person.

The interpersonal need for affection is defined behaviorally as the need to establish and maintain a satisfactory relation with others with respect to love and affection. Affection always refers to a two-person (dyadic) relation. "Satisfactory relation" includes (1) a psychologically comfortable relation with others somewhere on a dimension ranging from initiating close, personal relations with everyone to originating close, personal relations with no one; (2) a psychologically comfortable relation with people with respect to eliciting behavior from them on a dimension ranging from always originating close, personal relations toward the self, to never originating close, personal relations toward the self.

At the feeling level the need for affection is defined as the need to establish and maintain a feeling of mutual affection with others. This feeling includes (1) being able to love other people to a satisfactory degree and (2) having others love the self to a satisfactory degree.

The need for affection, defined at the level of the self-concept, is the need to feel that the self is lovable.

This type of formulation stresses the interpersonal nature of these needs. They require that the organism establish a kind of equilibrium, in three different areas, between the self and other people. In order to be anxiety-free, a person must find a comfortable behavioral relation with others with regard to the exchange of interaction, power, and love. The need is not wholly satisfied by having others respond toward the self in a particular way; nor is it wholly satisfied by acting toward others in a particular fashion. A satisfactory balance must be established and maintained.

INCLUSION, CONTROL, AND AFFECTION BEHAVIOR

Thus far these key terms have been discussed only from the standpoint of their status as interpersonal needs. Since the value of the theory is dependent to a large extent on the cogency and clarity of these terms, it is important to describe them as fully as possible. In later chapters many different ways of describing these terms will be introduced, including

1. *Examples;*
2. *Synonyms;*
3. *A description of aspects of these behaviors at various levels of personality;*
4. *A description of the interconnection between these terms and other terms in the theory, such as "compatibility";*
5. *A description of the relations between these areas and factors found by other investigators;*
6. *A description of these areas as applied to literary works; and*
7. *A measuring instrument FIRO—B (Fundamental Interpersonal Relations Orientation—Behavior), which measures two aspects of each of the three areas.*

Inclusion behavior is defined as behavior directed toward the satisfaction of the interpersonal need for inclusion.

Control behavior is defined as behavior directed toward the satisfaction of the interpersonal need for control.

Affection behavior is defined as behavior directed toward the satisfaction of the interpersonal need for affection.

In general, *inclusion behavior* refers to association between people. Some terms that connote a relation that is primarily positive inclusion are "associate," "interact," "mingle," "communicate," "belong," "companion," "comrade," "attend to," "member," "together," "join," "extravert." Some terms that connote lack of, or negative, inclusion, are "exclusion," "isolate," "outsider," "outcast," "lonely," "detached," "withdrawn," "abandoned," "ignored."

The need to be included manifests itself as wanting to be attended to, to attract attention and interest. The classroom hellion who throws erasers is often objecting mostly to the lack of attention paid him. Even if he is given negative affection he is partially satisfied, because at least someone is paying attention to him.

In groups, people often make themselves prominent by talking a great deal. Frequently they are not interested in power or dominance but simply prominence. The "joker" is an example of a prominence seeker, very much as is the blond actress with the lavender convertible.

In the extreme, what is called "fame" is primarily inclusion. Acquisition of fame does not imply acquisition of power or influence: witness Marilyn Monroe's attempt to swing votes to Adlai Stevenson. Nor does fame imply affection: Al Capone could hardly be considered a widely loved figure. But fame does imply prominence, and signifies interest on the part of others.

From another standpoint, behavior related to belonging and "togetherness" is primarily inclusion. To desire to belong to a fraternal organization by no means necessarily indicates a liking for the members or even a desire for power. It is often sought for its "prestige value," for increase of "status." These terms are also primarily inclusion conceptions, because their primary implication is that people pay attention to the person, know who he is, and can distinguish him from others.

This last point leads to an essential aspect of inclusion, that of identity. An integral part of being recognized and paid attention to is that the individual be identifiable from other people. He must be known as a specific individual; he must have a particular identity. If he is not thus known, he cannot truly be attended to or have interest paid to him. The extreme of this identification is that he be understood. To be understood implies that someone is interested enough in him to find out his particular characteristics. Again, this interest need not mean that others have affection for him, or that they respect him. For example, the interested person may be a confidence man who is exploring his background to find a point of vulnerability.

At the outset of interpersonal relations a common issue is that of commitment, the decision to become involved in a given relation or activity. Usually, in the initial testing of the relation, individuals try to identify themselves to one another to find out which facet of themselves others will be interested in. Frequently a member is silent for a while because he is not sure that people are interested in him. These behaviors, too, are primarily in the inclusion area.

This, then, is the flavor of inclusion. It has to do with interacting with people, with attention, acknowledgement, being known, prominence, recognition, prestige, status, and fame; with identity, individuality, understanding, interest, commitment, and participation. It is unlike affection in that it does not involve strong emotional attachments to individual persons. It is unlike control in that the preoccupation is with prominence, not dominance.

Control behavior refers to the decision-making process between people. Some terms connoting a relation that is primarily positive control are "power," "authority," "dominance," "influence," "control," "ruler," "superior officer," "leader." Some terms that connote primarily a lack of, or negative, control are "rebellion," "resistance," "follower," "anarchy," "submissive," "henpecked," "milquetoast."

The need for control manifests itself as the desire for power, authority, and control over others and therefore over one's future. At the other end is the need to be controlled, to have responsibility taken away. Manifestations of the power drive are very clear. A more subtle form is exemplified by the current magazine advertising campaign featuring the "influential." This is a person who controls others through the power he has to influence their behavior.

The acquisition of money or political power is a direct method of obtaining control over other persons. This type of control often involves coercion rather than more subtle methods of influence like persuasion and example. In group behavior, the struggles to achieve high office or to make suggestions that are adopted are manifestations of control behavior. In an argument in a group we may distinguish the inclusion seeker from the control seeker in this way: the one seeking inclusion or prominence wants very much to be one of the participants in the argument, while the control seeker wants to be the winner or, if not the winner, on the same side as the winner. The prominence seeker would prefer to be the losing participant; the dominance seeker would prefer to be a winning nonparticipant. Both these roles are separate from the affectional desires of the members.

Control behavior takes many subtle forms, especially among more intellectual and polite people. For example, in many discussion groups where blackboards are involved, the power struggle becomes displaced onto the chalk. Walking to the blackboard and taking the chalk from the one holding it, and retaining possession, becomes a mark of competitive success. Often a meeting is marked by a procession of men taking the chalk, writing something, and being supplanted by another man for a further message. In this way propriety is maintained, and still the power struggle may proceed.

In many gatherings, control behavior is exhibited through the group task. Intellectual superiority, for one thing, often leads to control over others so that strong motivation to achieve is often largely control behavior. Such superiority also demonstrates the real capacity of the individual to be relied on for responsible jobs, a central aspect of control. Further, to do one's job properly, or to rebel against the established authority structure by not doing it, is a splendid outlet for control feelings. Doing a poor job is a way of rebelling against the structure and showing that no one will control you, whereas acquiescence earns rewards from those in charge which satisfies the need to be respected for one's accomplishments.

Control is also manifested in behavior toward others controlling the self. Expressions of independence and rebellion exemplify lack of willingness to be controlled, while compliance, submission, and taking orders indicate various degrees of accepting the control of others. There is no necessary relation between an individual's behavior toward controlling others, and his behavior toward being controlled. The domineering sergeant may accept orders from the lieutenant with pleasure and gratefulness, while the neighborhood bully may also rebel against his parents; two persons who control others differ in the degree to which they allow others to control them.

Thus the flavor of control is transmitted by behavior involving influence, leadership, power, coercion, authority, accomplishment, intellectual superiority, high achievement, and independence, as well as dependency (for decision making), rebellion, resistance, and submission. It differs from inclusion behavior in that it does not require prominence. The concept of the "power behind the throne" is an excellent example of a role that would fill a high control need and a low need for inclusion. The "joker" exemplifies the opposite. Control behavior differs from affection behavior in that it has to do with power relations rather than emotional closeness. The frequent difficulties between those who want to "get down to business" and those who want to get to "know one another" illustrate a situation in which control behavior is more important for some and affection behavior for others.

In general, *affection behavior* refers to close personal emotional feelings between *two* people. Affection is a dyadic relation; it can occur only between pairs of people at any one time, whereas both inclusion and control relations may occur either in dyads or between one person and a group of persons. Some terms that connote an affection relation that is primarily positive are "love," "like," "emotionally close," "positive feelings," "personal," "friendship," "sweetheart." Some terms that connote primarily lack of, or negative, affection are "hate," "dislike," "cool," "emotionally distant."

The need for affection leads to behavior related to becoming emotionally close. An affection relation must be dyadic because it involves strong differentiation between people. Affectional relations can be toward parental figures, peers, or children figures. They are exemplified in friendship relations, dating, and marriage.

To become emotionally close to someone involves, in addition to an emotional attachment, an element of confiding innermost anxieties, wishes, and feelings. A strong positive affectional tie usually is accompanied by a unique relation regarding the degree of sharing of these feelings.

In groups, affection behavior is characterized by overtures of friendship and differentiation between members. One common method of avoiding a close tie with any one member is to be equally friendly to all members. Thus "popularity" may not involve affection at all; it may often be inclusion behavior, whereas "going steady" is usually primarily affection.

A difference between affection behavior, inclusion behavior, and control behavior is illustrated by the different feelings a man has in being turned down by a fraternity, failed in a course by a professor, and rejected by his girl. The fraternity excludes him and tells him, in effect, that they as a group don't have sufficient interest in him. The professor fails him and says, in effect, that he finds him incompetent in his field. His girl rejects him, and tells him, in effect, that she doesn't find him lovable.

Thus the flavor of affection is embodied in situations of love, emotional closeness, personal confidences, intimacy. Negative affection is characterized by hate, hostility, and emotional rejection.

In order to sharpen further the contrast between these three types of behavior, several differences may be mentioned.

With respect to an interpersonal relation, inclusion is concerned primarily with the formation of the relation, whereas control and affection are concerned with relations already formed. Basically, inclusion is always concerned with whether or not a relation exists. Within existent relations, control is the area concerned with who gives orders and makes decisions for whom, whereas affection is concerned with how emotionally close or distant the relation becomes. Thus, generally speaking, inclusion is concerned with the problem of *in or out*, control is concerned with *top or bottom*, and affection with *close or far*.

A further differentiation occurs with regard to the number of people involved in the relation. Affection is *always* a one-to-one relation, inclusion is *usually* a one-to-many relation, and control may be either a one-one or a one-many relation. An affectional tie is necessarily between two persons, and involves varying degrees of intimacy, warmth, and emotional involvement which cannot be felt toward a unit greater than one person. Inclusion, on the other hand, typically concerns the behavior and feelings of one person toward a group of people. Problems of belonging and membership, so central to the inclusion area, usually refer to a relatively undifferentiated group with which an individual seeks association. His feelings of wanting to belong to the group are qualitatively different from his personal feelings of warmth toward an individual person. Control may refer to a power struggle between two individuals for control over each other, or it may refer to the struggle for domination over a group, as in political power. There is no particular number of interactional participants implied in the control area.

Control differs from the other two areas with respect to the differentiation between the persons involved in the control situation. For inclusion and affection there is a tendency for participants to act similarly in both the behavior they express and the behavior they want from others; for example, a close, personal individual usually likes others to be close and personal also. This similarity is not so marked in the control area. The person who likes to control may or may not want others to control him. This difference in differentiation among need areas is, however, only a matter of degree. There are many who like to include but do not want to be included, or who are not personal but want others to be that way toward them. But these types are not as frequent as the corresponding types in the control area.

TYPES OF INTERPERSONAL BEHAVIOR

For each area of interpersonal behavior three types of behavior will be described: (1) deficient—indicating that the individual is not trying directly to satisfy the need, (2) excessive—indicating that the individual is constantly trying to satisfy the need, (3) ideal—indicating satisfaction of the need, and (4) pathological.

In delineating these types it is assumed that anxiety engendered by early experiences leads to behavior of the first, second, and fourth types, while a successful working through of an interpersonal relation leads to an individual who can function without anxiety in the area. For simplicity of presentation the extremes will be presented without qualifications. Actually, of course, the behavior of any given individual could be best described as some combination of behavior incorporating elements of all three types at different times, for instance, the oversocial, undersocial, and social.

Inclusion Types

The Undersocial. The interpersonal behavior of the undersocial person tends to be introverted and withdrawn. Characteristically, he avoids associating with others and doesn't like or accept invitations to join others. Consciously he wants to maintain this distance between himself and others, and insists that he doesn't want to get enmeshed with people and lose his privacy. But unconsciously he definitely wants others to pay attention to him. His biggest fears are that people will ignore him, generally have no interest in him, and would just as soon leave him behind.

Unconsciously he feels that no one ever will pay attention to him. His attitude may be summarized by, "No one is interested in me. I'm not going to risk being ignored. I'll stay away from people and get along by myself." There is a strong drive toward self-sufficiency as a technique for existence without others. Since social abandonment is tantamount to death, he must compensate by directing his energies toward self-preservation; he therefore creates a world of his own in which his existence is more secure. Behind this withdrawal lie anxiety and hostility, and often a slight air of superiority and the private feeling that others don't understand him.

The direct expression of this withdrawal is nonassociation and noninteraction with people, lack of involvement and commitment. The more subtle form is exemplified by the person who for one reason or another is always late to meetings, or seems to have an inordinate number of conflicting engagements necessitating absence from people, or the type of person who precedes each visit with, "I'm sorry, but I can't stay very long."

His deepest anxiety, that referring to the self concept, is that he is worthless. He thinks that if no one ever considered him important enough to receive attention, he must be of no value whatever.

Closely allied with this feeling is the lack of motivation to live. Association with people is a necessary condition for a desire to live. This factor may be of much greater importance in everyday interaction than is usually thought. The degree to which an individual is committed to living probably determines to a large extent his general level of enthusiasms, perseverance, involvement, and the like. Perhaps this lack of concern for life is the ultimate in regression: if life holds too few rewards, the prelife condition is preferable. It is likely that this basic fear of abandonment or isolation is the most potent of all interpersonal fears. The simple fear that people are not interested in the self is extremely widespread, but in scientific analyses it, too often, is included as a special type of affectional need. It is extremely useful, however, to make clear the distinction between inclusion and affection.

The Oversocial. The oversocial person tends toward extraversion in his later interpersonal behavior. Characteristically, he seeks people incessantly and wants them to seek him out. He is also afraid they will ignore him. His interpersonal dynamics are the same as those of the withdrawn person, but his overt behavior is the opposite.

His unconscious attitude is summarized by, "Although no one is interested in me, I'll make people pay attention to me in any way I can." His inclination is always to seek companionship. He is the type who "can't stand being alone." All of his activities will be designed to be done "together." An interesting illustration of this attitude occurs in the recent motion picture, "The Great Man." José Ferrer, as a newspaper man, is interviewing a woman about her reasons for attending the funeral of a television celebrity.

> *"Because our club all came together," she replies.*
> *"But," Ferrer persists, "why did you come here?"*
> *"I came here because the rest came here."*
> *"Were you fond of the dead man?"*
> *"Not especially," she replies, "but we always do things together."*

This scene (the dialogue is from memory) nicely illustrates the importance of being together presumably as an end in itself. The interpersonal behavior of the oversocial type of person will then be designed to focus attention on himself, to make people notice him, to be prominent, to be listened to. There are many techniques for doing this. The direct method is to be an intensive, exhibitionistic participator. By simply forcing himself on the group he forces the group to focus attention on him. The more subtle technique is to try to acquire status through such devices as name dropping, or by asking startling questions. He may also try to acquire power (control) or try to be well liked (affection), but for the primary purpose of gaining attention. Power or friendship, although both may be important (depending on his orientation in the other two interpersonal areas), is not the primary goal.

The Social. To the individual for whom the resolution of inclusion relations was successful in childhood, interaction with people presents no problem. He is comfortable with people and comfortable being alone. He can be a high or low participator in a group, or can equally well take a moderate role, without anxiety. He is capable of strong commitment and involvement to certain groups and also can withhold commitment if he feels it is appropriate.

Unconsciously, he feels that he is a worthwhile, significant person and that life is worth living. He is fully capable of being genuinely interested in others and feels that they will include him in their activities and that they are interested in him.

He also has an "identity" and an "individuality." Childhood feelings of abandonment lead to the absence of an identity; the person feels he is nobody. He has no stable figures with whom to identify. Childhood feelings of enmeshment lead to confusion of identity. When a child is nothing but parts of other people and has not had sufficient opportunity to evaluate the characteristics he observes in himself, he has difficulty knowing who he is. The social person has resolved these difficulties. He has integrated aspects of a large number of individuals into a new configuration which he can identify as himself.

Inclusion Pathology. Failure to be included means anxiety over having no contact with people. Unsuccessful resolution of inclusion relations leads to feelings of exclusion, of alienation from people, of being different and unacceptable, and usually the necessity of creating a phantasy world in which the nonincluded person is accepted. Inclusion, because it is posited to be the first of interpersonal relations to be dealt with by the infant, has strong narcissistic elements and other close similarities to the description by psychoanalysts of the interpersonal characteristics in the oral stage. Hence a pathological difficulty in the inclusion area leads to the most regressed kind of behavior, that concerned with belonging to people, being a significant individual. This syndrome is very much like the functional *psychoses*. In Ruth Munroe's description of the Freudian explanation of psychoses these points are made clear:

> *The essential feature of Freud's explanation of psychotic conditions may be stated as the greater depth of regression. The adult never lapses back to infancy all of a piece of course. . . . Freud felt, however, that the truly psychotic manifestations belong to the pre-oedipal period—indeed to the stage of narcissism before the ego has properly developed. The mechanisms of psychoses are the archaic mechanisms of the infant before secure object relations have been established.*[5]

The last line of this quotation is especially pertinent to demonstrating the close relations between the Freudian discussion of the psychosis and the area of inclusion. The phrase, "before secure object [interpersonal] relations have been established," certainly bears a close resemblance to the preceding discussion of the problems of becoming included in the social group.

It appears, then, that difficulty in establishing a satisfactory relation with other persons, with regard to inclusion or contact, when difficulty reaches a pathological state, leads to psychosis, especially schizophrenia. This statement does not mean that all conditions now called psychosis are caused by difficulties in the inclusion area, nor does it necessarily mean that all inclusion problems will, if pathological, become psychoses; nor does it even imply that there are "pure" inclusion problems uncontaminated with other areas. It implies only that there is a close relation between disturbance in the inclusion area and psychosis.

Psychosis, especially schizophrenia, appears to be related more to the undersocial pattern than the oversocial. The lack of identity and inability

[5]Ruth Munroe, *Schools of Psychoanalytic Thought* (New York: Dryden, 1956), p. 288.

to be alone, if carried to the extreme, would correspond to the pathological extreme of the oversocial.

Control Types

The Abdicrat. The abdicrat is a person who tends toward submission and abdication of power and responsibility in his interpersonal behavior. Characteristically, he gravitates toward the subordinate position where he will not have to take responsibility for making decisions, and where someone else takes charge. Consciously, he wants people to relieve him of his obligations. He does not control others even when he should; for example, he would not take charge even during a fire in a children's schoolhouse in which he is the only adult; and he never makes a decision that he can refer to someone else. He fears that others will not help him when he requires it, and that he will be given more responsibility than he can handle. This kind of person is usually a follower, or at most a loyal lieutenant, but rarely the person who takes the responsibility for making the *final* decision. Unconsciously, too, he has the feeling that he is incapable of responsible adult behavior and that others know it. He never was told what to do and therefore never learned. His most comfortable response is to avoid situations in which he will feel helpless. He feels that he is an incompetent and irresponsible, perhaps stupid, person who does not deserve respect for his abilities.

Behind this feeling are anxiety, hostility, and lack of trust toward those who might withhold assistance. The hostility is usually expressed as passive resistance. Hesitancy to "go along" is a usual technique of resistance, since actual overt rebellion is too threatening.

The Autocrat. The autocrat is a person whose interpersonal behavior often tends toward the dominating. Characteristically, he tries to dominate people and strongly desires a power hierarchy with himself at the top. He is the power seeker, the competer. He is afraid people will not be influenced or controlled by him—that they will, in fact, dominate him.

Commonly, this need to control people is displaced into other areas. Intellectual or athletic superiority allows for considerable control, as does the more direct method of attaining political power. The underlying dynamics are the same as for the abdicrat. Basically the person feels he is not responsible or capable of discharging obligation and that this fact is known to others. He attempts to use every opportunity to disprove this feeling to others and to himself. His unconscious attitude may be summarized as, "No one thinks I can make decisions for myself, but I'll show them. I'm going to make all the decisions for everyone, always." Behind this feeling is a strong distrust that others may make decisions for him and the feeling that they don't trust him. This latter becomes a very sensitive area.

The Democrat. For the individual who has successfully resolved his relations with others in the control area in childhood, power and control present no problem. He feels comfortable giving or not giving orders and taking or not taking orders, as is appropriate to the situation. Unconsciously, he feels that he is a capable, responsible person and therefore that he does not need to shrink from responsibility or to try constantly to prove how competent he really is. Unlike the abdicrat and autocrat, he is not preoccupied with fears of his own helplessness, stupidity, and incompetence. He feels that other people respect his competence and will be realistic with respect to trusting him with decision making.

Control Pathology. The individual who does not accept control of any kind develops pathologically into a psychopathic personality. He has not been adequately trained to learn the rules of behavior established for respecting the rights and privileges of others. Ruth Munroe says,

> *The major Freudian explanation for this condition is that there has been a serious failure of superego development. The practical image has not been adequately internalized in the form of conscience but remains the policeman at the corner—an external force. Truly, the behavior of the psychopath is childish without the limited experience of the child. When the resources of adulthood are used without the inner controls of adulthood the resultant behavior is very likely to be deplorable. Object relations generally are poor of necessity since good early object relations would have led to more adequate superego development.*[6]

Affection Types

The Underpersonal. The underpersonal type tends to avoid close personal ties with others. He characteristically maintains his dyadic relations on a superficial, distant level and is most comfortable when others do the same to him. Consciously, he wishes to maintain this emotional distance, and frequently expresses a desire not to get "emotionally involved"; unconsciously he seeks a satisfactory affectional relation. His fear is that no one loves him. In a group situation he is afraid he won't be liked. He has great difficulty genuinely liking people. He distrusts their feeling toward him.

His attitude could be summarized by the "formula," "I find the affection area very painful since I have been rejected; therefore I shall avoid close personal relations in the future." The direct technique for maintaining emotional distance is to reject and avoid people to prevent emotional closeness or involvement activity, even to the point of being antagonistic. The subtle technique is to appear superficially friendly to *everyone.* This behavior acts as a safeguard against having to get close to, or become personal with, any *one* person. ("Close" and "personal" refer to emotional closeness and willingness to confide one's most private concerns and feelings. It involves the expression of positive affection and tender feelings.) Here the dyadic relation is a threatening one. To keep everyone at the same distance obviates the requirement for treating any one person with greater warmth and affection.

The deepest anxiety, that regarding the self, is that he is unlovable. He feels that people won't like him because, in fact, he doesn't "deserve" it. If people got to know him well, he believes, they would discover the

[6] *Ibid.*, p. 292.

traits that make him so unlovable. As opposed to the inclusion anxiety that the self is of no value, worthless, and empty, and the control anxiety that the self is stupid and irresponsible, the affection anxiety is that the self is nasty and bad.

The Overpersonal. The overpersonal type attempts to become extremely close to others. He definitely wants others to treat him in a very close, personal way. His response may be summarized by the formula, "My first experiences with affection were painful, but perhaps if I try again they will turn out to be better." He will be striving in his interpersonal relations primarily to be liked. Being liked is extremely important to him in his attempt to relieve his anxiety about being always rejected and unlovable. Again, there are two behavorial techniques, the direct and the subtle. The direct technique is an overt attempt to gain approval, be extremely personal, intimate, and confiding. The subtle technique is more manipulative, to devour friends and subtly punish any attempts by them to establish other friendships, to be possessive.

The underlying dynamics are the same as those for the underpersonal. Both the overpersonal and the underpersonal responses are extreme, both are motivated by a strong need for affection, both are accompanied by strong anxiety about ever being loved, and basically about being unlovable, and both have considerable hostility behind them stemming from the anticipation of rejection.

The Personal. For the individual who successfully resolved his affectional relations with others in childhood, close emotional relations with one other person present no problem. He is comfortable in such a personal relation, and he can also relate comfortably in a situation requiring emotional distance. It is important for him to be liked, but if he isn't liked he can accept the fact that the dislike is the result of the relation between himself and one other person—in other words, the dislike does not mean that he is an unlovable person. Unconsciously, he feels that he is a lovable person who is lovable even to people who know him well. He is capable of giving genuine affection.

Affection Pathology. Neuroses are commonly attributed to difficulties in the area of affection. Ruth Munroe says,

> *The early bloom of sexuality, which cannot possibly come to fruition, is called the phallic stage to differentiate it from true genitality leading to mature mating and reproduction. At this period attitudes are formed which are crucial for later heterosexual fulfillment and good relations with people generally. For this reason it is the stage most fraught with potentialities for neurotic distortion.*[7]

The discussion of pathology in this chapter should be supplemented with discussion of the childhood origins of various adult behavior patterns. Combining the early experience and present behavior with the pathological classification will provide a more complete picture of the process of personality development and disintegration.

[7] *Ibid.*, p. 199.

SUMMARY

To summarize, difficulties with initiating interaction range from being uncomfortable when not associating with people ("can't stand to be alone"—the *oversocial*) to not feeling comfortable initiating interaction ("can't stand being with people"—the *undersocial*). Difficulties with controlling others range from not feeling comfortable controlling the behavior of anyone ("can't tell anyone what to do"—the *abdicrat*) to not feeling comfortable when unable to control everyone ("always have to be in charge"—the *autocrat*). Difficulties with originating close, personal relations range from being uncomfortable when unable to establish a sufficiently close, personal relation ('can't get close enough"—the *overpersonal*) to being uncomfortable when getting too close and personal with someone ("don't like to get emotionally involved with people"—the *underpersonal*).

This description could be stated in psychoanalytic terms with little if any difference in meaning. In the struggle between the id and the superego to determine the individual's behavior the excessive response in each area represents the triumph of the id. The restrained response results from the triumph of the superego. The ideal response represents the successful resolution of the id impulses, the demands of the superego, and external reality; it therefore corresponds to the triumph of the ego.

In each of the nonideal (extreme) types described there are anxiety, hostility, and ambivalence. (One outcome of this analysis is to suggest that each of these widely used terms could be divided profitably into three types.) Anxiety arises from a person's (a) anticipation of a nonsatisfying event (for instance, being ignored, dominated, rejected) and (b) fear of exposure, both to self and others, of what kind of person he "really" is—his inadequate self-concept. The anxiety indicates that these behavior patterns are inflexible, since anxiety usually leads to rigid behavior. The threat involved in changing behavior is too great to allow for much flexibility. Hostility also follows from anxiety; so the hostility, too, may arise in three ways.

Finally, ambivalence is also present in the nonideal behaviors, since the behavior pattern being utilized is necessarily unsatisfactory. In many instances an overpersonal individual, for example, will occasionally become underpersonal, and vice versa. Complete reversals are to be expected more than slight modifications, especially for the extreme behavior patterns. The characterization of a person's behavior can describe only his most usual behavior, not his invariable behavior.

Chapter 5
THE INTERPERSONAL ENVIRONMENT

Each of us has various needs for interpersonal communication as discussed in Chapter 3. We meet and "size up" another person in ways described in Chapter 4. Over time, our needs and our experiences in interacting with others combine to produce a general orientation toward other people (also discussed in Chapter 4). All of this does not take place in a vacuum; it occurs in one or another type of physical setting, imbedded in a social context.

The physical setting for interpersonal communication usually involves a suitable place, ordinarily a room or area of space somewhat shielded from the rest of the world. Usually this space includes chairs and tables; sometimes these are in the form of desks, counters, or bars. The social environment includes the influence of other people whether they are present or not. It involves our membership in groups, organizations, and cultures.

As we meet a person in our daily routine we may decide to stop for a chat or a conference. Together we look at our surroundings and go into an ecological huddle; we look for a place suited to our purpose. We note or ask about their commitments to others; do they belong to a group or an organization that limits our chance to talk at this time? This questioning goes on without our thinking very much about it because, as adults, we are accustomed to meeting limitations on our opportunities to talk with others; we have developed habits of accommodating our physical and social environment.

Our aim in this chapter is not to recount the obvious, nor is it to provide a catalogue of environmental factors that may inhibit or promote interpersonal communication. Our purpose here is to identify factors that most severely influence the communication process, calling attention primarily to those that, because they are so obvious or commonplace, may have been overlooked or given too little consideration. Our objective is to assist in the understanding of the process of interpersonal communication, suggesting ways in which environmental problems may be handled with greater effectiveness.

USING THE PHYSICAL ENVIRONMENT

Every teenager knows that there is a great deal of difference between being in one place or another with a boyfriend or a girlfriend. Walking home from school is one thing; "driving around" is another. Our interest here is not to explore the sexual overtones of meeting in a secluded spot, but to illustrate, in an introductory way, the significance of "places" on interpersonal communication. Certain physical environmental factors obviously influence the process of interpersonal communication. Let's suppose that you wish to "talk things over" with another person. The question arises: How can you best utilize the available environment? How can conditions be selected or arranged to serve your purpose best?

Rooms and Places

Different places have ways of giving us messages. Some places seem to say, "Sit down and enjoy yourself; talk things over if you wish." Other places are cold, formal, or barren, and contribute to difficulties in overcoming psychological distance between people. In many ways the physical elements influence the behaviors that can be expected in such a place.

When we wish to talk things over privately with another person, the size and shape of the room selected (or available) exercises significant influence. A large lobby in a hotel or dormitory suggests that strangers may meet, pass by each other, perhaps smile or nod, but in general exchange only minimum courtesies—what Erving Goffman calls "civil inattention."[1] Here acquaintances may pause briefly for a greeting; friends may greet and show each other calm affection. Lovers warmly embraced will appear out of place.

Interpersonal face-to-face interaction is facilitated by a small room, one no larger than necessary to provide a feeling of comfort for a few persons. A larger room tends to suggest that other persons foreign to this particular grouping might enter and diminish the atmosphere of privacy. To some extent we tend to feel that if there are only two or three of us we should not "tie up" the amount of space afforded by a large room.[2] In Mark Knapp's essay[3] following this chapter, special attention is given to the significance of room furnishings, carpeting, and draperies. There is some evidence showing that interpersonal communication is facilitated in rooms thought to be attractive; pleasing colors can enhance the effect of social interaction. For interpersonal communication we should seek a room that is not ordinarily used for some specific purpose such as table tennis or laboratory experiments. The usual behavior that occurs in such places

[1]E. Goffman, *Relations in Public* (New York: Basic Books, 1971), p. 209.

[2]Cf. A. H. Maslow and N. L. Mintz, "Effects of Esthetic Surroundings: I. Initial Effects of Three Esthetic Conditions Upon Perceiving 'Energy' and 'Well-Being' in Faces," *Journal of Psychology*, 41 (1956), 247–254.

[3]M. Knapp, "The Effects of Environment and Space on Human Communication," *Nonverbal Communication and Human Interaction* (New York: Holt, Rinehart and Winston, 1972). Reprinted in this volume, pp. 257–284.

tends to provide an atmosphere that distracts our attention, making it more difficult for us to note carefully both the verbal and nonverbal cues necessary for us to consider as we try to understand each other on something more than a surface level.[4]

By their very nature, rooms and places tend to imply a social contract between all persons who enter, a contract regarding the kind of interaction that is supposed to take place within their walls. Thus, semipublic (or semiprivate) places, such as cocktail lounges, have a special tone or atmosphere that suggests you may talk to your friends. But there is also a kind of piquant loneliness felt, such that if you have no friends, or none are present, you may talk to others who are similarly lonely. In such a place some persons are clearly observing the surface rule—talking with friends; others are more or less involved in hopes, fears, and actions that go beyond the surface rule—looking for a stranger with whom to be friendly.[5]

In our society restaurants provide a dilemma as a place for interpersonal communication. On the one hand, they are readily available and provide a minimal opportunity for interaction. On the other hand, there are interminable distractions—ordering food or drink; interruptions by waitresses or other people passing by; unwanted noises from kitchen, busboys, passing motorists, and recorded music. Despite these limitations the availability of cafes or restaurants tempts us to use them for serious interpersonal talk; frequently we find we are only partly able to accomplish this purpose.[6]

One of the advantages of being in the "management" class of persons working in many organizations is that for such people interpersonal communication is allowed, sometimes even encouraged. If an assistant manager is seen chatting with an employee it is supposed that he or she is doing a part of his/her job—"getting to know" the person, perceiving the employee's problems, gaining insight into his/her needs. An important status line in industry can be drawn on the basis of who may be allowed to "talk things over with others" or told to "get back to work." Persons who may be told to "get to work" may provide an outward show of activity along with surreptitious attempts to chat with other employees.[7]

In most rooms or places in our culture, interpersonal communication possibilities are institutionalized—that is, regulated and understood as conventional for that spot. Even if persons present are not quite aware of these conventions, they will sense something is sharply

[4] B. H. Westley and M. S. McLean emphasize the use of all sense modalities in "A Conceptual Model for Communications Research," *Journalism Quarterly*, 34 (1957), 31.

[5] Cf. Goffman, *op. cit.*, pp. 106–107.

[6] Cf. E. Goffman, *Behavior in Public Places* (New York: Free Press, 1963), p. 52.

[7] *Ibid.*, p. 56.

amiss if norms are violated. For optimal use of the process of interpersonal communication, one should find a place where face-to-face encounters without interruptions or distractions are common occurrences. Perhaps the best place of all is the living room in your home. For a college student away from home, a dormitory room may have to suffice. The fact that you sleep there may make it an awkward place. However, the dormitory lobby is equally unsatisfactory in other ways. It is probably true that part of the loneliness expressed by many college students is due to the fact that there is no place for personal, private communication available to them that does not have overtones of other activities. They generally have no equivalent of a living room in their own home.[8]

There is a vast amount of literature on the alienation of young people, particularly college students, with their sense of loneliness and separation.[9] Very little information is available about the impact on students of the unavailability of an equivalent of their living room at home—a place offering a sense of appropriateness for interpersonal communication of a private or semipersonal nature. Their usual available spaces are a dormitory lobby or their sleeping-study room. Of even less attraction are semipublic places such as a cafeteria, an empty classroom, or the lawn.

It is small wonder that college students away from home are lonely; they have no home, no place very suitable for interpersonal communication. Lobbies, as we suggested earlier, are characterized by interruptions of others walking by, coupled with a sense of lack of privacy. If something important and personal is said in a low voice so that others nearby can't hear, the simple act of leaning forward to hear produces a feeling that others will interpret this closeness as out-of-place intimacy, inappropriate behavior in a semipublic lobby. And, as in some colleges, even if boys may invite girls to their rooms (or vice versa), there are often confusing overtones of sexual involvement. Even if such involvement is not objectionable, these rooms are bedrooms, with the suggestion present of very private behavior—sleeping, changing clothes, private body functions and odors. This is hardly the place to encourage mere acquaintances to test the ground for friendship; too much is implied regarding a highly personal relationship. The two available alternatives—lobby or sleeping quarters—tend to provide either too little or too much for the start of an informal friendship. In part, it appears to us that many college students are lonely because they have no place to overcome their loneliness. Why don't dormitories rent sitting rooms to students for 25 cents an hour?

[8]See N. Sanford, *Self and Society* (New York: Atherton, 1966), pp. 48–51.

[9]See, for example, K. Keniston, *Young Radicals: Notes on Committed Youth* (New York: Harcourt Brace Jovanovich, 1968); see also G. B. Blaine, Jr., et al., *Emotional Problems of the Student* (Garden City, N.Y.: Doubleday, 1966).

Chairs and Tables

Time after time we have walked by the open door of a college classroom, barren except for its disordered array of empty chairs with their little side-saddle, arm-rest "desks"—a room empty save for two students, with chairs partly facing each other, each student trying to engage in interpersonal communication. With great concentration on each other they may be able to overcome the negative influence of the bare walls, empty chairs, and the feeling of the ambiguous presence of absent, unknown others. To some extent they may overcome the awkwardness of desk-chairs that suggest they should "take notes" on whatever is said.

Whether we are sharply aware of it or not, chairs and tables have a significant influence on the way we interact in face-to-face communication. Chairs have an effect in two ways: physical comfort and our psychological relationship to each other. In a similar fashion tables (including desks) provide physical convenience as well as psychological distance between us.

Chairs should be arranged in such a way that they encourage interpersonal communication, if that is the goal desired. They should be placed so that participants face each other and can easily see each other's eyes. As we suggested in Chapter 4, an interpersonal encounter starts with the eyes. The eyes provide information for the important first impression and can indicate answers to such questions as, "Does he/she really want to talk to me?" "Is his/her intention friendly, serious, sincere?" In his history of frontier life, R. F. Adams provides an amusing illustration of this point:

> *When nearin' 'nother person on a trail, etiquette required that a man approach within speakin' distance and pass a word before changin' his course unless, for a very good reason, he was justified in such a change. The West held that every person had the right to find out the intent of all other persons 'bout him. . . . If the stranger lit to cool his saddle, the other didn't stay mounted while carryin' on a conversation. The polite thing to do was dismount and talk with 'im face to face. This showed one wasn't lookin' for any advantage over the other.*[10]

There is a kind of "I-am-willing-to-talk-with-you" ritual that people use to start interpersonal communication. First they come into each other's presence. As they approach, their eyes are scanning the territory—the room, chairs, tables, and places where they may easily walk. When within a few paces of each other, their eyes connect. In the first flash of eye contact they recognize each other and *show this recognition.* Goffman, perhaps modern sociology's best-known "people watcher," thus describes the ritual for starting interaction:

[10]R. F. Adams, *The Old-Time Cowhand* (New York: Macmillan, 1961), pp. 57–58.

> *An encounter is initiated by someone making an opening move, typically by means of a special expression of the eyes. . . . The engagement properly begins when this overture is acknowledged by the other, who signals back with his eyes, voice or stance that he has placed himself at the disposal of the other for purposes of eye-to-eye activity. . . . There is a tendency for the initial move and responding "clearance" sign to be exchanged almost simultaneously.*[11]

In another of his writings, Goffman suggests that "when one individual meets the eyes of another he can indicate a position (attitude), perceive the other's response to his taking this position, and show his own response to the other's response all in a brief moment."[12]

The importance of eye contact in interpersonal communication can hardly be overemphasized. It is so significant that if held slightly too long at a time, it can be taken as an incursion on another's privacy. Staring or glaring can easily be taken as an offense.[13] It is somewhat amusing to observe that "topless" waitresses seldom look their customers in the eye, and in close serving frequently obtain a courtesy from their clients that keeps their eyes focused elsewhere, mainly on other clients.[14] Additional evidence of the importance of eye contact for personal interaction may be obtained by observing those who are alienated from those around them, particularly persons who are mentally ill; they commonly express their alienation through avoidance of eye contact.[15]

For interpersonal communication to become optimal, the eye contact used at the beginning of the relationship must be maintained. The persons involved must have full access to each other's feelings as expressed in visual contact. Studies have shown that the arrangement of chairs in a discussion circle influences interaction; persons adjacent to each other tend not to address each other except for side comments, but tend to direct their remarks to persons whose eyes they can see.[16] In any interpersonal encounter the arrangement of chairs can have either a damaging or an enhancing effect. Part of the popularity of cocktail lounges in airline terminals may be attributed to the circular arrangement of chairs around tables as compared to the rows of chairs formally arranged in terminal waiting rooms. Such formal arrangement discourages interpersonal communication and heightens

[11]Goffman, *Behavior in Public Places, op. cit.*, pp. 91–92.

[12]Goffman, *Relations in Public, op. cit.*, p. 18 (fn.).

[13]For a detailed treatment of such effect, see Goffman, *Relations in Public, op. cit.*, pp. 45–46, 59–60, 126–132.

[14]*Ibid.*, p. 45.

[15]See, for example, M. D. Riemer, "The Averted Gaze," *Psychiatric Quarterly*, 23 (1949), 108–115.

[16]For a report of experimental evidence, see B. Steinzer, "The Spatial Factor in Face-to-Face Discussion Groups," *Journal of Abnormal and Social Psychology*, 45 (1950), 552–555.

the traveler's isolated sense of loneliness—people, real people, are so near, yet so far.

The *distance* between participants in interpersonal communication is also of special significance. Perhaps there is no specific optimal distance; it will likely vary with the participants' attitudes toward each other. If convenient or appropriate, they may move their chairs close enough to feel comfortable while talking with each other; the distance thus chosen may define their perceptions of their relationship, a point to be considered in more detail below. If the available chairs are not easily moved, the distance thus dictated will have subtle influence on the participants' interaction.

In his book, *The Hidden Dimension,* Edward Hall has carefully observed distances commonly used for different kinds of human interaction.[17] A brief resume of his analysis is contained in his essay following Chapter 6.[18] Hall divides interaction space into four distances: intimate, personal, social, and public.

Intimate distance, close phase (touching) is the distance for lovemaking, comforting, and protecting (also struggling or fighting). Intimate distance, far phase (6 to 18 inches) is too close for interaction unless the participants enjoy an intimate relationship; it serves well for those who wish to comfort each other or get to know each other very well.[19] It is thus limited to the interpersonal communication of those who wish to become psychologically close—at least for most middle-class Americans.[20]

Personal distance ranges from 18 to 30 inches (close phase) and from 30 to 48 inches (far phase). These distances are used for interpersonal communication by persons who are friendly, favorably inclined toward each other.[21] The far-phase limit (48 inches) is the distance used to keep another person "at arm's length away," and marks the distance at which the dominance of one person by another is less effective. Those who are not afraid of being dominated may move within this range; those who are afraid will not.[22]

Social distance, according to Hall, ranges from 4 to 7 feet (close phase) and 7 to 12 feet (far phase). Close phase is the distance at which *impersonal* interaction generally occurs. It is commonly used by acquaintances attending an informal social gathering; the usual

[17]E. T. Hall, *The Hidden Dimension* (Garden City, N.Y.: Doubleday, 1969), pp. 113–129.

[18]Edward Hall and Mildred Hall, "The Sounds of Silence," *Playboy*, 18, No. 6 (June 1971). Reprinted in this volume, pp. 333–342.

[19]Hall, *The Hidden Dimension, op. cit.*, pp. 117–118.

[20]Hall's studies dealt primarily with middle-class subjects living in northeastern United States. He suggests that great care should be exercised in any attempt to generalize his findings to other geographical areas or ethnic groups.

[21]*Ibid.*, pp. 119–120.

[22]*Ibid.*, p. 121.

distance maintained by those who work together at impersonal tasks —executives and their secretaries, teachers and their students. Social distance, far phase is ordinarily employed for formal business or social transactions.[23] Incidentally, at this distance two people may work separately at different tables or desks.

Public distances, close (12 to 25 feet) and far (over 25 feet) are used on formal occasions involving public displays. Public figures—kings, presidents, governors, celebrities—may occasionally maintain this noninvolvement distance.[24] Conversely, politicians try to move in closer when seeking votes.

Hall's analysis of interaction distances provides special insight into the subtle influence of chairs and tables, particularly desks, on interpersonal communication. The uses of personal and social distances tend to vary from culture to culture, to some extent in a rather arbitrary fashion.[25] However, tables and desks almost universally provide distances that separate people psychologically and interfere with personal interaction. People ordinarily thought to be important usually have desks that keep visitors at the far phase (7 to 12 feet) of social distance. People talking across desks in modest offices are 9 to 10 feet apart. At this distance feedback from each other's eyes is significantly lost.[26] Not lost, however, is the impression of social distance separating the participants; a feeling that closeness, personal involvement, and a sense of interpersonal solidarity might be achieved only with special effort, if at all.[27]

Some chairs and tables (or desks) are personal territories, staked and claimed by an individual for his personal use. They may be the legal property of a company or institution, but personal territory from 8:00 A.M. to 5:00 P.M., assigned to an individual for his/her use. If in such a situation he/she meets an acquaintance, even an old personal friend, across such a desk that person is a "visitor" no matter how warmly he/she is greeted. The flow of interpersonal communication will be subtly influenced by these environmental conditions.[28] A university dean of our acquaintance comes out from behind his desk to meet his visitors and talks with them in a "conference corner" equipped with easy chairs, coffee table, side tables, rug, and the informal atmosphere of a living room in one's home. Such practices are

[23]*Ibid.*, pp. 121–123.

[24]*Ibid.*, pp. 123–124.

[25]See *ibid.*, pp. 128–164. See also R. Birdwhistell's comments cited in a symposium reported in B. Schaffner, ed., *Group Processes* (New York: J. Macy, 1959), pp. 184–185.

[26]*Ibid.*, p. 122.

[27]Cf. A. G. White, "The Patient Sits Down: A Clinical Note," *Psychosomatic Medicine*, 15 (1953), 256–257. See also K. B. Little, "Personal Space," *Journal of Experimental and Social Psychology*, 1 (1965), 237–247.

[28]Cf. Goffman, *Relations in Public*, *op. cit.*, pp. 28–32.

not unknown in industrial circles. For further discussion of this point see the essay by Mark Knapp following this chapter.[29]

Time

Perhaps you have not thought of time as a part of your physical environment. However, in our culture we are quite accustomed to regulating our behavior in terms of the relative amounts of time required. Work crews avoid starting a new task in the late afternoon if it cannot be completed that day. We tend to schedule our day's events with full attention to time available and time required. Similarly, our use of the process of interpersonal communication is influenced by our sense of available time.

An occasion such as a wedding, a senior prom, or a celebration may serve a special purpose and employ ritualistic use of language; even so, it is essentially a "time-person-space" event, with special consideration of *when* certain persons are brought together to use designated space in a certain way. It will not serve one's purposes for achieving interpersonal communication to violate these rituals of special occasions; in effect, the purposes of the occasion will take precedence over your purposes of getting to know someone better. For example, smiling and exchanging confidences in church will usually defeat such purposes. In this context we could review the protocol for many various occasions, but that does not seem to suit our purposes of describing the process of interpersonal communication. Most occasions involve primarily public communication, and our basic point here is that violating such protocol is usually to misuse the interpersonal communication mode.

We tend to "tell time"—note its passage—in three ways: by use of clocks; by events that transpire (for example, before or after lunch); and by the way people act. In an interpersonal encounter time available is frequently indicated by the way a person behaves. As he feels his time is being used for interaction that he doesn't desire, his hands may clasp and unclasp; his feet and legs move in subtle, inhibited "traveling" motions; his eyes wander to "not here, out there" distances; and his voice diminishes in interest-value cues. In nonverbal ways we are being told to move along. It is not by accident that a well-known beer advertisement proclaims that "If you've got the time, we've got the beer." Persons interested in initiating interpersonal communication might well take a lesson from this example.

The influence of the passing or availability of time on interpersonal communication has not received great attention from serious scholars. We are aware of the obvious, but little more. We are aware of the importance of talking with people "in time," meeting people

[29]See pp. 257–284.

"on time," and being careful of the ways we "spend our time." But the full impact of these environmental factors upon interpersonal communication has not been given careful study. On the surface it appears that their influence is considerable.

When we wish to engage a person in conversation, there is a kind of "access ritual" employed establishing that each is open to the other for at least a brief interchange.[30] Typically the two persons face each other and their eyes lock for a brief moment. Usually there is a smile of recognition, perhaps their eyes glisten or crinkle at the corners, and mutual pleasure is shown in some way. As they continue to show mutual willingness to talk with each other, a kind of "time-person-space" contract is subtly understood. In this access ritual the element of time is of fundamental importance. If either "lacks the time at this time," a different agreement is necessary if further interaction is to take place.

The passage of time is viewed differently by various people. To some extent the way one views the use of time appears to be an arbitrary, individual matter. Even so, its influence on human interaction deserves much more attention by serious scholars.

The practical point to be made on the basis of our observations is that when you desire to talk to someone in particular, you may easily overlook the fact that the other person may be viewing "his/her time" quite differently from the way you are viewing yours. He/she may wish to talk with you but have other commitments and needs for his time right now. Our recommendation is that as soon as the access ritual has taken place, you might well avoid misunderstanding and needless feelings of personal neglect or rejection if you courteously ask, "Are you sure you have time to talk with me? Perhaps there would be a better time for you?"

ADAPTING TO THE SOCIAL CONTEXT

In the environment there are things and people. Although other people may not always be present, much of our interpersonal communication takes place in the presence of persons other than the one or more with whom we are talking. These may be persons who can *overhear* what is said. In many cases they are members of a group, and for the most part we are actually talking with all of these group members. The presence of others, either those who overhear us or other members of a group with whom we interact, can have significant influence on our behavior in interpersonal communication.

Almost all of our interpersonal communication is influenced to some extent by the fact that we and others are members of various

[30]Cf. Goffman, *Relations in Public*, *op. cit.*, pp. 73–90.

organizations. When two people belonging to the same organization attempt to interact, the norms and regulations of that organization have at least a double impact on their behavior. The same is essentially true regarding the influence of a culture, although such influence may be relatively unnoticeable until we meet someone from a culture different from our own.

In this section we will look briefly at the influence of those who overhear as well as the factor of membership in groups, organizations, and cultures. Our objective will not be to review the nature of groups, organizations, or different cultures, but to focus on primary ways in which they influence our interpersonal communication.

In the Presence of Others

Interpersonal communication is a sufficiently clear-cut form of behavior so that a third person who is present must be either within the interaction or outside of it.[31] Imagine yourself with a close friend, lying on a beach, gazing at the water, and intermittently chatting with one another. A kind of bond of mutual trust and obligation has been established. You have laid yourself open to confidences and special privileges. In so doing you have made yourself available, to some extent, to special requests or expectations. In addition, although you may feel quite secure that they won't occur, there is the possibility—though faint—of demands, threats, insults, and false information. In this kind of situation your openness or availability will change considerably if an unknown person sits down near you and your friend. Perhaps you will feel like leaving the beach, hoping your friend will go along. Such feelings will likely be subtly conveyed to your friend even though they are not verbalized; in turn, however, he may not understand their source and suspect that you do not enjoy his conversation. In this way your interpersonal communication can be influenced by the presence of others not participating; unless such influences are well understood by both you and your friend, miscommunication and misunderstanding may occur.

The primary effect of the presence of persons who may *overhear* interpersonal communication is inhibition of openness and personal disclosures necessary for building friendship. We may conduct business in the presence of others as long as it does not involve personal affairs. We may exchange greetings and impersonal information if it does not impinge on our private feelings. In a word, we may be courteous but not personal when persons are present with whom we cannot trust our personal views or feelings. The usual resolution to this problem, of course, is to find a "private space," a room where nonparticipants in the interpersonal exchange can be excluded. Walls,

[31]Cf. Goffman, *Behavior in Public Places, op. cit.*, pp. 102–104.

even though sometimes thin as paper, are a social convention that provide a necessary feeling of privacy and are felt by most of us to exclude fairly effectively the influence of those who may be on the other side.[32]

There is a considerable body of experimental research to show that we tend to behave differently in the presence of even passive other persons.[33] Such presence tends to *impair* learning of new material[34] but *facilitates* performance of well-learned patterns of behavior.[35] In the presence of passive others our motivation to do well or "look good" is increased,[36] and exposure of our ideas or feelings that might make us "look bad" is inhibited.[37] In addition, there is significant evidence that behavior that is ordinary or habitual is much more likely to occur in the presence of others than is behavior that we use only rarely or on special occasions.[38] Thus we may quite reasonably conclude that making new friendships, exchanging information about our private thoughts, and, in general, opening up ourselves to others will likely be inhibited if we attempt interpersonal communication in the presence of persons not included in the interaction.

In and Out of Groups

Probably no phase of human behavior has received more study and careful research than human interaction in small groups.[39] Literally thousands of experimental studies have been reported[40] and their results compared.[41] Our interest here will not be to review, however briefly, the dynamics of group interaction. Rather, we will focus on those particular ways in which interpersonal communication is in-

[32]Goffman suggests that "the work walls do, they do in part because they are honored or socially recognized as communication barriers," even though they may not actually deter others from overhearing our conversations. See Goffman, *Behavior in Public Places, op. cit.,* pp. 152–153.

[33]For a review of this literature, see R. B. Zajonc, *Social Psychology: An Experimental Approach* (Belmont, Calif.: Wadsworth, 1966), pp. 10–15.

[34]J. Pessin, "The Comparative Effects of Social and Mechanical Stimulation on Memorizing," *American Journal of Psychology,* 45 (1933), 263–270.

[35]B. O. Bergum and D. J. Lehr, "Effects of Authoritarianism on Vigilance Performance," *Journal of Applied Psychology,* 47 (1963), 75–77.

[36]See R. B. Zajonc, "Social Facilitation," *Science,* 149 (1965), 269–274.

[37]Cf. D. Seidman et al., "Influence of a Partner on Tolerance for Self-Administered Electric Shock," *Journal of Abnormal and Social Psychology,* 54 (1957), 210–212.

[38]See K. W. Spence, *Behavior Theory and Conditioning* (New Haven, Conn.: Yale University Press, 1956).

[39]See, for example, D. Cartwright and A. Zander, eds., *Group Dynamics,* 3rd ed. (New York: Harper & Row, 1968).

[40]For a review, see J. E. McGrath and I. Altman, *Small Group Research* (New York: Holt, Rinehart and Winston, 1966).

[41]For a critical synthesis of this research, see G. Lindzey and E. Aronson, eds., *The Handbook of Social Psychology,* Vol. 4 (Reading, Mass.: Addison-Wesley, 1969), especially pp. 1–283.

fluenced by groups of which a participant is a member. In taking this focus we are viewing such groups as part of the social environment. Actually, a group's influence may be felt by persons engaging in interpersonal communication even though other members of such a group are not present—that is, if one or both of these participants are members of such a group. Thus your attention will be directed to ways in which your belonging to a group may influence your face-to-face interaction with others, including (but not only) other members of your group.

Perhaps before progressing further we should stop and give a brief definition of the term "group" as we are using it in this section, since many of us may refer to any loose collection of persons as a group. The most common definition of "small group" employed in research studies and sociopsychological literature today involves two factors: (1) a small number of persons in interdependent role relations who (2) have a set of values or norms that regulate behavior of members in matters of concern to each other.[42] Thus, in a group, as we are using the term, each member is aware of each other member's belonging to the group and is concerned to some extent about his/her behavior as it affects the group.

There are two major ways in which group membership influences interpersonal communication of its members: (1) *conformity* to the norms of behavior established by and for the group members, and (2) *task or goal commitments* made by such a group. These factors tend to influence the interpersonal communication of a group member even if he is talking with another person who is not a member of that group.

On the other hand, when a person is engaged in discussion with members of his/her own group, these two factors—conformity and goal commitments—exercise even greater influence. In such a circumstance a third factor also has considerable influence on interpersonal communication: the size of the group—the number of persons directly engaged in the discussion. These three factors will be discussed briefly in this section—with due apology to the thousands of researchers who have devoted extensive time and energy to many other variables shown to have some relevance. We have made this selection in recognition of the time available to our readers; for those who have greater need or interest we have prepared another book devoted to a detailed discussion of group interaction.[43]

Two other variables exercise great influence on the interpersonal

[42]Cf. K. Giffin, "The Study of Speech Communication in Small-Group Research," in J. Akin et al., eds., *Language Behavior* (The Hague: Mouton Press, 1970), pp. 138–162.

[43]B. R. Patton and K. Giffin, *Problem-Solving Group Interaction* (New York: Harper & Row, 1973).

behavior of members of groups: (1) *power* of one person over another, and (2) *personal attitudes* involving affection or hostility. However, these two variables are not in any sense uniquely a property of group interaction; they are the basic dimensions of any interpersonal relationship and may be easily observed in operation as two persons engage each other in interaction. They are significantly influential in the way a wife interacts with her husband or a child with his/her parent. They are, in fact, those primary variables that determine the specific nature of any interpersonal relationship.

There is a vast amount of literature on these two factors in reported studies of small groups. *Power* or influence is frequently discussed as a function of difference in social status, and *interpersonal relations* is often discussed under the rubric of *group cohesiveness*, sometimes that of *interpersonal attraction.* Because these two variables are not unique properties of groups and are pervasive in all interpersonal communication, we have chosen to discuss them in Chapter 7, The Interpersonal Relationship. To a large extent they are the primary concepts discussed in that chapter.

Long ago casual observation suggested that "Birds of a feather flock together." However, the degree to which people *change* to be like others with whom they associate was only conjectured. In 1952 Solomon Asch experimentally derived solid evidence for one of the most disturbing of all facets of human behavior.[44] In Asch's primary experiment college students were asked to look at a black line on a white card, then look at three other lines, and pick that one of the three that was the *same length* as the first one shown. In each case *one* of the "comparison" lines was *exactly the same length* as the original one. All lines were held in plain sight of the subjects. However, when the subject entered the experimental room several other students were present, and he was told that all present were there to perform the same task. Unknown to the "naïve" subject, the other students present were Asch's confederates, "planted" there to lead the subject astray. The experimental session consisted of twelve trials. In each trial the confederates were asked to make their judgments *first*; and unanimously they selected an incorrect line, erroneous as much as 1¾ inches. All choices were given orally—*and after the others had each individually voiced the unanimous but incorrect opinion, the* "naïve" subject gave his.

Asch's results were astounding. Control subjects working alone achieved about 93 percent accuracy on the same line judgments. However, "naïve" subjects exposed to erroneous social influence achieved only 67 percent accuracy, a drop of 26 percent. In further experiments confederates were instructed to give answers incorrect by as much as

[44] S. Asch, *Social Psychology* (Englewood Cliffs, N.J.: Prentice-Hall, 1952).

7 inches, the original line being 10 inches and the confederates' "choice" being only 3 inches. The results were almost the same. Control subjects were 98 percent accurate. "Naïve" subjects were 72 percent accurate—again a drop of 26 percent! Asch's comment was rather poignant:

> *We are appalled by the spectacle of the pitiful women of the Middle Ages who, accused of being witches by authorities they never questioned, confessed in bewilderment to unthought-of crimes. But in lesser measure we have each faced denials of our own feelings or needs.*[45]

The work of Asch and others confirms the principle of social conformity in very dramatic ways. The essential principle is that subjects agree to, or "go along with," conclusions of others—even decide to act upon them—when such decisions are contrary to evidence staring them in the face. There is really no way of estimating how many people conform to others' decisions that are contrary to their own beliefs and values if no clear evidence is available. Additional experiments have shown that conformity tends to increase as the topic for judgment becomes more difficult.[46] As few as three confederates giving unanimous but incorrect answers can produce this effect. And experimental evidence is in no way limited to American college sophomores. Studies have shown that American military officers "yielded" 37 percent; engineers, writers, scientists, and architects did about the same.[47] Norwegian students "yielded" 50 to 75 percent, and French students between 34 and 59 percent.[48]

It should be pointed out that in these studies the "groups" formed were not bound together by group norms or very much psychological cohesiveness—they were strangers prior to the experiments; nor were any attempts made to use personal power or influence—no "leaders" or status persons were identified or chosen. Under conditions where group norms, cohesiveness, status persons, or leaders are involved, we could expect even greater degrees of social conformity on the part of the group members. Some support of this conclusion is given in experiments where the experimenter (a sort of leader or status person) also made his/her choice known; when he/she also chose the erro-

[45] *Ibid.*, pp. 450–451.

[46] P. Suppes and M. Schlag-Rey, "Analysis of Social Conformity in Terms of Generalized Conditioning Models," in J. Criswell, H. Solomon, and P. Suppes, eds., *Mathematical Methods in Small Group Processes* (Stanford, Calif.: Stanford University Press, 1962), pp. 334–361.

[47] R. S. Crutchfield, "The Measurement of Individual Conformity to Group Opinion Among Officer Personnel," *Research Bulletin* (Berkeley: Institute of Personality Assessment and Research, University of California). See also R. S. Crutchfield, "Conformity and Character," *American Psychologist*, 10 (1955), 191–198.

[48] S. Milgram, "Nationality and Conformity," *Scientific American*, 205 (1961), 45–51.

neous stimulus picked by his/her confederates, the "naïve" subjects yielded about 60 percent![49] Studies of leadership and status influence further support this line of reasoning.

Conforming to the behavior of other members of a group is not necessarily undesirable, even when such behavior violates evidence in front of you; when people start to rush out of a building, you may not see the fire but save your life if you leave rather than decide they are crazy. "Blind conformity" can sometimes have survival value, and its practice can easily be observed in the animal world: One dog barks at a stranger in the dark, and dogs blocks away pick up the cry. However, in many cases *blind* conformity to group norms can be less than a proper use of one's intelligence.

If a collection of people can be characterized as a group, certain norms and conformity behavior may be identified. The concept of group norms was derived from long usage in sociopsychological studies. It identifies the ways members of a group behave and ways that are thought by them to be proper. Norms may be viewed as a set of directions bestowed by the group upon all its members concerning their behavior. Through interaction members find out the group's standards. For example, a young woman elected by her sorority as a representative to the student council may find that such membership is important because it improves her status and provides opportunities for influence. To be an effective member of the student council, she must first determine what is expected of members. This natural "period of adjustment" accounts for the fact that freshmen in the U. S. Senate are seen, but rarely heard.[50]

The relationship between norms and communication has received considerable attention by students of communication. Members who do not conform initially to group norms are the targets of greater amounts of communication, usually of an instructional nature; if they continue as nonconformists, the tendency is to give them rejecting communication and eventually little or none of any kind. The degree of rejection is a direct function of the cohesiveness of the group and the degree to which the nonconformist is deviant.[51] These results do not hold for just any collection of people, but for groups where belonging is attractive to its members. In some tightly knit, highly cohesive groups a nonconformist is almost immediately rejected upon detection, in which case communication is both minimal and rejective.

[49]E. E. Jones, H. H. Wells, and R. Torrey, "Some Effects of Feedback from the Experimenter on Conformity Behavior," *Journal of Abnormal and Social Psychology*, 57 (1958), 207–213.

[50]For a very detailed review of these studies, see B. E. Collins and B. H. Raven, "Group Structure: Attraction, Coalitions, Communication, and Power," in Lindzey and Aronson, eds., *op. cit.*, pp. 102–205; see especially pp. 168–184.

[51]S. Schacter, "Deviation, Rejection, and Communication," *Journal of Abnormal and Social Psychology*, 46 (1951), 190–207.

Such conformity to group norms is in actuality a yielding to group pressures, explicit or implicit. Conflict arises when the individual tends to react or respond in one way, but group pressures force him in another direction. Thus, when an individual has to express his opinion in a group on a particular issue and he knows his personal conviction is at variance with group attitudes, he may choose either to remain independent of group consensus and possibly suffer the consequences, or to conform.

Conformity to the norms of a group by one of its members tends to extend beyond the boundaries of the group; it will influence his/her interpersonal communicative behaviors toward persons who are not group members. It can affect the way one perceives others; it can influence how one talks as well as what one says. In a recent issue of a popular magazine there was a cartoon of a man talking to his wife. As a liberated woman she had entered politics. Her husband did not oppose her becoming a candidate, but was appalled that she would enter the race against "a brother Elk."

When a collection of people systematically gathers and forms a group, there is usually some common goal or task to be accomplished. If communication is poor within the group, there is no effective way of working toward the agreed-upon task. A person will work for a group goal only if he believes that its achievement will satisfy his/her own wants. Industrial studies of the relationship between worker morale and productivity emphasize the importance of the acceptance of group goals and the *perceived relevancy* of group goals to individual wants. The members must, in other words, see group goals as personally satisfying. The group is constantly challenged by problems of task or goal commitment. The feeling that members have toward their goals will not only affect their interaction with each other but also their interpersonal communication with persons outside the group.

Roles or role-functions are commonly conceptualized in the literature on small groups as a set of behaviors functionally related to the goals of the group. Research on experimental groups has demonstrated that roles tend to appear in a relatively short time, require different but specifiable sets of behaviors, and have performance criteria set by the group members. Factor analysis of a large number of alleged role-functions has revealed three major factors:

1. *Individual prominence—i.e., a higher amount of communication given and received;*
2. *Aiding group goal attainment—i.e., presentation of "best ideas" and general suggestions for guidance of group thinking; and*

3. *Sociability—i.e., the characteristics of being well liked by members and demonstrating emotional stability.*[52]

The relationship of these roles to communication is quite clear. The role of "prominent individual" correlates with amount of talking and being talked to by other group members.[53] The amount of verbalization is well correlated with best ideas and guidance; however, individuals who achieve the sociability role—that is, those who are well liked—generally do not give or receive as much verbalization and ordinarily do not present the best ideas for guidance of the thinking of the group.

Role-behaviors customarily performed by a member in a group are frequently observed in his communication behavior with persons outside of the group. This is especially true whenever the goals of the group are relevant.[54]

The variable of group size—number of members directly participating—may not have much effect on members' interaction outside the group; however, as members engage in interpersonal communication within the group, it has very significant influences. Researchers have typically found that as the size of the group increases, the most active participant becomes more and more identifiable as both a communication initiator and receiver; less-participative group members become even less differentiated in communicative amounts.[55] As size increases, the degree of feedback decreases, producing loss of communication accuracy and increased hostility.[56]

One study examined some correlates of group size in a sample of twenty-four groups ranging from two to seven members. These groups met four times to discuss problems in human relations. After each meeting members were asked to evaluate group size as it influenced group effectiveness. Members of five-person groups expressed most satisfaction; members of larger groups felt their groups wasted time and that members were disorderly, aggressive, too pushy and

[52]L. G. Wispe, "A Sociometric Analysis of Conflicting Role-Expectation," *American Journal of Sociology*, 61 (1955), 134–137.

[53]R. F. Bales and P. E. Slater, "Role Differentiation in Small Decision-Making Groups," in R. F. Bales et al., *Family, Socialization and Interaction Process* (New York: Free Press, 1955), pp. 259–306.

[54]See, for example, W. H. Crockett, "Emergent Leadership in Small Decision-Making Groups," *Journal of Abnormal and Social Psychology*, 51 (1955), 378–383.

[55]R. F. Bales, "The Equilibrium Problem in Small Groups," in T. Parsons, R. F. Bales, and E. A. Shils, eds., *Working Papers in the Theory of Action* (New York: Free Press, 1953), pp. 11–161; and P. A. Hare, "Interaction and Consensus in Different Sized Groups," *American Sociological Review*, 17 (1952), 261–267.

[56]H. J. Leavitt and R. A. Mueller, "Some Effects of Feedback on Communication," *Human Relations*, 4 (1951), 401–410.

competitive; members of groups with less than five members complained that they feared expressing their ideas freely through fear of alienating one another.[57]

These inferences were limited to decision-making tasks. However, other studies with "opinion" tasks tend to confirm these results; they also show communication behaviors different for odd-numbered versus even-numbered groups in degrees of disagreement and antagonism. An even-numbered opinion split in a small group of two, four, or six members may produce impasse, frustration, and unwarranted hostility. This difficulty was most marked in groups of only two members, a fact that should have relevance for marriage partners.[58]

How does group size influence productivity in creative groups? One researcher has found that larger groups produced a greater number of ideas, though not in proportion to the number of members; that is, there were diminishing returns from the addition of members. This may be due to the fact that as the size of the group increased, a larger and larger proportion of the group members experienced inhibitions that blocked participation. The researcher also noted that if he deliberately undertook to increase inhibitions by formalizing group procedures, a reduction in the number of ideas contributed was brought about.[59]

The Organization as Social Environment

There are many similarities between the ways our communication is influenced by our being members of groups and members of organizations, perhaps due to difficulty in distinguishing between a group and an organization. In this discussion we will be using the term "organization" to denote a combination of interrelated groups comprising an integrated social unity. This unit, like a group, has norms and conformity influence. In most organizations, those factors providing greatest impact on the communication behavior of their members are similar to those factors most influential in small groups: conformity and goal commitments. In actual operation they take these forms: (1) an emphasis on achieving the organization's goals—"getting the job done"; (2) suppression of discussion of interpersonal problems; (3) insensitivity regarding one's impact on the feelings of those around him; (4) avoidance of taboo topics; and (5) creation of a climate of distrust. Perhaps we can make these concepts less abstract by re-

[57] P. E. Slater, "Contrasting Correlates of Group Size," *Sociometry*, 21 (1958), 129–139.

[58] R. F. Bales and E. Borgatta, "Size of Group as a Factor in the Interaction Profile," in P. A. Hare, E. F. Borgatta, and R. F. Bales, eds., *Small Groups: Studies in Social Interaction* (New York: Knopf, 1955), pp. 396–413.

[59] C. A. Gibb, "Effects of Group Size and Threat Reduction upon Creativity in a Problem-Solving Situation," *American Psychologist*, 6 (1951), 324.

porting an interview recently held with one of our former students. Ten years ago Joe was hired as an executive trainee by a well-known corporation. He was interviewed a few months ago by one of the present authors in Chicago at a management institute. We later visited Joe's company at his invitation and found the following conditions.

In Joe's company it is believed that important communication should be concerned with the company's objective: *getting the job done.* Joe's communication is designed to be rational, objective, unemotional. He believes that his personal effectiveness will decrease if interpersonal attitudes are exposed and discussed; the keynote is, "Let's keep feelings out of our discussions." Joe keeps his communication with others impersonal through use of informal suggestions and little penalties.

In Joe's company the suppression of discussion of interpersonal problems has influenced Joe's interpersonal behavior. Joe has learned to hide, suppress, and disown his own interpersonal attitudes: "I didn't really mean it to sound that way." He has developed ways of keeping other people from discussing interpersonal problems: "Let's not get into personalities." Joe has difficulty in handling situations where personal attitudes are expressed; afterward he asks himself, "I wonder what he meant by that?" Joe avoids or refuses to consider new ideas involving human values: "I wouldn't want to get into that sort of thing." He tends to avoid *any* new idea for fear personal attitudes *might* become involved: "I never like to rock the boat." He avoids experimentation and risk-taking with new ideas that might involve value judgments: "Let's do it the safe way." He has become unaware of the impact upon other people of his own inner emotions and feelings. "I wonder why he thinks I don't like him." In Joe's branch of the company interpersonal problems go unresolved; they tend to reoccur and have been increasing over time. One of Joe's employees said, "Those people at the front office certainly don't like each other."

Joe is quite unaware of the impact of his personal attitudes toward other persons; he is also poor at predicting the impact upon himself of the personal attitudes of others toward him. Thus he occasionally shows the following:

1. *Surprised confusion: "Why did he get sore over that?"*
2. *Frustration: "How can you talk with a guy like that?"*
3. *Heroic attempts at "objectivity": "My plan is really very simple.*
4. *Mistrust of others: "You just can't trust people like that."*

Joe has adopted certain "play-it-safe" behaviors. He avoids intentional communication of his personal attitudes toward others. He ignores (or frowns at) communication of interpersonal attitudes by others. He tries to communicate "very clearly"; this means that he discusses only those ideas for which there is a very clear company policy. He affirms values thought to be held by his superiors: "Yes, I think Mr. ——— would see it that way." He gives only tentative commitments to any direct question, especially one involving a new idea. He has gathered around him a group of employees whose communication behavior is similar to his own. His support of his superiors lacks "commitment from within," which might involve personal warmth. As you can see, Joe is not winning personal regard or trust for himself.

In Joe's situation, mistrust, conformity, conditional commitment, and dependence have operated in a circular fashion and now feed upon themselves. Presentation of technical data is being substituted for exploration of interpersonal problems. Careful, close supervision and "sticking to the rules" has replaced any real attempts at teamwork on decisions and policies. Joe resists any suggestion of organizational change unless it is proposed by a superior; in such a case he gives an indefinite "Sir, I believe so." Joe makes no decisions or changes until absolutely necessary—that is, only when a crisis occurs. In such cases (two witnessed), Joe's communication of emotion was high—too high for the situations; Joe's emotional outbursts were only temporarily fruitful. Joe mistrusts his superiors and peers, and his *modus operandi* has become defensive behavior designed to avoid any possible crisis.

Perhaps you may think that Joe's organization and its influence on his interpersonal behavior is unique or unusual. Our observation, as well as careful studies, show that it is rather ordinary for older, established organizations.[60] There are many points we could emphasize here about organizational impact on interpersonal communication; however, we feel that they have been adequately identified in our description of Joe's company and his behavior. If you, the reader, believe you need further evidence of these influences, we feel quite safe in suggesting that you look closely at your own college or university. The odds are you will see supportive evidence all around you, with the exception of rare and special individuals such as, perhaps, your instructors in selected courses.

The Influence of One's Culture

The norms and traditions of a culture not only influence the way people behave, but they affect the use of space, rooms, and chairs. In addition, viewpoints may differ regarding the use of time. Thus, we could have included a consideration of cultural differences in our pre-

[60]Cf. C. Argyris, *Interpersonal Competence and Organizational Effectiveness* (Homewood, Ill.: Irwin, 1962), pp. 27–50.

vious discussion of the physical environment. We chose to discuss cultural use of these variables in this section because the *use* of space and time are *behaviors*, "people variables" more than "object variables." People from one culture can move into another, and even if their cultural objects are left behind and they are confronted with new ones, they tend to *use* them according to old ways. In effect, they carry their cultural use of physical items around with them.

Perhaps our culture is, in the long run, the most important environmental factor influencing our interpersonal communication. Like our clothing, we tend to carry our culture around on our backs. As long as we interact only with persons from our own culture, this influence may pass unnoticed; however, when we attempt interpersonal communication with persons from Europe, the Near East, or the Orient, we usually notice important differences. In this decade many college students are becoming personal acquaintances of students from these other cultures; in addition, many students personally visit these foreign places. In recent times cross-cultural differences have become for many of us not just an item of romantic interest but a part of our immediate interpersonal communication environment.

It seems to us that the most important aspect of cultural influences on our interaction are those behaviors of persons from other cultures that may surprise us or make us feel awkward. Similarly, we are interested in identifying our own usual, habitual behaviors that may be misinterpreted by, or prove embarrassing to, persons from foreign lands. For these reasons we believe that your interests can best be served if, in this section, we focus upon those cultural differences that directly relate to interpersonal communication. E. T. Hall, author of *The Hidden Dimension*,[61] is the outstanding authority on this topic, and to a large extent our review relies upon his careful observations.

Probably the most important cultural differences regarding the use of environmental factors is in the way people from Europe, the Orient, and America tend to utilize space. In the essay by Edward and Mildred Hall[62] following Chapter 6, the point is made that each individual surrounds himself with a "bubble of privacy," a small space that he feels is his own little territory; others must gain permission to enter unless they are willing to be perceived as intruding. To an American, a short distance is necessary for this "bubble"—perhaps 2 to 3 feet.[63] To a German, this distance must be much greater. Space is felt as an extension of the ego and is implicit in a German's use of the term *lebensraum*, a concept almost impossible to translate directly because of the emotional feelings implied. Hitler was able to use this

[61]E. T. Hall, *The Hidden Dimension, op. cit.*
[62]See pp. 333–342.
[63]Goffman, *Behavior in Public Places, op. cit.*, pp. 98–99.

feeling as a lever to move the Germans to combat. If an American pokes his head into an office or inside the screen door of a home to chat briefly, he is considered still "outside"; not so to a German—his privacy has been intruded upon if you can *see* inside his room.[64]

The German's ego is by American standards quite tender, and he will preserve his privacy with great effort. During World War II in one prison camp in the Midwest, German prisoners were housed four to a small hut. Out of any materials they could scrounge, they each built internal partitions so that each could have his own tiny private space.[65] A few years later during the Allied occupation when Berlin was in ruins and the housing shortage was indescribably acute, occupation authorities ordered Berliners with kitchens and baths to share them with neighbors—this arrangement had worked fairly well in Italy and France. The order had to be withdrawn in Germany when neighbors started killing each other over shared space.[66]

In office buildings Americans keep their doors open; Germans keep them closed. German doors are very important; usually they are very solid, fit well, and are often double in public buildings. To a German a closed door does not mean that the person behind it is doing something he shouldn't; it is his way of protecting the privacy of the individual. Hall describes the problem in one American overseas company where the German's use of doors had created a situation severe enough to have him brought in as a consultant: the Americans wanted the office doors open and the Germans wanted them closed. Hall reported that "the open doors were making the Germans feel exposed . . . closed doors . . . gave the Americans the feeling that there was a conspiratorial air about the place and that they were being left out."[67] The point we might make here is that if you want to get to know a student from Germany, don't try to hold interpersonal communication with him in a crowded bus or restaurant; find a room and close the door!

In this context (as has often been remarked regarding other factors), the English are quite different. To an American, space is a way of classifying people; large homes and yards indicate important owners. The Englishman is born into a social class and space has nothing to do with it; a Lord is a Lord even if he lives in a one-room apartment.

An Englishman may never have a "room of his own." As a child he will likely live with siblings in a "nursery"; as a schoolboy he may likely live in a dormitory with large communal eating and sleeping rooms; as a businessman he will likely share office space with numer-

[64]Hall, *op. cit.*, pp. 133–134.
[65]*Ibid.*, p. 135.
[66]*Ibid.*, pp. 135–136.
[67]*Ibid.*, p. 136.

ous colleagues. Even members of Parliament have no offices but often conduct their interviews in foyers or on a terrace.[68] The English are often puzzled by an American's need for enclosed private space; the English need no such device to protect their egos. Their social status bequeathed by their parents is their permanent birthright.

The typical Englishman's attitude toward personal space is very significant for interpersonal communication. When an American wants to be alone he goes into some room and shuts the door; for him to refuse to respond to someone else in the same room is to give them the "silent treatment," implying displeasure or lack of regard. When an Englishman wants to be alone he simply quits talking; in so doing he means no interpersonal disrespect—he simply wants to have time to think or be alone with his thoughts. Having never in his life used enclosed space or distance for this purpose, he is surprised when an American fails to understand this "common social convention." This factor holds much meaning for Americans wishing to hold interpersonal communication with the English: The more quiet or withdrawn the Englishman is, the more the American thinks something is wrong in the relationship, and the more he will press for assurances that all is well. The more he presses, the more he *intrudes* upon the Englishman's sense of privacy! Consequent tension will likely increase, lasting until one or the other perceives the other's true intentions.[69]

To many Americans the French appear to be from a world of their own, but they are fairly representative of that complex of cultures bordering the Mediterranean. In ways quite unlike the English and especially unlike the Germans, they live, breath, and eat in crowds. Crowded living is exemplified in their buses, trains, and cafes. They bundle a number of themselves into small cars that contrast sharply with Detroit iron. Their personal spheres of ego protection are relatively small.

In contrast to the Germans, their international neighbors, the French hold their conversations outdoors. Their homes are for the family—usually quite crowded; their cafes are for socializing. But even here they are quite crowded and are sensually very much involved with one another. If you wish to enjoy interpersonal communication with a student from France or Italy, you can expect him or her to stand or sit quite close, to touch you from time to time,[70] and to expect your full attention.[71]

The Arabian culture of the Near East provides some contrasts of a paradoxical nature with respect to the use of space. In their public places they are compressed and almost overwhelmed with crowd-

[68] *Ibid.*, p. 139.
[69] Cf. *ibid.*, pp. 139–140.
[70] See Goffman, *Behavior in Public Places, op. cit.*, p. 101.
[71] Cf. Schaffner, ed., *Group Processes, op. cit.*, p. 184.

ing, pushing, and shoving; however, inside their homes—at least in the upper and some middle classes—they rattle around in what suburban Americans would call too much space. The Arab dream is of a home with internal unlimited space, high vaulted ceilings, few items of furniture to obstruct one's "moving around," and a limitless view *from a balcony*. This home, however, is simply a protective wall to shield the family from the outside world.[72]

Within an Arab family and especially in public, there is no privacy as Americans know it; in fact, they do not even have a word for privacy.[73] In public it is quite acceptable to push, shove, and intrude on what Americans and Europeans regard as their "bubble" or personal sphere. An American "Pardon me" is surprising and confusing to an Arab, and, if meant as a request, usually ignored. Hall describes a personal experience when his privacy was violated in a public place; later, in his discussion of the incident with an Arabian friend, the Arabian regarded Hall's feelings as strange and puzzling. His conclusive comment to Hall was, "After all, it's a public place, isn't it?"[74] Perhaps it is no accident that there is no equivalent in Arabic for the English word "rape."

Where, then, is the Arabian's sense of privacy—his spatial shield for his ego? It is somewhere deep inside the body. This may partially explain why severing of a thief's hand is standard punishment in Saudi Arabia.[75] Paradoxically, although an Arab's ego is not violated by touching and pushing, it is not thus protected from words; a verbal insult is not something taken lightly.[76]

Arabs tend to breathe on each other when they talk; this is not accidental but a cultural pattern. To an Arab, smelling each other is a desirable way of being involved; good smells are pleasing and to smell one's friend, particularly his breath, is desirable. This does not mean that Arabs are careless about the way they smell—quite the contrary; they take special pains to enhance body odors and to use them in building human relationships.[77] This fact is significant for Americans in achieving satisfactory interpersonal relations with persons from the Near Eastern culture. Even more important, however, is the fact that to "deny one's breath"—that is, to refuse to interact closely enough so that your breath can be smelled—is to an Arab to act as if your are ashamed! Arabs are quite willing to tell each other when their breath smells badly; to avoid letting a friend smell your breath is an act denying friendship![78] Can you imagine, then, that

[72]Hall, *op. cit.*, pp. 158–162.
[73]*Ibid.*, p. 159.
[74]*Ibid.*, p. 156.
[75]*Ibid.*, p. 157.
[76]*Ibid.*, pp. 157–158.
[77]*Ibid.*, pp. 159–160.
[78]*Ibid.*, p. 160.

you, having been taught in America not to breathe in people's faces, are usually and overtly denying your friendship to an Arabian student, communicating shame to him when you are trying to be polite? If you really wish to be his friend, perhaps you might discuss these cultural differences with him.

At no time, in either public or private places, does an Arab like to be left by himself. He is used to crowds of people without physical privacy. How, then, does he achieve personal privacy, a sense of the integrity of himself as a person? Actually, it is easy: Like the Englishman, he just quits talking. If you inquire about his thoughts at this time he will regard you as a "pushy American"! Sometimes a member of an Arabian family may go for hours without saying a word and no one in the family will think anything of it. Now imagine an Arab exchange student who visited a Kansas farm; his hosts became angry at him and withdrew—gave him the silent treatment. He was actually unaware of their anger until they took him to town and forcibly put him on a bus! He was on his way home before he knew there was anything wrong![79]

At this time probably those representatives of the Orient most usually encountered by Americans are the Japanese. Crowding, sitting close, has special warm connotations to the Japanese. Deeply imbedded in their culture is the feeling of a family sitting close together around the *hibachi*, the "fireplace." This feeling has even stronger emotional overtones than the American concept of the hearth.[80] Hall quotes an old Japanese priest:

> *To really know the Japanese you have to have spent some cold winter evenings snuggled around the* hibachi. *Everybody sits together. A common quilt covers not only the* hibachi *but everyone's lap as well. In this way the heat is held in. It's when your hands touch and you feel the warmth of their bodies and everyone feels* together—*that's when you get to know the Japanese. That's the real Japan.*[81]

An American student may be surprised, even confused, by the emotional show of warmth on the part of a friendly Japanese student. In such a situation you may wish to take extra pains to overcome what, to a Japanese, may appear to be cold disinterest—the usual American use of interpersonal distance. But about the time these two persons get this spatial distance worked out to their satisfaction, a paradoxical problem may arise. It partially has to do with the Japanese way of regarding space and objects, but it realizes its full potential in the way the Japanese approach topics of special interest.

There is an ethic in the Japanese culture that encourages them *to*

[79]*Ibid.*, p. 159.
[80]*Ibid.*, p. 150.
[81]*Ibid.*, pp. 150–151.

help a friend discover something for himself rather than to tell him bluntly something he should know. This leads them to approach a subject *indirectly* rather than head-on. One American banker who had spent years in Japan voiced his greatest sense of frustration with the Japanese: "They talk around and around and around a point and never get to it."[82] They behave somewhat like a rancher "rounding up" cattle; the Japanese round up more or less related ideas until this "herd" with its size, shape, and related proportions is obvious to you or anybody—but this takes some time and patience. This way of behaving is illustrated dramatically in the way they treat space: They emphasize centers of population growth and ignore areas between; they name intersections (growth centers) rather than streets leading to them; houses are numbered in the order they are built (grow) rather than along a linear distance.[83] This causes travelers inestimable problems, but very well illustrates the way Japanese feel about relationships between objects, people, and ideas. People in close contact get to know each other well; peripheral areas relate somewhat. An area of concentration on the periphery will have *its own* center and focus; thus each "center" will have its own sense of unity and integrity. Similarly, with ideas, the circle or area is of greater importance than the linear or logical relationship between concepts. And the *feeling* one has about ideas is of greater value than their logical connections.

In talking with a Japanese friend, exercise time and patience; look for the feeling tones expressed rather than the logical rationale. Don't worry about "coming to the point," but sense your and his/her feelings about the general area of discussion as well as your feeling toward each other. And don't be surprised if you seem to sense an unexpected feeling of warmth and closeness. As the old priest said, "this is the real Japan!"

In this section on foreign cultures we would be remiss if we spoke only of space and interpersonal distance and failed to mention eye contact. Ways of using one's eyes in interpersonal communication is one of the most dramatic differences between cultures and carries considerable impact.

To get along without private rooms and offices the English have developed skill in paying strict attention, listening very carefully, and from about a distance of 6 to 8 feet they look you directly in one eye —or so it will feel to you.[84] In fact, an Englishman will likely fix an unwavering gaze upon you—*and blink his eyes to let you know he has heard you!* Once you have come to understand these social conventions, their meaning and source or derivation, you may come to

[82] *Ibid.*, p. 151.
[83] *Ibid.*, pp. 149–150.
[84] *Ibid.*, pp. 142–143.

use them—even appreciate their value in a crowded room. To misunderstand them is to increase confusion and minimize interpersonal understanding.

In like manner, as a Frenchman talks with you he really looks at you—in one eye, then the other eye, and then up and down. All French, especially the women, have grown accustomed to being looked at and will feel you are being cold or distant if you don't look at them in a direct manner.[85]

Arabs seem to be *unable* to talk without *facing* you at very close range (1 to 2 feet); to talk to a person while viewing him peripherally is regarded as impolite.[86] While talking, Arabs will look at you in a way that may seem to approach a stare or glare; sometimes this searching gaze appears to beseeching or demanding more attention than you wish to give. They frequently complain that Americans are aloof, "don't care."[87] Their searching gaze may at times seem hostile or challenging; some Arabs barely avoid fights with Americans because of the intensity and possible implications of this behavior.[88] If you have a friend from the Near East, think very carefully before you take offense at his close and intense look into your eyes as he talks with you; show him you mean to be his friend by looking him directly in the eye even though such behavior may seem awkward or uncomfortable to you at first. If you really want to be his friend and make him feel "at home" with you, this effort will have its reward.

Although in this section we have stressed differences between the American culture and those of Europe, the Near East, and the Orient, one of our more subtle purposes has been to give you some appreciation of the way your own American culture has conditioned you to the use of physical space in interpersonal behavior. From this discussion you should have gained some deeper understanding of the influence of one's culture on the use of the environment in interpersonal communication.

As you can easily see from your observation of Americans, not all of them are alike—neither are *all* English, French, Arabs, or Japanese. The behaviors we have described apply in a general way but will not be depicted by each individual. Even so, we believe that they apply well enough to be of value in your attempts to improve your interpersonal communication with persons from these cultures.

[85]*Ibid.*, p. 145.
[86]*Ibid.*, pp. 160–161.
[87]*Ibid.*, p. 161.
[88]*Ibid.*, pp. 161–162.

SUMMARY AND PREVIEW OF READINGS

In this chapter we have discussed environmental factors, physical and social, that have particular influence on interpersonal communication.

An enclosed space, a room or place where an atmosphere of privacy prevails, can favorably influence interpersonal communication. A room of modest size, pleasant furnishings, and attractive colors can have a positive effect. Tables and chairs can be helpful in terms of personal comfort and convenience; in addition, they can have a deleterious effect as psychological barriers. Restaurants and lobbies are usually available as places to attempt interpersonal communication, but they ordinarily lack a psychological atmosphere conducive to sharing personal information. In many cases they provide so many distractions that emotion cues and nonverbal messages are difficult to perceive.

Chairs and tables must not be allowed to interfere with eye contact as we attempt to engage others in interaction; messages carried by perceiving each other's eyes are perhaps almost as important as the verbal interchange; certainly these messages influence the interpretations of the relationship between people.

In our discussion of chairs and tables we noted the four "interaction distances" identified by E. T. Hall; these were briefly described along with their relative values for interpersonal communication. Further detail on rooms, chairs, tables, and interpersonal distances is given in Mark Knapp's essay following this chapter.

The way in which participants feel about the passage of time can significantly influence interpersonal communication; feelings of limited time or time poorly spent can subtly demolish the anticipated value of such interaction. Special occasions are essentially "time-person-place" arrangements wherein these environmental factors are controlled for specific purposes.

The social environment influences interpersonal communication in terms of four social contexts: the presence of other persons not currently engaged in the interaction, participants who are members of certain groups, interaction within an organization, and interpersonal customs within a culture.

Interaction within the presence of others who are not involved will likely be inhibited or limited; this will be particularly true if the participants hold allegiance of some sort to those who overhear.

Membership in groups tends to influence the interaction of its members both in and out of the group. Members tend to conform to group norms and adhere to group goal commitments; these factors may severely limit the interpersonal communication behavior of group members, even when talking with nonmembers. Within the group itself, interaction is significantly influenced by the size of the group (i.e., the number of persons attempting to interact).

Interaction within the boundaries of most older, established organizations will likely be influenced by these norms or practices: an emphasis on achieving the organization's goals, suppression of discussion of interpersonal problems, insensitivity to one's influence on the feelings of others, avoidance of taboo topics, and creation of a climate of distrust. The essay by Bormann et al. following this chapter discusses in some detail the ways in which an organization imposes environmental influence on interpersonal communication.

There are significant cultural differences between Americans, Europeans, Arabs, and Japanese. Those cultural differences having the most significant influence on interpersonal communication are social customs regarding use of space, interpersonal distance (sense of physical closeness), and use of eye contact. These practices will not be uniform for all members of these cultures, but the degree of difference *between* cultures is stable enough to be important as you try to improve your interpersonal communication with persons from these cultures.

SUGGESTED APPLICATIONS AND LEARNING EXPERIENCES

1. Note the environmental factors in your classroom. Can you determine the nature and extent of their influence on interaction in class? Discuss this issue with one or two of your classmates. Later, note any environmental influences at work in that discussion.

2. Think of the most successful discussion in which you have participated: Did it have an assigned leader? Was some organizational plan followed? Was everyone in the group active? Was the group able to achieve consensus? Determine some criteria for measuring the success of a group experience.

3. Attend a meeting in an organization outside of class (campus, church, community). Analyze the interaction in terms of the communication variables suggested in this chapter.

4. Read the book *Thirteen Days: A Memoir of the Cuban Missile Crisis* by Robert F. Kennedy (New York: Signet, 1969). Discuss the book with your classmates by considering the environmental and structural restraints imposed by the situation on the communication. How might the decision making have been improved?

5. In Knapp's article, "The Effects of Environment and Space on Human Communication," he discusses the influence of seating arrangements on behavior in small groups. He describes six different principles. Observe at least two meetings of a local campus policy-making or problem-solving group. Determine the degree to which each of these principles appears to be in effect.

6. Visit a local organization (a company, agency, or institution) and interview at least three of its members. Note any differences in communication behavior on the part of the three persons. Compare these differences with their status-position in the organization's hierarchy. Compare your conclusions with the description by Bormann et al. of communication in a hierarchy in their essay, "Speech Communication in the Organizational Context."

THE EFFECTS OF ENVIRONMENT AND SPACE ON HUMAN COMMUNICATION

Mark L. Knapp

> *Every interior betrays the nonverbal skills of its inhabitants. The choice of materials, the distribution of space, the kind of objects that command attention or demand to be touched—as compared to those that intimidate or repel—have much to say about the preferred sensory modalities of their owners.*
>
> *—Ruesch and Kees*

The ultimate influence on students of the student–teacher dialogue in America's classrooms is unknown. Few would disagree that this particular communication context is an extremely critical one for many students. What is the nature of the environment in which this important dialogue takes place? What difference does it make?

Most American classrooms are rectangular in shape with straight rows of chairs. They have wide windows which allow light to beam across the student's left shoulder. This window placement determines the direction students will face and thus designates the "front" of the classroom. Most classroom seats are also permanently attached to the floor for ease of maintenance and tidiness. Most classrooms have some type of partition (usually a desk) which separates teacher from students. Most students and teachers can provide a long list of "problems" encountered in environments designed for learning. Such complaints center around poor lighting, acoustics, temperature which is too hot or too cold, outside construction noises, banging radiators, electrical outlets which do not work, seats which do not move, gloomy, dull, or distracting color schemes, unpleasant odors, and so on. Why do they complain? Because they recognize that such problems impede the purpose for gathering in these rectangular rooms—which is to increase one's knowledge through effective student–teacher communication. The whole question of the influence of the classroom environment on student and teacher behavior remains relatively unexplored. One research project, however, provides us with some initial data on student participation in various classroom environments.[1]

Sommer selected six different kinds of classrooms for his study. He wanted to compare the amount of student participation in the different kinds of classrooms and to analyze the particular aspects of participatory

[1]R. Sommer, *Personal Space* (Englewood Cliffs, N.J.: Prentice-Hall, 1969): 110–19.

behavior in each type. The types of classrooms included seminar rooms with movable chairs—usually arranged in the shape of a horseshoe; laboratories (complete with Bunsen burners, bottles, and gas valves) which represented an extreme in straight row seating; one room which was windowless, and one which had an entire wall of windows. Undergraduate students acted as observers to record participation by the students. A distaste for the laboratory rooms and the windowless room was demonstrated through several attempts by instructors and students to change rooms or hold classes outside. Comparisons between rooms showed that in seminar rooms fewer people participated, but for longer periods of time. There were no differences between open and windowless rooms with respect to participation behavior.

When seminar rooms were analyzed separately, Sommer noted that most participation came from students seated directly opposite the instructor. Students generally avoided the two chairs on either side of the instructor—even when all other seats were filled. When a student did occupy the seat next to the instructor, he was generally silent throughout the entire period. In straight row rooms, the following observations were made: (1) Students within eye contact range of the instructor participate more. (2) There is a tendency for more participation to occur in the center sections of each row and for participation to generally decrease from the front to the back. This tendency, however, is not evident when interested students sit in locations other than those which provide maximum visual contact with the instructor. (3) Participation decreases as class size increases.

A related research project offers additional support for Sommer's observations on participation in straight row classrooms.[2] Adams and Biddle noted a remarkably consistent pattern of interaction in Grades I, VI, and XI which indicated most student participation comes from students sitting in the center of the room. Sixty-three percent of the 1176 behaviors observed came from students located in three positions, one behind the other, down the center of the room. Almost all pupil-initiated comments come from the shadowed area in Figure 1. In no instance did teachers select special students for placement in these locations. As the authors point out, "it is now possible to discriminate an area of the classroom that seems to be literally and figuratively the center of activity."

Sommer concludes his observations on classroom behavior and environmental influences by saying:

> *At the present time, teachers are hindered by their insensitivity to and fatalistic acceptance of the classroom environment. Teachers must be "turned on" to their environment lest their pupils develop this same sort of fatalism.*[3]

The preceding discussion of the classroom was used as an illustrative example of a specific context in which the *spatial relationships*, the *architecture*, and the *objects* surrounding the participants influenced the type of interaction which occurred. Before we examine each of these areas in

[2]R. S. Adams and B. Biddle, *Realities of Teaching: Explorations with Video Tape* (New York: Holt, Rinehart and Winston, 1970).

[3]Sommer, *Personal Space*, p. 119.

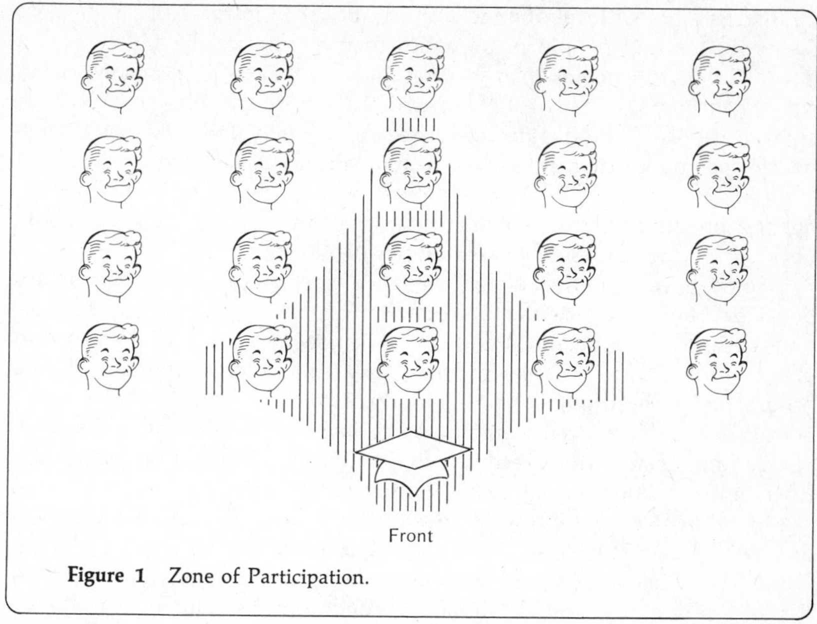

Figure 1 Zone of Participation.

greater detail, we should recognize that even geographic location and climate may have some bearing on how we interact with our fellow-men.

GEOGRAPHY AND CLIMATE

For many years, behavioral scientists have hypothesized that those who choose to live in urban rather than rural areas will have fewer close personal relations. In the United States, however, there is less and less evidence to support this theory. Greater mobility and the influence of the mass media tend to offset the possibility that these differences exist. There is evidence to suggest, however, that the more physical mobility you have in a city, the less social intimacy you will have within your own neighborhood. If you are a resident new to the community, you will very likely associate with your neighbors more than do the old residents who know more people in other parts of town. And if the neighborhood is fairly homogeneous in terms of religious beliefs, social class, political attitudes, etc., these close relationships will tend to persist.

Some descriptive research, comparing characteristics of city and rural environments, reveals additional differences in city and country life—from which one may develop hypotheses concerning the effects of differing environments on the interaction patterns of the inhabitants. For instance: (1) there appears to be more political and religious tolerance in cities than in rural areas; (2) there appears to be less religious observance in cities than in rural areas; (3) there are more foreign immigrants in cities than in rural areas; (4) there is more change in cities and more stability in the country;

(5) there is a higher level of education in cities than in rural areas; (6) there are fewer married people in the cities than in rural areas; (7) there is a lower birth rate in cities than in rural areas; (8) there is more divorce in cities than in rural areas; (9) there is more suicide in cities than in rural areas. In slums or ghettos in urban areas, one often finds a social climate which encourages or fosters unconventional and deviant behavior—or at least tolerates it. Thus, slum areas show a high incidence of juvenile delinquency, prostitution, severe mental illness, alcoholism and drug addiction, physical and mental disability, and crimes of violence.

Some have even speculated on the effects of the climate on man's behavior. There is considerable skepticism of this work—partially because climate (and moon positions and sun spots) seem too mystical to explain man's behavior, and partially because research studies conducted to date have generally used inadequate methods of scientific inquiry and control. Several pre-twentieth century authors hypothesized a relationship between climate and crime. More recently, the National Advisory Commission on Civil Disorders reported, in 1968, that the hot summer nights added to an already explosive situation which eventually resulted in widespread rioting in ghetto areas: "In most instances, the temperature during the day on which the violence erupted was quite high."[4] Griffitt varied heat and humidity under controlled laboratory conditions for students and confirmed a relationship to interpersonal responses. As temperature and humidity increased, evaluative responses for interpersonal attraction to another student decreased.[5] There may be more truth than fiction in the familiar explanation for a particularly unpleasant encounter, "Oh, he was just hot and irritable." Some research would even suggest air conditioning improves both student and teacher performance and attitudes toward the tasks they perform.

In the early twentieth century, Huntington advanced a seemingly bizarre theory that for mental vigour, an average outdoor temperature of 50 to 60 degrees is better than one above 70 degrees.[6] McClelland, in his analysis of folk stories in primitive societies, found that achievement motivation was highest in areas where the mean annual temperature ranged between 40 and 60 degrees Fahrenheit.[7] He also concluded that temperature variation was important in determining achievement motivation with at least fifteen degrees daily or seasonal variation needed for high achievement motivation. Lee speculates that tropical climates produce mental and physical lethargy:

> *Some loss of mental initiative is probably the most important single direct result of exposure to tropical environment. . . . Certainly, the usual pattern of life in tropical countries is more leisurely and less productive of material goods than that which is found in most temperate latitudes, and a case can*

[4]U.S. National Advisory Commission on Civil Disorders, "Report of the National Advisory Commission on Civil Disorders" (Washington, D.C.: U.S. Government Printing Office, 1968): 71.

[5]W. Griffitt, "Environmental Effects of Interpersonal Affective Behavior: Ambient Effective Temperature and Attraction," *Journal of Personality and Social Psychology* 15 (1970): 240–44.

[6]E. Huntington, *Civilization and Climate* (New Haven: Yale University Press, 1915).

[7]D. McClelland, *The Achieving Society* (New York: Van Nostrand Reinhold, 1961).

be made for at least some influence of climate in this respect. Man in the temperate zones has built up his civilization around the important demands created by cold weather for securing food and shelter in advance. In so doing, he has developed a culture in which activity and making provision for the future have high social values. In tropical populations, on the other hand, climate provides neither the social nor the psychological drive for activity and saving beyond the needs of the more or less immediate future. This difference in "spontaneous" activity marks one of the most important conflicts at the personal level between temperate and tropical modes of behavior.[8]

A final note—hardly worth reporting were it not for the fact that this author was born in July—some researchers have even argued that American babies born in the North, in the summer months, have slightly higher I.Q. scores in later life than those born at other times!

These reports on geography and climate provide us with little reliable and valid information. The fact that geographical location and atmospheric conditions do exert some influence on human interaction seems to be a reasonable assumption. The exact nature of this influence, under what specific conditions this influence occurs, and the degree of influence are still unknown.

THE ARCHITECTURE AND OBJECTS AROUND US

At one time in America's history, banks were deliberately designed to project an image of strength and security. The design frequently included large marble pillars, an abundance of metal bars and doors, uncovered floors, and barren walls. This style generally elicited a cold, impersonal reaction from visitors. Not too many years ago bankers perceived a need to change their environment—to present a friendly, warm, "homey" image where people would enjoy sitting down and openly discussing their financial problems. The interiors of banks began to change. Carpeting was added; wood was used to replace metal; cushioned chairs were added; potted plants were used in some cases for additional "warmth," along with other, similar changes designed to create the same effect. This is but one example of a situation in which it was recognized that oftentimes the interior within which interaction occurs can significantly influence the nature of the interaction. Night club owners and restaurateurs are aware that dim lighting and sound absorbing surfaces like carpets, drapes, and padded ceilings will provide greater intimacy and will cause patrons to linger longer than they would in an interior with high illumination and no soundproofing.

Sometimes we get very definite person-related messages from home environments. Our perception of the inhabitants of a home may be structured before we meet them—whether we think they decorated their house for themselves, for others, for conformity, for comfort, etc. We may be influenced by the mood created by the wallpaper, by the quality and apparent cost of the items placed around the house, and by many, many other things. Most of us have had the experience of being ushered into a living room which we perceive should be labeled an "unliving" room. We

[8]D. Lee, *Climate and Economic Development in the Tropics* (New York: Harper & Row, 1957), p. 100.

hesitate to sit down or touch anything because the room seems to say to us, "This room is for show purposes only; sit, walk, and touch carefully; it takes a lot of time and effort to keep this room neat, clean and tidy; we don't want to clean it after you leave." The arrangement of other living rooms seems to say, "Sit down, make yourself comfortable, feel free to talk informally, and don't worry about spilling things." Interior decorators and product promotion experts often have experiential and intuitive judgments about the influence of certain colors, objects, shapes, arrangements, etc., but there have been few attempts to empirically validate these feelings. Perhaps the best known empirical research into the influence of interior decoration on human responses were the studies of Maslow and Mintz.[9]

Maslow and Mintz selected three rooms for study—one was an "ugly" room (designed to give the impression of a janitor's storeroom in disheveled condition); one was a "beautiful" room (complete with carpeting, drapes, etc.), and one was an "average" room (a professor's office). Subjects were asked to rate a series of negative print photographs of faces. The experimenters tried to keep all factors, such as time of day, odor, noise, type of seating, and experimenter, constant from room to room so that any results could be attributed to the type of room. Results showed that subjects in the beautiful room tended to give significantly higher ratings to the faces than did participants in the ugly room. Experimenters and subjects alike engaged in various escape behaviors to avoid the ugly room. The ugly room was variously described as producing monotony, fatigue, headache, discontent, sleep, irritability, and hostility. The beautiful room, however, produced feelings of pleasure, comfort, enjoyment, importance, energy, and desire to continue the activity. In this instance, we have a well controlled study which offers some evidence of the impact of visual-esthetic surroundings on the nature of human interaction. Similar studies have tested recall and problem solving in rooms similar to those used by Maslow and Mintz. In both cases, more effective performance is found in rooms which are well appointed or "beautiful."[10]

Some pencil and paper research even associates specific colors with specific human "moods." Wexner presented eight colors and 11 mood-tones to 94 subjects. The results (see Table 1) show that for some mood-tones a single color is significantly related; for others there may be two or more colors.[11]

A real problem in interpreting such research concerns whether people

[9]A. H. Maslow and N. L. Mintz, "Effects of Esthetic Surroundings: I. Initial Effects of Three Esthetic Conditions Upon Perceiving 'Energy' and 'Well-Being' in Faces," *Journal of Psychology* 41 (1956): 247–54. Also: N. L. Mintz, "Effects of Esthetic Surroundings: II. Prolonged and Repeated Experience in a 'Beautiful' and 'Ugly' Room," *Journal of Psychology* 41 (1956): 459–66.

[10]H. Wong and W. Brown, "Effects of Surroundings Upon Mental Work as Measured by Yerkes' Multiple Choice Method," *Journal of Comparative Psychology* 3 (1923): 319–31 and J. M. Bilodeau and H. Schlosberg, "Similarity in Stimulating Conditions as a Variable in Retroactive Inhibition," *Journal of Experimental Psychology* 41 (1959): 199–204.

[11]L. B. Wexner, "The Degree to Which Colors (Hues) Are Associated with Mood-Tones," *Journal of Applied Psychology* 38 (1954): 432–35. Also, see D. C. Murray and H. L. Deabler, "Colors and Mood-Tones," *Journal of Applied Psychology* 41 (1957): 279–83.

Table 1 Colors Associated with Moods

Mood-Tone	*Color*	*Frequency of Times Chosen*
Exciting-Stimulating	Red	61
Secure-Comfortable	Blue	41
Distressed-Disturbed-Upset	Orange	34
Tender-Soothing	Blue	41
Protective-Defending	Red	21
	Brown	17
	Blue	15
	Black	15
	Purple	14
Despondent-Dejected-Unhappy-Melancholy	Black	25
	Brown	25
Calm-Peaceful-Serene	Blue	38
	Green	31
Dignified-Stately	Purple	45
Cheerful-Jovial-Joyful	Yellow	40
Defiant-Contrary-Hostile	Red	23
	Orange	21
	Black	18
Powerful-Strong-Masterful	Black	48

pick colors which are actually associated with particular moods or whether they are responding using learned verbal stereotypes. Another problem with some of the color preference research concerns the lack of association between colors and objects. Pink may be your favorite color, but you may still dislike pink hair. Nevertheless, we cannot ignore the body of educational and design literature which suggests that carefully planned color schemes seem to have some influence on improving scholastic achievement. Obviously, we cannot make any final judgments about the impact of color on human interaction until behavioral studies link differently colored environments with different types of verbal behavior or communication patterns. In short, what configuration of circumstances is necessary for environmental color to affect human interaction to any appreciable degree? Another study tested the effects of rooms of different sizes (150 cubic feet vs. 1600 cubic feet), different shapes (circular vs. rectangular), and different reverberation times (.8–1.0 seconds vs. .2–.3 seconds) upon a speaker's rate and intensity in reading aloud.[12] Generally, the data suggest that rate and intensity of reading were affected by the size of the room and the reverberation time—but not by the shape. Rate seemed to be slower in the larger and less reverberant rooms; vocal intensity was greater in smaller and less reverberant rooms; and intensity consistently increased as the subject read through the twelve phrases provided in the less reverberant rooms.

The architecture and arrangement of objects in various man-made

[12] J. W. Black, "The Effect of Room Characteristics Upon Vocal Intensity and Rate," *Journal of the Acoustical Society of America* 22 (1950): 174–76.

structures can suggest who shall meet whom, when, where, and perhaps for how long. In other words, objects can control actions.

> *The life of domestic animals is, among other things, controlled through the erection of fences, flap doors, or the placement of food and water in particular locations. Although the control of human situations is implemented through verbal and nonverbal actions, manipulation of barriers, openings, and other physical arrangements is rather helpful. Meeting places can be appropriately rigged so as to regulate human traffic and, to a certain extent, the network of communication.*[13]

In some cases, human interaction is inhibited or prohibited by environmental cues. Fences separating yards create obvious barriers—even if they are only waist high.

An experiment conducted in a doctor's office suggests that the presence or absence of a desk may significantly alter the patient's "at ease" state.[14] With the desk separating doctor and patient, only 10% of the patients were perceived "at ease," whereas removal of the desk brought the figure of "at ease" patients up to 55%. There seems to be little doubt that the location of a television set in a room has a definite influence on the positioning of chairs, and, in turn, on the pattern of conversations which occur in that room.

Less obvious barriers also exist. For instance, if you find a delicate objet d'art placed in front of some books in a bookcase you will likely feel hesitant about using the books. In at least one case, a furniture designer has deliberately designed a chair to exert disagreeable pressure on a person's spine when occupied for more than a few minutes. The Larsen Chair was originally designed to keep patrons from becoming too comfortable and remaining in seats which could be occupied by other customers.[15] Hotel owners and airport designers apparently are already aware of the "too comfortable" phenomenon. Thus, seating arrangements are deliberately made uncomfortable for long seating and conversations so patrons will "move along" and perhaps drift into nearby shops where they can spend some of their money. Some environments seem to have an unwritten code which prohibits interaction. The lone men entering, sitting, and leaving "girlie" movies without a word are a case in point.

Other environmental situations seem to facilitate interaction. Homes placed in the middle of a block seem to draw more interpersonal exchanges than those located in other positions on the block. Houses which have adjacent driveways seem to have a built-in structure drawing the neighbors together and inviting communication. Cavan reports that the likelihood of interaction between strangers at a bar varies directly with the distance between them.[16] As a rule, a span of three bar stools is the maximum distance over which patrons will attempt to initiate an encounter. Two men conversing with an empty bar stool between them are likely to remain that way since they would be too close if they sat next to each other. However, if a man is talking to a woman and there is an

[13]Ruesch and Kees, *Nonverbal Communication*, p. 126.

[14]A. G. White, "The Patient Sits Down: A Clinical Note," *Psychosomatic Medicine* 15 (1953): 256–57.

[15]Sommer, *Personal Space*, p. 121.

[16]S. Cavan, *Liquor License* (Chicago: Aldine Publishing Co., 1966).

empty stool between them, he will likely move onto it—to prevent someone else from coming between them. Some recent designs for housing elderly people have taken into consideration the need for social contact. These apartment dwellings have the doors of the apartments on a given floor open into a common entranceway. The probabilities for social exchange are then greatly increased over the situation in which apartment doors are staggered on either side of a long hallway so that no doorways face one another.

The whole question of physical proximity has received much attention from researchers concerned with human interaction. Stouffer comments:

> *Whether one is seeking to explain why persons go to a particular place to get jobs, why they go to trade at a particular store, why they go to a particular neighborhood to commit a crime, or why they marry the particular spouse they choose, the factor of spatial distance is of obvious significance.*[17]

Several studies have confirmed Stouffer's remark. For instance, students tend to develop stronger friendships with students who share their classes, or their dormitory or apartment building, or who sit near them, than with others who are geographically distant. Workers tend to develop closer friendships with those who work close to them. Some research concludes that increased proximity of white persons and blacks will assist in reducing prejudice.[18] Several studies show an inverse relationship between the distance separating potential marriage partners and the number of marriages. For example, in New Haven in 1940, Kennedy reports 76% of the marriages were between persons living within twenty blocks of each other and 35% were between persons living within five blocks of each other.[19] Obviously, proximity allows us to obtain more information about the other person, but some have even suggested that proximity, in and of itself, may facilitate attraction to another person—apart from any information it may provide about the other person. The inescapable conclusion seems to be that as proximity increases, attraction is likely to increase. One might also posit that as attraction increases, proximity will tend to increase.

Perhaps the most famous study of proximity, friendship choice, and interpersonal contact was conducted by Festinger, Schachter, and Back in a housing development for married students.[20] Concern for what the au-

[17]S. A. Stouffer, "Intervening Opportunities: A Theory Relating Mobility and Distance," *American Sociological Review* 5 (1940): 845–67.

[18]M. Deutsch and M. Collins, *Interracial Housing: A Psychological Evaluation of a Social Experiment* (Minneapolis: University of Minnesota Press, 1951). It is interesting that some attack social legislation designed to eliminate segregation because it does not change attitudes but only forces civil obedience. This study, and others, suggest there are times when bringing those of different races together in close proximity will indeed bring about corresponding, positive attitude changes. Caution should be exercised in the generalization of such an idea, however. If the two groups are extremely polarized, proximity may only serve to magnify the hostilities.

[19]R. Kennedy, "Premarital Residential Propinquity," *American Journal of Sociology* 48 (1943): 580–84.

[20]L. Festinger, S. Schachter, and K. Back, *Social Pressures in Informal Groups: A Study of Human Factors in Housing* (New York: Harper & Row, 1950). For another interesting example of how architecture structures interaction, see R. R. Blake, C. C. Rhead, B. Wedge, and J. S. Mouton, "Housing Architecture and Social Interaction," *Sociometry* 19 (1956): 133–39.

thors called "functional distance" led to the uncovering of some data which clearly demonstrated that architects can have a tremendous influence on the social life of residents in these housing projects. Functional distance is determined by the number of contacts that position and design encourage—e.g., which way apartments face, where exits and entranceways are located, location of stairways, mailboxes, etc. Figure 2 shows the basic design of one type of building studied.

The researchers asked the residents of seventeen buildings (with the design of Figure 2) what people they saw most often socially and what friendship choices they made. Among the various findings from this study, the following are noteworthy: (1) There seemed to be a greater number of sociometric choices for those who were physically close to one another —on the same floor, in the same building, etc. It was rare to find a friendship between people separated by more than four or five houses. (2) People living in apartments 1 and 5 gave and received from the upper floor residents more sociometric choices than the people living in any other apartment on the lower floor. (3) Apartments 1 and 6 exchanged more choices than apartments 2 and 7. Similarly, apartments 5 and 10 exchanged more choices than apartments 4 and 9. Although this represents the same physical distance, functional distance differed. (4) Apartment 7 chose 6 more than it chose 8; apartment 9 chose 10 more than it chose 8. This relationship did not hold true for corresponding first floor apartments. (5) Because of the mailboxes, apartment 5 chose more upper level friends —more of those choices being apartments 9 and 10. There are many ways of making friends, but functional distance seems to be highly influential —and functional distance is sometimes the result of architectural design.

The issue of proximity or distance, and its relation to interpersonal communication, brings us to the closely related area of the role of space in man's behavior.

THE SPACE AROUND US

The architecture and objects in our environment which we have discussed so far are defined by Hall as either fixed-feature space or semifixed-feature space.[21] *Fixed-feature* is space organized by unmoving boundaries (rooms of houses) while the term *semifixed feature* refers to the arrangement of moveable objects such as tables or chairs. Hall also defines a third category

[21] E. T. Hall, *The Hidden Dimension* (Garden City, N.Y.: Doubleday, 1966).

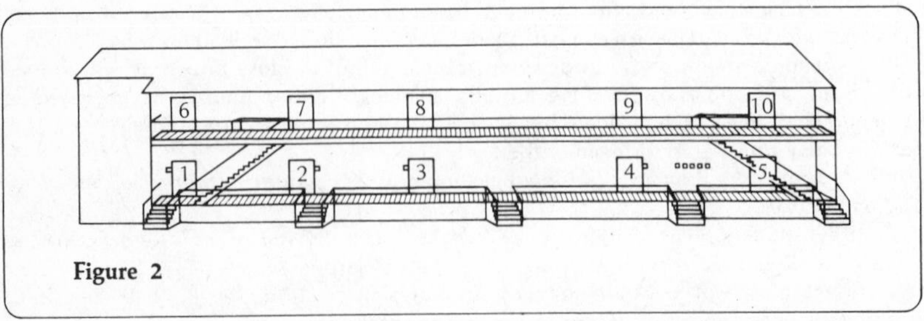

Figure 2

—informal space. Informal space is carried with each individual and expands and contracts under varying circumstances—depending on the type of encounter, the relationship of the communicating persons, their personalities, and many other factors. Hall further classified informal space into four subcategories: intimate, casual-personal, social-consultative, and public. According to Hall, intimate distances range from actual physical contact to about eighteen inches; casual-personal extends from one and a half feet to four feet; social-consultative (for impersonal business) ranges from four to twelve feet; public distance covers the area from twelve feet to the limits of visibility or hearing. Hall is quick to note that these distances are based on his observations of a particular sample of adults from business and professional occupations, primarily middle class, and native to the northeastern U.S., and that generalizations to various ethnic and racial groups in this country should be made with considerable caution. One of the premises upon which Hall's classification system is based is that it is the nature of animals, including man, to exhibit a behavior called territoriality. An understanding of the concept of territoriality is critical for understanding man's spatial behavior.

The Concept of Territoriality

The term "territoriality" has been used for years in the study of animal and fowl behavior. Generally, it has come to mean behavior characterized by identification with an area in such a way as to indicate ownership and defense of this territory against those who may "invade" it. There are many different kinds of territorial behavior, and frequently these behaviors perform useful functions for a given species. For instance, territorial behaviors may help coordinate activities, regulate density, insure propagation of the species, provide places to hide, hold the group together, provide staging areas for courtship, for nesting, or for feeding.

Most behavioral scientists agree that territoriality exists in human behavior, too, and that it is frequently an extremely important variable in a particular interpersonal transaction. However, many would not agree with Ardrey who feels it is a genetically inherited trait somehow related to man's innate aggressiveness.[22] Some territorial behaviors around one's home are particularly strong—"dad's" chair, or "mom's" kitchen, or "Billy's" stereo, or "Barbara's" phone. Gamblers sometimes determine odds on sporting events based not on the skill of the players, but on where the game is being played. If it is being played on one of the teams' home territory—where players are familiar with exactly how many steps it takes to perform a particular action, or how solid the turf is in a particular area, or how high the mound is, or a multitude of other peculiar characteristics of the home territory—the odds favor the home team if all other factors are relatively equal.

While territorial behavior seems to be a standard part of our everyday contact with other people, it is also very much in evidence when

[22]R. Ardrey, *The Territorial Imperative* (New York: Atheneum, 1966). For an excellent critique of Ardrey's position, see M. F. Ashley Montagu, ed., *Man and Aggression* (New York: Oxford University Press, 1968).

social contact is denied. Altman and Haythorn analyzed the territorial behavior of socially isolated and nonisolated pairs.[23] For ten days, two individuals lived in a small room with no outside contact while a matched group received outside contacts. The men in the isolated group showed a gradual increase in territorial behavior and a general pattern of social withdrawal. They desired more time alone. Their territorial behavior first evidenced itself with fixed objects (areas of the room) and personal objects (beds). Later the men began to lay claim to more mobile and less personal objects. Incompatibility of the two men living together with respect to characteristics such as dominance and affiliation resulted in high territoriality while incompatibility with respect to characteristics such as achievement and dogmatism did not have strong territorial outcomes.

Territoriality: Invasion and Defense

Instructions to police interrogators sometimes suggest sitting close to the suspect—not allowing a desk to intervene and provide any protection or comfort. This theory of interrogation assumes that invasion of the suspect's personal territory (with no chance for defense) will give the officer a psychological advantage. What happens when somebody invades "your" territory? For instance, how do you feel when the car behind you is "tail-gating"? How do you feel when you have to stand in a crowded theater lobby or bus? How do you feel when somebody sits in "your" seat? What do you do? Some researchers have asked similar questions, and their answers will help us to further understand how man uses the space around him.

Generally, an invasion of one's territory meets with defensive maneuvers of some type. Sometimes the defense is more aggressive than at other times—depending on the type of invasion, attachment to the territory, and the persons involved. Naturally, inanimate objects and persons who are not considered threatening do not provoke the defense that a stranger might. Some familiar methods for staking out territories and defending them include: (1) using "markers" such as umbrellas, books, coats, or magazines to identify "your" spatial area—in places which have a relatively low density, "markers" seem to be very effective over long periods of time; (2) tenure or simply staying in a certain place for long periods of time; and (3) asking a neighbor to help defend your territory—e.g., "Would you hold my seat while I go get some popcorn?" In an attempt to identify explicit kinds of territorial defense, Russo conducted a two-year study which consisted of invading the territory of female college students seated in a college library.[24] The study compared the responses of those invaded and a similar group which was not invaded. Several different invasion techniques were used—sitting next to subjects, across from them, etc. The quickest departure or flight was triggered when the researcher sat next to a subject and moved her chair closer (approximately one foot). After 30 minutes, about 70% of those approached at this distance moved. From

[23] I. Altman and W. W. Haythorn, "The Ecology of Isolated Groups," *Behavioral Science* 12 (1967): 169–82.

[24] Sommer, *Personal Space*, p. 35, 46–48, 64.

this study, a whole vocabulary of defense was developed. For instance, there were defensive and offensive displays which included the use of position, posture, and gesture. Position refers to location in the room; a newcomer to the room will interpret the situation differently if you have selected a corner position rather than a position in the middle of the room. Posture refers to such things as whether a person has his materials spread out "like he owned the place" or whether they are tightly organized. Gestures can be used to indicate receptivity or rejection of communication. Finally, although under some circumstances verbal defense is less apt to occur, verbal defenses such as profanity can be effectively used. Russo's work is summarized by Sommer:

> *There were wide individual differences in the ways victims reacted—there is no single reaction to someone's sitting too close; there are defensive gestures, shifts in posture, and attempts to move away. If these fail or are ignored by the invader, or he shifts position too, the victim eventually takes to flight. . . . There was a dearth of direct verbal responses to the invasions. . . . Only one of the eighty students asked the invader to move over.*[25]

Increasing the density of a species will also result in territorial violations. What happens when the population becomes so dense that one cannot exercise usual territorial behavior? The recent attention given to human overpopulation makes this a particularly important concern. First, let us look at some interesting examples of animal behavior under such conditions. For years, scientists were intrigued by the large scale suicides of lemmings, rabbits, and rats. Their interest was increased by the fact that at the time of the suicides, there seemed to be plenty of food, predators were not in evidence, and infection was not present. An ethnologist who had training in medical pathology hypothesized that such suicides were triggered by an endocrine reaction in the animals which resulted from stress built up during an increase of population.[26] This hypothesis was confirmed in a study of the deer population on James Island—an island one mile off the coast of Maryland in the Chesapeake Bay. Careful histological studies over a period of years showed that the deer on James Island died from overactive adrenal glands—resulting from stress. The adrenal glands play an important part in the regulation of growth, reproduction, and the level of the body's defenses. Thus, overpopulation caused death—not by starvation, infection or aggression from others—but by a physiological reaction to the stress created.

Calhoun's experiments go even further to suggest peculiar modes of behavior under conditions of overpopulation.[27] Calhoun noted that with plenty of food and no danger from predators, Norway rats in a quarter-acre outdoor pen stabilized their population at about 150. His observations, covering 28 months, indicated that spatial relationships were extremely important. He then designed an experiment in which he could maintain a

[25] *Ibid.*, pp. 35–36.

[26] J. J. Christian and D. E. Davis, "Social and Endocrine Factors Are Integrated in the Regulation of Mammalian Populations," *Science* 146 (1964): 1550–60.

[27] J. B. Calhoun, "Population Density and Social Pathology," *Scientific American* 206 (1962): 139–48.

stressful situation through overpopulation while three generations of rats were reared. He labeled this experiment a "behavioral sink"—an area or receptacle where most of the rats exhibited gross distortions of behavior. Some of Calhoun's observations are worth noting: (1) Some rats withdrew from social and sexual intercourse completely; others began to mount anything in sight; courtship patterns were totally disrupted and females were frequently pursued by several males; (2) nest building patterns—ordinarily neat—became sloppy or nonexistent; (3) litters of young rats became mixed; newborn and young rats were stepped on or eaten by invading hyperactive males; (4) unable to establish spatial territories, the dominant males would fight over positions near the eating bins; "classes" of rats shared territories and exhibited similar behaviors; the hyperactive males violated all territorial rights by running around in packs—disregarding any boundaries except those backed by force; (5) pregnant rats frequently had miscarriages; disorders of the sex organs were numerous; only one-fourth of the 558 newborns in the sink survived to be weaned; (6) aggressive behavior increased significantly.

Obviously such detailed and controlled studies have not been conducted with human subjects, but some consistencies were uncovered in a study of hospitalized children.[28] These children, brain damaged, autistic, and normal, were observed in a playroom in which the density was varied from less than six to more than 12. All groups showed deterioration of behavior, but normal children were least affected. As a function of group density, significant changes were found in three categories of behavior: aggressive/destructive, social, and boundary (withdrawal to the boundaries of the room). Autistic children usually reacted by withdrawing, while brain damaged and normal children reacted with increased aggressive/destructive behavior.

At this point it would be easy to conclude that density or crowding has an overwhelmingly negative effect on human behavior. Recent research by Freedman and his colleagues, however, should make us more cautious about generalizing from these studies of animal behavior.[29] Freedman observed groups of people from a wide range of age and ethnic backgrounds in crowded and uncrowded rooms during four one-hour periods of time. Certainly four one-hour periods cannot be compared to everyday living conditions, but the degree of crowding was also much greater than would normally occur. The results of Freedman's studies show density has apparently no effects on the performance of simple tasks; it does, however, seem to have profound effects on interpersonal behavior in groups of the same sex. For instance, men had generally negative reactions to the crowded situation. They liked other members less, considered them less friendly, gave more severe sentences to defendants in taped jury trials, and thought other members in the crowded rooms would make poor jury members. In short, they found the experience less pleasant, became more suspicious and

[28]C. Hutt and M. J. Vaizey, "Differential Effects of Group Density on Social Behavior," *Nature* 209 (1966): 1371–72.

[29]J. L. Freedman, "The Crowd: Maybe Not So Madding After All," *Psychology Today* 4 (1971): 58–61, 86.

combative. Women, on the other hand, were more lenient in their sentencing of defendants in the small room, found the experience more pleasant, other members more likable, friendlier, and better jury members. When men and women were mixed there seemed to be no negative effects on interpersonal behavior due to crowding. This research certainly suggests a note of caution in attributing only negative effects to crowded situations. In fact, Freedman and his associates hypothesize that it is not the density which causes negative reactions, but the number of persons who are forced to interact with one another which is the crucial factor producing these effects. The specification of how these two factors interact seems to be the next logical step for future research in this area.

Conversational Distance

We now shift our attention from spatial relationships in overcrowded conditions to those involved in a two-person conversation. You have probably had the experience (perhaps not conscious) of backing up or moving forward when speaking to another person. Sometimes this movement is caused by a need to find a comfortable conversational distance. In different situations, when discussing different topics, these "comfortable" distances vary. Is there any consistency to the distances chosen? Is there a specific distance most people select when talking to others? What factors modify the distances we choose?

Sommer, in an effort to answer some of these questions, studied people who were brought into a room and told to discuss various "impersonal" topics.[30] The two sofas in this room were placed at various distances and subjects were observed to see whether they sat opposite or beside each other. It was hypothesized that when they began to sit side by side, it would mean the conversational distance was too far to sit opposite one another on the two couches. From one to three feet, the subjects sat on different couches facing one another. After three and a half feet, people sat side by side. If one measures "nose to nose," this would make the participants 5½ feet apart when they started to sit side by side. In a follow-up study, Sommer used chairs and, hence, was able to vary side by side distance as well as distance across. Here he found that people chose to sit across from one another until the across distance exceeded the side by side distance—then they sat side by side. How generalizable are these findings? A critical look at this study immediately leads us to question what other variables may affect the distance relationship. For instance, this study was conducted with people who knew each other slightly, who were discussing "impersonal" topics, and who were in a large lounge. How would other factors affect the distance relationship? Argyle and Dean have theorized that distance is based on the balance of approach and avoidance forces.[31] What are some of these forces?

[30]R. Sommer, "Leadership and Group Geography," *Sociometry* 24 (1961): 99–110. Also: R. Sommer, "The Distance for Comfortable Conversation: A Further Study," *Sociometry* 25 (1962): 111–16.

[31]M. Argyle and J. Dean, "Eye Contact, Distance and Affiliation," *Sociometry* 28 (1956): 289–304.

1. Demographic Characteristics. Willis studied standing speaking distance of 775 people in a variety of contexts and recorded speaking distance at the beginning of the interaction.[32] Among his conclusions were the following: (1) speakers stood closer to women than men, (2) peers stood closer than did persons older than the listener, and (3) Caucasians stood closer to each other when speaking than did blacks, but Caucasians speaking to blacks kept a much greater distance. Robert Forston, however, recently conducted a study at Drake University in which he found no sex or race differences in conversational distance for seated triads. Distance measures were taken after about five minutes of discussion. There were no significant differences in the distances chosen by groups composed of all one race as compared to groups composed of black and white students. Having a member of a racial minority in one of these groups of three did not, apparently, have much impact on distance relationships.

2. Characteristics of the Interpersonal Relationship. Willis also found that strangers seemed to begin conversations further away than did acquaintances; women stood closer to close friends than did males, but further away from "just friends" (the author suggests this may be due to a more cautious approach used in making friends); and parents were found to be as distant as strangers! The range of distances measured in Willis' study was from 17.75 inches (close friends speaking to women) to 28 inches (Caucasian-black). Little, in a cross-cultural study, also found friends perceived as interacting closer together than acquaintances, and acquaintances closer than strangers.[33]

Also, in this culture status is associated with greater space or distance. Generally those with higher status have more and better space and greater freedom to move about. Theodore White, in *Making of the President 1960*, tells of an instance in which John Kennedy's status was emphasized by the distance his fellow campaign workers maintained on a particular occasion —said to be about 30 feet. Hall recounts a problem of status and distance in the military:

> *The Army, in its need to get technical about matters that are usually handled informally, made a mistake in the regulations on distance required for reporting to a superior officer. . . . Instructions for reporting to a superior officer were that the junior officer was to proceed up to a point three paces in front of the officer's desk, stop, salute, and state his name, his rank, and his business. . . The normal speaking distance for business matters, where impersonality is involved at the beginning of the conversation, is five and a half to eight feet. The distance required by the Army regulations borders on the edge of what we would call "far." It evokes an automatic response to shout. This detracts from the respect which is supposed to be shown to the superior officer. There are, of course, many subjects which it is almost impossible to talk about at this distance. . . .*[34]

Burns reports an experiment in which subjects consistently identified

[32]F. N. Willis, "Initial Speaking Distance as a Function of the Speaker's Relationship," *Psychonomic Science* 5 (1966): 221–22.

[33]K. B. Little, "Cultural Variations in Social Schemata," *Journal of Personality and Social Psychology* 10 (1968): 5.

[34]Hall, *The Silent Language*, p. 163.

a man's status according to spatial relationships.[35] Short films depicted a man at a desk sorting through a card index. He stopped to answer the phone. Then the film switched to another man who stopped, knocked on the office door, entered, and approached the man seated at the desk. The second man pulled out some papers, and the two men discussed them. Two actors switched roles throughout the films. Audiences were asked to rate the relative status of the two men. The caller was consistently rated subordinate if he stopped just inside the door and conversed from that distance with the man at the desk. Time between the knock and the man at the desk rising was also related to status—the longer it took the man to respond to the knock, the higher his status was judged. Mehrabian cites two studies which suggest "that the distance between two communicators is positively correlated with their status discrepancy."[36]

3. Setting for the Interaction. Obviously the social setting makes a great deal of difference in how far we stand from others in conversation. A crowded cocktail party demands a different distance than a comfortable evening in the living room while reading the paper. Some authors have hypothesized that as room size increases, people tend to sit closer together. Little had his subjects arrange actresses in certain settings to determine the interpersonal distances which were perceived as necessary in various situations.[37] Each student was a director and was to place the interactants in a street corner setting, an office waiting room, the lobby of a public building, and a campus location. The maximum placement distance was in the office while the closest placement was in the street scene.

4. Topic or Subject Matter Under Discussion. Earlier we noted that Sommer, in his efforts to examine the limits of conversational distance, tried to use "impersonal" topics—topics which would not obviously influence the distances chosen. Leipold's work demonstrates how anticipated treatment of the same general topic can influence conversational distance.[38] Students entered a room and were given either stress ("Your grade is poor, and you have not done your best"), praise ("You are doing very well and Mr. Leipold wants to talk with you further"), or neutral ("Mr. Leipold is interested in your feelings about the introductory course") comments. Students in the stress condition sat furthest from the experimenter and those given praise sat closest. Albert and Dabbs[39] found that a persuasive message on overpopulation had more influence on subjects at a distance of 14 to 15 feet than it had at two other distances tested—2 to 3 feet and 5 to 6 feet. Little asked subjects in several different countries to position

[35] T. Burns, "Nonverbal Communication," *Discovery* (October 1964): 31–35.

[36] A. Mehrabian, "Significance of Posture and Position in the Communication of Attitude and Status Relationships," *Psychological Bulletin* 71 (1969): 363.

[37] K. B. Little, "Personal Space," *Journal of Experimental Social Psychology* 1 (1965): 237–47.

[38] W. E. Leipold, "Psychological Distance in a Dyadic Interview" (Ph.D. diss., University of North Dakota, 1963).

[39] S. Albert and J. M. Dabbs, "Physical Distance and Persuasion," *Journal of Personality and Social Psychology* 15 (1970): 265–70.

dolls relative to one another for a variety of social situations and for pleasant, neutral, and unpleasant topics.[40] Pleasant topics clearly produced the closest placement of the figures, but neutral and unpleasant topic situations were not significantly different.

5. *Physical Characteristics.* A series of studies conducted by Kleck show that persons interacting with stigmatized individuals (a left leg amputation was simulated with a special wheel chair) choose greater initial speaking distances than with nonstigmatized or "normal" persons, but that this distance decreases as the length of the interaction increases.[41] Perceived epileptics elicited similar reactions.

6. *Attitudinal and Personality Characteristics.* Kleck's work also included situations in which the subject was told the other person was "warm and friendly" or "unfriendly." Not surprisingly, the subjects chose greater distances when interacting with a person perceived to be "unfriendly." Similarly, when told to enter into conversation with another person and to behave in a "friendly" way, subjects chose closer distances than when told to "let him know you aren't friendly." This "friendly-unfriendly" relationship to distance even seems to manifest itself with preschool children.[42] The number of unfriendly acts was directly related to the distance maintained by the recipient of such acts during free play situations. The distance could be reduced, however, by putting a prized toy near the aggressive child. An unpublished study mentioned by Patterson reveals we may make a whole host of interpersonal judgments about another person based on distance.[43] Subjects were told to interview others and secretly rate them on traits of friendliness, aggressiveness, dominance, extroversion, and intelligence. The interviewees were actually confederates who approached the interviewers at different distances and gave standard answers to the questions asked. The mean ratings for all the traits at four different distances were tabulated and revealed that the most distant position yielded significantly lower (less favorable) ratings. Mehrabian concluded his review of attitude-distance research by saying:

> *. . . The findings from a large number of studies corroborate one another and indicate that communicator-addressee distance is correlated with the degree of negative attitude communicated to and inferred by the addressee. In addition, studies carried out by sociologists and anthropologists indicate that distances which are too close, that is, inappropriate for a given interpersonal situation, can elicit negative attitudes when the communicator-addressee relationship is not an intimate one.*[44]

When we seek to win the approval of another person, there will also be a reduction in conversational distance as compared to instances when

[40]Little, "Cultural Variations in Social Schemata."

[41]R. Kleck, "Physical Stigma and Task Oriented Interaction," *Human Relations* 22 (1969): 51–60.

[42]M. G. King, "Interpersonal Relations in Preschool Children and Average Approach Distance," *Journal of Genetic Psychology* 108 (1966): 109–16.

[43]M. Patterson, "Spatial Factors in Social Interaction," *Human Relations* 21 (1968): 351–61.

[44]Mehrabian, "Significance of Posture and Position," p. 363.

we are deliberately trying to avoid approval. Rosenfeld's female subjects seeking approval maintained a mean distance of 57 inches; those trying to avoid approval averaged 94 inches. When the distance was held constant at five feet, approval seekers compensated by smiling more and engaging in gestural activity.[45]

Much has been written about the influence of introversion and extroversion on spatial relationships. It is difficult to draw any firm conclusions, however. Some find introverts tend to stand further away than extroverts—particularly in intimate situations. Some find that extroverts allow others to approach them more closely. Others find no differences in the distances which persons with these personality characteristics maintain when approaching others.

7. *Behavioral Factors.* There is some evidence that the direction from which a person approaches has something to do with comfort. Galvanic skin responses, thought by many to be an index of emotionality, were greatest when a person was approached frontally, next for approaches from the side, and least for approaches from the rear.[46] In other studies, by Argyle and Dean, it was found that if subjects approached photographs with intending to get close enough to "see well," they would stand closer to photographs of faces with eyes closed than to those with eyes open.[47]

Seating Behavior and Spatial Arrangements in Small Groups

In addition to studying man's spatial behavior in overcrowded situations and in conversation, some researchers have examined such questions in the context of the small group—particularly with regard to seating patterns. This work has come to be known as small group ecology. Results of these studies show that our seating behavior is not generally accidental or random. There are explanations for much of our seating behavior—whether we are fully conscious of them or not. The particular position we choose in relation to the other person or persons varies with the task at hand, the degree of relationship between the interactants, the personalities of the two parties, and the amount and kind of available space. Summaries of the findings about seating behavior and spatial positioning can be listed under the categories of leadership, dominance, task, sex and acquaintance, motivation, and introversion-extroversion.

1. *Leadership.* It seems to be a cultural norm that leaders are expected to be found at the head or end of the table. At a family gathering, we generally find the "head" of the household sitting at the "head" of the table. Elected group leaders generally put themselves in the head positions at

[45]H. Rosenfeld, "Effect of Approval-Seeking Induction on Interpersonal Proximity," *Psychological Reports* 17 (1965): 120–22. Also: H. Rosenfeld, "Instrumental and Affiliative Functions of Facial and Gestural Expressions," *Journal of Personality and Social Psychology* 4 (1966): 65–72.

[46]G. McBride, M. G. King, and J. W. James, "Social Proximity Effects on GSR in Adult Humans," *Journal of Psychology* 61 (1965): 153–57.

[47]Argyle and Dean, "Eye Contact, Distance and Affiliation."

rectangular tables, and the other group members try to position themselves so they can see the leader. Strodtbeck and Hook set up some experimental jury deliberations which revealed that a man sitting at the head position was chosen significantly more often as the leader—particularly if he was perceived as a person from a high economic class.[48] If the choice was between two people at each end, the one perceived as of higher economic status was chosen.

2. Dominance. The end positions also seem to carry with them a status or dominance factor. Russo found that people rating various seating arrangements on an "equality" dimension stated that if one person was at the head and one on the side, this was a more unequal situation in terms of status than if they were side by side or both on the ends.[49] In an analysis of talking frequency in small groups, Hare and Bales noted people in positions 1, 3, and 5 (at left) were frequent talkers.[50] Subsequent studies

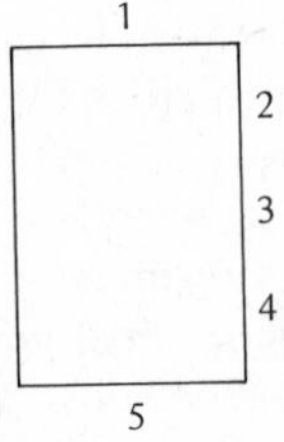

revealed that these people were likely to be dominant personalities, while those who avoided the central or focal positions (by choosing seats 2 and 4) were more anxious and actually stated they wanted to stay out of the discussion. While further study is necessary, some preliminary work by students at the University of Wisconsin-Milwaukee suggests that deliberately placing "nondominant" persons in focal positions and dominant persons in nonfocal positions will not radically change the frequency of their communications. In groups composed only of nondominant individuals, the results may be much different. Positions 1, 3, and 5 were also

[48] F. Strodtbeck and L. Hook, "The Social Dimensions of a Twelve Man Jury Table," *Sociometry* 24 (1961): 297–415.

[49] N. Russo, "Connotation of Seating Arrangement," *Cornell Journal of Social Relations* 2 (1967): 37–44.

[50] A. Hare and R. Bales, "Seating Position and Small Group Interaction," *Sociometry* 26 (1963): 480–86.

considered to be positions of leadership, but leadership of a different type—depending on the position. The two end positions (1 and 5) attracted the task oriented leader, while the middle position was determined to be for more of a socio-emotional leader—one concerned about group relationships, getting everyone to participate, etc.

3. Task. Sommer's observations of seating behavior in student cafeterias and libraries led him to study how students would sit in different task situations.[51] The same study was conducted by Cook in the United Kingdom (UK) with Oxford University students and a sample of nonstudents—civil servants, schoolteachers, and secretaries.[52] In each case, persons were asked to imagine themselves sitting at a table with a friend of the same sex in each of the following four situations:

Conversation: *Sitting and chatting for a few minutes before class. ("Before work" for nonstudents).*
Cooperation: *Sitting and studying together for the same exam. ("Sitting doing a crossword or the like together" for nonstudents).*
Co-action: *Sitting studying for different exams. ("Sitting at the same table reading" for nonstudents).*
Competition: *Competing in order to see who will be the first to solve a series of puzzles.*

Two types of tables were shown to each subject. One table was round and one was rectangular. Each had six chairs. The results of these two studies are presented in Table 2 for rectangular tables and Table 3 for circular tables.

There are many similarities between the different groups in terms of order of preference, but there are also some differences worth noting. For instance, it is interesting that the nonuniversity sample differs less from the U.S. student sample than does the Oxford University group. Conversations before class (or work) primarily involved corner or "short" opposite seating at rectangular tables and side by side seating at round tables. Oxford students seemed to be more favorable toward distant seating for conversation than other groups, but the value of closeness and visibility for this task seems to prevail. Cooperation seems to elicit a preponderance of side by side choices from everyone except the Oxford group. The author suggests that since Oxford students are encouraged to do most of their work alone, they may not have realized the question meant cooperating with another person. Even more doubt is cast on the validity of the Oxford responses to this question since their responses to the co-action question were similar. Co-action, studying for different exams or reading at the same table as another, necessitated plenty of room between the partici-

[51]R. Sommer, "Further Studies of Small Group Ecology," *Sociometry* 28 (1965): 337–48.

[52]M. Cook, "Experiments on Orientation and Proxemics," *Human Relations* 23 (1970): 61–76.

Table 2 Seating Preferences at Rectangular Tables

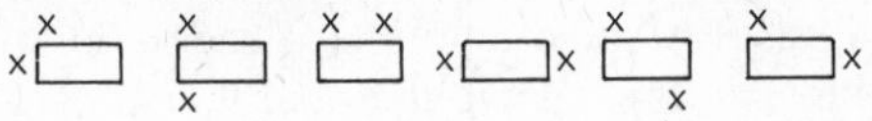

Conversation						
U.S. sample (151 responses)	42%	46%	11%	0%	1%	0%
U.K. (univ.) sample (102 responses)	51	21	15	0	6	7
U.K. (nonuniv.) sample (42 responses)	42	42	9	2	5	0
Cooperation						
U.S. sample	19	25	51	0	5	0
U.K. (univ.) sample	11	11	23	20	22	13
U.K. (nonuniv.) sample	40	2	50	5	2	0
Co-action						
U.S. sample	3	3	7	13	43	33
U.K. (univ.) sample	9	8	10	31	28	14
U.K. (nonuniv.) sample	12	14	12	19	31	12
Competition						
U.S. sample	7	41	8	18	20	5
U.K. (univ.) sample	7	10	10	50	16	7
U.K. (nonuniv.) sample	4	13	3	53	20	7

pants and the most distant seating positions were generally selected. The slightly different instructions for the nonuniversity sample may explain the greater variety of responses to the co-action question. Most persons wanted to compete in an opposite seating arrangement. However, the U.S. students wanted to establish a closer opposite relationship. Apparently this would afford them an opportunity not only to see how the other person is progressing, but would also allow them to use various gestures, body movements, and eye contact to "upset" their opponents. The more distant opposite position chosen by the United Kingdom samples would, on the other hand, prevent "spying."

In an attempt to replicate his work on seating arrangements and tasks with children, Sommer found that a widely used arrangement in adult groups, opposite seating, was infrequently used by children. The thirty-inch distance across the table was apparently a major factor. A related line of inquiry involved an attempt to determine the impact of discussion topics on seating arrangements. College women discussed topics ranging from very personal to very impersonal. The apparent lack of impact caused Sommer to conclude:

> *It seems apparent that it is the nature of the relationship between the individuals rather than the topic itself that characterizes a discussion as personal or impersonal. Two lovers discussing the weather can have an intimate conversation, but a zoology professor discussing sex in a lecture hall con-*

Table 3 Seating Preferences at Round Tables

	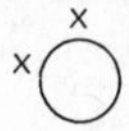 (adjacent, at corner)	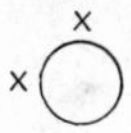 (adjacent, side by side)	 (opposite)
Conversation			
U.S. sample (116 responses)	63%	17%	20%
U.K. (univ.) sample (102 responses)	58	37	5
U.K. (nonuniv.) sample (42 responses)	58	27	15
Cooperation			
U.S. sample	83	7	10
U.K. (univ.) sample	25	31	44
U.K. (nonuniv.) sample	97	0	3
Co-action			
U.S. sample	13	36	51
U.K. (univ.) sample	16	34	50
U.K. (nonuniv.) sample	24	26	50
Competition			
U.S. sample	2	25	63
U.K. (univ.) sample	15	22	63
U.K. (nonuniv.) sample	9	21	70

taining 300 students would be having an impersonal session regardless of topic.[53]

4. *Sex and Acquaintance.* As the previous quote suggests, the nature of the relationship may make a difference in spatial orientation and, hence, in seating selection. Neither Sommer nor Cook found any differences between the sexes with respect to seat choices for different tasks; however, their studies were only concerned with the sex of the chooser. Perhaps

[53] Sommer, *Personal Space*, p. 65.

Table 4 Seating Preferences for a Bar or "Public House"

	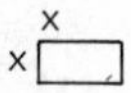 (corner)	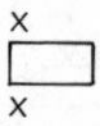 (opposite)	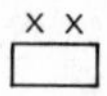 (side by side)	*Other*
Same sex friend	70%	25%	45%	2%
Casual friend of opposite sex	63	37	29	7
Intimate friend	43	11	82	4

Table 5 Seating Preferences for a Restaurant

	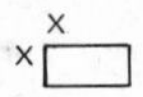	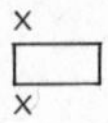	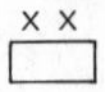	*Other*
Same sex friend	30%	73%	34%	4%
Casual friend of opposite sex	43	64	28	4
Intimate friend	40	53	46	2

cross-sex pairs choose differently. You may remember the previous studies were also concerned only with a "casual friend"; perhaps the degree of acquaintance will influence choices—e.g., intimate friends may move closer. Such questions prompted Cook to conduct another questionnaire study and to obtain some actual observational data of persons interacting in a restaurant and several bars.[54] Subjects in the questionnaire study were asked to select seating arrangements when: (1) sitting with a casual friend of the same sex; (2) sitting with a casual friend of the opposite sex; and (3) sitting with a boy or girl friend. The results for the "public house" or bar are found in Table 4 and results for the restaurant are found in Table 5.

The predominant seating pattern, as stated by questionnaire respondents using a bar as a referent, was corner seating for same-sexed friend and casual friends of the opposite sex. Intimate friends appear to desire side by side seating, however. In a restaurant, all variations of sex and acquaintance seem to select opposite seating—with more side by side seating occurring between intimate friends. There may be some very practical reasons for opposite seating in restaurants. For instance, others won't have to sit opposite you which might create some uncomfortable situations with respect to eye contact and overheard conversation. In addition, you won't poke the other person with your elbow while eating. The actual observations of seating in a restaurant, presented in Table 6, seem to validate the

[54]Cook, "Experiments on Orientation and Proxemics."

Table 6 Observations of Seating Behavior in a Restaurant

	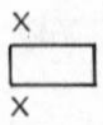		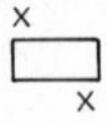
Two males	6%	0%	0%
Two females	6	0	1
Male with female	36	7	1
Total	48	7	2

questionnaire responses. Most people do select opposite seating in restaurants. However, the observations of people sitting in bars do not agree with the questionnaire study of seating preferences in bars. (See Table 7.) Although questionnaire preferences favored corner seating, actual observations show a marked preference for side by side seating. Cook suggests this may have been due to the fact that the bars were equipped with many seats located against the wall. Supposedly this allowed persons to sit side by side, not have their back to anyone, and have a good view of the other patrons. Thus, paper and pencil preferences were overruled by environmental factors. From this study we must conclude that sex and acquaintance with the other person do have an effect on one's actual and preferred seating positions.

5. *Motivation.* Earlier we mentioned the idea that one may regulate his intimacy with another through either increasing eye contact or decreasing distance. Of course you may do both. What we did not know prior to another study by Cook was what conditions prompt the use of distance and what conditions prompt the use of eye contact.[55] Again respondents made seating selections based on different types (positive and negative) and different levels (high, medium, and low) of motivation. For example, high-positive motivation was "sitting with your boy or girl friend" and low-negative motivation was "sitting with someone you do not like very

[55] *Ibid.*

Table 7 Observations of Seating Behavior in Three Bars

	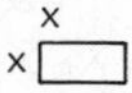 Corner (× at side and end)	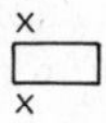 Opposite (× across table)	Side by side (× ×)
Bar A			
Two males	7%	8%	13%
Male with female	6	4	21
Total	13	12	34
Bar B			
Two males	1	0	9
Male with female	4	3	20
Total	5	3	29
Bar C			
Two males	0	11	7
Male with female	1	4	10
Total	1	15	17
Overall			
Two males	8	19	29
Male with female	11	11	51
Total	19	30	80

much and do not wish to talk to." He found that as motivation increased, persons wanted to sit closer or to have more eye contact; and when the motivation was affiliative the choice was to sit closer; when the motivation was competitive, the choice was one which would allow more eye contact. It seems, then, that the choice of eye contact or proximity depends on the motives of the interacting pair. It is quite permissible to sit close to another when there is high affiliative motivation; but when there are high levels of nonaffiliative motivation, such proximity is not as permissible, so eye contact is used.

6. *Introversion-Extroversion.* We have already discussed the possible influence of introversion and extroversion on conversational distance. Cook finds some relation between this personality variable and seating preference.[56] Extroverts chose to sit opposite (either across the table or down the length of it) and disregard positions which would put them at an angle. Many extroverts also chose positions which would put them in close physical proximity to the other person. Introverts generally chose positions which would keep them more at a distance, visually and physically.

Space and Culture

As a parting note, we should remind the reader that almost all the data collected on space relationships presented thus far has generally been obtained with white, middle class college students or adults. Volumes of folklore and isolated personal observations suggest that spatial relationships in other cultures with different needs and norms may produce very different distances for interacting. At present, however, the empirical evidence seems to be mixed. Watson and Graves found substantial and consistent differences between pairs of Arab students and pairs of American students in a conversational setting.[57] These differences included such things as (1) Arabs confronted one another more directly; (2) Arabs moved closer together; (3) Arabs used more touch behavior; and (4) Arabs were apt to look each other squarely in the eye—an event which occurred less frequently with American student pairs. They also found a tendency toward subcultural homogeneity among Arabs from four different nations and among Americans from four regions of the country. These results are tempered by the statistical tests used to measure the differences and by the small number of pairs used—16 pairs of subjects for each culture. In a much more extensive treatment of cross-cultural proxemics, Watson reports numerous observations on individuals representing "contact" and "noncontact" cultures.[58] *Contact* refers to interactants who face one another more directly, interact closer to one another, touch one another more, look one another in the eye more, and speak in a louder voice. Contact groups in Watson's study were Arabs, Latin Americans, and South-

[56]*Ibid.*

[57]O. M. Watson and T. D. Graves, "Quantitative Research in Proxemic Behavior," *American Anthropologist* 68 (1966): 971–85.

[58]O. M. Watson, *Proxemic Behavior: A Cross-Cultural Study* (The Hague: Mouton, 1970).

ern Europeans. Noncontact groups were Asians, Indians and Pakistanis, Northern Europeans, and Americans. In addition, two other studies provide little evidence of cross-national differences. Forston and Larson found that Latin American students did not necessarily exhibit the traditional space differences of sitting closer to one another than North Americans—in fact, their tendency was to sit further apart![59] Sommer found that when he asked students from five different countries to rankorder various seating arrangements according to degree of intimacy, there was agreement on the rank-order by all subjects.[60] Side by side seating was ranked most intimate; corner seating next; then face to face or opposite; followed by various distance arrangements. In an effort to study spatial differences in various ethnic and subcultural groups in the United States, Jones found no evidence of differences among these groups.[61] Obviously there is much work to be done in this area. The theoretical schema and observational data presented by Hall in his two books, *The Silent Language and The Hidden Dimension*, provide an excellent basis from which such work can begin.

SUMMARY

The environment in which people communicate frequently contributes to the overall outcome of their encounters. Where we live, the objects which surround us, the architecture, size and visual-esthetic dimensions of the situation, furniture arrangement, and possibly even the climate, operate in subtle ways to influence our communicative behavior. Even the space between two people may have its impact on the relationship. Naturally, as man's knowledge of these factors increases, he may deliberately use them to help him obtain the response he desires. In fact, this is the very point of a recent book by B. F. Skinner, perhaps the most renowned psychologist of this century.[62] Skinner believes we are a product of our environment and that if we want to change behavior we need only control the environment in which people interact. In recent years we have accumulated considerable information on man's spatial relationships. We know, for instance, that mere proximity is frequently an important factor in determining interpersonal contact and, in turn, interpersonal friendship; we know that some of man's spatial behavior can be explained by his need to maintain or stake out his territory; we know that man can get very aggressive on some occasions when this territory is invaded; animal experiments lead us to believe that the need for territory is an important variable in explaining the disruptive behavior which occurs during overcrowding; we know that each man seeks a comfortable conversational distance—a distance which varies depending on certain demographic characteristics, the relationship of the interactants, the context of the interaction, the topic being dis-

[59] R. F. Forston and C. U. Larson, "The Dynamics of Space: An Experimental Study in Proxemic Behavior Among Latin Americans and North Americans," *Journal of Communication* 18 (1968): 109–16.

[60] Sommer, *Personal Space*, p. 63–64.

[61] S. Jones, "A Comparative Proxemics Analysis of Dyadic Interaction in Selected Subcultures of New York City," *Journal of Social Psychology* 84 (1971): 35–44.

[62] B. F. Skinner, *Beyond Freedom and Dignity* (New York: Alfred A. Knopf, 1971).

cussed, certain physical and behavioral manifestations of the other person, and the attitudes and personality traits of the parties involved; we also know that distances chosen by members of small groups are not always accidental—that leaders and dominant personalities tend to choose specific seats and that seating will vary depending on the task at hand, the nature of the relationship between the parties, and certain personality variables; and finally, we know that spatial positioning varies in some way from culture to culture—the exact nature of this variance is yet to be determined. The major thrust of the research on spatial relationships thus far has focused on an individual's structuring of space toward another. Even the label used to describe such research reflects this interest—"*personal* space." Spatial behavior, however, like communication behavior, should be treated as a function of the behavior of both parties in the communicating pair. Constructs of group space may be a natural extension of the work to date, but as yet, such data are unavailable.

SPEECH COMMUNICATION IN THE ORGANIZATIONAL CONTEXT: THE CASE OF INFORMATION SYSTEMS, INC.

Ernest G. Bormann, William S. Howell, Ralph G. Nichols, and George L. Shapiro

Two months after Information Systems, Inc. moved to its new multimillion-dollar home office after years of being housed in an old four-story building in the center of town, five members of the procurement section resigned. President Herbert Moyers held a special meeting to deal with the crisis. Present were Bill Johnson, manager of the procurement section, Henry Wolfson, Bill's immediate superior, and the five disgruntled buyers.

President Moyers began the meeting by taking off his coat and loosening his tie. The men looked at one another with some surprise. They had never known the old man to open a meeting that way before. Moyers looked around the plush surroundings of his newly decorated board room and said, "I am deeply concerned about what is happening in the purchasing area. Now, I know we have a good manager in Bill Johnson and I know we have an able group of men for buyers. I want you to forget that I am president of the company and let's get this thing aired out. You men who have resigned have no reason to hold anything back, and I hope we can bring everything out here on the table, and if we do maybe we can iron things out. I'd like to see you men reconsider your resignations. Every one of you. I mean that."

There was a long painful silence as the five buyers slipped down lower in the upholstered chairs around the big shiny table. They looked at the heavy carpet on the floor and at the portrait of President Moyers on the wall and were silent. Again the president tried to get some response. Tension mounted. Finally, Harry Rider, who had been the ringleader behind the resignations, stood up and blurted out, "All right, I'll tell you what's wrong. Nobody tells anybody anything around here. We did not know until the ground was already broken that our desks—I can't say 'offices'—were to be in a bullpen like that."

"But certainly your facilities are much better than they were in the old plant," the president said.

"They are not. You can't do any work here. There's too much noise."

"The entire building is acoustically designed for low noise levels."

"Yeah, well you haven't tried working out there. There's no privacy."

"We have the conference rooms."

"They aren't available when you need them. Not only that, but you have to sign up for them and then take the group into a room away from your desk. That old way where we could meet right in our office was much better."

From Ernest G. Bormann, William S. Howell, Ralph G. Nichols, and George L. Shapiro, *Interpersonal Communication in the Modern Organization*, pp. 19–38.

"How do the rest of you feel about it?" the president asked.

Gradually the built-up resentment boiled over and the story was repeated. They were unable to work in the present conditions. It was bad enough trying to deal with engineers without having to go through all the red tape of signing up for and scheduling a meeting room.

George Nelson finally said, "Let me give you an example. Just Monday I was supposed to have a meeting with the vice-president of Norton's Tool and Die and their engineer and their salesman. When they got hung up over Chicago they came in an hour late and I couldn't find a meeting room available. Now there I am. Can I hold that meeting out in the bullpen?" Then fairly shouting with anger, George said, "You know what I finally did? Pete Wilson is the engineer who provides my specs. He invited us to his office over across the building. And we met in *his* office!"

"I bet you really had control of that meeting, didn't you," Harry said, "after demonstrating to that VP from Norton's that your own company treated you like a flunky."

"What do you mean by that crack?" Henry Wolfson asked.

"I just mean that I'm supposed to be in charge of buying certain items around here and I'm supposed to call and control these meetings and half the time the engineers have already made the decisions."

This brought the president to his feet and he demanded a further explanation.

"Simple enough," Harry said, "I don't blame the slide-rule boys. They want to build a new model so they sketch in the general design and then they call up a buddy who is an engineer for some vendor in the area and he draws up the specs for them. That way they can farm out half their work. 'Course when the time comes to let the contract these two guys have got the thing in the bag. I might just as well not bother to even put it out for bids."

"This is incredible," the president said. "We stopped this practice a year ago. As a matter of fact," he turned to Henry, "I gave you a specific responsibility to cut that practice completely when I established your division. Why wasn't I informed?"

"I didn't know myself," Henry said, mopping his brow. "I told them this practice was absolutely forbidden."

"Yeah," said Harry, "but did you tell them over in Research and Development?"

"Let's face it," said Bill, "nobody tells those engineers anything unless he's got that engineering degree. That's one of the troubles around here."

The incident related above suggests a faltering operation, a business so beset with difficulties that profits were low and expansion was grinding to a screeching halt. Such was not the case. To understand the significance of the dialogue just read, we must background the incident with relevant context.

Information Systems grew so rapidly that most organizational changes happened as a result of the need for more personnel to deal with more diversified and specialized tasks. The company was continually preoccupied with the pressing problems of fighting first for a toehold in the very competitive electronics industry and then delivering and expanding their product lines. Management never found time to rationalize organizational structure and procedures.

Originally Information Systems manufactured only one item—a small, efficient, and inexpensive data-processing system. There were few employees and many of them did several jobs. When the company decided to increase its line, the engineers who were developing new products tended to take their subcontracting problems to other engineers in small machining companies in the area. These men would then design the component and thus enable the Information Systems engineers to concentrate on the overall development of the equipment.

Information Systems was an amazingly successful firm. Within five years it had become a multimillion-dollar organization. As a result, the additional personnel required were added very rapidly. In some months as many as 30 per cent more people were added to the company roster. The new people were given a hasty orientation to their work and after a short interval—often less than a year—some were appointed to supervisory positions. Under these conditions most lower management people felt insecure. The problem was particularly crucial in the new division of buyers, established eight months before the move to the new headquarters building. The duties connected with subcontracting for component parts had become so time-consuming that the development engineers complained and excused some of their inability to meet target dates on that basis. Top management decided to establish a division of buyers modeled after the practice of several of the giant electronics firms in the area. This decision was reached after a thorough analysis by a management consultant firm.

The new division was to have the exclusive responsibility of making all purchases for the company. Everything from erasers and letterheads to the most complicated electronic component was to be purchased by the new procurement division. The typical procedure for large purchases was as follows: A buyer would first get the expert advice of an engineer, in regard to the specifications for the part to be purchased, and would then contact several firms to negotiate the purchase price, quality requirements, delivery rates, and so forth. The buyer often conducted the final negotiation session at the head office of Information Systems in the presence of one or more engineers from Research and Development, the salesman for the vendor, and an engineer, or, on occasion, an officer from the firm seeking the contract.

At the former offices the buying division was housed in a large open area, partitioned in such a way that each buyer had his desk in an office area 8 by 10 feet. His secretary's desk was located in the open passageway separating the rows of partitioned offices. The buyers held smaller conferences in these offices; for larger meetings they had two big conference rooms at their disposal.

The architects for the new building designed a separate area especially for the buying division. It consisted of a large open bullpen, airy, well-lighted, and spacious, for the buyers and their secretaries. Each buyer's desk and that of his secretary were side by side, and the acoustics assured a low noise level. A series of small meeting rooms and several larger ones bordered the bullpen area. The buyers scheduled their meetings in these rooms.

After the architectural plans were approved and the building underway, several consultations between representatives from the buyers, the interior decorators, and the architect were held to determine the buyers' wishes. At first the buyers expressed enthusiasm about moving into the spacious new building and were eager to offer suggestions to their representatives about furnishing details. But then word spread that the engineers who worked most closely with the buyers were to have individual offices measuring 10 by 12 feet. A number of disgruntled buyers got together and requested a meeting with Bill Johnson, their departmental manager. At the meeting they expressed their concern about the new arrangement. They suggested that Bill try to get the architect to provide them with at *least* the equivalent of the individual offices they had in the old office building. Bill was most reluctant to do so but finally agreed. When he approached his immediate superior, Henry Wolfson, he did so with considerable reluctance, since Wolfson habitually told him that he was an extremely busy man.

When Bill gingerly broached the subject of adding offices to the new plans, Wolfson immediately vetoed the idea. He insisted that it was much too late and that the buyers had known about the new building for months. Since construction was well underway, they could not possibly change design at this late date.

Bill was offended not so much by Wolfson's words as by his manner. Bill definitely got the impression that Wolfson thought he was a sorehead and should keep his mouth shut. Bill was so irritated by his reception that he told his boss that he did not feel that the men in his division had been given enough information about the new quarters and that they had not been consulted sufficiently in the planning stages.

Bill had interrupted Wolfson in the midst of a crisis over delay in the delivery of an important installation. Wolfson had been hearing charges from the production men all morning and he was frustrated by an apparently insoluble problem when he worked Bill into his schedule. When Bill blew up and talked to him in a completely uncharacteristic way Wolfson got up and began to pace the room. He said that while they were on the subject of Bill's division he might mention that he had been getting a lot of heat from the other sections because the buyers were not doing their jobs properly. Both Research and Development and Engineering had complained about the unnecessary delay in getting parts and materials.

Bill left the meeting shaking and sweating. He had never talked to Wolfson in this fashion before, nor had he ever gotten a dressing down like that before. He called his men into an emergency meeting immediately. During the course of the meeting he lost his temper, defended the decision of top management not to change the plans for the new quarters, and told his men that he was under a great deal of pressure from top management because of delays in procurement. During this same meeting Bill decided that Harry Rider would have to go. Not only was Rider a sorehead and troublemaker, but he was very influential with the men. They seemed to follow his lead in the matter under discussion, and when Harry said that he was not satisfied with Bill's answer and that the buyers should not take this thing lying down but should fight for their rights, he was supported by the men.

Buyer resentment mounted over the next few months and they made their move to the new offices; however, accumulated tension erupted finally when George Nelson had to schedule his meeting in the office of an engineer. When George and Harry and three others went to Bill with the suggestion that office partitions be erected in the area and were turned down, they resigned.

The case of "buyer's rebellion" in Information Systems illustrates a typical long, slow buildup of a serious organizational problem that is identified *for the first time* when a costly explosion occurs. We are not going to attempt to explain all the factors that contributed to the crisis in the procurement division of this firm. As you read, . . . turn back, and many reasons for puzzling bits of behavior in this narrative will become apparent. For the present we advance a simple summary generalization: *The problems of* INFORMATION SYSTEMS *were caused, predominantly, by management's failure to communicate effectively.*

THE ORGANIZATION AS A MESSAGE-PROCESSING SYSTEM

The modern organization is a message-processing system. A table of organization is an anatomical drawing that indicates the formal channel through which flow official and unofficial messages. Around the formal structure is an ever-changing and complicated network of informal communication channels. Through these veins flows the information that achieves a community of understanding to provide objectives, divide the work, develop morale, evaluate performance, and mobilize the resources of the organization. If the circulation of messages is good and the level of understanding high, the organization will be more effective.

Within the formal divisions, departments, projects, and units of an organization—whether it be governmental, commercial, industrial, scientific, educational, or religious—there are supervisors who must organize and divide the work for their people. These supervisors do not manhandle their subordinates and push them around. Supervision consists primarily of speaking and listening.

The smaller units within an organization are gathered together in larger clusters, and middle management divides the work of these larger units. The middle manager, too, must rely on speech-communication to do much of his job. Finally, all the parts of the organization must mesh together and upper management must organize the work of all and bring the resources of the total organization to bear upon the outside world. How well the organization meets the challenges posed by competition of similar groups and the pressures of other organizations is largely determined by the skill with which the total group handles information.

By 1950 our society had become so complex that the everyday citizen as well as the industrial leader had in a very real sense become a manager. Almost everyone today has management responsibilities of one kind or another. Some of us function as amateurs in the business of management, others become highly professional. But all depend heavily upon speech-communication in even their routine functions. Each day is filled with appointments, interviews, conferences, and meetings.

Within an organization a substantial part of our communication is for the purpose of keeping the operation on an even keel. But balance is seldom maintained for very long. Events are always disrupting operations. Pressures from competition or from other forces within or without challenge the organization to develop new working methods. Leaders must devote some of their communicating to changing the attitudes and actions of the personnel in their organization. They must bring their people to the point of accepting change. Becoming an agent of change requires that the leader have a clear understanding of the problem, that he sees new ways to meet the problem, and that his solution to the problem is effective in achieving the organization's objective. In addition, he must communicate with people in the organization in such a way that they are led to co-operate willingly with changes in their routines. In other words, change implies uncertainty. It causes each individual to doubt whether or not he and his organization will succeed in the new set of circumstances.

Every communication situation poses a challenge to those involved in it. Too often we face those challenges without thinking, relying on our habitual patterns of communication to help us to muddle through. Yet, every organizational setting provides an opportunity for vital choices in deciding how best to achieve results from our communicating. The possibility of choice creates the opportunity for rational decisions, the development of skills and competence, and the conscious attainment of effectiveness.

If we are to deal effectively with speech-communication in the modern organization, we must understand both the process of speech-communication and the organizational structure that furnishes its context. Our first task, therefore, is to describe the basic process of speech-communication and then investigate the interplay of organizational structure and human relationships that determine how messages are processed.

THE PROCESS OF SPEECH-COMMUNICATION

Most of us think of talking to another human being as an elementary, mechanical operation. We put an idea into vocalized words; the other person picks up the message and is thereby informed. Visualizing the sending and receiving of spoken messages in this fashion seems sensible but amounts to a drastic and deceptive oversimplification. The necessary further dimensions of the act of spoken communication can be seen in a model that represents *purposeful* use of speech from the point of view of the man with the message, the speaker. We wish to make clear that this is a PRESCRIPTIVE model, one that suggests what ought to be planned and implemented for optimum results. While the model is source-oriented, it may be said to be receiver-centered.

First let us look at the parts of our model in Figure 1 and their relations to each other. In the left margin are the three physical components

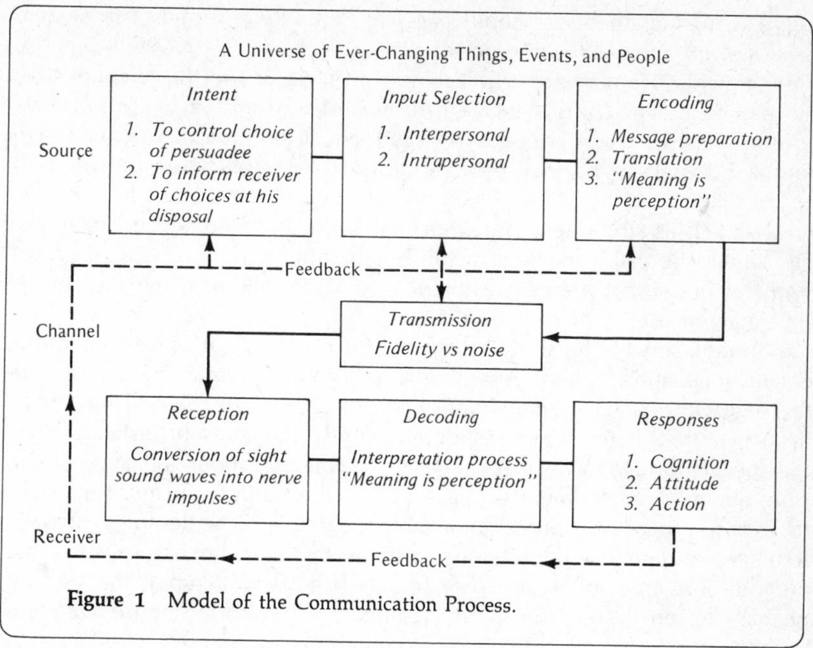

Figure 1 Model of the Communication Process.

involved in an act of communication, the SOURCE (speaker), the CHANNEL (speaking directly to the listeners with or without eye contact, public address system, telephone, radio, TV, and so forth), and the RECEIVER (the individual or group that is to hear the message and whose behavior or attitude is to be modified).

The Source

The direction of the solid arrows indicates both time sequence and the direction of development and movement of the message. Events in the "universe of ever-changing things, events and people" bring to the conscious mind of the communicator a need to communicate. Changing conditions produce stimuli that necessitate reinforcement of an existing purpose, or creation of a new purpose. The source begins the process of communicating by identifying an INTENT in the form of a statement of what he wishes to accomplish by the message. This purpose is as definite as he can make it, considering the situation, the person or persons who will receive it, and their attitudes, knowledge, and capabilities. If he wishes to produce an action response, his INTENT can be stated specifically in terms of desired terminal behavior (what he wants them to do).

Input Selection

Once his purpose is clear, the speaker plans the "inputs" for his message. He must make at least two strategy decisions: how he will transmit his message by light, sound, or electronic waves or telephone lines to his listener, and how his message will be conveyed from the ear and eye of the receiver to the audience member's centers of response and understanding. The first elements of input we will call *interpersonal.* The second series is *intrapersonal.* Interpersonally, a message source will choose among media. He may prefer to talk face-to-face, or use the telephone, or he may decide that this message can be best transmitted by radio, intercom system, or open- or closed-circuit television. He may go through formal channels or he may choose informal communication networks. If he decides to use a two-person or small group situation, he must decide how formal his structure of interpersonal interaction should be. For example, should he call a meeting in the board room or arrange a golf game? With telephone or intercom, should he plan to talk with the individuals separately or use a conference call?

Intrapersonally, he should make a choice that is not as obvious but is equally real and, perhaps, even more important. Human beings can be reached with messages that produce response through their critical faculties or via their conditioned responses (habits). In a present instance, does the speaker prefer to have his receivers deliberate about the facts of the case, about his recommendations, or would he consider it more effective to bypass critical responses to a large degree and settle for more automated, routine reactions? If he chooses the first, he has selected the intrapersonal input of *reasoned discourse.* If he decides upon the second, he has chosen to use the input leading to uncritical response we term *suggestion.*

Encoding

Never forgetting the unique individuals to whom he will speak, and being guided by his INTENT and choice of interpersonal and intrapersonal CONTEXT, the speaker ENCODES his message. He plans the main and supporting points he will make, the facts and illustrations he will use, and the language that will be most meaningful to his listeners. He adjusts to time limitations. Ordinarily, all encoding is tentative, amounting to a list of possibilities that the speaker can draw upon and rearrange during transmission. Only in the exceptional case does he write out the complete message, for he recognizes the rigidity a script imposes upon source output, as well as his own inability to predict precisely how well his listeners will understand him and how soon they will be ready to advance from point to point.

The "man with the message" is guided by two utilitarian concepts: the notion that he is *translating,* and the realization that whatever he wishes to send to another person is limited by the most basic empirical principle of communication, *meaning is perception.* Because his listener attaches his own meanings to words of the source, the sender must translate what he would communicate into what the receiver knows or is interested in. This is often as significant a change in the message as putting it into Chinese. And when his message is decoded, all results depend upon what the listener perceives, the meaning he thinks is there, no matter what the source intended. Thus selection of language and content in encoding are shaped largely by considerations of translation into terms the receiver is likely to interpret in predictable perceptions.

Transmission

The message becomes an event during TRANSMISSION. Sounds and visual stimuli are emitted by the speaker, and via selected channels either or both are conveyed to the receiver(s). The speaker's main concern is with "high fidelity" TRANSMISSION. If TRANSMISSION delivers to the receiver stimuli below the threshold of his sensory acuities, i.e., signals he is unable to see and hear clearly, distortions occur and *intelligibility* is lowered. Fidelity has deteriorated. Obviously, to the extent that fidelity is inadequate, communication fails.

A major problem in TRANSMISSION is noise. *Noise* is any physical or psychological distraction at the time of transmission that reduces the ability of the receiver to get the message. Speakers should assign a high priority to the control or elimination of *noise*.

The Receiver

The RECEIVER includes three discrete functions of message reception. Each function poses a different problem for the communicator. RECEPTION is satisfactory when a faithful copy of the source stimuli-pattern enters the nervous system of the listener. (If a source says "Wash out the lazy workers," and the receiver hears "Watch out for the daisy workers," the reception is poor.) RECEPTION depends upon the availability of above-threshold, high fidelity sights and sounds, plus properly functioning eyes and ears, plus the attention of the receiver on the message.

DECODING takes place in the brain of the receiver. Nervous impulses trigger habit and thinking activities necessary to the creation of meaning. When meanings are attached to sights and sounds received from a source, the listener has perceived the message. This fact accounts for the somewhat perplexing truism that "meaning lies not in the word, but in the mind of the hearer." Thus, the manager who hears his boss say, "Watch out for the daisy workers" and perceives that the meaning he attached to that sentence makes absolutely no sense in the context of the situation is likely to ask for clarification.

Only after meaning is developed is RESPONSE possible. If we respond to the meaning resulting from a unit of communication either by changing our opinion or by believing a controversial statement even more firmly than before, our response is one of *attitude*. If we do something we would not have done in the absence of the communication, our response is *action*. Change in attitude and action often indicates the impact of communication.

But much effective communication produces negligible attitude or action response. Information may be assimilated and understandings increased without the listener modifying any opinions or doing anything about it. *Cognition* refers to the acquisition of knowledge, the discovery of insights, and the extension of awareness. Cognition in and of itself is often a desired response of organizational speech-communication.

Feedback

FEEDBACK, represented in Figure 1 by the long, broken arrow connecting RESPONSE to INTENT, INPUTS, ENCODING, and TRANSMISSION, consists of collecting information about the receiver's reactions to the message and using that information to modify a current or subsequent message to make it more effective. "Feedback" is a term borrowed for our model from modern control systems. A simple example is furnished by the thermostat that controls the level of temperature in the room. Someone decides upon the desired level of temperature (intent) and sets the thermostat at that level. The thermostat takes a continuous reading on the actual level and feeds the information back to the furnace when the temperature departs from the desired level. This information causes the furnace to modify its behavior and turn off or on depending upon the information it receives from the thermostat. In this way the actual level of the temperature is brought on target to approximate the desired level. In the same way, the source of a message should take a reading on its effect on the receiver and modify subsequent stimuli.

In speech-communication almost continuous FEEDBACK is possible and desirable. The speaker can never know enough about the moment-to-moment reactions of his audience. Consequently, he becomes a "feedback detective," sensitive to all clues that tell him his listeners are reacting.

Along with continuous monitoring of the receiver(s) comes equally continuous modification of the message. Even the INTENT, what the speaker thought he could accomplish, may need to be revised in light of receiver reactions. The context, encoding, and transmission operations, all are candidates for change to better meet the current needs of particular listeners.

Delayed feedback, collecting information about response after the communication is complete, is useful to the planning of future messages, but too late to help a given communication event. Obviously, building continuous feedback mechanisms into a unit of communication becomes exceedingly important.

Our entire source-oriented process of communication is enclosed in a *Universe of Ever-Changing Things, Events and People*. This reminds us that the human and inanimate contexts of communication are never twice the same, that communication is an extraordinarily contingent phenomenon, and that which comes before and after an act of communication may profoundly influence its outcome.

Our model of the process of speech-communication is necessary because it makes explicit all of the significant variables and shows their interrelationships. The able practitioner of the process accounts for every element of the model in his planning. During the communication event he modifies various elements appropriately through continuous feedback. When communication fails he uses the model as an aid to diagnosis of the trouble. Usually one or two elements in the model will account for much of the failure. He can then modify his strategy for the next effort to correct the malfunctions and thus avoid repeating his mistakes. Occasionally the student of speech-communication will use the model to evaluate his successes not only for the personal gratification he receives from a good job but also because he can learn from success as well as from failure.

Our model of the process of speech-communication is a very general one and can be used to study a host of communication situations within as well as outside organizational settings. Now we must place the model within the context of the complicated message-processing system of the modern organization. When two members of an organization speak to one another, the very fact that they are members of a common structure influences the sending and receiving of messages, the fidelity of transmission, the perception that gives meaning to the message, and the cognitions that result. The organization also provides conditions that facilitate or impede feedback.

It may facilitate communication when two people are members of the same organization. Their shared experience in similar communicative situations often insures accurate reception of messages. If a person expects the message on the intercom to relate to the committee meeting, he is likely to decipher the words "Committee moved to room eight" properly rather than to receive them as "Committee moved to ruminate."

In the same fashion, a common jargon may standardize the meanings associated with certain terms so that the perception of the message is close to intent. The use of letters of the alphabet to designate groups within the organization, or different product lines, illustrates one such practice. In short, some of the organization's habits and traditions increase the fidelity of message transmission and promote effective feedback.

A number of factors in organizations inhibit communication, and these organizational barriers should be understood. To do so we need to examine both the anatomy and physiology of organizations. Anatomy separates the parts (organs) and discovers their position, relations, structure, and functions. Physiology, on the other hand, deals with the processes and dynamic interactions associated with the life of the organism. It relates to the various organs as they do their work in cooperation with all the other parts of the body.

THE STRUCTURE OF THE MODERN ORGANIZATION

Modern organizations have certain similarities whether they are concerned with the production of a product for profit, with the conduct of governmental business, with charitable enterprises, with the education of students, with the treatment of the ill, or with the defense of a country. Every manager must see that objectives are set, work clarified, performance reviewed, and problems solved. The manager's problems and the skills he needs to meet them remain essentially the same, thus it is not surprising that a successful army general often becomes a successful corporation president or that a successful corporation president often becomes a productive official of the Federal Government.

Formal Organizational Structure

What are the essential features that most organizations have in common? Organizations typically have a *formal* division of labor, authority, and responsibility; associated with the division of labor they have a *formal* division of status and prestige. Both sets of formal divisions are reflected in a hierarchical structure. That is, not only is the labor divided but some of the labor is formally judged to be more important to the organization, and hence is given a higher or more important place in the structure.

Figure 2 presents a typical anatomical diagram of the formal structure of an organization. Each block represents a *formal position* within the organization. The size and position of the block indicate its relative place in the hierarchy. The larger the block and the closer to the top of the diagram, the more important and influential the position, regardless of the abilities of the individual who might, at a given moment, be occupying it. Blocks of the same size and the same level of the diagram are judged equal in prestige, status, and importance. The anatomy of a typical organization also includes a formal specification of the share of the labor, responsibilities, and authority assigned to each position.

The blocks in Figure 2 are connected with heavy black lines that indicate not only who works for whom but also who reports to whom, who gets directions and orders from whom; in short, these lines indicate the formal channels set up by the structure to guide the flow of messages. Typically, a person in a block at the third level (e.g., D) is not allowed by the formal structure to talk about official matters to the top man (A). Rather, the person is supposed to go "through channels" and transmit official messages through his immediate superior (B) to upper manage-

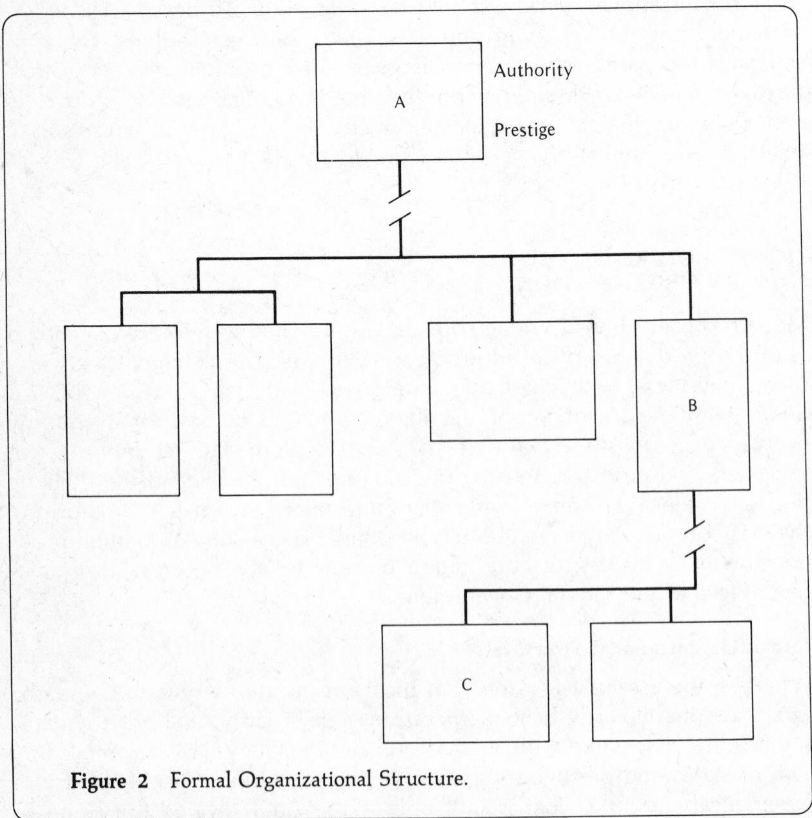

Figure 2 Formal Organizational Structure.

ment. Sending messages through channels assures that the man at position B is informed of developments in his unit.

The Human Factor

When one studies the diagram of the structure of an institution he learns something about its operation and about the communication patterns that accompany its function. Yet it is one thing to study the anatomy of the heart, and another to study a given individual and discover the way *his* heart functions, for it must be considered that he will have a unique history and hereditary background. Variables such as age, as well as the health, activity, and condition of other organs, will affect the functioning of the heart. Similarly, when an organization's formal structure is activated by a given complement of people, a new dimension is evident.

Figure 3 shows the addition of the human element. When individuals are placed within the formal positions, they begin to exercise their authority and thereby exert *power*. *Power* is the effective use of authority. Theoretically the allocation of authority in the formal structure divides the power as well, but actually it is the interaction of given individuals with certain amounts of assigned authority that determines how power is

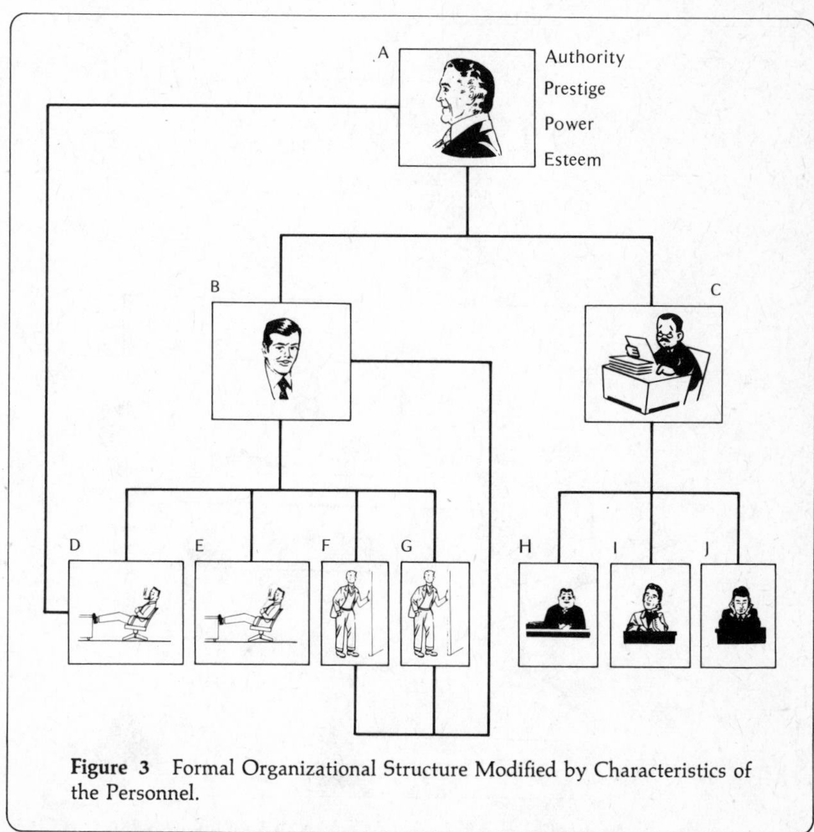

Figure 3 Formal Organizational Structure Modified by Characteristics of the Personnel.

divided. Conceivably, a person in position B may have more or less power than he has authority.

Esteem is also associated with persons. Prestige is influenced by location in the formal structure, but esteem is earned by the person who occupies a formal position. Again it is possible that a person in block B may have more or less esteem than he has prestige and status.

Figure 3 also indicates by the heavy lines that when the static structure of an organization is set in motion with a given complement of workers and managers, informal channels of communication develop. These channels may stem from a host of factors, such as previous acquaintance, familial ties, common hobbies and interests, shared irritations, sexual attraction, and congenial temperaments. If the individual in position D is the son-in-law of the member in block A, an important informal communication channel between the two may be established. If the persons in blocks B, F, G, and H frequently play golf together, they may establish another informal communication network.

Gatekeepers

Figure 4 adds an important factor to the communication channels, in this instance, a formal position called *executive secretary*. This person's duties

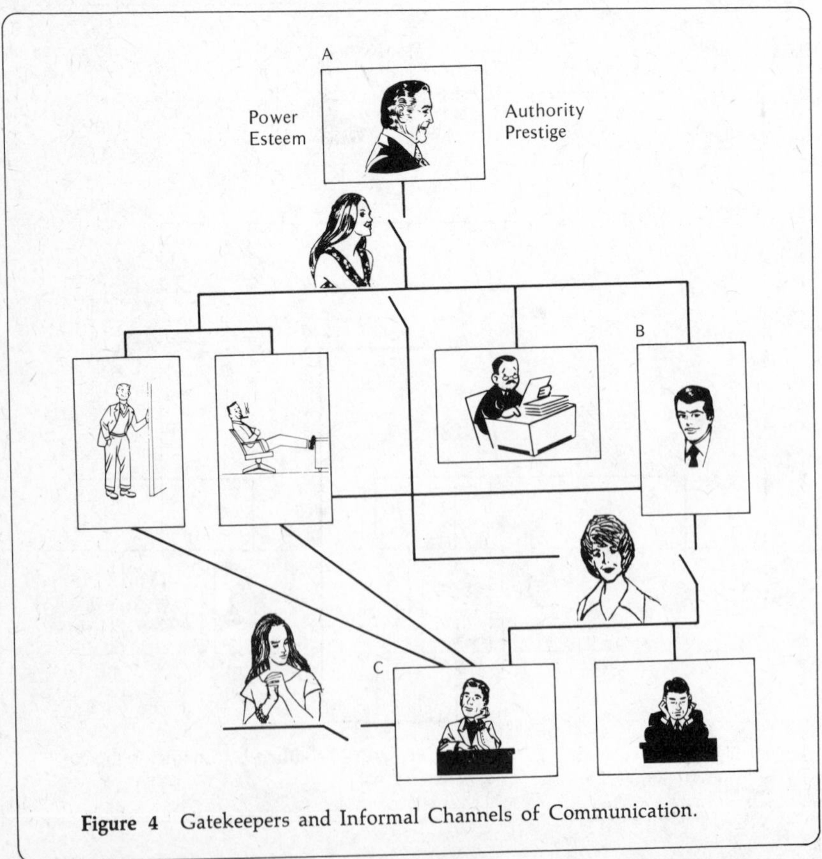

Figure 4 Gatekeepers and Informal Channels of Communication.

include the sifting of messages for individuals in positions A, B, and C. The executive secretary position shows how some people can act as valves turning off or on the flow of messages through the formal channels. Almost any person may do somewhat the same with the messages that flow through the grapevine, although some may be more adept and more highly motivated to ferret out rumors and information and thus play the informal role of gatekeepers. Other formal positions may afford a good opportunity to facilitate or impede communication, but few offer more such opportunities than does the position of secretary. The secretary may open the boss's mail and decide which letters need immediate attention. She may also control his appointment schedule and thus determine who gets in to talk to him. She may filter the telephone messages. Informally she is in an excellent position to establish lines of communication. If she has lunch with other secretaries in the organization, they can keep each other posted on what is going on.

A good deal of research has investigated the relationship between the flow of communication and the growth of influence in small laboratory groups. One of the implications of research into communication networks is that the individual who receives and controls communication grows in importance and influence in the group. Thus, if an artificial network is established as in Figure 5 so that all members can talk to A, and A can talk to all members, but no one else in the group can talk to anyone else, A soon becomes a key person. To some extent the gatekeeper in an organizational communication network experiences a similar increase in influence. The oft-noted instance where the "old man's secretary really runs things around here" illustrates the phenomenon.

Formal Channels

The formal channels influence the nature of messages in several important ways. Organizations tend to specify the nature of the messages that flow

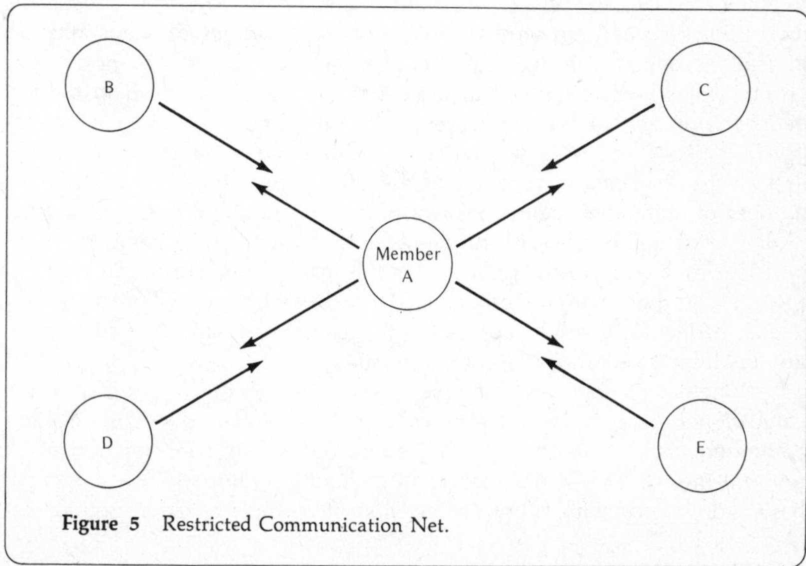

Figure 5 Restricted Communication Net.

through formal channels. They may even be routinized to such an extent that they are expected at a given time of the month or that they are to be presented on a standardized form. If they are speech-communication messages they may be expected on certain set occasions (department heads make oral reports in a monthly meeting with the plant manager), they may be restricted as to time (10 to 15 minutes), and they may be in a certain form (an oral presentation with slides, charts, etc., and a period for questions following). Messages sent through formal channels are often given greater consideration and more careful examination. They often take much longer to reach their destinations, and as they move from individual to individual up the levels they often experience the distortions common to messages handed on from one person to another. It is not uncommon for a person to wish that he might talk directly to someone several levels up the hierarchy rather than having to "work" through channels. Much of the so-called red tape and the delay that inhibits quick and decisive action in an organization stems from the cumbersome necessity of sending messages through formal channels.

Informal Channels

Often the messages that flow through informal channels, since they have no official sanction, are less carefully drafted and variously interpreted. Frequently they contain a high proportion of "scuttlebutt." Still, they furnish an effective medium. A few minutes with the boss on the golf course may break a barrier in the formal channels and bring key information to the attention of the organization for decision. To understand and use speech-communication in a modern organization, one must map formal and informal channels and make careful decisions about using either or both for a given communication purpose.

Communication in a Hierarchy

Successful communication among equals is difficult enough, but when a formal status ladder is clearly established and emphasized the difficulty is increased. We need not write an essay on the sociology of status and the indications of status in organizations because the subject is by now hackneyed. It has been discussed in industrial magazines, satirized in motion pictures (the key to the executive washroom), and studied by industrial psychologists. The reader will have no trouble listing the status indicators in a given organization. Location of the office, rugs and other furnishings, number of secretaries, eating and washing privileges, and the proper dress—all may serve to point up differences in status. Silly as some of these practices may seem to the outsider, to the insider they are useful clues to the prestige and status of others. In large organizations where a person needs to deal with other members who are relative strangers such clues are helpful in structuring the communication.

Nonetheless, *speech-communication among people with different organizational status is inhibited by that difference.* Good communication among equals is often characterized by honesty, ease, consideration of all relevant information, and a high level of feedback. But when a supervisor has a conference with subordinates, honest, complete, easy communication with adequate feedback is difficult to achieve simply because one person has authority over others and because he is in a position to control their fate.

We have now described our basic frames of reference. The process of speech-communication is fitted into the context of the modern organization. When a source initiates communication with a given intent and selects his channels, encodes his message, and speaks to his receivers, all elements occur within a human structure that divides work and assigns responsibility, authority, power, esteem, and prestige.

REFERENCES

Bass, Bernard M. *Leadership, Psychology, and Organizational Behavior.* New York: Harper & Row, Publishers, 1960.

Berlo, David K. *The Process of Communication.* New York: Holt, Rinehart, and Winston, Inc., 1960.

Blau, Peter M., and W. Richard Scott. *Formal Organization.* San Francisco: Chandler Publishing, 1962.

March, J. G., and H. A. Simon. *Organizations.* New York: John Wiley & Sons, Inc., 1958.

Chapter 6

SHARING IDEAS: INTERPERSONAL SEMANTICS

Most of us take our language so much for granted that we fail to note its impact on our lives. Stuart Chase has stated: "We live in an ocean of words, but like a fish in water we are not aware of it. There are close to 2½ billion of us on the planet today, and practically every one of us, except very young children, is constantly talking, listening to talk, learning to talk."[1] Language is so much a part of our environment that we hardly know it is there.

In a facetious manner, George du Maurier once wrote: "Language is a poor thing. You fill your lungs with wind and shake a little slit in your throat and make mouths, and that shakes the air; and the air shakes a pair of little drums in my head . . . and my brain seizes your meaning in the rough. What a roundabout way and what a waste of time."[2]

In Chapter 1 we noted some of the difficulties that we have in communicating common meanings. Symbolization is one of people's primary activities, and language is the systematised body of agreed-upon symbols. These symbols take the form of verbal and nonverbal messages. These messages, based on the mutual apprehension of common experiences of people, facilitate joint social action, make possible the formation of societies, and permit the bridging of time and cultures.

In this chapter we shall examine the verbal and nonverbal ways in which we attempt to share ideas. Semantics refers to the science of determining the relationship between symbols and meaning. We have used the term "interpersonal semantics" in an attempt to focus attention on the implications of our language usage on our interpersonal relationships. The words that we use as well as our behavior constitute important variables in our attempts to communicate.

CHARACTERISTICS OF LANGUAGE

The first fragmentary utterances of a small child who is just learning to speak indicate the interpersonal nature of human speech. Swiss psychologist Jean Piaget has distinguished two functions of speech for

[1]S. Chase, *Power of Words* (New York: Harcourt Brace Jovanovich, 1954), p. 3.

[2]Quoted from F. Davis, "How to Read Body Language," *The Reader's Digest*, December 1969, p. 130.

the child: the social and the egocentric. In social speech, "the child addresses his hearer, considers his point of view, tries to influence him or actually exchange ideas with him." In egocentric speech, "the child does not bother to know to whom he is speaking, nor whether he is being listened to. He talks either to himself or for the pleasure of associating anyone who happens to be there with the activity of the moment."[3] Other investigations have concluded that the bulk of the child's speech, approximately 90 percent, is social.[4] The work of the Russian psychiatrist Vigotsky suggests that even the monologues labeled by Piaget as "egocentric" are actually directed toward others. When Vigotsky placed a child who demonstrated the characteristics of "egocentric" speech (babblings, incomplete sentences) in isolation, in a very noisy room, or among deaf-and-dumb children, the child's speech dropped off considerably. Vigotsky concluded that the child believes his speech is being understood by others, and when external conditions make speaking difficult or when feedback is lacking, he stops speaking.[5] As we discussed in Chapter 3, the child does not initially clearly differentiate his/her perception of the world from the world as perceived by others. He/she seems to believe everyone else perceives and understands the world just as he/she perceives and understands it; thus, others must understand his/her highly idiosyncratic language. This tendency, as we shall see, is not completely restricted to the child, and lies at the heart of many communication problems. The most important point, however, is that according to available experimental data, all speech is a form of interpersonal behavior.

The child attaches meanings to visual and verbal phenomena and, in effect, works to "break the code." As we have noted, however, all language and all codes are arbitrary. Mutual understandings as to the meanings assigned to symbols are entirely by agreement and consent. There is no connection between the sound or series of letters in a word and the "thing" in reality except what is arbitrarily attached by human beings.

For purposes of clarity, semanticists have used the analogy of a *map* and the *territory* it represents to describe the relationship between our verbal symbols and the reality for which they stand. The basic aspect of words and nonverbal signals is parallel to the map-territory analogy. Words and nonverbal cues are symbols that stand for something. The fact that the meanings of many symbols are shared by many people allows communication to occur. We shall now examine

[3]J. Piaget, *The Language and Thought of the Child* (New York: Harcourt Brace Jovanovich, 1926), p. 26.

[4]G. A. Miller, *Language and Communication* (New York: McGraw-Hill, 1951), pp. 155–156.

[5]L. S. Vigotsky, "Thought and Speech," *Psychiatry*, 2 (1939), 29–54.

in some detail those characteristics of language that potentially cause us problems in our interpersonal communication.

1. Words Have Different Meanings to Different People

Generally we think of words as having two kinds of meaning or two kinds of definition. One is the connotative or associative definition. The other is the denotative or operational definition. The latter kind of meaning refers to the thing or event, a phenomenon to which the word refers. This denotative definition is what we would point to if asked to define a word without being able to speak or use any other words. Such denotative meanings are reasonably stable; they are common to science (H_2O), business (debit), industry (arbitration), and to each profession. They mean about the same to everyone, but problems can develop if agreements are not reached. For example, if someone asked you, "What class are you in?" it would be useless to respond unless you knew whether he was referring to class in school or social standing. As Irving Lee notes in the reading following this chapter, even in as restricted an area as parliamentary procedure, to "table" a motion in the United States means to put it aside, while in England the same phrase means "Let's bring it up for discussion."

Consider numerous possible meanings in the following story:

> *Struck by a sign in a plumber's window ("struck"?) reading "Iron Sinks," a wag went inside to inform the merchant that he was fully aware that "iron sinks." The storekeeper, ready to play the game, inquired, "And do you know that time flies, sulphur springs, jam rolls, music stands, Niagara Falls, concrete walks, wood fences, sheep run, holiday trips, rubber tires, the organ stops . . .?" But by then the wag had had enough and fled.*

Such multiple meanings inherent in our language force us to consider context and nonverbal cues to give us more exact meaning. The educated adult uses in daily conversation only about 2,000 of the more than 600,000 words in the English language. Of these 2,000, the 500 most-frequently used words have over 14,000 dictionary definitions. Even the term "meaning," which we have attempted to define, has eighteen groups of meanings in a recent dictionary. Further, our language is constantly changing, adding new words, and modifying definitions as usage changes. Figure 6.1 shows a dictionary definition ascribed to the word "love."

These dictionary definitions do not tell the complete story, however. Social psychologist Joost A. M. Meerloo has cited some of the potential meanings that the statement "I love you" may convey:

> *This is no essay on love and no profound treatise on the variations of feelings of tenderness. I only want to show how much semantic difficulty there is in the expression "I love you"—a statement that can be*

love (luv), *n.*, *v.*, **loved, lov·ing.** —*n.* **1.** the profoundly tender or passionate affection for a person of the opposite sex. **2.** a feeling of warm personal attachment or deep affection, as for a parent, child, or friend. **3.** sexual passion or desire, or its gratification. **4.** a person toward whom love is felt; beloved person; sweetheart. **5.** (used in direct address as a term of endearment, affection, or the like): *Would you like to see a movie, love?* **6.** a love affair; amour. **7.** (*cap.*) a personification of sexual affection, as Eros or Cupid. **8.** affectionate concern for the well-being of others: *a love of little children; the love of one's neighbor.* **9.** strong predilection or liking for anything: *her love of books.* **10.** the object or thing so liked: *The theater was her great love.* **11.** the benevolent affection of God for His creatures, or the reverent affection due from them to God. **12.** *Chiefly Tennis.* a score of zero; nothing. **13.** a word formerly used in communications to represent the letter L. **14.** **for love, a.** out of affection or liking; for pleasure. **b.** without compensation; gratuitously: *He took care of the poor for love.* **15. for the love of,** in consideration of; for the sake of: *For the love of mercy, stop that noise.* **16. in love (with),** feeling deep affection or passion for (a person, idea, occupation, etc.); enamored of: *in love with life; in love with one's work.* **17. make love, a.** to embrace and kiss as lovers. **b.** to engage in sexual intercourse. **18. no love lost,** dislike; animosity: *There was no love lost between the two brothers.* [ME; OE *lufu;* c. OFris *luve,* OHG *luba,* Goth *lubō*]
—*v.t.* **19.** to have love or affection for: *All her pupils love her.* **20.** to have a profoundly tender or passionate affection for (a person of the opposite sex). **21.** to have a strong liking for; take great pleasure in: *to love music; She loves to go dancing.* **22.** to need or require; benefit greatly from: *Plants love sunlight.* **23.** to make love to; have sexual intercourse with. —*v.i.* **24.** to have love or affection, esp. for one of the opposite sex. [ME *lov(i)en,* OE *lufian;* c. OFris *luvia,* OHG *lubōn* to love, L *lubēre* (later *libēre*) to please; akin to LIEF]
—**Syn. 1.** tenderness, fondness, predilection, warmth, passion, adoration. **1, 2.** LOVE, AFFECTION, DEVOTION all mean a deep and enduring emotional regard, usually for another person. LOVE may apply to various kinds of regard: the charity of the Creator, reverent adoration toward God or toward a person, the relation of parent and child, the regard of friends for each other, romantic feelings for one of the opposite sex, etc. AFFECTION is a fondness for persons of either sex, that is enduring and tender, but calm. DEVOTION is an intense love and steadfast, enduring loyalty to a person; it may also imply consecration to a cause. **2.** liking, inclination, regard, friendliness. **19.** like. **20.** adore, adulate, worship. —**Ant. 1, 2.** hatred, dislike. **19, 20.** detest, hate.

Figure 6.1 Definition of Love. (From *The Random House Dictionary of the English Language,* unabridged edition, p. 849. Copyright © 1971 by Random House, Inc. Reprinted by permission of the publisher.)

expressed in so many varied ways. It may be a stage song, repeated daily without any meaning, or a barely audible murmur, full of surrender. Sometimes it means: I desire you or I want you sexually. It may mean: I hope you love me or I hope that I will be able to love you. Often it means: It may be that a love relationship can develop between us or even I hate you. Often it is a wish for emotional exchange: I want your admiration in exchange for mine or I give my love in exchange for some passion or I want to feel cozy and at home with you or I admire some of your qualities. A declaration of love is mostly a request: I desire you or I want you to gratify me, or I want your protection or I want to be intimate with you or I want to exploit your loveliness. Sometimes it is the need for security and tenderness, for parental treatment. It may mean: My self-love goes out to you. But it may also express submissiveness: Please take me as I am, or I feel guilty about you, I want, through you, to correct the mistakes I have made in human relations. It may be self-sacrifice and a masochistic wish for dependency. However, it may also be a full affirmation of the other, taking the responsibility for mutual exchange of feelings. It may be a weak feeling of friendliness, it may be the scarcely even whispered expression of ecstasy. "I love you"—wish, desire, submission, conquest; it is never the word itself that tells the real meaning here.[6]

Even greater numbers of problems result from the connotative meaning of a word or expression than from the denotative. While the denotation gives sharpness and accuracy to a word, its connotations give it power. Our most familiar words are rich with connotations—mother, Vietnam, the President. The connotation may even be so strong that it erases the denotation, and for the individual only the connotation, then, has significance.

This connotative meaning of a word is the thought, feeling, or ideas that we have about the word, the things we say about the word when asked to define it. The words "factory worker" denote a person who earns his living by performing productive tasks in a building where many persons are organized to produce a product at a cost below what other people will pay for it. However, the words connote certain feelings and emotions. To some people, "factory worker" may mean a lazy, irresponsible, and apathetic person hostile to management. To others it may connote an honest, good man who is exploited, unjustly treated, and deprived of any freedom and opportunity to exercise responsibility and judgment. In the course of a lifetime, the denotations of words change but little, while our connotations alter with experience.

To some extent, the individual experiences of each of the approximately 30 million English-speaking people differ from all others. Every second of our lives we are experiencing something that is not exactly the same experience as any other we have had before, or that anyone else has had. Each individual has certain personal connotations derived from his/her experience with objects, persons, or ideas that are the referents of the words he/she uses. General connotations are those accepted as the typical reaction of a majority of people; thus most people in our society regard "war" with fear and abhorrence. This anticipated reaction with its fear overtones can be used then by some persons to manipulate others by simple reaction to the word.

Virtually all words have both denotative and connotative dimensions. The type and degree of reaction to words will vary from person to person. Meanings reside not in the words, but in the minds of people using them.

[6]J. A. M. Meerloo, *Conversation and Communication* (New York: International Universities, 1952), p. 83.

2. Words Vary in the Degree of Abstraction

A second major aspect of words and language is that words, like thought and conceptions, vary in degree of abstraction; words are symbols used to represent a generalized category of things, experiences, or ideas. The symbols vary from indicating a total class ("foreigners"), to a particular class ("Spaniards"), to a specific member of the class ("Juan Martinez"). S. I. Hayakawa has graphically depicted the principle of abstracting with his story of "Bessie," a cow. If we perceive in front of us a living organism, we respond, based on our previous experiences with other similar animals, by labeling the creature we are seeing a "cow." The cow is at the same time unique (different from all other living creatures in certain respects) and a member of a class ("cows"). This view of language is demonstrated in Figure 6.2, "The Abstraction Ladder." As the diagram shows, the object we see is an abstraction of the lowest level. As we ascend the ladder, the verbal categories become more general as "Bessie" is placed into broader categories in which we conceive some similarity.[7]

This characteristic of language permits people to avoid one another in arguments by retreating from one level of abstraction to another. Teachers and politicians are often adept at handling difficult questions by changing the level of abstraction when pushed as to specifics. The more abstract we become, the more we are relying upon "what is in our heads" rather than any sort of denotative reality.

When dealing with concrete empirical referents (denotative definitions)—like "book," "tree," "Illinois"—we have generally agreed-upon referents; highly abstract terms such as "justice," "obscenity," and "public welfare" are less likely to have common referents. In general, the more abstract a word, the greater the ambiguity, and the greater the chances of misunderstanding.

Hayakawa has cited a course in esthetics in a large midwestern university "in which an entire semester was devoted to Art and Beauty and the principles underlying them, and during which the professor, even when asked by students, persistently declined to name specific paintings, symphonies, sculptures, or objects of beauty to which his principles might apply. 'We are interested,' he would say, 'in principle, not in particulars.' "[8] When such people remain more or less permanently stuck at certain levels of the abstraction level, Wendell Johnson has labeled this linguistic phenomenon as "dead-level abstracting." As an example of a persistent low-level abstracting, he cites the following:

Probably all of us know certain people who seem able to talk on and

[7]S. I. Hayakawa, *Language in Thought and Action* (New York: Harcourt Brace Jovanovich, 1964), pp. 173–180.

[8]*Ibid.*, p. 189.

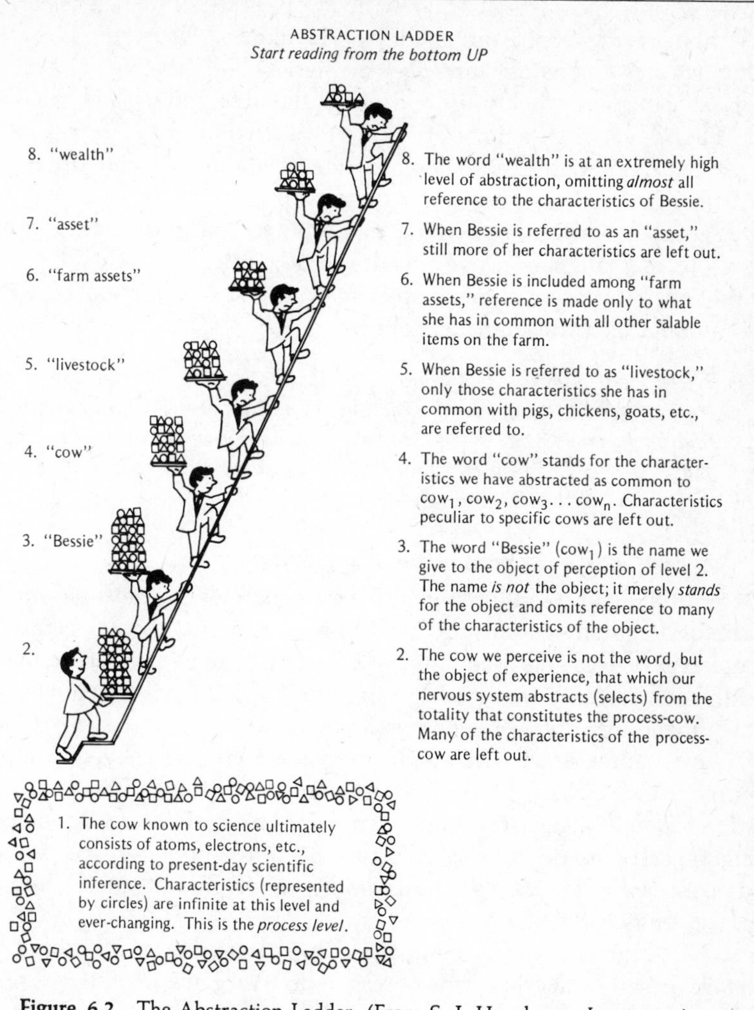

ABSTRACTION LADDER
Start reading from the bottom UP
8. "wealth"
7. "asset"
6. "farm assets"
5. "livestock"
4. "cow"
3. "Bessie"
2.
8. The word "wealth" is at an extremely high level of abstraction, omitting *almost* all reference to the characteristics of Bessie.
7. When Bessie is referred to as an "asset," still more of her characteristics are left out.
6. When Bessie is included among "farm assets," reference is made only to what she has in common with all other salable items on the farm.
5. When Bessie is referred to as "livestock," only those characteristics she has in common with pigs, chickens, goats, etc., are referred to.
4. The word "cow" stands for the characteristics we have abstracted as common to cow_1, cow_2, cow_3. . . cow_n. Characteristics peculiar to specific cows are left out.
3. The word "Bessie" (cow_1) is the name we give to the object of perception of level 2. The name *is not* the object; it merely *stands* for the object and omits reference to many of the characteristics of the object.
2. The cow we perceive is not the word, but the object of experience, that which our nervous system abstracts (selects) from the totality that constitutes the process-cow. Many of the characteristics of the process-cow are left out.
1. The cow known to science ultimately consists of atoms, electrons, etc., according to present-day scientific inference. Characteristics (represented by circles) are infinite at this level and ever-changing. This is the *process level*.

Figure 6.2 The Abstraction Ladder. (From S. I. Hayakawa, *Language in Thought and Action,* 2nd ed. Copyright 1941, 1949, © 1963, 1964 by Harcourt Brace Jovanovich, Inc. Reprinted by permission of the publisher.)

on without ever drawing any very general conclusions. For example, there is the back-fence chatter that is made up of he said and then I said and then she said and I said and then he said, far into the afternoon, ending with, "Well, that's just what I told him!" Letters describing vacation trips frequently illustrate this sort of language, detailing places seen, times of arrival and departure, the foods eaten and the prices paid, whether the beds were hard or soft, etc.[9]

[9]W. Johnson, *People in Quandaries* (New York: Harper & Row, 1946), p. 270.

This example contrasts sharply with the persistent, high level of abstraction of the professor cited by Hayakawa. Usually our speech demonstrates a constant interplay of higher- and lower-level abstraction, as we adapt quickly up and down the abstraction ladder.

High-level abstractions are quite useful when they are related to sense-data experience and demonstrate relationships and order. On the other hand, these abstractions can be dangerous as merely evocative terms standing for anything or nothing. The most highly valued terms in our language (love, beauty, truth, etc.) can either be maps without territories or point to specific experiences and feelings. Chase has summarized the point as follows:

> *When we use words as symbols for the abstraction that we "see," they are an abstraction of an abstraction. When we use generalizations like chairs-in-general, or "household furniture," we abstract again. The semantic moral is to be conscious of these abstraction levels, and not to lose sight of the original chair.*[10]

3. Language Is, by Its Very Nature, Incomplete

With millions of people reporting their experiences, the same meager store of accepted symbols are used to report to one another what they have experienced. Each common word symbol must, therefore, necessarily be used to cover a wide range of "meanings." Obviously, the categorized symbols omit details.

In Chapter 4 we discussed our perceptual tendency to simplify by the use of black-white categories and stereotyping. This characteristic of perception is reflected in our language. We are ill-equipped linguistically to describe gradations of differences, so we describe someone as either lazy or industrious, unable to categorize him/her in any unique fashion.

To be of any value, language must categorize and omit unique details, but this characteristic forces us to overgeneralize. If we fail to recognize that words are only generalized symbols, we are in danger of making certain invalid assumptions:

1. *We may assume that one instance is a universal example: "Nobody likes me." "All women are . . . ." "This always happens to me." "Nothing ever turns out right."*
2. *We may assume that our perceptions are complete: "Yes, I already know about that."*
3. *We may assume that everyone shares our feelings and perceptions: "Why didn't you do it the right way?" "Why would anyone eat in that horrible restaurant?"*
4. *We may assume that people and things don't change: "That's the way she is!"*

[10]S. Chase, *Power of Words* (New York: Harcourt Brace Jovanovich, 1954), p. 55.

5. *We may assume that characteristics we attribute to people or things are truly inherent: "That picture is ugly." "He's a selfish person."*
6. *We may assume that our message is totally clear to someone else. "You know perfectly well what I mean." "You heard me!"*[11]

While generalizations are potentially dangerous, they cannot be avoided, since language is a body of generalizations. Absolutely perfect interpersonal communication is impossible to achieve because our language is inherently incomplete. Yet there are degrees of incompleteness, and as communicators we should recognize that we are always functioning at levels of probability of understanding. The incomplete nature of our language makes it easy for us to misunderstand one another.

4. Language Reflects Not Only the Personality of the Individual but Also the Culture of His/Her Society

We have noted that an individual's language behavior necessarily reflects basic features of his/her personality, and that individual experiences and attitudes contribute to different reactions to words. Language, having developed in the context of a certain culture, of necessity reflects that particular culture. As a derived system of human solutions to recurring human events, experiences, and conditions, culture constitutes a system of social organization that differentiates and integrates human interaction and provides guides to behavior and motives to conform.

Language gives us innumerable insights into a culture. As an example of how language mirrors a culture, a study was made of the figures of speech in the language of the Palaun people of the western Pacific. Since figures of speech are a means of making the abstract concrete, such an analysis provides unique insights into a culture. To Palauns, a beautiful woman is a "comet." Since maternal descent is more greatly valued than paternal descent, superlative expressions reflect this organizational bias. "Largest" is *delad a klou* ("mother of large") and "highest" is *delad a ngarabub* ("mother of up").[12]

Even subcultures have language behaviors that distinguish one from another. While we tend to discount class differences in our own society, a team of investigators examined social-class speech differences of people surviving an Arkansas tornado. Ten people were classified as middle class by virtue of one or more years of college education and a moderate income. Ten other respondents were matched with them on such factors as age, race, and residence, but were able

[11]For other examples, see V. Satir, *Conjoint Family Therapy* (Palo Alto, Calif.: Science and Behavior, 1968), pp. 65–70.

[12]R. W. Force and M. Force, "Keys to Cultural Understanding," *Science*, 133 (1961), 1202–1206.

to be classified as lower class on the basis of income and inadequate education (no schooling beyond elementary school). Analyses of the transcribed tape-recorded interviews revealed the following differences:

1. *Almost without exception, descriptions by lower-class participants were given as seen through their own eyes, while middle-class respondents described the acts of others as the others saw them.*
2. *Lower-class respondents demonstrated a relative insensitivity to differences between their perspective and that of the interviewer. For example, surnames were used without identification, and pronouns like "we" and "they" had no clear referents. By comparison, the middle-class respondent used contextual clarification of his perspective in an attempt to consider the listener's role.*
3. *While middle-class respondents used overall frames to organize their entire account, lower-class respondents were basically disorganized, with segmental, limited accounts. Connections between incidents were obscure as respondents tended to wander from one incident to another.*

It could be concluded that lower-class respondents perceive in more concrete terms and that their speech reflects these more concrete cognitions. However, as the investigators ask:

> *Does his (the lower-class person) speech accurately reflect customary "concrete" modes of thought and perception, or is it that he . . . is unable to convey his perception? . . . One concludes that speech does in some sense reflect thought. The reader is perhaps best left at this point to draw his own conclusions. . . .*[13]

There is the great temptation to render value judgments on the language development and behavior of various subgroups, instead of viewing language differences as merely reflections of cultural differences. The imposition of linguistic rules formulating language into predictable sound patterns and a well-ordered grammatical structure and formal vocabulary facilitate analysis and description of the language, but do not provide a basis for qualitative judgments. A case of such a linguistic assumption can be noted in the following citation:

> *The syntax of low-income Negro children differs from standard English in many ways, but it has its own internal consistency. Unfortunately, the psychologist, not knowing the rules of Negro non-standard English, has interpreted these differences not as the result of well-learned rules but as evidence of "linguistic underdevelopment." He has con-*

[13]L. Schatzman and A. L. Strauss, "Social Class and Modes of Communication," *American Journal of Sociology*, 60 (1955), 329–338.

> *cluded that if black children do not speak like white children they are deficient. One of the most blatant errors has been a confusion between hypotheses concerning language and hypotheses concerning cognition. For this reason, superficial differences in language structures and language styles have been taken as manifestations of underlying differences in learning ability. To give one example, a child in class was asked, in a test of simple contrasts, "Why do you say they are different?" He could not answer. Then it was discovered that the use of "do you say," though grammatically correct, was inappropriate to his culture. When he was asked instead, "Why are they different?" he answered without any hesitation at all.*[14]

Such assumptions evolve because of misconceptions of what language is and how it functions.

Because language thus reflects a particular culture, problems abound when cross-cultural communication is attempted. Although words may mean different things to different people within a cultural grouping, at least some consensus and predictability is possible. The predictability is far less and the potential for misunderstanding is far greater in dealing with nonnative speakers. A young mother from the Middle East, for example, phoned a friend in extreme distress: Something must be wrong with her child because her two usual babysitters were *afraid* of her baby. She had called the sitters and both had told her, "I'm sorry, but I'm afraid I can't sit with your child tonight." If we fail to recognize the diverse ways in which the different peoples of the world have attempted to cope with the universal problems of adapting to their environment and the cultural basis for differences between cultures, we lay the groundwork for misunderstanding and conflict.

5. Language Creates a "Social Reality"

It is ridiculous to consider language a neutral medium of exchange. Specific words are selected for our use because they do affect behavior. Words call forth internal experiences as if by hypnotic suggestion. The role of language in contributing to people's problems and potential solutions can be shown to contribute to dangerous misconceptions and prejudices.

The color of a person's skin, for example, is tied to plus-or-minus words that inevitably condition our attitudes. The words "black" and "white" in Western culture are heavily loaded—"black" with unfavorable connotations and "white" with positive values. Ossie Davis, black actor and author, concluded after a detailed study of dictionaries and Roget's *Thesaurus* that the English language was his enemy. In the *Thesaurus* he counted 120 synonyms for "blackness" and noted

[14]J. C. Baratz, "The Language of the Ghetto Child," *The Center Magazine*, 1 (1969), 32.

that most of them had unpleasant connotations: blot, blotch, blight, smut, smudge, sully, soot, becloud, obscure, dingy, murky, threatening, frowning, foreboding, forbidden, sinister, baneful, dismal, evil, wicked, malignant, deadly, secretive, unclear, unwashed, foul, blacklist, black book, black-hearted," etc., as well as such words as "Negro, nigger, and darky."[15]

In the same book are cited 134 synonyms for the word "white" with such positive connotations as "purity, cleanliness, birth, shining, fair, blonde, stainless, chaste, unblemished, unsullied, innocent, honorable, upright, just, straightforward, genuine, trustworthy, honest," etc. Orientals fare little better than Blacks because "yellow" calls forth such associative words as "coward, conniver, baseness, fear, effeminacy, fast, spiritless, timid, sneak, lily-livered," etc.

Since these colors are not truly descriptive of races, color designations are more symbolic than descriptive. It seems reasonable and likely that our racial attitudes have been affected by our language. Our culture is not unique in this regard. In the Chinese language, while "yellow" is associated with "beauty, openness, flowering, and sunshine," "white" connotes "coldness, frigidity, bloodlessness, absence of feeling, and weakness." Similarly, in many African tongues "black" has associations of "strength, certainty, and integrity," while "white" is associated with "pale, anemic, untrustworthy, and devious."

Our language can also be shown to be sexist in nature. Feminist writer Jean Faust has observed:

> *All the titles, all the professions, all the occupations are masculine. They are weakened when they are made feminine by the addition of ess, ette. And man insists that these suffixes be used; he knows the power of language. He knows that language can control not only behavior, but thought itself. Words can determine the function, the very being of a person. Hence the awkwardness of lady novelist, sculptress, authoress, etc.* The New York Times *reached a low in its history when, on January 15, 1969, in the heat of the Great Jockey Controversy, it referred to girls who wish to ride horses in races as "jockettes." To insist on feminizing titles is to impress upon woman that she does not belong, that she cannot make a contribution equal to man's; that she performs only by man's sufferance.*[16]

One indication of the sexism of our language is in the grammatical use of personal pronouns. In most cases when the pronoun "he" is used, "he or she" is actually meant. To repeat the referent (e.g. "the speaker recited the speaker's speech") is extremely awkward; further, to state: "The speaker recited his or her speech" is confusing.

[15]This study of the effect of language on our prejudices was conducted at Pro Deo University in Rome. It is reported and evaluated by N. Cousins, "The Environment of Language," *Saturday Review*, April 8, 1967, p. 36.

[16]J. Faust, "Words That Oppress," *Women Speaking*, April 1970.

In this book we have made conscious efforts to attempt to include "he/she" and "his/her" references to people. Because of our awareness of the effect of language, we feel that such attempts are needed in lieu of a new glossary of personal pronouns.

The point is, the lack of a single pronoun for "he or she" forces a distinction in the case of an individual whose sex is not known and makes no difference. It forces emphasis upon differences between the sexes, instead of similarities, instead of accepting one common *humanity* (oops!). (Huwoman/manity?)

Language also provides a basis for grouping aspects of reality together. Linguist Benjamin Lee Whorf studied the ways in which languages express simple perceptions: Americans say "I am hungry"; Mexicans say "I have hunger"; Navajo Indians say "Hunger is killing me." He concluded that such differences in expression are connected with differences in cognition. He believed that different cultures perceive the world differently because of the restraints imposed by language.[17]

Whorf's hypothesis has been argued and contested by psychologists and linguists. The issue is whether language is a mold that determines the shape our thoughts and experiences take or the reverse, that language merely inventories and describes our perceptions of reality. The truth likely resides between the two extreme views. Since, as we have noted, our language is inherently inadequate to reflect all physical reality, a culture emphasizes the differences that are important to it. Thus Eskimos may have many words for snow and Bedouins many words for camel, while we have only one. If, however, kinds of snow or classes of camels were important to our lives, we could learn to pay attention to differences. As a child learns a language, he/she finds ready-made categories into which to fit his/her perceptions. The language, however, not only directs attention to selected features of the environment but also provides a biased basis for interpretations. Since language biases our perceptions, we need to be aware of the ways in which words condition our attitudes. If we can understand the basis of our prejudices, we are in a better position to cope with the effects.

NONVERBAL COMMUNICATION

In Chapter 4 we discussed the perceptual channels of sight, sound, and touch and noted Ruesch's three classifications of nonverbal codifications (sign language, action language, and object language). Although scholars disagree on definitional limits of verbal and nonverbal communication, we make the distinction to indicate that communica-

[17]B. L. Whorf, "Science and Linguistics," in J. B. Carroll, ed., *Language, Thought, and Reality* (New York: Wiley, 1956), pp. 207–219.

tion in addition to the words themselves occurs and has effects upon people.

For example, I may say the sentence, "I don't know where I'm going to have dinner tonight" in a variety of ways. I may be seeking information on good restaurants or I might be angling for an invitation. By my intonation, the context, the relationship between the two of us, and the various nonverbal cues I'm providing, you infer what I mean. Even "Good morning" can convey a number of meanings. One "Good morning" may indicate supplication, awareness of subordinate status, anxiety as to how the greeting will be received, etc. The other may convey condescension, awareness of power position, rejection, hostility, etc. The key is making sense out of the verbal and nonverbal messages to arrive at a congruent perception of a transaction.

Congruent messages contain information from a number of channels able to be combined harmoniously, agreeably, and consistently into one clear meaning. Messages from both verbal and nonverbal cues form redundant statements as clusters of behaviors reinforce and complement one another. For example, after a difficult task is completed, a woman might express a congruent message of relief by saying, "Thank heaven that's done!" relaxing her body as she eases into a chair, exhaling a full, audible sigh, and resting her limbs lightly beside her body.

When the verbal and nonverbal aspects of the message do not fit, the receiver must somehow translate the data into a single message. A husband—for example, one who has been working in the yard—comes into the house and says to his wife in an irritable tone of voice, "Damn it, the shovel handle broke!" The wife must then, with great agility and skill, go through the following process in her mind:

1. *He is reporting on the condition of the shovel.*
2. *I know that he is irritated. His "Damn it" and the tone of his voice make this clear.*
3. *Is he blaming me for the condition of the shovel? If he is criticizing me, what does he think I should do—apologize, help him, or what?*
4. *Maybe he is criticizing himself and is frustrated by the broken handle. If so, what is he asking me to do—sympathize, just listen, or what?*
5. *Since I know from living with him that he has little patience with malfunctions, he is probably just irritated at the situation and is asking me primarily to sympathize with him.*
6. *Now how can I communicate that I am genuinely sympathetic—listen quietly, offer to help, bring him coffee, offer suggestions? How can I best communicate my conscious concern and interest?*

Had the husband merely said, "I'm having a hard time in the yard; bring me a cup of coffee," the wife would have had little difficulty assessing the message. She is still in the position of deciding whether or not to agree to the husband's request, but at least she is not in doubt as to what he wants of her.[18]

Behavior in an interpersonal situation speaks louder than words and is more readily accepted. Such nonverbal communication similarly establishes the basis for interaction in the animal world and for animal interaction with humans. In research with bottle-nose porpoises, investigators have noted the unique way in which the porpoise attempts to establish a relationship with humans. The animal tries to take a person's hand in its mouth and gently squeeze the hand in its powerful jaws of razor-sharp teeth. If the human will submit to this demonstration, the porpoise seems to accept the act as a message of complete trust. Its next move is to reciprocate by placing the forward, bent portion of its body, roughly equivalent to the human throat—its most vulnerable area—upon the person's hand, foot, or leg, thereby signaling its trust in the friendly intentions of the person. Similarly, a cat routinely establishes a demonstration of trust through the ritual of throwing itself on its back, exposing its jugular vein to younger cats or cats from outside its own territory. The taking of the jugular vein in the jaw of the other cat establishes an "I-shall-not-attack-you" message that serves to define the relationship.[19]

While language can be used to communicate almost anything, however abstract, nonverbal behavior is rather limited in range. It is usually used to communicate feelings, likings, and preferences and to reinforce or contradict the verbal message. It may also add a new dimension to the verbal message, such as when a salesman describes his product to a client and simultaneously conveys, nonverbally, the impression that he likes the client.[20]

Nonverbal messages can, like linguistic ones, be misinterpreted. For example, a husband may find himself suspected of an unconfessed guilt if he spontaneously presents his wife with a bouquet of flowers. Sometimes we are confused in trying to interpret the meaning of growing pale, trembling, sweating, or stammering by a person who is being questioned. It can be interpreted as unmistakable proof of guilt, or it may merely be the behavior of an innocent person going through the experience of being suspected and realizing his fear may be interpreted as guilt. We add to the potential confusion by our propensity to "play games" with our outward manifestations of feelings. Some of

[18]This exchange and analysis is suggested by Satir, *op. cit.*, p. 79.

[19]P. Watzlawick, J. H. Beavin, and D. D. Jackson, *Pragmatics of Human Communication* (New York: Norton, 1967), p. 104.

[20]A. Mehrabian, "Communication Without Words," *Psychology Today*, February, 1968, 53.

us have become good "poker faces" and are temporarily able to conceal our genuine feelings.

The ways in which we interpret another person's reactions to us in the form of nonverbal messages determine our relationship with him/her. This person's acceptance of us in turn causes us to accept him/her. The cues are constantly being reinterpreted and reanalyzed at our subconscious level as the basis for future interaction. Since the nonverbal behaviors tend to be less conscious, we tend to believe them even more than the linguistic messages if the two are incongruent.

ACHIEVING INTERPERSONAL RAPPORT

As we attempt to elicit responses from other people, we seek to describe or "display" our thoughts in such ways that the receiver is able to identify with our thoughts. This process is dependent upon both effective transmission and effective reception of the messages.

The Sender

As the encoder of the message, the sender has certain responsibilities. Implicit in our discussion has been the assumption that words matter; the choice of words in the interpersonal relationship makes a difference to the people involved. If we want a child to move from a particular chair, we ask him/her to move. If at first our words and vocal emphasis do not impress him/her, we may try to cajole the child out of the chair, or, as a last resort, threaten or physically remove him/her. In our adult world, since most of the action we desire from others cannot be induced by the direct threat of force, we must rely upon words and nonverbal communication to achieve any manipulation of others.

Any attempts to manipulate people must be considered on ethical as well as pragmatic grounds. Interpersonal behavior depends to a great extent upon persuasive symbol manipulation designed to achieve certain actions from others, based on some kind of psychological consent. Such efforts might be viewed as unethical when we judge that the action called for will be advantageous to the persuader at the expense of the other person. Language was the instrument of achieving the outcomes in the mixed-motive situations discussed in Chapter 3. The information, if deliberately distorted, can be viewed as constituting unethical behavior.

Skilled salesmen become adept at selecting the key words that appeal to our motives, fears, and desires. Motivational selling has progressed to a fine art with near-scientific procedures. The encyclopedia salesman may induce us to buy because we think we are getting something for nothing, because we want an educated environment for our children, or because his product will make a significant contribution to our lives.

Word association is a common device in eliciting a desired response. A brewer was considering using the word "lagered" to describe his beer and conducted a word-association test. Only one-third of the people tested gave such responses as "ale," "beer," or "stout." Another third gave such responses as "tired," "drunk," "slow," and "dizzy," while the remaining participants had no response to the word. Thus the word was discarded.

Coined words are often the answer to an advertising campaign problem. Such words as "activated," "silicone," "sanforized," and "solium" are products of market researchers who have probed the public mind.

The "social reality" created by words can be used to control the minds of people. For example, a Soviet dictionary is reported to define "religion" as: "A fantastic faith in gods, angels and spirits . . . a faith without any scientific foundations. Religion is being supported and maintained by the reactionary circles. It serves for the subjugation of the working people and for building up the power of the exploiting bourgeois classes. . . . The superstition of outlived religion has been surmounted by the Communist education of the working class . . . and by its deep knowledge of the scientifically profound teaching of Marx-Leninism."[21]

In a similar vein, Hungarian Reds are reported to have taught their children the following Sovietized version of the Nativity:

> *There was once a poor married couple who had nothing to eat or dress in. They asked the rich people for help but the rich people sent them away. Their baby was born in a stable and covered with rags in a manger. The day after the baby was born, some shepherds who had come from Russia brought the baby some gifts. "We come from a country where poverty and misery are unknown," said the shepherds. "In Russia the babies grow in liberty because there is no unemployment or suffering." Joseph, the unemployed worker, asked the shepherds how they had found the house. The shepherds replied that a red star had guided them. Then the poor family took to the road. The shepherds covered the little baby with furs, and they all set out for the Soviet paradise.*[22]

Are any of us so very different from the Soviet propagandist as we entice, seduce, and coerce (all "loaded" words) others to view the world as we want them to see it? As individual senders of messages, we select the words designed to have the greatest desired effect on the listener. When we want to make a side trip, we tell our fellow traveler

[21] *Time*, January 29, 1951, 62.
[22] *Newsweek*, September 21, 1953, 62.

(a nonpolitical definition intended) that the trip is "only about 100 miles," while if we oppose the idea, we protest, "Why, that trip is over 100 miles!" Virtually every utterance that we make reflects a coloring of reality to reflect our feelings, attitudes, and values.

Our language usage creates attitudes and behaviors that would not otherwise occur. The exact words that we use at any particular time reflect our attitudes, feelings, and desires at that time. The same woman may be referred to as "young woman," "young lady," "miss," "hey-you," "girl," even "broad," or worse, depending upon the feeling and intent of the speaker.

Columnist Sydney Harris has frequently utilized what he has labeled "Antics with Semantics" to demonstrate how our attitudes determine the words we select:

> *The young nations which oppose our policies are "backward"; the neutral ones are "under-developed" and the ones supporting us are "developing." I lost the match because I was "off my form"; you lost because you were "over-confident"; he lost because he was "too cocky." The academic expert I agree with is a "scholar"; the academic expert I disagree with is a "pedant." When our statesmen say what they do not really mean, they are exercising "diplomacy"; when their statesmen say what they do not really mean, they are engaging in "guile."*[23]

One of the cruelest practices in our labeling process is the remark that tags a person—sometimes for life. Putting a label on a child can influence his entire life; for example, "piggy-fats," "brains," "porky," "gimpy," or "bat" can have either the effect of encouraging the victim to live up to the label or reject the title by changes in behavior. "Clumsy John" may be clumsy all his life unless he is able to forget his label. The label "juvenile delinquent" or "ex-con" may brand a person for life.

The Receiver

We spend far more time as receivers of messages than as senders. Just as the sender attempts to elicit a response from the receiver, the receiver must attempt to interpret the genuine meaning in the message. In the interpersonal verbal transaction, the receiver fulfills the role of listener.

We have become quite adept at not listening. In a society in which we are constantly bombarded with noise, we learn to close our minds to such distractions. Our brain picks and selects those cues having genuine significance. This capacity to shut out and ignore insignificant noise is a genuine blessing, but it can lead to listening

[23]S. Harris, "Last Things First," syndicated column appearing in the *Chicago Daily News*, December 18, 1962.

habits that can adversely affect the capability for interpersonal communication. The listener actually determines whether communication will take place. For any reason we can, as receivers, shut the speaker off mentally.

Part of the problem can be attributed to the disparity between our thought speed and the rate of a speaker. While we speak in the vicinity of 125–175 words per minute, our thought rate is far greater. We may use this spare time to "detour," to make brief excursions away from the subject, then come back to listen. Unlike the reader who loses his or her chain of concentration and rereads the section missed, however, the listener may have no opportunity for reiteration. The differential between thought speed and speech rate tempts us into the bad habits of daydreaming, shutting out the speaker, and impairing the flow of communication.

A leading authority on listening believes that much bad listening results from an emotional reaction to certain words or ideas that blot out the rest of the message. Consciously watch for the times when you tend to tune out a speaker because you fail to like his/her personality or ideas. Even if our goal is to argue the speaker down, we owe it to ourselves to listen fully. Notice the words or thoughts that make you stop listening. Today some people develop static when hearing words like "mod," "cool," "beat," "hippie," "Black Power." And there are special terms that jar persons involved in certain fields and distort their listening judgment. A man who has been having trouble with a newly purchased house may go "deaf" at the mention of leaks, termites, or contractor; his interest perks up, but he hears mainly his own jangled thoughts. Similarly, a person who has been speculating in the stock market may tune out anyone who mentions losses, sharp drop, or sell-off.[24] Thus, we filter incoming stimuli and perceive only those parts of the total pattern that fit our general or specific orientations (biases).

An additional problem for the listener is to distinguish between observational statements and statements of inference. A speaker may be reporting his/her perception of reality ("That man lives in a brown house") or drawing inferences from the data ("That man owns his home"). Observational and inferential statements are extremely difficult to distinguish because grammar, syntax, and pronunciation offer no clues to the differences. Likewise, the inference may be made with such vocal dynamics and certainty that the "truth" of the statement may go unquestioned. In Chapter 4 we noted the willingness of students to infer motives for the instructor's departure from the classroom ("He had another meeting"), and all were wrong. Inferences are

[24]R. G. Nichols and L. A. Stevens, *Are You Listening?* (New York: Hill, 1957), pp. 90–94.

necessary for our behavior and communication, but problems may develop when we tacitly assume statements of inference to be totally factual.

Feedback

The accomplishment of mutual understanding between encoder and decoder can only be determined by feedback. Because of the numerous sources of error and distortion in the message, it is often valuable to check back to see if understandings exist. Among the possible problems are:

1. *The encoded message may not be the same as the message intended by the speaker, or it may be garbled or unclear.*
2. *The receiver's perception of the speaker's motives or goals may influence the way the message is interpreted.*
3. *The words in the message may have different meanings to the receiver than to the sender, or they may have no meaning at all for the receiver.*
4. *The listener's attention might be diverted at a crucial time during transmission.*
5. *Expectations of the relationship may be confused.*

You can probably add to this list. The point is that there are so many pitfalls, we owe it to ourselves to provide adequate feedback to one another if we are to have any hope of gaining understanding and rapport.

SUMMARY AND PREVIEW OF READINGS

In every human relationship, words play an important part. They are among the tools used to establish bonds between people and may clarify or obscure ideas, unify or alienate people. In recent times we have noted that our nonverbal behaviors similarly provide bases for communication and may ultimately define a relationship.

In this chapter we have noted the characteristics of language that make communication difficult and the ways in which nonverbal signals further complicate matters.

The first article in this section, by the late Dr. Irving Lee of Northwestern University, is the result of keen observation, over a 5-year period, of people trying to work together in committees and conferences. He watched conflicts arise and noted the techniques used to avert problems. His findings provide a theoretical foundation for helping us understand how misunderstanding occurs.

The second article, by Edward and Mildred Hall, is a synthesis of the prolific research accomplished on nonverbal communication. We think the two articles together provide an excellent view of the problems of verbal and nonverbal communication.

SUGGESTED APPLICATIONS AND LEARNING EXPERIENCES

1. Meet in groups of five or six students. Have each group originate a word that has a justifiable meaning to the group. The members may choose, at random, one member of another group and give him the word to define. He may in turn immediately give the definition or take the option of conferring with other group members. The originating group may challenge his definition. Discuss criteria for judgment.

2. Have designated members of your group prepare brief, narrative stories. Send five members of your group out of the room and read someone's story. As the students return to the room one by one, have the story passed along, and note how the message changes. Ideas may be dropped, added, or modified. Discuss your capabilities as listeners and determine some of the causes for bad listening.

3. Collect some letters to the editor from your school and local newspapers. Observe the language usage and what it tells you about the sender of the message. As groups, generalize your reactions to the techniques employed.

4. Brainstorm a list of words that can cause communication problems between people of different reference groups (examples: "heavy," "gross," "chick," "dude," "hip"). To whom might these words cause difficulties—foreign students, older people? How do such words originate?

5. Compare your lists of potential problem words with Lee's analysis of misunderstanding in the reading that follows. Are Lee's suggestions for listening and clarifying realistic?

6. Observe and compare perceptions of the nonverbal communication of selected groups of people. Note the use of eye contact, postures, spatial distances, and possible cultural differences as suggested in the Hall and Hall article that follows. Share reports of your observations with the class.

THEY TALK PAST EACH OTHER

Irving J. Lee

"It takes," says Thoreau, in the noblest and most useful passage I remember to have read in any modern author, "two to speak truth—one to speak and another to hear."—Robert Louis Stevenson, "Truth of Intercourse," Virginibus Puerisque, *J. M. Dent & Sons, 1925, p. 32.*

HOW MISUNDERSTANDING HAPPENS

The one thing people tend to take for granted when talking to others is that they understand each other. It is rare, indeed, in a meeting to have someone hold up his own argument long enough to say, "I think you said. . . . Did you?" or "Was I right in thinking you meant . . . ?" We found people ever so eager to parry what a man says without ever wondering whether that is what the man said.

In the give-and-take of talk things go fast, and one is so busy organizing his reply that he doesn't take the time to make sure he knows what he is replying to. This is unfortunate because it often means that, instead of talking with others, people talk past or by-pass each other.

Note some by-passings.

1. The British Staff prepared a paper which they wished to raise as a matter of urgency, and informed their American colleagues that they wished to "table it." To the American staff "tabling" a paper meant putting it away in a drawer and forgetting it. A long and even acrimonious argument ensued before both parties realised that they were agreed on the merits and wanted the same thing.[1]

2. I remember a worrisome young man who, one day, came back from the X-ray room wringing his hands and trembling with fear. "It is all up with me," he said. "The X-ray man said I have a hopeless cancer of the stomach." Knowing that the roentgenologist would never have said such a thing, I asked, "Just what did he say?" and the answer was on dismissing him, the roentgenologist said to an assistant, "N.P." In Mayo clinic cipher this meant "no plates," and indicated that the X-ray man was so satisfied with the normal appearance of the stomach on the X-ray screen that he did not see any use in making films. But to the patient, watching in an agony of fear for some portent of disaster, it meant "nothing possible": in other words that the situation was hopeless![2]

[1]Winston Churchill, "The Second World War," Vol. III, Book II, *The New York Times*, February 28, 1950, p. 31.

[2]Walter C. Alvarez, *Nervousness, Indigestion and Pain*, Paul B. Hoeber, Inc., 1943, p. 74.

3. A foreman told a machine operator he was passing: "Better clean up around here." It was ten minutes later when the foreman's assistant phoned: "Say, boss, isn't that bearing Sipert is working on due up in engineering pronto?"

"You bet your sweet life it is. Why?"

"He says you told him to drop it and sweep the place up. I thought I'd better make sure."

"Listen," the foreman flared into the phone, "get him right back on that job. It's got to be ready in twenty minutes."

. . . What [the foreman] had in mind was for Sipert to gather up the oily waste, which was a fire and accident hazard. This would not have taken more than a couple of minutes, and there would have been plenty of time to finish the bearing. Sipert, of course, should have been able to figure this out for himself—except that something in the foreman's tone of voice, or in his own mental state at the time, made him misunderstand the foreman's intent. He wasn't geared to what the foreman had said.[3]

4. A lady recently ordered some writing paper at a department store and asked to have her initials engraved thereon. The salesgirl suggested placing them in the upper right-hand corner or the upper left-hand corner, but the customer said no, put them in the center. Well, the stationery has arrived, every sheet marked with her initials equidistant from right and left and from top and bottom.[4]

5. In a private conversation with Mr. Molotov, it became apparent that another difficult misunderstanding in language had arisen between ourselves and the Russians. At the San Francisco Conference when the question of establishing a trusteeship system within the United Nations was being considered, the Soviet delegation had asked Mr. Stettinius what the American attitude would be toward the assumption by the Soviet Union of a trusteeship. Mr. Stettinius replied in general terms, expressing the opinion that the Soviet Union was "eligible" to receive a territory for administration under trusteeship. Mr. Molotov took this to mean we would support a Soviet request for a trusteeship.[5]

In each case a word or phrase or sentence was used one way by the speaker and interpreted in another way by the listener. This is possible because words are versatile. Except for those intended for highly specialized purposes (like tetrasporangium, icosahedron, bisulfite), it is not unusual to find most words put to rather varied uses. A seventh-grade class in English was able to make up thirty sentences in which the word "set" was used differently each time. Even "word" is listed in sixteen different ways in *The American College Dictionary.*

The naïve speaker of a language usually has the feeling that, in general, words have a meaning, and he is seldom conscious of the great "area" of meaning for all except highly technical words. It is in this respect that the student's observation first needs widening and sharpening. Frequently we have tried to "build vocabularies" by adding more units or words. But to push first the addition of more vocabulary units in order to increase the number of words may interfere with, rather than help, effective mastery of language. This is the process that produces a Mrs. Malaprop. Most frequently the student needs first to know well the various areas of use of the units he is already familiar with; he needs to be made conscious of the great diversity of uses or meanings for commonly used words. He must be made aware, for example, that

[3]*The Foreman's Letter*, National Foreman's Institute, Inc., February 8, 1950, p. 3.

[4]"The Talk of the Town," *The New Yorker*, January 28, 1950, p. 21. Reprinted by permission. Copyright, 1950, The New Yorker Magazine, Inc.

[5]James F. Byrnes, *Speaking Frankly*, Harper & Row, 1947, p. 96.

the statement "The children did not count" can mean that they did not utter the words for the numbers in a series, or that the children were not considered. Ordinarily we just don't believe without considerable careful examination that for the five hundred most used words in English (according to the Thorndike Word Book) *the Oxford Dictionary records and illustrates from our literature 14,070 separate meanings.*[6]

At different times the same words may be used differently.

When Francis Bacon referred to various people in the course of his Essays *as indifferent, obnoxious, and* officious, *he was describing them as "impartial," "submissive," and "ready to serve." When King James II observed that the new St. Paul's Cathedral was amusing,* awful, *and* artificial, *he implied that Sir Christopher Wren's recent creation was "pleasing, awe-inspiring, and skilfully achieved." When Dr. Johnson averred that Milton's Lycidas was "easy,* vulgar, *and therefore* disgusting," *he intended to say that it was "effortless, popular, and therefore not in good taste."*[7]

The role of experience also affects the varieties of usage. Brander Matthews provided an example from a dinner-party conversation:

The second topic . . . was a definition of the image called up in our several minds by the word forest. *Until that evening I had never thought of forest as clothing itself in different colors and taking on different forms in the eyes of different men; but I then discovered that even the most innocent word may don strange disguises. To Hardy forest suggested the sturdy oaks to be assaulted by the woodlanders of Wessex; and to Du Maurier it evoked the trim and tidy avenues of the national domain of France. To Black the word naturally brought to mind the low scrub of the so-called deer-forests of Scotland; and to Gosse it summoned up a view of the green-clad mountains that towered up from the Scandinavian fiords. To Howells it recalled the thick woods that in his youth fringed the rivers of Ohio; and to me there came back swiftly the memory of the wild growths bristling up unrestrained by man, in the Chippewa Reservation which I had crossed fourteen years before in my canoe trip from Lake Superior to the Mississippi. Simple as the word seemed, it was interpreted by each of us in accord with his previous personal experience.*[8]

This conclusion about the range and possible uses of a word is easily verified. When it is forgotten, a listener just as easily comes to believe that (1) there is but one way to use a word—his—and (2) the speaker is doing with his words what the listener would were the listener doing the talking.

Can you see these beliefs at work in the examples given above?

In short, what you understand by any word or statement may not be what someone else intends to say. In a way, this is so obvious that most of us feel no obligation to think more about it. However, when one is aware of the fact it does not necessarily follow that he will act in terms of it. And there is some evidence that, unless people can be made sensitive to the possibility of by-passing, they make only meager efforts to stop it.

[6]Charles C. Fries, "Using the Dictionary," *Inside the ACD*, October, 1948, p. 1.

[7]Simeon Potter, *Our Language*, Pelican Books, 1950, p. 116.

[8]Brander Matthews, *These Many Years: Recollections of a New Yorker*, Charles Scribner's Sons, 1917, pp. 287–288. Quoted from the essay by Allen Walker Read, "Linguistic Revision as a Requisite for the Increasing of Rigor in Scientific Method," read at the Third Congress on General Semantics, July 22, 1949.

IT TAKES TWO TO MAKE COMMUNICATION

I have no wish here to give comfort to the bore who gets so much pleasure squelching discussions with his defiant "Define your terms." His maneuver results in shifting the burden in communication to the other fellow. Both must be brought into the act. We would have the listener work just a bit, too. So we urge him to state his notion of what was being said. Incidentally, that bore may sometimes be routed with this: "What definition of my words have you in mind? Perhaps we are thinking together after all."

The "plain-talk" and "say-it-in-simple-words" teachers have been in vogue but they haven't been especially helpful. They, too, tend to put the emphasis on one side of the communication line. Putting the burden for understanding on the speaker is a kind of implied invitation to the listener to sit back and contentedly assume he has nothing to do but wait his turn. And besides, even the simple words have uses which too frequently vary between man and man.

We once observed eight meetings of a group of nine men, who functioned as a standing committee in a corporation having wide public responsibilities. Five had taken one or more courses and had studied some of the books on "talking plainly." One of the items checked had to do with "the assumption of understanding." Can men be differentiated according to their readiness to believe they know what the other fellow is referring to? We looked in their replies for such indications as *questions* for assurance that the asker is "with" the speaker, *qualifications* like "If I understand what you say" "If I know what you mean . . . ," *invitations* like "Correct me if I'm off the beam" or "Tell me whether I answered what you intended to say. . . ."

We were hardly prepared to find that four of the "plain-talk students" did the least amount of questioning, qualifying, inviting, etc. This may, of course, be an accident. Before a conclusion worth much can be drawn we should have a broader sampling of the population. And before a cause can be assigned with confidence much more investigation would be needed. Nevertheless *these particular men*, knowing the ways to "plainness" and using them, tended to think they had done enough when they spoke so. They seemed to focus attention on *their* talking. They made no comparable effort to look to the character of what they heard.

I am not at all arguing that this finding in these particular cases means that training in plain talking makes for poor listening. I am trying to suggest only that training in the explicit effort at understanding may be a difficult sort of thing and may not automatically carry over from other training.

Cardinal Manning once said something relevant:

> *I have no doubt that I will hear that I am talking of what I do not understand; but in my defence I think I may say, I am about to talk of what I do not understand for this reason: I cannot get those who talk about it to tell me what they mean. I know what I mean by it, but I am not at all sure that I know what they mean by it; and those who use the same words in different senses are like men that run up and down the two sides of a hedge, and so can never meet.*

It is helpful to think of the radio in this. The performer in the studio can talk his heart out, but if the man in the easy chair is tuned in elsewhere it really makes no difference what is being said. Unless the receiver is on the same wave length, the character of what is sent out hardly governs the communication process.[9]

This is not to imply that a speaker cannot help by putting what he has to say in clear, listenable language. Anything he does to define, simplify, illustrate, is all to the good. But it is only part of the process. The listener has a job to do, too. He must make the effort to come to terms with the speaker to keep from assuming that he inevitably knows what the speaker has in mind. At the very least he might temper his arrogance with a question now and then just to make sure.

It takes two to make communication.

ARE YOU ON HIS COMMUNICATION LINE?

The preceding pages of this chapter were mimeographed and given to three groups, one meeting for study of the Bible, one considering matters of policy in a business corporation, and one working on problems in the administration of a college fraternity. Every member of each group read a portion out loud. We then talked about the main point—it takes two to make communication. We agreed that this was rather simple stuff and that we would try to talk with the possibility of by-passing in mind. We agreed, further, that no one of us would be insulted if asked to clarify or "talk some more" on any doubtful point. Nor would anyone feel hesitant about trying to get on the same wave length with anyone else. We gave each a small card with the inscription, "Are you on *his* communication line?"

What happened?

In each case the business of the meeting was slowed down. Only half as many items on the agenda could be covered. There was a certain amount of unfruitful wrangling about small points. Some members became tongue-tied in the face of so much freedom. Others became impatient with what seemed a waste of time, this trying to get to the speaker. The first sessions were always the worst. Most members felt comfortable only after the second or third.

And then we came upon something interesting. A man was being listened to. He found that others were actually waiting until he finished. He felt flattered in turn by the fact that another was trying to reach him rather than argue at him. He found himself trying to make his points so that his hearers would have less trouble with them. They were trying harder to read the cards he was putting on the table. The ornery member, normally so quick to doubt, stayed to question. The timid member found that the social pressure about the participation was all on his side.

We are inclined to think that the long-run results were worth time and trouble.

THE PURIST'S DOGMA

In a number of experimental discussion groups generous enough to submit to such instruction there was a curious resistance to this seemingly obvious

[9]This image is well developed in the article by Charles T. Estes, "Speech and Human Relations in Industry," *The Quarterly Journal of Speech*, April, 1946, pp. 160–169.

doctrine. I would be asked questions like these: Do you mean to say that a word doesn't have some definite, accurate meaning of its own regardless of the person who uses it? Isn't there a right or correct use for each word? If somebody fails to use a word exactly isn't he violating some rule in rhetoric or grammar?

How did these people come under the spell of the purist's dogma? Were they remembering some menacing drillmaster with a word list asking "What is the meaning of ———?" Or had they been badgered by vocabulary tests with entries like *glabrous heads: bald, over-sized, hairy, square, round; his stilted manner: irresolute, improper, cordial, stiffly formal* with instructions to circle the meaning? Or maybe they grew up when Alexander Woolcott was campaigning against certain current usage. He fought the use of "alibi" as a synonym for excuse; he wanted it saved for its "elsewhere" sense. He sneered when "flair" was used in the sense of knack or aptitude. He wanted it reserved for "capacity to detect." He and the traditional handbooks had a long list of such "reservations."

Or maybe they got their moorings from the pronouncements of Richard Grant White, who once said, "There is a misuse of words that can be justified by no authority, however great, and by no usage, however general." Or maybe they got no further in *Through the Looking Glass* than

> *. . . How old did you say you were?"*
>
> *Alice made a short calculation, and said, "Seven years and six months."*
>
> *"Wrong!" Humpty Dumpty exclaimed triumphantly. "You never said a word like it!"*
>
> *"I thought you meant 'How old are you?' " Alice explained.*
>
> *"If I'd meant that, I'd have said it," said Humpty Dumpty.*

Regardless of the source, they used this dogma as the basis for a theory of their own about the cause of misunderstanding. If a speaker didn't use a word correctly it was only natural if a listener who did know the exact meaning was misled. Just get people to use words in their right meaning and then everyone will understand everyone else.

Indeed, this might be a way—but how can we do it? Who has the authority to declare *the* correct use and who has the time to learn it? There are more than 600,000 words in the Merriam-Webster unabridged dictionary and perhaps half as many more in the technical vocabularies of medicine, engineering, law, etc. And when the dictionary gives several meanings, which is *the* one? And just how is anyone going to curb those who, like Humpty Dumpty, would have their own ways with words:

> *". . . Impenetrability! That's what I say!"*
>
> *"Would you tell me please," said Alice, "what that means?"*
>
> *"Now you talk like a reasonable child," said Humpty Dumpty, looking very much pleased. "I meant by 'impenetrability' that we've had enough of that subject, and it would be just as well if you'd mention what you mean to do next, as I suppose you don't mean to stop here all the rest of your life."*
>
> *"That's a great deal to make one word mean," Alice said in a thoughtful tone.*
>
> *"When I make a word do a lot of work like that," said Humpty Dumpty, "I always pay it extra."*

And what is more crucial, why do we look at words alone? Are words not most often used with other words in phrases, clauses, sentences? May not the setting affect the word?

We tried to get around this ill-advised zeal for exactness by suggesting that a word might be compared with a tool which can be used in a variety of ways. Thus, a screwdriver might be designed to drive screws, but once available it can be used to stir paint, jimmy a tight window, or, lacking any other weapon, to defend oneself with. You might, if you wish, insist that the screw function is the "right" or "correct" one and that a pistol is a much more effective weapon. But your insistence will hardly stop me from using the screwdriver in these other ways if I find it convenient or necessary to do so. A carpenter with a full rack of tools may have good reason for reserving each for but one use but if some other purpose is served there is nothing in the nature of the tool which could prevent that other use. The desire for the restriction, then, is personal rather than functional.

Within limits, especially in technical disciplines, it is possible to standardize word usage. One is usually safe in assuming that the workers in specialized areas will conform to some established, stipulated word usages. In the military establishment and in legal affairs, for example, it is often possible as well as necessary to insist that particular words be used in particular ways.

Once outside the range of the specialist's interests, however, we are wise if we expect words to be used variously. A speaker's concern at any moment is not to use a word but to make a statement. In his eagerness to speak his piece he is more concerned with his continuous expression than with his total effect. If he happens to range outside his listeners' conventional usage, they will get nowhere lamenting his lexicographical heresy. And if they do not get to his usage they are likely to assume that he said what he never intended to.

We have come to see wisdom in this advice: Never mind what words mean. What did *he* mean?

It may take time to find out what a man means. It may demand a patient listening and questioning. It may be an unexciting effort. But it should help to bring people into an area of awareness which they are too often on the outside of. Mr. Justice Jackson's experience in a situation more momentous than anything we were exposed to adds to our confidence in the advice:

> *It was my experience with the Soviet lawyers at Nürnberg that the most important factor in collaboration with the Soviet was patiently and persistently to make sure, when a proposition is first advanced, that it is thoroughly understood and that both sides are using their words to express the same sense. When this was done, the Soviet lawyers kept their agreements with us quite as scrupulously as American lawyers would. They may or may not regard that as a compliment, but my intentions are good. But it was my experience that it took infinite patience with them, as they thought it took infinite patience with us, to get to a point where there was a real meeting of minds as distinguished from some textual abstract formula which both could accept only because concretely it meant nothing or meant different things to each. And*

I have sometimes wondered how much misunderstanding could have been avoided if arrangement between the two countries had not often been concluded so hurriedly, in the stress of events, that this time-consuming and dreary process of reducing generalities to concrete agreements was omitted.[10]

[10]Excerpt from address by Mr. Justice Robert H. Jackson at the Bar Dinner of the New York County Lawyers' Association, December 8, 1949.

THE SOUNDS OF SILENCE

Edward Hall and
Mildred Hall

Bob leaves his apartment at 8:15 A.M. and stops at the corner drugstore for breakfast. Before he can speak, the counterman says, "The usual?" Bob nods yes. While he savors his Danish, a fat man pushes onto the adjoining stool and overflows into his space. Bob scowls and the man pulls himself in as much as he can. Bob has sent two messages without speaking a syllable.

Henry has an appointment to meet Arthur at 11 o'clock; he arrives at 11:30. Their conversation is friendly, but Arthur retains a lingering hostility. Henry has unconsciously communicated that he doesn't think the appointment is very important or that Arthur is a person who needs to be treated with respect.

George is talking to Charley's wife at a party. Their conversation is entirely trivial, yet Charley glares at them suspiciously. Their physical proximity and the movements of their eyes reveal that they are powerfully attracted to each other.

José Ybarra and Sir Edmund Jones are at the same party and it is important for them to establish a cordial relationship for business reasons. Each is trying to be warm and friendly, yet they will part with mutual distrust and their business transaction will probably fall through. José, in Latin fashion, moved closer and closer to Sir Edmund as they spoke, and this movement was miscommunicated as pushiness to Sir Edmund, who kept backing away from this intimacy, and this was miscommunicated to José as coldness. The silent languages of Latin and English cultures are more difficult to learn than their spoken languages.

In each of these cases, we see the subtle power of nonverbal communication. The only language used throughout most of the history of humanity (in evolutionary terms, vocal communication is relatively recent), it is the first form of communication you learn. You use this preverbal language, consciously and unconsciously, every day to tell other people how you feel about yourself and them. This language includes your posture, gestures, facial expressions, costume, the way you walk, even your treatment of time and space and material things. All people communicate on several different levels at the same time but are usually aware of only the verbal dialog and don't realize that they respond to nonverbal messages. But when a person says one thing and really believes something else, the discrepancy between the two can usually be sensed. Nonverbal-communication systems are much less subject to the conscious deception that often occurs in verbal systems. When we find ourselves thinking, "I don't know what it is about him, but he doesn't seem sincere," it's usually this lack of congruity between a person's words and his behavior that makes us anxious and uncomfortable.

Few of us realize how much we all depend on body movement in our conversation or are aware of the hidden rules that govern listening behavior. But we know instantly whether or not the person we're talking to is "tuned in" and we're very sensitive to any breach in listening etiquette. In white middle-class American culture, when someone wants to show he is listening to someone else, he looks either at the other person's face or, specifically, at his eyes, shifting his gaze from one eye to the other.

If you observe a person conversing, you'll notice that he indicates he's listening by nodding his head. He also make little "Hmm" noises. If he agrees with what's being said, he may give a vigorous nod. To show pleasure or affirmation, he smiles; if he has some reservations, he looks skeptical by raising an eyebrow or pulling down the corners of his mouth. If a participant wants to terminate the conversation, he may start shifting his body position, stretching his legs, crossing or uncrossing them, bobbing his foot or diverting his gaze from the speaker. The more he fidgets, the more the speaker becomes aware that he has lost his audience. As a last measure, the listener may look at his watch to indicate the imminent end of the conversation.

Talking and listening are so intricately intertwined that a person cannot do one without the other. Even when one is alone and talking to oneself, there is part of the brain that speaks while another part listens. In all conversations, the listener is positively or negatively reinforcing the speaker all the time. He may even guide the conversation without knowing it, by laughing or frowning or dismissing the argument with a wave of his hand.

The language of the eyes—another age-old way of exchanging feelings—is both subtle and complex. Not only do men and women use their eyes differently but there are class, generation, regional, ethnic and national cultural differences. Americans often complain about the way foreigners stare at people or hold a glance too long. Most Americans look away from someone who is using his eyes in an unfamiliar way because it makes them self-conscious. If a man looks at another man's wife in a certain way, he's asking for trouble, as indicated earlier. But he might not be ill-mannered or seeking to challenge the husband. He might be a European in this country who hasn't learned our visual mores. Many American women visiting France or Italy are acutely embarrassed because, for the first time in their lives, men really look at them—their eyes, hair, nose, lips, breasts, hips, legs, thighs, knees, ankles, feet, clothes, hairdo, even their walk. These same women, once they have become used to being looked at, often return to the United States and are overcome with the feeling that "No one ever really looks at me anymore."

Analyzing the mass of data on the eyes, it is possible to sort out at least three ways in which the eyes are used to communicate: dominance *vs.* submission, involvement *vs.* detachment and positive *vs.* negative attitude. In addition, there are three levels of consciousness and control, which can be categorized as follows: (1) conscious use of the eyes to communicate, such as the flirting blink and the intimate nose-wrinkling squint; (2) the very extensive category of unconscious but learned behavior governing where the eyes are directed and when (this unwritten set of rules dictates how and under what circumstances the sexes, as well as people of all status categories, look at each other); and (3) the response of the eye itself, which is completely outside both awareness and control—changes in the cast (the sparkle) of the eye and the pupillary reflex.

The eye is unlike any other organ of the body, for it is an extension of the brain. The unconscious pupillary reflex and the cast of the eye have been known by people of Middle Eastern origin for years—although most are unaware of their knowledge. Depending on the context, Arabs and others look either directly at the eyes or deeply *into* the eyes of their interlocutor. We became aware of this in the Middle East several years ago while looking at jewelry. The merchant suddenly started to push a particular bracelet at a customer and said, "You buy this one." What interested us was that the bracelet was not the one that had been consciously selected by the purchaser. But the merchant, watching the pupils of the eyes, knew what the purchaser really wanted to buy. Whether he specifically knew *how* he knew is debatable.

A psychologist at the University of Chicago, Eckhard Hess, was the first to conduct systematic studies of the pupillary reflex. His wife remarked one evening, while watching him reading in bed, that he must be very interested in the text because his pupils were dilated. Following up on this, Hess slipped some pictures of nudes into a stack of photographs that he gave to his male assistant. Not looking at the photographs but watching his assistant's pupils, Hess was able to tell precisely when the assistant came to the nudes. In further experiments, Hess retouched the eyes in a photograph of a woman. In one print, he made the pupils small, in another, large; nothing else was changed. Subjects who were given the photographs found the woman with the dilated pupils much more attractive. Any man who has had the experience of seeing a woman look at him as her pupils widen with reflex speed knows that she's flashing him a message.

The eye-sparkle phenomenon frequently turns up in our interviews of couples in love. It's apparently one of the first reliable clues in the other person that love is genuine. To date, there is no scientific data to explain eye sparkle; no investigation of the pupil, the cornea or even the white sclera of the eye shows how the sparkle originates. Yet we all know it when we see it.

One common situation for most people involves the use of the eyes in the street and in public. Although eye behavior follows a definite set of rules, the rules vary according to the place, the needs and feelings of the people, and their ethnic background. For urban whites, once they're within definite recognition distance (16–32 feet for people with average eyesight), there is mutual avoidance of eye contact—unless they want something specific: a pickup, a handout or information of some kind. In the West and in small towns generally, however, people are much more likely to look at and greet one another, even if they're strangers.

It's permissible to look at people if they're beyond recognition distance; but once inside this sacred zone, you can only steal a glance at strangers. You *must* greet friends, however; to fail to do so is insulting. Yet, to stare too fixedly even at them is considered rude and hostile. Of course, all of these rules are variable.

A great many blacks, for example, greet each other in public even if they don't know each other. To blacks, most eye behavior of whites has the effect of giving the impression that they aren't there, but this is due to white avoidance of eye contact with *anyone* in the street.

Another very basic difference between people of different ethnic backgrounds is their sense of territoriality and how they handle space. This is the silent communication, or miscommunication, that caused friction between Mr. Ybarra and Sir Edmund Jones in our earlier example. We know from research that everyone has around himself an invisible bubble of space that contracts and expands depending on several factors: his emotional state, the activity he's performing at the time and his cultural background. This bubble is a kind of mobile territory that he will defend against intrusion. If he is accustomed to close personal distance between himself and others, his bubble will be smaller than that of someone who's accustomed to greater personal distance. People of North European heritage—English, Scandinavian, Swiss and German—tend to avoid contact. Those whose heritage is Italian, French, Spanish, Russian, Latin American or Middle Eastern like close personal contact.

People are very sensitive to any intrusion into their spatial bubble. If someone stands too close to you, your first instinct is to back up. If that's not possible, you lean away and pull yourself in, tensing your muscles. If the intruder doesn't respond to these body signals, you may then try to protect yourself, using a briefcase, umbrella or raincoat. Women—especially when traveling alone—often plant their pocketbook in such a way that no one can get very close to them. As a last resort, you may move to another spot and position yourself behind a desk or a chair that provides screening. Everyone tries to adjust the space around himself in a way that's comfortable for him; most often, he does this unconsciously.

Emotions also have a direct effect on the size of a person's territory. When you're angry or under stress, your bubble expands and you require more space. New York psychiatrist Augustus Kinzel found a difference in what he calls Body-Buffer Zones between violent and nonviolent prison inmates. Dr. Kinzel conducted experiments in which each prisoner was placed in the center of a small room and then Dr. Kinzel slowly walked toward him. Nonviolent prisoners allowed him to come quite close, while prisoners with a history of violent behavior couldn't tolerate his proximity and reacted with some vehemence.

Apparently, people under stress experience other people as looming larger and closer than they actually are. Studies of schizophrenic patients have indicated that they sometimes have a distorted perception of space, and several psychiatrists have reported patients who experience their body boundaries as filling up an entire room. For these patients, anyone who comes into the room is actually inside their body, and such an intrusion may trigger a violent outburst.

Unfortunately, there is little detailed information about normal people who live in highly congested urban areas. We do know, of course, that the noise, pollution, dirt, crowding and confusion of our cities induce feelings of stress in most of us, and stress leads to a need for greater space. The man who's packed into a subway, jostled in the street, crowded into an elevator and forced to work all day in a bull pen or in a small office without auditory or visual privacy is going to be very stressed at the end of his day. He needs places that provide relief from constant overstimulation of his nervous system. Stress from overcrowding is cumulative and people can tolerate more crowding early in the day than later; note the increased bad temper during the evening rush hour as compared with the morning melee. Certainly one factor in people's desire to commute by car is the need for privacy and relief from crowding (except, often, from other cars); it may be the only time of the day when nobody can intrude.

In crowded public places, we tense our muscles and hold ourselves stiff, and thereby communicate to others our desire not to intrude on their space and, above all, not to touch them. We also avoid eye contact, and the total effect is that of someone who has "tuned out." Walking along the street, our bubble expands slightly as we move in a stream of strangers, taking care not to bump into them. In the office, at meetings, in restaurants, our bubble keeps changing as it adjusts to the activity at hand.

Most white middle-class Americans use four main distances in their business and social relations: intimate, personal, social and public. Each of these distances has a near and a far phase and is accompanied by changes in the volume of the voice. Intimate distance varies from direct physical contact with another person to a distance of six to eighteen inches and is used for our most private activities—caressing another person or making love. At this distance, you are overwhelmed by sensory inputs from the other person—heat from the body, tactile stimulation from the skin, the fragrance of perfume, even the sound of breathing—all of which literally envelop you. Even at the far phase, you're still within easy touching distance. In general, the use of intimate distance in public between adults is frowned on. It's also much too close for strangers, except under conditions of extreme crowding.

In the second zone—personal distance—the close phase is one and a half to two and a half feet; it's at this distance that wives usually stand from their husbands in public. If another woman moves into this zone, the wife will most likely be disturbed. The far phase—two and a half to four feet—is the distance used to "keep someone at arm's length" and is the most common spacing used by people in conversation.

The third zone—social distance—is employed during business transactions or exchanges with a clerk or repairman. People who work together tend to use close social distance—four to seven feet. This is also the distance for conversations at social gatherings. To stand at this distance from someone who is seated has a dominating effect (e.g., teacher to pupil, boss to secretary). The far phase of the third zone—seven to twelve feet—is where people stand when someone says, "Stand back so I can look at you." This distance lends a formal tone to business or social discourse. In an executive office, the desk serves to keep people at this distance.

The fourth zone—public distance—is used by teachers in classrooms or speakers at public gatherings. At its farthest phase–25 feet and beyond —it is used for important public figures. Violations of this distance can lead to serious complications. During his 1970 U.S. visit, the president of France, Georges Pompidou, was harassed by pickets in Chicago, who were permitted to get within touching distance. Since pickets in France are kept behind barricades a block or more away, the president was outraged by this insult to his person, and President Nixon was obliged to communicate his concern as well as offer his personal apologies.

It is interesting to note how American pitchmen and panhandlers exploit the unwritten, unspoken conventions of eye and distance. Both take advantage of the fact that once explicit eye contact is established, it is rude to look away, because to do so means to brusquely dismiss the other person and his needs. Once having caught the eye of his mark, the panhandler then locks on, not letting go until he moves through the public zone, the social zone, the personal zone and, finally, into the intimate sphere, where people are most vulnerable.

Touch also is an important part of the constant stream of communication that takes place between people. A light touch, a firm touch, a blow, a caress, are all communications. In an effort to break down barriers among people, there's been a recent upsurge in group-encounter activities, in which strangers are encouraged to touch one another. In special situations such as these, the rules for not touching are broken with group approval and people gradually lose some of their inhibitions.

Although most people don't realize it, space is perceived and distances are set not by vision alone but with all the senses. Auditory space is perceived with the ears, thermal space with the skin, kinesthetic space with the muscles of the body and olfactory space with the nose. And, once again, it's one's culture that determines how his senses are programmed—which sensory information ranks highest and lowest. The important thing to remember is that culture is very persistent. In this country, we've noted the existence of culture patterns that determine distance between people in the third and fourth generations of some families, despite their prolonged contact with people of very different cultural heritages.

Whenever there is great cultural distance between two people, there are bound to be problems arising from differences in behavior and expectations. An example is the American couple who consulted a psychiatrist about their marital problems. The husband was from New England and had been brought up by reserved parents who taught him to control his emotions and to respect the need for privacy. His wife was from an Italian family and had been brought up in close contact with all the members of her large family, who were extremely warm, volatile and demonstrative.

When the husband came home after a hard day at the office, dragging his feet and longing for peace and quiet, his wife would rush to him and smother him. Clasping his hands, rubbing his brow, crooning over his weary head, she never left him alone. But when the wife was upset or anxious about her day, the husband's response was to withdraw completely and leave her alone. No comforting, no affectionate embrace, no attention —just solitude. The woman became convinced her husband didn't love her and, in desperation, she consulted a psychiatrist. Their problem wasn't basically psychological but cultural.

Why has man developed all these different ways of communicating messages without words? One reason is that people don't like to spell out certain kinds of messages. We prefer to find other ways of showing our feelings. This is especially true in relationships as sensitive as courtship. Men don't like to be rejected and most women don't want to turn a man down bluntly. Instead, we work out subtle ways of encouraging or discouraging each other that save face and avoid confrontations.

How a person handles space in dating others is an obvious and very sensitive indicator of how he or she feels about the other person. On a first date, if a woman sits or stands so close to a man that he is acutely conscious of her physical presence—inside the intimate-distance zone—the man usually construes it to mean that she is encouraging him. However, before the man starts moving in on the woman, he should be sure what message she's really sending; otherwise, he risks bruising his ego. What is close to someone of North European background may be neutral or distant to someone of Italian heritage. Also, women sometimes use space as a way of misleading a man and there are few things that put men off more than women who communicate contradictory messages—such as women who cuddle up and then act insulted when a man takes the next step.

How does a woman communicate interest in a man? In addition to such familiar gambits as smiling at him, she may glance shyly at him, blush and then look away. Or she may give him a real come-on look and move in very close when he approaches. She may touch his arm and ask for a light. As she leans forward to light her cigarette, she may brush him lightly, enveloping him in her perfume. She'll probably continue to smile at him and she may use what ethologists call preening gestures—touching the back of her hair, thrusting her breasts forward, tilting her hips as she stands or crossing her legs if she's seated, perhaps even exposing one thigh or putting a hand on her thigh and stroking it. She may also stroke her wrists as she converses or show the palm of her hand as a way of gaining his attention. Her skin may be unusually flushed or quite pale, her eyes brighter, the pupils larger.

If a man sees a woman whom he wants to attract, he tries to present himself by his posture and stance as someone who is self-assured. He moves briskly and confidently. When he catches the eye of the woman, he may hold her glance a little longer than normal. If he gets an encouraging smile, he'll move in close and engage her in small talk. As they converse, his glance shifts over her face and body. He, too, may make preening gestures—straightening his tie, smoothing his hair or shooting his cuffs.

How do people learn body language? The same way they learn spoken language—by observing and imitating people around them as they're growing up. Little girls imitate their mothers or an older female. Little boys imitate their fathers or a respected uncle or a character on television. In this way, they learn the gender signals appropriate for their sex. Regional, class and ethnic patterns of body behavior are also learned in childhood and persist throughout life.

Such patterns of masculine and feminine body behavior vary widely from one culture to another. In America, for example, women stand with their thighs together. Many walk with their pelvis tipped slightly forward and their upper arms close to their body. When they sit, they cross their legs at the knee or, if they are well past middle age, they may cross their ankles. American men hold their arms away from their body, often swinging them as they walk. They stand with their legs apart (an extreme example is the cowboy, with legs apart and thumbs tucked into his belt). When, they sit, they put their feet on the floor with legs apart and, in some parts of the country, they cross their legs by putting one ankle on the other knee.

Leg behavior indicates sex, status and personality. It also indicates whether or not one is at ease or is showing respect or disrespect for the other person. Young Latin-American males avoid crossing their legs. In their world of *machismo*, the preferred position for young males when with one another (if there is no older dominant male present to whom they must show respect) is to sit on the base of their spine with their leg muscles relaxed and their feet wide apart. Their respect position is like our military equivalent; spine straight, heels and ankles together—almost identical to that displayed by properly brought up young women in New England in the early part of this century.

American women who sit with their legs spread apart in the presence of males are *not* normally signaling a come-on—they are simply (and often unconsciously) sitting like men. Middle-class women in the presence of other women to whom they are very close may on occasion throw themselves down on a soft chair or sofa and let themselves go. This is a signal that nothing serious will be taken up. Males, on the other hand, lean back and prop their legs up on the nearest object.

The way we walk, similarly, indicates status, respect, mood and ethnic or cultural affiliation. The many variants of the female walk are too well known to go into here, except to say that a man would have to be blind not to be turned on by the way some women walk—a fact that made Mae West rich before scientists ever studied these matters. To white Americans, some French middle-class males walk in a way that is both humorous and suspect. There is a bounce and looseness to the French walk, as though the parts of the body were somehow unrelated. Jacques Tati, the French movie actor, walks this way; so does the great mime, Marcel Marceau.

Blacks and whites in America—with the exception of middle- and upper-middle-class professionals of both groups—move and walk very differently from each other. To the blacks, whites often seem incredibly stiff, almost mechanical in their movements. Black males, on the other hand, have a looseness and coordination that frequently make whites a little uneasy; it's too different, too integrated, too alive, too male. Norman Mailer has said that squares walk from the shoulders, like bears, but blacks and hippies walk from the hips, like cats.

All over the world, people walk not only in their own characteristic way but have walks that communicate the nature of their involvement with whatever it is they're doing. The purposeful walk of North Europeans is an important component of proper behavior on the job. Any male who has been in the military knows how essential it is to walk properly (which makes for a continuing source of tension between blacks and whites in the Service). The quick shuffle of servants in the Far East in the old days was a show of respect. On the island of Truk, when we last visited, the inhabitants even had a name for the respectful walk that one used when in the presence of a chief or when walking past a chief's house. The term was *sufan*, which meant to be humble and respectful.

The notion that people communicate volumes by their gestures, facial expressions, posture and walk is not new; actors, dancers, writers and psychiatrists have long been aware of it. Only in recent years, however, have scientists begun to make systematic observations of body motions. Ray L. Birdwhistell of the University of Pennsylvania is one of the pioneers in body-motion research and coined the term kinesics to describe this field. He developed an elaborate notation system to record both facial and body movements, using an approach similar to that of the linguist, who studies the basic elements of speech. Birdwhistell and other kinesicists such as Albert Sheflen, Adam Kendon and William Condon take movies of people interacting. They run the film over and over again, often at reduced speed for frame-by-frame analysis, so that they can observe even the slightest body movements not perceptible at normal interaction speeds. These movements are then recorded in notebooks for later analysis.

To appreciate the importance of nonverbal-communication systems, consider the unskilled inner-city black looking for a job. His handling of time and space alone is sufficiently different from the white middle-class pattern to create great misunderstandings on both sides. The black is told to appear for a job interview at a certain time. He arrives late. The white interviewer concludes from his tardy arrival that the black is irresponsible and not really interested in the job. What the interviewer doesn't know is that the black time system (often referred to by blacks as C. P. T.—colored people's time) isn't the same as that of whites. In the words of a black student who had been told to make an appointment to see his professor: "Man, you *must* be putting me on. I never had an appointment in my life."

The black job applicant, having arrived late for his interview, may further antagonize the white interviewer by his posture and his eye behavior. Perhaps he slouches and avoids looking at the interviewer; to him, this is playing it cool. To the interviewer, however, he may well look shifty and sound uninterested. The interviewer has failed to notice the actual signs of interest and eagerness in the black's behavior, such as the subtle shift in the quality of the voice–a gentle and tentative excitement—an almost imperceptible change in the cast of the eyes and a relaxing of the jaw muscles.

Moreover, correct reading of black-white behavior is continually complicated by the fact that both groups are comprised of individuals—some of whom try to accommodate and some of whom make it a point of pride *not* to accommodate. At present, this means that many Americans, when thrown into contact with one another, are in the precarious position of not knowing which pattern applies. Once identified and analyzed, nonverbal-communication systems can be taught, like a foreign language. Without this training, we respond to nonverbal communications in terms of our own culture; we read everyone's behavior as if it were our own, and thus we often misunderstand it.

Several years ago in New York City, there was a program for sending children from predominantly black and Puerto Rican low-income neighborhoods to summer school in a white upper-class neighborhood on the East Side. One morning, a group of young black and Puerto Rican boys raced down the street, shouting and screaming and overturning garbage cans on their way to school. A doorman from an apartment building nearby chased them and cornered one of them inside a building. The boy drew a knife and attacked the doorman. This tragedy would not have occurred if the doorman had been familiar with the behavior of boys from low-income neighborhoods, where such antics are routine and socially acceptable and where pursuit would be expected to invoke a violent response.

The language of behavior is extremely complex. Most of us are lucky to have under control one subcultural system—the one that reflects our sex, class, generation and geographic region within the United States. Because of its complexity, efforts to isolate bits of nonverbal communication and generalize from them are in vain; you don't become an instant expert on people's behavior by watching them at cocktail parties. Body language isn't something that's independent of the person, something that can be donned and doffed like a suit of clothes.

Our research and that of our colleagues has shown that, far from being a superficial form of communication that can be consciously manipulated, nonverbal-communication systems are interwoven into the fabric of the personality and, as sociologist Erving Goffman has demonstrated, into society itself. They are the warp and woof of daily interactions with others and they influence how one expresses oneself, how one experiences oneself as a man or a woman.

Nonverbal communications signal to members of your own group what kind of person you are, how you feel about others, how you'll fit into and work in a group, whether you're assured or anxious, the degree to which you feel comfortable with the standards of your own culture, as well as deeply significant feelings about the self, including the state of your own psyche. For most of us, it's difficult to accept the reality of another's behavioral system. And, of course, none of us will ever become fully knowledgeable of the importance of every nonverbal signal. But as long as each of us realizes the power of these signals, this society's diversity can be a source of great strength rather than a further—and subtly powerful—source of division.

Chapter 7
THE INTERPERSONAL RELATIONSHIP

To negotiate satisfactory conditions with our social and physical environment, we must achieve cooperative, agreeable relationships with a number of our associates. Further, to achieve a deeply satisfying opinion of ourselves, it is essential to achieve a warm, personal relationship with at least one other person.

In recent times we have seen in our culture a new emphasis on seeking warm, personal relationships. Our complex, mobile, automated society has produced a heightened condition of impersonality. The yearning for closer personal ties is a major theme of our times. Without reservation we can conclude that for people in the 1970s, the most significant phase of the process of interpersonal communication is developing and maintaining a warm, personal relationship.

As two people interact, the relationship between them tends to stabilize, "freeze," become rigid and unchangeable. To improve an existing relationship or to achieve the most satisfying potential of a new one just developing, we must analyze it, then evaluate it, and eventually, if need be, change it if at all possible. In this chapter we shall focus on the process of analyzing, evaluating, and changing an interpersonal relationship.

ANALYZING A RELATIONSHIP

A relationship may be analyzed in terms of its (1) basic patterns of interaction and (2) degree of rigidity. Both are important to your understanding if changes or improvements are to be sought.

Identifying Basic Interaction Patterns

As you interact with another person, it is likely that you gain a general impression of "where you stand" with him or her. You seem to be fairly close, sympathetic with each other, and seem to like each other. Generally you cooperate, confide, and respect each other's wishes. The question we are raising here is this: Can the primary behavioral dimensions of a relationship be defined and identified? In how many *different* ways do people relate to each other? How many of these are really *important*, significant? In a given situation can these be observed and the *intensity* of each estimated?

Two decades of research support the conclusion that any interpersonal relationship has three primary dimensions: (1) the degree of involvement, (2) the emotional tone or feelings involved, and (3) the amount of interpersonal control. In the vernacular they have become known by some as "in or out," "near or far," and "top or bottom." These concepts were introduced in the article by Schutz[1] following Chapter 4. In his original work Schutz summarizes twenty years of research into the nature of interpersonal relationships.[2] He shows that sixteen studies of parent-child relations, three analyses of interpersonal behavior as "personality types," and ten major studies of interpersonal behavior in groups all converge in their findings to support the conclusion that there are these three basic dimensions. Each one is different and distinct enough to be useful; together, they provide a description of a relationship that covers the significant elements. Additional research by Schutz confirmed this conclusion.[3]

The dimension of *involvement* relates to the amount of interaction between the participants, but it actually refers to something more: the importance of the interaction to each of the participants. It indicates the extent to which a relationship actually exists. For example, we may work in an office building, at a desk 12 feet away from another person with whom we exchange impersonal greetings daily; we may even discuss with them weather and sports three or four times daily. And in so doing, we may feel little or no involvement, and not even miss them when absent. In such a case, there is little interpersonal involvement and not much of a relationship. Conversely, a father and daughter may live in different, distant cities, see each other rarely, and communicate infrequently, but enjoy a very meaningful relationship.

The degree of *involvement* between two persons is also a function of the amount of personal information exchanged. For someone to be important to you, you must know something about him/her that matters to you and that makes a great difference to you.[4] If you don't know much about the person, it is not likely that your acquaintance will amount to much of a relationship. If a rewarding relationship is desired, the other person will have to reveal something of himself/herself to you and you to himself/herself.[5]

Self-disclosure is a basic function of the degree of involvement between two people; there is a considerable body of research showing that when self-disclosure is high, interpersonal involvement is increased.[6] We may illustrate this principle with a common type of ex-

[1]See pp. 205–224.

[2]W. C. Schutz, *FIRO: A Three-Dimensional Theory of Interpersonal Behavior* (New York: Holt, Rinehart and Winston, 1958), pp. 34–54.

[3]*Ibid.*, pp. 54–56.

[4]Cf. J. Ruesch and G. Bateson, *Communication: The Social Matrix of Psychiatry* (New York: Norton, 1951), pp. 79–81.

[5]Cf. S. Jourard, *The Transparent Self* (New York: Van Nostrand Reinhold, 1964), pp. 19–39.

[6]See D. W. Johnson, ed., *Readings in Humanistic Social Psychology* (Philadelphia: Lippincott, 1972).

ample. Suppose Joe meets a girl, Susan, for the first time in a college cafeteria. Crowded conditions cause him to ask her to share her table. As they chat, he notices she is quite tense; however, the more they talk the more he is attracted to her. As they share information about each other, her anxiety leads to sharing of confidences. Joe learns that Susan has been ill, only recently returned to school, and last night experienced an attempted rape while going from the library to her dormitory. Joe is a bit shocked and sympathetic. In certain ways Susan has shown that (1) she likes Joe, and (2) she trusts him. Regardless of whether or not romantic interest may develop, Joe and Susan are now involved in each other's lives. They each care about what happens to the other. Such self-disclosure can be the start of a relationship; without some bits of important information, a relationship of any consequence is not likely to develop.[7]

As people disclose bits of information to each other—information about themselves—they tend to reach little agreements on what matters and what does not; what is relevant and what is not. They tend to develop a working consensus of mutual consideration and sympathy. In addition, they tend to unite their individual differences of opinion. As Erving Goffman says, a "shared definition" of their relationship comes to prevail.[8] This is what we mean by *involvement*: They interact in ways that are important to each other. They tend to care what happens to themselves when together, and to each other. If their *involvement* is high enough, a relationship is established.

In an active, established relationship the amount of interaction is ordinarily quite stable. It may vary somewhat from day to day, but such variations are usually expected and routine. In such a relationship the other two dimensions, *dominance versus submission* and *affection versus hostility*, are of greatest concern. Note that each of these dimensions is ambivalent; that is, each has a "zero" or neutral point in the center (see Figure 7.1). To illustrate, two people in a relationship could be highly affectionate, highly hostile, or somewhere in between, including neutral—neither affectionate nor hostile. In addition, one could be very dominant and the other very submissive or somewhere in between—neither one dominating the other.

In established relationships such as those in families or among members of work or task groups, these two basic dimensions are the primary ones needed to describe the relationship. In study after study attempts to detect those "differences that make a difference" in interpersonal relationships identify these two dimensions. In many cases they are tagged with different labels that essentially have the same meaning. This is not surprising, since more than thirty years ago All-

[7]Cf. D. W. Johnson, *Reaching Out* (Englewood Cliffs, N.J.: Prentice-Hall, 1972), pp. 9–13.

[8]E. Goffman, *Behavior in Public Places* (New York: Free Press, 1963), p. 96.

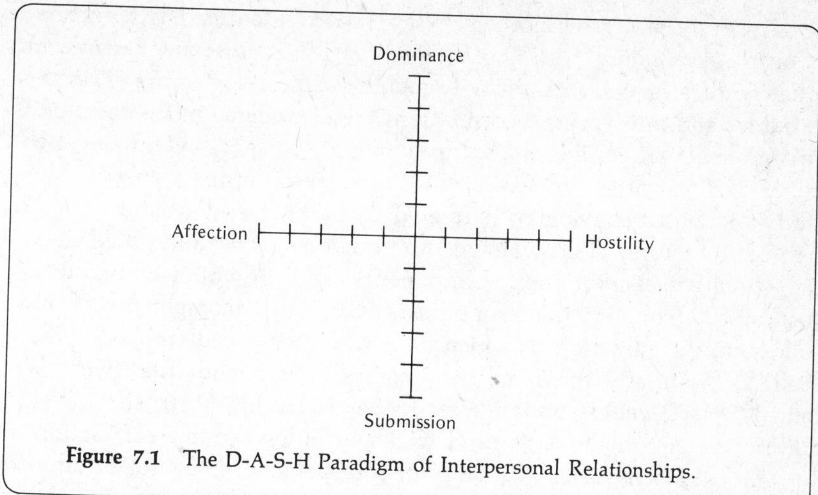

Figure 7.1 The D-A-S-H Paradigm of Interpersonal Relationships.

port and Odbert identified over 18,000 distinctive English words representing categories of human behavior.[9]

In an extensive study of relationships between psychotherapy patients and therapists, Timothy Leary and his associates developed a framework for analyzing interpersonal behavior.[10] Although they used only rough empirical data, their intuition and insight appear quite remarkable in view of findings of later studies. They identified two major factors ("Dominance-Submission" and "Hate-Love"); in addition, they represented variations of these computations on a wheel or "circumplex." Quadrants were divided into octants, and eight subcategories defined. The most interesting thing about the circumplex formulation is that the subcategories are ordered in an endless sequential circle, without severe breaks or any beginning or end. Thus, in such a formulation, *all* interpersonal relationships are included. In principle this formulation has been supported by data from subsequent studies.

A series of studies of students in small discussion groups identified two basic dimensions of member-relations: "Individual Assertiveness" and "Sociability."[11] The circumplex was used to describe relationship variations. An enlarged follow-up study later found similar results.[12]

[9]G. W. Allport and H. S. Odbert, "Trait Names: A Psycho-Lexical Study," *Psychological Monographs*, 47 (1936), 1–171.

[10]T. Leary, *Interpersonal Diagnosis of Personality* (New York: Ronald, 1957).

[11]E. F. Borgatta, L. S. Cottrell, and J. M. Mann, "The Spectrum of Individual Interaction Characteristics: An Interdimensional Analysis," *Psychological Reports*, 4 (1958), 279–319.

[12]E. F. Borgatta, "Rankings and Self-Assessments: Some Behavioral Characteristics Replication Studies," *Journal of Social Psychology*, 52 (1960), 297–307.

An early study of mother-child relations identified two factors: "Control-Autonomy" and "Love-Hostility."[13] A subsequent review of other studies of child behavior found the same two factors: Primary variables and intervariable correlations were arranged in the form of a circumplex.[14] A study analyzing parental behavior identified two factors: "Warmth-Coldness" and "Strictness-Permissiveness."[15] A study of child behavior as it related to parents and teachers found two basic factors: "Extraversion-Introversion" (containing a substantial *dominance-submission* component) and "Emotional Stability-Instability" (containing a strong *hostile-nonhostile* component).[16] In a follow-up investigation in which data were compared from six other studies, essentially the same two factors were found; they were labelled "Assertiveness-Submissiveness" and "Loving-Distrusting."[17] In addition, a circumplex was used to display intervariable correlations.

An extensive series of studies of interpersonal behavior of adults identified two major variables: "Dominance-Submissiveness" and "Affiliation-Aggression," with fifteen intervariable behaviors arranged in a circumplex.[18]

In a rather elaborate review of most of the relevant studies, Robert Carson arrived at this conclusion:

> *On the whole the conclusion seems justified that major portions of the domain of interpersonal behavior can profitably and reasonably accurately be conceived as involving variations on two independent bipolar dimensions. One of these may be called a* dominance-submission *dimension. . . . The poles of the second principal dimension are perhaps best approximated by the terms* hate *versus* love.[19]

Roger Brown is a scholar known for his interest in psychoseman-

[13]E. S. Schaefer, "A Circumplex Model for Maternal Behavior," *Journal of Abnormal and Social Psychology*, 59 (1959), 226–235.

[14]E. S. Schaefer, "Converging Conceptual Models for Maternal Behavior and for Child Behavior," in J. C. Glidewell, ed., *Parental Attitudes and Child Behavior* (Springfield, Ill.: C. C. Thomas, 1961), pp. 124–146.

[15]P. E. Slater, "Parent Behavior and the Personality of the Child," *Journal of Genetic Psychology*, 101 (1962), 53–68.

[16]W. C. Becker et al., "Relations of Factors Derived from Parent Interview Ratings to Behavior Problems of Five-Year-Olds," *Child Development*, 33 (1962), 509–553.

[17]W. C. Becker and R. S. Krug, "A Circumplex Model for Social Behavior in Children," *Child Development*, 35 (1964), 371–396.

[18]See M. Lorr and D. M. McNair, "An Interpersonal Behavior Circle," *Journal of Abnormal and Social Psychology*, 67 (1963), 68–75; M. Lorr and D. M. McNair, "Expansion of the Interpersonal Behavior Circle," *Journal of Personality and Social Psychology*, 2 (1965), 823–830; M. Lorr and D. M. McNair, "Methods Relating to Evaluation of Therapeutic Outcome," in L. A. Gottschalk and A. H. Auerbach, eds., *Methods of Research in Psychotherapy* (New York: Appleton, 1966), pp. 573–594.

[19]R. C. Carson, *Interaction Concepts of Personality* (Chicago: Aldine, 1969), p. 102. See especially Carson's chap. 4, "Varieties of Interpersonal Behavior," pp. 93–121.

tics—the psychological implications of language usage.[20] Working in an area quite removed from the research cited above, Brown studied the psychological implications of words used by one person to address another. Of particular interest, as you may guess, were practices involving languages where the equivalent of "you" allows more than one choice—for example, the Spanish *tu* and *usted*, one a term of familiar affection and the other denoting polite respect. From his study of such practices around the world, Brown concluded that forms of address "are always governed by the same two dimensions: solidarity and status."[21] Brown further noted that

> *Solidarity and status appear to govern much of social life. They lie behind the great regularities of everyday behavior: the way in which similarity generates liking and interaction which in turn produce more similarity; the way in which differential status confers power and privilege.*[22]

It seems clear that here Brown is suggesting the same two basic dimensions described above: *Affection-Hostility* and *Dominance-Submission.* He suggests that these two factors permeate all interpersonal relationships and are obvious, "probably because we have all had to work them out in order to get along with others."[23]

One other extensive series of studies should be mentioned in this context for two reasons: A tremendous amount of sophisticated research has been involved, and on the surface the results may appear to disallow our conclusion. For over 25 years Robert Bales has been analyzing interpersonal relations in various problem-solving or task-oriented groups.[24] The results of his research provide identification of three basic dimensions of interpersonal behavior: "Up-Down"; "Positive-Negative," associated with interpersonal liking or group cohesiveness; and "Forward-Backward," a dimension less-clearly defined[25] but generally related to forward motion in the problem-solving process.[26] It is easy to see that Bales' first two dimensions generally refer to our categories of *Dominance-Submission* and *Affection-Hostility* discussed above. His third category, we believe, is a result of data derived entirely from *task-oriented* groups. This is, in fact, suggested by Bales: "The conceptual scheme of this book associates the forward direction . . . with task-orientation, that is, with task-

[20]See R. Brown, *Words and Things* (New York: Free Press, 1958).
[21]R. Brown, *Social Psychology* (New York: Free Press, 1965), p. 52.
[22]*Ibid.*, p. 53.
[23]*Ibid.*, p. 53.
[24]See R. F. Bales, *Interaction Process Analysis: A Method for the Study of Small Groups* (Reading, Mass.: Addison-Wesley, 1950); and R. F. Bales, *Personality and Interpersonal Behavior* (New York: Holt, Rinehart and Winston, 1970).
[25]See Bales, *Personality and Interpersonal Behavior, op. cit.*, pp. 395–398.
[26]*Ibid.*, pp. 30–50; see especially Figures 3.1, 3.2, and 3.3, pp. 33–35.

seriousness. . . . It is assumed that the group to which the system is applied is in a task-oriented phase."[27] In essence, we can conclude that Bales' research supports our position and suggests an additional dimension especially valuable for analyzing relationships among persons in problem-solving or task-oriented groups.

The value of the D-A-S-H paradigm to us as we attempt to analyze our own interpersonal relationships is that it makes our work easier and more efficient. It gives us primary targets for our analysis. Instead of saying to ourselves such things as "We are usually friendly toward each other but I always feel uncomfortable and my feelings get hurt," we can review our interpersonal behavior with another person *in toto*; in so doing we can usually arrive at a satisfactory summary of the relationship in terms of the two dimensions: Am I *generally* dominant or submissive; are we mostly affectionate or hostile (or in between)? In arriving at answers to these questions we review prior interpersonal behavior and observe more carefully interaction events as they transpire from day to day. We look for evidence of our tentative conclusions—smiles, disagreements, squeezes of a held hand, a smile unreturned, frowns, "hard looks," and many other such behaviors that Goffman calls "tie-signs," indications that the relationship is affectionate or hostile, that we are dominating or being dominated.[28]

The D-A-S-H paradigm can be useful to you as you attempt to summarize your relationship with another person. The *essential* characteristics of any interpersonal relationship can be graphed on this model. For example, relationships between you (Y) and any other person (P) might be summarized in one of the ways shown in Figure 7.2. Note that the degree of *Dominance, Submission, Affection*, or *Hostility* is shown by the distance of Y or P from the center of the D-A-S-H axis.

[27]*Ibid.*, pp. 395–396.

[28]E. Goffman, *Relations in Public* (New York: Basic Books, 1971), pp. 194–199.

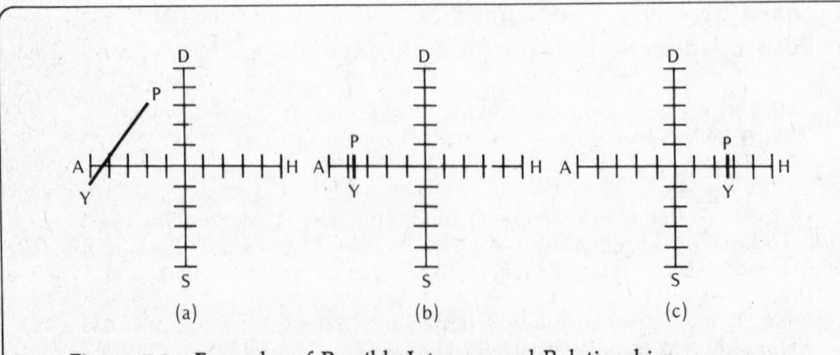

Figure 7.2 Examples of Possible Interpersonal Relationships.

As you have been reading along, undoubtedly you have also been thinking about one of your own interpersonal relationships. Perhaps it is the one you have with your father. After giving it some thought, you may conclude that your relationship with him resembles the one in Figure 7.1(b), involving considerable mutual affection but containing some dominating efforts by your father to which you give small tokens of submission. On the other hand, now that you have entered adult life, 7.1(c) may more closely resemble the current power-struggle between you and your father.

As you consider your relationship with another person, graph it as best you can on a D-A-S-H model. Reflect for a while; compare this relationship with other relationships of your own or with some you have observed on the part of other couples or groups. Make a tentative assessment and plot it on a graph as we did above. Then pay special attention to interaction events that transpire between you and the other person over a number of days. See if your tentative summary tends to be supported; if not, change it to comply with your observations.

As you attempt to summarize your relationship with another person, you may find some difficulty with what has been called "punctuation" of on-going interaction behavior.[29] As we interact with others we are usually aware of little interaction events, encounters, or communication sequential units. For example, we meet, they smile, we respond, they tell us some news, we show what we think of it, we talk, then we note we must move along to do other things, so we show our pleasure regarding this meeting and we say we will meet again at some specified time. What happened first, second, third, etc., may be collectively viewed as an interaction unit or encounter.

In an on-going series of such events or encounters, we tend to find one event overlapping with another. We may "pick up where we left off" or relate back to some midpoint item. It may be difficult, even a bit arbitrary, to decide when any particular sequence of communicative acts started, who did what first, who "responded" to whom, etc. Even so, as we reflect back on such happenings, we usually have an impression of what behavior preceded another, and what response it received. The way we reflectively or cognitively break up a series of on-going, reoccurring actions into units may be termed our "punctuation" of such an on-going series. Although this concept of "punctuation" may seem to you to be vague or complex, we bring it up because it can have considerable significance as you attempt to analyze your relationship with another person. The way you "punctuate" your interaction with him/her can make a difference in the way you view the relationship.

Frequently the identification of such communication units is in

[29]Cf. Watzlawick et al., *Pragmatics of Human Communication* (New York: Norton, 1967), pp. 54–59.

terms of interpersonal roles. For example, we may have a view of our relationship with our employer, identifying him as leader and ourselves as followers: When he speaks, we respond; and as we respond, we expect him to speak again and us to respond again. If, however, boss and employee are in disagreement about who is responding to whom, difficulty is likely to arise.

The "punctuation" made by one of the interacting persons may be quite different from that made by the other person in the relationship; differences in "punctuation" can thus produce confusion and misunderstanding. Consider a couple having marital difficulties. Suppose that the husband generally shows passive withdrawal and then reentry into the communication situation. In explaining the couple's disagreements and frustrations, he will indicate that withdrawal is his only defense against her nagging. He will indicate that she nags, he withdraws; he goes back into the situation, she nags, and he withdraws. The wife's interpretation of the interaction sequences, however, will very likely be that he withdraws, and she has to nag to get him back into talking with her. Their two interpretations have been identified as:

a. "I withdraw because you nag."
b. "I nag because you withdraw."[30]

Seldom, however, do people recognize such a problem or talk about these things. The point to be noted here is that in analyzing your relationship with another person, your own "punctuation" of communication events or encounters should be made as accurately as possible. We suggest that you seek the help, if possible, of a trusted observer outside the relationship.

As you attempt to analyze your relationship with another person, you may note discrepancies and contradictions between their verbal statements and their nonverbal behavior. They may say they like or love you, but neither look nor act as if this were true. This problem is discussed in greater detail in Haley's article at the end of this chapter.[31] In such a situation you need to arrive at some overall assessment of the relationship. *The general rule is that in such contradictory situations, nonverbal behavior ultimately defines the relationship.* This principle is widely supported by common belief, folkways and folklore: "Actions speak louder than words." To our knowledge there is very little formal research on this issue.[32]

There are a number of currently popular schemes that may be used to assist in analyzing interpersonal relationships. One of these is commonly known as "Transactional Analysis," originated by Eric

[30]Watzlawick et al., *op. cit.*, p. 56.
[31]See pp. 368–373.
[32]See, for example, Watzlawick et al., *op. cit.*, pp. 62–67.

Berne.[33] This analytic scheme was originally devised for analyzing relationships between psychotherapists and their patients. It was extended to apply to ordinary persons (nonpatients) in a book by T. A. Harris, *I'm OK—You're OK.*[34] Numerous trained persons now demonstrate its method in clinics and counseling situations. An extremely popular application of the principles involved was made by Berne in his well-known book, *Games People Play.*[35]

Transactional Analysis is based on ego psychology; that is, it gives primary emphasis to an individual's psychological needs, sometimes called "ego needs." A basic postulate is that each person has inside himself/herself three ego states: the *Parent*, the *Adult*, and the *Child*. The *Parent* state reflects what we've been taught about life—our attitudes toward things in terms of the way they *ought* to be. The *Adult* state unemotionally and objectively looks at the facts, gathers information, and makes decisions. The *Child* state shows feelings of joy, sadness, fear, anger, and love.

The basic principle is that you can identify which "ego state" a person is in by his/her behavior. Demonstrations of Transactional Analysis ordinarily present two people interacting; a counselor or therapist observes and now and then suggests to one or the other, "Now you're in a *Parent* state," or "That sounded like a *Child* state to me," etc.

It seems to us that this analytical scheme can have considerable value in helping a person to be more aware of his/her own behavior, noting more clearly when he/she is behaving as an "adult" and when he/she is not, etc. There are some obvious parallels between our D-A-S-H paradigm and the suggested ego states. As we observe interpersonal communication, noting carefully what one person is trying to do to the other, the behavior usually classed as the *Parent* state is employed for interpersonal *control*. In most such cases the discussion is focused on how to view information, to determine if such and such is true, and if it is the way it *ought* to be. The *Child* state is directly concerned with like and dislike, involving attendant feelings of joy and anger, love and hate. This concept, of course, suggests the dimension of interpersonal relations we identified above as *Affection-Hostility*.

It should be noted that in the Transactional Analysis scheme the very labels employed (Child, Adult, Parent) in this context have evaluational connotations. One grown person does not like to have another treat him as a "Parent." Labeling one's behavior thus is perceived as degrading. In similar fashion, labeling a grown person's behavior as

[33]E. Berne, *Transactional Analysis in Psychotherapy* (New York: Grove, 1961).

[34]T. A. Harris, *I'm OK—You're OK* (New York: Harper & Row, 1967).

[35]E. Berne, *Games People Play* (New York: Grove, 1964).

that of a "Child" is also degrading—one does not like the subjective implication of being "childish." In our opinion greater objectivity can be achieved by use of the D-A-S-H paradigm; in effect, we like the scheme we have suggested better than that of Transactional Analysis for reasons that we hope have been made clear.

In our opinion it is particularly unfortunate that *expression of emotions in human interaction* should be characterized as "childish." Childish behavior suggests interaction that is immature or unreasonable. We believe that the expression of emotion, showing our true feelings, is an important part of life and that their value should be fully understood and appreciated. In a desirable, healthy relationship, they should be known, disclosed by one person to another, without an implied sense of condemnation. To enjoy being together, we must disclose our feelings as well as our more "rational" thoughts. Their expression should be encouraged if a healthy relationship is to be achieved. This principle is the major thesis of the article by Bach and Wyden presented at the end of this chapter.[36]

Despite these criticisms, we are convinced that Transactional Analysis can have considerable value in helping us to be more aware of our attempts to *control* one another; its primary emphasis and value seems to us to relate to this interpersonal dimension. Berne's analysis of the games people play is also very much concerned with the dimension of interpersonal *control*, even though in many cases the objective of such control is to produce a display of affectionate behavior.[37] (In passing, we should note the "sick" aspect—the unsatisfying, self-defeating quality—of forced or manipulated "displays of affection.")

A typical game as analyzed by Berne is one he calls "Corner." Berne shows that it essentially consists of a delayed refusal to follow another's ploy to produce a show of affection. In this game, a wife suggests to her husband that they go to a movie; he agrees. She makes an "unconscious" suggestion that maybe they shouldn't because the house needs painting. He has previously told her that they don't have the money to paint the house right now; therefore, this is not a "reasonable" time to relate such an expensive consideration to the price of a movie. The husband responds rudely to the house-painting remark. His wife is "offended" and says that since he is in a bad mood, she will not go to the movie with him and *suggests that he should go alone.* This is the critical artificial ploy of the game. He knows very well from past experience that he is not supposed to take this suggestion seriously. What she really wants is to be "honeyed-up" a bit, told everything will be all right. Then they could go off happily to the

[36]See pp. 374–387.
[37]See Berne, *Games People Play, op. cit.*

movie together. *But he refuses* to show her this affectionate attention; he leaves, feeling relieved but looking abused; she is left feeling resentful. In this instance the husband won this game because all he did was to do as she suggested—literally. Berne's conclusion is: "They both know this is cheating but since she said it, she is cornered."[38] As suggested above, this is a cruel game played to achieve a *show* of affection; its target is manipulation or control of another person; its interpersonal attitude beneath the surface—no matter who wins—is not affection but *hostility*. If playing of such games were standard interaction for two persons, their relationship would have to be plotted in the *Dominant-Hostile* quadrant of the D-A-S-H model, with *both persons'* behavior represented in this way: The person most often winning could be shown a little *above* the other (more dominant), but *both* seeking to dominate.

It is extremely interesting to read Berne's analyses of games that people sometimes play. To us it is even more enlightening to plot such players' interpersonal relationships on the D-A-S-H model. What they are doing to each other is just as interesting to us as how they do it.

Determining the Degree of Rigidity in a Relationship

The degree of rigidity, the established routine, is an important consideration in analyzing your relationships. It provides a basis for estimating the possibility of change and improvement, a primary issue in a relationship's value to us.

In the early work of Leary and his associates, sometimes known at that time (1957) as the Kaiser Foundation Group,[39] it is intriguing to note how their basic conceptualization of interpersonal behavior has been supported by subsequent research. However, an additional feature of their work that we have not yet mentioned is their principle of *interpersonal behavior reflex*. In his studies of interpersonal communication, Leary arrived at this conclusion: A large percentage of interpersonal behaviors simply involve a reflex—an automatic response.[40] Such behaviors are so automatic that they are often unconscious and even at variance with the individual's own perception of them; they are involuntary responses to the behavior of the other person. It is important to note that these behaviors are *reflexes, not general interpersonal orientations* discussed in Chapter 4.

We now need to look once again at the D-A-S-H paradigm. Affectionate or hostile behavior tends to produce similar behavior. If one

[38]*Ibid.*, pp. 91–92.

[39]For a brief summary and evaluation of the work of this group, see Carson, *Interaction Concepts of Personality, op. cit.*, pp. 103–116.

[40]See T. Leary, "The Theory and Measurement Methodology of Interpersonal Communication," *Psychiatry*, 18 (1955), 147–161.

person in a relationship is highly affectionate toward the other, that other person ordinarily responds with at least moderate affection. In like manner, hostility generally generates hostility. On the other hand, dominant or submissive behavior tends to produce its *reciprocal*. Ordinarily, if a relationship survives over time, dominant behavior elicits passive or submissive responses. The reverse is also true: Passivity tends to reinforce and thus produce dominant behavior on the part of the other person. Of course, in the event two dominant people try to relate to each other, a power-struggle usually ensues; it may last for years, and may often involve manipulative games such as "Cornering" previously described. In some cases, such as in families, such a power-struggle may never be resolved but may continue endlessly, as suggested in Haley's article following this chapter.[41] In other cases, however, if neither person's behavior changes, the relationship may dissolve because *reciprocal* responses cannot be established.

To a very large extent the effect of one person's behavior can be explained, even predicted, on the basis of these principles: Affection or hostility elicits *similar* behavior, and dominance or submissiveness elicits *reciprocal* responses. As two people interact, one person's behavior produces responses by the other; these responses in turn produce responses on the part of the first person. Responses produce responses that produce responses. As time goes on, the two persons tend to work out a "shared definition" of their relationships.[42] The first "starting" behavior may be forgotten; perhaps it was never consciously perceived or analyzed; perhaps it was misperceived due to an erroneous expectation. Nevertheless, once in motion, responses to responses tend to produce what may be called a "lock-step" effect. Once such a "lock-step" series has been established, it is difficult to change. A rather interesting account of the way this principle works in the control dimension has been given by W. F. Whyte in his description of the behavior of the capable restaurant waitress:

> *The first point that stands out is that the waitress who bears up under pressure does not simply respond to her customers. She acts with some skill to control their behavior. . . . The skilled waitress tackles the customer with confidence and without hesitation. . . . She greets him, says, "May I change the cover, please?" and, without waiting for an answer, takes his menu away from him so that he moves back from the table, and she goes about her work. The relationship is handled politely but firmly, and there is never any question as to who is in charge.*[43]

Some people tend to respond to all other people in nearly the

[41]See pp. 368–373.

[42]See Goffman, *Behavior in Public Places, op. cit.*, p. 96.

[43]W. F. Whyte, "When Workers and Customers Meet," in W. F. Whyte, ed., *Industry and Society* (New York: McGraw-Hill, 1946), pp. 132–133.

same way because of their narrow, rigid orientation toward all or nearly all other people, as we discussed in Chapter 4. This singular response, once given, tends to elicit a singular response from the other person, and the lock-step effect goes into full swing. On the other hand, many persons have a wider *repertoire* of responses, and can appropriately react in different ways to different interpersonal behaviors. *The range of a person's response repertoire will tend to determine the degree of rigidity of his/her interpersonal relationships.* This is the third major point derived from Leary's research.[44] As we view two persons interacting, the degree of rigidity in their relationship to each other will be a function of the variety in the response repertoires of the two individuals.

To test the degree of rigidity in one of your own interpersonal relationships, you can "try out" new responses to the other person's behavior. Be prepared for his/her surprise—even shock, confusion, or disgust! Note the degree to which you are able to employ a wider repertoire of responses; note, also, the other person's responses, especially any new ones. This procedure can give you some kind of index of the degree of rigidity in the relationship.

EVALUATING A RELATIONSHIP

In order to assess one of your own interpersonal relationships, we suggest that you first determine its nature in the manner suggested in the previous section. The issue then becomes: Are you happy with what you have? The answer to this question, of course, depends upon what you like. In the long run, only you can decide what is satisfying to you. For example, you may feel that you need to be dominated, told what to do; that without such direction your life is too puzzling, that problems overwhelm you. The question still remains: By what process do you arrive at such a decision? How does a person evaluate a relationship? What procedures are involved?

Calculating the Cost/Reward Ratio

In 1959 Thibaut and Kelley, two well-known social psychologists, summarized available research evidence and developed a theory regarding the evaluation of interpersonal behavior as two people interact, calling it "a theory of interaction outcomes."[45] Their major conclusion was that a relationship is evaluated by comparing the rewards received with the costs incurred. Working independently but at about the same time, George Homans developed a similar "theory of social

[44]See Leary, "The Theory and Measurement of Interpersonal Communication," *op. cit.*, 152–161.

[45]J. W. Thibaut and H. H. Kelley, *The Social Psychology of Groups* (New York: Wiley, 1959); see especially pp. 80–99.

exchange."[46] Although the two theories differ in some details, they agree remarkably in essential principles.[47]

Once an initial contact is made with another person, the survival of the relationship will depend upon the cost/reward ratio for either one of the participants. If, for either one, the perceived costs significantly exceed the perceived rewards, the relationship is not likely to endure.[48] In the initial phase of a relationship, we tend to explore the possible outcomes. We experience samples of what may happen, and we forecast trends, arriving at what might be called *an estimation of the relationship potential.*

Various interaction sequences or encounters in a relationship will have different resultant cost/reward ratios or values.[49] Thus, over time, we tend to arrive at a general evaluation of the relationship in terms of costs versus rewards. At times, for some of us, a single interaction event can be a determinant. Our anger or disgust can be so great, our quick-step estimate of the relationship potential can be so convincing, that we conclude: "I'll never talk to that miserable mocker-nut again! No way!"

Rewards accrue in terms of building a desired self-image or obtaining needed control over our environment.[50] Costs consist of investment of our time or energy. Anxiety, embarrassment, and anger are examples of psychological costs. Punishment of either a physical or psychological nature is to be considered.[51]

Behaviors that are rewarded are repeated; costly behaviors are eliminated.[52] If a relationship consists largely of costly behaviors on our part, we tend to discontinue the interaction and the relationship deteriorates into an acquaintanceship.[53] Homans described this process as based on the principle of "distributive justice"—we don't like to give more than that equal to what we receive.[54] If the relationship continues, we tend to assess our overall costs and rewards.[55] In addition, we consider the possible potential value of alternative relationships. We ask: Can we spend our available time interacting in a more satisfying relationship with some other person or persons?[56] If our

[46]G. C. Homans, *Social Behavior: Its Elementary Forms* (New York: Harcourt Brace Jovanovich, 1961).

[47]For a summary and evaluation of these two theories, see M. E. Shaw and P. R. Costanzo, *Theories of Social Psychology* (New York: McGraw-Hill, 1970), pp. 69–103.

[48]See Homans, *op. cit.*, pp. 54–55; see also Thibaut and Kelley, *op. cit.*, p. 20.

[49]Thibault and Kelley, *op. cit.*, pp. 12—13.

[50]*Ibid.*, pp. 97–101.

[51]Cf. Homans, *op. cit.*, pp. 57–61.

[52]Thibaut and Kelley, *op. cit.*, p. 63.

[53]Cf. Homans, *op. cit.*, pp. 54–55.

[54]See *ibid.*, p. 75.

[55]Thibaut and Kelley, *op. cit.*, p. 81.

[56]*Ibid.*, p. 21.

answer appears to be affirmative, we tend to break off interaction and terminate the less-satisfying relationship.

The *sequential connection* between our behavior and the behavior of the other person is also a significant factor in evaluating a relationship.[57] Suppose you can govern your behavior so that the other person gains reward by behaving in ways that then heighten your own rewards. Put into different words, this is the interaction sequence: Y rewards P so that P rewards Y. In such a case a *fair exchange* is achieved, but more important to Y, he *initiated* the exchange and thus has some *control* over his rewards. This is more satisfying to Y than relationships in which rewards seem to be obtained by caprice, by chance, or in a random fashion. Even if we gain satisfaction from a relationship, if we are unable to see any logical, sequential *connection* between our behavior and the behavior of the other person, we tend to become uncomfortable in the relationship. We wonder how dependable such a relationship may be, and we tend to feel a bit guilty over "getting something for nothing."[58]

Deciding to Terminate, Maintain, or Change a Relationship

As you determine the cost/reward ratio of a relationship and note the degree of causal connections between your behavior and that of the other person, you have three possible alternatives. First, you may terminate the relationship if you see fit; you avoid or at least stop seeking out this person. Second, you may maintain the relationship as it is, perhaps fairly satisfied with it as it exists. Third, you may give serious thought and effort toward improving the relationship. This decision will be made on the basis of your estimates of the cost/reward ratio and the alternative relationship opportunities available to you.

Although your own interpersonal relationships will have to be assessed by you individually, we believe that it may be of some help to you to consider what students of human relations have advanced as basic elements of a desirable relationship.

We agree with Bennis and his colleagues that a desirable relationship contains interdependence, that each person exercises influence on the other, and that the degree exercised is well balanced.[59] Each individual should determine, without coercion by the other, the degree of dependence on the other person he desires. Differences of opinion should be faced and evaluated; decisions, when finally determined, should be reached by consensus. Conflict should be resolved by considerations credible to both parties.

[57]*Ibid.*, p. 101.

[58]*Ibid.*, p. 85.

[59]See W. G. Bennis et al., eds., *Interpersonal Dynamics*, rev. ed. (Homewood, Ill.: Dorsey, 1968), pp. 663–664.

In the tradition of ancient rhetoricians—those philosopher-scholars of public speaking—we hold that a desirable relationship employs communication that maximizes clarity. This concept was given heavy emphasis by Quintilian, a first-century critic of public speaking; his concept of a great orator was *a good man speaking well.* By a good man he meant one who used communication in an honest, responsible manner. Today this implies a relationship wherein communication is not used to mislead; wherein reality is not distorted; where, in this special sense, one person does not "manipulate" another. Although "manipulators," as described by Shostrum in his article following Chapter 8,[60] are often encountered in our society, we would rather enjoy relationships with persons who do not try to exploit us as "things."

We believe with Jourard that personal security is achieved not by hiding oneself but by being more fully known by another person, and consequently by coming to know the other more fully.[61] In a desirable relationship the participants openly express their feelings and sense, with accuracy, one another's attitudes. This point is elaborated in Jourard's article following Chapter 9.[62]

We hold, with Allport, that a desirable relationship is one that is "open"; that is, one that shows awareness of its social and physical environment.[63] It recognizes unexpected events, negotiates with external constraints, and accommodates its social ecology.

Lastly, we believe, as does Rogers, that being in an ideal relationship with another person means that we care very much what happens to them as well as to us.[64] As he suggests in his article following Chapter 9,[65] a relationship is of greatest value when it helps us to give and to accept affection and regard.

If you have a fairly rewarding relationship but would like it to be a little better, a little more in the ideal directions suggested above, this question then becomes pertinent: How can one go about trying to improve a relationship?

IMPROVING A RELATIONSHIP

To improve an existing relationship three things may be done: (1) Make optimum use of the process of interpersonal communication as

[60]See pp. 416–422.

[61]S. M. Jourard, *Disclosing Man to Himself* (New York: Van Nostrand Reinhold, 1968).

[62]See pp. 456–465.

[63]G. Allport, *Personality and Social Encounter* (Boston: Beacon, 1960), pp. 42–43.

[64]See, for example, C. R. Rogers, *On Becoming a Person* (Boston: Houghton Mifflin, 1961), pp. 50–58.

[65]See pp. 466–477.

detailed in Chapters 3 through 7, (2) give special attention to the use of self-disclosure as described in Chapter 9, and (3) work with the other person as suggested in the final section of this chapter.

Using the Interpersonal Communication Process

No one particular relationship is exactly like another. In one, certain aspects of the interpersonal communication process may be functioning well while other aspects are not. In another relationship various other parts of the communication process may need attention. In Chapter 8 we focus on special problems that occur most frequently. As you analyze a particular relationship, we suggest you keep in mind the procedures described in Chapters 3 through 5 and determine which aspects of the process need to be improved. In addition, you may review the special problems discussed in Chapter 8 to see if one or another is involved.

In many cases it is somewhat difficult to observe accurately our own behavior. We suggest that the observations of "third parties" not involved in the relationship may be useful if such persons are in a position to observe your behavior and if they can be trusted to give you honest feedback.

Using Self-Disclosure and Feedback

If a relationship is to be improved, self-disclosure on your part is essential. In many cases tactful expression of your feelings—joys, worries, elation, and anger—can help a relationship to be more rewarding. Disclosure of your intentions, motives, hopes, and expectations can help the other person to understand you better and respond more in tune with your desires and needs. Such exposure should not ordinarily be started all at once. You should work in this direction a little at a time until a new climate is established and you feel confident of the results.

Achieving new levels of openness will not come easily. The overt help of the other person or a training group may be needed. Even so, a determined effort on your part, tactful and with small attempts at first, can be a start toward the goal described in more detail in Chapter 9.

Working with the Other Person

Obtaining the cooperative help of the other person in the relationship is usually about the only way possible to achieve any significant change. The "lock-step" of patterned responses to responses usually dooms to failure the lone effort of a single member of the relationship. Together with the other person you may "try out" new behaviors and note the responses. Deliberate role playing may be found useful; however, be careful of adopting roles that are not true to your own personal feelings. In most cases, artificiality in interpersonal behavior can create greater problems than the original undesirable behavior.

In some cases you may find a relationship nearly impossible to change. The other person may be entirely unwilling to cooperate. Whether or not he/she is agreeable, there are three kinds of behavior on your part that can be helpful. By showing appropriate empathy for the other person, by demonstrating nonpossessive warmth or personal regard, and by being genuine or sincere, you can help to provide what Gibb has called a "climate of trust formation," a social environment conducive to personal growth and change.[66] These behaviors need some further explanation, but first let's emphasize what you should *not* do.

The other person in your relationship may resent the idea that any changes are needed. You may make the mistake of trying to point out to him/her the need for such changes. If such changes are discussed, the person is likely to fear exposure of his/her ideas and feelings. What he/she actually fears, of course, is possible damage to his/her self-image as a result of such exposure. If you try to point out the behaviors that are causing difficulty, it will tend to increase his/her anxiety. Many times this is what people do who want to be helpful but who are not very knowledgeable.

What can you do to be helpful? What is known about empathy, warmth, and genuineness in interpersonal relations? Studies of counselors and therapists, summarized by Truax and Carkhuff,[67] indicate differences in relationships between various counselors and clients. Specifically, counselors vary as to characteristics of accurate empathy, nonpossessive warmth, and genuineness. These studies have demonstrated that counselors who show higher degrees of these particular characteristics have greater success in relating with clients. The studies include both individual and group counseling approaches. These findings appear to have direct application in all interpersonal communication situations involving a need for improvement.

Accurate empathy is the ability to sense the other person's view of the world as if that view were your own. However, to demonstrate accurate empathy requires ability to *communicate* this understanding to the other person.[68] You need to be sensitive to his/her current feelings and emotions, even his fear of letting you develop a closer relationship with him/her. You do not need to *feel* the same fear or anx-

[66]See J. R. Gibb, "Climate for Trust Formation," in P. Bradford, J. R. Gibb, and K. D. Benne, eds., *T-Group Theory and Laboratory Method: Innovation in Re-Education* (New York: Wiley, 1964), pp. 279–309.

[67]C. B. Truax and R. R. Carkhuff, *Toward Effective Counseling and Psychotherapy* (Chicago: Aldine, 1967).

[68]*Ibid.*, p. 46.

iety that the other one does, but you must have an *awareness* and *appreciation* of these emotions. Such empathy is communicated by the language you use and also by your vocal qualities and behavior. Your posture, gestures, and entire attitude should reflect the other person's point of view and depth of feeling. Your behavior must show awareness of shifts in his/her emotional attitudes, his/her subtle fears and anxieties. At all times the message of accurate empathy is: "I am with you; I understand."

Nonpossessive warmth is a demonstration of unconditional positive regard, involving caring about the other person without imposing conditions. The attitude you communicate should be warm acceptance; there should be no expression of dislike, disapproval, or *conditional* warmth in a selective or evaluative way. You will need to show willingness to share the other person's joys and aspirations as well as his anxiety and despair. It may be difficult for you to understand how you can really show warmth and affection for a person who has ways or habits you dislike; this is indeed a serious problem and becomes the heart of the matter in trying to be helpful to others. What is actually required is caring about that person's potential, a warm feeling about him as a person—a human being. Hopefully, you can face the problem *together*, behavior that both of you dislike. But it is imperative that he feels you will be *for* him, even if he fails in his attempt to change. He will need to feel that you care about him in spite of your dislike of some of his behavior.

The attitude described here may not be very clear to you; indeed, in working with problems in human relations it is the most complicated concept we have faced. However, it is also the most important. Let us note it once again: *Nonpossessive warmth* involves unconditional caring about a person *as a person with valued potential* irrespective of some behaviors you do not like. You must show that you care for him even though you may not care for some of his ways. This caring is much like the loyalty and affection shown by supporters of a football team even when that team is having problems and losing games; these fans want the team to win, but they still love it when it loses—they love it for trying and for its *potential.* If you wish to help another person, you must show him acceptance as a human being who has both human frailties and human potential.

Genuineness consists of being open and frank at all times; it involves being yourself. You must be willing not only to express your feelings, but never to deny them.[69] There must be no façade, no defensive communication, no show of emotion followed by denial of that emotion. Your responses to the other person must be sincere, never phony. It does not mean that you need to show *all* of your

[69]*Ibid.*, p. 58.

feelings or emotions; but once one is shown, it must not be denied—your behavior must be consistent. You need not disclose your total self, but whatever is shown must be a real aspect of yourself, not behavior growing out of defensiveness or an attempt to *manipulate* the other person. Glib attempts to persuade or efforts to convince him/her are dangerous pitfalls. A "professional" façade—"Now, let us take our medicine"—can be disastrous. In view of the discussion of nonpossessive warmth in the preceding paragraph, it should be noted that your show of warmth must be genuine. This combination of requirements makes it extremely difficult to help another person if you really do not care about him/her. What you think are clever strategies will likely be viewed with suspicion. You must learn to be true to yourself if you wish to be helpful to others.

SUMMARY AND PREVIEW OF READINGS

In this chapter we have suggested that a significant phase of the interpersonal communication process is developing, maintaining, and improving a warm personal relationship. In recent years we have seen a new emphasis on seeking such a relationship with at least one other person.

To improve an existing relationship or to achieve the most satisfying potential of a new one we must analyze it, then evaluate it, and eventually, if need be, change it.

A relationship can be analyzed in terms of its (1) basic patterns of interaction, and (2) degree of rigidity. Interaction behavior has three basic dimensions: (1) degree of involvement, (2) emotional tone, and (3) amount of interpersonal control.

In an established relationship where the degree of involvement has stabilized, the other two dimensions are of greatest concern. Such a relationship can be described in its *essential characteristics* by determining the interpersonal behavior of the two persons on two independent, bipolar dimensions: *Dominance-Submission* and *Affection-Hostility*. We have presented these two dimensions as forming an axis in a D-A-S-H paradigm.

In determining each person's degree of *Dominance* versus *Submission* and amount of *Affection* versus *Hostility* in a relationship, we have noted that affectionate or hostile behavior on the part of one participant tends to elicit *similar* behavior on the part of the other. Conversely, dominant behavior tends to produce its *reciprocal*, submissive behavior and submissiveness tends to encourage dominance. Taken together, these two principles tend to produce a "lock-step" effect of responses that produce responses. Once set in motion, such a behavior pattern is difficult to change. The possibility of change can be estimated by noting the variety of the participants' response repertoire—to what extent they tend to respond differently to different behaviors.

Evaluation of a relationship is accomplished by calculating the ratio of individual costs to personal rewards and by comparing this ratio to estimates of relationship potential for any available alternative relationships. Decisions to terminate a relationship are based primarily on the cost/reward ratio but may also consider the potential value of available alternate relationships. A decision to attempt to improve a relationship is ordinarily based on a comparison of what exists with an ideal version of what might be. Five characteristics of a desirable human relationship have been presented.

Improving a relationship ordinarily requires determined effort on the part of both members. Procedures for improvement include optimum use of the process of interpersonal communication, special emphasis on self-disclosure followed by feedback, and working with the other person. Cooperation of the other person may be facilitated by showing accurate empathy, nonpossessive warmth, and genuineness.

The readings that follow this chapter support our discussion in two ways. The article by Jay Haley, "Establishment of an Interpersonal Relationship," details problems of mutual definition of the relationship by the participants. The article by Bach and Wyden, "Why Intimates Must Fight," suggests ways in which *excessive* tensions and frustrations in a relationship can be exposed and reduced. "Fighting" by their rules thus becomes therapeutic and growth producing.

SUGGESTED APPLICATIONS AND LEARNING EXPERIENCES

1. Select one of your most important interpersonal relationships and analyze it as suggested in this chapter. Use the D-A-S-H model; check your analysis by noting your own and the other person's behaviors in a number of subsequent encounters. If you trust the other person sufficiently, talk over your conclusions with them. Note especially your "punctuation" of interaction events.

2. In one of your interpersonal relationships, attempt to broaden your "response repertoire." Try to respond in various ways (new to you) to the other person's behaviors. Note his subsequent responses. Determine if possible the degree to which the "lock-step" effect influences your and their behaviors.

3. To give you more personal insight into helping others, we offer the following suggestion. Determine which one of your friends or classmates would like to work with you on improving his ways of relating to others; this person will likely be one who has participated with you on one of the applications or learning experiences previously suggested in this book. Have that person meet with you and a third person for lunch. During this time have your friend do his best to employ effective interpersonal communication with this third person, while you act primarily as an observer. Later meet with your friend and give him open, frank, honest feedback on his behavior while talking at lunch. Then ask your friend to evaluate your communication behavior during the present discussion with respect to his perceptions of your empathy, nonpossessive warmth, and genuineness. Discuss these aspects of yourself with him at some length, being careful to listen more than talk. Later, when you are alone, reflect on this feedback, recalling as best you can your own interpersonal communication behavior. Decide what specific behaviors you would like to change. Then arrange another sequence of experiences with two other persons. See if you can achieve feedback that is more desirable from your own point of view.

4. Identify the person who has shown you the greatest amounts of empathy, warmth, and genuineness while working with friends or classmates on applications and learning experiences suggested in this book. Ask him to meet with you and a third person for lunch. During this lunch period, do your best to use effective interpersonal communication with the third person, while your special friend acts mainly as an observer of your communication behavior. At a later meeting with your friend, ask him for open and honest feedback regarding your behavior. Now, note very carefully your personal feelings as you listen to this friend criticize your effectiveness. Note any feelings of yours that are negative or evasive. Note: Do you look your friend in the eye as you receive this feedback? Note carefully any defensive communication on your part, identified either by you or by him. Thank your friend sincerely for his efforts to be of help to you. At a later time—the next day or in days to follow—determine for yourself your own capability for accepting and utilizing such help from other people.

5. In his essay, "Establishment of a Relationship," Jay Haley emphasizes the problem of incongruent verbal and nonverbal messages, particularly with respect to our defining our relationship with another person. Have you experienced such a problem? With one of your classmates discuss your and his/her experiences with this type of problem. After you have discussed the topic to your satisfaction, discuss with this person a lack of congruence either one of you has felt on the part of the other. Note carefully any feedback that you thus obtain.

6. In their article, "Why Intimates Must Fight," Bach and Wyden describe specific rules for a "fight exercise." With one of your close friends experiment with this exercise and later discuss with them the value derived from it.

ESTABLISHMENT OF AN INTERPERSONAL RELATIONSHIP

Jay Haley

When two people meet for the first time and begin to establish a relationship, a wide range of behavior is potentially possible between them. They may exchange compliments, insults, sexual advances, statements that one is superior to the other, and so on. As the two people define their relationship with each other, they work out together what sort of communicative behavior is to take place in this relationship. From all the possible messages they select certain kinds and reach agreement that these rather than others shall be included. Their agreement on what is and what is not to take place can be called a mutual definition of the relationship. Every message they interchange either reinforces this definition or suggests a shift in it. If a young man puts his arm around a girl, he is indicating that amorous behavior is to be included in their relationship. If the girl says, "No, no," and withdraws from him, she is indicating that amorous behavior is to be excluded. The relationship they have together, whether amorous or platonic, is defined by the kind of messages they mutually agree shall be acceptable between them. This agreement is never permanently worked out but is constantly in process as one or the other proposes a new sort of message or as the environmental situation changes and provokes change in their behavior.

If human communication took place at only one level, the working out, or defining, of a relationship would be a simple matter of the presence or absence of messages. In that case there would probably be no difficulties in interpersonal relationships. However, human beings not only communicate, but they also communicate about that communication. They not only say something, but they also qualify or label what they say. In the example above, the young lady says, "No, no," and also withdraws from the young man. Her physical withdrawal qualifies, and is qualified by, her verbal statement. Since the qualification affirms her message, there is no particular difficulty. She is making it clear that amorous behavior does not belong in their relationship. But suppose she had said, "No, no," and moved closer to the young man. By snuggling up to him she would have qualified incongruently, or denied, her statement. When a message is qualified incongruently, then a relationship becomes more complex than when a message is simply present or absent. A classification of human behavior must take into account at least *two levels* of communication. To describe interpersonal behavior one must deal not only with communicative behavior but the qualifications of that behavior by the participants.

From Jay Haley, "An Interactional Description of Schizophrenia," *Psychiatry* 22 (1959), 321–332.

Any communicative behavior interchanged between two people does not exist separately from other behavior which accompanies and comments upon it. If one person says, "I'm glad to see you," his tone of voice qualifies his statement and is qualified in turn by it and by other qualifying messages that might also be present. Communication between people consists of (1) the context in which it takes place, (2) verbal messages, (3) vocal and linguistic patterns, and (4) bodily movement. As people communicate, their relationship is defined as much by the qualifications of their messages as by the presence or absence of messages. A person may make a criticism with a smile or a frown. The smile or frown as much as the criticism defines the relationship. An employee may tell his boss what to do, thus defining their relationship as one between equals, but he may qualify his statement with a self-effacing gesture or a weak tone of voice and thereby indicate that it is a relationship between unequals. If people always qualified what they said in a congruent way, relationships would be defined clearly and simply, even though two levels of communication were functioning. However, when a statement indicating one sort of relationship is qualified by a contradictory communication, difficulties in interpersonal relations become inevitable.

It is important to emphasize that one cannot *not* qualify a message. A person must speak a verbal message in a particular tone of voice, and if he says nothing, that, too, is qualified by the posture he presents and the context in which his muteness appears. Although the meanings of some qualifying messages are obvious, as when one pounds one's fists on the table when making a statement, subtle qualifications are always present. For example, the slightest upward inflection on a word may define a statement as a question rather than an assertion. A slight smile may classify a statement as ironical rather than serious. A minute body movement backwards qualifies an affectionate statement and indicates that it is made with some reservations. The absence of a message may also qualify another message. For example, if a person is silent when he is expected to speak, the silence becomes a qualifying message, and if a man neglects to kiss his wife good-bye when she expects it, the absence of this movement qualifies his other messages as much as, if not more than, the presence of it.

People tend to judge whether others are being sincere or deceitful, whether they are serious or joking, and so on, by whether they affirm what they say by congruent qualifications. And when one person responds to another with his own definition of the relationship between them, this response is to all levels of messages.

CONTROL IN A RELATIONSHIP

When one person communicates a message to another, he is maneuvering to define the relationship. The other person is thereby posed the problem of accepting or rejecting the relationship offered. He can let the message stand, thereby accepting the other person's definition, or counter with a maneuver defining it differently. He may also accept the other person's maneuver but qualify his acceptance with a message indicating that he is *letting* the other person get by with the maneuver.

For example, if a young man spontaneously puts his arm around a young lady, she must either accept this message, thereby letting him define the relationship, or oppose it, thereby defining the relationship herself. Or she might have controlled the definition by inviting this behavior. She may also accept it with the qualification that she is *letting* him put his arm around her. By labeling his message as one permitted by her, she is maintaining control of the relationship.

Any two people are posed these mutual problems: What messages, or what kinds of behavior, are to take place in this relationship? And who is to control what is to take place in the relationship and thereby control the definition of the relationship? It is hypothesized here that the nature of human communications requires people to deal with these problems, and interpersonal relations can be classified in terms of the different ways in which they do deal with them.

It must be emphasized that no one can avoid being involved in a struggle over the definition of his relationship with someone else. Everyone is constantly involved in defining his relationship or countering the other person's definition. If a person speaks, he is inevitably indicating what sort of relationship he has with the other person. By whatever he says, he is indicating, "This is the sort of relationship where this is said." If a person remains mute, he is also inevitably defining a relationship, because by not speaking he is circumscribing the other person's behavior. If a person wishes to avoid defining his relationship with another and therefore talks only about the weather, he is indicating that their communication should be neutral, and this defines the relationship.

A basic rule of communications theory proposed by Bateson[1] maintains that it is difficult for a person to avoid defining, or taking control of the definition of, his relationship with another. According to this rule all messages not only report but also influence or command. A statement such as, "I feel bad today," is not merely a description of the internal state of the speaker. It also expresses something like, "Do something about this," or "Think of me as a person who feels bad." Even if one remains silent, trying not to influence another person, the silence becomes an influencing factor in the interchange. It is impossible for a person to hand over to another the entire initiative regarding what behavior is to be allowed in the relationship. If he tries to do this, he is controlling the relationship by indicating that it is one in which the other person is to determine what behavior is to take place. For example, a patient may say to a therapist, "I can't decide anything for myself; I want you to tell me what to do." By saying this, he seems to be telling the therapist to control the relationship by directing the behavior in it. But when the patient requests that the therapist tell him what to do, he is telling the therapist what to do. This paradox can arise because two levels are always being communicated—for example: (1) "I am reporting that I need to be told what to do," and (2)

[1]Gregory Bateson and Jurgen Ruesch, *Communication, the Social Matrix of Psychiatry*, p. 179, Norton, New York, 1951.

"Obey my command to tell me what to do." Whenever a person tries to avoid controlling the definition of a relationship, at a different level he is defining the relationship as one in which he is not in control. A person who acts helpless controls the behavior in a relationship just as effectively as another who acts authoritarian and insists on a specific behavior. Helplessness will influence the other person's behavior as much as, if not more than, direct authoritarian demands. If one acts helpless, he may in one sense be controlled by the person caring for him, but by acting helpless he defines the relationship as one in which he is taken care of.

It should be emphasized here that "control" does not mean that one takes control of another person as one would a robot. The emphasis here is not on a struggle to control another person's specific behavior but rather on a struggle to control *what sort of* behavior is to take place in the relationship and therefore to define the relationship. Any two people must inevitably work out what sort of relationship they have, not necessarily prescribing behavior, but at least circumscribing what behavior is to take place.

AVOIDING CONTROL IN A RELATIONSHIP

I have said that it is difficult for anyone to avoid working out what sort of relationship he has with another person. However, there is one way in which a person can avoid indicating what is to take place in a relationship, and thereby avoid defining it. He can negate what he says. Even though he will be defining the relationship by whatever he communicates, he can invalidate this definition by using qualifications that deny his communications.

The fact that people communicate on at least two levels makes it possible to indicate one relationship, and simultaneously deny it. For example, a man may say, "I think you should do that, but it's not my place to tell you so." In this way he defines the relationship as one in which he tells the other person what to do, but simultaneously denies that he is defining the relationship in this way. This is what is sometimes meant when a person is described as not being self-assertive. One man might respond to his wife's request to do the dishes by saying, "No, I won't," and sitting down with his newspaper. He has asserted himself in the sense that he has defined his relationship with his wife as one in which he is not to be told what to do. Another man might respond to a similar demand by saying, "I would like to do the dishes, but I can't. I have a headache." He also refuses to do the dishes, but by qualifying his message in an incongruent way. He indicates that *he* is not defining the relationship by this refusal. After all, it was the headache which prevented the dishwashing, not him. In the same way, if a man strikes his wife only when drunk, the act of striking her is qualified by the implication that *he* isn't responsible; the effect of the liquor is. By qualifying his messages with implications that *he* isn't responsible for his behavior, a person can avoid defining his relationship with another. These incongruent qualifying messages may be verbal, such as, "I didn't mean to do it," or they may be conveyed by a weak voice or a hesitant body movement. Even the context may negate a maneuver to define a relationship—for example, when one boy invites another to fight in church where a fight is not possible.

To clarify the ways in which a person might avoid defining his relationship with another, suppose that some hypothetical person decided to entirely follow through with such an avoidance. Since anything he said or did not say would define his relationship, he would need to qualify with a negation or a denial whatever he said or did not say. To illustrate the ways in which he could deny his messages, the formal characteristics of any message from one person to another can be broken down into these four elements:

1. *I*
2. *am saying something*
3. *to you*
4. *in this situation*

A person can avoid defining his relationship by negating any or all of these four elements. He can (1) deny that *he* communicated something, (2) deny that something was communicated, (3) deny that it was communicated *to* the other person, or (4) deny the context in which it was communicated.

The rich variety of ways in which a person can avoid defining a relationship can be summarized briefly.

1. To deny that *he* is communicating a message, a person may label himself as someone else. For example, he may introduce himself with an alias. Or he may indicate that he personally is not speaking, but his status position is, so that what he says is labeled as coming from the boss or the professor, for example. He may indicate that he is only an instrument transmitting the message; he was told to say what he did, or God was speaking through him, and therefore he is not the one who is defining the relationship.

A person may also deny that *he* is communicating by labeling what he says as effected by some force outside himself. He may indicate that *he* is not really talking, because he is upset or deranged by liquor, or insanity, or drugs.

He may also label his messages as being the result of 'involuntary' processes within himself, so that *he* isn't really the one communicating. He may say, "You aren't upsetting me; it's something I ate," and deny that his sick expression is a message from him about the relationship. He may even vomit or urinate and indicate that these things are organically caused and not messages from *him* which should be taken as comments on a relationship.

2. The simplest way in which a person can deny that he *said* something is to manifest amnesia. By saying, "I don't remember doing that," he is qualifying an activity with a statement negating it. He may also insist that what he says is being misunderstood, and that therefore the other person's interpretations do not coincide with what he really said.

Another way to deny that something is said is to immediately qualify a statement with one which contradicts it. This negates everything said as irrelevant nonsense that is therefore not a comment on the relationship. Or a person may make up a language, simultaneously communicating and negating that communication by the very fact that the language cannot be understood by the other person. In another variant, a person can indicate that his words are not means of communication but things in themselves. He may make a statement while discussing the spelling of the words in the statement, and so indicate that he has not communicated a message but has merely listed letters of words.

3. To deny that what he says is addressed *to* the other person, a person may simply indicate that he is talking to himself. He may also label the other person as someone else. For example, he can avoid talking to the other person by talking to the person's status position rather than to him personally. One can be sarcastic with a salesman at the door without defining one's relationship with that person, if the comments are about salesmen in general.

Or, if a person wishes to go to an extreme, he can say that the friend he is talking to is not really a friend but is secretly a policeman. Everything he says is then labeled as a statement to a policeman and therefore cannot define his relationship with his friend.

4. To deny that what he says is said in this situation, a person can label his statements as referring to some other time or place. He can say, "I used to be treated badly and I'll probably be treated badly in the future," and these temporal qualifications deny his implication that he is treated badly at the present moment. Similarly, he can say, "A person I used to know did such and such," and by making it a past relationship he denies that his statement is a comment on the present relationship.

To negate a situational statement about his relationship most effectively, he can qualify it with the statement that the place is some other place. He may label a psychiatrist's office as a prison and thereby deny that his statements are about his relationship with the psychiatrist.

In summary, these are ways of avoiding a definition of the relationship. When everything a person says to another person defines the relationship with that person, he can avoid indicating what sort of relationship he is in only by denying that he is speaking, denying that anything is said, denying that it is said to the other person, or denying that the interchange is occurring in this place at this time.

WHY INTIMATES MUST FIGHT

George R. Bach and Peter Wyden

Verbal conflict between intimates is not only acceptable, especially between husbands and wives; it is constructive and highly desirable. Many people, including quite a few psychologists and psychiatrists, believe that this new scientific concept is an outrageous and even dangerous idea. We know otherwise, and we can prove it. At our Institute of Group Psychotherapy in Beverly Hills, California, we have discovered that couples who fight together are couples who stay together—provided they know how to fight properly.

The art of fighting right is exactly what we teach couples who come to us for marriage counseling. Our training methods are not simple and cannot be successfully applied by everyone. They require patience, good will, and the flexibility to adopt some challenging and unconventional ways for dealing with humanity's most personal drives. Most of all, they demand hearts and minds that are open—open to reason and to change. The great majority of our clients master the art of marital combat quickly. For them, the payoffs are warmly rewarding, and we believe that any couple with honest and deep motivation can achieve the same results.

When our trainees fight according to our flexible system of rules, they find that the natural tensions and frustrations of two people living together can be greatly reduced. Since they live with fewer lies and inhibitions and have discarded outmoded notions of etiquette, these couples are free to grow emotionally, to become more productive and more creative, as individuals in their own right and also as pairs. Their sex lives tend to improve. They are likely to do a better job raising their children. They feel less guilty about hostile emotions that they harbor against each other. Their communications improve and, as a result, they face fewer unpleasant surprises from their partners. Our graduates know how to make the here-and-now more livable for themselves, and so they worry much less about the past that cannot be changed. They are less likely to become victims of boredom or divorce. They feel less vulnerable and more loving toward each other because they are protected by an umbrella of reasonable standards for what is fair and foul in their relationship. Perhaps best of all, they are liberated to be themselves.

Some aspects of our fight training shock trainees when they first begin to work with us. We advocate that they fight in front of their friends and children. For many couples we recommend fighting before, during, or after sexual intercourse. Some people who learn about our work by way of hearsay get the impression that we encourage trainees to become expert at the sort of sick and chronic insult exchanges that proved so readily recognizable to audiences of Edward Albee's play and movie, *Who's Afraid of Virginia Woolf?* But this we never, never do. People fight in the *Virginia Woolf* style before we train them, not afterward.

The wild, low-blow flailing of *Virginia Woolf* is not an extreme example of fighting between intimate enemies; in fact, it is rather common in ordinary life. Let's listen in on a fight that we have heard, with variations, literally hundreds of times during nearly 25 years of practicing psychotherapy. We call this a "kitchen sink fight" because the kitchen plumbing is about all that isn't thrown as a weapon in such a battle.

Mr. and Mrs. Bill Miller have a dinner date with one of Bill's out-of-town business associates and the associate's wife. Mrs. Miller is coming in from the suburbs and has agreed to meet Bill in front of his office building. The Millers have been married for 12 years and have three children. They are somewhat bored with each other by now, but they rarely fight. Tonight happens to be different. Bill Miller is anxious to make a good impression on the visiting firemen from out of town. His wife arrives 20 minutes late. Bill is furious. He hails a taxi and the fun begins:

He: Why were you late?

She: I tried my best.

He: Yeah? You and who else? Your mother is never on time either.

She: That's got nothing to do with it.

He: The hell it doesn't. You're just as sloppy as she is.

She (getting louder): You don't say! Who's picking whose dirty underwear off the floor every morning?

He (sarcastic but controlled): I happen to go to work. What have *you* got to do all day?

She (shouting): I'm trying to get along on the money you don't make, that's what.

He (turning way from her): Why should I knock myself out for an ungrateful bitch like you?

The Millers got very little out of this encounter except a thoroughly spoiled evening. Trained marital fighters, on the other hand, would be able to extract from this brief volley a great deal of useful information. They would note that while the trigger for this fight was legitimate (the lady *was* very late), it was also trivial and not indicative of what was really troubling this couple. The aggression reservoir of the hapless Millers was simply so full that even a slight jar caused it to spill over. Both partners had been keeping their grievances bottled up, and this is invariably a poor idea. We call this "gunny-sacking" because when marital complaints are toted along quietly in a gunny sack for any length of time they make a dreadful mess when the sack finally bursts.

Our graduates would also be able to point out that Bill Miller quite unfairly reached into the couple's "psychiatric museum" by dragging the totally irrelevant past (his mother-in-law's tardiness and sloppiness) into the argument; and Mrs. Miller added to the destruction when she escalated the conflict by going out of her way to attack Bill's masculinity. She did this when she castigated him as a poor provider (we call this "shaking the money tree").

Obviously, both of these fighters would benefit from the principal recommendation we make to our trainees: to do their best to keep all arguments not only fair but up-to-date so that the books on a marriage can be balanced daily, much as banks keep their debits and credits current by clearing all checks with other banks before closing down for business every evening. Couples who fight regularly and constructively need not carry gunny sacks full of grievances, and their psychiatric museums can be closed down.

By studying tens of thousands of intimate encounters like this one between the Millers, we designed a system for programming individual aggression through what we call constructive fighting. Our system is not a sport like boxing. It is more like a cooperative skill such as dancing. It is a tool, a way of life that, paradoxically, leads to greater harmony between intimates. It is a somewhat revolutionary notion, but we believe that it can serve not only to enrich the lives of husbands, wives, and lovers; it could become the first step toward controlling the violent feelings that lead to assassinations and to aggressions between entire peoples. A Utopian dream? Perhaps. But we submit that humanity cannot cope with hostilities between nations until it learns to hammer out livable settlements for hostilities between loved ones.

About eight years ago our Institute pioneered in the management of intimate aggression. We have worked successfully with more than 250 couples, and many therapists throughout the United States and abroad now use our system. But, since our methods are still widely misunderstood, we would like to emphasize that our kind of "programming" is neither as precise nor as rigid as the type achieved by computers. Anyone who tries to "program" people in a machinelike way is either kidding himself or trying to play God.

Our system amounts to a set of experimental exercises. We suggest format, but not content; the frame, but not the picture. The picture is filled in by each couple as they fight. This is known as the heuristic approach to education, a system that trains students to find out things for themselves. We train attitudes and suggest directions for further inquiry through trial and error. We formalize and civilize impulsive or repressed anger, but we preserve the spontaneity of aggressive encounters. This is vital because no fight is predictable and no two are alike.

We will describe the at-home fight exercises that we offer our clients; when, where, and how to start a fight; when and how to finish it when it has gone far enough; how couples can regulate their "closeness" to each other while they are between fights; how to score 21 kinds of results of an intimate battle. Our program does not, however, offer hard-and-fast recipes in cookbook style. It can be tried, always with due consideration for the vulnerability of the partner, by anyone without a therapist. But when a therapist is present, as is always the case at our Institute, he is no distant father figure. He participates as trainer, coach, referee, cheerleader, model, and friend.

Some readers may wonder whether all this adds up to complicated machinery constructed by psychologists who cannot bear to keep things simple. Our clinical experience suggests otherwise. Many intelligent, well-to-do trainees tell us of fights that are so abysmally crude and hurtful that it is impossible to doubt the need for fight training. But these kitchen-sink fighters are not the ones who are worst off. We have far more clients who live in a style that can be infinitely more threatening to intimate relationships. Again paradoxically, these unfortunates are the partners who fight rarely or not at all.

Although the Bill Millers, for example, sustained painful emotional injuries in their taxicab fight, they became aggressors ("hawks") under pressure. This is a point in their favor, not against them, for even this destructive encounter produced one positive result. In its way, the taxicab fight gave the Millers a rough—very rough—idea of where they stood with each other, which is the essential first step toward the improvement of any relationship. This knowledge placed them way ahead of many couples. Approximately 80% of our trainees start out as natural nonfighters or active fight-evaders ("doves"), and these people usually know much less about each other than the Millers did. After their fight the Millers knew at least how far apart they were and how far each would go to hurt the other.

In intimate relationships ignorance is rarely bliss. At best it leads to the monumental boredom of couples who are living out parallel lives in a state of loneliness *à deux*. The quiet that prevails in their homes isn't really peace. Actually, these people are full of anger much of the time, like everyone else on earth. After all, what is anger? It's the basic emotional and physiological reaction against interference with the pursuit of a desired goal; and an expression of strong concern when things go wrong. When partners don't fight, therefore, they are not involved in an intimate relationship; honest intimates can't ignore their hostile feelings because such feelings are inevitable.

One typical evening in the home of nonfighting pseudo-intimates began like this:

He (yawning): How was your day, dear?
She (pleasantly): OK, how was yours?
He: Oh, you know, the usual.
She: Want your martini on the rocks?
He: Whatever you want to fix, dear.
She: Anything special you want to do later?
He: Oh, I don't know . . .

In this fight-phobic home nothing more meaningful may be exchanged for the rest of the evening. Or practically any evening. For reasons to be discussed shortly, these partners won't level with each other. Their penalty is emotional divorce.

There is another group of fight-evaders who do exchange some important signals with their mates, but usually with unfortunate results. We call them the pseudo-accommodators. Here is one such husband who is about to dive into appalling hot water:

Wife (settling down comfortably for a sensible discussion): Mother wants to come visit from New York.

Husband (shrinking away and accommodating): Why not?

The dove-husband in this case was saying to himself, "Oh, my God!" He did not say it out loud because he "can't stand hassling." So his mother-in-law arrives and the fights triggered by her presence are far more terrible than the original fight with his wife which the husband managed to avoid. This husband was also practicing another technique that is popular among intimates. He expected his wife to *divine* how he really felt about the mother-in-law's visit. He was saying to himself, "If Emmy loves me she will know that I don't want her mother to come until later in the year when I'll have less pressure on my job." Too bad that most people are not talented in the extrasensory art of divining. But they're not, and many intimates therefore never really know "where they're at."

Surprisingly few couples seem to realize how their failure to level with each other can lead to a totally unexpected, dramatic marriage crisis and perhaps even to divorce. This is what happened to another pair of doves, Mr. and Mrs. Kermit James. While making love, many husbands and wives pretend more passion than they really feel. In some marriages, both partners engage in this charade. In the case of the James family, the wife was the one who did the pretending. True intimates would confess their sex problems to each other. Pseudo-intimates, on the other hand, just go on pretending. The trouble is that unless two partners are really beyond the point of caring what happens to their union, the pretending eventually wears dangerously thin.

The Jameses had been married for eight years. One night after they had sexual intercourse Mr. James patted himself innocently on the back for his skill at love-making. Mrs. James happened to be furious at him because at dinnertime he had refused to discuss an urgent financial problem and later he had left his clothes strewn messily all over the floor. Normally she ignored such provocations just to keep things peaceful. This time, her anger at her husband got out of control. She was ready to "let him have it." She had been gunny-sacking so many additional grievances for such a very long time, however, that she reached unthinkingly for the trigger of an atomic bomb. The danger of a nuclear explosion hovers over every nonfighting marriage. Mrs. James unleashed the lethal mushroom cloud when she casually said:

"You know, I never come. I fake it."

Marriages have split up with less provocation. The Jameses gradually repaired their relationship by entering fight training at our Institute. One of the first bits of advice we gave them, incidentally, is that wise marital combatants always try to measure their weapons against the seriousness of a particular fight issue. Nuclear bombs shouldn't be triggered against peashooter causes; or, as we sometimes warn trainees: "Don't drop the bomb on Luxembourg!"

Fight-evading can also lead to disaster without any blowup whatever. A somewhat extreme example are Mr. and Mrs. Harold Jacobson, a prosperous suburban couple who had been married for more than 20 years.

They had raised two children and were socially popular. Everybody thought they had a fine marriage. Mr. Jacobson was a sales manager with an income of well over $20,000. His wife dressed well, played excellent bridge, and did more than her share for local causes. Both were considered well-informed conversationalists in their set, but at home Mr. Jacobson rarely said much. Peacefully, he went along with whatever his wife wanted to do.

Shortly after their younger child went off to college, Mr. Jacobson packed his clothes while his wife was out shopping and left home without leaving a note. It took Mrs. Jacobson some time to discover through her husband's lawyer that he meant to leave for good. As usual, he just hadn't felt like arguing about it. His wife was incredulous and then horrified. Their many friends were flabbergasted. None would have believed that this marriage could break up. Over a period of weeks, several of them brought sufficient pressure to bear on the Jacobsons to enter our fight-training program.

Mr. Jacobson was persuaded to start first. He joined one of our self-development groups, along with eight other individuals who were involved in marital crises but were not yet ready to work on their problems in the presence of their mates. The senior author of this book was the therapist. Together the group convinced Mr. Jacobson that the "silent treatment" which he had given his wife was not cooperation or strength but non-cooperation or something worse: hostility camouflaged by phony and misleading compliance. He admitted that he had never leveled with his wife, and never clearly communicated his feelings about the way she dominated most of the family decisions; it riled him no end when she decided what they should do to "have fun," to "be creative," and all the rest. Almost invariably he went along, even though he resented it terribly in what we call the "inner dialogue" (conversations and fights which all of us keep going within ourselves). On the few occasions when Mr. Jacobson did protest mildly—always without making the true depth of his feelings clear—he found that his wife became even more assertive when she was resisted. So he became even more quiet.

At first Mr. Jacobson resisted fight training. He said that it would be "undignified" to let himself go and engage his wife in "useless" arguments. It was against his "values." It turned out that his German-born mother had taught him the virtue of the old adage, *"Reden ist Silber, aber Schweigen ist Gold"* (Talk is silver, but silence is golden). Mr. Jacobson still lived by this peasant saying, which was useful in feudal times when speaking up was indeed dangerous for serfs. He therefore believed that self-control was more virtuous than his wife's "noisy dominance."

In the course of six weekly sessions, the group thawed out this typical case of "etiquette-upmanship." We were able to convince Mr. Jacobson that speaking up in a good cause is more effective and valuable than "golden silence" that leads only to hopelessness, In his therapy group he then practiced "speaking up" and "fighting back" on a particularly domineering lady who became, in effect, a substitute for his wife. He reasoned with her. He argued. He refused to be squelched. He was elated when finally he succeeded in getting through to her, and boasted that she was "much worse than my wife."

Then Mr. Jacobson entered a second type of group. Here, four to six married and unmarried intimates work at their problems not as individuals but as couples. Having learned the value of asserting himself aggressively in the self-development group, Mr. Jacobson found that he could now face Mrs. Jacobson on a new basis. During the group sessions he noticed that the wife whom he had always considered overwhelmingly argumentative and domineering could be managed, even tamed. To his surprise, he discovered that she actually *preferred* him to speak up assertively and to share the responsibility for family decision making. It also made him generally more attractive and stimulating to her, with pleasing sexual fringe benefits for both.

Eventually, Mr. Jacobson, like most intelligent people, came to enjoy the give-and-take of true intimacy. He dismissed his divorce lawyer and, most likely, will carry on his marriage for another 20 years, but on a fresh, realistic basis. We felt that the Jacobsons had gained a brand-new marriage without a divorce.

Like most people today, Mr. Jacobson considered "aggression" a dirty word, just as "sex" used to be. Most people feel secretive about their anger and their fights. When we first initiated fight training, we asked couples to put some of their fights on tape at home and bring us the tapes for interpretation and discussion. This system did not work too well. Some partners were too clever; they turned on the tape recorder only when it was to their supposed "advantage" and turned it off when they felt like acting as censors. Other couples resisted the tape-making at home simply because they were too embarrassed to put their anger on record and then listen to it.

The fact is that anger is considered taboo in modern society. It isn't "gentlemanly." It isn't "feminine." It isn't "nice." It isn't "mature." This is supposed to be the age of sweet reason and "togetherness." The very word "fighting" makes most people uncomfortable. They prefer to talk about "differences" or "silly arguments." And they will go to considerable lengths to maintain the quiet that isn't peace.

Partners say, "Darling, I love you too much to fight with you; you're not my enemy!" But they usually say this in their inner dialogue, not out loud to their partner. Then, when they get angrier, their next step may be a demand, also directed toward the partner but still usually unspoken: "Act nice, no matter how angry you feel!" When an intimate feels even more threatened, he may finally speak up with a plea: "Don't get angry with me!" Or he may demand to turn the partner off: "I can't take you seriously when you're angry!" In an extremity, he may link his demand to a threat: "Don't raise your voice—or else!" All this is part of the strategy of "peace at any price."

The wish to be above personal animosity is fed by many mistaken beliefs. Control of anger, rather than its expression, is considered "mature." Hostility feelings toward an intimate are not only considered the antithesis of love ("If you really love me you should tolerate me as I am"); often such "hate" emotions are considered "sick," requiring psychiatric care. If an angry partner is not seriously enough afflicted to be led away to the head doctor, he is considered at least temporarily irrational. After all, everybody "knows" that what is said in anger cannot be taken seriously; a "mature" partner discounts it as the gibberish of an emotionally upset person, much like the ranting of a drunk.

Nonfighting marital stalemates are rooted in the romantic belief that intimates should take one another as they are. Folklore and etiquette insist that one should not try to change the beloved but accept him or her, warts and all, and "live happily ever after." Once one somehow acquires the magic ability to accept the other's frailties, automatic bliss is supposed to ensue. This charming idyll is promoted not only in fiction and on the screen but even by some marriage counselors and other professionals.

The dream of romantic bliss is an anachronistic hangover from the Victorian etiquette that tried to create gentlemen and gentleladies by social pressure. But the notion that a stress- and quarrel-free emotional climate in the home will bring about authentic harmony is a preposterous myth, born in ignorance of the psychological realities of human relationships. Fighting is inevitable between mature intimates. Quarreling and making up are hallmarks of true intimacy. However earnestly a mature person tries to live in harmony with a partner, he will have to fight for his very notions of harmony itself and come to terms with competing notions—and there are always competing interests.

Everybody has his own ideas about what makes for harmonious living. Being human, one likes one's own ideas to prevail except perhaps in cases of aggression-phobic fight-evaders or excessively submissive partners who act like doormats. The mature partner may yield some of his notions, but usually not without a fight. The classic battle about where to take the family on vacation is a perfect example of such an authentic encounter.

"The mountains are most relaxing," shouts the husband.

"The beach is more fun," shouts the wife.

Such conflicting notions make it perfectly natural for everybody to be angry at his mate some of the time.

Yet many couples still consider intimate conflict revolting. "We never fight," they tell us indignantly. They are, in truth, afraid of fighting. Sometimes they fear just the stress of "hassling"; few couples know about the modern research that shows stress is valuable for keeping the nervous system toned up in the psychological sense. More likely, intimates fear that anger is a Pandora's box. They fear they "can't afford to fight" because they have so many years invested in each other. They worry that if one partner raises his voice, the other must raise his. There might be tears. The fight might escalate out of control. It could lead to rejection, even separation!

As a matter of fact, our trainees find that they tend to feel closest after a properly fought fight. Only our newest recruits wonder whether we're being facetious when we tell them, "A fight a day keeps the doctor away."

Fascinating new experiments document this paradoxical-sounding thesis. In one famous series, Dr. Harry Harlow of the University of Wisconsin reared several generations of monkeys and showed that an exchange of hostilities is *necessary* between mates before there can be an exchange of love. Harlow's calm, mechanical, totally accepting and nonfighting monkey mothers raised offspring who grew up "normal" except that they couldn't and wouldn't make love.

Another distinguished researcher, Konrad Lorenz, made similar observations about "bonding" (loving) behavior: "Among birds, the most aggressive representatives of any group are also the staunchest friends, and the same applies to mammals. To the best of our knowledge, bond behavior does not exist except in aggressive organisms. This certainly will not be news to the students of human nature. . . . The wisdom of old proverbs as well as that of Sigmund Freud has known for a very long time how closely human aggression and human love are bound together." Indeed, one of the leading theorists on emotional maturity, Erik Erikson of Harvard University, blames the failure to achieve human intimacy on "the inability to engage in controversy and useful combat."

Oddly enough, anger can be useful just *because* it pours out with a minimum of forethought. Unless a partner hides it behind a falsely neutral or false-friendly (and ulcer-producing) façade, his anger—like spontaneous laughter or spontaneous sexual arousal—cannot be dishonest. Making a person angry is the surest way to find out what he cares about and how deeply he cares. Since intimates keep measuring and remeasuring how much they care for one another ("Are you getting bored with me?"), they can make each other angry in normal but usually unconscious tests of the depth of their involvement.

The process starts right in the early phase of courtship when one partner tries to get the other "sore," not necessarily to "pick a fight," but just to "tease," to test the other out. How far can he go? What does she care enough about to get her "good and angry"? These fight games can be informative if they are played fairly and in a spirit that seeks not to inflict hurt but to resolve realistic conflicts. Lovers also find out by this process that affection grows deeper when it is mixed with aggression. Both feelings then become part of a natural, genuine relationship that allows for expression of the bitter as well as the sweet side of emotional involvement.

We believe, then, that there can be no mature intimate relationship without aggressive leveling; that is, "having it out," speaking up, asking the partner "what's eating" him and negotiating for realistic settlements of differences. This does cause stress, but our successful trainees learn to accept one of the realities of the human condition: the pain of conflict is the price of true and enduring love. People simply cannot release all their love feelings unless they have learned to manage their hate.

"Hate" sounds like too strong a word, but it isn't. When a partner performs according to one's expectations, one is "turned on" and feels love. When these expectations are frustrated, one is "turned off" and feels hate. This is what people recognize as the ups and downs of marriage. We call it "the state of marital swing." Unfortunately, it is usually a state viewed with vast resignation; hence the saying, "You can't live with 'em and you can't live without 'em." This hopelessness is unwarranted. At our Institute we discovered: (1) It is not a partner's sweet and loving side that shapes his bond with an intimate; it is the talent for airing aggression that counts most. And (2) aggression management not only can be learned; it can be used to *change* a partnership constructively.

Contrary to folklore, the existence of hostility and conflict is not necessarily a sign that love is waning. As often as not, an upsurge of hate may signal a deepening of true intimacy; it is when neither love nor hate can move a partner that a relationship is deteriorating. Typically, one partner then gives up the other as a "lost cause" or shrugs him off ("I couldn't case less"). Indifference to a partner's anger and hate is a surer sign of a deteriorating relationship than is indifference to love.

The problem of regulating personal aggression is rarely discussed. It hovers too uncomfortably close to home for most people. Almost everybody has a greater or lesser "hangup" about admitting hostile feelings, even to himself. It is part of humanity's embarrassment about its inborn aggressive side. Frequently, therefore, people displace their hostilities onto others. We call this "blamesmanship" or "scapegoating," and intimates usually find the process baffling and infuriating.

Suppose it's Wednesday night. Mrs. Jones has had a trying day. She doesn't feel like making love and has decided to withhold sex from her husband. Instead of negotiating with him, she contaminates the situation with an extraneous issue and engages in blamesmanship between the sheets.

She: Not tonight, dear. Besides, I can't ever feel anything anyway. Your stomach is in the way.

He: That's just your excuse. It all depends on the position.

She (heatedly): You know perfectly well that I can't make it with those acrobatics. Everything would be very simple if you'd just stop stuffing yourself.

He (furious): I'm comfortable the way I am and you're not going to take my gourmet tastes away from me.

She (icily): Well, something's got to give.

He (angry but resigned): Oh hell, there we go again. . . .

Children are a favorite target when intimates displace their own fights onto other people. Most parental fights about children, for example, are not about children at all. The disagreement is between the parents; the child is only the battleground. Tom and Myra Robinson learned this when they conducted the following fight before one of our training groups:

She: You simply must start to enforce discipline around here and make the kids toe the line.

He: Why me?

She: Because I want you to be the power in this house!

He: I like to be and I am.

She: No, you're not—I am! I have to be!

He: No, you don't have to be, and you're not!

She (getting angrier): Don't be stupid! Who disciplines the kids? Me! Who takes all the responsibility for discipline—me!

He (pacing and pulling hard on cigarette): I am glad you do, but that just makes a cop out of you . . . it doesn't really impress the kids at all.

She (very red in the face): You're driving me out of my mind! That's my point! You let me do all the dirty work. That makes me a "mean mother" in the eyes of the kids. You get all the goodies: you're their loving "super daddy." I don't like it!

He (flopping resignedly into an armchair): Why shouldn't you like it when the kids and I have a terrific relationship? I don't understand you. That's one of the main attractions for coming home. I love those kids and you'll never make a "heavy" out of me!

She: OK! But I can't do it all! You have to back me up and you never do! Listen to what they just did today. . . .

He (disgusted with her but not with his children): Cut it out!

She (totally exasperated): Why? Don't you want to hear? Don't you want to be part of this family? Don't you want to take any responsibility?

He (getting up again to counterattack): I take enough responsibility earning our living. And I don't like you when you tattle on the kids! In fact, I can't stand it. . . .

The Robinsons thought they were battling about their ideas of "parental authority," "doing a good job of raising the kids," and the role of the "man of the house." But these are only superficial cultural stereotypes. Once the therapy group began to probe what was really bothering Tom and Myra, we discovered some much deeper intimate issues which the couple did not dare confront.

It developed that Myra was jealous of Tom's love for the kids because he was not making enough passionate love to her. Tom, in turn, was not making love to Myra because since the kids came she had been a disappointment to him. She did not conform to his definition of a "good mother." What turned him off completely was her tattling because this aroused a strong memory of ugly, angry emotions from his past. His mother used to tattle to his father about his own misdeeds, and his father used to beat discipline into him every Saturday morning after his mother, behind the boy's back, had presented the father with a list of misdeeds!

Myra is also bitter because, since the kids came, the husband turned off loving her. She thinks that he thinks that she thinks: "I love kids more than him. I only used the man to have a father for my kids, who are my joy and pride and who fulfill me." She therefore thinks: "He is jealous of my love for the kids and punishes me by withholding his love from me. He does not want to share me with anybody."

In our training group this spiral of misconceptions collapsed as the facts were exposed. By using techniques . . . the Robinsons learned to level about their real feelings, wants, and expectations. The issue of disciplining the children never came up again. It was spontaneously handled by one partner or the other, as the situation demanded.

Another popular way to divert aggressive feelings is to repress them as "irrational" in one's personal life but to express them by directing (displacing) them onto such *symbols* as President John F. Kennedy, Senator Robert F. Kennedy, the Reverend Dr. Martin Luther King—or onto the anonymity of large, faceless groups: perhaps "kooks" or the Cosa Nostra or other criminals, or the Viet Cong and other "enemies." This displacement of hostility ultimately enables political leaders to engage in the most catastrophic form of aggression: war.

Not that politicians are the only ones who are busy manipulating human aggression. Spokesmen for the Judeo-Christian religions have urged people to pray it away. Psychiatrists have tried to analyze it or rationalize it away. The late Emily Post and other etiquette devotees would have liked to smile it away. Nothing has worked, and for the most logical reason. Anger is part of the personality, like the sex drive. It can be displaced, channeled, modified, or repressed. But it cannot go away. This is why our efforts are designed to make people face it and decontaminate it as sensibly as human fallibility permits.

We believe that the inability to manage personal conflicts is at the root of the crisis that threatens the structure of the American family. Communications between children and parents are breaking down. More and more young people are "tuning out" by escaping into the world of drugs and other short-lived emotional kicks. One out of every three marriages ends in divorce. In our largest and most "advanced" state, California, the figure is approaching an almost incredible one out of every two.

Millions of other couples continue to live together physically and legally, yet emotionally apart. Atrophy, boredom, casual infidelities, and false-front façades "for the children's sake" are no longer exceptional. No one knows how many couples are emotionally divorced. We do know that millions of husbands and wives live in card houses held together by fantasy; by social, religious, economic, or legal pressures—or by the fear of change.

The philosophers say modern man is alienated, trapped by loneliness, yet hostile to those who might come too close. They blame this sense of alienation for the anxieties of most people, for humanity's daily failures of heart and nerve. But the philosophers have stated the problem backward. It is not alienation that is becoming unbearable. It is intimacy.

We have entered a psychological ice age. Except for occasional bursts of warmth, often fueled by sex after a few cocktails, truly intimate encounter has begun to disappear from civilized Western life. Closeness has become a paradox: longed for, but increasingly intolerable. Without the sweet anesthesias of role playing, libido, or liquor many people can no longer find each other or stand each other. Sustained closeness between man and wife, parents and child, and friend with friend, is in danger of becoming extinct. We believe that this quiet private threat endangers civilization as severely as the public threats of nuclear incineration, automation, urbanization and others that are constantly talked about.

Why should this be happening today, of all times? Again, the answers are so close that it is easy to overlook them. Not so long ago, the family was not a small unit but a tribe. Tribal people rubbed shoulders constantly. Everybody used to know everybody else's business. There was less privacy but more opportunity for sharing failures and unhappiness, to get attention and help from friendly souls. The things that matter in life were more visible and understandable. Today, as everybody knows, the family is segmented. We no longer witness many happenings; we merely talk *about* them. And much of the talk has become specialist's talk that only other specialists can grasp. Who can readily share the joys and ulcers of a husband who comes home from his work as a missile expert?

These trends have turned individuals into faces within a "lonely crowd," who worship privacy and autonomy as the supposedly ideal way of coping with intimate problems. Marriage, therefore, is more of a closed-circuit affair than ever. The burden on mates and lovers is heavier; they must fulfill vital functions (reacting, sharing, etc.) that used to be the job of more than one other person. No wonder that the circuits of so many marriages are becoming overloaded, and that mates are tuning each other out and playing games with each other.

When Dr. Eric Berne's book, *Games People Play*, became a runaway bestseller, publishing experts were surprised. They shouldn't have been. America's living rooms and bedrooms are full of partners who are too weak or frightened or not sufficiently knowledgeable to tolerate authentic encounters with their supposed intimates. They recognized their own camouflaging rituals in Dr. Berne's somewhat cynical and overly flip but essentially accurate descriptions. Remember "Uproar," the pointless fight that is provoked by a husband or wife early in the evening merely to avoid sex later? It is all but a national pastime. So are such marital games as "If it weren't for you" and "Look how hard I've tried."

Dr. Berne performed a valuable service because he made game-players aware of what they are doing. However, we believe he was too pessimistic in appraising their potential capacity to drop their masks and become authentic persons capable of intimacy.

Our own clinical experience indicates that most couples would dearly like to stop playing games. They often realize that the camouflaged life is needlessly tiring and anxiety-arousing. Game-players never really know "where they're at." The more skillful they are, the less they know, because their objective is to cover up motives and try to trick their partners into doing things. The game-player's life is loaded with uncertainties, and human beings are poorly equipped to withstand uncertainty.

Unfortunately, one can't simply command game-players: "Stop Playing Games!" Something better must fill the void. People have to manage their emotions somehow, especially their aggressions. (Games are actually aggression that camouflage the desire to exploit a partner, manipulate or weaken him, do him in, etc.)

Constructive fighting makes for game-free living. It is a liberating, creative alternative that works. Since we introduced fight training, the rate of reconciliation among our Institute's problem couples has increased sharply. Follow-up studies indicate that most of our graduates are living much more satisfying (if perhaps noisier) lives than before. And for the most tragic victims of our psychological ice age, the children, the benefits are incalculable. For them, a sense of genuine family closeness is as important as food and drink. When a "nest" cools or disintegrates, children can grow only amid enormous handicaps. Young children especially thrive on intimacy and starve emotionally when they cannot share and learn it. We regard the neglect of intimacy and the absence of intimate models within many families as principally responsible for the current "generation gap." Those who are deprived of an intimate nest may never care to build or to protect one for themselves.

For intimate partners, perhaps the richest payoff of well-managed conflict comes with yielding after a fight. Any intimate relationship implies some readiness to yield one's own self-interest when it clashes with that of the partner. Everybody knows that the give-and-take of trying to get along with someone often means bending one's own will to the wishes of the other. This is never easy because the psychological price of yielding to another is a loss (however temporary and partial) of one's own identity. Realistic intimates find that this is a small price as long as it is part of an equitable, mutual process and leads to an improved relationship.

The final benefit of yielding is the tremendous feeling of well-being that comes from making a beloved person happy. This is why it feels so delicious to make one's wife or husband laugh. It also explains why "It is better to give than to receive." In true intimacy, it really is. Which is one more reason why intimacy is worth fighting for.

Section Three
IMPROVING INTERPERSONAL COMMUNICATION

In this section our purpose is to provide specific suggestions for improving your use of the process of interpersonal communication. It appears to us that two approaches could be useful. We recommend that you use both as you analyze your own communication choices and habits.

One approach is to identify what you may be doing poorly. You can do this by noting interpersonal communication barriers or problems that seem to plague most people; then you can determine, perhaps with the help of your close friends or classmates, the extent to which these common barriers pose problems in your own interaction. To assist you in this program of personal improvement, we have identified and discussed a selected group of such barriers in Chapter 8.

A second approach that may be used to improve interpersonal communication behavior is suggested in Chapter 9. In this chapter we have attempted to challenge you to transcend your former ambitions—to raise your sights, so to speak. In our discussion of self-actualization we have tried to accentuate the positive, to encourage you to reach for the limits of your unknown, untapped potential. In our discussion of interpersonal trust we have suggested that, without becoming another per-

son's dupe, you should search for a new plateau of interpersonal relationships—one on which you build with others new foundations of trust and rapport.

In this section our ultimate goal is to challenge you to attempt to become the kind of person you personally have always wanted to be—and then be better.

Chapter 8
BARRIERS TO INTERPERSONAL COMMUNICATION

One way of achieving successful human communication is by overcoming potential barriers. We have previously discussed some of the environmental conditions that can limit or deter interpersonal communication, such as cultural differences (Chapter 5). Now that we have examined the elements in the interpersonal communication process, we wish to focus on problems of a personal nature that frequently limit the effectiveness of human interaction. Three significant problem areas of interpersonal relations will be discussed: (1) interpersonal distrust, (2) "gaps" between people, and (3) feelings of alienation. To the extent that these problems can be avoided or resolved, our interpersonal communication can be greatly enhanced.

INTERPERSONAL DISTRUST

Probably the foremost problem in relating well to other people is distrust—and its counterpart, defensive interpersonal behavior. The basic cause of defensiveness is inherent in one's unmet interpersonal needs. We have suggested in Chapter 3 that we need supportive feedback from valued others to achieve a satisfactory self-image. When this need remains unmet, a general feeling of anxiety is produced. Unresolved anxiety generates defensive tactics when we are with other people. Defensive behavior may simply be a show of fear, including postural, facial, or verbal signals that warn the other person to be careful. Or defensive behavior may involve small signs of desire to withdraw: Verbal hesitancies, stepping backward, turning sideways, or simply paying more attention to some other person. These defensive behaviors are real, and not very devious; thus, the other person perceives them directly as signs of anxiety or fear.

A more disagreeable strategy of defensiveness is the deliberate distortion of the message received. All of us have heard exchanges such as the following: (She) "Will you please shut the door; I feel cold." (He) "Why don't you just say you don't want me coming in and bothering you?"

A most serious form of defensive strategy is direct, personal attack. A severe problem arises when the person attacked is unaware that in some way he or she is perceived as a threat; in such a case he or she will likely view the attack as pure, unprovoked aggression.[1] A

[1]P. Watzlawick, J. H. Beavin, and D. D. Jackson, *Pragmatics of Human Communication* (New York: Norton, 1967), pp. 80–93.

brief example may serve to illustrate the complexity of this type of behavior. Recently one of our students went home to visit her parents who were having marital strife. Approximately at the time of her arrival, her mother was "leaving" to go to her mother's home. The mother asked the girl to go with her, and upon their arrival at the grandmother's home, the girl telephoned her father that they had arrived safely. Her mother asked her why she had done so; the girl replied, "I knew he would be worried." Her mother accused: "Why have you turned against me?" In talking about the incident, the girl interpreted her mother's attack as unprovoked aggression, although she made some allowance for her highly emotional condition at that time. Even so, her resentment of her mother's attack was clearly unresolved.

Communication Behaviors That Generate Defensiveness

Sometime we find ourselves distrusting a person without quite knowing how it came about. Knowledge about communication behavior that tends to produce or increase distrust may help us forestall our signal reactions of defensiveness. Investigation of such incidents has identified the following contributory conditions, or causes, of defensive behavior:

1. *Evaluation by expression, manner of speech, tone of voice, or verbal content, perceived by the receiver (listener) as criticism or judgment, will produce defensive behavior.*
2. *Communication perceived by the recipient as an attempt to control him/her will produce defensiveness; it is interesting to note that if speech can be said to be a social "tool," the implication is that the recipient has been "tooled."*
3. *Stratagems that are perceived as clever devices produce defensiveness; partially hidden motives breed suspicion. Persons seen as "playing a game," feigning emotion, withholding information, or having private access to sources of data will stimulate defensive responses.*
4. *An appearance of lack of concern for the welfare of a person will heighten his/her need for defensiveness. Such "neutrality" may be necessary at times, but people strongly need to be perceived as valued persons. A clinically detached or impersonal manner (not caring) is usually feared and resented.*
5. *An attitude of superiority arouses defensive behavior; any behavior that reinforces the recipient's feelings of inadequacy is a source of disturbance.*
6. *Dogmatism is a well-known stimulus of defensive behavior; if you know something "for certain," it is wise to determine*

whether or not anyone else wants to hear it from you, and whether they want your answer to be offered tentatively or with final certainty.[2]

In his essay following this chapter, Everett Shostrum identifies other ways in which people try to manipulate people, and, when detected, how they thus tend to increase suspicion and defensive behavior.[3]

Requisite Conditions for Reducing Defensive Behavior

About a quarter of a century ago Carl Rogers began to report a movement toward a nondirective approach to psychotherapy. These practices culminated in his client-centered approach. The relevant point here is his emphasis on the patient's need for personal trust in the therapist and his communication behavior. Rogers emphasized acceptance or psychological safety in psychotherapy groups.[4]

Rogers' approach was a forerunner of Gibb's concept of supportive climate in the communication process. Starting a long-range research effort in 1953, Jack Gibb focused his efforts on the reduction of defensive behavior in groups. This defensive behavior seemed to be caused, in part, by lack of interpersonal trust. In later work he began to focus on trust and its development, associating trust with interpersonal acceptance.[5] According to his findings, defensive behavior is reduced by interaction that is perceived by the individual as (1) descriptive rather than evaluative or critical, (2) oriented toward solving of mutual problems rather then oriented toward personal control, (3) spontaneous rather than strategic, (4) empathic rather than neutral, (5) indicative of an attitude of equality instead of superiority, and (6) expressive of provisionally held viewpoints instead of dogmatic certainties.[6] Additional studies by Gibb tend to corroborate these findings.[7]

Effects of Reducing Defensiveness

As interpersonal trust increases, interpersonal relationships are changed so that there is (1) increased acceptance of legitimate influence by others, (2) decreased suspicion of motives of others, (3) increased tolerance for deviant behavior of others, (4) increased sta-

[2]J. R. Gibb, "Defensive Communication," *Journal of Communication*, 11 (1961), 141–148.

[3]See pp. 416–422.

[4]C. R. Rogers, *Client-Centered Therapy* (Boston: Houghton Mifflin, 1951), pp. 515–520.

[5]J. R. Gibb, "Climate for Trust Formation," in L. P. Bradford et al., eds., *T-Group Theory and Laboratory Method* (New York: Wiley, 1964), pp. 279–309.

[6]Gibb, "Defensive Communication," *op. cit.*

[7]J. R. Gibb, "Dynamics of Leadership," *Current Issues of Higher Education* (Washington, D.C.: American Association for Higher Education, 1967).

bility when one is not trusted by others, (5) shifting of emphasis to control over the group interaction process rather than control over individuals, and (6) further increase in interpersonal trust.[8]

Changes in personality characteristics are not easy to produce; changes in behavior that seem to indicate changes in personality structure may be only temporary. Even so, studies tend to indicate that, as defensive behavior decreases and interpersonal trust increases, two very important personality changes can occur: (1) We tend to achieve heightened feelings of personal adequacy (improved self-image), and (2) we achieve easier acceptance of our temporary feelings of internal conflict (less anxiety). Reducing defensive behavior and increasing interpersonal trust appear to be extremely valuable goals in terms of effective interpersonal communication.

"GAPS" BETWEEN PEOPLE

Dwight D. Eisenhower is said to have typified the simple virtues of the heartland of his nation. Even so, as he saw it, the most important message he could leave with the people of his boyhood "hometown" was that not even the people of Abilene, Kansas, could ever again afford to think that the way in which people thought and acted in other parts of the world would not directly influence their lives. A major problem today is that of overcoming communication barriers between different groups and groupings of people. Gaps need to be bridged between members of different reference groups, different generations, and different cultures and minority subcultures.

Barriers Between Members of Different Reference Groups

In order to be adequate socially we must achieve personal beliefs, attitudes, and convictions that help us to function well with those people who surround us. Conflicts over norms of behavior and belief usually prove to be threatening. If our personal standards and norms seriously conflict with those of people in our immediate environment, the experience is likely to be painful because our very basis of existence is at stake.

When we identify with a group such as the people in our community, we almost inevitably adopt and defend the standards and behavior of that group. A group with which we thus identify is sometimes called a "reference group." This process of identification introduces a certain degree of narrowness or distortion into our perceptual field; this limiting and distorting of our perception of "foreigners" (persons not in our reference group) then becomes a major source of breakdown in communication.

[8]Cf. K. Giffin, "Interpersonal Trust in Small-Group Communication," *Quarterly Journal of Speech*, 53 (1967), 224–234.

Since each of us accepts our own perceptions as "reality," the customs and attitudes of our own reference group are judged to be superior when they are different from those of other groups. Other people and other groups are then judged according to these standards. Americans commonly place a high value on houses with modern plumbing. As a result, many American soldiers consider that the Germans are superior to the French. If you say, "Well, they are!" then you have illustrated the point at issue—you have made a judgment based on a standard derived from your American reference group.

A boy whom we shall call George has identified with a predelinquent gang. He has a different system of prestige values from Charles, who has identified with the Boy Scouts. Not only do the two boys admire different institutions, but they also respect different individuals and types of "success." It is not enough to say that they "don't talk the same language." Such may be the case, and if so, communication is hampered; but even if they know and agree on the same meanings for words, their system of values is different—Charles will think the predelinquent boy is wrong, and George will judge Charles to be naïve and ignorant. This kind of problem is not uncommon; in fact, two such boys may even live within the same city block. Even so, bridging the communication gap in this rather common setting is not at all easy.

In the larger social sense, the insular thinking described above is one of the principal barriers to intercultural cooperation. People of almost all cultures sincerely desire a better world and a better society; the barrier consists of lack of agreement among the various groups as to *what constitutes a good society*. Members of each culture consider their own version of society as fundamentally right because it (more or less) satisfies their personal needs as they see them. Thus, they believe that the better society can only arise from a further development and modification of their own. This is true for Iranians, Hindus, Berbers, Eskimos, Russians, and Americans.[9] When members of different reference groups or subcultures try to communicate, it frequently seems that their actions are chiefly intended to hinder or obstruct another group's efforts to create their version of a "better" world. In his essay following this chapter, R. D. Laing describes the ways in which concepts of *us* and *them* are generated in groups and cultures; his analysis of how we behave in response to what "we" think "they" are thinking is a bit involved but extremely enlightening.[10]

How can such gaps ever be bridged? In a way, every individual bridges a similar gap whenever he tries to contact and "get to know" any other single individual. We start by accepting and even adopting

[9]A. W. Combs and D. Snygg, *Individual Behavior*, rev. ed. (New York: Harper & Row, 1959), pp. 341–344.

[10]See pp. 423–432.

a few behaviors of others that help us to satisfy some personal need. As we accept or adopt behaviors, we later modify our attitudes, beliefs, and value systems. For example, the white man's alcohol was a boon from heaven in the eyes of the Plains Indians, who viewed the world as a place where man became great ("successful") and held power over others through dreams and delirium. On the other hand, the Hopi, living in a world of fragile order and regularity where a small mistake could bring personal hardship, saw alcohol as a great menace and rejected it.

This process of acceptance of the ways, attitudes, and beliefs of others is speeded up if the other person has some acceptable source of status, or if the behavior satisfies some immediate and important personal need.[11] New ways of doing things that otherwise fit our customary pattern of behavior are easily accepted and adopted. Once the change is made, we quickly find additional reasons why it was a good idea; thus we reduce the cognitive dissonance imposed by the new behavior.[12]

The primary tool in this process of bridging gaps between reference groups is, of course, getting them to look at each other without perceptual distortion. The real barrier is the *a priori notion that just because a person is a member of another group his behavior and his beliefs will be inferior.* People who fail to conform to our standards tend to be viewed as ignorant or perhaps evil. Such prejudgment—judgment without taking an objective, open-minded, inquisitive look to see first and judge later—is properly called prejudice. People of no nation, religion, or group have been entirely free of this problem. Even a teacher, who ordinarily is a severe critic of his own educational system, will have difficulty giving objective consideration to the suggestions of those who are not a part of the system. However, such objectivity is the true basis of tolerance and makes possible the bridging of gaps between members of different reference groups.

The Generation Gap

For most of the twentieth century there have usually been identifiable differences between the folkways, attitudes, and beliefs of two consecutive generations; technological advances in machines, factories, automobiles, telephones, etc., have produced differences in ways of communicating and interacting with others. However, the cultural gap today between persons in their forties and beyond and persons in their twenties is much greater than in previous times. This is true for two reasons.

In the first place, technological advancement has a way of self-

[11]R. Linton, "*The Cultural Background of Personality* (New York: Appleton, 1945), pp. 39–74.

[12]S. Feldman, *Cognitive Consistency* (New York: Academic, 1966), pp. 43–57.

accelerating; each single advancement paves the way for a number of new developments, until the speed of additional technological changes is tremendous. We have reached the point in this change process where for those of us who are forty, very little happened in the first twenty years of our lives to prepare us very well for the last twenty. In fact, much of what we did then is now outmoded. The second reason for the current generation gap is the advent of the "affluent society." The so-called Protestant ethic, the idea that work is good and leisurely idleness is bad, served a frontier society very well. Today the need for it does not seem critical. As the authors of this book work overtime in its preparation, the children of one of the authors say, "Dad, you don't need to work that hard; it'll be all right. Come on and go to the movies with us—we have the money!" And of course they do —they always have more cash than their Dad!

We could well afford to take our technological advances and enjoy them; we could accept our young folks' advice and relax our way of life. Many members of the younger generation are sincerely questioning attitudes and beliefs generally accepted by the older one, especially issues of social justice versus law and order, and social welfare versus capitalism. In addition, the problem described in the previous section traps us: Each generation is convinced that the folkways and value system of the other generation are inferior. We focus on the differences and ignore the similarities; we see only beards and sandals or bald heads and worried frowns.

The writers of this book are convinced that there is a strong, abiding ethic in our American culture that will keep us from letting the generation gap become a severe social problem—it is simply this: Throughout their history the American people have had a strong regard for the value of the individual person. Our most severe national crises have each been settled with a favorable consideration of this principle. Perhaps we should all remember that when someone makes his plea to be allowed just to "do his thing"—grow a beard, wear ragged jeans, or work at night trying to write a book—he is simply asking for an old American privilege: to be himself as an unhampered individual. As suggested in the section above, an openminded, objective look at a person of the "other generation" can be the start toward bridging the generation gap on an interpersonal level.

Gaps Between Cultures and Minority Subcultures

We have been vaguely aware of the problem of communication between segments of cultures or subcultures ever since it was discovered in Boston that Lowells talked only to Cabots and Cabots talked only to God. Today the need for communication between members of different subcultures is more urgent. Our primary concern in this section is with interpersonal communication barriers between representatives of different cultures or subcultures; such problems are brought to light at the "interface" between cultural groups.

Communities that pride themselves on tolerance and absence of prejudice almost always have only a few members of a minority group in their midst. Minority groups become threatening to majority groups only when they are large or powerful. When a group feels threatened its members tend to accentuate or idealize the reference group's characteristics. When individuals are threatened, two negative effects upon their perceptual processes occur: (1) Their perceptions tend to be narrowed to the object of threat so that it is difficult to see broadly and clearly, and (2) they tend to be much more rigidly defensive of their existing perceptions.[13] As a general principle, the psychological effects of intergroup threat or conflict are felt at the lower socioeconomic levels of these groups, especially if persons at these lower levels are the victims of domination or aggression within their own group.[14] For example, in the South, the most violent reactions to school integration have occurred among the "poor white" lower economic classes.

The point of greatest potential for bridging intercultural gaps is at the interface between cultures—that is, the personal, face-to-face interaction between official and unofficial representatives of those cultures. Such persons are generally better educated, more broadly experienced, and feel less personally threatened by representatives of the other culture. At this interface a common language capability is helpful but not the major problem. For example, in the earlier periods of World War II, American soldiers and Russian soldiers found ways of overcoming the language problem. The need for action in a common cause made individuals from the different cultures important to each other; there was even a certain pleasure in getting acquainted with new allies. Americans were pleasantly surprised at the great physical stamina and courage of the Russian soldier.

What is severely needed by intercultural representatives at this interface is objectivity of perception, as suggested in previous sections. Intercultural conflict is always carried on by individuals who think of their antagonists as members of the other group rather than as individual human beings. Intergroup conflict at the cultural interface can be diminished by increasing the capability of the representative members to differentiate one another as individuals.[15]

[13]Combs and Snygg, *op. cit.*, pp. 165–189.

[14]D. Snygg, "The Relative Difficulty of Mechanically Equivalent Tasks: I. Human Learning," *Journal of Genetic Psychology*, 47 (1935), 299–320.

[15]B. Kutner, C. Wilkins, and P. Yarrow, "Verbal Attitudes and Overt Behavior Involving Racial Prejudice," *Journal of Abnormal and Social Psychology*, 47 (1952), 649–652.

Increased interaction between such representatives is helpful; it fosters the capability of these persons to see each other as individuals rather than as "Blacks" or "Whites," Germans or Jews, Russians or Americans.[16] A very interesting procedure developed by R. D. DuBois has been shown to be an effective means of promoting better relationships between such representatives of different groups. Instead of talking about intergroup or intercultural problems and differences, they are asked to talk about pleasant childhood memories.[17] Members of both groups talk about their experiences in smelling and tasting enjoyable foods, playing games, and participating in athletic events. After awhile they feel as if they have had similar experiences, somewhat similar childhoods, and are first of all members of the common human race. Shared experiences make possible a common feeling; further, shared experiences provide a more personal, human view of a member of another group or culture.

The objective view of one another, a view focused on the other person as an individual human being rather than as a specimen of a strange cultural type, is the basis for effective interpersonal communation between intercultural representatives. Such effective communication behavior is highly useful in reducing intergroup conflict for the following reasons: (1) It maximizes human capability for tolerance of differences and acceptance of new or different folkways and attitudes, and (2) it minimizes the degree of fear and feelings of threat imposed by the other group, race, or culture.

FEELINGS OF ALIENATION

In comments on current social problems, the term "alienation" is frequently used. Sometimes these comments are about the "alienated teenager" or the "alienated generation." Since there are many persons in our society who appear to hold negative attitudes toward other persons in their immediate social environment, the problem deserves special consideration.

In common parlance the term "alienated" usually refers to persons who are estranged or withdrawn from other persons whom they would ordinarily be expected to associate with, or to admire—even to love. A student who has turned away from his teachers—that is, who has ceased to talk with them in the way that they expect or desire—may sometimes be called "alienated." When a large number of persons "under thirty" appear to be distrustful of all persons "over thirty," it is time to look carefully at the possible causes.

[16] J. W. Thibaut and J. Coules, "The Role of Communication in the Reduction of Interpersonal Hostility," *Journal of Abnormal and Social Psychology*, 47 (1952), 770–777.

[17] R. D. DuBois, *Get Together, Americans* (New York: Harper & Row, 1943).

The Problem of the Alienated Person

The term "alienated" has two usages pertinent to our discussion. The first simply refers to a person who withdraws from or avoids another person or persons. This withdrawal behavior has been identified as *social alienation,* and is defined by Hajda, a representative authority in this area, as follows:

> *Alienation is an individual's feeling of uneasiness or discomfort which reflects his exclusion or self-exclusion from social and cultural participation. It is an expression of non-belonging or non-caring, an uneasy awareness or perception of unwelcome contrast with others. It varies in scope and intensity. It may be restricted to a few limited situations, such as participation in a peer group, or it may encompass a wide social universe, including participation in the larger society. . . . In this sense, alienation is a general social phenomenon, a feeling that may be experienced in some fashion by any member of a given society. It cannot be understood apart from its opposite, the feeling of belonging, sharing, or participation which follows from the individual's inclusion or integration into the social collectivities.*[18]

Although here we will be using the term "alienation" to refer to social alienation, it should be noted that common usage of the term connotes an implication of mental disturbance. This connotation comes from the technical use of the term in psychiatry. In their *Psychiatric Dictionary,* Hinsie and Campbell give the psychological definition of mental alienation as follows:

> *The repression, inhibition, blocking or dissociation of one's own feelings so that they no longer seem effective, familiar or convincing to the patient.*[19]

Thus whenever a person is said to be alienated, there is a connotative suggestion of personal maladjustment.

Alienation does not mean simple disagreement with another person, even if the disagreement is violent, as long as interaction continues. When one ceases overt communication with another person or persons and withdraws from interaction, social alienation, in the sense we are using the term, has occurred. In this way one can become alienated from a person or a group—a brother, sister, mother, father, husband, wife, teacher, peer group, school, reference group, or even an entire culture or social system. Alienation thus involves a conclusion that one's attempts to communicate with a person (or persons) are pointless. At this point functional withdrawal from interaction begins.

[18]J. Hajda, "Alienation and Integration of Student Intellectuals," *American Sociological Review,* 26 (1961), 758–759.

[19]L. E. Hinsie and R. J. Campbell, *Psychiatric Dictionary,* 3rd ed. (New York: Oxford University Press, 1960), p. 26.

Alienation of a person from another can be partial; one can be convinced that he will be denied the opportunity for communication on certain topics or at certain times or under certain conditions. As long as he/she is allowed to communicate on most topics most of the time, the degree of alienation is only slight. The severity of alienation increases as a person perceives an increase in the relative number of times or topics on which his/her communication is denied.

Alienation can occur between a person and one or more other people. Complete alienation from one other person may not matter very much; complete or nearly complete alienation between a person and many others can make his life miserable. William James once said, "No more fiendish punishment could be devised, even were such a thing physically possible, than that one should be turned loose in society and remain absolutely unnoticed by all members thereof."[20]

Alienation does not occur between a person and someone whom he/she has never known. It does occur most noticeably when a person withdraws from interaction with someone he/she has known well or ought to know well, such as a parent, wife, or husband.

As described above, alienation from another person does not necessarily mean neurotic behavior; when confronted with denial of one's attempts to communicate, it is perfectly rational to conclude (1) "He won't talk with me (on those topics, now, or under those conditions)" or (2) "It is not worth my time to try to talk with him (on those topics, now, or under those conditions)." Neurotic alienation begins when *reality* is ignored—that is, when the above conclusions are drawn in the face of identifiable evidence to the contrary. It becomes critical when a person denies his/her own feelings that are at the same time expressed in obvious behavioral ways.

Of course, social alienation does not meet the given criteria for mental alienation. However, it is sometimes viewed by parents and even by others in society as mental disturbance. This confusion in thinking occurs as follows: (1) The socially alienated person may appear to parents to be repressing, inhibiting, blocking, or denying expected or desired warm feelings about them, and (2) these expected or desired feelings no longer seem to be operative in producing "appropriate" responses to the overtures of the parents. This breakdown of such a relationship can be analyzed in terms of communication theory; that is, it constitutes a refusal to utilize a communication channel generally thought to be available and useful. An important question for the student of communication behavior is thus exposed: What kinds of communication behavior tend to produce alienation?

Tangential questions are as follows: Is it possible that "the alien-

[20]Quoted by R. D. Laing, *The Self and Others: Further Studies in Sanity and Madness* (London: Tavistock, 1961), p. 89.

ated" are realistically responding to communication events in an intelligent way? Can such alienating communication events be described in a way that will provide insight and understanding of this socially relevant problem? Are "the alienated" mistakenly withdrawing from social interaction that would be very useful to them? Have parents or teachers or other important persons unknowingly or thoughtlessly provided excellent causes for such social withdrawal?

An exploratory study of this problem was made through analyses of interviews with college students who appear to be alienated from teachers and peer groups. The data tend to indicate that certain prior communication events have transpired. These events can be identified as misuse or misunderstanding of one or more of the basic principles of interpersonal communication.[21] We will give this problem detailed consideration here, because we have found that young people of our acquaintance are concerned about it.

Speech Anxiety

In the study of speech communication, tendencies to withdraw from interpersonal communication have been variously called communication apprehension,[22] reticence,[23] and speech anxiety.[24] Essentially such tendencies are a response to interaction conditions that produce fear or tension.[25] This attitude is a situation-specific anxiety, and will be identified here as *speech anxiety*.[26]

A major part of our research work in The Communication Research Center at the University of Kansas has been focused on persons who exhibit tendencies toward general withdrawal from social interaction. For three years we have offered such students a special program designed to improve their interpersonal communication behavior and reduce their speech anxiety.[27] Students are identified for invitation to participate in this program on the basis of a high degree

[21]For a more detailed report of studies completed and those in progress, see K. Giffin, "Social Alienation by Communication Denial," *Quarterly Journal of Speech*, 56 (1970), 347–357.

[22]J. C. McCroskey, "Measures of Communication-Bound Anxiety," *Speech Monographs*, 37 (1970), 269–277.

[23]G. M. Phillips, "Reticence: Pathology of the Normal Speaker," *Speech Monographs*, 35 (1968), 39–49.

[24]K. Giffin and S. M. Gilham, "Relationships Between Speech Anxiety and Motivation," *Speech Monographs*, 38 (1971), 70–73.

[25]M. Heider and K. Giffin, *The Influence of Situation Variables on Reported Approach or Avoidance of Communicative Interaction, Research Report* R-37 (Lawrence, Kan.: Communication Research Center, University of Kansas, 1971).

[26]Cf. D. H. Lamb, "Speech Anxiety: Toward a Theoretical Conceptualization and Preliminary Scale Development," *Speech Monographs*, 39 (1972), 62–67.

[27]For further details see K. Giffin, *A Program in Counseling for Speech Anxiety* (Lawrence, Kan.: Communication Research Center, University of Kansas, 1967).

of speech anxiety.[28] The most marked difference in behavior of these students (in comparison with the average University of Kansas freshman or sophomore), however, is not a poor ability to communicate, but the tendency to avoid or withdraw from interaction situations. Our research efforts have identified what might be termed a speech anxiety syndrome for students exhibiting withdrawal tendencies. They have a significantly higher-than-average degree of speech anxiety. They have lower self-image and lower trust of others,[29] as well as higher motivation to avoid failure and lower motivation to achieve success.[30] They also indicate that they have experienced significantly greater suppression of their childhood communicative efforts by their parents[31] and a significantly greater-than-average degree of communication denial from persons held by them to be important.[32]

The introspective pattern of low self-image, low trust of others, high speech anxiety, high motivation to avoid failure, low motivation to achieve success, along with indications of parental suppression of communication and communication denial by important others, all point to the probability of a significantly high degree of social alienation—and this is what we have found.[33]

It is tempting to guess that the reported childhood communication suppression and/or experience of communication denial have produced this syndrome; this, of course, we have not experimentally verified. We have only established significant correlation coefficients; however, because it would be unethical to produce experimentally

[28]See K. Giffin and G. Friedrich, *The Development of a Baseline for Studies of Speech Anxiety*, Research Report 20 (Lawrence, Kan.: Communication Research Center, University of Kansas, 1968).

[29]K. Giffin, M. Heider, B. Groginsky, and B. Drake, *A Study of the Relationships Among Four Variables: Speech Anxiety, Self-Concept, Social Alienation, and Trust of Others, Research Report* 24 (Lawrence, Kan.: Communication Research Center, University of Kansas, 1970).

[30]See K. Giffin and S. Masterson, "A Theoretical Model of the Relationships Between Motivation and Self-Confidence in Communication," in Lee Thayer, ed., *Communication Spectrum* (Flint, Mich.: International Communication Association, 1968), pp. 311–316; see also K. Giffin and S. M. Gilham, *A Study of the Relationships Between Speech Anxiety and Two Types of Motivation: (1) Motivation to Achieve Success, and (2) Motivation to Avoid Failure, Research Report 24* (Lawrence, Kan.: Communication Research Center, University of Kansas, 1969).

[31]See K. Giffin and M. Heider, "A Theory of the Relationship Between Adult Speech Anxiety and Suppression of Communication in Childhood," *Psychiatric Quarterly Supplement, II* (1967), 311–322; see also M. Heider, "An Investigation of the Relationship Between Speech Anxiety in Adults and their Indication of Parental Communication Suppression During Childhood," unpublished M.A. thesis, University of Kansas, 1968.

[32]See Giffin and Groginsky, Research Report 20, and Giffin and Groginsky, Research Report 31 (Lawrence, Kan.: Communication Research Center, University of Kansas, 1969).

[33]K. Giffin and B. Groginsky, *A Study of the Relationship Between Social Alienation and Speech Anxiety*, Research Report 27 (Lawrence, Kan.: Communication Research Center, University of Kansas, 1970).

such an undesirable syndrome, we will continue to pursue this problem mainly through case studies and clinical reports. In the meantime, we suspect that the causal relationship does exist.

Communication Behaviors Related to Social Alienation

It has been our experience that an understanding of the ways in which basic principles of interpersonal communication may be ignored or violated can lead to a better understanding of one's feelings of alienation. In addition, such insights can provide the basis for changes in one's communication behavior that may lead to the reduction of the feeling of alienation. Your own insights and your changes in use of interpersonal communication techniques may or may not change the behavior of those persons from whom you feel alienated, but such additional insight can at least help you to understand yourself and others better.

The first principle of interpersonal communication that appears to be related to social alienation is this: We communicate on two levels. The first level is that of message sending; the second level is that of providing information about the message. When the message itself is in conflict with, or contradictory to, the communication about the message, a natural response is confusion and at least a partial attempt at withdrawal from further interaction. If parents say, "We really do love you, John," *but say it in a way that shows distrust, suspicion, anger, or hostility*, social alienation is a reasonable result from John's point of view. This problem of incongruency was discussed in Chapters 4 and 6.

The second principle that appears to be related to alienation is that in an interpersonal situation one cannot refuse to communicate. A refusal to interact with another person is a communication in and of itself. When another person simply refuses to talk to you (perhaps for a reason thought to be excellent by that person), the message given to you is conclusive: He/she does not wish to talk with me. Such a conclusion provides an excellent reason for withdrawal from later interaction unless it is absolutely necessary. This principle was discussed in Chapter 3.

The third related principle (discussed in Chapter 6) is that nonverbal communication ultimately establishes the nature of an interpersonal relationship. Many times we actually receive verbal messages from another person telling us how he/she perceives our interpersonal relationship with him/her: "I like to be with you"; or "I enjoy talking with you." Sometimes we believe what we hear; however, *if the other person's nonverbal behavior is in conflict with such a verbal message, we usually recall the old adage that "actions speak louder than words."* In the final analysis, a person's perception of his relationship with another is determined by the latter's nonverbal communication. In many interviews we have been told by students that "my parents said they loved me, but they didn't act like it." Such behavior appears to us to be reasonable justification for diminishing interaction.

The fourth related principle is that the degree to which two persons similarly perceive their relationship will heavily influence the interpretation of communication between the two. Different perceptions of their relationship by two persons can lead to serious and even violent disagreement between them regarding what one has really "said" to the other. There is a case study of the husband and wife who frequently participated in violent quarrels. An example occurred one day when the husband received a phone call from a friend who was in town for a few days. The husband immediately invited the friend to stay at their home when he arrived in town. When he told his wife, a bitter quarrel arose over the desirable and undesirable characteristics of this friend. Finally the wife agreed that an invitation to the friend was the appropriate and natural thing, but concluded with this comment: "Well, you may be right, but you are wrong because you are arguing with me." In actual fact the real conflict was over the husband's right to take such initiative without consulting his wife; this concerned their perceptions of the nature of their interpersonal relationship. In their quarrel this couple committed a common mistake in their communication. They *argued* about the characteristics of a third person while actually *disagreeing* about their treatment of each other, failing completely to resolve the confusion between their two perceptions of their own interpersonal relationship.[34]

At this point we can briefly summarize the potential impact of the four principles of interpersonal communication given: In an interpersonal situation, nonverbal communication usually establishes the nature of an interpersonal relationship, which in turn heavily influences interpretations of communication by both persons in the relationship.

Alienation by Communication Denial

As we noted in Chapter 3, the initiation of any communication act carries with it an implied request: "Please validate me." This plea can be in the form of a request for recognition of one's ideas as worthwhile. Even in such a case, however, there is an obvious implication regarding the value of oneself personally.

There are three ways in which a person can respond to the implied request for validation of another person: (1) agreement—a person or his idea is responded to as somewhat worthwhile or valid; (2)

[34]Watzlawick, Beavin, and Jackson, *Pragmatics of Human Communication*, *op. cit.*, pp. 80–81.

disagreement—the person or his idea is responded to as more or less invalid; and (3) denial of the existence of the question. This denial (that is, an attempt to refuse to give any response at all) not only denies the existence of the request "Please validate me," but by implication denies the existence of the other person on a functional, interpersonal, or communicational level.

Little Johnny, age five, comes home from kindergarten and says, "I have a girl friend." His mother says, "Eat your soup, Johnny." This constitutes a denial of Johnny's capability of discussing girl friends (at that time)—perhaps an event of no great consequence. Ten years later John says, "Dad, Joe Smith is taking his folks' car to the school picnic Saturday." Dad says, "Finish your homework, John." This is an example of a denial of John's right to talk about using the family car—that is, a denial of John's existence on this communicational level. Two such instances in ten years are inconsequential; two instances per day for ten years is another matter. Also, denial of communication on one isolated topic may not pose a severe threat to an individual's self-validation. Remember, however, that the question of his validity is implied with every statement John ever makes, and that in any interpersonal situation the other person cannot refuse to respond to it: A refusal becomes at least a temporary or partial denial of John's self-identity.

The impact of such denial depends upon the value a person places on the other person or persons, perhaps upon the value he places upon his relationship with them. Consistent and continued denial of a child by his parents can cause severe damage. Ronald Laing has given the following description of what happens when a child is denied in this manner:

> *The characteristic family pattern that has emerged from the study of families of schizophrenics does not much involve a child who is subjected to outright neglect or even to obvious trauma, but a child whose authenticity has been subjected to subtle, but persistent, mutilation, often quite unwittingly.*[35]

In another paragraph Laing poignantly describes the effect on the child:

> *The ultimate of this is . . . no matter how a person feels or how he acts, no matter what meaning he gives his situations, his feelings are denuded of validity, his acts are stripped of their motives, intentions and consequences; the situation is robbed of its meaning for him so that he is totally mystified and alienated.*[36]

In commenting on our society, Martin Buber wrote as follows:

[35]Laing, *op. cit.*, p. 91.
[36]*Ibid.*, pp. 135–136.

> *At all its levels, persons confirm one another in a practical way, to some extent or other, in their personal qualities and capacities, and the society may be termed human in the measure to which its members confirm one another. . . . The basis of man's life with man is two-fold and it is one; the wish of every man to be confirmed as what he is even as what he can become, by men, and the innate capacity of man to confirm his fellow men in this way; that this capacity lies so immeasurably fallow constitutes the real weakness and questionableness of the human race; actual humanity exists only where this capacity unfolds.*[37]

We should note that the implied request, "Validate me," may be put by an individual, a group, a subculture, or even a nation; also the responses—agreement, disagreement, or denial of existence—may be made by another individual, a group, a subculture, or a nation. Perhaps not in the last year, but certainly in previous years, most of us have seen an adult black person attempt to ask a sincere, intelligent question about how to perform a part of his job, only to be given a response of this order: "Boy, bring me that board over there!" Looking backward, it seems to the present writers that much of the observed communication of white people with black people has carried a denial of the latters' capability to interact with others as worthwhile human beings.

There are two major ways an individual can respond to the denial described: (1) He can refuse to accept it as a denial, or (2) he can accept the idea that he does not exist on that communication level. Communication behaviors exhibiting a refusal to accept such a denial include (1) repetition of the request, (2) escalation of the tone or manner of the request, and (3) overt verbal communication about the denial.

Repetition of the request simply involves continuation of any verbal communication with its attendant implied request, "Please validate me." Escalation can involve changes in vocal tone or intensity, threatening posture, violent gestures, or, on a larger scale, demonstrations, riots, etc. Overt communication would likely be something like this: "Dad, why don't you talk with me about my using the family car on the picnic?" It should be noted that such overt communication is rarely initiated by the person in the weaker, "one-down" position who feels threatened, and, of course, such denial of one's existence (on any level) by a valued other will produce a feeling of threat.[38]

Acceptance of the implication of denial of oneself is more common than many people believe; many persons accept the idea that they are unworthy of talking to "better" people, people with more

[37]M. Buber, "Distance and Relation," *Psychiatry*, 20 (1957), 97–104.
[38]Watzlawick, Beavin, and Jackson, *op. cit.*, pp. 86–90.

influence, more education, more experience or just more self-assurance. This phenomenon is not uncommon; the acceptance of this implication is frequently a constituent of the process of social alienation.[39]

The "Double Bind"

A particularly interesting problem arises when communication denial occurs and at the same time the denied person cannot withdraw from a situation because of the value he/she places on a potential relationship with that specific other person. In an analysis of the communication environment of schizophrenia, Bateson and his asssociates[40] coined the term "double bind" to identify a communication situation in which these elements occur: (1) For certain important reasons a person cannot withdraw from the scene; for example, for his own moral reasons he must continue to try to talk things over with his parents, or for his own religious reasons he must continue to try to talk with his wife; (2) messages are sent by the other person on the verbal and nonverbal levels that are internally contradictory; that is, the subject is validated by a verbal message and invalidated by nonverbal behavior—those cues as to how he is to interpret the verbal message; and (3) his attempts at overt communication about the contradiction are denied; that is, he is not allowed to initiate discussion about the internal contradiction posed between the verbal message that validates him and the nonverbal communication that invalidates him.

An attempt to justify the denial of opportunity to communicate about this contradiction—that is, denial of opportunity to engage in overt communication about it—is frequently based on rather unreasonable grounds. Moral ground-rules may be invoked: "It is not right (moral) for you to question your mother this way." Such morality is seldom expressed in overt verbal communication; rather, the horrified stare or the hurt expression usually carry the message of infraction of moral boundaries. In other cases an ethic is invoked; for example, in business circles it is sometimes claimed to be unethical to "deal in personalities." Thus, a request for overt communication about the contradiction may be construed as an attack on the other person's status or position of authority. Once again, refusal of overt communication about the contradiction will likely be indicated by a cold stare or nervous fidget rather than by forthright verbal communication. If for his own reasons a person cannot "leave the field" and is also denied the opportunity to initiate overt communication with the other person, he is confronted with an undecidable problem. If he addi-

[39]Laing, *op. cit.*, pp. 135–136.

[40]G. Bateson et al., "Toward a Theory of Schizophrenia," *Behavioral Science*, 1 (1956), 251–264.

tionally feels it is morally wrong to question the source of this contradiction—for example, if he actually believes it is immoral to question his mother about her confusing messages—he truly is in a double bind. If he acts upon the apparent implication of the verbal message ("You are a worthwhile person or have a good idea," etc.), he will run the risk of antagonizing his mother. On the other hand, if he accepts the apparent implication of his mother's vocal tone and general manner, he will infer that she thinks his idea is worthless, and thus, again, will run the risk of antagonizing her by acting as if his mother did not "properly" care about her son. The point is, he is in trouble; he is "damned if he does and damned if he doesn't."

There is no way out of this dilemma; the doorways out—leaving the field, or initiating overt communication—have been closed. In such a case the individual usually does one of three things: (1) He scans the interpersonal horizon—that is, his mother's behavior—for some message or clue that he must have missed or overlooked; (2) he ignores all or most communication from her, or he interprets all or most of her communication as confusing and of slight value or meaning; (3) he may overreact, jumping inside his skin when his mother says, "How's my boy tonight?" Such is the way in which the double bind can produce an unhappy relationship between two more or less well-meaning people who, according to the notions of many of us, should mean a great deal to each other.

It is of the highest importance to note that the double bind is not life's ordinary difficult situation in which one must choose between two mutually exclusive but equally desirable alternatives—for example, choosing between getting married or staying single—with both alternatives holding attraction, but once one is chosen, the other cannot then be enjoyed. The double bind is not the same dilemma; it is not a case of simply finding out that you cannot have your cake and eat it too. Rather, in the case of the double bind, *both choices are poor*. The double bind *bankrupts choice itself*; neither alternative is tenable and the dilemma is complete—the situation is a true paradox.

Matina Horner made an insightful examination of such a condition:

> *A bright woman is caught in a double bind. In achievement-oriented situations she worries not only about failure but also about success. If she fails, she does not live up to her own standards of performance; if she succeeds she is not living up to societal expectations about the female role. College women students who feared success aspired to traditional female careers: housewife, mother, nurse, schoolteacher. Girls who did not fear success aspired to graduate degrees and careers in such scientific areas as math, physics, and chemistry.*[41]

[41]M. Horner, "A Bright Woman Is Caught in a Double Bind," *Psychology Today* (1969), 36–38, 62.

Where double binding is of long-lasting duration, it will produce habitual suspicion regarding the general nature of human relationships. This suspicion leads to a self-perpetuating pattern of mistrust of communication. It can lead to alienation, not only toward others, but eventually toward oneself.[42]

There may be times when we cannot or should not respond to the overtures of another person. At times we may be tired, mentally exhausted, or have nothing to say that has not already been said over and over. At other times, for our own survival or peace of mind we may deem it necessary to ignore the presence of another person. Even so, the point to be noted here is that in such a case we should be aware of what is happening: If we are with another person, and they believe we are aware of their presence, to ignore them is to deny their implicit request for validation as a person. Even more, to remain silent in response to an *overt request* to talk with us is prima facie evidence that, for us, they do not, at this time, functionally exist.

Interpersonal Communication with Alienated Persons

There are few things more difficult than to try to overcome the effects of misuse of interpersonal communication principles outlined above; interaction with persons who have been alienated from their social environment is never easy. Of course, the primary requirement is that someone must want to make the effort. It is also helpful to provide the alienated person with insights into the process that has contributed to the alienation; sometimes this insight plus that person's own attempts to reach out and establish new contacts with people around him/her tend to reduce the problem. Most certainly, covert denial of communication must be avoided if interaction with alienated persons is to be achieved.[43]

It has been our observation that people who alienate people and then are surprised at their alienation do not seem to understand the basic principles of interpersonal communication. One can raise the following questions: When people alienate other people in the ways described above, are they really surprised by the results? Or are they perhaps subconsciously aware of what they are doing?

It should be emphasized that the purpose of the present analysis has not been to untangle the problems of all teenagers, much less the snarls of the generation gap. Our purpose here has been simply to shed light on the way in which some persons are alienated from those who seem to be surprised when it happens. It is our belief that new

[42] D. Jackson, "Psychoanalytic Education in the Communication Processes," *Science and Psychoanalysis*, 5 (1962), 129–145.

[43] K. Giffin and K. Bradley, "An Exploratory Study of Group Counseling for Speech Anxiety," *Journal of Clinical Psychology*, 25 (1969), 98–101.

insight into such a problem shows ways in which the problem can be reduced. Our suggestions regarding ways in which basic principles of interpersonal communication have been ignored or violated identify possible change in communication behavior that can sometimes provide more desirable results—warmer and more satisfying interpersonal relationships.

SUMMARY AND PREVIEW OF READINGS

Out of the many potential barriers to interpersonal communication, at least three are important enough to deserve special consideration. In this chapter we have discussed (1) interpersonal distrust and its consequence—defensive communication behavior, (2) prejudicial gaps between groups and cultures, and (3) social alienation along with attendant speech anxiety.

We have suggested ways in which defensive behavior can be increased as well as reduced. In the essay that immediately follows this chapter, "The Manipulator," Everett Shostrum describes techniques of manipulation of people that are commonly found in our society. We suggest that you think carefully about the possible influence on defensive behavior that such manipulative practices may have. In addition you should assess their possible impact on the process of interpersonal communication.

We have suggested that cultural prejudice and gaps between groups and cultures are natural but not necessary. Certain ways of overcoming prejudice are available to those who wish to reduce this barrier. Such achievement is rarely easy; in any case it will take determination and strong resolve. In the essay "Us and Them," R. D. Laing describes the psychological process by which the concepts of "we" versus "they" are developed, exaggerated, and solidified. He gives a fairly involved description of the effect on our behavior when we respond to what we think "they" are thinking. Although this process is somewhat complex, we think you will find it interesting and helpful in understanding human behavior.

In the final section of this chapter we described the way individuals are sometimes influenced to withdraw from interaction with others. We discussed this process in terms of social alienation as well as speech anxiety, and indicated some close relationships between the two concepts. In addition, we suggested that such withdrawal can be the result of prior communication experiences, particularly that of continued communication denial.

In this chapter we have described three personal and basic barriers to effective interpersonal relations: lack of trust (defensiveness), prejudice between reference groups, and social alienation. We have explained ways in which such barriers are formed and have suggested interpersonal communication techniques that can be used to reduce these barriers. Appropriate changes in one's communication behavior are more easily achieved if one has good insight into the need for such changes. In this chapter we have attempted to provide the basis for such insight.

SUGGESTED APPLICATIONS AND LEARNING EXPERIENCES

1. Obtain permission to observe a routine problem-solving discussion such as that frequently occurring in a dormitory, student living group, or student organization. Note very carefully any defensive behavior that occurs. Also note the immediately preceding interaction that seemed to generate this defensiveness, and compare it with Gibb's findings reported in the preceding chapter. Share your observations with a small group of your classmates.

2. Select a person of your acquaintance who is at least twenty years older than you; arrange to have lunch together "to discuss the generation gap." During your lunch period do the following two things: (1) Ask this person to identify ways in which he/she believes you think differently from the ways he/she thinks (suggest possible difference in values and motivations), and (2) ask him/her to temporarily "exchange places with you" as you and he/she role-play each other in a brief additional discussion of these human values and motivations. Identify new information thus obtained about the "older generation" and report it to your classmates. Note especially any changes of attitude (positive or negative) on your part as a result of this experience.

3. Determine in your own mind the degree to which you feel alienated from some particular person who is supposed to be (expected by society to be) important to you. This may be a wife, husband, mother, father, sister, brother, teacher, counselor, advisor, or department chairman. Arrange a meeting with such a person and note very carefully any evidences of communication denial on the part of this person; note also the nature of your responses to such denial. Carefully but deliberately attempt to discuss with this person your perception of his/her communication denial and what the two of you might be able to do about it. Share your findings with your classmates.

4. If for any reason (geographic distance or no feelings of alienation on your part) you cannot comply with suggestion 3 above, select a member of another race and follow the instructions given.

5. In the article "The Manipulator," Everett Shostrum describes eight types of manipulative behavior. Observe a campus group in at least two of their meetings and note the types of manipulative behavior evidenced. Discuss these observations with the other members of your class.

6. In his article "Us and Them," R. D. Laing suggests a way of analyzing degrees of interpersonal understanding. Meet with one of your classmates and discuss Laing's procedure for analyzing (1) agreement, (2) understanding, and (3) realization of understanding. After you have discussed Laing's suggestions to your satisfaction, reflect back on your discussion. With your classmate attempt to determine the amount of understanding that is going on between you. Focus precisely on selected parts of your interaction at first; then try to arrive at an overall assessment of your discussion with this other person. Discuss the principles Laing describes as they may apply to the "Watergate Incident."

THE MANIPULATOR
Everett L. Shostrom

A manipulator is a person who exploits, uses, or controls himself and others as "things" in self-defeating ways. I would say further that the modern manipulator has developed from our "scientific" emphases as well as from our marketplace orientation, which sees man as a thing to know about, to influence, and to manipulate.

Erich Fromm has said that things can be dissected or manipulated without damage to their nature, but man is not a thing.[1] He cannot be dissected without being destroyed; he cannot be manipulated without being harmed. Yet the very objective of the marketplace is to achieve this "thingness" in people!

Here, man is no longer a man but a customer. To the sales manager he is a prospect, to the tailor a suit, to the bond salesman a bank account; even at the beauty parlor, which performs a rather intimate personal service, madame is a generality, "the patron." All of this tends to depersonalize us and deprive us of our individuality, and we resent it. I don't want to be a "head" to my barber; I want to be Everett Shostrom, a live and vibrant person. We all want particularity, but that is not what we have when we're hooked by systems of commercial thought which tend to destroy that very quality. When the con artists of the selling game cajole us with stock phrases, meaning not a bit of it, we resent it, and them.

Since there is some of the manipulator in all of us, let's see if we can't bring him into clearer focus. I would say that there are some fundamental types of manipulators, as illustrated in Figure 1. Paradoxically, Figure 1 is a picture of a typical therapy group and also a picture of each of us with our various self-defeating manipulative techniques. Let me describe each of them:

1. The *Dictator* exaggerates his strength. He dominates, orders, quotes authorities, and does anything that will control his victims. Variation of the Dictator are the Mother Superiors, Father Superiors, the Rank Pullers, the Boss, the Junior Gods.

2. The *Weakling* is usually the Dictator's victim, the polar opposite. The Weakling develops great skill in coping with the Dictator. He exaggerates his sensitivity. He forgets, doesn't hear, is passively silent. Variations of the Weakling are the Worrier, the "Stupid-Like-a-Fox," the Giver-Upper, the Confused, the Withdrawer.

[1]See Erich Fromm, "Man Is Not a Thing," *Saturday Review*, March 16, 1957, pp. 9–11.

Figure 1 The Manipulative Types. (The internal dimensions of this figure are adapted from Timothy Leary, *The Interpersonal Theory of Personality,* New York: The Ronald Press Company, 1957.)

3. The *Calculator* exaggerates his control. He deceives, lies, and constantly tries to outwit and control other people. Variations of the Calculator are the High-pressure Salesman, the Seducer, the Poker Player, the Con Artist, the Blackmailer, the Intellectualizor.

4. The *Clinging Vine* is the polar opposite of the Calculator. He exaggerates his dependency. He is the person who wants to be led, fooled, taken care of. He lets others do his work for him. Variations of the Clinging Vine are the Parasite, the Crier, the Perpetual Child, the Hypochondriac, the Attention Demander, the Helpless One.

5. The *Bully* exaggerates his aggression, cruelty, and unkindness. He controls by implied threats of some kind. He is the Humiliator, the Hater, the Tough Guy, the Threatener. The female variation is the Bitch or Nagger.

6. The *Nice Guy* exaggerates his caring, love, and kills with kindness. In one sense, he is much harder to cope with than the Bully. You can't fight a Nice Guy! Curiously, in any conflict with the Bully, Nice Guy almost always wins! Variations of the Nice Guy are the Pleaser, the Nonviolent

One, the Nonoffender, the Noninvolved One, the Virtuous One, the Never-Ask-for-What-You-Want One, the Organization Man.

7. The *Judge* exaggerates his criticalness. He distrusts everybody and is blameful, resentful, slow to forgive. Variations of the Judge are the Know-It-All, the Blamer, the Deacon, the Resentment Collector, the Shoulder, the Shamer, the Comparer, the Vindicator, the Convictor.

8. The *Protector* is the opposite of the Judge. He exaggerates his support and is nonjudgmental to a fault. He spoils others, is over-sympathetic, and refuses to allow those he protects to stand up and grow up for themselves. Instead of caring for his own needs, he cares only for others' needs. Variations of the Protector are the Mother Hen, the Defender, the Embarrassed-for-Others, the Fearful-for-Others, the Sufferer-for-Others, the Martyr, the Helper, the Unselfish One.

The manipulator over-exaggerates any one or combination of these types. Usually when we are most strongly one type, we project its opposite onto others around us, making them our targets. Weakling wife, for instance, often chooses a husband who is a Dictator and then controls him by her subversive devices.

So each of us, paradoxically, is such a group, with all these manipulative potentials, and any therapeutic group is each of us turned inside out! This is why, as we shall see later, group therapy is so effective in helping the manipulator to see himself in others. The reason we seem different to different people is that we expose only certain manipulations to some and other manipulations to others. This is the reason that we must be careful not to judge another by other peoples' opinions, for, too often, they have seen only certain sides of the person.

CAUSES OF MANIPULATION

I would agree with Frederick Perls that a basic cause for manipulation lies in man's external conflict between self-support and environmental support. There is a good deal of this in employer-employee relationships. The employer, for example, creates the sales manual (a dastardly thing!) as a substitute for individual thinking. He patently does not trust the individual salesman to approach the customer with his own individuality, to size him up, and then to *be* what comes naturally. Instead, the salesman must make his approach within the limited framework of the prefabbed manual of thought provided by the boss and thus receives insult to his personal integrity and, in turn, is an insult to the customer.

The employee in our modern society, on the other hand, tends to be a freeloader, a fringe-benefit-getter. He demands certain rights and privileges without having made an effort to demonstrate his ability and performance. I had a firsthand example of this not long ago while interviewing an applicant for work to be done on a small commercial project. He wasn't at all interested in showing me what he could contribute; instead, he first demanded a contract. With it he wanted participation in the profits although he hadn't been part of the project at its beginning.

Not trusting himself for self-support, man believes his salvation lies in trusting others. Yet, not trusting the other person completely, modern man manipulates the other in an effort to support himself in the process. It is as if he rides the coattail of the other person and then attempts to steer him at the same time; or, to use a more modern analogy, he is the backseat driver refusing to drive, yet driving the driver! The word that describes this cause of manipulation is "distrust." We cannot really *trust* the natural organismic balance each of us has, which would allow us to live our lives simply and feelingly. In great part this is a fruit of childhood, in which we are taught that our organism is like a wild horse which we must ride and never let go of, which we must control vigilantly.

Erich Fromm has suggested a second cause for manipulation in modern man. He reasons that the ultimate relationship between man and man is that of love, and that love is knowing a human being as he is and loving his ultimate essence. The world's great religions admonish us to love our neighbor as we would ourselves, but here unfortunately, we run into an operational snag. How many people know how? Most aren't even aware that we can't love our neighbor *until we love ourselves.*

We seem to assume that the more perfect we appear—the more flawless—the more we will be loved. Actually, the reverse is more apt to be true. The more willing we are to admit our weaknesses as human beings, the more lovable we are. Nevertheless, love is an achievement not easy to attain, and thus the alternative that the manipulator has is a desperate one —that of complete power over the other person, the power that makes him do what *we* want, feel what *we* want, think what *we* want, and which transforms him into a thing, *our* thing.

A third suggestion for the causes of manipulation is posed by James Bugental and the existentialists. Risk and contingency, they point out, are on every side of us, as though our every act were a stone dropped in a pond. The number and potentialities of the things that may happen to us at any minute are beyond our knowing. Modern man feels powerless when he faces this existential situation. According to Bugental, the *passive manipulator* says, " 'Since I can't control everything that will determine what happens to me, I have no control at all.' Experiencing the unpredictability of his life, the patient gives up and enacts this feeling of having no possibility of affecting what happens to him. He makes himself totally an object."[2] The passive manipulator thereupon lapses into an inertia which accentuates his helplessness. To the layman it might appear that the passive manipulator now becomes automatically a victim of the active manipulator. Not so. This is a sneaky trick of the passive manipulator. As Perls has shown, in any encounter between top-dog and under-dog in life, the under-dog most always wins. An example of this is the mother who gets sick because she can't handle her children. Her helplessness causes them to become subservient to some degree and to give in, even though they don't want to.

The *active manipulator*, on the other hand, "victimizes other people, capitalizing on their powerlessness, and apparently gaining gratification by

[2] J. F. T. Bugental, *The Search for Authenticity* (New York: Holt, Rinehart & Winston, 1965), p. 298.

exercising gratuitous control over them. Parents who are oppressed by the dread of powerlessness often need to make their children excessively dependent upon them and to defeat the child's efforts to gain independence."[3] Usually the parent is the top-dog and the child the under-dog, and we see the use of the "If-Then" technique. "*If* you eat your potatoes, then you may watch television." "*If* you do your homework, then you may use the car." Naturally the modern child soon learns the technique too. "If I mow the lawn, then how much do I get?" "If Jim's father lets him use the car every weekend, then why can't I?"

The truly active manipulator might simply roar: "Do as I say and no questions!" We see it in business: "I own fifty-one percent of the stock, and they will wear this uniform because *I* want them to." Even in education. The founder of the college where I once taught used to say: "I don't care what color the buildings are, so long as they are blue."

A fourth possible cause for manipulation is suggested in the writings of Jay Haley, Eric Berne, and William Glasser. Haley, in his work with schizophrenics, has found that the schizophrenic is intensively afraid of close *interpersonal relationships* and so tries to avoid such relationships. Berne suggests that people play games in order to regulate their emotions and thereby avoid *intimacy*. Glasser suggests that one of the basic fears of people is their fear of *involvement*. In effect, then, a manipulator is a person who ritualistically relates to people in an effort to avoid intimacy or involvement.

A fifth suggested cause for manipulation comes from the work of Albert Ellis. He writes that each of us learns, in the process of growing up, certain illogical assumptions about living. One of them is that it is a dire necessity to be approved by *everyone*.[4] The passive manipulator, Ellis suggests, is a person who refuses to be truthful and honest with others and instead tries to please everyone because he is basing his life on this foolish assumption.

GAMES VS. MANIPULATION

It should be made clear that when I refer to manipulation I mean something more than "playing games," as developed in Berne's *Games People Play*. First, manipulation is a *system* of games or a *style of life*, as opposed merely to *playing* an individual game to avoid involvement with another person. Manipulation is more akin to what Berne refers to as "a script," which is a recurrent pattern of games that characterizes a lifetime system of dealing with people. Secondly, the manipulator uses games along with other maneuvers to exploit or control *himself* as well as others. Thirdly, manipulation is a pseudo-philosophy of life, not just a trick. As we proceed, these distinctions between game playing and manipulation will be seen more clearly.

For instance, Weakling Wife, the manipulator, has turned her whole

[3] *Ibid.*, p. 299.

[4] Albert Ellis, "New Approaches to Psychotherapy," *Journal of Clinical Psychology, Monograph Supplement*, 1955, p. 11.

existence into a subtle campaign to make her Dictator Husband responsible for her life's woes. To some extent, this pattern exists in most marriages, yours and mine included, although the roles may be reversed. Berne, on the other hand, by pinpointing her individual games, such as "Kick Me," "Harried," "Look How Hard I've Tried," and "Now I've Got You, You S.O.B.," helps us to understand her modus operandi. After she has seduced him into kicking and abusing her, she tries to convince him he is a louse for having done it. Her manipulative system, which is bigger than the sum of all the games, may be called "injustice collecting."

A rather attractive young lady of twenty-five, bleached blonde and shapely, sat in my office one day. She hoped to impress me with the fact that she was "a nice girl"—the feminine counterpart of the Nice Guy manipulator—and that she was constantly having to fight off attempts by men (the Bullies in her life) of making improper advances. I observed the low-cut dress, the high-riding hemline, and the green light in her glance. In her story I recognized that she habitually had played what Berne calls the "Rapo" game with men many times, but what I really saw was a life-style of flirtations followed by rejections when the man rose to the bait. She was, of course, denying the Bully in herself. She was winning every encounter, not losing it, as she was implying. Her hostility was expressed in her naïveté, and she refused to admit it. The object of therapy would be to help her recognize her Bully and then use both her strength and weakness to quit playing this continuing manipulative system of "seek-and-go-hide."

SUMMARY OF MANIPULATIVE SYSTEMS

A manipulative system may be described as a pattern of manipulations or games. At this writing, there appear to be four basic types:

1. The *active* manipulator attempts to control others by active methods. He avoids facing his own weaknesses by assuming the role of the powerful one in a relationship. Usually he does this with some institutional affiliation or rank (parent, top sergeant, teacher, boss). He plays "top-dog" and gains gratification but capitalizes on others' feelings of powerlessness to gain control over them. He uses such techniques as creating obligations and expectations, pulling rank, pushing people around like puppets.

2. The *passive* manipulator is the reverse of the active. He decides, since he cannot control life, that he will give up and allow the active manipulator to control him. He feigns helplessness and stupidity and plays the "under-dog." Whereas the active manipulator wins by winning, the passive manipulator, paradoxically, wins by losing. By allowing the active manipulator to do his thinking and work for him, in a sense, he wins out over the top-dog by his passivity and deadness.

3. The *competitive* manipulator sees life as a constant game of winning and losing in which he has to be the vigilant fighter. To him, life is a battle, and all others are competitors or enemies, real or potential. He sees all men as "racing dogs" in the game of life. He alternates between top-

dog and under-dog methods and so may be seen as somewhat of a mixture between the active and passive manipulator.

4. A fourth basic form of the manipulative system is that of *indifferent manipulation*. The manipulator plays hopeless, indifferent to, and withdraws from his contact with another. His stock phrase is "I don't care." He treats the other as if he were dead—a puppet who has lost the capacity for growth and change. His methods are also both active and passive, sometimes playing the Nagger, Bitch, or Martyr, or Helpless. His secret, of course, is that he still cares and has not given up, or he would not continue to play the manipulative game. Husbands and wives often play this game with each other. As one treats the other like a puppet, the attitude of indifference creates a puppetlike quality in himself. This is why the system is self-defeating. The "Divorce Threatening Game" is an example by which the manipulator secretly hopes to win back his partner, rather than to truly separate from him.

Having now examined the philosophy and systems of the manipulator, we see more clearly that he always regards himself and others as objects. The basic philosophy of the active manipulator is to maintain control at all costs; of the passive manipulator, never to offend; of the competitive manipulator, to win at all costs; and of the indifferent manipulator, to deny caring. Obviously, the manipulator can never be himself, nor can he ever relax because his system of games and maneuvers requires that he always play a role rather than be himself.

Turning next to an examination of the actualizor, we will see a suggested system or philosophy of life which pays greater dividends in the living. Again there must be a caution that a book can only be like the white line down the road on a foggy night. To change over from manipulating to actualizing requires having some kind of experience and, unfortunately —and perhaps sounding a little like Gertrude Stein—an experience is not an experience unless you experience it.

Even then, the ways of human nature aren't always predictable. I think of a story I heard recently about a small town little theater group which got down to its last member in casting a play. He wasn't much of an actor but the part called only for a walk-on, when a gun would fire and he had his single line: "My God, I am shot!" Alas, the man wasn't quite up to it. No matter how many times they rehearsed, the line came out rigidly mechanical. He wasn't *experiencing* the shock of a bullet. The director decided finally on a ruse. He would load the gun secretly with rock salt, hoping that when it hit, the wooden actor would "feel" his role. Came the night of the performance and the duffer's scene. He walked on, the gun fired, the rock salt stung. Then he saw blood. "My God!" he shrieked, "I really *am* shot!"

But of course that wasn't the line.

US AND THEM
Ronald D. Laing

Only when something has become problematic do we start to ask questions. Disagreement shakes us out of our slumbers and forces us to see our own point of view through contrast with another person who does not share it. But we resist such confrontations. The history of heresies of all kinds testifies to more than the tendency to break off communication (excommunication) with those who hold different dogmas or opinions; it bears witness to our intolerance of different *fundamental structures of experience*. We seem to need to share a communal meaning to human existence, to give with others a common sense to the world, to maintain a *consensus*.

But it seems that once certain fundamental structures of experience are shared, they come to be experienced as objective entities. These reified projections of our own freedom are then introjected. By the time the sociologists study these projected-introjected reifications, they have taken on the appearance of things. They are not things ontologically. But they are pseudo-things. Thus far Durkheim was quite right to emphasize that collective representations come to be experienced as things, exterior to anyone. They take on the force and character of partially autonomous realities, with their own way of life. A social norm may come to impose an oppressive obligation on everyone, although few people feel it as their own.

At this moment in history, we are all caught in the hell of frenetic passivity. We find ourselves threatened by extermination that will be reciprocal, that no one wishes, that everyone fears, that may just happen to us "because" no one knows how to stop it. There is one possibility of doing so if we can understand the structure of this alienation of ourselves from our experience, our experience from our deeds, our deeds from human authorship. Everyone will be carrying out orders. Where do they come from? Always from elsewhere. Is it still possible to reconstitute our destiny out of this hellish and inhuman fatality?

Within this most vicious circle, we obey and defend beings that exist only insofar as we continue to invent and to perpetuate them. What ontological status have these group beings?

This human scene is a scene of mirages, demonic pseudo-realities, because everyone believes everyone else believes them.

How can we find our way back to ourselves again? Let us begin by trying to think about it.

We act not only in terms of our own experience, but of what we think *they* experience, and *how* we think they think we experience, and so on in a logically vertiginous spiral to infinity.[1]

Our language is only partially adequate to express this state of affairs. On level 1, two people, or two groups, may agree or disagree. As we say, they see eye to eye or otherwise. They share a common point of view. But on level 2 they may or may not think they agree or disagree, and they may or may not be correct in either case. Whereas level 1 is concerned with agreement or disagreement, level 2 is concerned with understanding or misunderstanding. Level 3 is concerned with a third level of awareness: what do I think you think I think? That is, with realization of or failure to realize second-level understanding or misunderstanding on the basis of first-level agreement or disagreement. Theoretically, there is no end to these levels.

In order to handle such complexity more easily we can use a shorthand. Let A stand for agreement and D for disagreement. Let U stand for understanding and M for misunderstanding. Let R stand for realization of understanding or misunderstanding, and F for failure to realize understanding or misunderstanding. Then R U A U R can mean, when applied to husband and wife, that husband realizes his wife understands they are in agreement, and that she realizes that he understands.

Thus

Husband	Wife		Husband	Wife
R	U	A	U	R

On the other hand

Husband	Wife		Husband	Wife
F	M	D	M	F

would mean: that husband and wife disagree; they both misunderstand each other, and both fail to realize their mutual misunderstanding.

There are many ramifications to this scheme that have been gone into in some detail elsewhere.[2]

The possibilities of the three levels of perspective can be put together as follows:[3]

	Realization		*Failure of Realization*	
	Understanding	Misunderstanding	Understanding	Misunderstanding
Agreement	RUA	RMA	FUA	FMA
Disagreement	RUD	RMD	FUD	FMD

[1]Elsewhere I have worked out a scheme to try to think about some of these issues. This is based on theories of a number of thinkers, notably Durkheim, Sartre, Husserl, Schultz, Mead and Dewey. See R. D. Laing, H. Phillipson and A. R. Lee, *Interpersonal Perception: A Theory and a Method of Research* (London: Tavistock Publications, 1966; New York: Springer, 1966).

[2]Laing, Phillipson and Lee, *op. cit.*

[3]The sociologist Thomas Scheff has pointed out that, whereas all these cells are empirically possible in two-person relations, two of them may be null cases in group conditions, viz. R M A and R M D.

It makes a difference, presumably, to many people whether they think they are in agreement with what most people think (second level); and whether they think that most people regard them as like themselves (third level). It is possible to think what everyone else thinks and to believe that one is in a minority. It is possible to think what few people think and to suppose that one is in the majority. It is possible to feel that They feel one is like Them when one is not, and They do not. It is possible to say: I believe this, but They believe that, so I'm sorry, there is nothing I can do.

THEM

Gossip and scandal are always and everywhere elsewhere. Each person is the other to the others. The members of a scandal network may be unified by ideas to which no one will admit in his own person. Each person is thinking of what he thinks the other thinks. The other, in turn, thinks of what yet another thinks. Each person does not mind a colored lodger, but each person's neighbor does. Each person, however, is a neighbor of his neighbor. What They think is held with conviction. It is indubitable and it is incontestable. The scandal group is a series of others which each serial number repudiates in himself.

It is always the others and always elsewhere, and each person feels unable to make any difference to Them. I have no objection to my daughter marrying a Gentile *really*, but we live in a Jewish neighborhood after all. Such collective power is in proportion to each person's creation of this power and his own impotence.

This is seen very clearly in the following inverted Romeo and Juliet situation.

John and Mary have a love affair, and just as they are ending it Mary finds she is pregnant. Both families are informed. Mary does not want to marry John. John does not want to marry Mary. But John thinks Mary wants him to marry her, and Mary does not want to hurt John's feelings by telling him that she does not want to marry him—as she thinks he wants to marry her, and that he thinks she wants to marry him.

The two families, however, compound the confusion considerably. Mary's mother takes to bed screaming and in tears because of the disgrace—what people are saying about the way she brought her daughter up. She does not mind the situation "in itself," especially as the girl is going to be married, but she takes to heart what everyone will be saying. No one in their own person in either family (". . . if it only affected me . . .") is in the least concerned for their own sake, but everyone is very concerned about the effect of "gossip" and "scandal" on everyone else. The concern focuses itself mainly on the boy's father and the girl's mother, both of whom require to be consoled at great length for the terrible blow. The boy's father is worried about what the girl's mother will think of him. The girl's mother is worried about what "everyone" will think of her. The boy is concerned at what the family thinks he has done to his father, and so on.

The tension spirals up within a few days to the complete engrossment of all members of both families in various forms of tears, wringing of hands, recriminations, apologies.

Typical utterances are:

Mother (to Girl): Even if he does want to marry you, how can he ever respect you after what people will have been saying about you recently?

Girl (some time later): I had finally got fed up with him just before I found I was pregnant, but I didn't want to hurt his feelings because he was so in love with me.

Boy: If it had not been that I owed it to my father for all he had done for me, I would have arranged that she got rid of it. But then everyone knew by then.

Everyone knew because the son told his father who told his wife who told her eldest son who told his wife . . . etc.

Such processes seem to have a dynamism divorced from the individuals. But in this and every other case the process is a form of alienation, intelligible when, and only when, the steps in the vicissitudes of its alienation from each and every person can be retraced back to what at each and every moment is their only origin: the experience and actions of each and every single person.

Now the peculiar thing about Them is that They are created only by each one of us repudiating his own identity. When we have installed Them in our hearts, we are only a plurality of solitudes in which what each person has in common is his allocation to the other of the necessity for his own actions. Each person, however, as other to the other, is the other's necessity. Each denies any internal bond with the others; each person claims his own inessentiality: "I just carried out my orders. If I had not done so, someone else would have." "Why don't you sign? Everyone else has," etc. Yet although I can make no difference, I cannot act differently. No single other person is any more necessary to me than I claim to be to Them. But just as he is "one of Them" to me, so I am "one of Them" to him. In this collection of reciprocal indifference, of reciprocal inessentiality and solitude, there appears to exist no freedom. There is conformity to a *presence* that is everywhere *elsewhere.*

US

The being of any group from the point of view of the group members themselves is very curious. If I think of you and him as together with me, and others again as not with me, I have already formed two rudimentary syntheses, namely, *We* and *They*. However, this private act of synthesis is not in itself a group. In order that *We* come into being as a group, it is necessary not only that I regard, let us say, you and him and me as *We*, but that you and he also think of us as *We*. I shall call such an act of experiencing a number of persons as a single collectivity, an act of rudimentary group synthesis. In this case *We*, that is each of Us, me, you and him, have performed acts of rudimentary group synthesis. But at present these are simply three private acts of group synthesis. In order that a group really jell, I must realize that you think of yourself as one of Us, as I do, and that he thinks of himself as one of Us, as you and I do. I must ensure furthermore that both you and he realize that I think of myself with you and him, and you and he must ensure likewise that the other two realize that this We is ubiquitous among us, not simply a private illusion on my, your or his part, shared between two of us but not all three.

In a very condensed form I may put the above paragraph as follows.

I "interiorize" your and his syntheses, you interiorize his and mine, he interiorizes mine and yours; I interiorize your interiorization of mine and his; you interiorize my interiorization of yours and his. Furthermore, he interiorizes my interiorization of his and yours—a logical ingoing spiral of reciprocal perspectives to infinity.

The group, considered first of all from the point of view of the *experience* of its own members, is not a social object out there in space. It is the quite extraordinary being formed by each person's synthesis of the same multiplicity into *We*, and each person's synthesis of the multiplicity of syntheses.

Looked at from the outside, the group comes into view as a social object, lending, by its appearance and by the apparent processes that go inside it, credence to the organismic illusion.

This is a mirage; as one approaches closer there is no organism anywhere.

A group whose unification is achieved through the reciprocal interiorization by each of each other, in which neither a "common object" nor organizational or institutional structures, etc. have a primary function as a kind of group "cement," I shall call a *nexus*.

The unity of the nexus is in the interior of each synthesis. Each such act of synthesis is bound by reciprocal interiority with every other synthesis of the same nexus, insofar as it is also the interiority of every other synthesis. The unity of the nexus is the unification made by each person of the plurality of syntheses.

This social structure of the completely achieved nexus is its *unity as ubiquity*. It is an ubiquity of *heres*, whereas the series of others is always elsewhere, always *there*.

The nexus exists only insofar as each person incarnates the nexus. The nexus is everywhere, in each person, and is nowhere else than in each. The nexus is at the opposite pole from Them in that each person acknowledges affiliation to it, regards the other as coessential to him, and assumes that the other regards him as coessential to the other.

We are all in the same boat in a stormy sea,
And we owe each other a terrible loyalty.

G. K. Chesterton

In this group of reciprocal loyalty, or brotherhood unto death, each freedom is reciprocally pledged, one to the other.

In the nexal family the unity of the group is achieved through the experience by each of the group, and the danger to each person (since the person is essential to the nexus, and the nexus is essential to the person) is the dissolution or dispersion of "the family." This can come about only by one person after another dissolving it in themselves. A united "family" exists only as long as each person acts in terms of its existence. Each person may then act on the other person to coerce him (by sympathy, blackmail, indebtedness, guilt, gratitude or naked violence) into maintaining his interiorization of the group unchanged.

The nexal family is then the "entity" which has to be preserved in each person and served by each person, which one lives and dies for, and which in turn offers life for loyalty and death for desertion. Any defection from the nexus (betrayal, treason, heresy, etc.) is deservedly, by nexus ethics, punishable; and the worst punishment devisable by the "group men" is exile or excommunication: group death.

The condition of permanence of such a nexus, whose sole existence is each person's experience of it, is the successful reinvention of whatever gives such experience its *raison d'être*. If there is no external danger, then danger and terror have to be invented and maintained. Each person has to act on the others to maintain the nexus *in them*.

Some families live in perpetual anxiety of what, to them, is an external persecuting world. The members of the family live in a family ghetto, as it were. This is one basis for so-called maternal overprotection. It is not "over"-protection from the mother's point of view, nor, indeed, often from the point of view of other members of the family.

The "protection" that such a family offers its members seems to be based on several preconditions: (i) a fantasy of the external world as extraordinarily dangerous; (ii) the generation of terror inside the nexus at this external danger. The "work" of the nexus is the generation of this terror. This work is *violence*.

The stability of the nexus is the product of terror generated in its members by the work (violence) done by the members of the group on each other. Such family "homeostasis" is the product of reciprocities mediated under the statutes of violence and terror.

The highest ethic of the nexus is reciprocal concern. Each person is concerned about what the other thinks, feels, does. He may come to regard it as his *right* to expect the others to be concerned about him, and to regard himself as under an obligation to feel concern towards them in turn. I make no move without feeling it as my right that you should be happy or sad, proud or ashamed, of what I do. Every action of mine is always the concern of the other members of the group. And I regard you as callous if you do not concern yourself about my concern for you when you do anything.

A family can act as gangsters, offering each other mutual protection against each other's violence. It is a reciprocal terrorism, with the offer of protection-security against the violence that each threatens the other with, and is threatened by, if anyone steps out of line.

My concern, my concern for your concern, your concern, and your concern for my concern, etc. is an infinite spiral, upon which rests my pride or shame in my father, sister, brother, my mother, my son, my daughter.

The essential characteristic of the nexus is that every action of one person is expected to have reference to and to influence everyone else. The nature of this influence is expected to be reciprocal.

Each person is expected to be controlled, and to control the others, by the reciprocal effect that each has on the other. To be affected by the others' actions or feelings is "natural." It is not "natural" if father is neither proud nor ashamed of son, daughter, mother, etc. According to this ethic, action done to please, to make happy, to show one's gratitude to the other, is the highest form of action. This reciprocal transpersonal cause-effect is a self-actualizing presumption. In this "game," it is a foul to use this interdependence to hurt the other, except in the service of the nexus, but the worst crime of all is to refuse to act in terms of this presumption.

Examples of this in action are: Peter gives Paul something. If Paul is not pleased, or refuses the gift, he is ungrateful for what is being done for him. Or: Peter is made unhappy if Paul does something. Therefore if Paul does it he is making Peter unhappy. If Peter is made unhappy, Paul is inconsiderate, callous, selfish, ungrateful. Or: if Peter is prepared to make sacrifices for Paul, so Paul should be prepared to make sacrifices for Peter, or else he is selfish, ungrateful, callous, ruthless, etc.

"Sacrifice" under these circumstances consists in Peter impoverishing himself to do something for Paul. It is the tactic of *enforced debt*. One way of putting this is that each person *invests in the other*.

The group, whether We or You or Them, is not a new individual or organism or hyperorganism on the social scene; it has no agency of its own, it has no consciousness of its own. Yet we may shed our own blood and the blood of others for this bloodless presence.

The group is a reality of some kind or other. But what sort of reality? The We is a form of unification of a plurality composed by those who share the common experience of its ubiquitous invention among them.

From outside, a group of Them may come into view in another way. It is still a type of unification imposed on a multiplicity, but this time those who invent the unification expressly do not themselves compose it. Here, I am of course not referring to the outsider's perception of a We already constituted from within itself. The Them comes into view as a sort of social mirage: The Reds, the Whites, the Blacks, the Jews. In the human scene, however, such mirages can be self-actualizing. The invention of Them creates Us, and We may need to invent Them to reinvent Ourselves.

One of the most tentative forms of solidarity between us exists when we each want the same thing, but want nothing from each other. We are united, say by a common desire to get the last seat on the train, or to get the best bargain at the sale. We might gladly cut each other's throats; we may nevertheless feel a certain bond between us, a negative unity, so to speak, in that each perceives the other as redundant, and each person's metaperspective shows him that he is redundant for the other. Each as other-for-the-other is one-too-many. In this case, we share a desire to appropriate the same common object or objects: food, land, a social position, real or imagined, but share nothing between ourselves and do not wish to. Two men both love the same woman, two people both want the same house, two applicants both want the same job. This common object can thus both separate and unite at the same time. A key question is whether it can give itself to all, or not. How *scarce* is it?

The object may be animal, vegetable, mineral, human or divine, real or imaginary, single or plural. A human object uniting people, for instance, is the pop singer in relation to his fans. All can possess him, albeit magically. When this magic confronts the other order of reality, one finds the idol in danger of being torn to shreds by the frenzy of fans seeking any bit of him they can tear off.

The object may be plural. Two rival firms engage in intense competitive advertising, each under the impression that they are losing their consumers to the other. Market research sometimes reveals how riven with fantasy is the scene of such social multiplicities. The laws governing the perception, invention and maintenance of such social beings as "the consumers" are undiscovered.

The common bond between Us may be the Other. The Other may not even be as localized as a definable Them that one can point to. In the social cohesion of scandal, gossip, unavowed racial discrimination, the Other is everywhere and nowhere. The Other that governs everyone is everyone in his position, not of self, but as other. Every self, however, disavows being himself that other that he is for the Other. The Other is everyone's experience. Each person can do nothing because of the other. The other is everywhere elsewhere.

Perhaps the most intimate way We can be united is through each of us being in, and having inside ourselves, the same presence. This is nonsense in any external sense, but here we are exploring a mode of experience which does not recognize the distinctions of analytic logic.

We find this demonic group mysticism repeatedly evoked in the prewar speeches at Nazi Nuremberg rallies. Rudolf Hess proclaims: We are the Party, the Party is Germany, Hitler is the Party, Hitler is Germany, and so on.

We are Christians insofar as we are brothers in Christ. We are in Christ and Christ is in each one of us.

No group can be expected to be held together for long on the pure flame of such unified experience. Groups are liable to disappear through attacks from other groups, or through inability to sustain themselves against the ravages of starvation and disease, from splits through internal dissensions, and so on. But the simplest and perennial threat to all groups comes from the simple defection of its members. This is the danger of evaporation, as it were.

Under the form of group loyalty, brotherhood and love, an ethic is introduced whose basis is my right to afford the other protection from my violence if he is loyal to me, and to expect his protection from his violence if I am loyal to him, and my obligation to terrorize him with the threat of my violence, if he does not remain loyal.

It is the ethic of the Gadarene swine, to remain true, one for all and all for one, as we plunge in brotherhood to our destruction.

Let there be no illusions about the brotherhood of man. My brother, as dear to me as I am to myself, my twin, my double, my flesh and blood, may be a fellow lyncher as well as a fellow martyr, and in either case is liable to meet his death at my hand if he chooses to take a different view of the situation.

The brotherhood of man is evoked by particular men according to their circumstances. But it seldom extends to all men. In the name of our freedom and our brotherhood we are prepared to blow up the other half of mankind, and to be blown up in turn.

The matter is of life or death importance in the most urgent possible sense, since it is on the basis of such primitive social fantasies of who and what are I and you, he and she, We and They, that the world is linked or separated, that we die, kill, devour, tear and are torn apart, descend to hell or ascend to heaven, in short, that we conduct our lives. What is the "being" of "The Reds" to you and me? What is the nature of the presence conjured up by the incantation of this magic sound? Are we sympathizers with "the East"? Do we feel we have to threaten, deter, placate "it" or "her" or "him"? "Russia" or "China" have "being" nowhere else than in the fantasy of everyone, including the "Russians" and "Chinese": nowhere and everywhere. A "being" fantasied by "The Russians" as what they are in and which they have to defend, and fantasied by the non-Russians as an alien super-subject-object from whom one has to defend one's "freedom," is such that if we all act in terms of such mass serialized preontological fantasy, we may all be destroyed by a "being" that never was, except insofar as we *all* invented her or it or him.

The specifically human feature of human groupings can be exploited to turn them into the semblance of nonhuman systems.

We do not now suppose that chemical elements combine together *because* they love each other. Atoms do not explode out of hatred. It is men who act out of love and hatred, who combine for defense, attack, or pleasure in each other's company.

All those people who seek to control the behavior of large numbers of other people work on the *experiences* of those other people. Once people can be induced to experience a situation in a similar way, they can be expected to behave in similar ways. Induce people all to want the same thing, hate the same thing, feel the same threat, then their behavior is already captive—you have acquired your consumers or your cannon-fodder. Induce a common perception of Negroes as subhuman, or of whites as vicious and effete, and behavior can be concerted accordingly.

However much experience and action can be transformed into quantitatively interchangeable units, the schema for the intelligibility of group structures and permanence is of quite a different order from the schema we employ when we are explaining relative constancies in physical systems. In the latter case, we do not, in the same way, retrace the constancy of a pattern back to the reciprocal interiorization of the pattern by whatever one regards as the units comprising it. The inertia of human groups, however, which appears as the very negation of praxis, is in fact the product of praxis and nothing else. This group inertia can only be an instrument of mystification if it is taken to be part of the "natural order of things." The ideological abuse of such an idea is obvious. It so clearly serves the interests of those whose interest it is to have people believe that the status quo is of the "natural order," ordained divinely or by "natural" laws. What is less immediately obvious, but no less confusing, is the application of an epistemological schema, derived from natural systems, to human groups. The theoretical stance here only serves to intensify the dissociation of praxis from structure.

The group becomes a machine—and that it is a man-made machine in which the machine is the very men who make it is forgotten. It is quite unlike a machine made by men, which can have an existence of its own. The group is men themselves arranging themselves in patterns, strata, assuming and assigning different powers, functions, roles, rights, obligations and so on.

The group cannot become an entity separate from men, but men can form circles to encircle other men. The patterns in space and time, their relative permanence and rigidity, do not turn at any time into a natural system or a hyperorganism, although the fantasy can develop, and men can start to live by the fantasy that the relative permanence in space-time of patterns is what they must live and die for.

It is as though we all preferred to die to preserve our shadows.

For the group can be nothing else than the multiplicity of the points of view and actions of its members, and this remains true even where, through the interiorization of this multiplicity as synthesized by each, this synthesized multiplicity becomes ubiquitous in space and enduring in time.

It is just as well that man is a social animal, since the sheer complexity and contradiction of the social field in which he has to live is so formidable. This is so even with the fantastic simplifications that are imposed on this complexity, some of which we have examined above.

Our society is a plural one in many senses. Any one person is likely to be a participant in a number of groups, which may have not only different memberships, but quite different forms of unification.

Each group requires more or less radical internal transformation of the persons who comprise it. Consider the metamorphoses that one man may go through in one day as he moves from one mode of sociality to another —family man, speck of crowd dust, functionary in the organization, friend. These are not simply different roles: each is a whole past and present and future, offering differing options and constraints, different degrees of change or inertia, different kinds of closeness and distance, different sets of rights and obligations, different pledges and promises.

I know of no theory of the individual that fully recognizes this. There is every temptation to start with a notion of some supposed basic personality, but halo effects are not reducible to one internal system. The tired family man at the office and the tired businessman at home attest to the fact that people carry over, not just one set of internal objects, but *various internalized social modes of being,*[4] often grossly contradictory, from one context to another.

Nor are there such constant emotions or sentiments as love, hate, anger, trust or mistrust. Whatever generalized definitions can be made of each of these at the highest levels of abstraction, specifically and concretely, each emotion is always found in one or another inflection according to the group mode it occurs in. There are no "basic" emotions, instincts or personality, outside of the relationships a person has within one or another social context.[5]

[4]See "Individual and Family Structure," in *Psychoanalytic Studies of the Family,* edited by P. Lomasz (London: Hogarth Press, 1966).

[5]This chapter, in particular, owes a great deal to *Critique de la Raison Dialectique* (1960) by J.-P. Sartre. It is summarized in *Reason and Violence* (London: Tavistock Publications, 1964), by R. D. Laing and David Cooper.

There is a race against time. It is just possible that a further transformation is possible if men can come to experience themselves as "One of Us." If, even on the basis of the crassest self-interest, we can realize that We and They must be transcended in the totality of the human race, if we in destroying them are not to destroy us all.

As war continues, both sides come more and more to resemble each other. The uroborus eats its own tail. The wheel turns full circle. Shall we realize that We and They are shadows of each other? We are They to Them as They are They to Us. When will the veil be lifted? When will the charade turn to carnival? Saints may still be kissing lepers. It is high time that the leper kissed the saint.

Chapter 9

GUIDELINES FOR IMPROVING INTERPERSONAL COMMUNICATION

Basic to your improvement of interpersonal communication is a sincere desire to become a better person—"better" according to your own criteria gained from personal experience. Embodied in this concept of a better person is the possibility of your becoming the very best person you can within your own biological capabilities and psychological potential. This improvement not ony includes becoming the best you have ever dreamed of for yourself, but also involves, as we see it, the vision of becoming something even better—a person who desires eventually to *transcend* your present highest hopes for yourself.

When we speak of improving ability in interpersonal communication, we do not have in mind a person who just talks better; rather, we envision a better person talking. As we see it, improvement in interpersonal communication involves achieving a healthier, more functional personality. We might look at a person engaged in business; let's think of this person in the role of a manager. As this person strives to improve his/her interactions with others in the organization, he/she is striving to become a better person. In writing on the process of manager development in the *Harvard Business Review*, Paul Brouwer makes this point: Improvement in one's management behavior requires improvement in the whole person. Management development is self-development.[1]

Improvement in interpersonal communication is not just the acquisition of a skill like learning to type or use shorthand. It involves the psychological interior of a person, his/her way of thinking about himself/herself as well as his/her way of relating to others.

In Chapter 3 we have suggested that our needs for interpersonal communication are twofold: first, for self development, and second, for negotiation with others to control our physical and social environment. Our primary need is the first—self-development; improved achievement in negotiating with others follows from changes in ourselves. These changes in ourselves may be identified as personal growth. The first thing involved is a change in the image of our potential, at least to the extent that we can envision or imagine ourselves being different—not just doing something *in addition* to what we do already. Personal growth inherently involves changes in self-concept.

[1]P. J. Brouwer, "The Power to See Ourselves," *Harvard Business Review*, 42 (1964), 156–163; see especially 158–159.

Similarly, improvement in interpersonal communication also involves changes in one's self-concept.

Great people have always held a concept of themselves as unique, set apart from the ordinary—Michelangelo, fighting political pressures to achieve his art; Beethoven, composing even when deaf; Milton, writing even though blind. Such people had a vision of themselves fulfilling their destiny. The difference between a great person and one who is not great is not always ability, for many clerks have keen intelligence; it is not ambition, for many ambitious people somehow defeat themselves. The primary difference is in self-concept: How valuable is my life? What do I want to do with it? What must I do to be myself?[2]

THE PROCESS OF SELF-ACTUALIZATION

There is a great deal of interest today in what is sometimes called "The Third Force" in psychology.[3] This movement, also sometimes labelled Humanistic Psychology,[4] is especially interested in people's human potential, particularly in terms of how we may develop better ways of relating to each other.[5] The essay by Jack and Lorraine Gibb following Chapter 3 is written in this vein. Probably the best known advocate of this emphasis is Abraham Maslow, and the key concept he employs is *self-actualization*, the process of becoming that which is inherent in one's potential.[6] According to Maslow, self-actualization involves "acceptance and expression of the inner core of self," and putting into operation "these latent capacities and potentialities." Implicit in this concept is minimal presence of neurosis or psychosis and optimal use of "the basic human and personal capacities."[7] Achievement in the sense of personal accomplishment is also involved in this concept—achievement according to one's unique innate capabilities.[8]

Carl Rogers has significantly contributed to the movement toward humanistic emphasis in psychology. From his personal experience he has come to place special emphasis on a person's being of value to

[2]Cf. C. R. Rogers, "Toward Becoming a Fully Functioning Person," in *Perceiving, Behaving, Becoming: A New Focus for Education: 1962 Yearbook* (Washington, D.C.: Association for Supervision and Curriculum Development, 1962), pp. 21–33.

[3]See, for example, F. G. Groble, *The Third Force* (New York: Pocket Books, 1971).

[4]Cf. J. F. T. Bugental, *Challenges of Humanistic Psychology* (New York: McGraw-Hill, 1967).

[5]See, for example, Rollo May, *Psychology and the Human Dilemma* (New York: Van Nostrand Reinhold, 1967).

[6]See A. H. Maslow, *Toward a Psychology of Being* (New York: Van Nostrand Reinhold, 1962).

[7]*Ibid.*, p. 184.

[8]See A. H. Maslow, *The Further Reaches of Human Nature* (New York: Viking, 1971), p. 43.

other people, and this concern is elaborated in his essay following this chapter.[9] A relationship with another person in such a way that both persons benefit is essential to Rogers' thinking about a fully functioning, self-actualized person.[10]

Self-Actualization and Interpersonal Communication

Inherent in the *process* of self-actualization is interpersonal communication. For a person to get to know himself well, to understand how he/she might become better, to envision himself/herself *being* better, and to change his/her ways almost always requires interaction with helpful others.[11] This is especially true when one is trying to improve his/her ways of relating to other people.[12] Inherent in this process is disclosure of one's thoughts and feelings to another person. Perhaps the clearest exponent of this process is Sidney Jourard; his essay, which follows this chapter, is representative of his writings.[13] According to Jourard, the process of self-actualizing includes self-disclosure, feedback from a trusted person, self-examination, and personal change.[14]

For self-actualization Jourard emphasizes disclosure of one's thoughts and feelings to a trusted listener.[15] In one of his earlier writings, Jourard gives this illustration of an interchange between a person and someone he trusts:

> *I have never told this to a soul, doctor, but I can't stand my wife. My mother is a nag, my father is a bore, and my boss is an absolutely hateful and despicable tyrant. I have been carrying on an affair for the past ten years with the lady next door, and at the same time I am a deacon in the church.*[16]

Jourard has the doctor respond in a sympathetic manner, making no particular evaluation except to appreciate that all this poses a problem.

Such self-disclosure may take the form of statements about oneself; however, much more valid and useful are actions. In either case the true feelings must be displayed; the use of masks, subterfuge, and deceit must be minimal. Achieving this level of disclosure is not easy,

[9]See pp. 466–477.

[10]See, for example, his treatment of this principle in C. R. Rogers, *Becoming Partners: Marriage and Its Alternatives* (New York: Delacorte, 1972).

[11]See, for example, the evidence summarized in C. B. Truax and R. R. Carkhuff, *Toward Effective Counseling and Psychotherapy* (Chicago: Aldine, 1967).

[12]Cf. R. R. Carkhuff, *Helping and Human Relations*, Vol. 1 (New York: Holt, Rinehart and Winston, 1969).

[13]See pp. 456–465.

[14]See S. M. Jourard, *The Transparent Self* (New York: Van Nostrand Reinhold, 1964); see especially pp. 19–30.

[15]S. M. Jourard, *Disclosing Man to Himself* (New York: Van Nostrand Reinhold, 1968), p. 47.

[16]Jourard, *The Transparent Self*, *op. cit.*, p. 21.

and for some may take special instruction and assistance of trained persons.[17]

Our twentieth-century society tends to strip each of us of our personal identity characteristics. Organizations and bureaucracy seem to be intent on reducing each of us to an interchangeable unit. This "sociological sheep-shearing" is often accomplished by removing or ignoring all identifiers not needed to help us fit a certain slot: student, teacher, doctor, patient, etc. In most cases this procedure starts with "admissions" and is called "training."[18] When this process is completed, quite often a person does not know what he/she is really like —what his own feelings and desires actually are—or if he/she has any! Jourard argues in *Disclosing Man to Himself* that interpersonal communication, involving self-disclosure and feedback, can recapture for people this ability to know themselves.[19]

Feedback: An Essential Element

Self-actualization requires feedback from a person you trust. Validation of your self-concept can produce belief in yourself.[20] It can supply encouragement and support when it is most needed. On the other hand, negative feedback can stimulate self-examination; the twin needs of self-esteem and self-evaluation can produce dissonance that leads to a desire for personal change.

Self-actualization requires *vision* on the part of the individual involved—vision in the older, perhaps Bibilical, sense of creative imagination. Nowhere in the literature of the human potential movement have we seen this concept of vision better portrayed than in *Man's Search for Meaning*, by Victor Frankl.[21] During World War II Frankl, a Jew, was in a Nazi prison camp. He saw relatives and friends tortured and killed; he went through years of extreme physical and psychological suffering. His book is a psychological treatise on what keeps a person going under such conditions and how some survive and some do not. After describing an almost endless series of depraving and traumatic experiences, Frankl approaches the question of why some men gave up—"broke"—and others did not. The difference between these men was that some were able to *transcend* the most pitiful conditions and horrible experiences. It required a vision of oneself being able to suffer anything and live through it:

[17]See, for example, the results of an experimental study by J. W. MacDoniels, "Factors Related to the Level of Open Expression in Small Group Laboratory Learning Experiences," unpublished doctoral dissertation, University of Kansas, 1972.

[18]Jourard, *The Transparent Self*, *op. cit.*, p. 149.

[19]Jourard, *Disclosing Man to Himself*, *op. cit.*; see especially pp. 43–51.

[20]Z. A. Pepitone, "An Experimental Analysis of Self-Dynamics," in C. Gordon and K. J. Gergen, eds., *The Self in Social Interaction* (New York: Wiley, 1968), p. 350.

[21]V. E. Frankl, *Man's Search for Meaning* (Boston, Mass.: Beacon Press, 1963).

> *Any attempt at fighting the camp's psychopathological influence on the prisoner by psychotherapeutic or psychohygienic methods had to aim at giving him inner strength by pointing out to him a future goal to which he could look forward. Instinctively some of the prisoners attempted to find one on their own. . . . I remember a personal experience. Almost in tears from pain (I had terrible sores on my feet from wearing torn shoes), I limped a few kilometers with our long column of men from the camp to our work site. Very cold, bitter winds struck us. I kept thinking of the endless little problems of our miserable life. What would there be to eat tonight? If a piece of sausage came as extra ration, should I exchange it for a piece of bread? Should I trade my last cigarette, which was left from a bonus I received a fortnight ago, for a bowl of soup? How could I get a piece of wire to replace the fragment which served as one of my shoelaces? Would I get to our work site in time to join my usual working party or would I have to join another, which might have a brutal foreman? What could I do to get on good terms with the Capo, who could help me to obtain work in camp instead of undertaking this horribly long daily march?*
>
> *I became disgusted with the state of affairs which compelled me, daily and hourly, to think of only such trivial things. I forced my thoughts to turn to another subject. Suddenly I saw myself standing on the platform of a well-lit, warm and pleasant lecture room. In front of me sat an attentive audience on comfortable upholstered seats. I was giving a lecture on the psychology of the concentration camp! All that oppressed me at that moment became objective, seen and described from the remote viewpoint of science. By this method I succeeded somehow in rising above the situation, above the sufferings of the moment, and I observed them as if they were already of the past. Both I and my troubles became the object of an interesting psychoscientific study undertaken by myself.*[22]

Under other, much more pleasant conditions, Paul Brouwer has analyzed the characteristics of people that make some of them good managing executives and that cause some never to make it. He has come to the same conclusion: The major difference lies in self-concept —vision of themselves meeting the requirements of the job![23]

It is our belief that any attempt to improve a relationship with another person—a parent, teacher, wife, husband, friend—requires this same kind of vision of ourself *behaving* in a new way, acting in a different manner. If it doesn't come to us easily, we must think about it and try hard. As Frankl said about those men who survived the prison camp by gaining a concept of themselves being different from their former selves—some of them had to work at it![24]

In his book on becoming partners in a marriage, Carl Rogers reports a case of a young married couple who became involved in a

[22]*Ibid.*, pp. 116–117.
[23]Brouwer, "The Power to See Ourselves," *op. cit.*, pp. 162–163.
[24]Frankl, *op. cit.*, pp. 123–127.

"triangle."[25] The husband, Roy, fell in love with another young woman, and the survival of his marriage was seriously at issue. Through talking with others and his wife, Roy achieved a vision of himself being open and sharing with his wife—being her true friend and companion in ways never before achieved. Rogers quotes Roy's evaluation of their new relationship as follows:

> *There has always been movement and development in our marriage but never like the last two years—moving from a small town to a large city, children both in school, women's liberation, sexual liberation in the youth culture—all have had a profound impact. As the kids grew, Sylvia increasingly began to search out her own identity. I really affirmed that. I wanted a stimulating relationship of co-equals. Increasingly we spent time together talking—exploring wishes—my listening and drawing out her thinking about herself and what she wanted to become. It works. Now she does this for me too. It's great to have someone to help you explore your own mind.*[26]

As we see it, personal growth involves self-disclosure in words and actions, feedback from a trusted person, self-evaluation, a vision of what one might become, attempts to achieve those changes, followed by further feedback, self-evaluation, etc. This use of interpersonal communication can provide a self-revelation, *not just what you are* (as suggested in Jourard's essay following this chapter), *but a vision of what you can become.* It can stimulate self-improvement by stirring your imagination, opening new horizons, new ideas, new appreciation of the needs of others, along with a desire to meet those needs. This process of "getting involved" with others can give you a new vision of yourself relating to them in new ways.[27]

Jourard has presented some evidence that through the process of interpersonal communication involving self-disclosure to trusted others, a person can achieve a healthier personality; by contrast, he shows that nondisclosers tend to get sick—alienated, mentally disturbed.[28]

Breuer, a Viennese physician, escaped fame only by a small margin. He discovered that when his hysterical patients *talked about their suppressed feelings,* their hysterical symptoms disappeared. Breuer backed off from reporting discoveries that would have made him Freud's colleague in psychiatry's hall of fame. Apparently he became scared because some of his female patients (in Victorian times) disclosed themselves to be quite sexy; worse yet, they felt quite sexy toward him! From such discoveries, however, Freud did not flinch.

[25]Rogers, *Becoming Partners: Marriage and Its Alternatives, op. cit.,* pp. pp. 53–70.

[26]*Ibid.,* pp. 54–55.

[27]Cf. Jourard, *Disclosing Man to Himself, op. cit.,* p. 47.

[28]Cf. *ibid.,* pp. 37–51.

He found that neurotic people were struggling toward being themselves, admitting their feelings to themselves, and being known fully to others.[29] Without some opportunity to let their true selves develop and be known to others, these persons allowed their problems to multiply and become severe. And, indeed, we sometimes find ourselves surprised to encounter and confront an infant inside the skin of someone playing the role of an adult!

Throughout recorded time there has existed a struggle between the self-actualizers and the nondisclosers. We now know the nonself-actualizers as persons who tend to hide their thoughts and ideas, people who wear masks and distort reality. In severe cases they actually achieve cognitive separation from reality—they become sick. In the past decade we have heard much about a "sick society," containing people who would keep their consciousness within limits of traditional views—the status quo. This struggle is now sharper than ever before; as we write this book we feel we are on the side of those who try to find reality through self-disclosure plus feedback from honest people.

INCREASING INTERPERSONAL TRUST

Central to the process of self-actualization through self-disclosure plus honest feedback is the factor of interpersonal trust—on the part of both the discloser and the person giving feedback. In their essay on personal growth in groups (following Chapter 3), Jack and Lorraine Gibb emphasize the importance of trust. According to their studies, growth of the individual in ways relevant to human relations relies heavily on developing with others a climate of interpersonal trust.

The importance of trust in all human relations has received considerable attention in the literature of social science, religion, and philosophy. Gordon Allport's theory of personality development through social encounter places trust at the foundation of a satisfying interpersonal relationship.[30] The essays of Erich Fromm on the art of loving[31] and of Martin Buber on the nature of warm human relationships[32] place personal trust at the center of their theories. Such essays are penetrating and exceedingly insightful, and the importance of personal trust in our relations with others is hardly to be questioned. However, thoughtful and discerning as they are, such essays leave us personally wistful for ways to achieve such relationships with those around us. How can *we*, who are not blessed with interpersonal genius, achieve a relationship that is full and spontaneous, open and frank? How can we go about achieving the relationship described by

[29]Cf. Jourard, *The Transparent Self, op. cit.*, pp. 21–22.
[30]G. W. Allport, *Personality and Social Encounter* (Boston: Beacon, 1960).
[31]E. Fromm, *The Art of Loving* (London: Allen and Unwin, 1962).
[32]M. Buber, *I and Thou* (Edinburgh: T. & T. Clark, 1957).

Fromm in which people care for, show responsibility toward, have respect for, and understand each other?[33] What are the conditions for development of trust?

In an attempt to determine the nature of an effective helpful relationship between psychiatrist and patient, Carl Rogers developed his theory of client-centered therapy. To him, a sense of "psychological safety" was necessary for the patient, and this trusting relationship could be produced by the therapist only if he gave complete acceptance to the patient.[34] Rogers has used the same approach to the problem of helping ordinary people (i.e., those who are not mentally ill) to improve their daily relationships with others. If you wish other people to trust you more readily, Rogers would have you give them acceptance and a sense of nonthreatening empathy, warmth, and genuineness.[35]

In a long-range (1953–1964) series of analyses of behavior in human relations training groups ("sensitivity" or t-groups), Jack Gibb explored the relationship between interpersonal trust and primary dimensions of group behavior.[36] His emphasis on the need for a supportive climate is very similar to Rogers' requirement of a sense of psychological safety. In 1964 Gibb reported that, according to his research, people in groups were inevitably concerned with four basic goals: gaining personal acceptance, exchanging information, achieving a group goal, and controlling each other.[37] He reported that the acceptance goal is primary to the others—that is, it must be obtained before the other goals can be achieved; and that the achievement of a climate of acceptance hinges on the development of interpersonal trust. Gibb's work demonstrated that attempts at persuasion in the early life of a group produced distrust, cynicism, and suspicion. On the other hand, communication that was descriptive (not evaluative), problem oriented (not oriented toward interpersonal control), spontaneous (not strategic), empathic (not insular), equality oriented (not indicative of superiority), and expressive of provisionally held views (not dogmatic) produced a climate of interpersonal trust.

The Nature of Trust

Trust is here defined as an attitude in the sense of involving perceptions, feelings, and behavior tendencies. It involves cognition of a

[33]Fromm, *op. cit.*, p. 25.

[34]C. R. Rogers, *Client-Centered Therapy* (Boston: Houghton Mifflin, 1951).

[35]C. R. Rogers, *On Becoming a Person* (Boston: Houghton Mifflin, 1961).

[36]See pp. 143–155.

[37]J. Gibb, "Defensive Communication," *Journal of Communication*, 11 (1964), 141–148.

situation,[38] degrees of positive or negative feelings,[39] and a potential for action under certain conditions.[40]

It appears to us that in an interpersonal relationship, trusting behavior involves these conditions:

1. *A person (P) is relying upon another person or persons.*
2. *P is risking some potential loss.*
3. *P is attempting to achieve some goal or gain.*
4. *This desired goal is viewed by P as uncertain.*
5. *P's potential loss if his trust is violated is greater than his potential gain if his trust is fulfilled.*

Trust in Interpersonal Communication

Trusting behavior in the communication process can be defined as reliance upon the communication behavior (speaking and/or listening) of a person while you are attempting to achieve a desired but uncertain objective in a risky situation. A theoretical formulation of the trust paradigm in the communication process includes both interpersonal and intrapersonal trust:[41]

1. *Trust of a speaker by a listener, called ethos by Aristotle and source credibility by Hovland, Janis, and Kelley;*[42]
2. *Trust of a listener by a speaker, called sense of psychological safety by Rogers,*[43] *perceived supportive climate by Gibb,*[44] *and speech confidence (rather than anxiety) as described by Giffin and Bradley;*[45]
3. *Trust of oneself as a speaker–a person's perception of himself/herself as a communicator capable of achieving a desired goal in a situation perceived as "risky" or threatening (the opposite of speech anxiety);*
4. *Trust of oneself as a listener—a person's perception of him-*

[38]T. M. Newcomb, "An Approach to the Study of Communicative Acts," *Psychological Review*, 60 (1953), 393–404.

[39]L. L. Thurstone, "Comment," *American Journal of Sociology*, 52 (1946), 39–70.

[40]A. L. Edwards, *Techniques of Attitude Scale Construction* (New York: Appleton, 1957), pp. 5–9.

[41]K. Giffin, "Interpersonal Trust in Small Group Communication," *Quarterly Journal of Speech*, 53 (1967), 224–234.

[42]C. Hovland, I. L. Janis, and H. H. Kelley, *Communication and Persuasion* (New Haven, Conn.: Yale University Press, 1953), p. 21.

[43]Rogers, *Client-Centered Therapy, op. cit.*, p. 41.

[44]J. Gibb, "Climate for Trust Formation," in L. P. Bradford et al., eds., *T-Group Theory and Laboratory Method* (New York: Wiley, 1964), p. 298.

[45]K. Giffin and K. Bradley, "Group Counseling for Speech Anxiety: An Approach and a Rationale," *Journal of Communication*, 19 (1969), 22–29.

self/herself as a listener capable of achieving a desired goal in a situation perceived as risky or threatening.

Trust both influences and is influenced by various elements in the communication process. For example, our trust of a person is influenced by his/her reliability as we perceive it. On the other hand, the degree of trust we have for this person influences the communication behavior of both of us as well as the results of our interaction. The relationship between these variables is reflexive—as trust increases, certain interaction patterns change; and in turn, their change tends to increase the degree of interpersonal trust.

The manner in which one person's perception of another influences personal trust has been of major concern to many scholars; however, interest has been focused primarily on the first element of the trust paradigm described above: trust of a speaker by a listener (ethos or source credibility). Although the evidence is not entirely clear, trust of a speaker appears to be influenced by a listener's perceptions of the following characteristics of a speaker:

1. *Expertness relevant to the topic under discussion; this expertise may be in the form of quantity of pertinent information, degree of ability or skill, or validity of judgment.*
2. *Reliability; this may be perceived as dependability, predictability, consistency, or intentions of the trusted person regarding the goals or objectives of the person doing the trusting.*
3. *Dynamism; that is, behavior perceived as more active than passive and more open or frank than closed or reserved.*[46]

Further evidence has been obtained to demonstrate that these three dimensions constitute the attitude elements of personal trust.[47] These three characteristics of a person are perceived directly by another person, and each may influence interpersonal trust. If you wish to have others trust you, you should adopt behaviors that will demonstrate that you are expert, reliable, and dynamic.

Self-Concept and Trust of Others

One's cognition of oneself is obtained, in part, by personal sensory perception and also, in part, by checking with other people. According to this line of reasoning, a person needs to communicate with others in order to verify his/her own view of himself/herself. However, if there is considerable question in mind about our social capabilities, we

[46]K. Giffin, "The Contribution of Studies of Source Credibility to a Theory of Interpersonal Trust in the Communication Process," *Psychological Bulletin*, 68 (1967), 104–120.

[47]K. Giffin, *An Experimental Evaluation of the Trust Differential: Research Monograph R/19* (Lawrence, Kan.: Communication Research Center, University of Kansas, 1968).

are not likely to expose ourselves via communication with others. In fact, we will likely fear communication situations. Research evidence tends to support this line of reasoning.[48]

Both Heider's balance theory and Festinger's theory of cognitive dissonance would lead us to suspect that a person with a very high concept of self would not fear exposure in his/her interaction with others, and even if an attack upon his/her self-image occurred, he/she she would likely disparage the source of the attack. Very likely he/she would filter such information, accepting only that with which he/she tended to agree. Exactly the same reasoning would lead us to suspect that a person with a *low* concept of self would reject information that would tend to raise the concept. There is research support for this line of reasoning. Bergin has demonstrated that when (1) a person's self-concept is low, and (2) the information received from another person is favorable about his/her behavior, he/she will tend to resolve this dissonance *by discrediting the source.*[49] An experiment by Deutsch and Solomon indicated that persons with low concept of self will tend to accept only information congruent with their concept; such subjects viewed *low* evaluations of themselves from others more favorably than high evaluations.[50]

In our culture, having a low concept of self is not a pleasant experience. Confirmation of it, even if valid, is likewise not pleasant. Thus, the individual with low self-esteem will pay more attention to information that confirms his low concept, but not be happy about it. He/she actually *fears confirmation of his/her fears.* In terms of interpersonal relationships, the protection of one's self-image is closely linked with trust of those with whom one interacts. Self-confidence in interpersonal relations can be conceptualized as willingness to expose one's self-concept to evaluation by others.

In a summary of the literature on the self-concept, Roger Brown concluded that there is a strong relationship between a broad conception of oneself and one's conception of others with whom one interacts (or, if I like people, I tend to like me).[51] Recent research has provided direct evidence in support of this line of reasoning.[52]

Rogers has argued that when an individual interacts with trusted others, he is then able to form new and more favorable perceptions

[48]H. Gilkinson, "A Questionnaire Study of the Causes of Social Fears Among College Speech Students," *Speech Monographs,* 10 (1943), 74–83. See also E. Bormann and G. Shapiro, "Perceived Confidence as a Function of Self-Image," *Central States Speech Journal,* 13 (1962), 253–256.

[49]A. E. Bergin, "The Effects of Dissonant Persuasive Communications upon Changes in a Self-Referring Attitude," *Journal of Personality,* 30 (1962), 423-438.

[50]M. Deutsch and L. Solomon, "Reactions to Evaluations by Others as Influenced by Self-Evaluations," *Sociometry,* 22 (1959), 93–112.

[51]R. Brown, *Social Psychology* (New York: Free Press, 1965), p. 650.

[52]Rogers, *Client-Centered Therapy, op cit.,* pp. 515–524.

of himself; that is, he can afford exposure of his self-concept for possible self-evaluation.[53] There is limited research evidence that exposure of oneself can help to increase one's trust of his/her listeners.[54]

In view of the findings cited above, the following principles may be stated: (1) Self-confidence in a given interpersonal communication situation is a function of perceived acceptance by valued others; and (2) there is an interaction between three types of trust, all three of which are functionally related to self-confidence in a given interpersonal communication situation: (a) trust of oneself, (b) trust extended toward others, and (c) perceived evidence of trust extended by others.

Increasing One's Trust of Others

If speech anxiety and tendency toward withdrawal from communication situations are related to one's trust of others, it is a natural question to ask: How can one's trust of others be increased?

It should be acknowledged that, in some cases, increasing a person's trust of others may be dangerous; some dupes are altogether too trusting. However, if a person is abnormally distrustful of other persons—that is, if he/she has unrealistic or irrational fear of others in social or communicative situations—then attempts on his/her part to increase his/her general level of trust of other people seem warranted. By achieving a more objective perception of others, one can hope to raise his/her own self-concept and reduce his/her speech anxiety.[55]

Interpersonal trust can best be achieved in a climate of perceived acceptance of the individual by others with whom he/she interacts. Personal change in a socially desirable way, and in a way desirable for the individual, requires a climate of acceptance and support. This climate of acceptance is sometimes found in t-groups (sensitivity training groups) and in therapy groups. From his work with normal subjects who were attempting to make their interpersonal relations more effective, Gibb has drawn the following conclusion:

> *A person learns to grow through his increasing acceptance of himself and others. Serving as the primary block to such acceptance are the defensive feelings of fear and distrust that arise from the prevailing defensive climates in most cultures. In order to participate consciously in his own growth, a person must learn to create for himself, in his*

[53]Rogers, *On Becoming a Person*, *op. cit.*, pp. 39–58.

[54]Giffin, "The Contribution of Studies of Source Credibility," *op. cit.*, 104–120.

[55]See evidence cited by K. Giffin and M. Heider, "A Theory of the Relationship Between Speech Anxiety and the Suppression of Communication in Childhood," *Psychiatric Quarterly Supplement*, 2 (1967), 311–322.

dyadic and group relationships, defensive-reductive climates that will continue to reduce his own fears and distrusts.[56]

It seems somewhat obvious that a key variable in increasing a person's trust of others is the behavior of those others. Studies of counselors, summarized by Truax and Carkhuff,[57] indicate variation in the relationship between counselors and clients. Specifically, counselors vary as to characteristics of accurate empathy, nonpossessive warmth, and genuineness. A large number of studies cited in their review have demonstrated that counselors who show above-average amounts of empathy, warmth, and genuineness have above-average success with psychoneurotic clients in psychiatric hospitals, psychiatric outpatient clinics, veterans' clinics, college counseling centers, and juvenile delinquency institutions. These studies include both individual and group counseling approaches.

The following line of reasoning thus emerges: (1) Speech anxiety involves low concept of self and distrust of others; (2) irrational distrust of others is significantly reduced by interaction with others and by counselors who show empathy, warmth, and genuineness; thus the inference—an environment that can measurably increase interpersonal trust is one in which a person is shown high degrees of these elements of rapport.

This inference makes logical sense; an anxious person can cope more easily with a communication environment in which he receives empathy, warmth, and genuineness. Successful coping with this communication environment may provide additional interpersonal confidence.

MAKING OPTIMAL USE OF THE PROCESS OF INTERPERSONAL COMMUNICATION

Advice is rarely popular, especially when it is not requested. Up to this point we have attempted to be primarily explanatory and descriptive, relying upon available research conclusions on interpersonal communication. In this section, however, we shall be primarily prescriptive; advice and suggestions will be offered based on theories and concepts presented in previous chapters.

Obviously, you as an individual must use sound judgment in applying the ensuing suggestions. Interpersonal communication should never be mechanistic or routine. A suggestion that might be generally useful may not apply specifically to your own communication with your father, mother, teacher, or particular friend. The value of the

[56]Gibb, "Climate for Trust Formation," *op. cit.*, p. 279.

[57]C. B. Truax and R. R. Carkhuff, *Toward Effective Counseling and Psychotherapy* (Chicago: Aldine, 1967).

suggestions presented here is to increase your awareness of choice in interpersonal encounters. The educated person should be cognizant of the communication choices available and the potential consequences.

1. Note Very Honestly Your Own Interaction Needs

Many of our individual needs can only be satisfied through social interaction; these include our personal development, personal growth, clarification of our relationships with others, and ways of negotiating our disagreements.

In our personal development we must deliberately search for new ways of gaining social approval. As our social environments change, we need to check on those elements in them that earn approval. As we should avoid straight, narrow, ritualized ways of behaving, we should also avoid trying to hide a part of ourselves, or acting as if we are something we are not. An open, frank, and genuine approach to others in our communication is our best avenue of self-identity.

We must build confidence in our ability to achieve and maintain self-esteem. This is accomplished as we expose a bit of ourselves to someone and note and evaluate the feedback we receive. As we find that we can profit from such exposure and feedback, we then disclose ourselves a little more. When we find a person whom we can trust to be open, frank, and accepting, we can gain honest and genuine feedback. As we communicate in this fashion with another, we may achieve the pleasure of shared personal growth. When we find that we can be comfortable in shared silence, we have achieved a level of interpersonal growth that is fully worth the effort.

When we have associated with other individuals over a period of time, there is a temptation to take the relationships for granted. In a work group, it is often useful to ask the other people how they feel about the way the members work together. A conflict area or basis of confusion may be revealed. We should seek to establish a pattern whereby every now and then we seek to clarify our relationships with those with whom we come in constant contact.

We should negotiate disagreements by attempting to achieve a level of mutual satisfaction. Ethically, we should avoid deliberate efforts to manipulate or distort the perceptions of others. They may see things differently than we do, but we should allow this to occur and attempt to understand it. The bases for our varying perceptions should be communicated and mutual revision accomplished, particularly if our needs and desires are obscuring reality. A compromise is sometimes necessary; usually it can be satisfactorily achieved through open, accurate, and honest exposure of the different viewpoints.

2. Try to Achieve Accurate Perceptions of Others

We should attempt to avoid use of pigeonhole categories and oversimplification in our perceptions of other people. We must expect and note complexities and differences instead of simple similarities. We should expect our perceptions of another person to change from time to time, and avoid "once-and-for-all" conclusions. Two-valued orientations, such as "clear-dirty" or "young-old," and status perceptions, such as "high-low," should not filter our views of others.

It is important to watch for subtle visual cues as we try to get to know others better. It will be necessary to look beyond such surface characteristics as use of cosmetics, long hair, and dress; as we avoid misleading stereotype casting we should watch closely for visual expressions and slight changes in posture and eye contact that give us more significant messages. Such nonverbal communication can help us understand the emotions and true feelings of the other person. We may deliberately have to explore the ways in which he/she wishes to relate to us, or the "game" he/she is attempting to play.

It is important that we try to understand the ways in which we ordinarily orient ourselves toward others. Such an orientation may serve our own personal needs for interaction, but greater flexibility may serve them even better. One of the major considerations is to determine if our willingness to interact with others is congruent with our desire to be included in their activities. Occasionally we find an unhappy person who, for one reason or another, is unwilling to include others in his/her life or activities, and who simultaneously feels that others seem to pass him by. The "Golden Rule" would seem to apply, for if we wish others to include us in their activities, we will have to show the same interest in including them in ours.

We must determine if we are willing to share control of a group in which we participate. We must see if our desire to control others is balanced by a willingness to be controlled at times by them. If we attempt to control others and feel that we can be happy only if we are in control of the situation, we may find conflict with those who are unwilling to let us control all of the time. It is probably beneficial to adopt a balanced approach—to be willing to be controlled as well as to take control when others seem to feel that it is appropriate.

Similarly, we should determine if our needs to receive attention and affection are approximately equal to our tendencies of showing affection to others. The area is critical in interpersonal orientations. In our culture many of us, especially males, find it difficult to show affection toward others. At the same time, however, most men and boys find it pleasant and rewarding to receive attention and affection. The point is this: If we want affection from others, we will probably have to be willing to show it toward them at appropriate times. Such displays of affection may be so foreign to our habits of thinking as to be awkward or even embarrassing, but they may be necessary if our interpersonal relations are to be mutually pleasant and satisfying.

If we feel that we are left out of groups or given too little affection by others, we can do the following:

1. *Make a special effort to include others in our circle of associates;*
2. *Show more readiness to accept the leadership and suggestions of others;*
3. *Sincerely show others the genuine affection we feel for them.*

We must try to make our behavior toward others congruent with the interpersonal behavior we would like to have them extend to us.

3. Constantly Consider Environmental Conditions

Teachers of public speaking have for many years requested students to note the requirements of the "occasion" or the situation confronting a speaker. In like manner, in an interpersonal situation the other person expects us to interact in certain ways; these expectations will be related to the specific environment and the chain of events or interactions that have led to this specific encounter. We typically respond without reflecting on the basis for our situational conditions.

Here we are concerned with situations that call for discriminating choice, for fine distinctions. For example, you are going to accuse your roommate of misusing your typewriter; at the time you meet him he is standing on a street corner talking to an acquaintance. "Now is probably not the right time to bring it up, but . . ." is a poor way to deal with the situation if we want optimum response. There may never be a perfect time to open a discussion about personal disagreements, but the usual mistake is that they are not brought up under optimum conditions. A presentation of such problems should take advantage of conditions that are at least somewhat favorable.

Certain situational guidelines are available for work in groups. You should hope to work with groups that provide optimum conditions for the accomplishment of a given task as well as maintaining positive group relations:

1. *The group task should be clear and relevant to your interests;*
2. *There should be the possibility for you to achieve a desirable status in the group;*
3. *The group's norms should be known and acceptable to you;*
4. *The power structure of the group should offer you an opportunity to participate in controlling other members as well as being controlled and influenced;*
5. *Group cohesiveness should be present or potentially possible;*
6. *Leadership roles should be shared and they should be reasonably attractive to you—that is, few members should exhibit excessive anxieties or need to dominate others.*

In joining and working with groups, it may take some time to learn each of these group characteristics, and when you have done so, some elements may not be to your liking, since, like people, no group is perfect. However, if you are to work well with the group and achieve satisfaction, you will want most of the above characteristics to be present or attainable.

4. Try to Achieve Interpersonal Rapport

If we are to gain maximum information from our interactions, we have to avoid making fast assumptions that we "know what he means." Whereas verbal communication and nonverbal signals provide clues to the other person's intended meanings, we should ask for additional information when the cues are in conflict or if we are unsure of what is intended. We must make every attempt to make certain that our conceptual maps are known to one another and that they fit the territory they profess to represent.

We should pay special attention to the intended meaning of another person when he/she uses words describing such strong feelings as love, dislike, hurt, sympathy, understanding, and fear. When a person says that he/she is "unhappy" with someone, we must not automatically assume we know what he/she means. Our own experiences and feelings may make empathy difficult.

Sudden shifts in the levels of abstraction should be noted. Suppose we ask a friend, "Did you have a good time at the party last night?" and he responds, "I met a lot of new people." Since we asked for an evaluative response and received a statement of fact, what conclusions can we draw?

Since language can be used as an instrument for interpersonal manipulation, we should be alert to the ways in which we are influenced and persuaded. Consider the ways in which many adults talk to children: basic premises are implied but not stated openly; value systems are evoked but not discussed; general statements are made about observed data, behaviors, and events but are not allowed to be questioned. For example, a child may want to wear his hair long, and his mother states: "Boys don't look well with long hair; men don't wear long hair; only beatniks and hippies run around with hair hanging down on their shoulders; I don't want to discuss it further." Such a statement negates the possibility of discussion of such questions as: (1) Long hair looks bad to whom? (2) Has long hair never been worn by some admirable men? (3) Are beatniks and hippies all "bad"? An open invitation to discuss the relative importance of adherence to social customs would be a mature, ethical way to approach this example of interpersonal conflict or disagreement. Avoidance of such discussion on grounds that the child is "too young" for such interaction voids the opportunity to help him grow and develop; it also denies the actual facts of the situation that initiated the conflict.

Such uses of language are manipulative and produce responses that may be unthinkingly submissive, resentful, alienated, or hostile. Interpersonal relationships are damaged rather than improved. Although it may be true that language is a social tool, care must be exercised that you or someone else is not thus "tooled."

Listening to others ordinarily requires deliberate effort. It should include a sincere attempt to understand the viewpoint of the other person: his/her value system; the source of his/her basic premises that frequently are implied but not openly stated; his/her generalized notion of observable facts, including his/her limited ability to observe objectively—sometimes called "personal prejudice"; and his/her limited linguistic ability to express his/her ideas in ways easily understood by others.

True listening is hard work. We may decide that in many cases it may not be worth all that much effort; but to make such a decision with full knowledge of the potential loss of understanding is one thing, and to allow such loss through neglect is quite another. When we really desire a lasting relationship with someone, listening to him/her is a necessary investment.

The point of this discussion is this: A rewarding relationship with another person seldom occurs by chance; we can't expect such a relationship to "just happen." If we really want to enjoy being with another person, we have to *work at* "being with" him or her. A starting point is to try to listen, to hear with "ears like theirs" instead of ours.

5. Build the Best Possible Human Relationships

Without allowing ourselves to become dupes for "confidence men," we should strive to increase our trust in other people. Increased trust in ourselves is vital; we must be willing to expose our thoughts and ideas to others and listen to their responses to these ideas. Our trust of others will increase as we learn to profit from their responses. An open and frank expression of what we think and how we feel about it will be an excellent start toward increasing interpersonal trust.

Our confidante must be selected with care. By easy stages we can achieve greater candor and disclosure of our feelings—our fears, anxieties, hopes, and pleasures. We should not worry about "saying things just right"; the other person's responses should guide us in determining how well we have expressed ourselves. As trust increases, we learn that the correction of misinterpretation is not only possible but relatively easy; it does require, however, that we listen carefully to the other person's responses and reflections upon our thoughts.

The most valuable thing for us to learn as our trust of others is increased is that *we do not ordinarily lose self-esteem by self-disclosure and relevant feedback*; rather, the opposite is true: The surest way to increase self-esteem is to listen and to evaluate feedback about ourself from someone we trust, making changes in our behavior when desirable and possible. In this way increased interpersonal trust serves our own personal needs and purposes.

SUMMARY AND PREVIEW OF READINGS

This chapter has focused on improving interpersonal communication by becoming a better person. A challenge was presented to fulfill your own human potential, not by just adding a few behaviors to those already practiced, but by achieving a new vision of yourself as a human being and then working toward self-actualization in terms of that vision. Special emphasis was placed upon *self-disclosure* to a trusted person and utilization of *feedback* thus obtained.

Self-disclosure requires interpersonal trust. In the communication setting, trust of a speaker is influenced by our perception of his/her expertness, reliability, and dynamism. Trust of a listener is influenced by our perception of his/her accurate empathy, nonpossessive warmth, and genuineness. Our trust of ourselves, trust *of* others, and perceived trust *by* others are all three interrelated; as one goes up or down, the others appear to be influenced.

Increased trust of others can be beneficial if one guards against being a dupe—offering trust when there is solid evidence that it will be misused. To increase our trust of others, we must first increase our interaction, and, second, increase our self-disclosure. Usually these overtures will achieve rewarding responses from others; if they do not, we must find associates who respond with consideration, sincerity, and warmth.

The final section of this chapter presented direct suggestions for improving interpersonal communication. These incorporated a very brief review of the essential elements of the process of interpersonal communication discussed in Chapters 3 through 7.

In the essay following this chapter, "Growing Awareness of Growth," Sidney Jourard makes a strong case for self-disclosure as a means of achieving a healthy personality. In his essay, "Being in Relationship," Carl Rogers presents his view of the ideal interpersonal relationship. Stress is placed on being real or genuine as a means of achieving one's full human potential.

SUGGESTED APPLICATIONS AND LEARNING EXPERIENCES

1. Meet with one of your close friends and, in more detail than you have ever done before, describe the kind of person you would really like to be. Listen carefully to his/her feedback; request it in more depth and more detail than usual. Note its effect on you and discuss this with your friend.

2. With one of your close friends, reverse the procedure described in No. 1 above; this time you take the role of listener and encourage your friend to describe the kind of person he/she would like to be. As best you can, help this friend to gain an imaginary picture or "vision" of themself actually behaving in ways that meet and even transcend his/her hopes or aspirations. With your friend discuss the value of this interaction.

3. With one of your classmates take a "trust walk." Do it this way: Close your eyes and have the other person lead or guide you out of the room, outside, and around at least two objects such as a building and a tree. On the return trip have the other person close his eyes and you guide him/her. During this walk note very carefully two things: (1) ways in which the other person "takes care of you" and actually shows that he/she cares about you; (2) your own thoughts and feelings while the other person is dependent upon you. Discuss these observations with a small group of your classmates after they have returned from a similar "trust walk." Determine for yourself personally the extent to which you have perhaps previously been needlessly distrustful of other people or careless about trust placed in you by others.

4. Meet with two or three of your best friends and, with their help, attempt to create a climate of acceptance and trust formation. No one should behave in ways that are insincere; do not try to show feelings that are not genuine. However, special efforts should be made to be as accepting of one another as possible without being artificial. Talk about your personal aspirations for becoming a better person. After some time spent in this way, together assess the degree of interpersonal trust among all of you. Has it increased? If so, do you and they think the experience has been valuable? Together decide to what extent attempts should be made, through similar experiences, to increase one's trust of others not present. Discuss with them where "one should draw the line" in increasing one's interpersonal trust.

5. In his essay "Growing Awareness and the Awareness of Growth," Sidney Jourard discusses one's awareness of self and its contribution to personal growth. After reading this article, reflect for awhile on your concept of yourself. After doing this, think about your experiences relating to elements of your self-concept. To what extent can you *experience* a transition taking place in the way you look at yourself? Do you believe, as Jourard does, that such meditation will change your behavior? If not, look over Jourard's article once again to see if you may have missed something.

6. Note in Roger's article, "Being in Relationship," his emphasis

on communicating realness to others and encountering it from them. With one of your friends discuss the degree of realness that they see you communicating to them; request and encourage honest feedback. Note the degree of realness in you that they perceive. Also note very carefully your willingness to accept and encourage realness in their feedback. Be specific in deciding what, if anything, you are going to do as a consequence of this discussion.

GROWING AWARENESS AND THE AWARENESS OF GROWTH

Sidney M. Jourard

Everything looks different when I visit the neighborhood where I grew up. The stores and houses look smaller, decayed, less imposing than I remember them to have been. My old school chums are balder, fatter; some look defeated and resigned, and others are smug, more self-satisfied than I knew them to be years ago. Their change appears to me as a kind of fall, a failure to realize many of the dreams which I knew animated them in their younger days. My own change (which I become acutely conscious of at times like these) feels to me like growth. I feel I have grown, while they have just grown older.

What is growth? What is my growth? How does it appear from the outside, from the point of view of another? Do I experience my growing? Or do I only see a difference, say, between old and more recent pictures of myself, and conclude that I have changed? Indeed, I have heard tape recordings of my speech, and have seen moving pictures of myself, made several years ago, and seeing how I looked and sounded makes me almost nauseous. I do not recognize myself as the source of those impressions. I experience myself from the "outside" and cannot recapture the "feel" of the person I was. Yet at times I have undergone some engrossing experience and, in a flash, realize I am changed. I experience myself and the world in new dimensions, as if a veil has suddenly been lifted.

What is the essence of this change? Is it growth? What brings it about? Can I help it along or hinder its occurrence? Can another person bring it on? Prevent it? I am going to speak here of growth from an "inside" point of view, of the growth of experience, and the changed experiencing that is growth. There are many accounts available about growth as it appears on the "outside," as recorded by instruments, or by scientific observers, but few about growing awareness. Since I *am* my awareness, an account of growing, changing awareness must at the same time be an account of my growth.

Growth is the dis-integration of one way of experiencing the world, followed by a reorganization of this experience, a reorganization that includes the new disclosure of the world. The disorganization, or even shattering, of one way to experience the world, is brought on by new disclosures from the changing being of the world, disclosures that were always being transmitted, but were usually ignored.

From Herbert A. Otto and John Mann, eds., *Ways of Growth*, pp. 1–15.

I

Change is in the world. The being of the world is always changing. My body is in the world, and it changes from instant to instant. Things and other people are in the world, and they metamorphose swiftly, or ever so slowly. I may not be aware of the change that *is* the world. The world-for-me may not appear to change, but rather it may seem congealed, constant, fixed. I may also experience my own being as unchanging.

In fact, people *strive to construct* a stable world, a world they can control and get their bearings in. A view of the world as constant is an achievement, a *praxis*, not a "given." A naive view of the world sees it both as a "buzzing, blooming confusion" and as stable and "structured." We simply cannot navigate in a world that is swiftly changing. And so we "freeze" it by pledging not to notice change until it has reached some critical degree, until it has gone on so far that it can no longer be ignored. Then, we might acknowledge it. If everything changed, during the night, so that you awakened to a new experience of yourself and the world, you might be terrified. But if suddenly the world froze, so that as everything now is, it would remain for eternity, you would be horrified. It would be hell. A hell of perfect predictability and boredom.

This disclosure of change is going on all the time. Change is *experienced*, however, only at moments. The awareness of change is frequently the experience of *surprise;* the unexpected has just been presented to us. The world, and my own bodily being, are not as I had believed them to be. My expectations about being, my concepts and beliefs about the world, have just been disconfirmed. The awareness that things are different is not growth, though it is a necessary condition of growth. A growth *cycle* calls for (a) an acknowledgment that the world has changed, (b) a shattering of the presently experienced "world-structure," and (c) a restructuring, re-totalization of the world-structure that encompasses the new disclosure of changed reality.

The retotalization of experience that consummates a growth cycle happens when a person sets goals and projects for himself, when he envisions a possibility and sets about trying to bring it to fruition. In fact, the growth cycle is often tripped off by a *failure* in goal-seeking. As one sets about trying to make or do something, he finds that his initial concepts and beliefs about what and how things *are*, are false. Faced with failure, he must then suspend his present beliefs and let the world disclose itself to him as it *now* is. If he does this, he can revise his concepts and get on with his project.

A growth cycle can also be triggered when goals and projects turn stale, when money can no longer buy anything that the person wants, when the fame that was once the person's glory has turned to ashes, and when the love of that woman long pursued is now experienced as cloying, suffocating possessiveness. The lack of fulfillment when long-sought goals are achieved signifies, however indirectly, that *our personal being* has changed, unnoticed by us. Our *concept of ourselves* as the person who would be fulfilled by this pleasure or made happier by that success, *has gotten out of touch with the reality of our being*. We are in for some surprises. The boredom signifies the imminence of growth. The time is ripe for the experience both of new goals and of new unfoldings of our being. It is time to let the world and ourselves disclose their being to our experience. We may undergo this new experience (if we let it happen) in delight, or in the terrifying realization that we are going out of our minds.

II

The world is full of Being, of many beings—some human, some animal, some inanimate. Being has many forms. Every being in the world can be likened to a kind of broadcasting station, transmitting signals of its being to other beings in the world. This transmission is ceaseless. As people and things and animals exist, they change, and they broadcast the fact of this change into the world. You and I are both beings, but beings of a special kind. We have (or are) awareness. We are embodied consciousness. We experience the transmissions that originate in our bodies, and through our bodies we experience some of the transmissions of being that originate elsewhere.

As human beings, we originate transmissions of our being, and we receive transmissions from other beings. My being discloses itself to me—I experience my own being—and it is disclosed to you through my appearance and behavior. *My* experience of *my* being is different from *your* experience of *my* being. And my experience of the being you disclose to me differs from your experience of your own being.

Man is a *concept-maker*. He forms *concepts* of the being of the world, and of his own self-being. A concept is an abstraction from what *is*. From a phenomenological and existential perspective, *a concept is a commitment to stop noticing the changing disclosures (disclosures of change) incessantly being transmitted by the beings in the world*. When I identify something as a cow, I rubricize it. I let it disclose enough of its being for me to classify it into the category *cow*. Then I stop receiving, though the cow hasn't stopped sending. It is a cow. It is this very cow, Bossie. Bossie is that cow which presents itself to me as black and white, of the kind "Holstein," with a big chip flaked off her left front hoof. I know Bossie. I can anticipate what she will do, on the basis of her past disclosures to me, and my awareness of these disclosures. I can get milk from Bossie. She will kick me if I approach her from the right side. And so on. But Bossie is continually changing, and these changes are continually revealed to the world. So long as I think of Bossie as I always have, I ignore these disclosures. I address Bossie as though she has not changed. Indeed, for the purposes I pursue in my transactions with Bossie, these changes may not make any difference until enough change has occurred that my predictions about Bossie are not borne out and my purposes are thwarted.

I start milking Bossie, and no milk comes. I say, "Something's wrong. Bossie is different. She has changed. She is not the Bossie I knew." Of course she isn't. She never is. No sooner did I form a *concept* of Bossie (stop perceiving her disclosures) than it was out of date. When I say, "Bossie has changed," all I am doing is belatedly acknowledging a change that has been inexorable and continuous. For my purposes (getting milk out of her), she did not change. When my purposes were thwarted, I was forced to expand my awareness of Bossie, to suspend my concept of her being, and let her being address me. My concept of Bossie (which terminated my perception of the multiple disclosures of her changing being) enabled me to fulfill my milking project. When the project was stymied, my concept became perceptibly incongruent, out of date with the actuality of Bossie's being. In fact, if I propose some new projects that involve Bossie, I may find my concept of her being requires revision. I may wish to enter her in a race. I believe she is a fast runner and can win me a prize. I test her—I put her in a situation where she can disclose her running ability. I find her slow. My concept of Bossie's being must now include the assertion, "She is slow."

III

Enough of cows, and enough of Bossie. I am going to contend that when my concepts of myself, of you, of cars, of cows, trees and refrigerators, are shattered; and when I again face the world with a questioning attitude; when I face the being in question and *let it disclose itself to me* (it always has, but I paid it no attention after I conceptualized it); and when I reform my concept on the basis of this newly received disclosure—then, *I have grown*. I will suspend my concepts when my projects in life (which depend on accurate concepts of reality for their fulfillment) are thwarted, when my predictions about how things will act or react prove wrong. Then, if I adopt the attitude of "Let the world disclose itself to me," I will receive this disclosure and change my concepts, and I will have grown.

My concepts of being can change under more pleasant circumstances than failure. In those rare moments when I have gratified all of my urgent needs—I have done my work, I feel good and fulfilled, and I want nothing out of the world just now—then the world will disclose all kinds of new faces to me. I am letting the world be itself, for itself. I may then notice all kinds of things about my friends, trees, the sky, animals, whatever is there, things that call upon me to enlarge my previous concepts of those same beings. Thus, success and gratification can open up my world for me, and let me experience it in new dimensions.

IV

You may notice that I seem different from the last time you saw me. My behavior and my verbal disclosures will show a change to you. You will say of me, "He has changed, he has grown." You will have to modify your concept of me at that time. *If you do, then you will have grown*. Your action toward me will reflect your changed concept of me, your changed experience of me. And I will then say to you, "You have changed, you have grown." You will feel confirmed in your being. You will feel understood. You will feel that the disclosure of your changed being—in words and actions—has been received and acknowledged by me.

V

I have a certain concept of my being, of myself. This is my *self-concept.* It is my belief about my own being. My being discloses itself to me, in the form of my intentional experience of myself. I experience the feel of my body's existence. I experience my own action from the inside. I form a concept of myself—what I am like, how I react, what I am capable of and what I cannot do, on the basis of this self-experience. You may also tell me what and who you think I am, on the basis of your experience of the outside of my being, and I take your belief into account. We may agree that I am thus and such a kind of person—a man, a psychologist, kind, strong, able to play a fair game of handball, unable to sing in key, etc. Once I have formed this concept of who and what I am, I proceed to behave in the world as if that is all and everything I am or can be. My behavior, my self-disclosure, endlessly confirms my self-concept. It is as if I have taken a pledge to show this and only this as my being.

VI

In fact, my being, like all Being, *is change.* This change discloses itself to me through my experience, and to others through my behavior. But if you and I have formed a concept of my being, neither of us pays attention to the ceaseless transmission of my changing being. It is transmitted, but no receiver is tuned in to acknowledge the change. Things can get more complicated: I may notice the changes and change my concept of myself accordingly. You may not notice the changes. You treat me as if I were the same person. I do not recognize myself as the one you believe I am. I feel you are talking to somebody else, not me.

Or, you may notice the changes before I do and change your concept of me accordingly. Again, I may not recognize the "me" that you seem to be addressing. Your concept of me is disjunctive from my self-concept.

Or, I may display and disclose the newly experienced facets of my being to you. You may say, "I don't recognize you. You are not yourself today. I don't like the person you seem to be. I'll come see you when you have gotten back into your right mind." If you thus disconfirm my newly experienced and tentatively disclosed being, and if I am unsure of myself, I may try to suppress and repress my newly emerged being and seek to appear to you and to me as the person I was. If I do this chronically and successfully, I may become mad.

There is also another way in which I might grow through a relationship with you. I may have a fixed concept of you and hence behave toward you in an habitual, stereotyped way. My action toward you is predictable. I always become aggressive in your presence. I experience you as a source of harm to me, and I attack first, to protect myself. My concept of you is that you are menacing, that you harbor ill will toward me. *When I experience you, I may not be undergoing a perceptual experience, but rather an imaginative experience of your being.* I tune out your disclosed being and replace it by an imaginative experience. Imagination veils perception. In fact, much of our experience of the people in our lives, even when they are face to face with us, is *not* perceptual, but *imaginative.*

The perceptual mode of experiencing entails the readiness to receive revealing inputs from the other, so that one's awareness of the other is constantly changing. But the imaginative mode of experiencing tunes out fresh disclosures. My image of you remains fixed, unchanged by your disclosures, because I do not pay them any attention. Now, if you can break through my imaginative experience of you, if you can catch my attention, by a shout, a blow, a scream of pain or joy, I may, as it were, wake up from my daydreamlike experience of your being, and undergo a fresh perceptual experience of you. You will surprise me. If you do this, if you get me "un-hung" from fixation on one *mode* of experiencing you—the imaginative mode—so I can now perceive you, I will have grown. My consciousness of you will have expanded. My awareness will have grown, and where I had previously been aware of you only as an image (though I didn't know this was an image), now I can experience you perceptually. If my consciousness expands, so I can experience you or the world in many more modes than I could hitherto: imaginatively, perceptually, recollectively, in the mode of fantasy, then I have grown; I *am* my awareness, and if my awareness expands, I have grown.

My world of awareness may not only be fixed in one *mode* of experiencing, e.g., the abstracting, conceptual mode or the imaginative mode; *my world may also be confined to some one or two sensory 'channels' of awareness*. For example, I may limit my clear awareness to only visual and auditory impressions and exclude the worlds of smelling, tasting, or the feel of my own body. If you can "turn me on" to my feelings, to smells, to tastes; if you can wake up my imagination; if you can get me to experience the feel of my body, you will have expanded my awareness and helped me to grow. You could back-rub me out of my mind and into my experience of my body.

VII

If I, from time to time, suspend my concept of myself, and "tune in" on my being; if I meditate, or reflect on my experience, then I must re-form my self-concept. I will believe myself to be different. I will act differently. I *am* different. Moments of meditation are the times (rare in our culture) when we try to let the changing flux of our being disclose itself to us. Meditation, if we learn how to do it, or let it happen, can give us the *experience* of transition in our being and can yield transitional experiences. In meditation we also let the world disclose more of its changing being to us, and we may find ourselves experiencing more of the variety in the world.

VIII

But meditation is not the only occasion when our self-concepts are put into question and temporarily suspended. Whenever we are unselfconscious, whenever our attention is fully focused upon some task, some project, our being changes; and our changing experience of our changed being goes on spontaneously. We let our personal being *happen*. We do not try to monitor and control it so it conforms to a concept. Fascinated engagement with *anything* can let change happen and be experienced, such that the next time I reflect upon myself, I find my experience of myself different from how I remember it the last time I reflected. And my concept of myself will have to be changed to encompass the new experiencing I have undergone. Challenge, fascination, total involvement in some task or project such that self-consciousness and self-conceptualizing is *not* the mode of experience, will permit the changed self-being to be experienced.

IX

If I engage in conversation with you, in dialogue; and if you disclose your experience of yourself and of me to me in truth; and if I receive your continuing disclosure; and if I disclose my experience of myself and of your disclosure to you in truth, *then I must be letting change happen and be disclosed to us both*. If I reflect upon my experience of the dialogue, I must notice that I am different from the way I was when we began the dialogue. But if I have (as it were) pledged myself to appear before you and to myself as *this* kind of man and no other, then my intentional disclosures to you will be very selective. Perhaps I will lie to you, to preserve your present concept of me, or at least *my* concept of *your* concept of me. Indeed, if my pledge of sameness is made to myself, then every time my *actually* changed being discloses itself to me, I will feel threatened, and repress it. I will pretend to myself I did not have the experience of hatred, or of anxiety, or of lust. And I will believe my own pretense to myself. Then, I will not grow. My concept of myself will become increasingly estranged from the ongoing change of my being. If my self-concept is too discrepant from actuality, the disclosure to me of my changed being will become more insistent. I will then have to pretend and repress much harder. If the change is too great, the experience of change will no longer be repressible. It will declare itself in my experience, and perhaps in my behavior. I may become terrified, and feel I have "gone out of my mind." Actually, I have, if by "mind" we mean "self-concept." If I still insist on trying to appear to you as the same person I *was*, I may develop neurotic symptoms. Or if I am terrified enough, I may become psychotic.

X

You can help me grow, or you can obstruct my growth. If you have a *fixed* idea of who I am and what my traits are, and what my possibilities of change are, then anything that comes out of me beyond your concept, you will disconfirm. In fact, you may be terrified by any surprises, any changes in my behavior, because these changes may threaten your concept of me; my changes may, if disclosed to you, shatter your concept of me, and challenge you to grow. You may be afraid. In your fear, you may do everything in your power to get me to un-change, and reappear to you as the person you once knew.

But if you suspend any preconceptions you may have of me and my being, and invite me simply to be and to disclose this being to you, you create an ambience, an area of "low pressure" where I can let my being happen and be disclosed, to you and to me simultaneously—to me from the inside, and to you who receive the outside layer of my being.

If your concept of my being is one that encompasses more possibilities in my behavior than I have myself acknowledged; if your concept of my being is more inclusive and indeed more accurate than my concept of my being, and if you let me know how you think of me; if you let me know from moment to moment how you experience me; if you say, "Now I think you dislike me. Now I think you are being ingratiating. Now I think you can succeed at this, if you try"; if you tell me *truly* how you experience me, I can compare this with my experience of myself, and with my own self-concept. You may thus insert the thin edge of doubt into the crust of my self-concept, helping to bring about its collapse, so that I might re-form it. In fact, this is what a loving friend, or a good psychotherapist, does.

XI

There is another way you can help me grow, and that is through challenging me and encouraging me to attempt new projects. We actually construe and conceptualize the world and ourselves in the light of the projects we live for. It is our commitment to these which "structures" our world. The beings in the world, including our own being, reveal different facets of themselves to us, depending upon the projects we are pursuing at the moment. The trees in the forest reveal their timber footage to the lumber merchant, the bugs in their trunks to the insect-collector, their colors to the painter. My muscular strength or weakness reveals itself to me as I try to chop the forest down, and I form a concept of my muscular strength. I may never come to question or doubt this estimate I made. My self-concept gets frozen if my projects are frozen and if I become too skilled at fulfilling them.

Suppose, when I find my existence dull and boring, I decide to try some new project—to write a book, climb a mountain, change jobs. I tell you of this faint resolve. I am afraid to try, because, as I presently think of myself, I don't believe I have the capacity to succeed. If you encourage me to try, and encourage me and support me when the going gets rough, so I stick with the project with more and more single-mindedness, I discover in myself transcendent powers I never experienced before, and never imagined I had. I do not and cannot transcend my *possibilities*; I don't know what these are and won't know until I stop living. I only transcend my *concept* of what my possibilities might be. You can help me transcend my self-concept by challenging and supporting me in new projects that I mount.

Even the decision to *attempt* something new results in a new experience of myself and the world, *before* I actually get going. If I decide to start a new book, I begin to experience friends as interferences in this project; movies and television, formerly very inviting, become dull and boring. The whole world and my experience of myself change with the change in projects. If you help me give up old projects which are no longer satisfying, delightful or fulfilling, and encourage me to dare new ones, you are helping me to grow.

XII

Growing entails going out of our minds and into our raw experience. Our experience is always of the disclosure of the world and of our own embodied being. When we function smoothly, habitually, and effectively in the world, our concepts are confirmed, and we do not receive new disclosure. When we meet impasse and failure in the pursuit of our projects, then our habits and concepts (a habit can be seen as the "outside" of a concept) are challenged. Failure of our projects gives us a whiff of the stink of chaos, and this can be terrifying. Our concepts get cracks in them when we fail. Through these cracks, the encapsulated experience "contained" by the concept might leak or explode; or through the crack there may occur an implosion of more being. When there are no concepts, there is nothing, no-thing, we can grapple with, get leverage on, in order to get on with the projects of living. There is the threat of pure chaos and nothingness. If we experience the pure nothingness, we panic, and seek quickly to shore up the collapsing world, to daub clay into the cracks in our concepts. If we do this, we don't grow. If we let the concepts explode or implode, and do not re-form them veridically, we appear mad, and are mad. If we reform them, to incorporate new experience, we grow.

XIII

Once again we must consider projects, this time in relation to integration, a vital and crucial phase of growth. When our projects are obstructed because our concepts are out of phase with being, the concepts must explode, or become fractionated, differentiated into parts. We experience chaos. Our commitment to the old projects, or recommitment to new projects, serves as the field of force that organizes the fractionated experience of being into meaningful wholes, concepts, gestalten. Growth is our experience of our concepts and percepts being detotalized and then retotalized into newly meaningful unities.

XIV

I know I am ready to grow when I experience some dissonance between my beliefs, concepts, and expectations of the world, and my perception of the world. I am also ready to grow when I experience boredom, despair, depression, anxiety or guilt. These emotions inform me that my goals and projects have lost meaning for me; that my being has gotten too big, too out of phase with my concepts of my being. I have a choice at such moments, if indeed I can experience the emotions. I may have become so unaccustomed to and maladept at reflection and meditation that I simply don't notice these "all is not well" signals, and continue to pursue my projects and believe my beliefs as if experience were confirming them.

But if I do acknowledge the signals, my choice is: either to meditate, suspend my concept and preconception of self, and let my changed being disclose itself to me even when it hurts (it frequently does); or to affirm the project of being the same (an impossible project, but one that many people try to live). If I decide to try to be the same, then I will repress my experience of change, of the "all is not well" signals. I will have resolved, really, to stop perceiving myself.

Since nothing *definite* is possible, purposeful action is impossible. Yet, if a person can endure this voyage within his own experience, he can emerge from it with a new concept of his being and with new projects; the new concept of being will include more of his being in it. But this new integration will last only so long, and then the entire process must be repeated again. A sentient life is an endless series of getting out of one's mind and concepts, only to re-enter, and depart again.

The experience of surprise is also a sign of one's readiness to grow. Amazement and wonder signify that one's concepts of self and of the world and of other people are "loose," ready to be re-formed. The "know-it-all," the "cool" one, has pledged himself never to be surprised. Everything that the world discloses is no more than an unfolding of what he has expected and predicted, or so he tries to convey to others. But when a man can be dumbfounded and surprised at what comes out of him, or what his friend or spouse is capable of doing and disclosing, he is a growing person.

In fact, if I intentionally adopt the "set" that all of my concepts are tentative and provisional, I invite others, myself, and the world to reveal new facets of their being to me, so that even my daily life can be an unfolding of newness, where simply perceiving the world or the self is a source of endless variety and surprise.

If I am with you, and I have wilfully adopted the set that I do not know and cannot ever fully know all your possibilities, my very presence embodies an invitation to you to surprise me, to show off, to transcend your (and my) previous concepts of your being. I can tell when I am in the presence of a person with a closed mind. I feel constrained to shut off most of my possibilities. But in the presence of a wonderer, I feel an absence of prejudgment, a permissive acceptance, and my terror and self-consciousness about revealing surprises are diminished.

In short, if you and I both retain our capacity for surprise, we aid and confirm one another's growth.

BRING IN RELATIONSHIP

Carl R. Rogers

Just as it was an awesome thing to face a sea of a thousand faces so early in the morning, so I have the same feeling, something akin to panic, whenever I start a chapter. . . . What possible way is there in which I can make real *contact* with a multitude of unknown readers, whose background, expectations, and attitudes are all unknown to me? Especially is this concern a deep one when I want to talk about interpersonal relationships. I don't believe a scholarly, abstract chapter will make that contact. Furthermore, I have no desire to instruct my readers, or impress you with my knowledge in this field. I have no desire to tell you what you should think or feel or do. How can I meet this dilemma?

The only solution I have come up with is that perhaps I can share something of myself, something of *my* experience in interpersonal relationships, something of what it has been like to be me, in communication with others. This is not an easy thing to do. But if I can do it, if I can share something of myself, then I think you can take what I say, or leave it alone. You can decide whether it is relevant to your own job, your career, your profession, your life. You can respond to it with the reaction, "That's just what *I've* felt and what *I've* discovered," or equally valuably, "I feel *very* differently. My experience has taught me something entirely different." In either case, it may help you to define *yourself* more clearly, more openly, more surely. That I *do* regard as worthwhile, and as something I hope I can facilitate.

So I'm going to share with you a somewhat miscellaneous bag of learnings, things I have learned or am learning about this mysterious business of relating with other human beings, about communication between persons. I'm going to share some of my satisfactions and my dissatisfactions in this area. The reason I call it a mysterious business is that interpersonal communication is almost never achieved except in part. You probably never feel fully understood by another, and neither do I. Yet I find it extremely rewarding when I have been able, in a particular instance, truly to communicate myself to another. I find it very precious when, for some moment in time, I have felt really close to, fully in touch with, another person.

From Carl R. Rogers, *Freedom to Learn*, 1969, pp. 231–237. Reprinted by permission of Charles E. Merrill Publishing Company, Columbus, Ohio.

This paper is a revised version of a highly personal talk I gave to a recent conference of the American Personnel and Guidance Association in Dallas. I was dumbfounded that the auditorium, holding several thousand persons, was crammed full at 8:30 in the morning (!) to hear a talk on interpersonal relationships.

I LIKE TO HEAR

So the first simple feeling I want to share with you is my enjoyment when I can really *hear* someone. I think perhaps this has been a long standing characteristic of mine. I can remember this in my early grammar school days. A child would ask the teacher a question and the teacher would give a perfectly good answer to a completely different question. A feeling of pain and distress would always strike me. My reaction was, "But you didn't *hear* him!" I felt a sort of childish despair at the lack of communication which was (and is) so common.

I believe I know why it is satisfying to me to hear someone. When I can really hear someone it puts me in touch with him. It enriches my life. It is through hearing people that I have learned all that I know about individuals, about personality, about psychotherapy, and about interpersonal relationships. There is another peculiar satisfaction in it. When I really hear someone it is like listening to the music of the spheres, because beyond the immediate message of the person, no matter what that might be, there is the universal, the general. Hidden in all of the personal communications which I really hear there seem to be orderly psychological laws, aspects of the awesome order which we find in the universe as a whole. So there is both the satisfaction of hearing this particular person and also the satisfaction of feeling oneself in some sort of touch with what is universally true.

When I say that I enjoy hearing someone I mean, of course, hearing deeply. I mean that I hear the words, the thoughts, the feeling tones, the personal meaning, even the meaning that is below the conscious intent of the speaker. Sometimes, too, in a message which superficially is not very important, I hear a deep human cry, a "silent scream," that lies buried and unknown far below the surface of the person.

So I have learned to ask myself, can I hear the sounds and sense the shape of this other person's inner world? Can I resonate to what he is saying, can I let it echo back and forth in me, so deeply that I sense the meanings he is afraid of yet would like to communicate, as well as those meanings he knows?

I think, for example, of an interview I had with an adolescent boy, the recording of which I listened to only a short time ago. Like many an adolescent today he was saying at the outset of the interview that he had no goals. When I questioned him on this he made it even stronger that he had no goals whatsoever, not even one. I said, "There isn't anything you want to do?" "*Nothing* . . . Well, yeah, I want to keep on living." I remember very distinctly my feeling at that moment. I resonated very deeply to this phrase. He might simply be telling me that, like everyone else, he wanted to live. On the other hand he might be telling me, and this seemed to be a distinct possibility, that at some point the question of whether or not to live had been a real issue with him. So I tried to resonate to him at all levels. I didn't know for certain what the message was. I simply wanted to be open to any of the meanings that this statement might have, including the possible meaning that he might have at one time considered suicide. I didn't respond verbally at this level. That would have frightened him. But I think that my being willing and able to listen to him at all levels is perhaps one of the things that made it possible for him to tell me, before the end of the interview, that not long before he had been on the point of blowing his brains out. This little episode constitutes an example of what I mean by wanting to really hear someone at all the levels at which he is endeavoring to communicate.

I find, in therapeutic interviews, and in the intensive group experiences which have come to mean a great deal to me in recent years, that hearing has consequences. When I do truly hear a person and the meanings that are important to him at that moment, hearing not simply his words, but *him*, and when I let him know that I have heard his own private personal meanings, many things happen. There is first of all a grateful look. He feels released. He wants to tell me more about his world. He surges forth in a new sense of freedom. I think he becomes more open to the process of change.

I have often noticed, both in therapy and in groups, that the more deeply I can hear the meanings of this person the more there is that happens. One thing I have come to look upon as almost universal is that when a person realizes he has been deeply heard, there is a moistness in his eyes. I think in some real sense he is weeping for joy. It is as though he were saying, "Thank God, *somebody* heard me. Someone knows what it's like to be me." In such moments I have had the fantasy of a prisoner in a dungeon, tapping out day after day a Morse code message, "Does anybody hear me? Is there anybody there? Can anyone hear me?" And finally one day he hears some faint tappings which spell out "Yes." By that one simple response he is released from his loneliness, he has become a human being again. There are many, many people living in private dungeons today, people who give no evidence of it whatever on the outside, where you have to listen very sharply to hear the faint messages from the dungeon.

If this seems to you a little too sentimental or overdrawn, I would like to share with you an experience I had recently in a basic encounter group with fifteen persons in important executive posts. Early in the very intensive sessions of the week they were asked to write a statement of some feeling or feelings which they had which they were *not* willing to tell in the group. These were anonymous statements. One man wrote, "I don't relate easily to people. I have an almost impenetrable façade. Nothing gets in to hurt me but nothing gets out. I have repressed so many emotions that I am close to emotional sterility. This situation doesn't make me happy but I don't know what to do about it." This is clearly a message from a dungeon. Later in the week a member of my group identified himself as the man who had written that anonymous message, and filled out in much greater detail his feelings of isolation, of complete coldness. He felt that life had been so brutal to him that he had been forced to live a life without feeling, not only at work, but in social groups, and saddest of all, with his family. His gradual achievement of greater expressiveness in the group, of less fear of being hurt, of more willingness to share himself with others, was a very rewarding experience for all of us who participated.

I was both amused and pleased when, in a letter a few weeks later he included this paragraph. "When I returned from (our group) I felt somewhat like a young girl who had been seduced but still wound up with the feeling that it was exactly what she had been waiting for and needed! I am still not quite sure who was responsible for the seduction—you or the group, or whether it was a joint venture, I suspect it was the latter. At any rate I want to thank you for what was an intensely meaningful experience." I think it is not too much to say that because several of us in the group were able genuinely to hear him, he was released from his dungeon and has come out, at least to some degree, into the sunnier world of warm interpersonal relationships.

I Like To Be Heard

Let me move on to a second learning which I would like to share with you. I like to *be heard*. A number of times in my life I have felt myself bursting with insoluble problems, or going round and round in tormented circles or, during one period, overcome by feelings of worthlessness and despair, sure I was sinking into psychosis. I think I have been more lucky than most in finding at these times individuals who have been able to hear me and thus to rescue me from the chaos of my feelings. I have been fortunate in finding individuals who have been able to hear my meanings a little more deeply than I have known them. These individuals have heard me without judging me, diagnosing me, appraising me, evaluating me. They have just listened and clarified and responded to me at all the levels at which I was communicating. I can testify that when you are in psychological distress and someone really hears you without passing judgment on you, without trying to take responsibility for you, without trying to mold you, it feels *damn good*. At these times, it has relaxed the tension in me. It has permitted me to bring out the frightening feelings, the guilts, the despair, the confusions that have been a part of my experience. When I have been listened to and when I have been heard, I am able to reperceive my world in a new way and to go on. It is amazing that feelings which were completely awful become bearable when someone listens. It is astonishing how elements which seem insoluble become soluble when someone hears; how confusions which seem irremediable turn into relatively clear flowing streams when one is understood. I have deeply appreciated the times that I have experienced this sensitive, empathic, concentrated listening.

I have been very grateful that by the time I quite desperately needed this kind of help, I had trained and developed therapists, persons in their own right, independent and unafraid of me, who were able to go with me through a dark and troubled period in which I underwent a great deal of inner growth. It has also made me sharply aware that in developing my style of therapy for others, I was without doubt, at some unconscious level, developing the kind of help I wanted and could use myself.

When I Can Not Hear

Let me turn to some of my dissatisfactions in this realm. I dislike it in myself when I can't hear another, when I do not understand him. If it is only a simple failure of comprehension or a failure to focus my attention on what he is saying, or a difficulty in understanding his words, then I feel only a very mild dissatisfaction with myself.

But what I really dislike in myself is when I cannot hear the other person because I am so sure in advance of what he is about to say that I don't listen. It is only afterward that I realize that I have only heard what I have already decided he is saying. I have failed really to listen. Or even worse are those times when I can't hear because what he is saying is too threatening, might even make me change my views or my behavior. Still worse are those times when I catch myself trying to twist his message to make it say what I want him to say, and then only hearing that. This can be a very subtle thing and it is surprising how skillful I can be in doing it. Just by twisting his words a small amount, by distorting his meaning just a little, I can make it appear that he is not only saying the thing I want to hear, but that he is the person I want him to be. It is only when I realize through his protest or through my own gradual recognition that I am subtly manipulating him that I become disgusted with myself. I know too from being on the receiving end of this how frustrating it is to be received for what you are not, to be heard as saying something which you have not said and do not mean. This creates anger and bafflement and disillusion.

When Others Do Not Understand

The next learning I want to share with you is that I am terribly frustrated and shut into myself when I try to express something which is deeply me, which is a part of my own private, inner world, and the other person does not understand. When I take the gamble, the risk, of trying to share something that is very personal with another individual and it is not received and not understood, this is a very deflating and a very lonely experience. I have come to believe that it is that experience which makes some individuals psychotic. They have given up hoping that anyone can understand them and once they have lost that hope then their own inner world, which becomes more and more bizarre, is the only place where they can live. They can no longer live in any shared human experience. I can sympathize with them because I know that when I try to share some feeling aspect of myself which is private, precious, and tentative, and when this communication is met by evaluation, by reassurance, by denial, by distortion of my meaning, I have very strongly the reaction, "Oh, what's the use!" At such a time one knows what it is to be *alone*.

So, as you can see, a creative, active, sensitive, accurate, empathic, non-judgmental listening, is for me terribly important in a relationship. It is important for me to provide it. It has been extremely important especially at certain times in my life to receive it. I feel that I have grown within myself when I have provided it. I am very sure that I have grown and been released and enhanced when I have received this kind of listening.

I WANT TO BE REAL

Moving on to another area of my learnings, I find it very satisfying when I can be real, when I can be close to whatever it is that is going on within me. I like it when I can listen to myself. To really know what I am experiencing in the moment is by no means an easy thing but I feel somewhat encouraged because I think that over the years I have been improving at it. I am convinced, however, that it is a lifelong task and that none of us ever is really able to be comfortably close to *all* that is going on within his own experience.

In place of the term *realness* I have sometimes used the word *congruence*. By this I mean that when my experiencing of this moment is present in my awareness, and when what is present in my awareness is present in my communication, then each of these three levels matches or is congruent. At such moments I am integrated or whole, I am completely in one piece. Most of the time of course I, like everyone else, exhibit some degree of incongruence. I have learned, however, that realness, or genuineness, or congruence—whatever term you wish to give to it—is a fundamental basis for the best of communication, the best of relationships.

What do I mean by being real? I could give many examples from many different fields. But one meaning, one learning is that there is basically nothing to be afraid of when I present myself as I *am*, when I can come forth nondefensively, without armor, just me. When I can accept the fact that I have many deficiencies, many faults, make lots of mistakes, am often ignorant where I should be knowledgeable, often prejudiced when I should be openminded, often have feelings which are not justified by the circumstances, then I can be much more real. And when I can come out wearing no armor, making no effort to be different from what I am, I learn so much more—even from criticism and hostility—and I am so much more relaxed, and I get so much closer to people. Besides, my willingness to be vulnerable brings forth so much more real feeling from other people who are in relationship to me, that it is very rewarding. So I enjoy life *much* more when I am not defensive, not hiding behind a façade, just trying to be and express the real me.

Communicating the Realness in Me

I feel a sense of satisfaction when I can dare to communicate the realness in me to another. This is far from easy partly because what I am experiencing keeps changing in every moment, partly because feelings are very complex. Usually there is a lag, sometimes of moments, sometimes of days, weeks, or months, between the experiencing and the communication. In these cases, I experience something, I feel something, but only later do I become aware of it, only later do I dare to communicate it, when it has become cool enough to risk sharing it with another. Yet it is a most satisfying experience when I can communicate what is real in me at the moment that it occurs. Then I feel genuine, and spontaneous, and alive.

Such real feelings are not always positive. One man, in a basic encounter group of which I was a member, was talking about himself in ways which seemed to me completely false, speaking of the pride he took in maintaining his front, his pretense, his façade, how skillful he was in deceiving others. My feeling of annoyance rose higher and higher until finally I expressed it by simply saying, "Oh, nuts!" This somehow pricked the bubble. From that time on he was a more real and genuine person, less a braggadocio, and our communication improved. I felt good for having let him know my own real angry feeling as it was occurring.

I'm sorry to say that very often, especially with feelings of anger, I'm only partly aware of the feeling at the moment, and full awareness comes later. I only learn afterward what my feeling *was*. It is only when I wake up in the middle of the night, finding myself angrily fighting someone, that I realize how angry I was at him the day before. Then I know, seemingly too late, how I might have been my real feeling self; but, at least, I have learned to go to him the next day, if need be, to express my anger, and gradually I'm learning to be more quickly acquainted with it inside myself. In the last basic encounter group in which I participated, I was at different times very angry with two individuals. With one, I wasn't aware of it until the middle of the night and had to wait until morning to express it. With the other, I was able to realize it and express it in the session in which it occurred. In both instances, it led to real communication, to a strengthening of the relationship, and gradually to a feeling of genuine liking for each other. But I am a slow learner in this area.

Encountering Realness in Others

It is a sparkling thing when I encounter realness in another person. Sometimes in the basic encounter groups which have been a very important part of my experience these last few years, someone says something which comes from him transparently and whole. It is so obvious when a person is not hiding behind a façade but is speaking from deep within himself. When this happens I leap to meet it. I want to encounter this real person. Sometimes the feelings thus expressed are very positive feelings. Sometimes they are decidedly negative ones. I think of a man in a very responsible position, a scientist at the head of a large research department in a huge electronics firm, very "successful." One day in such a basic encounter group he found the courage to speak of his isolation, to tell us that he had never had a single friend in his life. There were plenty of people whom he knew but not one he could count as a friend. "As a matter of fact," he added, "there are only two individuals in the world with whom I have even a reasonably communicative relationship. These are my two children." By the time he finished he was letting loose some of the tears of sorrow for himself which I am sure he had held in for many years. But it was the honesty and realness of his loneliness which caused every member of the group to reach out to him in some psychological sense. It was also most significant that his courage in being real enabled all of us to be more genuine in our communications, to come out from behind the façades we ordinarily use.

My Failures To Be Real

I am disappointed when I realize—and of course this realization always comes afterward, after a lag of time—that I have been too frightened or too threatened to let myself get close to what I am experiencing and that consequently I have not been genuine or congruent. There immediately comes to mind an instance which is somewhat painful to reveal. Some years ago I was invited to spend a year as a Fellow at the Center for Advanced Study in the Behavioral Sciences at Stanford, California. The Fellows are a group chosen because they are supposedly brilliant and well-informed scholars. It is doubtless inevitable that there is a considerable amount of one-upsmanship, of showing off one's knowledge and achievements. It seems important for each Fellow to impress the others, to be a little more assured, to be a little more knowledgeable than he really is. I found myself several times doing this same thing—playing a role of greater certainty and of greater competence than I really felt. I can't tell you how disgusted with myself I was as I realized what I was doing. I was not being me; I was playing a part.

I regret it when I suppress my feelings too long and they burst forth in ways that are distorted or attacking or hurtful. I have a friend whom I like very much but who has one particular pattern of behavior that thoroughly annoys me. Because of the usual tendency to be nice, polite, and pleasant I kept this annoyance to myself for too long a time. When it finally burst its bounds it came out not only as annoyance but as an attack on him. This was hurtful and it took us some time to repair the relationship.

I am inwardly pleased when I have the strength to permit another person to be his own realness and to be *separate* from me. I think that is often a very threatening possibility. In some ways I have found it sort of an ultimate test of staff leadership and of parenthood. Can I freely permit this staff member or my client or my son or my daughter to become a separate person with ideas, purposes, and values which may not be identical with my own? I think of Kahlil Gibran's poem on marriage,[1] which includes the lines:

> Let there be spaces in your togetherness,
> And let the winds of the heavens dance between you.
> Love one another, but make not a bond of love:
> Let it rather be a moving sea between the shores of your souls. . . .
>
> Give your hearts, but not into each other's keeping.
> For only the hand of Life can contain your hearts.
> And stand together yet not too near together:
> For the pillars of the temple stand apart,
> And the oak tree and the cypress grow not in each other's shadow.

From a number of these things I have been saying I trust it is clear that when I can permit realness in myself or sense it or permit it in the

[1]Reprinted from *The Prophet*, by Kahlil Gibran with permission of the publisher, Alfred A. Knopf, Inc. Copyright 1923 by Kahlil Gibran; renewal copyright 1951 by Administrators C.T.A. of Kahlil Gibran Estate, and Mary G. Gibran.

other, I find it very satisfying. When I cannot permit it in myself or fail to permit a separate realness in another it is to me very distressing and regrettable. I find that when I am able to let myself be congruent and genuine it often helps the other person. When the other person is transparently real and congruent it often helps me. In those rare moments when a deep realness in one meets a deep realness in the other it is a memorable "I-thou relationship," as Martin Buber, the existential Jewish philosopher, would call it. Such a deep and mutual personal encounter does not happen often but I am convinced that unless it happens occasionally we are not human.

UNLEASHING FREEDOM FOR OTHERS

There's another learning. I like it when I can permit freedom to others, and in this I think I have learned, and developed considerable ability. I am frequently, though not always, able to take a group, a course, or a class of students, and to set them psychologically free. I can create a climate in which they can be and direct themselves. At first, they are suspicious; they're sure that the freedom I'm offering them is some kind of a trick, and then they bring up the question of grades. They can't be free because in the end I will evaluate them and judge them. When we have worked out some solution, in which we have all participated, to the absurd demand of the University that learning is measured by grades, then they begin to feel that they are really free. Then curiosity is unleashed. Individuals and groups start to pursue their own goals, their own purposes. They become explorers. They can try to find the meaning of their lives in the work they're doing. They work twice as hard in such a course where nothing is required as in courses with requirements. I can't always achieve this atmosphere and when I cannot, I think it is because of some subtle holding back within myself, some unwillingness for the freedom to be complete. But when I can achieve it, then education becomes what it should be, an exciting quest, a searching, not an accumulation of facts soon to be outdated and forgotten. These students become persons living in process, able to live a changing life. Of all the learnings I have developed, I think this climate of freedom which I can frequently create, which I can often somehow carry with me and around me, is to me one of the most precious parts of myself.

ACCEPTING AND GIVING LOVE

Another area of my learning in interpersonal relationships has been slow and painful for me. It is most warming and fulfilling when I can let in the fact, or permit myself to feel, that someone cares for, accepts, admires, or prizes me. Because, I suppose, of elements in my past history it has been very difficult for me to do this. For a long time I tended almost automatically to brush aside any positive feelings which were turned in my direction. I think my reaction was, "Who, me? You couldn't possibly care for me. You might like what I have done or my achievements but not *me*." This is one respect in which my own therapy helped me very much. I am not always able even now to let in such warm and loving feelings from others, but I find it very releasing when I can do so. I know that some people flatter me in order to gain something for themselves. Some people praise me because they are afraid to be hostile. Some people, in recent years, admire me because I'm a "great name," or an "authority." But I have come to recognize the fact that some people genuinely appreciate *me*, like me, love me, and I want to sense that fact and let it in. I think I have become less aloof as I have been able really to take in and soak up those loving feelings.

I have found it to be a very enriching thing when I can truly prize or care for or love another person and when I can let that feeling flow out to him. Like many others, I used to fear that I would be trapped by this. "If I let myself care for him he can control me, or use me, or make demands on me." I think that I have moved a long way in the direction of being less fearful in this respect. Like my clients I, too, have slowly learned that tender, positive feelings are *not* dangerous either to give or receive.

Here I could give examples from my own experiences, but, as I thought this over, it seemed to me that it would be almost too personal and might reveal the identities of others, so I'm going to give an illustration in which I have helped two other people to go even further than I could, I think, in the giving of love. The story has to do with two friends, both of them priests, whom I will call Joe and Andy. Joe participated in a basic encounter group that I conducted and he was deeply affected by it. Later, Andy was also a member of a group with which I was associated. Some months later, I received this letter from Andy. It said:

> *Dear Carl:*
>
> *I've been trying to get a letter off to you ever since the workshop. I keep thinking I'm going to have some leisure time when I can sit down and really collect my many impressions of those three days. I can see that the leisure time is a dream so I'd like to get at least a note to you.*
>
> *Perhaps, I can best tell you what that workshop meant by describing an incident that happened not too long after.*
>
> *Joe [the other priest] had been working with a severely neurotic woman with schizophrenic tendencies, very suicidal and very guilty. She had spent a fortune on psychiatrists and psychologists. One afternoon he asked me to come down to her home with him to meet her, sing and play my guitar and talk. As Joe hoped, it turned into a basic encounter. At one point, she said that her hands really contained her. When she is angry, her hands are angry; when she is happy, her hands are happy; when she is dirty, her hands are dirty. As she was speaking and gesturing, she was sitting near me on the couch. I had the sudden urge to take her hand. I just couldn't buy the concept that she was dirty. So I did. Her first reaction was, "Thank you." Then she went into a type of seizure, shaking and crying. We learned later she was reliving a frightening and traumatic experience from her past. Joe had his arm around her shoulders. I held onto her hand for dear life. Finally, she relaxed. She put my hand in hers, turned it over and looked at it. She remarked, "It is not cracked and bleeding, is it?" I shook my head. "But it should be, I'm so dirty." About ten minutes later in the course of the encounter, she reached out and took my hand.*
>
> *A while later her little girl, a third grader, was screaming. The girl is very emotional and has a lot of problems. I excused myself and went in to see her. I sat on her bed, talked with her and sang. Before long I had her in my arms, holding her and kissing her and rocking her. When she quieted down,*

I put her under the covers and got her Mom. She told me later that when she kissed Mary good night, on a new inspiration, she leaned over and kissed her again on the cheek. "This was for Father Andy." Mary looked up, smiled, and said, "You know Mommy, he loves me kind of special, doesn't he?" Then she turned over and went to sleep.

I wanted to tell you about these incidents, Carl, as the workshop with you helped me to respond in each case freely and trustingly with my own instinctive reactions. I have had the words for years. In theory, I have strongly held that that is how I think a man—a Christian—a priest most truly acts. But I have had a hard struggle getting to the point where I could be that free, without hesitation or worry. I left your workshop really *knowing that I couldn't just say to people that I love them or that they are loveable, especially when they need to be shown this. Since then, many times, I have in some way or another* shown *where before I would have* said. *This has brought much more joy and peace to many like this mother and daughter and to myself.*

So often I think gratefully about our group. As you might imagine, I can quite vividly remember the love and warmth of the members of the group as I was struggling so hard to be truly honest with myself and you. For an experience like that, it is difficult to say thank you. May a life more free, more honest, and more loving say it for me. I still get tears in my eyes when I think of the last few hours, all of us sharing deeply and warmly, without any urgency, of ourselves. I can't ever remember being so deeply touched by anything–nor have I felt more true love for a group of people. I could go on but I think you see how truly grateful I am for the workshop, for the group, for you. I just pray that I can help give to others what you and the others gave me. Thank you.

I'm not at all sure that I could have gone as far as those two men did, but I'm very pleased that I have had a part in helping someone go beyond where I am. I think it is one of the exciting aspects of working with younger people.

It is also very meaningful to me that I can vouch for the truth of this account. Since the time of this letter I have come to know both Andy and Joe much better. I have also had the privilege of becoming acquainted with the woman whose psychological life they quite literally saved. So I feel confirmed in my view that prizing, loving feelings are *not* basically dangerous to give or receive, but are instead growth-promoting.

I Am More Able to Appreciate Others

Because of having less fear of giving or receiving positive feelings, I have become more able to *appreciate* individuals. I have come to believe that this is rather rare. So often, even with our children, we love them to control them rather than loving them because we appreciate them. I have come to think that one of the most satisfying experiences I know—and also one of the most growth-promoting experiences for the other person—is just fully to *appreciate* this individual in the same way that I appreciate a sunset. People are just as wonderful as sunsets if I can let them *be*. In fact, perhaps the reason we can truly appreciate a sunset is that we cannot control it. When I look at a sunset as I did the other evening I don't find myself saying, "Soften the orange a little on the right hand corner, and put a bit more purple along the base, and use a little more pink in the cloud color." I don't do that. I don't *try* to control a sunset. I watch it with awe as it unfolds. I like myself best when I can experience my staff member, my son, my daughter, my grandchildren, in this same way, appreciating the unfolding of a life. I believe this is a somewhat oriental attitude, but for me it is the most satisfying one.

So in this third area, prizing or loving and being prized or loved is experienced by me as very growth-enhancing. A person who is loved appreciatively, not possessively, blooms, and develops his own unique self. The person who loves non-possessively is himself enriched. This at least has been my experience.

I VALUE INTERPERSONAL COMMUNICATION AND RELATIONSHIPS

Let me close this chapter by saying that in my experience real interpersonal communication and real interpersonal relationships are deeply growth-promoting. I enjoy facilitating growth and development in others. I am enriched when others provide a climate which makes it possible for me to grow and change.

So I value it very much when I am able sensitively to hear the pain and the joy, the fear, the anger, the confusion and despair, the determination and the courage to be, in another person. And I value more than I can say the times when another person has truly been able to hear those elements in me.

I prize it greatly when I am able to move forward in the never-ending attempt to be the real me in this moment, whether it is anger or enthusiasm or puzzlement which is real. I am so delighted when a realness in me brings forth more realness in the other, and we come closer to a mutual I-thou relationship.

And I am very grateful that I have moved in the direction of being able to take in, without rejecting it, the warmth and the caring of others, because this has so increased my own capacity for giving love, without fear of being entrapped and without holding back.

These, in my experience, are some of the elements which make communication between persons, and *being in* relationship to persons, more enriching and more enhancing. I fall *far* short of achieving these elements, but to find myself moving in these directions makes life a warm, exciting, upsetting, troubling, satisfying, enriching, and above all a worthwhile venture.

POSTSCRIPT

In the play *Our Town,* Thornton Wilder develops a scene in which young Emily Webb, who has died prematurely at the age of 26, is allowed to return to earth from heaven for one day. She chooses her twelfth birthday. To her father and mother this is just another day in their lives, but to Emily it is the only day that she has. With her new insights Emily is distressed by the family's lack of genuine communication and by the distracted, matter-of-fact manner of her mother. Finally in desperation she cries out:

> *"Oh Mama, just look at me one minute as though you really saw me . . . just for a moment now we're all together. . . . Let's look at one another."*

Like Emily, our time on earth is also limited. We should not have to accept indefinitely the alienations, the undue hostilities, the misunderstandings, and the distrust and impersonality between people of good faith. It is our hope that through improved interpersonal communication each of us can contribute toward a world in which we can, like Emily Webb in Grover's Corners, New Hampshire, "look at one another."

INDEXES

AUTHOR INDEX

SUBJECT INDEX

127